Civility and Politics in the Origins of the Argentine Nation

Sociabilities in Buenos Aires, 1829–1862

UCLA Latin American Studies

VOLUME 88

PILAR GONZÁLEZ BERNALDO DE QUIRÓS

Civility and Politics in the Origins of the Argentine Nation

Sociabilities in Buenos Aires, 1829–1862

Translation by Daniel Philip Tunnard

UCLA LATIN AMERICAN CENTER PUBLICATIONS
UNIVERSITY OF CALIFORNIA, LOS ANGELES

Civilité et politique aux origines de la nation Argentine:
Les sociabilités à Buenos Aires, 1829–1862
Publications de la Sorbonne, Paris, 1999

To my parents, Ángel and Julia, and to my brothers and sisters, Julio, Ignacio, Ángeles, Gloria, Martín, Diego, Rodrigo, Fernán and Julia, who inhabit my personal memory of Buenos Aires

Cover illustration: *El Mosquito,* March 1864

Designer/Production Manager: Brenda Johnson-Grau

UCLA Latin American Center Publications
University of California
Los Angeles, CA 90095-1447

Library of Congress Cataloging-in-Publication Data

Gonzalez-Bernaldo, Pilar.
[Civilité et politique aux origines de la nation Argentine. English]
Civility and politics in the origins of the Argentine nation : sociabilities in Buenos Aires, 1829-1862 / Pilar Gonzalez Bernaldo de Quirós ; translation by Daniel Philip Tunnard.
p. cm. -- (UCLA Latin American studies ; v. 88)
Includes bibliographical references and index.
ISBN-13: 978-0-87903-089-6 (pbk. : alk. paper)
ISBN-10: 0-87903-089-5 (pbk. : alk. paper) 1. Social networks--Argentina--Buenos Aires--History--19th century. 2. Political culture--Argentina--Buenos Aires--History--19th century. 3. Buenos Aires (Argentina)--Social conditions--19th century. I. Title.
HN270.B8G65 2007
306.20982'11--dc22 2006036445

Contents

Preface

There are works whose fame precedes their publication. Since her defense of her doctorate thesis at the Sorbonne in 1992, the work of Pilar González Bernaldo de Quirós has become a reference both for those who have had the pleasure of reading it and for the many people around the world who were aware of its existence. The publication of this translation allows a wider public to appreciate its qualities and, no doubt, apply its methods to other countries and periods.

This book sits at an intersection of various roads of research essential for understanding the nineteenth century: the mutations of sociability and social practices, the birth of modern politics and nation-building. The most original aspect of the work lies in its fundamental intuition that provides its unity: the three aspects are inseparably connected in a causal relationship that, while complex, is nonetheless unquestionably true.

To break down and demonstrate this connection may seem a considerable task, more fitting of a vast historiographical synthesis than the work of a single researcher. However, another approach is possible: finding a geographic framework limited enough to illustrate how these variables interact, with the condition that the framework's relationship with the nation be determinant and that the period in question be sufficiently prolonged. Between 1829 and 1862 the city of Buenos Aires met these conditions admirably because of its place in the construction of an Argentina with which, for many, it would ultimately identify. This was not always the case, quite the contrary, in fact, because during the sixty years following independence the relationship between the port city and the provinces of the interior was the central problem of the River Plate; it continues to be one of the most controversial aspects in the memory and historiography of Argentina.

In this context, limited but capital in the strictest sense of the word, this critique is developed. For the first time on this scale, a vivid and concrete description of spheres and forms of sociability goes hand in hand with a comprehensive deliberation and conceptual analysis. In this way, we can observe the procession of all types of sociability, of varied finalities and foundations, both formal and informal, elitist and popular: fraternities, African "nations" and societies, reading rooms, literary and philanthropic societies, friendly societies, Masonic lodges, leisure associations, electoral clubs. Cartography comes to the assistance of qualitative analysis to show hidden developments. The dominant sociabilities of the first period are undoubtedly old-fashioned, originating in the primary ties of the neighborhood, in guild solidarity and ethnic belonging. In the tightly woven fabric of the *pulperías*, concentrations around parishes stand out. Only a few modern elitist sociabilities—cafés, reading rooms, student and merchant societies—begin to specialize the urban space. We then see their growth, which was not continuous but dependent on political developments, with rhythms and modalities which give credence to the hypothesis of their close relationship with modern politics. After a peak in the early 1820s, during the Rivadavia era, came slow growth or lethargy during the Rosas regime, and lastly the associative boom following the fall of the *caudillo*. In mid-ninteenth century Buenos Aires, the economic peak and the abundance of leisure activities were not in contradiction with the hectic political activity accompanying the rebirth of the representative regime, in fact quite the opposite is true.

However, and surprising though it may seem, the quantitative and spatial correlation proves insufficient. It is also necessary to show the existing connection between sociability, associative practices and the exercise of power. The prosopographic analysis of a vast corpus which includes politicians and journalists allows us to advance a step further. Above all, it counters the socioeconomic interpretation of politics still dominant in Argentine historiography. Juan Manuel de Rosas' controversial regime was not the expression of a ruralization of political life nor a coup by the large landowners (*estancieros*). The makeup of the governing elite shows, on the contrary, the significant place occupied by the traditional urban elites: the old administrative elite and the large families of diverse interests, with the sole though significant difference, that this ruling group had very little involvement in the new sociability and was based rather on old-fashioned networks. Rosas himself garnered a large part of his strength from clientele ties with the urban masses, particularly from African societies.

Quite different was the relationship that the post-Rosista generation maintained with modern associative practices. For almost all those involved, these were a necessary stage in their personal itineraries, be it as the sphere of initiation into modern opinion and politics or as a means of widening and setting their area of influence. In this sense, the nascent minority student sociability of the 1830s was in fact the seed of the modern population, and its proscription by Rosas "the exile of opinion" or "the nation in exile."

Given that—and here we reach the nucleus of the work—the new sociocultural associations and their new relational practices entailed a new way of thinking and of imagining collectivity (the social bond, authority, behaviors), this interpretative way of thinking, which gradually gained a foothold in the new history of politics, met here with a resounding confirmation. Modern sociability went hand in hand with the individual's involvement, the valuing of contractual bonds, the ideal of equality, the empire of opinion, the sovereignty of collectivity. In this previously-unheard-of constellation, the sociability on which the author so insists occupied a central, ambiguous place. The civilized, courteous and pacified relationships of the elites in the new relationship spaces prepared and foreshadowed the civil society of modern politics. In this River Plate, which precisely at this time began to think in terms of the "civilization and barbarity" opposition, civility was at once a school of citizenship and criterion of social distinction, given that it was also urbanity and the rejection of coarse rural customs. As in the rest of the western world, marked by a Greco-Roman inheritance, politics belongs to the *polis*, civility and civilization are inseparable from the *civitas* and the *cives* and urbanity is part of the *urbs*. Without doubt the old city–countryside divide did not disappear from the minds of the elites but was reformulated in order to make the new urban sociability practices the basis of a new society. In this sense, even though they were not the only ones to embark on this path, the Buenos Aires elites were effectively the "origins of the Argentine Nation." The modern nation was a new way to exist for a human community: a collectivity founded on a new bond between men and on new values and imageries.

This does not make it any less true that the new city—as well as the capital and the nation—was and would remain to be for a long time more an ideal than a consummate reality, an ideal with an extraordinary transforming power but which coexisted for a long time with the old ideal. From this, it can be deduced that the road to the creation of a public sphere is neither straightforward nor lineal. The modern elites were at once the prefiguration of the future nation and its pedagogues (because of urbanism, commemorative places, symbolism and later school) but also the administrators of a city still structured by old belongings.

This ambivalence was present everywhere and accounts for many oddities of nineteenth-century politics, made up of hybrids and discrepancies between resolutely modern imageries and practices and others that sank their roots into a past that these rejected. A ubiquitous presence in countries that attempted to break abruptly with the *ancien régime*, this distance was particularly important in Spanish America. Independence was not only the break with Spain and sectors of the old monarchy but also, and perhaps above all, the immediate and definitive establishment of a sovereignty in which the adjective "national" poorly masked incertitude as to the nature of the nation. This uncertainty refers as much to territorial elements—a particularly patent problem in the United Provinces of the River Plate—as to the tie between elemental components in the nation. It is true that references to the citizen abound and in Buenos Aires male suffrage was universal from an early stage. Nevertheless, in practice, it was not only elections that manifested the will of the people but also the gathering of crowds and the occupation of the street, physical pressure on adversaries. From here arose the phenomenon of the popular movement that occupied such an important place in the city, from plebiscites during the Rosas regime to the manipulation of the vote by notable people, as will be seen below. The existence of different representative logics only reflected the heterogeneity of a society far from being made up of freely associated individuals and civilized customs.

Revealing the complexity of apparently aberrant phenomena is the best proof of the validity of an explanatory model. This is undoubtedly the case with this work, far from a falsely modest history that, under the pretext of letting the sources speak and vanish before the complexity of what is real, leads to the accumulation of case studies or an overall interpretation introduced surreptitiously by undeclared premises. The hypotheses on which this work is founded are clearly enunciated, the variables used are explained and the connections of the exposition are clearly shown. One might discuss them, complete them, or reformulate them, but such an approach makes a debate possible on the great logics in action in History and is evidence of the ambition of the historian to approach a general vision of what is real.

FRANÇOIS-XAVIER GUERRA
University of Paris-I-Sorbonne
March, 1998

I was, in the primitive sense of the metaphor before it took shape, a bag of nerves. From where, I wonder, the will to transgress that goads me ceaselessly, and that constantly felt desire of a lost race, one last break, to bring about an end to the violence that haunts me and that, even now, disciplines the way I use this pen; and from where, that which might appreciate above the whole system of precautions, manners and courtesies perfected by men with the passing of the centuries in order to kill each other less, in which I am confined and with which I blindfold myself. I fear myself; I obey myself.

HÉCTOR BIANCIOTTI
What The Night Tells The Day

INTRODUCTION

Ask any historian to imagine a world without the dimension of time and you will see in their face signs of vexation and anguish comparable to the reaction of a nineteenth-century intellectual conceiving of a society without a nation. The nation is so essential to modern political thought that we of the late twentieth century—who have rushed to proclaim the end of the nation—experience singular difficulties in making a historical object of it. There, however, is no shortage of studies, interpretations, and even operating instructions. This is not to say that we don't continue to feel the same uneasiness when faced with a reality that like the dimension of time, is as indisputable to the historian as it is difficult to apprehend. Did not E. Renan answer the question "What is a nation?" by confessing that its existence depended on forgetfulness and even historical error?[1] So what is the point in trying to historically discern a nation? Our uncertainty is all the greater, in this case, for the fact that in trying to approach the nation as it is presented historically in Argentina, the complexity of the issues surrounding the process of the organization of the national State obscures the few clues that would allow us an easier approach.

However, I decided to take up the gauntlet—not only to understand nineteenth-century Argentina but also, as the press insists on reminding us daily, because the question seems so essential. The history that I propose here is not, however, a history of national institutions or of the idea of nation. It is not a political history of the formation of the Argentine State nor is it a history of the establishment of a city as capital of the nation. Although all these questions are part of this investigation, I focus here on the relational practices of the population of the city of Buenos Aires, a sector of which (distinguishable as cultural elites) would play an incontrovertible role in the creation of an Argentine nation.[2] Was this, in short, an epiphenomenon with regards to the greater historical process mentioned here? Admittedly the point of view taken is incomparable to the size of the problem. It does however argue that everyday relational experiences are not unrelated to the overall political process of constitutional organization of the former Spanish provinces as a representative republic. With the focus fixed on the city of Buenos Aires and the sociability practices of its elites, this study is not intended to give an unequivocal answer. Even less does it claim to have found the key to explain a process that implies different dimensions of reality and consequently different levels of analysis. This approach, however, must uncover dimensions unknown until now, rendering this political process at once more complex and in certain aspects more understandable.

The Starting Point: The Problem of the Creation of a Nation in Argentina

Paradoxical as it may seem, until very recently it was absurd to raise such a question for one simple reason. Since the first accounts on the origins of the nation, historians have reiterated the theory formulated by the creators of the Argentine nation. The undisputed author of this theory is Bartolomé Mitre, who between 1857 to 1859 and 1877 developed his theory on the "the republican revolution" and turned the process begun in May of 1810 into the result of a long and not-always-silent struggle for national independence.[3] In Mitre's judgment, independence involved the development of an alternative economy contradictory to Spain's interests, a new awareness among the Argentines arising from this shift and a local society characterized by a lengthy democratic tradition. From then on, the problem of the nation was assimilated with that of independence. Thus, all historians in the second half of the nineteenth century, with few exceptions, maintained that the Argentine Nation was born—Porteño[4] and republican—in 1810.[5] This theory was taken up and enhanced by the new conceptual methods that characterized twentieth-century historiographical work. The emphasis was placed on the economic and social aspects that had led to the revolution, considered the fruit of national maturity. Attempts were made to prove that the birth and development of a capitalist economy and national bourgeoisie required a break with Spanish domination in order to ensure its own survival.[6] In both cases, the basis was a prior notion of the existence of a nation and a national sentiment in the origin of independence (in the nineteenth century the emphasis was more on the political side, whereas in the twentieth century it was on the economic). In this perspective, however, the long period of bloody civil wars that broke out between the presumed birth of the nation in 1810, year zero in Argentine history and the beginning of the definitive organization of a national State remained difficult to explain. For some, it was a matter of a step backwards, as in Rosas' theory of feudal power; for others, it was the consequence of a native anarchic trend attributable to "national idiosyncrasy," as in Sarmiento's theory on the origin of the *caudillos*.

The last twenty years have been rich in new writing, both from colonial history specialists revising the relationship between Spain and her colonies on the eve of independence and from nineteenth-century specialists challenging the classic theory of the "nationalist" origin of independence and proposing provincial societies and economies as the only coherent unit of the period.[7] These recently opened paths allow an entirely different approach to nineteenth-century Latin America. I therefore based my study on these new investigations to invert the terms of classic theory. I started this study with the opposite hypothesis, that of an insurrectional movement which, rather than resolving the problem of the nation, raised it, a first step in formulating a number of new questions as to the creation of the nation.

It is by no means excessive to introduce some clarifications in regard to the sense and use of a notion with a high level of generality and abstraction and whose strong ideological and political component converts it into an object of power in societies founded on the principle of the sovereignty of the nation and the self-determination of its peoples. There cannot be an exact or "aseptic" definition of the nation. It is often forgotten that the two definitions which today are universally accepted were two political responses to notions that had turned into projects for political power. Fichte wrote his *Addresses to the German Nation* in 1806 after Prussia's defeat at the hands of Napoleon. In turn, Renan gave his lecture at the Sorbonne in 1882 after the French defeat at the hands of Germany. In current studies that attempt to connect the sense of the nation with that of the civic nation, it is easy to discern a response to the present reawakening of nationalisms, which, because of intense ethnic and xenophobic connotations, are on the whole worrying.[8] It is therefore futile to resolve from the outset the exact definition of a strongly polysemous concept. Its sense should instead be found in the different semantic combinations that are produced in the struggle for power. Thus, the question will rather entail finding out how certain sectors of the cultural elites historically positioned the nation as a foundation of power with the representation of a community of belonging. This is a necessarily reductionist perspective, as it is a matter of representations whose possible declinations were almost as varied as the populations in question but with the exception that these elites would go on to monopolize the public space and the representative institutions out of which a discourse on the nation was formulated and which could be used to legitimize the construction of the State, a project undertaken by those same elites.

The idea of nation tied to political independence from Spain appeared in the River Plate above all in a political context: in the laws of the provisory governments, in the Declaration of Independence, in different constitutional projects and during debates in constituent assemblies that the official or opposition press communicated to the public sphere. In this case there was a clearly political definition: the nation as sovereign subject. The community notion of the nation is problematic in the River Plate and in the Americas as a whole, as the actors in the uprising were *criollos*, people born in Latin America but of European ancestry, and the foundations of their identity lay precisely in their belonging to metropolitan culture. Thus, in the young Spanish American republics it was the constitutional act that essentially created the nation. However, the problem in the River Plate lay precisely in that the founding pact of the political community could not take shape. Before the Constitution of the Argentine Confederation was written in 1853, proclaiming a national union in which the province of Buenos Aires (which split with the rest of the territory and created its own constitution in 1854) did not participate, four constituent assemblies had already met, in 1813, from 1816 to 1819, from 1824 to 1826 and in 1828, and adopted two constitutional texts, that of the United Provinces of South America in 1819 and the Constitution of the Argentine Republic in 1826, both of which were doomed to failure. Only in 1862, after two armed confrontations between Buenos Aires and the Argentine Confederation, would national unity be established in all of what is today the Argentine Republic—with the exception of Patagonia and the territory of the Chaco, which were both controlled by rebellious indigenous tribes. Another twenty years would pass before the nation finally put an end to indigenous rebellion and the autonomist whims of Buenos Aires.

The nation, however, continued to be used as a pretext. A nation which, to a certain degree, was everywhere and nowhere: acclaimed ceaselessly in legislative texts and constitutional projects, invoked during intellectual gatherings in literary societies; invoked by Lavalle's men in 1828 to 1829 to denounce the "horde" that intended to replace the people; embodied by either Catholics or Freemasons in their claims. Hence, in the River Plate the sense of nation was furtively displaced from the State to society, a semantic displacement that placed society and its representation at the heart of projects for political power.

The History of Sociabilities as a Way of Approaching the Nation

My interest in the object of "sociability" has its primary historiographic source in the investigations of Maurice Agulhon, whose importance in this field has long been vital.[9] The reading of his work was as determinant a factor in the choice of subject as in the analytic perspective. In particular, I adopt here the meaning of sociability in the sense of associativity, which Agulhon identifies with a number of egalitarian social and cultural practices that facilitated the reception of republican ideas in the Var *département* of Provence.

More essentially, Maurice Agulhon paved the way for a sociocultural approach to politics, which the rebirth of political history made possible.[10] His theory of association as the framework for the transformation of sociabilities would arouse, furthermore, a special interest among historians studying the advent of the democratic era.[11] Sociability thus became the meeting point of two historiographic streams that contributed to the renovation of political history: the history of mentalities and problem-oriented historical inquiry.[12] In this precise territory, Furet's rereading of Cochin coincides with the groundwork laid by Agulhon. These two authors do fall into two different historiographic streams. Their evaluation of the role of some associative practices in the advent of democracy differs from medium to medium. For Cochin, it is a practice that drives the people away from power, especially through the production of the democratic ideology; for Agulhon, they are forms of popular participation. In one case, associative practice leads to totalitarianism; in the other, to a kind of democratization of democratic institutions. Both currents, which proceed from different conceptual matrices, begin, however, with the same assumption: relational practices are at the heart of politics as social practice. In my study I took this idea and became interested in the nation as a category that diminishes the importance of social practice. A third school of thought, which would later overwhelm the field of sociability, can be described as "history of the public sphere"; it maps out a new path between sociocultural history and political history.[13] I consider these issues in order to place the question of social spaces and community representations at the heart of the problem of the construction process of a national sociability.

This work is a tributary of a second theory of Agulhon's that was valued among historians of mentalities: a theory that postulates sociability as an historical object. I do not refer here to the fact that from Agulhon's works sociability garnered the status of an "object of scientific interest," to be incorporated into university history that has since seen the multiplication of monographs on different forms and spheres of sociability. Although important for historical knowledge, Agulhon's primary contribution has been in making behaviors a possible historical subject.[14] One phrase, though apparently anodyne, sums up the extent of his contribution:

> Any human group, whether defined in space, time or social hierarchy, possesses its own sociability, to a certain extent by definition, the specific forms of which it is important to analyze. Given this, it can no longer be said that the inhabitants of a small town like Gap in the *département* of Hautes-Alpes are less sociable than the people of Marseille, rather that they are sociable in a different way.[15]

This appreciation is evidence of a concept heretofore uncommon in sociability theory: a sociability that would not be related to one's degree of perfection of customs.[16] The notion of sociability as a "principle of relationships between people" or "aptitude of men to live in a society" indicates for Agulhon any human relationship:

> Man is born and he dies, he eats and drinks, throws himself into love and combat, works or dreams and—equally essentially as these major functions—is constantly running into his peers, talking to them, getting close to them or running from them; in short, he is constantly establishing relationships with them.[17]

It is understood, then, that brutality and affability alike are forms of sociability and possible subjects of history.[18] Agulhon thus allows sociability to be thought of as outside of the conceptual and ideological framework that it had previously had and that associated it with the process of civilization.[19] Since the sociability object is not constructed in opposition to "associability," it is possible, however, to consider as arbitrary the analogy between sociability and civility—that is, to approach sociability as a historical object. It can be argued that this particular sense of sociability was an undeniable tool in the internalizing device of self-obligation that ensured for the State a monopoly over the legitimate use of violence. Elias speaks less of a process of civilization than of a tool in this process.

Based on practices of associative sociability, it can be seen that in the nineteenth century in the River Plate, a discourse circulated among the Porteño elites on "sociability" that was associated with the idea of "civil" relationships as constitutive of the social bond. It is not strange to find, in articles from the periodic press or political texts from the first half of the nineteenth century, the word "sociability" used to refer to characteristics that we would now call "nationality."[20] The former would thus be less the beginning of the relationship than the result of the latter: the nation. Sources, however, rarely use the term "civility," preferring the term "cultured sociability" or, as in the case of Sarmiento, "civilized sociability" or "public sociability."[21] These different references coincide with the notion of civility in the two senses of the word, courtesy and civic responsibility, which were profoundly interwoven at the time.[22] According to these, civility would be the daily support of civilization as a dynamic of a superior culture that underlies the liberal definition of the nation as a unit of possible development.

The idea and practice of civility, thus associated with the constitutive principle of the social and political bond, placed such practices at the heart of the process of constructing a national representation of the community of belonging. The nucleus of the theory can be expressed in a few lines: the modern associative movement and more generally the forms of contractual sociability were transformative factors in society and in the representations that society had of itself. In this sense, these factors worked to mobilize a new representation of collectivity as a "national society." In the course of my research I became aware of the complexity of this relationship, which affected both the sphere of the imaginary and that of actors and power relations. In effect, the associationist discourse was used frequently by cultural and political elites to conceptualize the social bond; the association was conceived by them as a form of civic pedagogy through which the citizen learned of the public sphere, which was constitutive to the political community; associative practice, which exceeded the sphere of these elites, fell into the network of relationships which broke with the local referential context and established a new relationship space in which society was conceived of as an extension of rational individuals and the social bond as the product of a voluntary contract. These practices decreased the sense of belonging to a nation defining itself as a "civil society," in the double sense of democratic and civilized. This investigation proposes exploring this extraordinary confluence of questions within the same object: sociability.

Method of Analysis

To explore in all its complexity the relationship between the establishment of the nation as the basis of power and representations of the community of belonging, I chose the city of Buenos Aires as the context of observation. This decision, however, does not imply a deductive reasoning that led to the conclusion that the question of the construction of a national representation of society was resolved in this city. In any event, the choice of Buenos Aires was not random. The question takes on particular importance in this city, because of three interrelated factors, and above all because of a reason of inheritance. The city of Buenos Aires was already the capital of the viceroyalty of the River Plate and due to Bourbon reforms enjoyed a centralized administrative structure. For this reason, from the 1810 insurrectional movement onwards, the Porteño elites regularly asserted the directorial role of the city over its old territory and saw in the creation of the modern nation a way of affirming this historical inheritance. The combination of modern models for the organization of the nation and the confirmation of colonial power in the city explains the importance of this question in the port city. Furthermore, the international economic situation favored the development of the coastal region of the River Plate and gave Buenos Aires a new dominance over other regional economies. In this first half of the nineteenth century, the city and its area of influence experienced economic and technical developments which assured the region's elites of the material conditions to establish themselves in any possible, albeit primitive, national organization of regional economies. These circumstances explain why the city and its elites associated the nation with the conditions of their political and economic dominance over the rest of the territory. The third factor was partially a consequence of the economic boom that Buenos Aires experienced after independence. Indeed, the economic development of the region led to the multiplication of cultural exchanges between Buenos Aires and the world of the Atlantic. These exchanges, with the intensification of transatlantic migration, favored the transformation of the sociability habits of a Porteño population, which, as will be seen throughout this work, was closely related to the national potential of the political and cultural action of city elites.

One place, then, and a three-sided methodological perspective. Firstly, the aim is a study of sociability, as my objective here is to tackle the study of political and cultural identities in and because of social practices. To do so, I have dedicated myself to an analysis of sociability practices among the population of Buenos Aires during the first half of the nineteenth century. In this I have principally used three types of sources: private archives, particularly those of the associations; police archives, testimony above all to the everyday lives of a population submitted to the constant watchful eye of the law; and the periodic press, which informs us at the same time of the gatherings of the crème de la crème of Buenos Aires and public forms of sociability. For this analysis, I favored associative forms of sociability because their degree of institutionalization makes them easy to circumscribe. Indeed, associations for the most part come complete with regulations and therefore additional sources. Unfortunately, the archives themselves proved to be far less revealing. Nevertheless, a certain amount of unpublished information on associative life—particularly of Freemasonry, whose archives I was able to access—is presented here. Police archives provided priceless information, particularly on sociability among the black population.

Experimental cartography, as proposed to me by Françoise Vergneault, provided the second methodological perspective.[23] This approach employed cartography and graphs not only as visual modes of expression but also as a method of analysis and research procedure. This procedure, complementary to the first, allowed me to circumscribe in space the transformation that occurred in the sphere of sociabilities and social imagination.[24] I embarked on my investigation without really raising this question. On discovering in the new relationships of civility a specific form of sociability that tied the individual to the modern nation, I began to wonder as to the existing tie between the new context in which sociabilities were established and the modalities of their establishment in space, which led me to carry out a study into the organization of the urban social space.

Prosopography, the third methodological perspective, is a method based on comparing biographies. However, the procedure for constructing the group for analysis differs from more customary practices. Indeed, it was not fixed beforehand in accordance with socioprofessional or political criteria but was the result of the crossing of three computerized archives on associative personnel: the Porteño ruling class and the world of opinion, the press. Finding relationship modalities between these three fields of action using the evidence left by the actors' biographies was the objective. This approach, which is complementary to those outlined above, allowed me to show the correlation between the development of new sociability habits and the identification of the cultural elites with a certain representation of the nation.[25]

The investigation is situated at the crossroads of three approaches: the compared biography, sociability and interaction among the population, and the urban space. Over the eight chapters, it explores the places where individuals gathered, urban sociability, and the political process of national organization.

The choice of the chronological limits in which to explore this problem can be easily explained. Rosas came to power in the province of Buenos Aires after the failure of the attempt at national organization by the Porteño liberals around governor Bernadino Rivadavia. The year 1829 thus marks the liberals' exit from the provincial government and the abandonment of attempts at a constitutional organization of the nation. In turn, 1862 was the date of the creation of the definitive constitution of the Argentine nation under the leadership of the Porteño liberals, who after coming to power in the province of Buenos Aires in 1852 organized around this future task. This moment was crucial in the process of national organization, wherein the different representations of the community of belonging went hand in hand with various political projects for national organization. Anything seemed possible in these years. From an uncertain denouement, the political organization of a territory unified in the form of a representative republic. This form was a justified choice, but at the same time unsatisfactory, as it confines the investigation in a teleological device that gives these practices a political dimension that they would only acquire later. Historians, however, cannot turn into actors. We are invariably condemned to know how the story ends. In this backwards journey, our gaze tends to rest on and expand certain events that later prove to be determining factors. But while these events are used here as chronologic markers, the goal is to better articulate their connections with other, less prominent experiences, from the lives of the actors: sociability practices, relational codes and values, social representations.

NOTES

1. E. Renan, "Qu'est-ce qu'une nation?," lecture at the Sorbonne, 11 March 1882, *Discours et Conférences* (Paris: Calmann-Lévy, 1887), 277–310.
2. The concept of cultural elites coincides with two notions of the period: that of the "well-to-do" and that of the "neighbors" (*vecinos*). It shares with the "neighbors" the relationship with the public sphere and with the "well-to-do" societal recognition

because of education, good manners, and kinship ties. The expression "cultural elites" adds to these two phenomena the idea of a position of preeminence stemming from their identification with the public sphere, at first literary and later political.

3. Bartolomé Mitre, "Biografía de Belgrano," in José María Gutiérrez, *Galería de celebridades argentinas* (Buenos Aires, 1857; third complete edition with the title *Historia de Belgrano y de la Independencia argentina*, 1876/1877); Bartolomé Mitre, *Historia de San Martín y de la emancipación sudamericana* (Buenos Aires: Félix Lajouane, 1890).
4. The name given to the inhabitants of the city of Buenos Aires.
5. On the reconstruction of the national past by this first generation of historians the classic works are Ricardo Rojas' *Historia de la literatura argentina*, Buenos Aires, 1922, and Rómulo Carbia's *Historia crítica de la historiografía argentina (desde sus orígenes en el siglo XVI)* (Buenos Aires: Coni, 1940). On the intellectual origins of this first generation, see in particular the works of Natalio Botana: *La tradición republicana* (Buenos Aires: Sudamericana, 1984), and *La libertad política y su historia* (Buenos Aires: Sudamericana, 1991). Fernando Devoto offers an overall reflection on this question in "Idea de nación, inmigración y cuestión social en la historiografía académica y en los libros de texto en Argentina," *Estudios Sociales*, 2/3 (1992): 9–30,
6. There are numerous works of varying quality, and it is difficult to summarize them in one footnote. Such a list is proposed in Noemí Goldman and the present author's, "Treinta años de historiografía política argentina," in Comité Internacional de Ciencias Históricas, Comité Argentino, *Historiografía argentina 1958–1988. Una evaluación crítica de la producción histórica argentina* (Buenos Aires, 1990), 293–302. For a non-Marxist perspective, see John Lynch, *The Spanish-American Revolutions 1808–1826* (London, 1976; Barcelona: Ariel, 1983).
7. We have based this on the latest works by José Carlos Chiaramonte, "La cuestión regional en el proceso de gestación del Estado nacional argentino. Algunos problemas de interpretación," in Marco Palacios (comp.), *La unidad nacional en América Latina, del regionalismo al nacionalismo* (Mexico City: El Colegio de México, 1983); J. C. Chiaramonte, "Formas de identidad en el Río de la Plata luego de 1810," *Boletín del Instituto de Historia Argentina y Americana "Dr. E. Ravignani"* (Buenos Aires) 1 (third series, first trimester, 1989): 71–92; Tulio Halperin Donghi, *Revolución y guerra: formación de la élite dirigente en la Argentina criolla* (Buenos Aires: Siglo xxi, 1972); T. Halperin Donghi, *Reforma y disolución de los imperios ibéricos 1750–1850* (Madrid: Alianza, 1985; Colección Histórica de América Latina, vol. 3); T. Halperin Donghi, *Guerra y finanzas en los orígenes del Estado argentino (1791–1850)* (Buenos Aires: Editorial de Belgrano, 1982); François-Xavier Guerra, "Révolution française et révolutions hispaniques: filiation et parcours," in *Problèmes d'Amérique Latine. Notes et études documentaires*, no. 94 (Paris: La Documentation Française, 1989), 3–26. For an overview of the different positions of Latin American historians on this question, see Buisson et al., *Problemas de la formación del Estado y de la nación en Hispanoamérica* (Bonn: Inter Nationes, 1984); Annino *et al.*, *América Latina: Dallo Stato coloniale allo stato nazione (1750–1950)*, 2 vols. (Milan: Franco Angeli, 1987).
8. The definition of nation given is a clear political response to this problem, as seen in the notion of "constitutional patriotism" proposed by J. Habermas to bring together the definition of the nation and that of the political community. See Jürgen Habermas, *Écrits politiques* (Paris: Cerf, 1990). In France, D. Schnapper associates equally the modern nation and the idea of civic nation. See Dominique Schnapper, *La Communauté de citoyens. Sur l'idée moderne de nation* (Paris: Gallimard, 1994).

9. The bibliography on this question is considerable. We will indicate here one of Agulhon's principal works and refer the reader to the bibliography at the end of this volume. See Maurice Agulhon, *La Sociabilité méridionale. Confréries et associations en Provence orientale dans la deuxième moitié du XVIIIe siècle*, 2 vols. (Paris, 1966; published two years later with the title *Pénitents et francs-maçons de l'ancienne Provence)*. See also the 1984 edition, with an important preface by Maurice Agulhon (Paris: Fayard, 1984). For a primary critique of the bibliography of sociability, see Giuliana Gemelli and Maria Malatesta, *Forme di sociabilità nella storiografia francese contemporanea* (Milan, 1982). A more recent revision of European historiographic writing can be found in Jordi Canal i Morell, "El concepto de sociabilidad en la historiografía contemporánea (Francia, Italia y España)," *Siglo XIX (*second period) 13 (January/June): 5–25.
10. Political history, formerly "battle history," is thus fed by a renewed reflection of politics as a place of the social sphere. Revolution is at the heart of this reflection, which in France was developed through an intense debate on the French Revolution, begun by Richard Cobb and which François Furet would later confirm with *Penser la Révolution Française*. But this reflection owes much to political philosophy and particularly to the thinking of Claude Lefort, Cornelius Castoriadis, and Marcel Gauchet (René Rémond, ed., *Pour une histoire politique* [Paris: Seuil, 1988]), an indication can be found of the impact of this reflection in political history, which continues to expand its field of study.
11. See, for example, Ran Halevi's study, *Les Loges maçonniques dans la France d'Ancien Régime. Aux origines de la sociabilité démocratique* (Paris: A. Colin, 1984).
12. See François Furet, "De l'histoire-récit à l'histoire-problème," in *L'Atelier de l'histoire*, Paris, Champs-Flammarion, 1982. I believe François-Xavier Guerra's research should be included in this stream. In any event, it is an essential element in the renewal of political history that this author constantly urged. See François-Xavier Guerra, "Pour une nouvelle histoire politique: acteurs sociaux et acteurs politiques," in *Structures et cultures des sociétés ibéro-américaines* (Paris: CNRS, 1990), 245–260.
13. The way Habermas was received was particularly important among culture historians, especially among eighteenth-century specialists. See Keith Michael Baker (ed.), *The French Revolution and the Creation of Modern Political Culture*, vol 1. (Oxford and New York: Pergamon, 1987); K. M. Baker, *Au tribunal de l'opinion. Essais sur l'imaginaire politique au XVIIIe siècle* (Paris: Payot, 1993); K. M. Baker, "Defining the Public Sphere in Eighteenth Century France: Variations on a Theme by Habermas," in Craig Calhoun (ed.), *Habermas and the Public Sphere* (Cambridge, MA, and London: MIT Press, 1992); D. Goodman, "Governing the Republic of Letters: The Politics of Culture in the French Enlightenment," in *History of European Ideas* 13 (1991): 183–199; Roger Chartier, *Les Origines culturelles de la Révolution française* (Paris: Seuil, 1991).
14. Agulhon was preceded in this sense by P. Ariès, whom the former recognizes as the true founder of the history of collective mentalities in France. See Maurice Agulhon, "Préface," in *Pénitents et francs-maçons*.
15. See Agulhon, "Préface," in *Pénitents et francs-maçon*, vii.
16. This is the notion that Halevi, borrowing from Agulhon, gives to sociability. See R. Halevi, *Les Loges maçonniques*.
17. Maurice Agulhon, "La sociabilité est-elle objet d'histoire?," in François Étienne (dir.), *Sociabilité et société bourgeoise en France, en Allemagne et en Suisse (1750–1850)* (Paris: Ed. Recherches sur les Civilisations, 1986), 18.
18. With few exceptions, the problem of violence in social relationships is the blind spot in

research into sociability. There are few researchers who, like Alain Corbin and Arlette Farge, consider violence as a form of social relationship. This can be explained, in my judgment, by the idea that sociability implies the internalization of certain behavioral codes and rules which civilize human relationships. There is no doubt that sociability implies the existence of prohibitions—N. Elias spoke quite rightly of impulsive economy—without which no society would be possible, but the rules are historically variable and, as Elias notably demonstrates elsewhere, the impulsive economy can be related to forms of exercising power. In associating the idea of sociability with the existence of certain mechanisms of self-obligation, one of the possible meanings of the notion of sociability is established.

19. As is the case with G. Simmel or N. Elias. See Georg Simmel, "La sociabilité. Exemple de sociologie pure ou formelle," in *Sociologie et épistémologie* (1918); Norbert Elias, *Über den Prozess der Zivilisation* (Frankfurt am Main: Auflage, 1939); N. Elias, *Die höfische Gesellschaft* (1969).

20. This allowed Bartolomé Mitre to speak of Argentine sociability and Francisco Bilbao of Chilean sociability. See Francisco Bilbao, "Sociabilidad chilena," in *El Crepúsculo*, 20 June 1844; Bartolomé Mitre, "La sociabilidad argentina," in *Historia de Belgrano*.

21. Sarmiento goes as far as to speak of "disassociation" of sociability not born from public interest. See Domingo Faustino Sarmiento, "Asociación. La pulpería," in *Civilización y barbarie. Vida de Juan Facundo Quiroga, i aspecto físico, costumbres i hábitos de la República Argentina* (Santiago de Chile: Imprenta del Progreso, 1845).

22. The explanation for this contradiction apparently resides in the very concept of civilization that these young men discussed and the model of which came from French society. The originality of the contribution of Norbert Elias consists precisely in showing this aspect of the formation of the concept of civilization in France. In *La Civilisations des mœurs*, the author shows how, from a singular historical process, French bourgeoisie assimilated itself with the courtesan nobility, and explains that when the former took on the fate of the nation, many elements from courtesan society would survive the profound mutation of the Revolution and become part of the national character. See N. Elias, *La Civilisations des mœurs*. For the meaning of this notion in the Hispanic world, see the *Diccionario de la lengua castellana en que se explica el verdadero sentido de las voces, su naturaleza y calidad y las fraces o modos de hablar, los proverbios o refranes y otras cosas convenientes al uso de la lengua* (1737) (Madrid: Gredos, 1969), vol. 3, 133. For eighteenth-century Spain, see Pedro Álvarez de Miranda, "Palabras e ideas: el léxico de la ilustración temprana en España (1680–1760)," in *Boletín de la Real Academia Española* (Madrid) 1992, 395–410.

23. The maps and graphs were worked out with Françoise Vergneault-Belmont. Her work has been the object of a recent publication: *L'Œil qui pense* (Paris: L'Harmattan, 1998).

24. See Pilar González Bernardo (PGB), *La Création*, vol. 3, appendix 4, "La démarche graphique."

25. To do so, I created first an archive of the ruling class of the province of Buenos Aires between 1829 and 1862. I incorporated all those who held an institutional function in the power structure of the province. Therefore, this archive includes all those who occupied elective posts and those of high positions taken by designation, for a total of 1,503 people occupying 4,293 posts. The archive on associative belonging was made up of all the members of associations existing in Buenos Aires during the period in question. In this case, the selection criteria were more random, that is, dictated in part by the existence or nonexistence of sources. Nevertheless, I have data concerning

the principal associations of the period, which represents a total of 2,282 persons and 3,653 memberships. The third archive, dedicated to the press, covers a total of 433 publications that either appeared in Buenos Aires or were published by Porteños in exile; these totaled 250 people. A more detailed explanation of the procedure of putting together this database can be found in PGB, *La Création*, vol. 3, appendix 1, "Base de données.,"

PART I
Nationless Peoples
(1820–1852)

The political regime inaugurated by Juan Manuel de Rosas in 1829 was the first to establish, with the organization of the Rosista Confederation, a de facto "national" power and, at the same time, one that would be revoked by the "nation." The following analysis is an attempt to understand this paradox at the center of the process of shaping national representation, a process that accompanied the fall of the Empire and with it monarchical legitimacy.

The Fall of the Colony and the Establishment of the Provincial Republic in Buenos Aires (1810–1827)

Before tackling the specific issues of this investigation, some preliminary observations are necessary, firstly with regards to the River Plate. This region was peripheral in the Empire, both from an economical and demographical/cultural point of view. The crown showed relatively late interest in the region, and even the creation of the Viceroyalty of the River Plate depended to a great extent on Lima. The new viceroyalty established in 1776 covered a vast territory from Alto Peru to Tierra del Fuego, or at least theoretically given that a large part of the area, particularly south of Buenos Aires, was under the control of rebellious Indians. It nevertheless included the rich provinces of Alto Peru, torn from the grasp of the Viceroyalty of Peru, and the provinces of Cuyo, formerly part of the General Command of Chile. Buenos Aires, the capital of this new administrative area, was to control an enormous territory without any of the political or economic authority that Lima and Mexico had over their respective viceroyalties.

The Viceroyalty of the River Plate therefore did not constitute a territorial community configured by time, comparable to those of Peru, Mexico, or the Kingdom of Chile. Nor did it have a single, central, irrefutable political unit. When the insurrections began, Buenos Aires had only been the capital for thirty years and was far from stamping its authority on the whole of this vast region.

Napoleon I's invasion of Spain was a crucial event for Spanish America as a whole. Fernando VII's forced abdication brought about a crisis in the monarchy that contributed to the weakening of already tenuous colonial ties. The situation, however, had its unlikely aspects, for while events triggered the eruption of latent tensions between royal administrators and local powers, the power vacuum placed the Spanish colonies in a revolutionary political position. As a result, the insurrection of the Viceroyalty of the River Plate, which originated in the crisis in Spain, not only jeopardized colonial ties but also introduced the problem of the legitimacy of power. The disappearance of the king left the place of power vacant. Local elites entered into a struggle—the likes of which had never been seen—for this authority. Colonial political structures and networks were intermixed with new principles regulating the mechanisms to access these structures and networks.

The collapse of the ideological foundations of royal authority brought in its wake the problem of the breakup of the colonial unit. To denounce the illegitimacy of royal power in the name of the sovereignty of the people was to challenge the viceroyalty as a coherent territorial entity. The first to highlight this problem was the city of Asunción del Paraguay, which split with the revolutionary government of Buenos Aires in 1811 for the same reason that it split with Spain, in the name of the sovereignty of the people. This inevitably raised the question of inheritance. Who should inherit authority? Undoubtedly, the *patria* should, but which one? Former colonies on the other side of the Atlantic, the territory of the nascent viceroyalty, the old "Government of Buenos Aires," the region of the River Plate, the city and its hinterland? This ambiguity was evident in the various constitutions of the "United Provinces" of the former viceroyalty and can also be found in the polysemy of the words *pueblo* and *pueblos ("Pueblo/pueblos" on one level means "people" but has a connotation of "the people/population of one nation"–Translator),* a term that in Spanish refers both to the source of democratic legitimacy and the city as a territorial political community. As recent research has shown, this polysemy placed the liberal concept of the nation side by side with an organic concept from which grew a pre-absolutist representation of the monarchy, encouraging the process of territorialization of sovereignty, which was responsible itself for the breakup of viceroyalty territory.[1]

It is feasible that this confusion was owing to the presence, in the early days of the revolution, of the king figure (the proverbial mask of Fernando VII), which allowed the perpetuation of a plural representation of the nation. However, this confusion lasted throughout the Constituent Congress of 1824 to 1827, which after the failure of the constitutional attempt of 1819 intended to reunite the different provinces as a national State. Given these circumstances, the sovereignty of the nation and the sovereignty of the *pueblos* were then evoked, which raised serious constitutional problems (often highlighted by the representatives of Buenos Aires) and led conclusively to a new constitutional setback.[2] Hence, after ten years of revolution and war and because of the successive failures at constitutional organization, the territory of the viceroyalty was reduced to the only coherent economic and social unit, the city and its hinterland, which from 1820 made up the "provincial State."[3] The lengthy period of civil wars that followed is a story of conflicts and alliances between these different powers to organize a national power. From the attempt by G. Artigas to form a republic including Uruguay and the provinces of Entre Ríos, Corrientes, Santa Fe, and Córdoba to the 1831 Federal Pact, which ultimately led to the origin of the Rosista Confederation, the projects were numerous and based on diverse geo-economic spaces.

Many difficulties arose from the organization of a national State. From an economic point of view, the organization of a common market had to resolve the problem of regional incompatibilities, which implied sacrificing some economies for the benefit of others.[4] In addition to this were specific questions of the organization of the State, a matter of conflict between Unitarians and Federals.[5] If the conflict between supporters of a centralist state and those of a federal state was, however, lengthy and bloody, this was because this conflict of ideas concealed the not inconsiderable political problem of the inexistence of an unquestionable, supralocal power structure capable of ending of the inclination towards sovereignty among the old political entities.

Juan Manuel de Rosas appears to have understood this problem, rejecting any political organization not founded on provincial reality after a failed attempt at national organization following the promulgation of the constitution of 1826. Rosas learned two lessons from the Rivadavian government. First, the interests of Buenos Aires did not favor a commitment to the constitutional organization of a national State. The only way Rosas had of ensuring a leading place for the province of Buenos Aires over the "United Provinces" group was through the social and political stability of the province, an indispensable condition of the region's economic development. Second, the legitimacy of a national government depended on how much society identified with the authority. Rosas then sought to establish himself as the de facto national "authority," with the help of personal alliances with different local authorities, both those of traditional entities and the new authorities emerging from these entities' representative or independent institutions, such as in the case of some regional *caudillos*. In this way, Rosas dressed his power in a "national" legitimacy that was not established along constitutional lines.[6] However, due to the same process dissolving colonial ties, only the constitutional act could provide the nation with the republican legitimacy to which the modern nation tied its fate. This returns us to the problem raised by the collapse of the Spanish Empire. On the one hand, the community structures that had previously lent coherence to the territorial unit but that subsequently pertained to a political community that was no longer legitimate (the group of entities that made up the Spanish monarchy) survived; On the other hand, the modern nation, whose very existence of which depended on the presence of the sovereign subject but which lacked the social subject, was proclaimed: at once nationless peoples and a peopleless nation.

The failure of different attempts at constitutional organization is irrefutable evidence of the difficult transition from a colonial society to a national society. However, around these attempts a public culture developed which was one of the principal spaces for diffusing a new representation of social ties and of society as a product of a contract between individuals. These were representations that corresponded to the idea of a civic nation as a source of legitimacy and criterion of belonging. Thus the government of Bernadino Rivadavia (1821–1827) was at the same time the result of a failed project to organize a national State and the institution of a new civil culture that emerged in the context of the public sphere and thus inaugurated a space from which it became possible to imagine the nation as the product of these new social ties. While refusing to become embroiled in constitutional attempts, Juan Manuel de Rosas accepted these relational forms that conveyed new community representations, a strange inheritance for his government.

The Cultural Inheritance of the Republican Patria: Civility

Contained in this chapter are two prior assumptions. The first, in slight disagreement with the classical perspective, is that there was a continuity in the form of inheritance between the liberal government established by Bernadino Rivadavia (the period from 1821 to 1827) and the first period of Juan Manuel de Rosas' conservative regime (from his first government in 1829 to the political crisis of 1838 to 1840). The second and more controversial assumption is that this inheritance was civility. This declaration is strange, to say the least, for a historiography that unanimously recognizes the ruralization of the urban world as one of the effects of the collapse of central power in 1819.

What, however, do historians mean exactly when they speak today of ruralization? In Tulio Halperin Donghi's example, it means firstly that those who wielded power in the province from 1820 owed it to their economic influence, derived from raising livestock, hence the verdict of a rural basis for Porteño power.[7] Thus expounded, this theory can be immediately challenged. Was the capital from rural production really different from the capital of urban traders? Who dominated rural production?[8] The theory of the ruralization of political life is nevertheless founded on irrefutable data. There is no doubt that with the organization of an independent power a rural society (or even various rural societies), previously governed by a power that by definition was urban, could become incorporated into political life.[9] In this sense, the integration of the rural population into nascent representative institutions can effectively be considered as an element of ruralization in political institutions.[10] When writers speak of this ruralization, however, they do not refer only to this new political presence from the countryside but also to its consequences: the extinction of urban customs, the *civitas*, by the presence and primacy of the coarse and violent ways typical of the lack of social convention or public spirit that characterized the countryside.[11] T. Halperin Donghi alludes not only to power bases but also to a "way of doing politics" and even a way of doing thing in general that he connects, together with the ruralization of the foundations of power, with a vaster phenomenon, qualified as "barbarization." In Halperin Donghi's opinion, this "barbarization" was the result of the ruralization of power bases, the political fragmentation after 1820, and the absence of an institutional framework in which political life should take place.[12] The author goes further in connecting the lack of internal cohesion in political order with the absence of a network of affinities and alliances on which the new system could stand. The advance of brutality represented, in his opinion, a degradation of the relationship network that had previously characterized the cohabitation of members of the elite. Such diagnosis is also expressed by Mark Szuchman in his recent research, which attempts to show the familial strategies implemented to tackle this turbulence.[13] With "barbarization" the city would give up the ghost, and Rosista violence becomes nothing more than a manifestation of this phenomenon.

A close look at relationships of sociability in the city of Buenos Aires after 1820 nevertheless reveals the faults in this interpretation because, above all, many of the aspects used to describe the "barbarization" of the *civitas* were in fact features of a capital still living at the pace of a colonial city.[14] In addition, this vision does not take into account the growth of the urban population's relationship practices or, at least, those of the sector of the population one can qualify as cultural elites. However, in this sphere in this period, one finds significant modifications in the structure of urban sociability that instituted a public space where manners considered decent, moderate, courteous, and urbane were developed to reestablish the relationship with others and to place the individual rational being at the center. The specific way in which one understood how to be decent, moderate, and courteous evolved, naturally, with society's values.[15] It goes without saying that relationships of civility did not always imply contractual relationships likely to produce a civic culture. And here lies all the interest of the question: The spirit of civility that is revealed as this work progresses came up against what, in principle, should have been its support: politics as the citizens' sphere of action. This meant all the difference between civility understood as a quality of decency and relationships of civility that indicated membership in a political community founded on freedom and equality. In the first case, public life was identified with the sociable virtues of worthy men; in the second, relationships of civility, while persisting within the same class, served as the framework and support for a new representation of the nation as the foundation of democratic power.

NOTES

1. Since the completion of this investigation, many others have cast some light on the question. See François-Xavier Guerra, *Modernidad e independencias* (Madrid: Mapfre, 1992); Antonio Annino (ed.), *Historia de las elecciones en Iberoamérica, siglo XIX* (Buenos Aires: Fondo de Cultura Económica, 1995); Véronique Hébrard, *Le Venezuela indépendant. Une nation par le discours 1808–1830* (Paris, L'Harmattan, 1996); José Carlos Chiaramonte, "El federalismo argentino durante la primera mitad del siglo XIX," in Marcello Carmagnani (ed.), *Federalismos latinoamericanos: México, Brasil, Argentina* (Mexico: El Colegio de Mexico/Fondo de Cultura Económica, 1993), 81–132. Geneviêve Verdo will shortly defend a thesis on this question in the Sorbonne.
2. During the debate on the possibility of mortgaging state lands of the territory of the union as a guarantee of national debt, for example, the deputies of the provinces opposed it, claiming that these territories were their own property. The government minister intervened in the debate to highlight the profound contradiction of the provincial deputies' position in a national representation. See Constituent Assembly, session of 15 February 1826, in Emilio Ravignani (ed.), *Asambleas Constituyentes argentinas* (Buenos Aires: Instituto de Investigaciones Históricas, 1937), vol. 2, 674–675.
3. On the formation of the provinces, see José María Rosa, *Del municipio indiano a la provincia argentina, 1580–1852* (Madrid: Instituto de Estudios Políticos, 1958).
4. On these questions, see Juan A. Álvarez, *Las guerras civiles argentinas* (Buenos Aires, 1912; Buenos Aires: Eudeba, 1984); M. Burgin, *Aspectos económicos del federalismo argentino* (Cambridge, MA: Harvard University Press, 1946; Buenos Aires: Solar, 1975); Jonathan Brown, *A Socioeconomic History of Argentina, 1776–1860* (Cambridge: Cambridge University, 1979).
5. Usually Unitarians supported a centralist State and Federals a federal State, but in practice both denominations covered clearly distinct institutional political currents. On this question, see Enrique Barba, *Unitarismo, federalismo, rosismo* (Buenos Aires: Pannedille, 1972).
6. The different provinces had delegated Buenos Aires as the representative of the nation abroad.
7. John Lynch uses a more demographic argument that partly challenges the ideas of José Luis Romero, for whom the ruralization of the city was only apparent; rural society was gradually reduced to the thinking of urban society. See in particular T. Halperin Donghi, *Revolución y guerra*, 378–385; John Lynch, *Argentine Dictator Juan Manuel de Rosas, 1829–1852* (Buenos Aires: Emecé, 1984), 127; José Luis Romero, *Latinoamérica, las ciudades y las ideas* (Buenos Aires: Siglo XXI, 1976), 179–196.
8. Diana Balmori shows that family networks covered the city and the countryside and

that in this case it is difficult to distinguish one urban elite from a presumably rural one. Recent research into the rural world, furthermore, highlights the social and in certain cases productive importance of low and medium level farming, and invites a revision of the theory of the postcolonial State as the expression of the interests of large landowners. See Diana Balmori, *Casa y familia. Spacial Biographies in Nineteenth-Century Buenos Aires*, Ph. D. diss., University of California, 1973; Diana Balmori et al., *Notable Family Networks in Latin America* (Chicago: University of Chicago Press, 1984). For new research into the rural world, see "Discontinuidades y permanencias: el Río de la Plata pampeano en la primera mitad del siglo XIX," *Anuario IEHS* (Universidad de Tandil) 12 (1997).

9. In a relatively limited geographic space, various types of societies effectively cohabited. In reference to this question, see the author's analysis in "El levantamiento de 1829: el imaginario social y sus implicaciones políticas en un conflicto rural," *Anuario IEHS* 2 (1987): 137–176.
10. Various Argentine researchers are currently working on this question. See in particular the works of Carlos Cansanello, Marcela Ternavasio y Ricardo Salvatore. See *Anuario IEHS* 12 (1997); A. Annino (coord.), *Historia de las elecciones.*
11. According to the Littré dictionary, *civilité* ("civility") is a usage originating in the seventeenth century, meaning a "decent, moderated and courteous manner of acting and conversing with others." This would be specific of the *civitas*, given that according to Furtière, "only peasants, coarse people, lack civility." In this sense, while sociability was to some extent "spontaneous" in the countryside, it was necessary to succeed in the city, something that demanded that the population learn extra-familiar relational codes, which we call codes of urbanity. The Littré distinguishes the natural character of courtesy with regards to a civility "which has its forms and rules which correspond to convention." *Le Dictionnaire Universel d'Antoine Furetière* (1690) (Paris: SNL Robert, 1978–1984, facsimile edition). For an analysis of the notion of civility, see François Bourricaud, "Civilité," in *Encyclopedia Universalis*, Corpus 5 (1989), 948–951.
12. T. Halperin Donghi, *Revolución y guerra*, 377–385.
13. See Mark Szuchman, *Order, Family and Community in Buenos Aires, 1810–1860* (Stanford, CA: Stanford University Press, 1988).
14. For example, Szuchman attributes political turbulence to a break in community morals, which he deduces from the number of arrests in the city. However, eighteenth century cities give numerous other examples of licentiousness. In any event, discourse on depravation of urban customs and the necessary repression of these practices is typical of Bourbon reformism. On the moralizing discourse of the Bourbon era, see Juan Pedro Viqueira Albán, "Diversiones públicas y cultura popular en la ciudad de México durante el siglo de las luces," *Anuario de Estudios Americanos* 44 (1987): 195–228.
15. The meaning of the notion evolved with time. As Chartier shows, it had a moralizing normative meaning in the sixteenth century, then was associated in the following century with the idea of social courtesy, which explains its devaluation in the eighteenth century. For example, the *Diccionario de la lengua castellana* of 1726 defined the notion of civility using two antithetic meanings. It meant "sociability, urbanity" but also "poverty, meanness." See *Diccionario de la lengua castellana…*; Roger Chartier, "Distinction et divulgation: la civilité et ses livres," in *Lecture et lecteurs dans la France d'Ancien Régime* (Paris: Seuil, 1987), 45–86.

CHAPTER 1

Public Sociability Spaces in Buenos Aires

No human society can exist without sociability. As found in the vast majority of contemporary dictionaries, the primary meaning of sociability is "the ability to live in society." It has, however, taken a long time and the work of one historian with exceptional ethnological sensitivity to turn this evidence into an object of history. In this sense, the historiography of the last twenty-five years is enormously indebted to Maurice Agulhon: The notion of "sociability" has now won over the university establishment, although problems still arise in the discipline because trivialization and a decline in scientific precision sometimes accompanies proliferation. Thus, in France a two-sided phenomenon can be seen: On the one hand, there has been an increase in use of the term in historical writing; on the other, a decrease in specific historical research, to the extent that "sociability" in contemporary history writing becomes a catchall word, its very mention making certain phenomena appear more intelligible. Evidently, this does not simplify our task, all the more so because to consider a historical study of "sociabilities" in a port city and capital of a vast territory–even when the city, as was the case in Buenos Aires in the early nineteenth century, had scarcely more than forty thousand inhabitants–entails a range of difficulties, particularly that of circumscribing the object of our study.[1] In principle, anything is valid as study material, as any relationship with another concerns the history of sociability. In this perspective, writing a history of sociability in Buenos Aires, admittedly as I first imagined it, meant simply writing a history of the life of men. This temptation was rejected immediately, and I opted instead to record the practices of sociability that were on the whole institutionalized, the first of which would be associations.[2] This choice was not dictated solely by reasons of research strategy, in that associations are more likely to leave written evidence and even archives but also by the heuristic hypothesis of this work.

It was necessary to find the most salient features in the practices of relationships in Buenos Aires, without which the lines of a study of the associative world would become blurred. There was therefore a need to consider the study from the perspective of meeting places. This raised the question of how to draw a complete picture of the places in which the inhabitants of Buenos Aires met in the course of any given day: the doors of the parish church, the portico of the *cabildo* (the municipal administration building), the market, the port, the tree-lined avenues, the public baths, the cafés, the street corners, and the *pulperías* (a kind of tavern-cum-general store). The list of public places where people periodically met would be endless. Further, even if we were to devote ourselves, with the patience of an entomologist, to drawing up an inventory of these places, it would also be necessary to consider the choice of meetings and the connections that these imply. While the existence of this multitude of meeting places provides us with a hint as to the vitality of social life, it tells us little about the nature or the intensity of these relationships.[3] Nonetheless, one can find at least some of the elements that characterize the diversity of relationships of public sociability in the city of Buenos Aires. To do so, priority is given to what one might call ordinary exchanges, leaving aside more solemn exchanges that accompany the multiple festivities and public ceremonies, which have their own temporal rhythm and demand other methods of analysis. For similar reasons, I have also ruled out another important aspect of informal urban sociability, public entertainment, which often formed part of ceremonies and feast days: bullfights, equestrian contests, horse races, *pato* (a local variation of polo) matches, *carreras de sortijas* (horseback relays), theater and public spectacles, cockfights, games of chance, and *bolos* (a kind of skittles) matches, to name but a few.[4] Nevertheless, we will come across some of these more playful forms of sociability in periodic meetings at taverns and cafés, since after the Bourbon reforms of the second half of the eighteenth century these popular events tended to be strictly controlled and confined to closed spaces.[5] For the analysis of ordinary exchanges, I will focus on two types of places: the city as the setting for public sociability and the favored places— liquor stores, *pulperías,* and cafés—of spontaneous male sociability.

The City of Buenos Aires as a Place of Public Sociability

The urban space constitutes one of the settings for sociability. It is often associated with a specific type of sociability whose definition varies according to the period but which—from the modern era and up to the appearance of metropolises or, to use Ariès' term, agglomerations—is based around notions of urbanity, civility. and courtesy.[6] These notions help to define urban behavior, but we can imagine that around these exchanges will appear "reference groups" that delineate the spaces of urban sociability. Here we confine ourselves more to these reference groups than to networks of relationships, as the former appeal more to the space—physical, symbolic, or imaginary—within which the relationship falls, rather than the latter, which can naturally cross over various reference groups—while recognizing that individuals may belong to a variety of groups that will not necessarily coincide with their network of relationships.[7] In order to highlight the organization of social spaces in the postcolonial city, some observations are needed.

THE COLONIAL CITY IN SOUTH AMERICA

> As a notable feature of the physiognomy of this country, one could indicate the confluence of navigable rivers that meet in the east, from all points on the horizon, to meet in the Plate and venerably bestow their stupendous tribute to the ocean, which receives it on the flank, not without visible signs of turbulence and respect.…At its mouth are two cities: Montevideo and Buenos Aires, today alternately reaping the advantages of their enviable position. Buenos Aires is destined one day to be the greatest city of both Americas. With a benign climate, mistress of the navigation of the hundred rivers that flow at her feet, leisurely reclining over an immense territory, and with thirteen provinces with no other way to export their products.…She alone, in the vast expanse of Argentina, has the European nations within her reach; she alone can exploit the advantages of foreign commerce; she alone has power and income.[8]

In 1845, the writer and journalist Domingo Faustino Sarmiento considered a description of the geography of the River Plate an apt way to begin his history of *Civilization and Barbarism*.[9] The decision to begin his work in this way, which at first glance might be categorized as prototypically Braudelian, was in fact part of a considerably different political design. When Sarmiento wrote these lines, the "Argentine Nation" as such was no more than a pipe dream championed by a sector of intellectual elites. In using the geographical argument, Sarmiento tried to prove two things: that a natural national geography existed and that the city of Buenos Aires was at its heart. This insistence on showing that geographical determinism confirmed a governing role over a vast territory for the city rankled all the more given that such determinism was not a historical fact. Indeed, the "physical geography" that made Buenos Aires the gateway for the flow of commerce and culture from different provinces to world markets and vice versa was not even a century old. Until the mid-eighteenth century the coastal region of the River Plate had occupied only a marginal role in an economy and society established around Peru and the Pacific Ocean. Nevertheless, Sarmiento was right to place the city in a space that had previously been limited to exchanges between the port and the vast territories along the road to the silver mines of Potosí. Sarmiento's text is instructive on this point, because it shows that even in the nineteenth century the city of Buenos Aires could not be conceived of outside of the spatial context that had marked it from the previous century, but whose unity was apparently based now on Buenos Aires and the power of an Atlantic economy. The history of urban sociability, and of Argentina in the nineteenth century, cannot be understood without taking into account the history of the city in its regional context.

Buenos Aires was twice founded by the Spanish. The first settlement in 1536 did not long withstand attacks from the Querandí Indians. It was abandoned until 1580, when Juan de Garay took possession of the land and founded the city for the second time, with a population of three hundred souls.[10] The chosen location was the banks of the broad, low-lying basin formed by the estuary of the rivers Paraná and Uruguay. The city stretched out over a plain, bordered to the south by a river which was to act as a port for small boats and river traffic. Twenty years later, the "city" was little more than a poor village, an inferior defense of Alto Peru *(Alto Peru, or Upper Peru, refers to the silver-rich area south of Peru with its center at Potosí, in an area which is modern-day Bolivia.–Translator)* and the last military advance into a territory of rebellious Indians in the extreme south of the continent, home to eighty-one soldiers and their families and some twenty religious folk.[11] The reason for its port location was at the time more strategic—to protect the rearguard of the Viceroyalty of Peru—than economic.

The city soon took advantage of its location. From early in the seventeenth century, the settlement went from being engaged in some port activity—partly from smuggling but also the result of concessions granted by the crown—to a fortified town whose survival depended on communication and exchanges through the port.[12] On this foundation of trade and military activities, the city developed in the course of the seventeenth century as a center of consumption and supply and of storage and forwarding of merchandise, which brought the city into the economic sphere of Alto Peru.[13] This development strengthened the central population of just over seven thousand inhabitants, offering local residents—mostly soldiers, missionaries and bureaucrats—the means to ensure their subsistence and even prosper through merchant activity. In spite of its shabby border town appearance, the "city" appeared to be finally establishing its political function in the midst of a network of colonial cities acting as staging posts for the power of the crown. This may explain why the crown "ennobled" the city in 1716, conferring on it the title of "very noble and loyal."[14] Born on the periphery of the rich Viceroyalty of Peru and having grown up in Lima's shadow, Buenos Aires was able towards the late seventeenth century to consolidate a local economy from its established connections with the Atlantic economy and the road to Alto Peru and the lucrative market of Potosí.[15] In this regional context, it is easier to understand the particular place of Buenos Aires and why, later in the nineteenth century, the city would resist submission to the capital.

The eighteenth century was to confirm Buenos Aires' place in the interregional and Atlantic economy with the creation of the Viceroyalty of the River Plate, which removed the rich provinces of Alto Peru from the jurisdiction of the Viceroyalty of Peru. With the formation of the viceroyalty, Buenos Aires witnessed a growth in its bureaucratic and administrative roles, notably in the establishment of the court of the Real Audiencia in 1783 and the Consulado de Comercio in 1794, allowing Buenos Aires to make the leap from the central city of a government to an actual capital city. In 1778, immediately after the creation of the viceroyalty, the Spanish crown authorized the opening up of the port. The city became the principal Atlantic port for overseas trade in the southern region of the empire, gaining equal footing with Lima, which had heretofore regarded Buenos Aires as a secondary or alternative port for overseas trade.

As a result, Buenos Aires witnessed the greatest demographic growth among Latin American cities.[16] According to Johnson and Socolow's figures, between 1778 and 1810 the population increased 63 percent, or slightly more if Besio Morenio's figures are to be believed.[17] In 1810 there were 44,371 inhabitants, four times the population of 1744.[18] The main reason for this growth was the forced immigration of slaves. Between 1742 and 1806, according to a study by Elena F. S. de Studer, 25,933 slaves legally entered the port of Buenos Aires, a number equivalent to the total population of the city around 1780.[19] This figure modified the characteristics of the urban population considerably, because of a greater presence of blacks and mulattos. This part of the population represented 16.6 percent of all Buenos Aires inhabitants in 1744, rising to 28.4 percent in 1778 and reaching 33 percent in 1810. In addition to this notable demographic growth, from the mid-eighteenth century there was a flow of farmworkers and craftsmen from outside Buenos Aires, attracted by the rapid expansion of agriculture and livestock rearing in the region.[20] Naturally, these workers headed for the surrounding countryside, but some workers may have resided on the outskirts of the city, at least temporarily when work was unavailable in the countryside, since the city could offer alternative means of subsistence.[21]

With the opening up of the port, the city's commercial activities grew, as did the number of people working in this field. Among these, a group of Spanish merchants from Cantabria and Catalonia attained a hegemonic position in the trade circuit.[22] These major traders represented an essential element in liaisons between the regional market and the Atlantic economy. While imports of what were known as "goods from Castile" and metal currency exports from Alto Peru were still predominant, regional products also began to be traded.[23] The intensity of port activity, partly due to the increase in the urban population, allowed the development of complementary activities, such as small businesses, handicrafts, and farming aimed at feeding a rapidly growing urban population.[24] Notably, the most apparent aspects of urban growth can be discerned: a city asserting itself as a center of economic exchange and as the administrative and political head of a vast region, now known as the Viceroyalty of the River Plate, experiencing considerable population growth and becoming one of the most important centers of consumption while offering a concentration of labor.

BUENOS AIRES AND POST-INDEPENDENCE STATUS PROBLEMS

The breakup of the economic and political space of the viceroyalty after the war of independence brought with it considerable changes in the city of Buenos Aires. From an economic perspective, the war meant the loss of the rich provinces of Alto Peru, restructuring the regional economic space and transforming the economy of the province of Buenos Aires, which henceforth would be based on farm production aimed at foreign markets via the port of Buenos Aires. Commercial elites, whose economic interests embraced a wide-ranging market from Potosí to Buenos Aires and from Paraguay to Santiago de Chile, were now more inclined towards overseas trade, cattle raising and the financing of production activities. The global economic situation favored Buenos Aires and its farms enormously, triggering an economic prosperity unheard of in war-torn Latin American economies. From the political perspective, the result of the break with colonial ties was more moderate. Following the insurrectional movement of May 1810, Buenos Aires hoped to inherit the position of capital of the old viceroyalty, but the revolution raised old jurisdictional conflicts between different authorities within the city itself, and between other cities and head mayoralties, checking Buenos Aires' power over viceroyalty territory. After various attempts at constitutional organization, the city of Buenos Aires gave in to the strength of these competing cities' arguments and accepted the organization of the old cities as autonomous provinces.

With the loss of its position as capital of a vast territory, Buenos Aires sought to restructure political institutions in line with changes in its relations with neighboring areas. In 1821, the government of the nascent province of Buenos Aires established a House of Representatives, bringing political representation to the countryside and opening up a divide between city and countryside, which fed new discourse concerning the urban role, simultaneously aimed at affirming the preeminence of the city over the rest of the territory and regaining its position as capital.[25]

However, it is necessary to imagine a city—or large village, in the words of many a disappointed traveler—with an insalubrious climate and 60,471 inhabitants at the time Juan Manuel de Rosas came to power.[26] If travelers' tales are to be believed, Buenos Aires in 1829 was surprising to say the least, in that luxurious tastes alternated with a lack of creature comforts that shocked even the most hardened adventurers.[27] All this added to the paradox of a port city that did not even have a real port. In addition, the shallowness of the River Plate, covered in sandbanks and lashed by strong winds from the pampas, made navigation dangerous, further complicating the approach to Buenos Aires and on occasion forcing boats to anchor thirty miles off the west coast. Crew and goods would then have to be transferred to smaller boats for a second attempt at reaching the port. Lastly, cart drivers would have to drive their carts into the river to pick up passengers where the boats ran aground. While undoubtedly providing a livelihood for a humble population of cart drivers, drovers, and other odd jobbers, the cost of transport was thereby substantially increased, leaving a notoriously bad impression on foreign travelers. In this respect, French traveler Arsène Isabelle's words are most eloquent:

> It is most shameful for Buenos Aires, for such an important town, for the only port in the Argentine Republic…it is shameful, say I, that those very foreigners upon their arrival should come into contact with the greatest rudeness, the most barefaced impertinence from the people of Buenos Aires. It is quite pitiful to be exposed to insults, to the vile epithets of *gringo*, *carcamán*, *godo*, or *sarraceno* which the cart drivers accompany with a thousand obscenities.…There is nothing more ridiculous, nothing more unpleasant, nothing more barbaric than this manner of arriving on a cart mounted on two enormous wheels, the size of our windmills.[28]

Foreigners were all the more disappointed with how little the city resembled the image advertised on pamphlets distributed by liberal Porteños to attract immigrants to the River Plate, which reached risible levels in the cartography of Buenos Aires circulating in this period.[29] We can cite the exemplary case of the map that Rivadavia commissioned from the engineer Bertrès in 1822. Apart from being a good example, this map symbolizes a regime. A sketch on a grid in which each line was presumably a street, finished off with a Marianne *(Most prominent symbol of the French Republic–Translator)* and dedicated to Bernadino Rivadavia, this map was more of a programmatic vision of what the future capital of a republic ought to be rather than a genuine topographic plan of urban structure.[30] The disappointment was all the greater, given that the disillusionment caused by the mediocre urban spectacle cast grave doubts on the status of the city and of the republican regime. Indeed, for new arrivals from the old continent, the image of a free republican society was at odds with the rustic appearance that still characterized the city of Buenos Aires. In this sense, the disappointment revealed by the Englishman John Miers is revealing. The homes of Porteños, he explains, "judging by their appearance of neglect and their miserable exterior seemed more like dungeons than the rooms of an industrious, civilized and free people."[31] Similar feelings inspire F.B. Head's description of the extravagance of Buenos Aires sociability. This English engineer passed through Buenos Aires on business during what he calls the "illusion" of Rivadavian liberalism. In his memoirs he lambastes the absence of *savoir-vivre*, in opposition to the good airs of Buenos Aires society: "In Buenos Aires, men and women rarely walk together; in the theater they are entirely apart; and it is not so jolly to see all of the ladies seated in the boxes while the men sit in the stalls – slaves, simple sailors, soldiers and tradesmen, all members of the same republic."[32] The irony of these observations clearly show the features of Buenos Aires sociability that our engineer found most shocking: the fact that in these public spaces the sexes were segregated while within this segregation the classes were mixed together. Hence it is difficult to see what is it that bothered him the most, the primitive customs and the resulting lack of comfort, or the democratic features that this entailed, as if in his mind one thing did not imply the other, given that unlike Miers, the model from which Head condemns Buenos Aires sociability is very much an aristocratic kind of sociability.

Notwithstanding the credence that we might grant the impressions of these gentlemen in search of exoticism, they steadfastly evoke the dissimilarity between life in Buenos Aires and the city as seen on maps, almanacs and pamphlets circulating both in the River Plate area and in Europe. However, the Rivadavian "happy experience," an expression with which historiographers have baptized this period, had introduced—along with the new discourse of the city—real modifications in the ordering of the urban space.[33] The *Manual de Buenos Aires* gives an example of this. In this manuscript, intended to compliment Bertrès' 1822 map but not ultimately published, the author speaks of the need to administer a city whose growth and melting pot of a population rendered old communication methods ineffective:

> From some years round these parts there has been a need felt in Buenos Aires for all the streets to have different names, for all the houses to be numbered, and that all should have some comfortable and easy means to acquire this knowledge. When a town is small, when its population is scarce, the ease of its inhabitants to walk all the streets, the frequency with which they see each other, and with which they have contact or hear each other named, this alone provides all of the means necessary for their mutual communication....In a

town as large, populated and busy as is Buenos Aires today, these means make such a way impossible; and there is always a considerable number of residents who are unfamiliar with practically all but one part of the city; who look lost in neighborhoods or quarters where they've never been and where they know nobody...[34]

Urban Sociability: Parochial Order in the Social Space

In spite of the efforts of the Rivadavia government,[35] the city of Buenos Aires still gave the impression of a large village in which face-to-face relationships prevailed. Although the *Manual de Buenos Aires* is testimony to transformations which discouraged people from frequenting the city in its entirety, the need to rationalize the urban space seems related, above all, to the imperatives of the urban role with which the city then wished to identify, more than the need to repair the social fabric.[36] From the *Manual* it is possible to distinguish the existence of small units of neighborhood sociability—designated by the name of the most notable inhabitants or the nearest church—with frequent interrelations between inhabitants.[37] Regardless, the fact that people met in church, at the market, or in the corner store does not mean that these were the same social space. I can certainly concur with José Luis Romero on the phenomenon of "interpenetration" of different social groups in everyday encounters in these public spaces, but with the condition that we attend carefully to these terms. The fact that the Plaza de la Victoria was frequented by different sectors of urban society does not provide evidence for the existence of bonds of sociability.[38]

We may take social microspaces—made up of the family and the relational network of individuals interacting with each other—as a clear starting point. Research into the history of the colonial family has tended to highlight the impact of family networks over the spatial and social structure of the urban space.[39] However, based on our own knowledge it seems difficult to deduce the existence in the city of Buenos Aires of neighborhoods based on family lineage, as in the model described by G. Delille.[40] We are rather more inclined to believe that other forms of spatial organization connected these social microspaces. As the *Manual de Buenos Aires* suggests, the 1822 population was itself divided into small neighborhood units. Numerous sources refer to the existence of these *barrios* and the importance of neighborly ties in social relationships.[41] We need to discover the limits of these neighborhood community spaces, in the context of which urban sociability ties were formed.[42] To avoid the a priori use of analytical categories, we can start from the observation of elements that organized the urban space: urban structure, principal axes of movement, and meeting points (figure 1). In observing the map of the city's urban structure, the grid design, characteristic of

Spanish cities in the Americas, is the first noticeable aspect. In accordance with the typology of urban forms in Ibero-American cities, Buenos Aires, exemplifies a classic model except in the location of its central square, which in the interests of port access was not centrally positioned;[43] this observation is true of most of the squares and markets. Although on the whole they were distributed evenly around the urban space, they tended to be close to the river. This is a city, therefore, whose organization of space was equally regulated by an established Spanish model and by geographic specifics. It can also be noted that both the squares and markets tended to be located near to the principal axes of movement, the most important of which was the east-west route connecting the city with the other provinces of the former Viceroyalty of the River Plate (the former royal road from the west, called "calle de la Federación" during the Rosas government and from 1857 "Bernadino Rivadavia"), and the road from the south leading to the port at the mouth of the River Riachuelo.[44] Around these axes we find the marketplaces that were as important for social transactions as for commercial transactions.[45] Traders arriving from the country would park their carts here to sell their products and could remain here during their entire stay in the city. These squares, which brought together economic and social functions, were important centers in attracting inhabitants.[46] Churches and their entrance areas also played a part as an organizing element of social space because of their importance in community life, through births, weddings, deaths; in urban sociability, through participation in associations, public festivities, and even education; and in economic life, not only because religious congregations were economic actors but also because they could participate in corporate organization with their brethren.

To some extent, these different urban, economic, and cultural factors conditioned social relationships in the city, in stimulating and facilitating encounters between residents in spaces whose boundaries were unavoidably vague. There were, however, other elements intervening in the structure of spaces of sociability, such as the jurisdictional divisions of different authorities regulating the lives of the people. Some of the various units of influence over the structure of social spaces included parishes and ecclesiastic divisions; the districts of justices of the peace; the area of influence of the *alcaldes* (mayors), themselves dependent on police precincts; judicial districts, to which justices of the peace were assigned under the authority of the examining magistrates; and police districts delimiting the boundaries of city precincts.[47]

The conclusions that can be garnered from figure 2 are quite revealing in terms of the organization of the urban space. First, the boundaries of each of the divisions were not superimposed entirely on each other, most probably for administrative reasons. But if one compares the areas with the meeting points around which

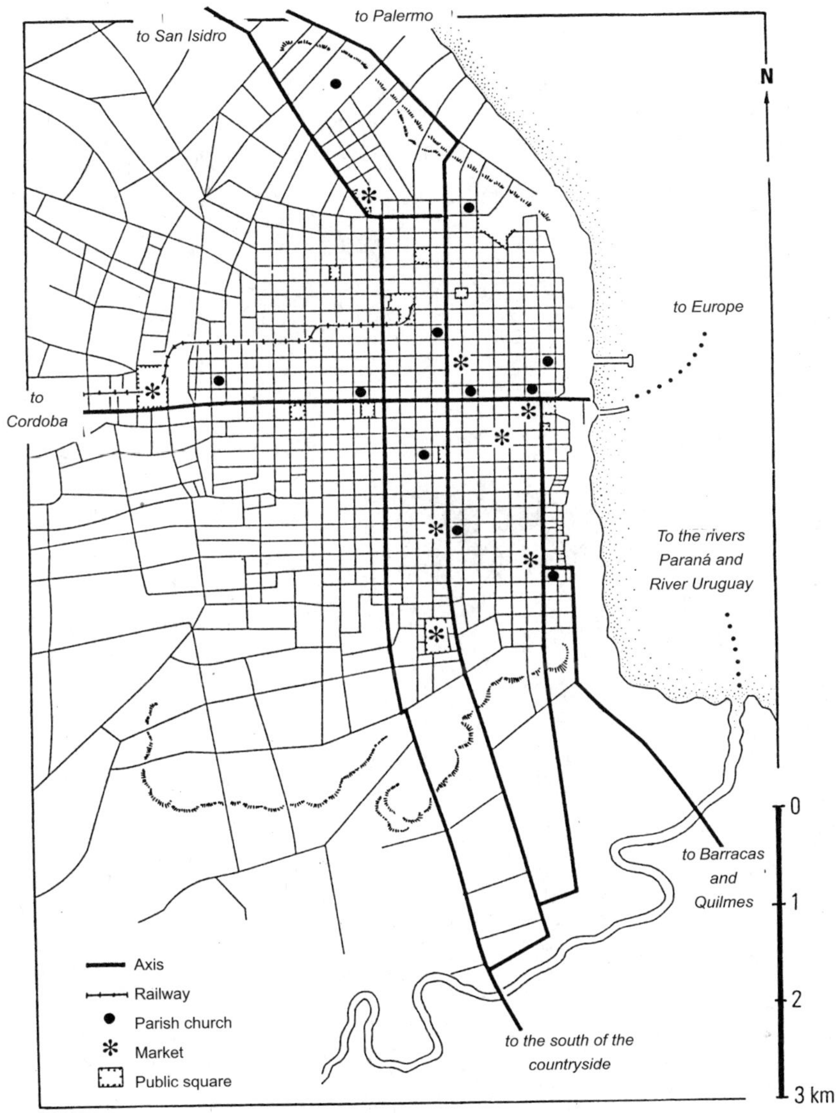

Figure 1. Buenos Aires: Location and Urban Structure

Principal axes of movement and meeting points (1820–1862)

Cartography by Pilar González Bernaldo and Françoise Vergneault, EHESS, 1990

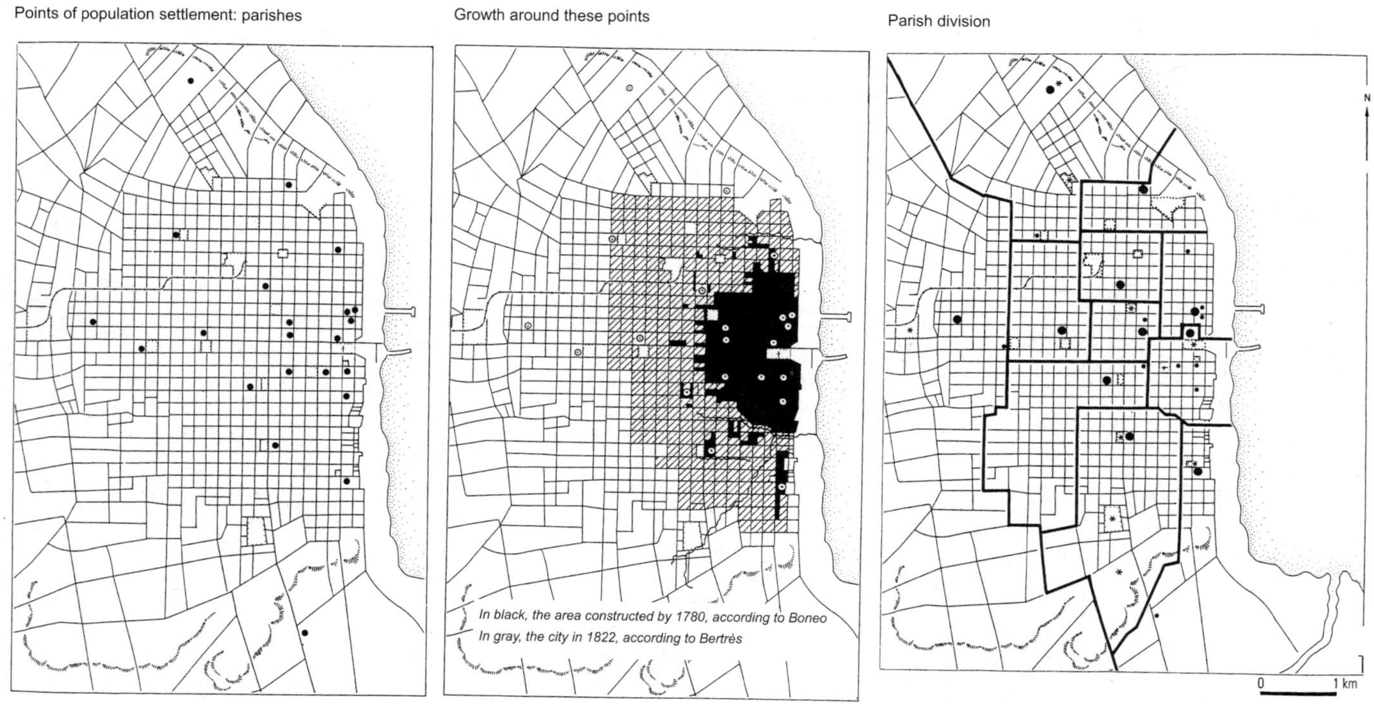

Figure 2. The religious community and the origin of neighborhood sociability

A. The organization of the urban space around parish churches.

Source: Taullard, *Los planos más antiguos de Buenos Aires* (Buenos Aires, 1940).

B. Other divisions of the urban space (1829-1862)

Source: Manuel R. Trelles, *Registro estadístico del Estado de Buenos Aires,* 1858, vol. 1, Buenos Aires, *La Tribuna,* 1859.

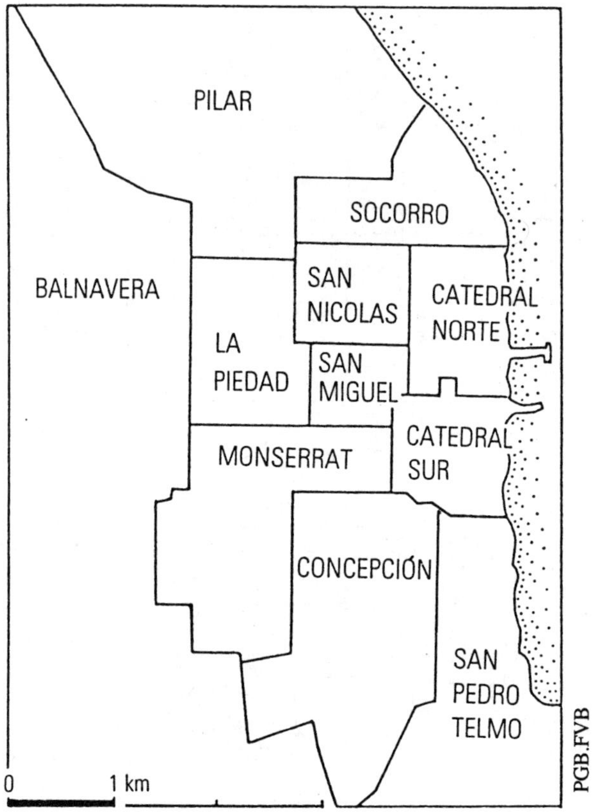

C. The parishes and their names

social life was organized, such as squares and markets, one notices that parochial divisions best account for the spatial distribution of the neighborhood community, essentially because it was the parish that grouped in the most homogenous way the different meeting places into more or less coherent units. A comparison of the grid design and the size of the different districts allows one to reach this conclusion. How else can one interpret the fact that, in such a geometric city, a strange irregularity in the plan allows Catedral al Sur parish to incorporate the block where the Catedral de Buenos Aires is located? This was the *barrio* where the city's most notable figures resided, and it is well known that these well-to-do folk benefited from the prestige surrounding the cathedral. By the same token, in comparing the different maps in question, one notices the variation in size of the different areas: the parochial division shows a disparity in the size of the districts with regards to the limits of the *cuarteles* or police districts. Furthermore, the parish boundaries best reflect the growth rate of the city of Buenos Aires.

Indeed, the oldest parishes, which are also the smallest, are found in the city center. The further the parish is from the center, the greater its size (figure 2a). The second map shows the built area and the hydrography of the city of Buenos Aires in 1780 according to the data from Boneo's map and the same aspects of the city in 1822 from Bertrès' map. Superimposing this information onto the urban structure of 1859 highlights the mode of urban development in Buenos Aires:[48] The city grows along its principal axes (the royal road from the west and the old port road); this expansion is accompanied by the creation of new churches, which would later become parish churches. Hence, along the port road to the south the most built-up area is around the church of San Pedro de Telmo, which became a parish church in 1813. To the west we can distinguish the beginnings of urban development around the churches of Monserrat and Nuestra Señora de la Piedad, both parish churches since 1769.

Furthermore, parish limits are the only ones that take into account geographic features, which at the same time are quite revealing as to the social use of physical space. Hence the limit between the parish of the Catedral al Sur and that of San Pedro Telmo follows the course of a stream crossing the south of the city and flowing into the River Plate. Likewise, to the north, the border between the parishes of Nuestra Señora del Socorro and Catedral del Norte follows the course of another stream. In times of rains and rises in the water level, the course of these waters functioned as genuine geographic boundaries.

In this analysis we find a first indication of the organization of the urban space as a neighborhood community administered by the parish. In the structure of these spaces the characteristics of the urban structure come into play as much as the role of the different parochial authorities. Among these, the influence of the priest and the justice of the peace, who resolved disputes and acted as a conciliator between the inhabitants of a parish, seems to have had decisive importance in the structure of spaces of social interaction, which although not closed or fixed by genuinely set boundaries could nevertheless function as a reference group.[49] The task then consists of evaluating the vitality of this religious community, which at the same time is a community of places, with regards to other spheres of sociability of Buenos Aires' inhabitants.

CELLS OF NEIGHBORHOOD SOCIABILITY: THE PULPERIAS

According to some etymologists, the word *pulpería* is a derivation of *pulque*, a Mexican term of uncertain origin, possibly from the Nahuatl *puliuki*, the name of a fermented drink made from the juice of certain agave plants, namely the *maguey* or the *zabila*;[50] the *pulquería* (in Mexico) or *pulpería* (in Argentina) came to be the place where *pulque* or other alcoholic drinks were sold. Among the advocates of this "Americanist" thesis, there are some regional variations. In the River Plate area some claim that *pulque* is a derivation of the Mapuche term *pulcú*, the name Patagonian natives gave to the local *aguardiente*, a kind of liquor.[51] Others, such as the eminent Spanish etymologist J. Corominas, defend the "Hispanicist" thesis. This thesis argues that *pulpería* derives from the word *pulpa* (pulp), from the Latin *pulpa*. Hence in the Americas, the word *pulpería* was used to describe any place selling fleshy fruits, characteristic of the tropics, and by extension the trade in foods.[52] Underlying the etymologists' argument is another issue not tackled in this debate, that of social practices, given that these theses refer to two quite contrasting practices. In the "Americanist" thesis, the *pulpería* was a place selling the indigenous alcoholic *pulque* drink. For the Hispanicists, it was a place of exchange, frequently with bartering, established after the arrival of the Spanish (*pulpa*). In the first case, the *pulpería-pulquería* is a place of popular sociability which presumably originated from an autochthonous custom of "drinking in public," while the second theory indicates a place of exchange tied to the world of the conquistadors and which does not necessarily imply a meeting place.

The function of the *pulpería* such as we find it in Buenos Aires in the nineteenth century corresponds to both definitions, insofar as it was at once a liquor store and general store. The *pulpería* hosted periodic social gatherings—*tertulias*—based on a more or less regular male clientele drinking alcohol.[53] However, unlike the *pulquerías* of Mexico, where the *pulque* drinking was part of a representation of a world in which alcohol and drunkenness play very important ancient ritualistic and sacred roles, the sociability woven around the drinking of wine or *aguardiente* belonged to a highly distinct Judeo-Christian culture.[54] Spanish sources, on the other hand, clearly distinguish between these two meeting places in cases pertaining to controlling a practice that authorities considered the cause of all kinds of disturbances.[55] In the eyes of the Spanish authorities, the *pulperías* of the River Plate seem to be part of the tradition of sociability in taverns, which implied a specific type of control and repression.[56]

BUSINESS AND PLEASURE IN BUENOS AIRES

It is surprising how these businesses and places of sociability grew in the city of Buenos Aires. The earliest references date from the early seventeenth century; by 1682 the town's governors were already expressing concern about the development of the *pulperías*.[57] However, we have no testimony as to the *pulpería* as a meeting place up until the order of the governor José Bermúdez de Castro in Buenos Aires in 1715.[58] The "city," which at the time had a mere 8,908 inhabitants, had

300 *pulperías* over a built area of one square kilometer, that is, one *pulpería* per 30 inhabitants, with a density of 2.88 *pulperías* every 10,000 square meters—an enormous number.[59] For the late eighteenth century, Johnson and Socolow count 428 *pulperías* in a city of 26,165 inhabitants, one per 61 inhabitants. In 1813 a government census listed 457 *pulperías* for a city of around 40,000 inhabitants (1/87); thirteen years later, Blondel's almanac listed 464, while Kinsbruner suggests the figure was 502 *pulperías*, one per 119 inhabitants. From the eighteenth century on the proportion of *pulperías* to inhabitants fell from 1/30 to 1/119, but these are still considerable figures in comparison with such businesses in other cities of the empire.[60] These figures must be compared with the economic potential of the city.[61] Nevertheless, they indicate the intensity of an urban sociability, or at least its potential, all the more so given that in Buenos Aires these stores were also liquor stores and meeting places.[62]

The first colonial reference to the sale of alcohol in the *pulperías*, according to Rodríguez Molas, dates from 23 March 1600, twenty years after the second founding of the city of Santa María de los Buenos Aires. At that time a *pulpero* (*pulpería* owner) was fined for selling wine to Indians.[63] Throughout the seventeenth century, but especially in the second half of the century, the Cabildo introduced a multitude of measures aimed at checking the provision of wines and *aguardiente*, in addition to controlling prices, but we have no testimony as to the *pulpería* as an established meeting place until the order of governor José Bermúdez de Castro. From this moment on there is an abundance of references to "gatherings of vagrants" and laws aimed at bringing such affairs under control. It is clear that, as Viqueira Albán shows in the case of Mexico, the increase in reports and complaints must also have been related to a manifest will of social control characteristic of the politics of the Bourbons, accentuated in some regions of the empire because of a chronic lack of laborers.[64] The "counter" conflict that broke out in the late eighteenth century shows clearly that by this time the practice was well established in the urban environment.

The "counter" dispute began in 1788 when the attorney general of the city, Francisco José de Ugarte, prohibited gatherings of people and guitars in *pulperías*, while protecting the purely commercial roles of these businesses. Ugarte then ordered the mostly Spanish proprietors to place their counters in the street, which had the double advantage of bothering a clientele susceptible to prolonging their stay beyond their commercial transactions and facilitating checks on these gatherings around a drink and a guitar. The measures were not at all to the liking of the proprietors, who opposed them vehemently, arguing that they were more at risk from robberies. Indeed, if clients could make their purchase without dismounting from their horse, there was nothing to stop them from

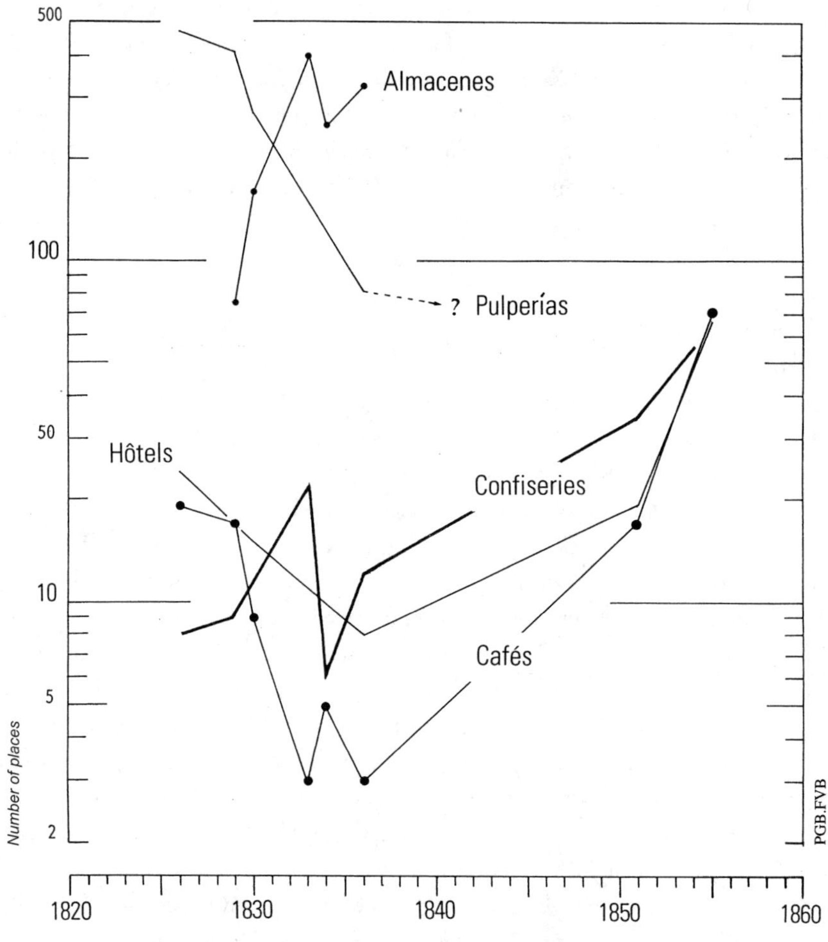

Figure 3. Development in the Number of Liquor Stores and Meeting Places in Buenos Aires (1825–1855)

Source: *Almanaque de comercio*, 1825, 1829, 1830, 1834, 1836, 1851, 1855

(*"Almacenes" are a type of general store; "confiterías" are a type of well-to-do teahouse and cake shop.–Translator)*

leaving without paying the bill. The proprietors also argued that given the new conditions, consumption on the premises would be considerably diminished. The "counter" dispute was to keep *pulperos* and the colonial authorities at loggerheads for some time.[65] In the absence of any immediate solutions, the counters stayed in place and the prohibition was maintained for "any gathering of persons, guitars or card games in the *pulperías*."[66] This result indicates not only the vitality of the practice and power of the association but also the will of the city authorities to put an end to them.

The conflict continued after Buenos Aires ceased to be a colony. Two years after the insurrection in the city of Buenos Aires, the issue of the counters reappeared. This time it was the revolutionary government that wished to put an end to certain practices of sociability, which, in their judgment, encouraged vagrancy, alcoholism and delinquency. Still, this did not deter the government from taking advantage of them for the revolutionary cause, particularly given the impossibility of putting an end to such deep-rooted habits. So it was that an edict from the Cabildo of Buenos Aires dated 19 August 1812 suggested that, in place of obscenities, paeans might be sung for freedom and the fatherland.[67] This edict, however, is the exception that proves the rule. Indeed, the revolutionary government tended to distrust these kinds of gatherings, which encouraged alcoholism and social disorder and above all incited disobedience. Hence it was to these meeting places that the powers that be went in search of "patriotic volunteers" for the war of independence. Then when this voluntary patriotism missed its appointment, the application of vagrancy laws assured a less spontaneous though equally effective recruitment. In fact, or at least according to legislation, anyone not in possession of a *papaleta de conchabo* was in the eyes of the law a vagrant, and the law provided that such vagrants could be press-ganged into the army for two to five years. Such was the connection between public pastimes and delinquency: It is hard to imagine conversations and songs in the *pulperías* in praise of the government.[68]

Unable to prevent a widespread practice among the urban population, the liberal Rivadavia government attempted to at least move it away from the center. Rivadavia introduced a regulation establishing five kinds of licenses for businesses in Buenos Aires. According to this regulation, the cost of a *pulpería* license was tripled for businesses in the center, with the owner's prices no doubt suffering a similar fate.[69] The persuasive power of these measures was patently limited. In 1826 there were 464 *pulperías*. While they would later decrease in number between the first Rosas government of 1829 and the second of 1835, this type of business and place continued to exert a deep-rooted influence in the city of Buenos Aires.[70]

A place of leisure, of the depravation of the urban masses, if authoritative reports are to be believed, the *pulpería* also constituted one of the gears in the local socioeconomic system. The phenomenon of multifunctional meeting places is one of the characteristic features of spontaneous sociability, most marked in popular sectors.[71] In the case of the *pulperías,* however, there was a notable feature worth investigating, which lay in the kind of exchanges associated with this form of popular entertainment. Indeed, drunkenness constituted what is known as nonequivalent commercial exchange, characteristic of transactions whereby the salesman bases a part of his profits on the fact of his monopoly position. Applied to the world of the abattoir worker, this meant that payment—if there was a monetary payment—passed directly into the hands of the *pulpero*, who became the worker's creditor, through a subtle combination of the provision of victuals on credit and the consumption of alcohol on the premises. The worker could always try to pay off his debt by selling certain products, at a price fixed by the *pulpero*. In certain cases, the *pulpero* was also the employer, examples of which abounded in the countryside; in others, the worker came to an arrangement with the *pulpero* to draw his wage.[72] In this way, sale on credit in the *pulpería* could work as the missing link in merchant credit forms, which in the absence of metallurgy or a genuine labor market contributed to strengthening the dominance of commercial capital.[73] For the authorities, however, the presumed culprit in the people's debts was gambling and not the kind of exchange between customer and *pulpero*.[74]

This allows us to outline better the complexity of relationships surrounding these practices and the difficulties into which the authorities could run in reconciling such opposed interests. Indeed, how do you reconcile the will of social order with the commercial interests of those who demanded such order? Furthermore, the authorities could condemn outright those gatherings that encouraged vagrancy. However, these customs could be used to their advantage, both as a way of legally and freely replacing scarce labor and guaranteeing electoral triumph. From all this we can conclude that popular sociability in the *pulperías* was profoundly rooted in the socioeconomic and political dynamic of local society, which explains the vigor of these practices until the mid-nineteenth century. Their disappearance indicates an important transformation in socioeconomic structures and urban sociability.[75]

THE LIQUOR STORE AND ITS CLIENTELE

Sources indicate on numerous occasions the social background of the *pulperías*' regular customers. Police reports used the term "vagrants" to refer to the clientele in search of leisure at the bottom of a glass. This appellation gives us little in the way of information as to social background, as long as we accept that the "vice" of drinking in public was not exclusive to the lower classes, as would appear to be the case in one report by police captain Elías Bayala. He writes that "rowdy parties and public festivities where commoners participate" were frequented by "idle persons and good-for-nothings, in addition to the sons of both noble and common families, who leave their houses furtively and without parental permission and pervert themselves with all kinds of vices, which lead to thefts, deaths and other things."[76]

It would seem, nevertheless, that throughout the nineteenth century the well-to-do tended to disapprove of these meeting places or, at least, the authorities were inclined to associate this manly pleasure more with plebeian vice than bourgeois idleness.[77] Be that as it may, this does not allow us to form a conclusion as to the popular nature of practices and clientele, above all because in these meeting places we can find elements belonging to the cultural universe of the well-to-do, such as the drinking of wine and the presence of the press.[78] We also find less "noble" cultural objects such as the guitar, although this is an instrument associated with Hispanic culture, unlike the *tamboril* drums used by African Argentines and which were scarcely found in urban *pulperías*.

Sources appear to identify *pulpería* clientele as members of the neighborhood. For example, due to a decree of November 1829, the *pulpero* Martín Canon was convicted for "having a gathering on his corner on November 11th,"[79] a Sunday, which was prohibited by the decree. Canon responded to the accusations, denying that he had "had a gathering of drunkards, as the individuals who were there were Don Manuel Rodríguez, owner of the land, Don José Cabral, next-door neighbor, Don Doroteo Campusano and Don José Maria Ramos, the latter two friends of mine who had just come in to visit when the watchman opened the door, and who assert that there was no gathering and that they were not drinking but in conversation."[80] The reference to the presence of an individual from the neighborhood allows for two differing interpretations. It may be an indication of the quality of the clientele in these meeting places, or alternatively it may be that the owner makes use of the reference to his neighborhood to prove that this was not a "gathering of drunkards," for which *pulperías* were suspected of being a cover. This interpretation does not contradict the first, rather it leaves us to suppose that there were two kinds of possible clientele: neighbors, supposedly more prudent and moderate—or rather, less inebriated—and the others, the strangers who would visit the *pulpería* only to drink and who were the root of all kinds of trouble. These worried less about the authorities, given that they were "passing through" and therefore considered to be of no fixed address, feared police repression less and were more inclined towards violence.

On this point we find more precise indications from the police captain responsible for law and order in the city, dated 31 January 1833. The captain informs his superior, Bernardo Victorica, of results attained "after cleaning up one neighborhood of dangerous men and vagrants..." To do so, our captain naturally went to pick them up at the *pulpería*.[81] In March of the same year, the captain of the fourth precinct (Catedral al Sur parish) gave information about one *pulpería* which was found to be open at half past one in the morning and "in which a gathering was taking place." The owner, José María Benavente, refused to close the bar and, according to the police captain, responded in a very unfriendly tone, which earned him a place on police records. The defense lawyer requested that the plaintiff be acquitted, claiming "that the *pulpero* José M. Benavente was probably not alone in his *pulpería* open at half past one in the morning, or that perchance he had opened it in order to let in fresh air on a hot night, in which case it is difficult to deprive a neighbor of relief in such silent hours if furthermore this did not harm public order."[82] Another reference appeared in 1838 in the trial of Antonio Pérez on charges of inconveniencing the *pulpero* and speaking publicly against Juan Manuel de Rosas."[83] The dispute began with a disagreement over prices between the client and the proprietor. According to the *pulpero*, the client, having drunk more than his fair share, considered that he had been overcharged on his check. Thus began one of many classic conflicts between the *pulpero*, generally protected by a grille separating the counter from the saloon, and the customer, in which the remainder of those present—though this was not the case here—frequently joined in, according to the authorities because of drunkenness, and possibly because they saw the opportunity to argue their own debts. For the clientele, such disputes promised a magnificent free-for-all. At times—indeed often—the dispute ended in a far less friendly manner, with a kind of knife duel (*cuchillada*) which, pardoning the pun, cut short any kind of argument. One of the witnesses in the Pérez case stated: "Pérez began to insult the *pulpero*, who said to him: 'sir, you keep cursing me, neighbors though we are,' but he kept cursing him."[84] This testimony confirms the existence of a clientele made up of the neighboring community but also suggests, as we have indicated, the presence of a more feared clientele from further afield, made up of residents from the outskirts of the city and outlying areas who traveled to the city to buy provisions and sell products from their small holdings from time to time, and of cart drivers and muleteers who regularly visited the *pulpería*.

Nevertheless, the frequency of the gatherings at a *pulpería* did turn some occasional clients into regulars. It is common to find in the *clasificaciones*—a kind of register of police records which Rosas used to understand the political mood of the population—the mention of the *pulpería* of which the person was a "regular visitor." To cite one of many examples, a notice of imprisonment of three muleteers not resident in the city, gives the following information: "they tend to go opposite Mr. José María Benavente's place, to the *pulpería* de la Salomé."[85] While for locals the *pulpería* reinforced primary ties around the notion of a community of places, in the same way as the marketplace or parish church,"outsiders" could join this network through secondary ties, ties of sociability.[86] The network of relationships is constructed nevertheless in the social space of neighborhood sociability, as the analysis of the urban location appears to suggest.

The diagrams of the positions of the *pulperías* (figure 4) show that these were distributed fairly evenly around the city.[87] Nevertheless, a more notable development can be detected around the principal roads which also coincided with the locations of markets. This is the case of the first point on the map, corresponding to the street leading to the River Riachuelo and the old city port (diagram B). From here came the wares transported mainly by river from the Mesopotamian region *(In Argentina, this refers to the region north of Buenos Aires between the rivers Iguazú, Paraná and Uruguay, consisting of the provinces of Entre Ríos, Corrientes and Misiones.–Translator).* The street also led over the Barracas bridge to the area of abattoirs and meat-curing plants. The roads crossing the bridge led to the Plaza del Comercio in San Telmo parish, one of the most important markets in the city. The second point, from south to north, is the Plaza de la Concepción. The third, situated towards the Monserrat barrio, was the most popular and populous, and where the majority of the black population lived. This was also the heart of the city. The same observations apply to the north side of the city (diagram A, 1826). In diagram B, from 1826, but from north to south, the positioning on the principal roads is clearer. In 1930 the trends seen on the geo-graph of 1826 continued. On almost all of the streets there was at least one *pulpería.* Nevertheless, it is interesting to note that these were more numerous at crossroads and commercial exchanges. In diagram A (1830) three points can clearly be seen which coincide with Plaza del Comercio, Plaza Monserrat and Plaza San Miguel and Plaza de la Victoria. In diagram B, the street with the highest concentration of *pulperías* is Bolívar, which leads from the rural area in the south to the city. From the north side it is Artes, which joined the roads from the wheat growing area of San Isidro.[88] If we compare the diagrams corresponding to 1826 and 1830, we can generally distinguish a uniform growth of *pulperías* in the urban space as a whole. This confirms the popularity of this practice and sheds light on the nature of the clientele from a different perspective. Taking into account the evenness of *pulpería* distribution throughout the city, it clear that the regulars of each *pulpería* were most probably its very neighbors. It is most likely that the *pulpería*, often called the corner, was in the same concept as the neighborhood square and parish church, the space where a form of neighborly sociability took place.

A New Urban Phenomenon: Café Gatherings

While the origins of public gatherings in *pulperías* apply to the oldest forms of public sociability and therefore are difficult to date, the beginnings of the fashion for gatherings in café salons offers a more accurate chronology. The first legal reference to the existence of this type of business in the city of Buenos Aires dates, according to Bossio, from 1764: The "Viejo Almacén del Rey."[89] The first regulation applied to cafés, again according to Bossio, dates from 1779, when Viceroy Vértiz passed a decree allowing the detention of "any vagabond found in *pulperías, casas de truco (Places where the popular card game truco was played.–Translator),* cafés or other places of gaming with cards, or other prohibited games."[90] The same year saw the opening of the "Café de los Catalanes," in which, according to Vicente Fidel López, the first meetings against the viceroy were held.[91]

A significant change appears to have come about in these places in the early nineteenth century. At this time, gatherings in cafés tended to differ clearly from other forms of leisurely sociability. In this aspect it is interesting to note that the first regulations aimed at controlling meetings in *pulperías* were simultaneous with the specific social nature acquired by gatherings in cafés; indeed, it is possible to see a correlation between the two phenomena. The well-to-do who previously only visited the drinking establishments of their own neighborhood when inclined towards gambling and gentlemen's meetings, could now find a place that offered the same advantages but with a more select clientele in cafés. As a result, the *pulperías* became more dangerous in the eyes of the authorities, and at the same time, easier to control due to the absence of more influential customers.

If the account of the traveler Beaumont is to be believed, meetings in cafés were widespread practice among men, at least between 1826 and 1827 during Beaumont's stay in the city. In his memoirs he indicates that "the cafés of Buenos Aires are popular places. A large part of the public meets there every night to play cards and billiards.... There are six considered as principal cafés, and many others of a lower order, all of which contributes, most unfortunately, to a lack of homely habits among the male population."[92] Gálvez confirms and expands on these impressions in his memoirs, acknowledging distinctions between the clientele of different cafés, which nonetheless in all cases concerned members of the well-to-do class.[93] Some places received students, others tradesmen or members of the military. Hence, the Café de la Victoria, in the square of the same name in the wealthiest parish of the city, attracted a more "aristocratic" clientele who rarely dabbled in political plotting, while the Café de los Catalanes, located in the north of Buenos Aires, attracted a more "democratic" clientele. Occasionally one café might become the meeting place of different groups. Gálvez gives the example of the famous café de Marco. While the young newspaper owners met in the central salon, "the magnates of the time did their business in the immense patio, around a multitude of tables, as there was no stock exchange."[94]

These different testimonies mention the coexistence of these public forms of male sociability with the traditional social gatherings, or *tertulias*, in family houses but also point out the simultaneous development of the custom of meeting in cafés, particularly among young bachelors.[95] This would contradict Mark Szuchman's idea of the well-to-do as people retired in their private space and with no participation in the diverse forms of public entertainment, except in activities associated with religious or patriotic festivities.[96] Naturally, it is important to bear in mind the different degrees of intensity in practices of public sociability.[97] Szuchman's affirmation is probably based on the evidence of the liveliness of popular sociability during periodic meetings in *pulperías* in comparison with the cafés, which were yet to establish themselves.[98] Blondel's almanac of 1826 indicates that in Buenos Aires there were 19 cafés and 470 *pulperías*. These differences are nevertheless logical if one bears in mind that the *pulpería* was also a general store and that its number should be related to the need for supplies of the whole population of the city. Furthermore, as the popular classes accounted for far more of the population than the elite, it is only natural that their meeting places should outnumber those of the elite. In any case it can be agreed that the popularity of public sociability in *pulperías* is not in itself an indication of the reclusion of the elites in private spaces.

Nevertheless, temporal variations between the habits of sociability of the elites and of the popular sectors are of some interest, namely the hours each sector kept for public sociability were not the same. The urban masses met in *pulperías* on days of rest—Sundays and public holidays—but also during the obligatory daily siesta when police control was most lax. At this time of the day the well-to-do slept in their homes, fearing the deserted streets and the risk of breaking decorum, preferring the morning or the evening for their public meetings. On Sundays and public holidays they would leave the city for country walks and frequent stays at country houses. Both Beaumont and Isabelle inform us of these variations in the calendar of the everyday sociability of the inhabitants of Buenos Aires. Beaumont recounts, for example, that among the elites

> the gentlemen, having slept the siesta (a nap of some two or three hours after lunch) smoke their cigars and go to cafés, where they play cards or billiards, or visit the theatre....The ladies, after the siesta, make their visits with very little etiquette and spend the afternoon in small *tertulias*, in animated conversation, where they receive favor from all of the suitors who can enter this circle; but a young man, unless he is in love, rarely devotes his time to *tertulias*...[99]

The evening, as Isabelle reports, was the time when high society showed itself off: ladies and gentlemen strolling along the avenues, gentlemen gathering in the cafés, and ladies in the *tertulias* of their family homes.[100] This division of time could function as a social border marking a particularly elite public space, which would otherwise be shared between the well-to-do and the urban masses.

CAFE SOCIABILITY: A NEW DEFINITION OF PUBLIC ENTERTAINMENT

Like the *pulperías*, cafés were liquor stores where a drink could be enjoyed along with a game of billiards or the ever-popular card matches. However, cafés offered no opportunities for stocking up on other consumer goods. Musical entertainment was also present in cafés but influenced by the tastes of a more educated audience: evening concerts with nobler instruments now replaced popular songfests accompanied by the Spanish guitar. At first sight it might be said that here was the same need for male sociability directed at a clientele of distinct social extraction. However, there are differences in the way entertainment was conceived. As the *tertulia* was possible in either of the two places, gatherings in cafés appear to have been predisposed towards a specific type of public culture: public opinion.

The relationships between the development of a new clientele and this kind of sociability are evident from the establishment of the first cafés in Buenos Aires. A month after opening of the Café de Marco, for example, there was already a group of "young doctors," regular customers who included promoters of the first newspaper published in the city, the *Telégrafo Mercantil*, which appeared the same year.[101] The role of this circle of intellectuals, self-proclaimed the "club del café de Marco," in the Buenos Aires insurrection is too well known for us to dwell on here.[102]

Perhaps it is enough to remember the disturbing character that these meetings rapidly acquired, which ultimately convinced the "revolutionary" government of the city of the need to prohibit them. But more than evoking the specific features of the insurrection of the *cabildos* of the region, the important issue here is to highlight the relationship between sociability in cafés and the new revolutionary power, critical to the emergence of a space for public opinion. The Café de Marco is an undoubtedly magnificent example but is not the only one.[103] During the "Rivadavian" period and even up to the second Rosas government, there were glimpses of what, from 1852, would be a marked trend: the establishment of a modern political structure using the institutions of public sociability as the basis of political power. Forms of sociability such as gatherings in cafés were identified increasingly with the new political power to the extent that they became a public sphere themselves, more literary during the first Rosas government, more political afterwards. They were frequently associated with the publication of a newspaper and later with "political parties."[104]

Seemingly, those most attracted to these practices were understandably young men of a high cultural level. A clientele of students entails a certain age group, which in turn indicates that they were bachelors without family responsibilities.

This facilitated the development of a practice, which at the time was perceived as harmful to family morals. It remains to be seen whether these young students of the "principal families," among whom the habit of gathering in cafés became common, satisfied their new needs for sociability within the context of the community of places or whether these practices left them outside of the traditional structure of urban sociability.

CAFE CLIENTELE IN THE URBAN SPACE

The cafés' geographic locations confirms the relationship between sociability in cafés and cultural activity. Figure 4 shows that of the nineteen recorded cafés in Buenos Aires in 1826, thirteen were on the south side of the city and centered around the Manzana de las Luces, a ten-thousand-square-meter block of buildings where Porteño social life was concentrated: the University of Buenos Aires, the Museum of Natural History, the City Public Library, and such private schools as the Escuela Argentina, the Ateneo de Señoritas, the Ateneo, and the Escuela de Comercio. It was also close to the center of power: the seat of the governor, the provincial legislature, and the Supreme Court. This was also in the wealthiest and most frequented parish of the time, Catedral al Sur. In the diagrams of 1830 it is possible to see clearly the concentration of cafés around these places of culture. At this date there were nine cafés, of which five were around the Manzana de las Luces, which gives another indication as to the type of clientele these places were likely to receive: principally the students who frequented the neighborhood. One might also consider the neighbors of the parish. However, it is important to note that there was a great difference with regards to spaces of sociability in general stores and liquor stores. While *pulperías* were distributed homogeneously throughout the city, cafés were grouped together. This concentration implies a specialization in the urban space, and therefore of a clientele which by necessity was not resident in the area.

In fact, when we speak of specialization of urban space, we take into account the dimensions of the city of Buenos Aires, which leads one to think more of one large *barrio*. Indeed, even considering urban structure in one of the later maps (1859), it can be seen that the distance between the suburbs and the center never exceeds four kilometers. If we take the city as it is shown on Bertrès' map or in the reproduction ordered by Rosas in 1840, the distances are as short as one and a half to two kilometers. That is, in spite of the notable increase in urban surface, it was possible to walk to any point in the city in one hour. As Szuchman noted, Buenos Aires is a city of small dimensions.[105] However, these dimensions do not themselves constitute an argument against the existence of a neighborhood life.[106] The size of the city is an indication of the existence of time and space to facilitate human relationships and ultimately the speed with which they could be

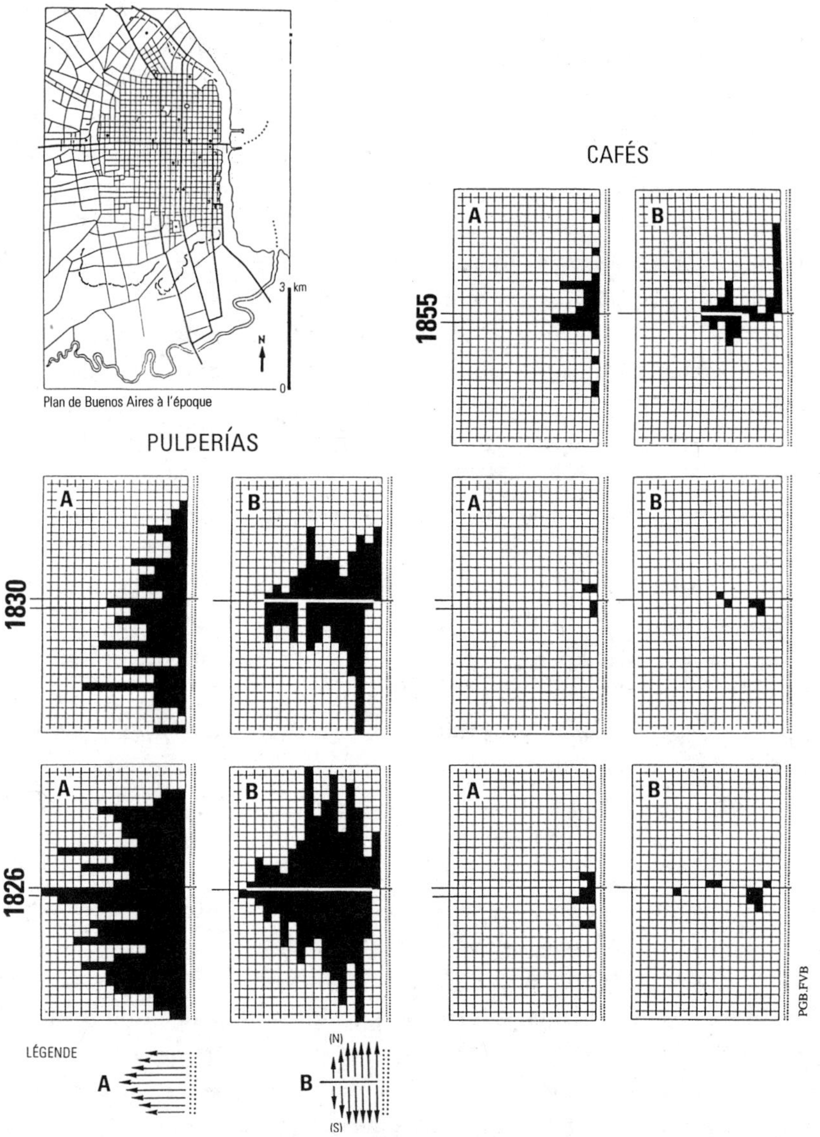

Figure 4. Geo-graphs of the development of places of sociability in the city between 1826 and 1855

The diagrams repeat the topological structure of the city, with each black square corresponding to an establishment. In A, the squares are placed on a horizontal grid, starting from the estuary. In B, they are placed from up (north) to down (south), from one side to the other of the principal horizontal axis leading from the estuary to the west.

established, but it does not tell us in any way about the configuration of social spaces. It is necessary to know whether it was enough for men to rub shoulders with each other in their own neighborhood or whether they had to move across the city to satisfy the need for sociability. The concentration of cafés in one part of the city suggests a specific kind of clientele and, at the same time, a break with the traditional context of neighborhood sociability. Once the community network of blood ties and place has been breached, what identifies this male population of most privileged origin? It is their relationship with the public sphere, a feature of culture, given that in these gatherings, secondary ties are formed, which in turn implies a common sense of belonging defined in political and cultural terms.

At the start of this chapter, we set out to find forms of public sociability in the city of Buenos Aires. At its end, we discover that although this public sociability is not a class feature, this idea holds significant variations in meaning, according to whether it is inscribed in the spatial framework of the culture community or breaks with it. In this way, at the heart of the traditional urban community, we see the emergence of a new notion of the public, which may reveal a break with traditional solidarities.

NOTES

1. I am not the first to establish this. In this aspect, the criticism drawn from the work of Maurice Agulhon—in addition to the author's own responses to and criticism of his work—have contributed to the present work. See Maurice Agulhon, "Les Chambrées en Basse-Province: histoire et ethnologie," *Revue Historique* (Paris) 497 (January-March 1971): 337–368; Michel Vovelle, "Dix ans de sociabilité méridionale," in *Idéologies et mentalités* (Paris: Maspero, 1982), 177–188; Rémy Ponton, "Une histoire de la sociabilité politique. À propos de l'ouvrage de Maurice Agulhon *Les cercles dans la France bourgeoise 1810–1848*," *Annales ESC* (Paris) 6 (1980): 1269–1280; Jean-Claude Chamboredon, "Compte rendu de l'ouvrage de Maurice Agulhon et Maryvonne Bodiguel: Les Associations au village," *Annales ESC* (Paris) 1 (January-February 1984): 52–58.
2. For this study, I have used the following sources: police records, trade almanacs, memoirs from the period, travelers' accounts, local press, and the records of associations, wherever these were available. I have classified this information with criteria previously used by both sociologists and historians of sociability but have introduced some modifications that take into account specific aspects found in the society analyzed. In this way I have distinguished different types of sociability according to the space in which they developed, the forms around which these relationships were based, the bonds implied by these relationships. and the social origin of its members, as well as the objectives, explicit or implicit, of these encounters. This process led me to differentiate between sociability evident in public places and in private places; typically urban forms and typically rural forms; relationships formalized in associations and more or less informal relationships; relationships that implied primary bonds and those that were formed from secondary bonds; and lastly, practices that identify the well-to-do and practices specific to the masses. This framework gives an idea of the chronology and scope of the phenomenon. See "Développement du mouvement associatif à Buenos Aires (ville et province) de 1800 à 1862," in PGB, *La Création*, addendum 3, "La vie associative."

3. The author agrees with J.C. Mitchell that a high frequency of contacts does not imply a high intensity in social relationships. See *Social Networks in Urban Situations* (Manchester: U of Manchester Press, 1969), ch. 1.
4. For a description of these activities, see José Torre Revello, "Fiestas y costumbres," in Academia Nacional de la Historia, Historia de la Nación Argentina, vol. Iv, sec. 1, 409–420.
5. See J. P. Viqueira Albán, "Diversiones públicas."
6. For a thought-provoking evocation, see Philippe Ariès, "L'enfant et la rue, de la ville à l'antiville" (1979), in *Essais de mémoire 1943–1983* (Paris: Seuil, 1993), 233–255.
7. In the colonial period, the "reference group" is often found in the domain of discourse around which community representations are built. Naturally, the group is connected to a relational reality which discourse attempts to restrict while simultaneously being redefined by it. A notable analysis of this question can be found in Maurizio Gribauldi, *Itinéraires ouvriers: espaces et groupes sociaux à Turin au début du XXe siècle* (Paris: Éditions de l'École des Hautes Études en Sciences Sociales, 1987); M. Gribauldi, "A proposito di linguistica e storia," *Quaderni Storici*, 46 (1981).
8. See D. F. Sarmiento, *Civilización i barbarie.*
9. For the urban elites, what made the city of Buenos Aires the head and capital of the territory was "geographic determinism." See D. F. Sarmiento, *Civilización i barbarie.*
10. The details of the foundation of Buenos Aires and this primary stage feature in Rómulo Zabala & Enrique de Gandía, *Historia de la ciudad de Buenos Aires 1 (1536–1718)* (Buenos Aires: Municipalidad de la Ciudad de Buenos Aires, 1937).
11. Calculated from a military census held in Buenos Aires in 1602. See Nicolás Besio Moreno, *Buenos Aires. Puerto de la Plata, capital de la Argentina. Estudio crítico de su población, 1536–1936* (Buenos Aires, 1939), chapter 8.
12. On the issue of the development of port activity in Buenos Aires in the seventeenth century, see Zacarías Moutoukias, *Contrabando y control colonial en el siglo XVII* (Buenos Aires: Centro Editor de América Latina, 1988).
13. The question of interregional markets is developed in the now-classic work by Carlos Assadourian, "Integración y desintegración regional en el espacio colonial. Un enfoque histórico," in *El sistema de la economía colonial* (Lima: Instituto de Estudios Peruanos, 1982); Juan Carlos Garavaglia, *Mercado interno y economía colonial* (Mexico: Grijalbo, 1983).
14. The question of ennobling cities was evoked by Demelas. In the case of Spain, see Adeline Rucquoi, "Des villes nobles pour le Roi," in *Realidad e imágenes de poder. España a fines de la Edad Media* (Valladolid: Ámbito, 1988), 195–214.
15. Zacarías Moutoukias shows one particular dynamic of Buenos Aires in the regional domain: the more the city intensified its connections with the Atlantic market, the greater its dependence on the regional economy. With regards to these issues, see Guillermo Céspedes del Castillo, Lima y Buenos Aires. Repercusiones económicas y políticas de la creación del Virreinato del Plata (Sevilla: Escuela de Estudios Hispanoamericanos, 1947); Jorge Gelman, Économie et administration locale dans le Rio de la Plata du XVIIe siècle, doctorate thesis third cycle, Paris, Ehess, 1983; Z. Moutoukias, Contrabando y control colonial.
16. See Lyman Johnson & Susan Socolow, "Población y espacio en el Buenos Aires del siglo XVIII," *Desarrollo Económico* 20: 79 (October-December 1980), 329–349.
17. According to Besio Moreno, in 1774 the city had 11,572 inhabitants, twice that of a little more than thirty years earlier. Besio Moreno adjusts the 1810 figures of the

census, estimating two thousand more inhabitants. See N. Besio Moreno, *Buenos Aires. Puerto de la Plata.*

18. Figures revised by Jonson & Socolow in "Población y espacio."
19. To these figures, it is necessary to add illegal immigrants, which might double or triple the final total. See Elena F. S. de Studer, *La trata de negros en el Río de la Plata durante el siglo XVIII* (Buenos Aires: Facultad de Filosofía y Letras, 1958), 324–325.
20. See Juan Carlos Garavaglia & José Luis Moreno (ed.), *Población, sociedad, familia y migraciones en el espacio rioplatense. Siglos XVIII y XIX* (Buenos Aires: Cántaro, 1993).
21. Construction provided an urban alternative to work in the fields, as can be inferred from Fernando Aliata's research into the evolution of buildings in Buenos Aires during the period from 1821 to 1827. In his memoirs, Juan Manuel Beruti also refers to the mobility of a semi-urban, semi-rural population. See Fernando Aliata, "Edilicia privada y crecimiento urbano en el Buenos Aires posrevolucionario, 1824–1827," *BIHAA-E. Ravignani,* third series, first semester, 1993, 59–92; Juan Manuel Beruti, Memorias curiosas de los sujetos que han sido gobernadores y virreyes de las provincias del Río de la Plata, en Biblioteca de Mayo (Buenos Aires: Senado de la Nación, 1960), vol. IV, 3814–3815.
22. See Susan Socolow, *Los mercaderes del Buenos Aires colonial: familia y comercio* (Buenos Aires: Ediciones de la Flor, 1991).
23. For more on trade, see S. Socolow, *Los mercaderes;* Juan Carlos Garavaglia, "El Río de la Plata en sus relaciones atlánticas: una balanza comercial (1779–1784)," *Moneda y Crédito* 141 (1977): 75–101.
24. These activities provided employment for a considerable number of inhabitants, especially the city's slaves. According to estimates by García Belsunce, artisanal activities accounted for 12% of the free population in 1810, while commercial activities (large and small businesses) employed 17.63%, with the military accounting for 12 percent of inhabitants. See César A. García Belsunce (ed.), *Buenos Aires. Su gente, 1800–1830* (Buenos Aires: Emecé, 1977), vol. 1, "Su gente," 109.
25. Hence, during the government of Rivadavia, which coincided with the period of political organization of the Province of Buenos Aires (1821–1824), a project was presented to reorder the city with a view to rationalizing and regulating the urban space. Rivadavia's words in his speech to the legislature are unmistakable with regards to this point: "Buenos Aires must yield to herself, improve her interior administration in all respects; by her example call to order sibling towns, and with the resources she possesses within her borders, find that importance with which she must stand when the ideal opportunity arises to found a nation." See "Discurso del ministro de Gobierno en la sesión del 1° de mayo de 1822," in *Acuerdos de la Honorable Junta de Representantes de la Provincia de Buenos Aires* (La Plata: Archivo de la Provincia de Buenos Aires, 1932), cited by Fernando Aliata, "La ciudad regular. Arquitectura edilicia e instituciones durante la época rivadaviana," in *Imagen y recepción de la Revolución Francesa en la Argentina* (Buenos Aires: Comité Argentino para el Bicentenario de la Revolución Francesa/Grupo Editor Latinoamericano, 1990), 159–179. For this new definition of the city as an administered place, see Bernard Lepetit, *Les Villes dans la France moderne (1740–1840)* (Paris: Albin Michel, 1988), 52–81.
26. This figure corresponds to 1829. For demographic estimates, I use Besio Moreno's figures, as his calculations are the most reliable and also have the advantage of covering the whole period under review. See Besio Moreno, *Buenos Aires. Puerto de la Plata.*

27. See F. B. Head, *Las Pampas y los Andes* (London, 1826; reprinted Buenos Aires: Hyspamérica, 1986), 27
28. See John Miers, *Viaje al Plata 1819–1824* (London, 1826; reprinted Buenos Aires: Solar Hachette, 1968), 20; Arsène Isabelle, *Voyage à Buenos Aires et à Porto Alegre de 1830 à 1834* (Havre: Imp. de J. Morlent, 1835), 134–135.
29. The most important text is that of Ignacio Núñez, *Noticias históricas, políticas y estadísticas de las Provincias Unidas del Río de la Plata, con apéndice sobre la usurpación de Montevideo por los gobiernos portugueses y brasileros* (London: R. Ackermann, 1825). This was translated into French one year later by M. Varaigne and published by Poutheu, Paris, 1826. At the time, this was the only work of its kind available in France. See A. Isabelle's reference in his travel memoirs, *Voyage à Buenos Aires.*
30. This map is reproduced in PGB, *La Création* appendix 4. For an analysis of the map and its author, see María H. Marín, Alberto De Paula and Ramón Gutiérrez, *Los ingenieros militares y sus precursores en el desarrollo argentino (hasta 1930)* (Buenos Aires, 1976); Alfredo Taullard, *Los planos más antiguos de Buenos Aires, 1580–1880* (Buenos Aires: Peuser, 1940), 124–129.
31. J. Miers, *Viaje al Plata,* 21.
32. F. B. Head, *Las Pampas y los Andes,* 28.
33. On this issue, see the works cited by Fernando Aliata, in addition to "Ciudad o aldea. La construcción de la historia urbana del Buenos Aires anterior a Caseros," *Entrepasados* II:3 (1992): 51–70.
34. See *Manual de Buenos Ayres. Explicación del Plano Topográfico que manifiesta la distribución y nuevos nombres de las principales calles de esta Ciudad, Plazas, edificios públicos y Cuarteles. Con Agregación del sistema que se ha seguido en la nueva numeración. 1823* (anonymous manuscript, 1823; first edition, with preface and paleographic transcription by Professor Jorge Ochoa de Eguileor [Buenos Aires: Municipalidad de Buenos Aires, 1981]), 19–21.
35. By government of Rivadavia I include the period when he was minister of Government and Foreign Relations under Colonel Martín Rodríquez (1821–1824) and later president of the National Executive (1826–1827).
36. See *Manual de Buenos Ayres.*
37. "To remedy these disadvantages the people have found a certain method, dividing the town into certain parts, called 'barrios,' and giving them the names of Temples, establishments and most notable and known private houses, which are found in each respective part; and with this a considerable effect is achieved." See *Manual de Buenos Ayres,* 21
38. See J. L. Romero, *Latinoamérica, las ciudades.*
39. See Linda Greenow, "Microgeographic Analysis as an Index to Family Structure and Networks," *Journal of Family History* 10: 3 (1985), 272–283.
40. See Gérard Delille, Famille et propriété dans le royaume de Naples (xv–xix) (Paris: EHESS-École Française de Rome, 1985).
41. See below for the customers of *pulperías* (taverns). The research of Ricardo Cicerchia offers us an example of criminal trials concerning urban families for the period from 1800 to 1810, in which 80 percent of testimony was given by persons of the neighborhood. See "Vida familiar y prácticas conyugales. Clases populares en una ciudad colonial, Buenos Aires, 1800–1810," *BIHAA-E. Ravignani* (third series) 2 (first semester, 1990): 91–109.

42. It has proved useful here to take into consideration geographical research, particularly in the relationship between the structure of community life and reference groups. See Paul Claval, *La Logique des villes. Essai d'urbanologie* (Paris: Litec, 1981), 470.
43. See Jorge E. Hardoy, "Las formas de la ciudad colonial," in *Estudios sobre la ciudad iberoamericana* (Madrid: CSIC/Instituto Gonzalo Fernández de Oviedo, 1983), 319–322. For an analysis of the most recent research into the city, see Woodrow Borah, "Trends in Recent Studies of Colonial Latin American Cities," *Hispanic American Historical Review* 63: 3 (August 1984), 535–554.
44. After independence, this road, known as the "old port road," was renamed "Defensa" in recognition of the courageous defense of the city by its inhabitants during the English invasions of 1806 and 1807. See Vicente O. Cutolo, *Buenos Aires. Historia de las calles y sus nombres*, 2 vols. (Buenos Aires: Elche, 1988).
45. On the role of the square in Spanish and Ibero-American cities, see Publicaciones de la Casa de Velázquez, *Forum et Plaza Mayor dans le monde hispanique*, Recherches en Sciences Sociales, no. IV (Paris: E. de Boccard, 1978).
46. There are various testimonies from the lithographs of the period. See Bonifacio del Carril, *Monumenta iconográfica. Paisajes, tipos, usos y costumbres en la Argentina, 1536–1860* (Buenos Aires: Emecé, 1964); B. del Carril, *Iconografía de Buenos Aires. La ciudad de Garay hasta 1852* (Buenos Aires: Municipalidad de Buenos Aires, 1982).
47. The limits vary with time. The oldest divisions are ecclesiastic. Until 1769 one single parish was responsible for parochial services for the entire population of the city. This parish was then divided into six, then into eleven in 1859. Administrative divisions also saw various modifications. The oldest was the division by *cuartel.* Later on, judicial and police districts were created. See A. Taullard, *Los planos*; Ricardo Figueira, "La gran aldea," in J. L. Romero (comp.), *Buenos Aires, historia de cuatro siglos* (Buenos Aires: Abril, 1983), vol. I, 285–303.
48. The original can be seen in PGB, *La Création,* appendix 4, "La démarche graphique."
49. The concept of "community" is not used here in the sense that anthropologists give the word—that is, a closed territorial group—but as a conceptual tool that allows us to distinguish strong ties of a communitarian nature from weak ties of an associative nature. Our reference for this distinction is F. Tönnies. In Alan Macfarlane, "History, anthropology and the study of community," *Social History* 5 (May 1977), a critical analysis can be found of the study of community. The author has explored this question previously in "Sociabilidad, espacio urbano y politización" in Sabato, H, Lettieri, A (ed.) *La vida política. Armas, votos y voces en la Argentina del siglo XIX* (Buenos Aires: FCE, 2003).
50. The first reference to this appears in a letter written by Hernán Cortés and dated 1524. See Joan Corominas, *Diccionario crítico etimológico de la lengua castellana* (Berna: Francke, 1954), vol. III, 919–920.
51. See Jorge A. Bossio, *Historia de las pulperías* (Buenos Aires: Plus Ultra, 1972), 13–23.
52. See J. Corominas, *Diccionario crítico*, 919–920. The origin of this word is uncertain, but many authors have faithfully followed Solórzano y Pereyra, who in *Política indiana* affirms that "it was ordered that there be introduced and designated into each city or town a signposted shop, which in Castile are known as 'abacería' and in the Indies as '*pulperías*' or 'pulquerías' of 'pulque.'"

53. In addition to drinking, there would often be card games and singing accompanied by a Spanish guitar and, later in the nineteenth century, the reading of newspapers.
54. On the role of alcohol in Mexico, see William B. Taylor, *Drinking, Homicide and Rebellion in Colonial Mexican Villages* (Stanford: Stanford University Press, 1979); Serge Gruzinski, *La Colonisation de l'imaginaire. Sociétés indigènes et occidentalisation dans le Mexique espagnol XVI–XVIIIe siècle* (Paris: Gallimard, 1988), 189–261; Sonia Corcuera de Mancera, *El fraile, el indio y el pulque. Evangelización y embriaguez en la Nueva España (1523–1548)* (Mexico: Fondo de Cultura Económica, 1991).
55. See "Informe sobre Pulquerías y Tabernas el año de 1784," *Boletín del Archivo General de la Nación* (Mexico) XVIII (1947): 3 & 4, 198–236, 368.
56. In "Informe sobre Pulquerías," one can find an example of different treatment.
57. See Ricardo Rodríguez Molas, "La pulpería rioplatense en el siglo Xvii (ensayo de historia social y económica)," Universidad (Universidad Nacional del Litoral, Santa Fe) 49 (1961): 99–134. See also, by the same author, "Las pulperías," in Lugares y modos de diversión (Buenos Aires: Centro Editor de América Latina, 1985), Cuadernos de historia popular argentina, 1–20.
58. The order of 5 December 1715 prohibited card and dice games and established a policy of control over any such gatherings. See J. A. Bossio, *Historia de las pulperías*, 69–70.
59. The population figures for Buenos Aires are Besio Moreno's. The size of the city is calculated from Besio Moreno's proposed map and Lyman Johnson and Susan Socolow's estimates for the city in the late eighteenth century. See L. Johnson and S. Socolow, "Población y espacio."
60. In the early nineteenth century, Mexico City had a proportion of 1/548, Puebla 1/372 and Caracas 1/393, according to Jay Kinsbruner's estimates in *Petty Capitalism in Spanish America: The pulperos of Puebla, Mexico City, Caracas and Buenos Aires* (Westview Press, 1987) Dellplain Latin American Studies, no. 21.
61. Kinsbruner sees in this the beginnings of petty capitalism, in *Petty Capitalism*. Z. Moutoukias argues that soldiers in the garrison were, because of their post and the nature of their role, in an excellent position to participate in the commercial life and the city and owned a large number of these businesses. See Z. Moutoukias, *Contrabando y control colonial.*
62. In Caracas or in Mexico, a *pulpería* did not necessarily function as a liquor store, for which special authorization was required. Hence in Mexico there were *pulperías* and *pulperías tabernas*, and in Caracas *pulperías* (authorized to sell alcohol) and *bodegas* (not authorized). See J. Kinsbruner, *Petty Capitalism.*
63. See R. Rodríguez Molas, "La *pulpería* rioplatense."
64. See J. P. Viqueira Albán, "Diversiones públicas," 195–228.
65. On the "counter dispute" ("pleito de los mostradores"), see J. A. Bossio, *Historia de las pulperías*, 26–40.
66. Trade regulation pronounced by Viceroy Arredondo in 1790. See J. A. Bossio, *Historia de las pulperías*, 65–96.
67. See Acuerdo del Extinguido *Cabildo* de Buenos Aires del 19 de agosto de 1812 en Archivo General de la Nación, *Acuerdos del extinguido Cabildo de Buenos Aires*, series IV, vol. III, books LXII, LXIII, and LXIV, and vol. IV, 1810–1812 (Buenos Aires: G. Kraft, 1927). These revolutionary songs were compiled in part and published by Ramón Díaz in *La lira argentina* (Buenos Aires, 1824).
68. There are numerous references to police officers being verbally abused or even stabbed. See AGN. AP. X 16-3-5.

69. Pedro de Angelis, *Recopilación de Leyes y Decretos promulgados en Buenos Aires desde el 25 de mayo 1810 hasta el fin de diciembre 1835* (Buenos Aires: Imprenta del Estado, 1837), vol. I, 422.
70. It is likely that the decrease in *pulperías* in existing sources did not correspond to a real reduction; it is more likely the consequence of a changed classification, which included these under *almacenes* (warehouses).
71. Maurice Agulhon has indicated this with regards to workers' sociability in "Classe ouvrière et sociabilité," in *Histoire vagabonde 1. Ethnologie et politique dans la France contemporaine* (Paris: Gallimard, 1988), 60–97.
72. Emilio Sereni, in *Capitalismo y mercado nacional* (Barcelona: Crítica/Grijalbo, 1980), develops the theory of nonequivalent commercial exchange. José C. Chiaramonte's research show that Sereni's analysis can be applied to the socioeconomic situation of the River Plate during the first half of the nineteenth century. See J. C. Chiaramonte, "La cuestión regional" (recently republished in *Mercaderes del litoral. Economía y sociedad en la provincia de Corrientes, primera mitad del siglo XIX*, Buenos Aires, Fondo de Cultura Económica, 1991).
73. This phenomenon has been demonstrated by J. Gelman for the late colonial period, which, taking into account the economic problems in the River Plate after independence could last into the early decades of the nineteenth century. See Jorge Gelman, "El gran comerciante y el sentido de la circulación monetaria en el Río de la Plata colonial tardío," *Revista de historia económica* 5: 3 (Autumn 1987), 485–508,
74. Even the French traveler A. Isabelle was of the same opinion: "often they gamble the shirts off their own backs; it is most fortunate if the game might end without disputes! Otherwise, disputes are settled in the very place, with a long knife with which they are always armed." See A. Isabelle, *Voyage à Buenos Aires*, 236.
75. See chapter 5.
76. See ANG.IX 7-9-5, loose leaf. Quoted in C. A. García Belsunce (ed.), *Buenos Aires. Su gente*, vol. II, 213.
77. There are some references to "honest folk" among the clientele in the *pulperías* of Santiago de Chile. See José Zapiola, *Recuerdos de treinta años 1810–1840* (Santiago de Chile: Guillermo Miranda Editor, 1902). The idea of "idle folk" and "working folk" was widespread in the nineteenth century. For the former, idleness was necessary for a pleasant life; for the latter, it was synonymous with laziness. On this question, see Centre de Recherches d'Histoire Sociale de l'Université de Picardie, *Oisivité et loisir dans les sociétés occidentales au XIXe siècle*, coloquio multidisciplinario, Amiens, 19 y 20 de noviembre de 1982 (Abbeville: Imp. F. Paillart, 1983), particularly the contribution by A. Kremer Marietti, "Les avatars du concept de loisir au XIXe siècle dans la société industrielle et dans la philosophie sociale," 31–39; and the work of Maurice Agulhon, especially *Le Cercle dans la France bourgeoise 1810–1848. Étude d'une mutation de sociabilité* (Paris: Armand Colin, 1977).
78. Nonetheless, the presence of the written press is accompanied by a practice of public reading, which does not appear to correspond to the public sociability practices of "well-to-do folk." On the question of shared cultural practices, and more generally for a revision of the cultured–popular opposition, see R. Chartier, *Lecture et lecteurs*, particularly 7–19.
79. AGN. AP. X.L 36-1829, 32-11-6.
80. "Corner" was another name for the *pulpería*, referrring to its location.
81. AGN. AP. X 16-3-5.

82. AGN. AP. X 16-3-5.
83. AGN. AP. X 31-10-1.
84. AGN. AP. X 31-10-1.
85. AGN. AP. X 43-7-5. Benavente, whom we have already come across in police records, was also a pulpero. See AGN. AP. X 16-3-5.
86. I follow here the definition of sociability ties as given by Lemieux: "We can call sociability ties the ties of identification and differentiation in which the relationship is more important than the connected terms and which usually follow from belonging to primary groups (relatives, friends, neighbors, or co-workers). Sociability per se cannot be satisfied in spite of relating the likes of occupation, property, information, and ends. It finds it in the identification with a like person, in the singular emotional relationship that unites two actors. See Vincent Lemieux, *Réseaux et appareils. Logique des systèmes et langage des graphes* (Quebec: Edisem, 1982), 13–14.
87. To find the number of *pulperías* and their location, the principal source was trade almanacs. In all cases it is possible to raise the same criticism with regards to the accuracy of the data. The author of the almanacs extracts them from the register of commercial licenses. This means that the number of actual places of business was undoubtedly higher than that given in the almanacs. The almanacs do, however, give us a uniform series that allows us to compare the data of 1826, 1829, 1830, 1833, 1834, 1836, 1851, 1853, and 1855. The almanacs give the name of the owner and the address of the business. However, the city at the time did not have a continuous numbering system, which leads to some irregularity between the numerical order and the actual numbering of the establishments, which makes it harder to accurately indicate the location of the address given. To mitigate these difficulties I have constructed, with the help of F. Vergneault, "geo-graph" diagrams that reproduce the topological structure of the city. The comparison of the forms of these diagrams allows a comparative and diachronic reflection as to the use of urban space and the place of sociability within this. See J. Blondel, *Almanaque de comercio de la ciudad de Buenos Aires para el año 1826* (Buenos Aires: Imprenta del Estado, 1825; reprinted in Buenos Aires: Ediciones de la Flor, 1968); *Almanaque de la ciudad de Buenos Aires* (Buenos Aires, 1851); Manuel R. Trelles, *Registro estadístico del Estado de Buenos Aires* (Buenos Aires: Imprenta del Pueblo, 1854); *Almanaque comercial. Guía del forastero para el estado de Buenos Aires* (Buenos Aires: Imprenta de la Tribuna, 1855).
88. The reader can find these streets using the "Cultural Life in Buenos Aires" map, document no. 7.
89. Very little research has been devoted to the history of gatherings in cafés. The most extensive study is by Bossio, although it uses data somewhat impressionistically. Other extant research is more general and refers to Buenos Aires cafés of the late nineteenth and early twentieth centuries. See Jorge A. Bossio, *Los cafés de Buenos Aires* (Buenos Aires: Schapire, 1968), 29–33; José Barcia, *Los cafés* (Buenos Aires, 1982); Juan Carlos Giusti, "Los cafés," in *Lugares y modos de diversión*, 1–20; Migue Ángel Scenna, "Los cafés, una institución porteña," *Todo es Historia* (Buenos Aires) 21 (1967): 48–56.
90. J. A. Bossio, *Los cafés*.
91. See Vicente Fidel López, "La gran semana de 1810. Crónica de la Revolución de Mayo," in *Evocaciones históricas* (Buenos Aires: Jackson, 1945), 61.
92. Beaumont repeats here the principal fear that these new places represented for male public sociability: harming traditional family life. John Beaumont, *Viajes por Buenos Aires, Entre Ríos y la Banda Oriental (1820–1827)* (Buenos Aires: Hachette, 1957; Spanish translation by J. L. Busaniche), 112–113.

93. Aside from the first reference in 1779, there is no indication for the whole of the first half of the nineteenth century as to the existence of working-class cafés. See Víctor Gálvez, *Memorias de un viejo. Escenas y costumbres de la República Argentina* (1888) (Buenos Aires: Pieusen, 1889), vol. 1, 256–257.
94. Gálvez, *Memorias de un viejo.*
95. In Spanish, *tertulia* means a "friendly conversation." It is not associated with an exact place; it might take place in a private home, as in the salons of France, or in a café. The word refers not to any given form of sociability but to sociability per se. Nor is the word specific to any one class: Both the well-to-do and the "masses" might participate in a *tertulia.* It does imply, however, the existence of friendly ties between those taking part. In other words, the *tertulia* implies a bond of sociability that presumably fits into a network of relationships. It must be noted nevertheless that the connotations of the word vary from one country to another. See Julio Casares, *Diccionario ideológico de la lengua española* (Barcelona: Gustavo Gili, 1988).
96. See M. Szuchman, *Order, Family,* 9.
97. Szuchman nevertheless raises the problem of social variations in the intensity of public sociability, an extremely interesting point as this entails important implications for many aspects of the political culture of the urban population.
98. According to García Belsunce, there were 364 *pulperías* and 24 cafés in Buenos Aires in 1810, but it is likely that the number of cafés was slightly smaller, as the figure may include other drinking establishments. See C. A. García Belsunce, *Buenos Aires. Su gente,* vol. 1, 120.
99. See J. Beaumont, *Viajes por Buenos Aires,* 115. This source is an extremely rich one, as a traveler generally pays great attention to a country's customs.
100 A. Isabelle, *Voyage à Buenos Aires,* 238–239.
101. In June 1801, the newspaper makes an explicit reference to cultural activities in the gatherings at the café de Marco: "'What do they say of this newspaper (the *Telégrafo Mercantil*) there in the café de Marco?' one student asks a regular. The latter replies: 'May the University say, for there are many men of letters there…'" See "Aborto intelectual del autor de la carta no. 12. Conversata entre un palangana y un estudiante," in *Telégrafo Mercantil, Rural, Político-económico e Historiográfico del Río de la Plata* (Buenos Aires: Imprenta de los Niños Expósitos, 1801–1802, facsímil dirigido por la Junta de Historia y Numismática Americana, Buenos Aires, 1914–1915, no. 27, 8 June 1801).
102. The memoirs of the young Núñez and Beruti are an invaluable source for showing the establishment of these new places and forms of sociability. There are equally valuable references for the first regulars of the café in the *Telégrafo Mercantil.* See Ignacio Núñez, *Noticias históricas, políticas y estadísticas de las Provincias Unidas del Río de la Plata, con apéndice sobre la usurpación de Montevideo por los gobiernos portugueses y brasileros* (London: R. Ackermann, 1825; Buenos Aires: La Cultura Argentina, 1952), vol. II, 140–145; J. M. Beruti, *Memorias curiosas,* 3784–3788. I have also published the results of my own research on this matter in "La Revolución Francesa y la emergencia de nuevas prácticas de la política: la irrupción de la sociabilidad política en el Río de la Plata revolucionario (1810–1815)," in Ricardo Krebs y Cristián Garmuri, *La Revolución Francesa y Chile* (Santiago de Chile: Editorial Universitaria, 1990), 111–135.
103. The identification between sociability in the cafés and the new power of opinion transcends the insurrectional crisis. See various references in Senado de la Nación, *Biblioteca de Mayo, Diarios y crónicas.*
104. This provides one answer to the question of the decrease in number of cafés during the Rosas government. Evidently, visiting a café was not an expression of politically

neutral sociability, even when the intention was merely culture entertainment. See chapter 3.

105. No data is available as to the built-up area; I therefore consider as an urban sector the area in which the drawing of the streets maintains a certain regularity.

106. See for example the case of Paris from the Middle Ages up to the eighteenth century, in R. Descimon and J. Nagle, "L'espace parisien. Les quartiers de Paris du moyen âge au XVIIIe siècle. Évolution d'un espace plurifonctionnel," *Annales ESC* 34: 5 (September-October 1979), 956–975.

CHAPTER 2

New Relational Forms
ASSOCIATIVE SOCIABILITY

Having described "sociability" in its broadest sense, this study will now focus on a more restricted sense of associative sociability, following particularly Maurice Agulhon's proposal to analyze association as the intermediate sphere between the family as a primary group and the nation as a community of political belonging.[1] This approach has the great advantage of allowing us to simultaneously study individuals in their relational life and society through one of its particular groups. This is not a matter, naturally, of attempting to find in the association an equivalent or even a substitute for community as an elemental form of society. Agulhon's perspective not only makes it possible to take up an issue that was, as M. Vovelle has noted, a bastion of conservative sociology at the time, but by situating the associative world in this intermediate space between family and State, one can also raise the question of the specificity of modern political culture: whether these new social and cultural practices were perceived as the basis for the elaboration of and early attempts at democracy, as Agulhon and R. Huart argue, or whether, as Habermas suggests, they were the foundations of a new sphere from which emerged a free, autonomous and sovereign public.[2]

It is important to clarify that analysis by associative forms is considered here as a medium for tackling the study of sociability relationships and not as a model for analyzing society understood as a crossroads in relational networks.[3] It is true that associative ties are weak and whose communicative effectiveness can in no way be compared with the primary ties that are central to the construction of ego-centered networks.[4] But from my point of view, associative relationships are of particular interest, given the ritualized characteristic these introduce and the extent of their development among the urban population. Through these, we can pinpoint the social representations conveyed by associative ties.

Map of Associative Movement in the City of Buenos Aires

Associative practice was not specific to the independent city. Colonial cities experienced considerable growth in forms of religious organization, such as brotherhoods and Third Orders. This associative model, of Spanish origin, developed fairly rapidly in the Americas. In 1619, the city of Lima already had sixty brotherhoods, shared among the three main ethnic groups, for a population of 14,262 inhabitants.[5] In the case of Buenos Aires, Torres Revelo lists for 1609 the existence of two brotherhoods, at a time when the "city" had 540 inhabitants. Fourteen years later, thirteen brotherhoods were busy saving the souls of some two thousand Porteños.[6] Unfortunately, the history of the establishment and development of these organizations in the River Plate region is one of the lesser known accounts of the empire. However, indirect references indicate the vitality of this form of relationship in the city of Buenos Aires, even in the early nineteenth century.[7] This type of relationship practice seems to have declined later; it is feasible that this decrease came about because of new, secular associative practices.

In order to better understand the extent of this phenomenon, it is useful to first map out these practices by charting catalog associations according to criteria that take into account the forms, objectives and types of ties. In particular I use the distinction established by classical sociology—especially that of Ferdinand Tönnies—between primary and secondary ties.[8]

THE BEGINNING OF A MUTATION: FROM COLONIAL CITY TO LIBERAL CITY (1800–1827)

During the insurrectional movement of the American *cabildos,* we see the emergence of associations in a small circle of men committed to the revolutionary cause, as was the case with the patriotic societies of Caracas and Buenos Aires or in the *Lautaro* lodges in the River Plate, Chile and Peru. The history of the modern associative movement did not begin, however, with these forms of revolutionary sociability. Its genealogy takes us to early eighteenth-century Europe, the moment of the creation of the first Masonic lodges and other societies known by the generic name of "free-thinking societies."[9] The chronology of the development of these modern associative forms, however, varies from one region to another and presents some significant differences in the Spanish-speaking world. Although regular Freemasonry was established fairly late in the territory of the empire, with the first lodges dating from the early nineteenth century, the region developed a specific type of associative form with its "Societies of Friends of the Country" or "Patriotic Societies of Friends of the Country."[10]

In the city of Buenos Aires the first reference to new associative forms dates from 1801, when a group of men involved in the publication of the first newspaper

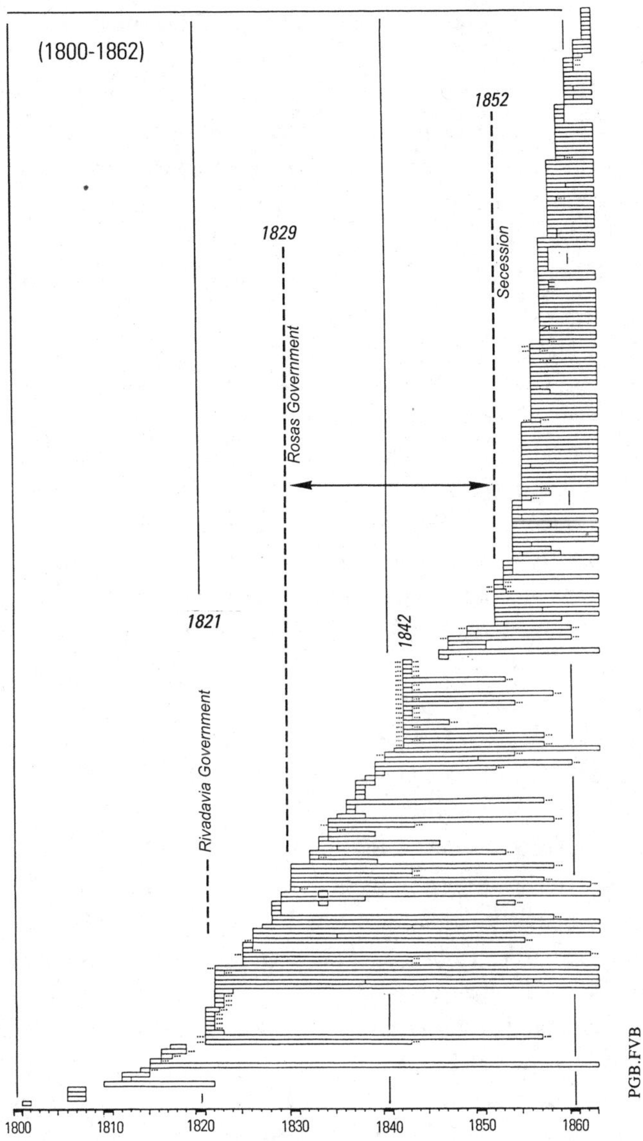

Figure 5. Chronology of Associative Movement in Buenos Aires (1800–1862). *Each horizontal bar represents an association and the duration of its existence. From bottom to top, the associations follow the chronology of their appearance. The line of dots preceding or following the bar indicates uncertain or incomplete information.*

to be printed and published in the city, *El Telégrafo Mercantil*, planned the creation of a "Patriotic, Literary and Economic Society." We have no conclusive proof that this society ever saw the light of day. There is nevertheless evidence of a project to set up the society and the list of its promoters, all members of the colonial elite. Among them were great Spanish traders such as Miguel de Azcuénaga and Juan Antonio Santa Coloma. Furthermore, there were representatives of high colonial office such as Juan de Almagro, Martín José de Altolaguirre, Matías de Bernal, Pedro José de Ballesteros, Antonio Carrasco, Manuel Gallegos and Antonio Olaguer Feliú, among others.[11] Their presence eliminates any suggestion that the appearance of the new modern form of association represented the birth of revolutionary objectives within the colonial elite. However, the composition of this list does not correspond entirely to that of a coterie of men of letters, which leads one to believe that the recruitment of these associations indicates a certain separation from the colonial intellectual model. Further, in spite of a tentative reconciliation of this project with the laws of colonial society, the project broke with the principle of a society of castes by establishing "the free association of individuals with common interests" as a principle of organization.[12] Nevertheless, it is important to point out that these societies were often developed by government initiative and can as a result be distinguished from societies of ideas created by private initiative and often opposed to the government. Notwithstanding, the two kinds of society shared certain characteristics: they were associated with the publishing of a newspaper and tended to combine meetings with more informal gatherings among friends, *tertulias*, in which they could develop a critical opinion as regards the authorities of the land.[13]

It is not surprising, then, that during the American revolutionary process one sees the development of new forms of political sociability, now tied to a will to break with colonial ties emerging from this new relational universe that introduced the notion of a contractual bond based on interests not strictly tied to one body or class. In practically all cities where *criollo* elites participated in the insurrection, loosely formalized political societies took root, calling themselves clubs, patriotic societies, lodges, or simply *tertulias*.[14]

In Buenos Aires, between these first traces of free association and the rise of the associative movement during the liberal government of Rivadavia (1821–1827), two intermediate points must be fixed. The first came in 1806 to 1807 when the first military lodges appeared among the English troops occupying successively Buenos Aires and Montevideo.[15] According to several testimonies from the period, interest in this new kind of association quickly caught on, especially among the city's educated public.[16] The second stage is the period leading from the insurrection of Buenos Aires in 1810 up to the declaration of independence in 1816. These six years witnessed the birth of various sociocultural associations. Their creation must no doubt be seen in the context of the new freedom that accompanied the insurrectional movement but also with the new political situation, given that initiatives not only came from civil society but also from the revolutionary government, which saw in the creation of this new type of organization a means for consolidating the revolution among local elites sympathetic to new ideas.[17]

With the advent of the new liberal order established during the Rivadavia government, however, the associative movement developed considerably. These were organizations with diverse aims and content, but who all received their support from voluntary participants. While limited in number, this development was indicative of transformations in the forms of organization in community life, in which various factors appear to have come into play. Firstly, there was an expansion of the regional economy in the wake of the breakup of the former colonial territory in 1819. Economic growth in the province of Buenos Aires provided the Rivadavia government with the means to undertake various projects aimed at reorganizing urban infrastructure and developing cultural institutions.[18] Political/cultural factors, tied to the break with the religious regimentation of collective life, which the new liberal regime encouraged, likewise benefited the rise of new associative forms—although not accompanied by any new legislation concerning the right of association. Until 1854, associative life developed because of a climate of de facto liberty, which was not reflected in any specific laws with regards to the associations. Various constitutional attempts implied a right of association, but none led to the enactment of a corresponding law. It was not until 1854 that the province of Buenos Aires declared freedom of association. Until this date, the associative movement operated under the outdated assumption that it was reliant on implicit or explicit government authorization.

During what came to be known as "the happy experience" of the liberal government, associative practices appeared above all among the well-to-do, with a preponderance of associations of a cultural nature such as the Lancastrian Society of Buenos Aires, founded in the city by Diego Thompson on the 5th of February, 1821, with the aim of introducing the Lancastrian teaching system into the River Plate.[19] The new associative movement was not limited, however, to the political/cultural sphere. Other associations for the dissemination of leisurely culture appeared, such as the Philharmonic Society and the Academy of Song and Music, both of which aimed to provide secular music lovers with performances of the best lyric repertoires of the period.[20] The new relational practices also spread to other sectors of the urban population, as revealed by the appearance of the "African Societies" created from the traditional "African nations," on which more is to come.

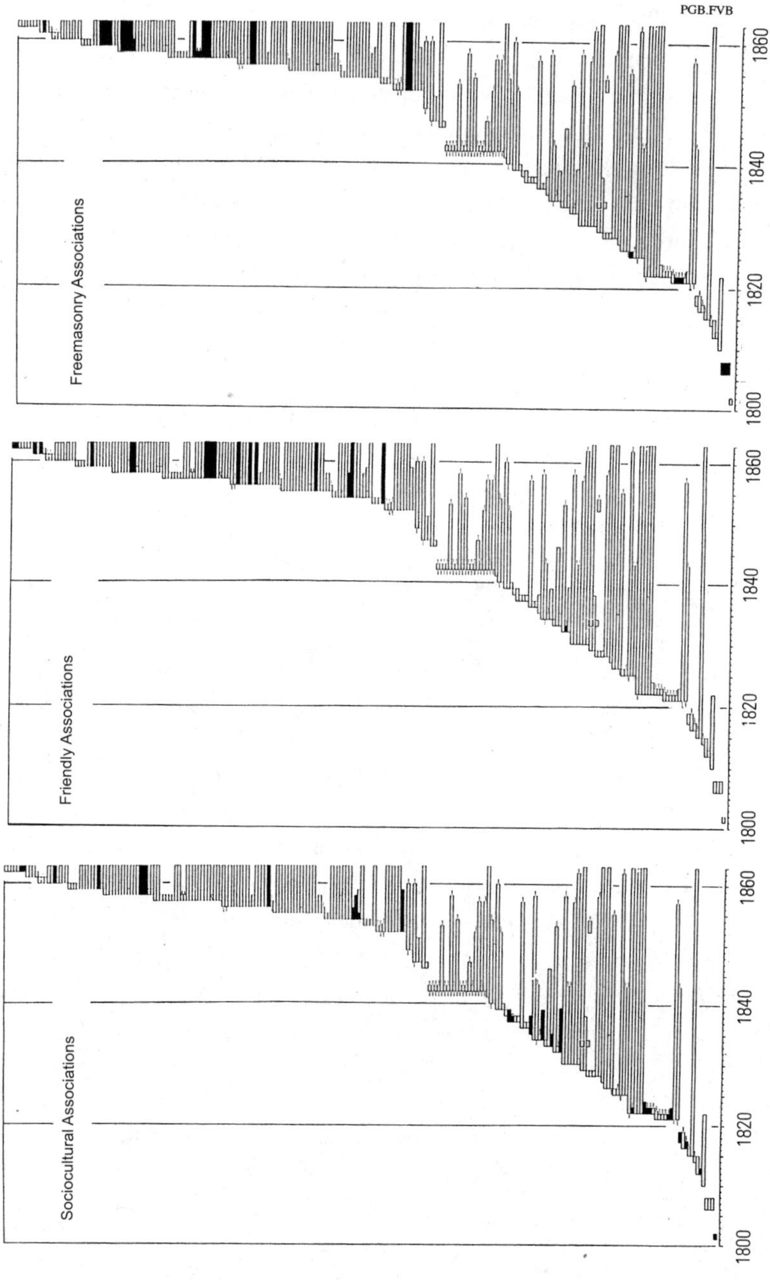
PGB.FVB
Freemasonry Associations
Friendly Associations
Sociocultural Associations
1800
1820
1840
1860

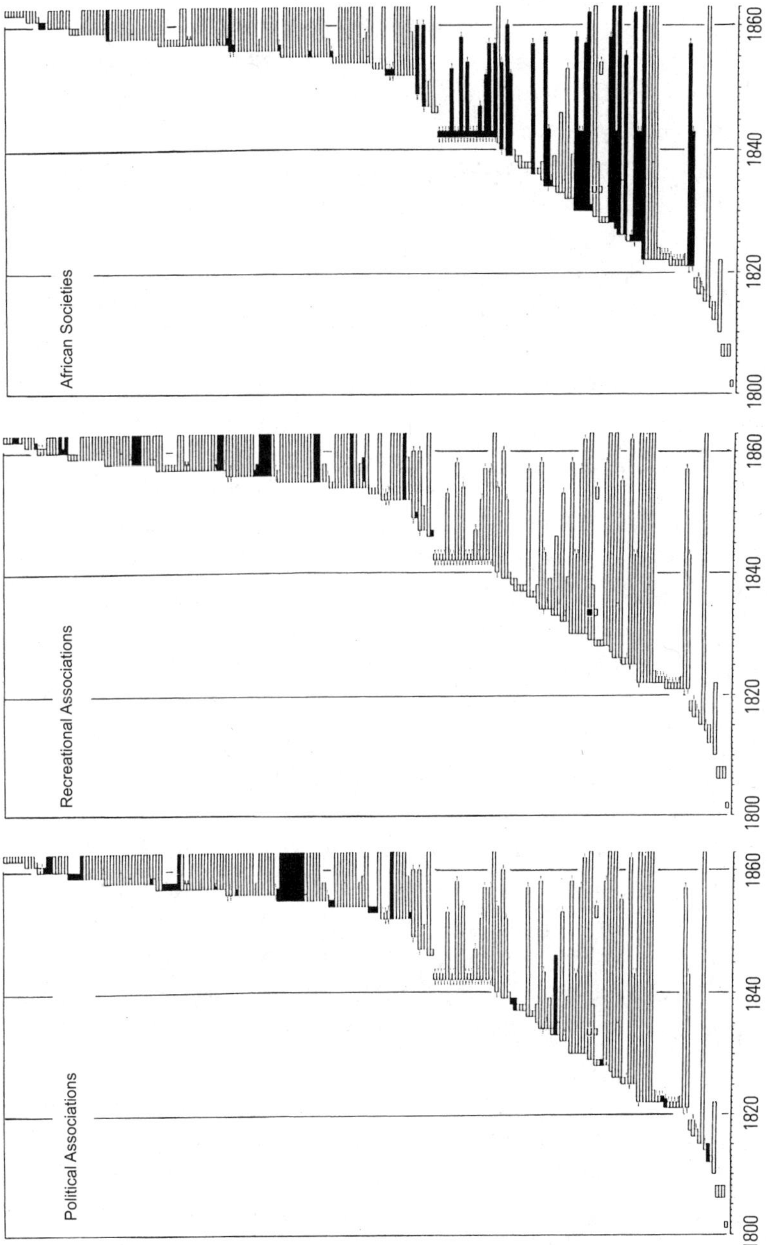

Figure 6. Typology of the Associative Movement (1800-1862)
In each graph, the association corresponding to each title is highlighted in bold.

A TREND CONFIRMED: ASSOCIATIVE LIFE IN THE POST-RIVADAVIAN CITY

The impression that the establishment of liberalism constituted a positive experience for the province of Buenos Aires gradually faded with the intensification of internal and external conflicts and chronic inflation which swept away any remaining memories of Rivadavian euphoria. Between 1829, when Rosas came to power in the province, and 1839, the city's people suffered three political uprisings (in 1829, 1833 and 1839), war against the Peruvian-Bolivian Confederation[21] (1837–1838) and a blockade of the port by the French Navy (1838), in addition to the internecine war that pitched Unitarians against Federalists and wrought havoc on society.[22] In spite of the fragility of social life that such conflict might imply, Porteños' tendency to join a variety of associations did not disappear with Rosas' arrival, according to what can be gathered from the chronology graph of the associative movement in Buenos Aires (figure 5) which shows the same growth curve between 1822 and 1839.[23] An initial moment can be distinguished during the first year for the first Rosas government (1829–1830), characterized by a considerable amount of growth in African societies and socioeconomic societies. Sociocultural forms prevailed between 1832 and 1838, a period corresponding to the *Rosista* interregnum and the first years of Rosas' second government. Between 1838 and 1839, the associative movement became politically polarized: on the one hand, the mostly pro-government African societies; on the other, cultural, political and secret societies aligned against Rosas.

It can therefore be seen that there were different cycles in the development of the movement, which when correlated with political history presents significant contradictions given that from the point of view of the history of the associative movement, it is not possible to distinguish between "before" and "after" Rosas. In fact, it would appear that until 1839 the associative movement followed the rhythm set by the liberal Rivadavia government. Only after this latter date can any significant change be noted.[24]

Let us now see how this phenomenon influenced the social use of the urban space.[25] An overview of the map showing the sites of the associations in the city shows two kinds of locations, one concentrated around the central square of the University of Buenos Aires and the other reaching the suburban areas (figure 7). In the second case, it is possible to distinguish two areas of attraction: to the southeast, in the Monserrat and Concepción parishes, near to the two axes of movement crossing the city from south to north, and the street Buen Orden (09) and its continuation along Artes (9), and the street San José (013) and its continuation along Uruguay (13). A second zone is formed by the Campo de Marte and Plaza del Parque, both in the north of the city. In these areas we find the African societies, recreational societies organized around ties of ethnic solidarity. In these suburban areas we also find some of Buenos Aires' theaters, a coincidence that allows us to trace some early reflections as to how the space was used. With the suburban spread of dance societies and entertainment halls, there is a noticeable concentration of sociocultural associations in the center, in the Catedral al Sur parish, around the university, and in the Catedral al Norte parish, near the cathedral and the port. In the south, the cultural attraction of the university was as inarguable as it was novel. Around the block of houses surrounding the older Jesuit buildings, now converted into a university site, an intense cultural life was to develop: a public library, bookshops, publishing houses and cafés were concentrated within a space of two hundred meters, logically bearing the name "La Manzana de las Luces" ("the Block of Enlightenment," streets O and Q between 05 and 03). To the north are located certain associations, almost entirely socioeconomic and part of the "entertainment" of trader circles. Their location can be easily explained by their clientele, principally found in the foreign trader sphere. It is hardly surprising that they should be found near the port, in the neighborhood with a high concentration of "business" functions. Far from the center but within an older populated area, we find the location of the Mutual Society of French Artisans, created in 1832. Although this was to have a somewhat ephemeral existence, it set the location of future friendly associations established after 1852.

It can therefore be seen that different types of association were distributed by area: sociocultural in the south, socioeconomic in the north, ethnic in the southwest and mutual societies in the northwest. The religious associations were the only ones not to follow this scheme, brotherhoods and Third Orders being fairly homogeneously distributed around the city. Like the *pulperías*, these associations appear to have belonged to a different social space, that of the parishes. The development of new forms of organization entailed considerable transformations in the organization of collective life. These forms primarily indicated an organization quite distinct from the sociability space and a break with the traditional framework of neighborhood sociability. Above all, the new forms brought about other transformations in the representations of social ties and led to a redefinition of the community of belonging.

Civility by Association

The eighteenth century witnessed an expansion in the semantic field of all matters social. The terms "society," "social," "sociable," and "sociability" were used far more frequently than heretofore.[26] In the River Plate, at the time of the 1810 insurrection, some of these notions took on particular importance. This was the case with "sociability," which appeared at the center of the debate on the nature of new social bonds.

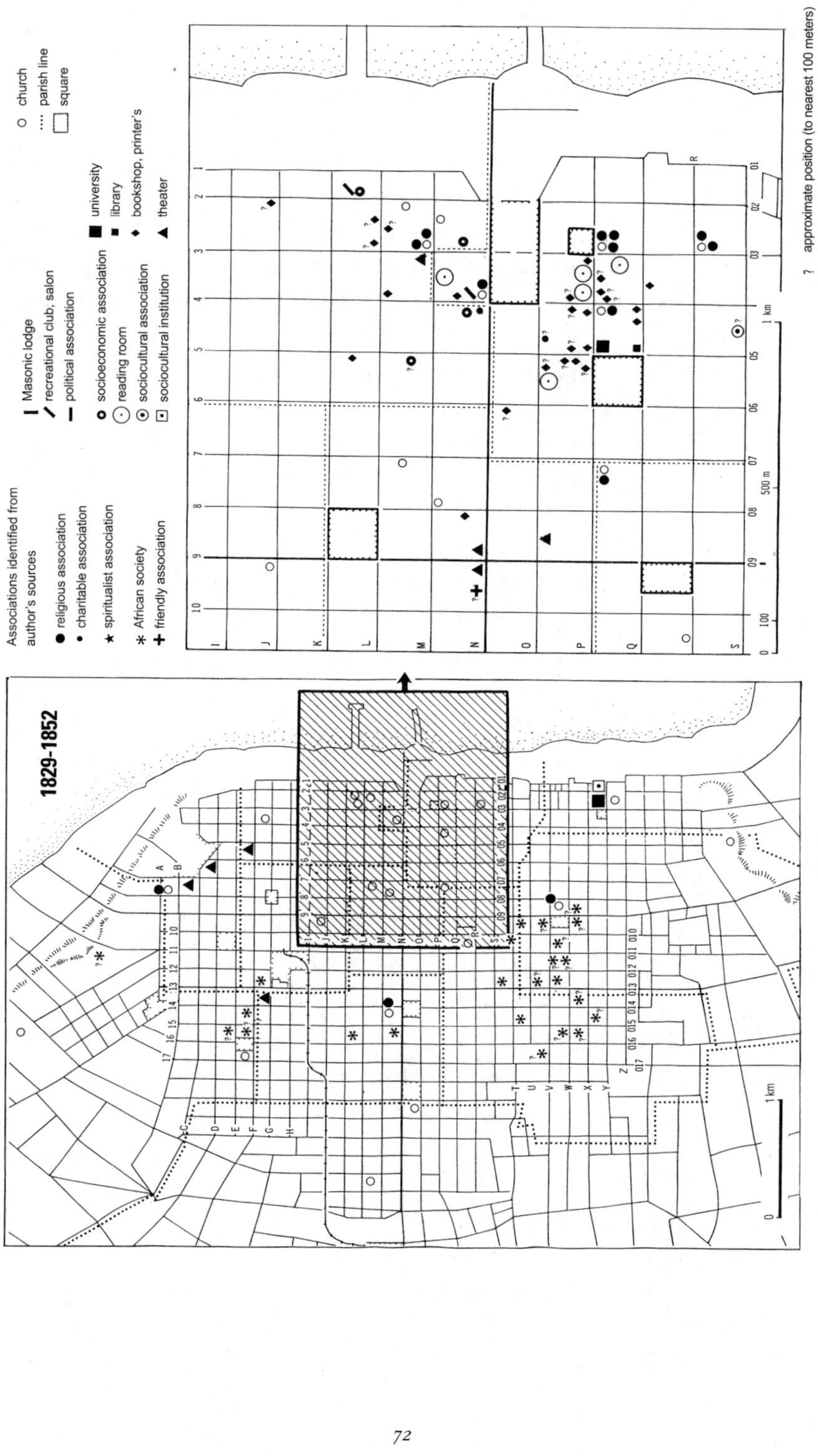
1829-1852
Associations identified from author's sources
religious association
charitable association
spiritualist association
African society
friendly association
Masonic lodge
recreational club, salon
political association
socioeconomic association
reading room
sociocultural association
sociocultural institution
university
library
bookshop, printer's
theater
church
parish line
square
? approximate position (to nearest 100 meters)
1 km
500 m

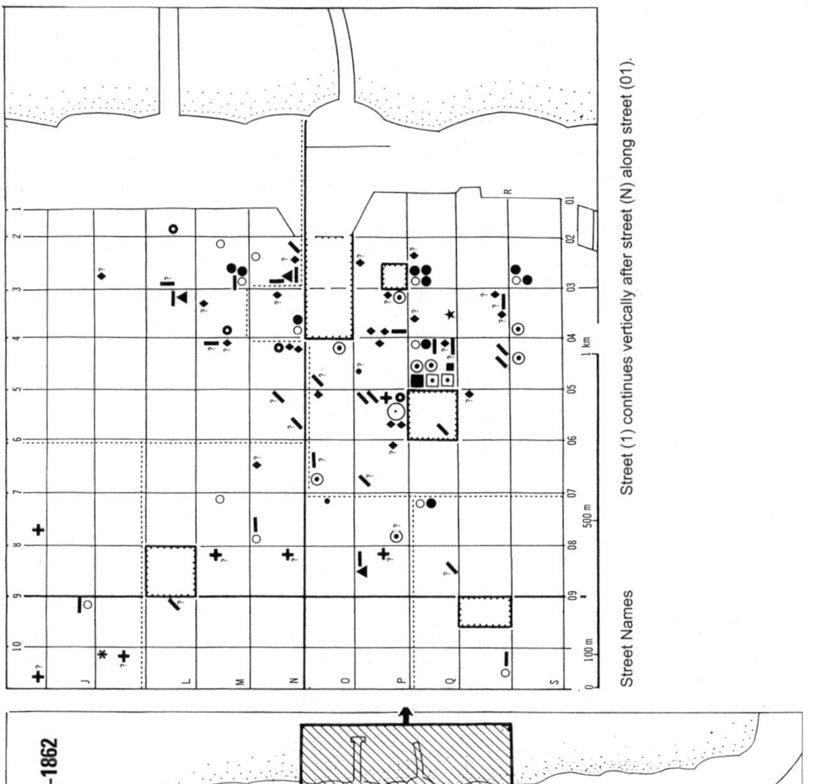

Figure 7. Cultural life in Buenos Aires (1829-1862)

For the genealogy of the concept of "sociability" used by young intellectuals it is necessary to return to the beginning of the eighteenth century.[27] Along with the theories of natural law, the concept was associated with individuals' rational choice, although this did not challenge the king's sovereignty, belonging to the sphere of society's constitutive pact.[28] This is the meaning given in the *Encyclopédie.* In Jaucourt's 1765 article on the word, "sociability" is defined as: "benevolence towards other men, disposition to do good, to conciliate our happiness with that of others and subordinate our own advantages to the greater good."[29] Jaucourt affirmed that all laws of society were derived from the principle of sociability, citing Pufendorf, whose work had been translated in 1706.[30] It is important to consider that from this we find an amalgam of the notion of the rational bond and polite language. In the same article we can observe a differentiation between "sociable" and "polite," which merits quoting: "the sociable man has suitable qualities for the good of society, and by this I refer to mildness of character, humanity." The sociable man, the article concludes, is a true citizen. In contrast, the polite man "is most indifferent to the greater good, cares for nobody, pleases all and is often scorned." We see here the difference between one presumably artificial or even antisocial kind of politeness and another courtesy essential to the *res publica.*

Towards the late eighteenth century, once revolution had breached the barrier separating society from sovereignty, the word "sociability" took on two meanings in the River Plate. One referred to private virtue, which might imply both a Christian reference of charity to fellow men and a more sociable reference related to the idea of civility.[31] The other meaning made sociability a virtue of public morals in relation to the idea of association, understood as learning from life in society.[32] As recent research on this question shows, the distinction is not merely formal given that the new public sphere emerged from the private sphere.[33] Civility, a relational code in courtesan society, henceforth proved to be useful in defining relationships in the private sphere, because of the value placed on conversation that had allowed the emergence of a public sphere in the private domain. In the River Plate, polite discourse carried out these two functions.

The first explicit reference found in the press of the River Plate (although more systematic research is necessary) dates from 1817 and appears to be tied, precisely, to the notion of contract and etiquette. It is an unsigned article from the newspaper *El Censor*, probably written by Friar Camilo Henríquez and titled "The Private Societies," with the intention of praising the benefits of the associations.[34] Sociability appears here as a foundation of the communal life that the association developed. It is possible to see an interesting combination of the notion of rational ties and courtesy as a constituent piece in social ties. The text also allows a glimpse of a distinction that sociability permits between society as a group of rational individuals, which can be identified with the public sphere, and the plebs or rabble, to use the terms of the period, governed by passions: stubbornness, intolerance and a lack of moderation and calm in discussion.

The first advocates of the associative movement in the city of Buenos Aires identified their social practices with the new discourse of sociability. Hence, in the introduction to the minutes of the Literary Society of Buenos Aires, founded in 1822, secretary Ignacio Núñez highlights the usefulness of the enterprise in these terms: "The association makes man leave his state of savage isolation.... Friendship, trust, reciprocal benevolence can only spring from men with frequent communication."[35] From this communication and not from the ties of political obedience previously uniting the king with his subjects, a society would emerge founded on contractual ties between individuals.[36] The same contractual representation of society was found in relationship practices that associated sociability, as a social state, with the language of courtesy. While at first this aspect concerned a limited number of associations, which, like the Literary Society, had close ties to power and whose essential aim was to transform society, this discourse contrasted with the new cultural associations relating "cultivated sociability" to civic virtue in both senses of the word: good citizenship and politeness.

A NEW SPHERE OF EXCHANGE: STUDENT SOCIABILITY

The University of Buenos Aires was founded by Bernardino Rivadavia in 1821 and was to be the only university in the *litoral* region *(Region of Argentina, comprising the city of Buenos Aires and the provinces of Buenos Aires, Corrientes, Chaco, Entre Ríos, Formosa, Misiones and Santa Fe.–Translator)* until the foundation of the University of La Plata in the province of Buenos Aires.[37] Previously, the inhabitants of Buenos Aires who wish to continue in further education in the Americas had to move to Córdoba (500 miles from Buenos Aires), Santiago de Chile (900 miles) or even contemplate the possibility of a journey of over 1200 miles to the University of Charcas in Alto Perú. The foundation of the University of Buenos Aires in 1821 changed much of the cultural landscape of the city, not because the university was an important center of original scientific output—in this aspect I share Halperin Donghi's view—but rather because a cultural life previously scattered among various university cities would come to be concentrated around the University of Buenos Aires.[38] Nevertheless, its significance was not limited to determining a topographic specification for urban cultural space, as important as this was for the concentration of new spaces of cultural sociability. In fact, the university extended and completed the public literary sphere, from which would emerge a new political consciousness.

The actors in this process were young men defined as much by their cultural level as by their belonging to this new institutional framework which allowed them to exist as a group. In all, the influence of this student population on the cultural life of Buenos Aires was not quantitative, for, in this period, a mere thirteen degrees were awarded by the university.[39] Even counting the students who only followed preparatory courses (the first two years of study) and those who did not graduate, the student population was still fairly small. In his memoirs, López remembers attending in 1832 Mariano Guerra's course in Latinity, a first-year course common to all disciplines, and there being 86 students, and this class was one of the more popular. Naturally, these figures should be seen in relation to the equally low number of individuals able to attain this cultural level.[40] The importance of the student population is better measured by the potential of their relationships than by their numbers.

Indeed, this age group was the most open to extrafamilial relationships. According to sociologists' studies, at least, the young population appears to be the one most susceptible to an increased number of encounters with others.[41] Within this population relationships are more open and diversified. If the students' cultural level is added, it is expected that the new practices of associative sociability of a sociocultural nature were considerably developed among them. Further, judging by the decree of 26 December 1822, student sociability developed with a speed and intensity which was soon noticed by the government. According to this text, the danger was not political but disciplinary. The decree sanctioned students' fondness for sociability, a preference exercised, it adds, outside of the university, something that the authorities considered incompatible with the rigor of one's studies. In other words, there was a suspicion that students would skip courses in search of amusement elsewhere. The decree attempted to put an end to the students' bothersome custom of being seen "in streets, summer houses, cafés and other public places."[42] And it is to be believed that the custom was fairly widespread, to the extent that the government felt obliged to punish such behavior with a 24-hour prison sentence.[43]

To be fair to the students, their natural fondness for sociability relationships was not always at odds with their education. Quite on the contrary, these informal gatherings and discussions, even those with undeniably leisurely purposes, often complemented university education by integrating other issues and knowledge that, for various reasons, was not covered by university curricula. Students, as a result, also developed a liking for social exchanges, through which they satisfied newfound intellectual interests. This was undoubtedly the case among first-year Porteño students, not least with a group whose intellectual interests—deeply stimulated by their mentor and philosophy professor, Diego Alcorta—

exceeded the level set by the university authorities. Recognizing a compatible intellectual authority, students undoubtedly found their interests to be shared and "socializable." But because of a common need for student sociability, extensively developed in informal meetings during classes, breaks or outside of the university, in cafés or family homes, this socialization took shape and finally came to life in the organization of voluntary associations.[44]

During the period in question, it is possible to find in Buenos Aires two associative forms that originated in relationships of student sociability and that had a crucial bearing on cultural and associative life: the Association of Historic and Social Studies, founded by university students in 1833, and the Literary Salon of 1837. The former was a study association with generally cultural aims formed from the relationship network of university students. López writes that the association, "which was organized according to the new French school," had one rule obliging all members to write an essay for each meeting. The meetings were held on Saturday nights, first at the home of one Miguel Cané, later in a specially rented room on Calle Venezuela, two hundred yards from the university.[45] At the origins of this association were the young fellow students of Vicente F. López and contemporaries of the 1830 liberal revolution, who would usually meet at the home of one Santiago Viola. A man of questionable schooling, Viola nevertheless possessed the great merit of being a young heir and "having recently ordered from Paris, for the sum of twenty five thousand francs, all of the most celebrated books, translated from French, Italian and German, and complete volumes of the *Paris Revue* and the *British Review.*"[46] López, with the disdain and arrogance Bartolomé Mitre claimed were characteristic, calls Viola "a simple *aficionado* who lacks depth of reflection but manages to excel." It can be added that his "talent" consisted also of a well-stocked library. López writes that all of his friends would meet, "like flies to a feast," around the library.[47] This observation reveals the extent of the thirst for new ideas at the time but shows also how difficult it was for this sector to afford the cost of their educational aspirations.

It is interesting to note that from the fairly standard practices of meeting at a family home and borrowing books from a friend, a study association was founded which formalized these gatherings, organized discussions and perhaps even developed rules for book loans. The formalization process can be clearly outlined: regulations, rented meeting rooms and probably therefore a subscription fee, and regularity of meetings. In terms of the network of relationships, this is known to have been sufficiently solid as to continue in Sastre's Literary Salon.[48] Here is a classic example of a public institution from private origins: first, gatherings of friends in private spheres; next, the institution of discussions, firstly of a literary nature, then political; lastly, formalization through a contractual association and the publication of a newspaper to publicize the group's opinion.[49] The success of this initiative can be accounted for in part by the fact that the formula of public reading corresponded to the needs of a student population, having the double advantage of permitting access to costly works and satisfying the marked needs for sociability in these young men.

The second associative form which originated from student sociability relationships was the Literary Salon of 1837. In this case, students' gatherings in Marcos Sastre's reading room ultimately led to the formalization of the Literary Salon, whose foundation was due to some extent to the initiative of this study association, but which went on to incorporate a far broader strata from both the perspective of age and socioprofessional category.

Without intending to establish a direct, causal relationship between the cultural practices of student sociability and the introduction of new customs of culture consumption in the city, it is necessary to show that with the foundation of the university and the cultural renewal of Buenos Aires, this type of student sociability attained undeniable primacy in the world of urban cultural exchanges, stimulating a "learned sociability" in which "Society" became an issue of public interest.[50] Student sociability, born of specific ties within a certain age group and culture level, built around it a world of new relationships based on equality of exchanges, freedom of expression, communion in and from the exchange of ideas. In this sense, it was symptomatic of transformations in the social and cultural life in the city of Buenos Aires.

THE NEW CULTURAL PRACTICE OF PUBLIC READING AND THE DEVELOPMENT OF ASSOCIATIONS OF INTELLECTUAL ENTERTAINMENT

The profitability of certain cultural practices of students may have motivated their rapid establishment among the well-to-do people of the city, as these new forms of socialization of culture adapted well to new bourgeois values as seen in the establishment of traders' circles. This explains the appearance during this decade of such businesses and areas of sociability as reading rooms, a process in which the student population played an important role.

Reading Rooms in Buenos Aires: The first reading circle was founded in Buenos Aires under the initiative of English-speaking immigrants. An announcement in *La Gaceta Mercantil* informs of the existence of "a library, reading room of the Union open in the month of August 1831 and visited by Englishmen and North Americans."[51] Another announcement in the same newspaper reveals that this was in fact a circle for members of the British community with the aim of keeping them informed of events at home and abroad. The announcement, published in English and signed "The Commission," was directed at the "reading community" and proposed that they "join the association" as shareholders, or simply visit the reading room, subject of course to payment of a subscription fee. In return, a collection not exceeding five hundred volumes was offered, along with the guarantee of principal English-language newspapers and magazines.[52] The emphasis on information rather than on strictly literary consumption speaks volumes about the characteristics of the clientele and the purpose of the meetings: foreigners connected generally to the business world but also foreigners far from home who felt the need to meet other compatriots, to obtain up-to-date information or simply have a conversation. While this association called itself a reading room, it had more in common with a literary salon or circle than a reading room in the classic sense of the business initiatives of a bookseller.

The second reference to a reading room also concerns the foreign community, this time a French subject, Théophile Duportail. Unlike the first case, this was clearly a book business, opened some time between 1827 and 1829,[53] and according to the trade almanac one of the five existing bookstores in Buenos Aires in 1830. According to Arsène Isabelle, who visited the city between 1830 and 1835, this bookstore was the only one in the city with a reading room, hence it is correct to place its foundation around this five year period.[54] From what is known, Duportail was a bookseller and supplier.[55] We have no complementary information, except that in 1836 the Duportail brothers sold their collection to the Uruguayan bookseller Marcos Sastre. The reasons for the sale are unknown, but if Arsène Isabelle is to be believed, it was due to commercial bankruptcy, attributable to the insignificance of cultural life in Buenos Aires: "this apathy observed in them, this kind of aversion to any serious reading whatsoever, and these insurmountable obstacles to the constitution of the country, the inevitable consequence of the scant progress of the political sciences."[56] Isabelle's observations may well have been fair, but they do not explain how one year later Sastre was able to make an entirely profitable business out of the same collection. The problem undoubtedly lay elsewhere. It is true that the business of selling and renting books was a wholly novel practice and never is it easy to enter a new market, all the more so in Buenos Aires where no specialized book-selling activity existed. Books could be found both in small shops and in *pulperías*.[57] Furthermore, accounts suggest that this kind of business struggled to establish itself.[58] Difficulties could prove insurmountable if, in addition, the trader misjudged his clientele, aiming a product at people unlikely to become consumers, a far greater risk for the arriving foreigner with the consumer habits of his country of origin. Thus, T. Duportail's misfortune perhaps stemmed from applying what was an effective commercial strategy in France but which failed to respond to the practices of meeting and consumption among

Porteños. His error may also have been in aiming predominantly literary and political philosophy works at a clientele more accustomed to reading newspapers at public gatherings.[59]

Five years on, the Uruguayan bookseller Marcos Sastre took up Duportail's formula.[60] Sastre, who had settled in Buenos Aires for political reasons in 1833, shortly later opened a bookstore on Calle Reconquista.[61] He had two advantages over Duportail. Most importantly, he was a classmate of other University of Buenos Aires students. He had started his studies at the University of Córdoba, but registered at Buenos Aires in 1830 to follow courses in jurisprudence, at a time when fellow students included Marco Avellaneda, Vicente Fidel López, Juan Bautista Alberdi, Miguel Cané and many other young men who were later prominent in Sastre's literary salon.[62] Knowledgeable of student sociability practices, Sastre had better chances than Duportail of building up a reading clientele. The presence of young students in his bookstore was one more ace up his sleeve, as the shop became a contact point for the young Porteño intelligentsia, the network of relationships effectively constituting another sales product. His second advantage over Duportail was that as well as a bookseller, Sastre was a man of letters with publishing experience, making him an excellent source for literary, cultural and, of course, political news. In his memoirs, López describes him thus:

> Sastre was very well-known and enjoyed much popularity among students. He was most erudite and was the first bibliophile of his time. He had opened, many years earlier, a bookstore on Defensa Street, between Belgrano and Moreno, opposite the houses of Plomer, where we lived, and therefore immediately round the corner from the University. Before long, his bookstore became a place we would visit daily…and not only students, but people of greater import would visit; for he not only had an abundance of merchandise but also gave news, of where, how and in what way, etc., the work one was seeking could be found or ordered.[63]

As can be seen, Sastre had the profile of the bookseller in whose bookstore one pauses and swiftly becomes a customer. He rapidly took advantage of his reputation, moving to larger premises in January 1835 and opening a "Reading Room or Public Library" in the bookstore, baptized with patent opportunism "Librería Argentina." What better name to arouse the interest of schoolboys and students, swept away by romanticism, in search of a national literature?

According to a press announcement from the period, Sastre did not offer book loans: the only possibility was to read in the reading room itself, which was open until the late hour of 10 PM.[64] This highlights the importance of the availability of a meeting place in the cultural trade of Buenos Aires and explains why the reading room was advertised as a library. Nevertheless, in 1836 when Sastre purchased Duportail's collection, he included a home loan system in his business.[65] Weinberg reports that many other bookstores began to follow suit, no doubt with the hope of making their activities more profitable. We have no quantitative data as to the importance of this system in Porteños' commercial cultural habits. It is known that the system did not bring about the disappearance of the custom of reading in the bookstore. In Sastre's store, for example, home loans never attained the commercial success of in-store reading. The ever-scowling bookseller Ortiz opposed gatherings in his bookstore because "visitors hinder sales," though Gálvez in his memoirs puts this down rather to a lack of sociability, a trait which nevertheless did not prevent Ortiz from opening a reading room in his shop in 1837 where "for a few *reales* he rented out or lent books to read."[66] In all likelihood this particular bookseller had finally discovered the benefits of in-store gatherings of young men, which suggests that for the few book-based businesses in Buenos Aires it was more profitable to offer a meeting space, and with it, acquire a network of relationships through which to rent out books and newspapers. In other words, what sources term "reading rooms" in fact resembled bourgeois circles far more than businesses linked to the world of publishing. In the three cases of bookstores opening reading rooms, it is evident that what attracted and won over the clientele's loyalty was the meeting place rather than the renting of books.

Upon payment of a fee clientele were permitted reading and entrance to the salon, where the members would find themselves among readers and customers. The clientele visited the reading room, to read, to bring themselves up to date and even to better themselves, but it was also the need for sociability that got them to leave the private. Although people went to bookshops to read, they stayed there longer out of the pleasure of a gathering during which certain civil rules were supposedly observed: to respect the reading choices of others, to handle the works with care, to remain silent but also to at times engage in conversation. While many of these relationship codes were already de rigueur in refined relationships in Porteño salons, they now defined a kind of civil behavior which established the public sphere as a new space of social relationships.

The practice of conversation may have been on the whole established and, depending on the place where it took place, passed from one form to another. Hence, when reading was followed by a discussion on literature, it passed to another form: the literary salon.

Marcos Sastre's Literary Salon: During the period in question here, Buenos Aires saw only one literary salon, inaugurated by Marcos Sastre in June 1837.[67] According to

López, Sastre's idea had been to transfer the informal discussions, which university students had held in private houses for some time, to his premises. But the mode of operation and the nature of the link denaturalized the form and objectives found in the origins of these meetings. The literary salon set up at the back of Sastre's store was, according to López, "a club for discussion, conversation and reading." More so than in the case of the reading room, an emphasis was placed here on intellectual entertainment, which explains the use of the word "club" to define the activity.

According to the announcement published in the press, the salon's meetings took place twice or three times a week at the end of the working day, which made it easy for professionally active members to attend.[68] The purpose of the meetings was "the reading and discussion of literary works presented in the salon." Everyone could express their opinion and make any comments that seemed pertinent but, the announcement added, at these meetings "frankness, cordiality and good humor must prevail," which indicates the extent to which civil relationships were becoming a prime necessity in gatherings among educated Porteños.

The primary difference with the association of students was that anybody could join it, subject to a subscription fee. In this sense, the salon resembled the formula of the reading room already in operation in the same bookstore. But inasmuch as the reading room brought with it the possibility of widening the network beyond the previous limits of the student sphere, the subscription fee restricted the clientele to the more well-to-do social stratum. As F. Parent writes of Paris, while literary salons and reading rooms worked in the same way, their positions were quite dissimilar.[69] The Sastre salon subscription fee was soon three times that of the reading room, rising from twenty to sixty pesos.[70] It is easy to imagine the kind of clientele for whom the salon was reserved. In prime position were students participating in the association of literary and historical studies. Some, namely those from wealthy families, could afford the cost of subscription, but other less fortunate members were no doubt admitted in exchange for their erudite participation which became indispensable for the success of the business. This was surely the case of Echeverría and Gutiérrez, the salon's promoters. For this reason, the subscription of new members from the business sphere undoubtedly became essential. Lopez's memoirs refer explicitly to this, stating that the project was able to overcome difficulties due to the membership of the city's wealthy traders, among them Porteños, naturally but also "very Argentinized" foreigners, adds López, such as the German Federico von Shenteim or the Englishman Hughes. In terms of the establishment of associations it can also be observed that this was the first bookstore to move away from the university area in order to be nearer the business district.[71] It is not clear whether this was a deliberate move by Sastre to extend his clientele, but it can be inferred that the location facilitated the widening of the member network, which according to Mangel du Mesnil was as large as five hundred members, no mean sum for a city of around 65,000 inhabitants.[72] Unfortunately, the register of subscriptions has not been preserved, hence to study who visited the reading room I have based my research almost exclusively on the information provided by F. Weinberg. According to this information, the clientele was generally young, with an average age of 23. Among these, nine out of ten had a university degree, almost all from the University of Buenos Aires. When the salon was founded the majority had already graduated and to a great extent did so in the same year. However, a significant third were finishing their studies upon joining the salon, which suggests that the network of relationships within the salon may have coincided with previously existent networks probably established during university lectures.[73]

In many aspects, the organization of the salon resembled that of the Literary Society of 1822. In both cases, the object of the meetings was to read aloud and to discuss and share opinions through the press and the publication of works. However, while the Literary Society had precise political objectives which limited its clientele and closed off the network, the Literary Salon was much closer to the formula of the bourgeois circle specializing in intellectual dissemination, which anybody who could afford the subscription could join. Although politics was present in debates, this salon, unlike the Literary Society of 1822, emphasized the poet and thinker acting in an autonomous literary sphere.[74] In this aspect the salon of 1837 broke with the tradition of the Societies of Friends of the Country as an attempt to reform society through the medium of the State.[75] This was now a private initiative, but the objectives and the political scope of the movement placed it in this new public sphere.[76]

This phenomenon was not limited to the Literary Salon of 1837, nor was the formula of public reading and discussion reduced to the medium of the cultural elites. The city of Buenos Aires had other meeting points which were also public reading spaces, as was the case with reading rooms in the premises (circles) of traders, in which similar relationships of sociability tied to reading and discussion could be developed.

Reading Salons in Traders' Circles: It is not surprising to discover that traders' circles, undeniably bourgeois clubs with an emphasis on the commercial aspects of the meetings, were developed principally by the foreign population with its ties to the export trade. It is even less surprising that these should be British subjects, among whom such forms of association were highly developed. Once again, it can be seen that the foreign community had close ties with innovations in local sociability practices.

The oldest of these circles was the Sala Comercial Inglesa (English Commerce Room), founded in Buenos Aires in 1810 and occupying the same premises until 1822. After this date the association operated in the homes of its members until 1829, when it was reorganized by the Englishman Thomas Lowe, secretary of the association from 1822.[77] According to an English traveler who visited the city, this was an English club whose aim, aside from sociability and entertainment, was information. Gálvez describes the club as: "a center which brought together coastal trade crews, the owners of small boats and anybody connected to river commerce." The English Salon was at the time, in Gálvez's words, "the sailors' club, a place to meet, watch and relax for those involved in foreign trade."[78] Its members had a reading room at their disposal where they could consult the local press and principal foreign newspapers. It has also been seen that the British Friendly Society operated within the English Salon, proof if it was ever needed of the importance of sociability practices in the choice of public consumption of culture. The British influence was seen again in 1829 as a result of the trade treaty signed with Great Britain in 1825, which had reactivated commercial exchange between the two countries, and local traders picked up on this. In 1929 Lowe established the "Buenos Aires Commercial Room," intended for local traders refused entry to the English Club, an initiative which undoubtedly allowed Lowe to profit from the English circle's collection of books and periodicals. This circle provided a wide selection of documents for consultation on the premises, subject to a subscription fee. The French trader Isabelle writes, "one could read all of the principal European and American newspapers."[79] The room was in operation until at least 1838, after which no references have been found.

In these circles and clubs, reading was related to intellectual diversion and business. The profitable aspect was to be found not only in lucrative information but also from relationships established in the reading room. This was an essential aspect for foreigners yet to integrate with local society but also for Porteños who could widen, consolidate and even build a network of relationships aimed at facilitating mercantile exchanges through this medium. To study the usefulness of such a network, it is vital to place it in the general context of an individual's network of relationships. However, from the present perspective it is important to highlight the specificity of this form of relationship, which undoubtedly traversed an enormous variety of networks, but which nevertheless fell within a general trend of transformation in forms of urban sociability which must surely have brought modifications to the structure of relationship networks. This tendency to establish a contractual relationship model affected other relationship spheres indirectly related to intellectual diversion. It is here that the impact on society was apparently significant. While it is possible to express serious reservations as to the potential of these institutions, operating in the public space, to establish an autonomous public sphere critical of the country's leaders, they nevertheless introduced changes in relationship practices which appear to have gone hand in hand with considerable mutations in social and economic life.

The Scope of the Associative Relationship Model: The associative contractual model was primarily tied to the world of cultural elites, to such an extent that one might define the association as a practice stemming from the cultural exchanges of the well-to-do. However, other sectors were found in which this associative organization model was present. Far from exhaustive, a chart of the relational field where new associative practices were developed might include: charity work, at first by the Church but later as the aim of secular associations, traditional networks of commercial exchange aiming to structure themselves on a foundation of conventional rules adapted to the conditions of societies by contract, and the old trade guilds which tended to metamorphose into friendly associations.

The first lay association with charitable aims was created in 1822. Established under the initiative of the Rivadavia government, the Sociedad de Beneficencia (Charity Society) was made of "good society" ladies and managed the city's different education, charity and health institutions. In so doing, the Society took on many roles previously covered by religious groups and the Cabildo, such as the running of the principal charitable institution created by Viceroy Vértiz, the Hospicio de Niños Expósitos (a foundlings' hospice).[80] The association's organizational form was adopted, but in a tradition of community management typical of colonial society. However, the introduction of the associative contractual principle had its consequences in the representation of community action and even in the community itself. Under an 1828 governmental initiative, the short-lived Philanthropic Society was created with a view to complementing the work of the Sociedad de Beneficencia; that year's political crisis was probably the reason for its rapid disappearance. It was reestablished by an 1833 decree, but once again political crisis brought about its swift demise, while attempts to revive the society in 1852 foundered in the hands of a municipal organization. These organizations, like the Consejo de Beneficencia Pública (Public Welfare Council) created in 1833, all formed part of the context of secularization of community life and shared the same characteristic of being halfway houses between associations and public institutions. They were connected to the State apparatus in that they were created by government initiative with a view to carrying out roles considered to be of public interest and funded by the State.

The emergence of new social ties concerned economic relationships in equal measure. In this sphere, three types of associations appeared: the socioeconomic associations seen above, socioeconomic institutions,[81] and commercial societies. While the latter two fall outside of the sphere of sociability, they merit some brief attention.

These societies were developed with purely commercial ends, and sociability was not a value emphasized either in their roles or their exchanges. Nevertheless, these entities were indicative of a transformation in forms of social organization. Indeed, unlike the exchange circles of traditional family network-based societies, in these entities exchanges had to be adapted by contract to the conditions of the societies.[82] In emphasizing rationality in exchanges and the contractual nature of the relationship, these societies broke with the socioeconomic structure of exchanges in the region.[83] It can be seen that even in the sector of farmers close to the regime, societies were share-based.[84] Between 1836 and 1837 three share-based societies were set up with the aim of developing sheep farming, bringing together men whose families already had ties with livestock rearing, such as Lucio Mansilla, Luis Dorrego, Isidoro Peralta, Simón Pereyra, Tomás and Nicolás Anchorena, Juan Cano, Zenón Videla and Idelfonso Ramos Mejía, among others who alternated between sheep and cattle rearing.[85] These associations provide much information about transformations in the relationship sphere of a population which exceeded the medium of cultural elites opposed to Rosas, at least up to 1839. Furthermore, these examples confirm the continuity between the liberal period and the first decade of the Rosas government, at least in terms of relational practices.

To complete this brief overview, it is important to mention the appearance during this period of friendly societies, the first of which was created in 1832 by French artisans.[86] On October 4th of this year, to be precise, the Sociedad Mutual de Beneficencia de los Artesanos Franceses (French Artisans' Friendly Welfare Society) requested authorization from the government to hold their meetings on the first Sunday of each month at the home of the administrator, a Monsieur Mandain.[87] The organization of this association raised diplomatic problems between the French General Consul in Buenos Aires, Monsieur de Mendeville, the French community resident in the city and the province government, a conflict on which abundant documentation is to be found in the archives of the Quai d'Orsay.[88] It appears that the French authorities in Buenos Aires, as a result of these conflicts, decided to support the creation of another association which would take up the same charitable aims but extend them to include all members of the community, which modified the associative form. Fearful that the Sociedad Mutual de Beneficencia might veer off its political course, the French authorities proposed in its place the creation of a charitable association controlled by the French Consulate in Argentina. According to a report from the French Consul in Buenos Aires to the Minister of Foreign Affairs, dated 25 August 1835, the new Sociedad Filantrópica Francesa (French Philanthropic Society) had around four hundred members and capital of twenty thousand piasters, a sum with which "the Society may bring relief to many unfortunate souls. It has already repatriated various wretches who would have died in poverty, and attended to many sick people, be it at the hospice or in their homes,"[89] As for the origin of the capital, in addition to contributions from French subjects and funds from a lottery organized with this end, there were some contributors, of whom very little is known.[90] In any event, the society maintained a close relationship with the French Consulate which managed its funds. It was to enjoy a lengthy existence, as it was still operating in 1853.[91] This does not appear to have been the only case. Another charitable association was set up by North Americans in 1836, the North American Benevolent Society, of which unfortunately we have very little information.

These examples show a slow transformation of relational practices, whose consequences for social representations remain to be seen in their entirety. Without intending to attribute to these associations a similar relational structure, a common purpose or a like catalog of shared values, it is clear that all were founded on a kind of associative tie to which cultural elites attached a discourse of the nation as a new society of individuals.

The Cultural Limits of Associative Civility: Ethnic Sociability

It is notable that in this period the most developed associations among the population of Buenos Aires were those pertaining to the black population, considering that what scant research there is into associative life in the city refers strictly to the elite white associations.[92] While it is true that elite sociocultural associations were the first contractual forms of associative sociability to take root in the River Plate at the start of the century, after 1821, and with the creation of "African societies," it was the population of African origin that most used the associative form of organization of community life. These associations remain relatively unknown in Argentine historiography. Until presently, and with a single exception, they were studied solely by folklore historians. The exception is the research of George Reid Andrews, a North American historian of "African-Argentines," who has studied these associations in greater depth. Nevertheless, to date not a single work—not even Andrews'—has attempted to analyze the development of African societies in the global associative movement.[93] To understand the particularities of this associative movement it is necessary to firstly take into account the principal specific aspects of the population of African origin.

THE BLACK POPULATION IN THE CITY OF BUENOS AIRES

The scarcely visible mark that the African population has left on present-day Buenos Aires makes it easy to forget that, during the first half of the nineteenth century, more than 30 percent of the population of Buenos Aires was of African origin. From historiography's "forgetfulness" was born the "enigma" of Buenos Aires' African population.[94] The present chapter does not intended to decipher but simply to recall the principal aspects of the history of the African population in the city of Buenos Aires that might help to explain the development of ethnic associations.

The history of the black population in Buenos Aires must be seen in the context of the rise of the slave trade in the modern age but also the economic development of the region. Indeed, although the port city of Buenos Aires, like other territories of the Spanish kingdom, had witnessed the slave trade, the flow of slave labor to the city was relatively limited until the mid-eighteenth century. Besio Moreno's figures show an African population of only 233 in Buenos Aires in 1595. In fact, the growth of the slave trade in the region began with the opening of the port in 1778. Elena Studer claims that between 1742 and 1806 around 25,000 slaves legally entered Buenos Aires, although the figure is most likely to be twice this amount if we include those slaves illegally smuggled into the port.[95] Half of the slaves were imported from Brazil and the other half from Africa, especially the west coast and particularly from "bamboo peoples" such as the "Bengalis," the "Congos," the "Luandans," as well as other peoples known as "Angola caste," such as the "Mina," the "Ashanti," the "Mandinga," the "Volo," the "Revolo," the "Camandú," and the "Yumbé."[96] Although three-quarters of those slaves who arrived in Buenos Aires continued on to other parts of the viceroyalty, between 1744 and 1810 the percentage of the black population of the city increased more rapidly than that of the white population.[97]

To establish a more accurate idea of the numerical importance of the African population in the postcolonial city, we must refer to the results of Marta Goldberg's demographic study of the censuses of 1810, 1822, 1836 and 1838.[98] These figures represent the minimum base of the real numbers of the African population in Buenos Aires, taking into account the tendency of those of mixed ethnic origin to claim "whiteness" in order to escape prejudice aimed at African-Argentines.[99] In any case, it should be kept in mind that for the period in question an average proportion of around 24 percent of the population were recognized as being of African origin.

The presence of this population was more noticeable in certain parts of the city. While this was not a case of ethnic segregation in the urban space, sources often refer to the "*barrio de los tambores*" (the tambour neighborhood) to refer to the area of the city with the highest concentration of the black population.[100] The map of population distribution in the city of Buenos Aires in 1836 nevertheless shows a greater concentration of "African-Argentines" in the parish of Monserrat, but a third of the slaves, and a similar proportion of emancipated slaves, still lived in barrios in the center and often shared their place of residence with well-to-do people.[101] However, there was a tendency for many African-Argentines, upon gaining their freedom, to live in certain neighborhoods on the outskirts of the city, something which Miguel Ángel Rosal appears to confirm in former slaves' real estate transactions.[102] Therefore, to speak of an ethnic neighborhood it is necessary to see the cycle of integration of the free black population. Available data give a fixed image of the patterns of urban settlement without taking into account the spatial cycle of each inhabitant.[103]

The Legal Situation of the African Population: In the nineteenth century, to be black was not synonymous with slavery, nor was this the case during the colonial period. There were numerous possibilities for emancipation: freedom could be purchased from the owner, granted freely by the owner, or given by the state in recognition of services to the country.[104] In the case of manumission in colonial Buenos Aires, L. Johnson suggests that the majority of slaves, nearly 70 percent, paid for their own freedom.[105] According to Johnson, this may explain the importance to slaves in participating in artisanal activities, which allowed them to accumulate the necessary capital to buy their freedom.[106]

With the break with colonial ties and the introduction of a republican regime in the region, the number of slaves diminished noticeably. While, according to García Belsunce, slaves represented 86.41 percent of the "African-Argentine" population in 1810, by 1822 they made up no more than 12 percent.[107] This change does not appear to be so much the consequence of abolitionist methods as the result of African-Argentines' participation in the wars of independence, or simply from purchasing their own freedom, an operation which was now more affordable for slaves due to funds loaned by the "African nations." Indeed, in spite of the first abolitionist measures in 1812, there was a notable gap between formal declarations and slaves' actual situation.[108] The reverse situation cannot even be detected, declarations of principles notwithstanding, nor explicitly refuted.[109] This was the case, for example, with the declaration of 12 September 1827 aimed at regulating the entry of Brazilian slaves acquired as spoils of war. Although the article recalls "the inalterable principle that sustains that all slaves arriving at the port of the Republic are free ipso facto, from the moment they set foot on our beaches," the regulation guaranteed slaves, on their arrival on Argentine soil, a status of freedom which was in fact closer to slavery. The decree assured the privateer in possession of the spoils the right to patronage over "his" slaves. Thus, although legally converted into free men, these immigrants were obliged to serve the privateer for a period of between five and ten years, according to the age of the slave. In short, the transactions revolved around the right to patronage which would guarantee slave labor in the prime of life. In other words, this right assured a captive labor force during the period of greatest labor profitability, after which the slave was at liberty to find himself a means of subsistence until the end of his days.[110] The situation appears to have begun to change in 1840 when Rosas signed the antislavery treaty with Great Britain.[111] However, it was only in 1853 that slavery was legally abolished by the Constitution of the Argentine Confederation. Taking into account that the province of Buenos Aires did not vote in this constitution until seven years later, slavery can be said to have existed in the city of Buenos Aires until 1860, around the same time as when African-Argentine communities began to disappear. The reality of slavery accounts for the vitality of an associative movement which counted among its principal aims that of loaning money for the emancipation of its members.

African-Argentines in the Urban Economy: From the colonial period onwards, slave labor was used for several tasks, the best known of which was domestic work in elite Argentine families.[112] Slave labor was also found in minor urban jobs: transporting water, exterminating insects and even peddling goods were some activities commonly carried out by the black population, whether slaves or free.[113] Blacks also worked in various areas of production: baking bread, building furniture, or making hats.[114] As seen earlier, however, the slaves' most important presence—both in quantity and the place of their work in the economic and social structure of the city—was in the various artisanal trade activities. Their presence was owing to the significance of the system for renting slave labor in capital investment, widespread particularly among widows and unmarried women. Because of chronic labor shortages, this type of investment proved sufficiently lucrative to convince a considerable and fairly heterogeneous number of slave owners to opt for hiring out a day-to-day basis.[115] Lyman Johnson writes that of the 1,137 people working as artisans in 1780 in the city of Buenos Aires, 12 percent were of African origin, of which 57 percent were not free.[116] Various authors see the strong presence of slave labor or former slaves' labor in artisanal trades as one of the reasons for the scant development of guild organizations in the city of Buenos Aires, as racial discrimination against black artisans led to a social devaluation of manual jobs identified with slavery.[117] Indeed it is difficult to imagine any organization aimed at consolidating guild interests and creating ties of solidarity within a guild made up of slaves and free men in a society governed by a system of legal inequality.[118] This could also explain the rise of ethnic associations aimed at replacing trade guilds, which were harder to establish.

Having considered all of these aspects, we can first highlight the quantitative importance of the African-Argentine population in the city, which facilitated the regrouping of individuals of like ethnic origin into societies of "nations."[119] It is necessary to outline the particularities of the legal status of the black population after independence, which serves to illustrate the usefulness of maintaining previous forms of solidarity: since declarations of principles inseparable from natural law did not radically change the fate of slaves in the region, it is not unreasonable to imagine that they continued to adopt old methods of manumission. Their place in the local economy could also constitute another element of response. In short, all of these reasons lead one to consider these societies more as a continuation of old organizational forms than as a break with prior practices and representations. Nevertheless, the vitality of associative life can also be explained by the republic's will to control this potentially rebellious population.[120] The problem with the continuity and breaks between the "nations" of the colonial period and of the "African Societies" is in fact quite complex and deserves further attention.

THE AFRICAN NATIONS BEFORE 1821

There is some confusion as regards the black population's practices of sociability. African associations were indistinctly named "Nations," "African Societies," "Guilds," and even "Friendly Societies," when in fact these different denominations corresponded to quite distinct forms of sociability at different moments in time.[121] G. Andrews and R. Rodríguez Molas thus link the African Societies of the Rivadavian period to the *candombes*. Andrews dates the first testimony to the existence of the nations in 1770, while Rodríguez Molas dates their appearance to 1813. Rossi, on the other hand, establishes total continuity between the African ethnic association and the societies of the nineteenth century.[122]

During the colonial period, there appear to have been two forms of sociability typical of the African community: those brought from the people's countries of origin, most frequently manifested in dances around a drum (known as *candombes*); and those acquired in the River Plate viceroyalty, principally religious brotherhoods. Naturally, this distinction does not exclude notable cultural syncretisms, but it will be seen that in at least one transcendent aspect this distinction is not only useful but also necessary.

Candombe and Brotherhoods in the Colonial City: In almost all colonial cities with a strong black population, whether slaves or free, there is much testimony of dances or *candombes*.[123] *Candombe* refers to both the dance and the gathering at which the dance takes place. That is, the same word refers at once to the form and the place of the gathering. By extension, *candombe* and even *tambor* indicate the group who gathers to dance; in other words, the relationship network consolidated by ethnic sociability ties. We have thus arrived at the meaning of "African Nation," which

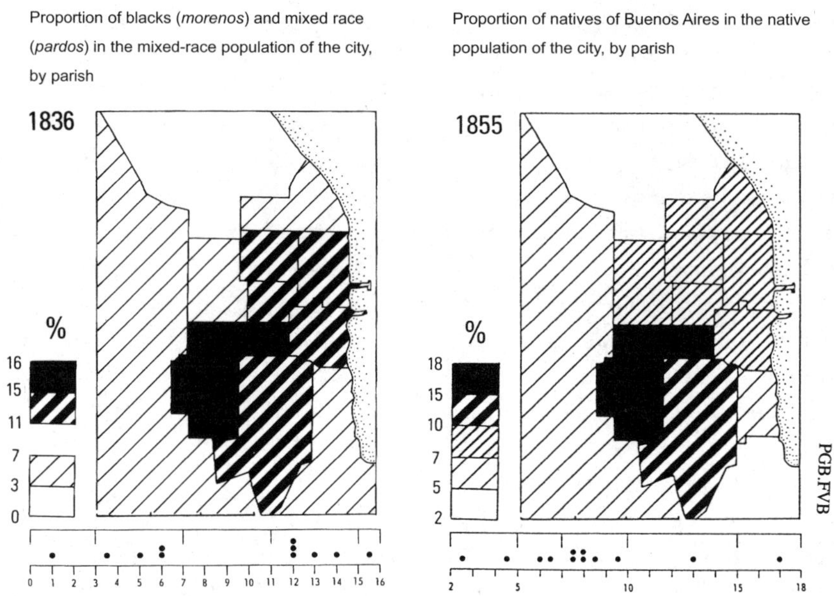

Figure 8. Distribution of the black and mixed-race population in the city of Buenos Aires (1836-1855)

refers to the tendency of African-Argentines to group together according to their "nation" of origin. Hence, colonial sources mention "blacks of the Conga Nation" or of the "Cambunda Nation" who organized their dances to the rhythm of the tambour.[124] According to Rodríguez Molas, the first historical reference to these collective practices dates from 1649. A century later, "dancing gatherings" appear to have developed considerably, to the extent that they were a point of concern for the authorities. The edict of 1770 of the then Governor and later Viceroy Vértiz prohibiting "dances practiced by blacks" permits a deduction that the reason for their proscription was that they took place without permission.[125] To this was added the indecency of the physical movements in public places and also the fact that other activities prohibited by the Crown might take place, such as games of chance or frightful manifestations of paganism. Such is the message from 1779 of priest Francisco Javier Zamudio of the Piedad parish: "[the blacks'] lack of public respect for the Church, when they begin to dance before its doors their typical obscene dances, on the afternoon of Saint Balthazar's Day and Easter Sunday."[126] In 1791, the city Attorney General reported how while walking through the parish of Concepción one Sunday, "he observed in many houses a number of black men and women enclosed therein and playing the tambour."[127] It is well known that the dances could often occur in closed spaces, which suggests that controls on these were not necessarily due to the attack on morals in the streets.

As we approach the nineteenth century, a time of important demographic growth for the black population in Buenos Aires, references to African sociability become increasingly numerous. It can be agreed that between "dance" and the existence of an "African Nation" there is a relationship which, as logical and conceptual as it may be, is no proof of the historical existence of an organizing structure regrouping African-Argentines according to their ethnic origin. There are no known sources confirming the pre-independence existence of an organizational structure founded on ethnic solidarity objectives. It would appear that in spite of the propagation of practices, the informal type of gathering prevailed. The colonial administration especially ensured respect for the calendar of festivals and the decency of gestures, while showing evidence of a certain tolerance for periodic dance gatherings. This tendency appears to have continued into the early nineteenth century, when repressive measures do not appear to have occurred, according to sources. Furthermore, it can be assumed that the Cabildo was increasingly indulgent with Africans' entertainment forms, when the insurrection in the city against the Spanish authorities made the latter's loyalty to the revolutionary cause a necessity. Already, in view of African-Argentines' participation in the defense of Buenos Aires in 1806 and 1807, a series of initiatives by the Cabildo had set out to reward their loyalty to the crown and to the city.[128] It was also during these years that the Africans of the Conga Nation were to acquire land for the first time, in barrio 15 in the parish of Nuestra Señora de Pilar, in order to perform their "tango dance."[129] But until the 1821 regulation, dance-based sociability does not appear to have gone hand in hand with a formalized organizational structure. Nevertheless, it can clearly be distinguished from spontaneous sociability in *pulperías*: there was apparently no alcohol or guitars, both sexes attended, the clientele were of the same ethnic origin, there was no fixed meeting place and dancing was de rigueur. The sociability of the *candombe*s can, then, be clearly distinguished from the sociability of *pulperías*. Furthermore, periodic collections during the gatherings to guarantee dances during festivals required the existence of a recognized authority to administer the money, and often to arrange a meeting place. The same person was also responsible for the organization of the dances, including arranging the musicians and choreographers. These differences made gatherings in *pulperías* a form of sociability that was more permeable to new relational codes and values disseminated by the associative movement.

The black population in the city also participated in another form of associative sociability often confused with *candombe*s: brotherhoods. It is true that there is a gray area between *candombe* and brotherhood gatherings. In this respect, colonial references to the former are quite wrong and lead to this confusion. For some it was the same community organization which presumably took on different shapes, while for others there was an evolution in the tradition of community organization which accounted for the transition first to brotherhoods and then to societies of nations.[130] It is undoubtedly difficult to distinguish between religious festivity and the *candombe*, especially as the same people took part, such as on the day of the Epiphany, one of the most important dates in the *candombe* calendar and at the same time the date of the procession of the Saint Balthazar brotherhood. Significantly, it was precisely the Saint Balthazar brotherhood that came into most conflict with its priest, which suggests a confusion between two commemorations that the priest attempted to remedy.[131] Nevertheless, a formal distinction can be made between *candombe*s and brotherhoods. While the latter were religious associations in which African-Argentines were organized according to trade bodies, in *candombe*s organization was by ethnic origin. Further, the brotherhoods had a formal organization, while *candombe*s, being a form of recreational sociability, did not have a genuinely formalized structure. Aside from this distinction, it must be clarified that there are few data as to these African-Argentine brotherhoods in Buenos Aires.[132] According to research by Miguel Angel Rosal, these associations appear to have been firmly rooted among the black population of colonial Buenos Aires. The same author sustains that with the development of "African societies" the black population tended to leave the brotherhoods in order to join these new associative forms.[133]

The "African Societies," a Creation of Rivadavian Liberals

The rise of African associations coincided with the Rivadavia government, more precisely between 1821 and 1823, when a series of instructions from the government to the chief of police with regards to public dancing led to the regulation of these gatherings and the creation of "African Societies." The first of these regulations dates from 30 November 1821. Previously, the decree of 8 November of the same year had set up the observation of African dances, with the intention of eventually establishing "a regulation to fix a method for society to observe." The liberal government thus intended to legalize "tango dances" while at the same time prohibiting dancing in the street.[134] The definitive regulation which would apply to all African societies was that of August 1823, after a series of measures passed between 1821 and the same year by the Chief of Police of the City of Buenos Aires, Joaquín de Achával, with the intention of establishing a regulation and legal definition of tambour dances or *candombe*s.[135] As a result an important African-Argentine associative movement can be seen to have appeared and developed in the city.

The objectives of these new associations were explicitly set by the regulations: to aid the emancipation of its members through loans with a 5 percent annual interest rate, safeguard the morals, education and industry of the members and organize a monthly mass so that the souls of its deceased might rest. Among these objectives it is possible to recognize roles typical of trade brotherhoods, such as the welfare of men and their souls. Nor did the society abandon the role of educator, but the hierarchical structure characteristic of technical teaching in the brotherhoods disappeared. The regulation also contained a series of articles which recall the secular associative forms built up according to the contractual principle of relationships and authority: equality among members, election of authorities, possibility of revoking mandates by members of the association and the loss of the religious authorities' control over the associative movement of black men. It is not unreasonable to suppose that the will to create a new associative form, which would assure assistance in the African community, fell within the context of the policy of secularization of assistance, of which the creation of new charity institutions/associations were another aspect.[136] Yet, in secularizing the "assistance role" in the African-Argentine commerce, the liberal Rivadavian government created a new associative form inexistent until then: the ethnic association. It is true that the regulation of 1823 did not institute networks of relationships particular to the ethnic community, nor did it invent solidarity among members. Nonetheless, it formalized these through a new associative practice organized according to old forms of sociability in the African population. In spite of the apparent liberality of Achával's administration, the full sense of these measures must not be mistaken. Rather than wishing to put an end to old restrictions burdening freedom of association, the liberal Rivadavia government in fact intended to bring in stricter vigilance.[137] Nonetheless, it has to be said that this initiative by the liberal government facilitated the development of an associative experience which preserved old features but fell within a new logic.

THE FATE OF THE AFRICAN SOCIETIES AFTER RIVADAVIA

To a certain extent, it is now possible to see the history of these associations because of police control. Indeed, in spite of the explicit directive of the regulations with regards to the archives that each society must have had, this documentation, supposing that it was written at the time, has now disappeared entirely, hence all available information on the African Societies comes solely from police files.[138]

From this body of evidence, one can produce a chronological picture of the associations' development over the period in question.[139] The graph (figure 6) allows us to show firstly the continuous and fairly regular development of African associations, which nevertheless shows two salient points in 1825 and 1830.[140] In the first five years following the regulation a considerable number of associations were founded, with the objective of legalizing gatherings as a result of the new possibilities provided by the government. This was the case of those of the Conga Nation previously mentioned, as well as the Benguela, Cabunda, Mina, Mondongo, Mongolo, Moros, Lubolo, Mozambique, Angola, Carabari and Huombe nations. The interpretation of the second salient point, which indicates a notable rise in the number of societies in 1830, is more controversial. It can be associated with the previous phenomenon, but can also be explained by other causes. Firstly, there is a possibility of an exceptional influx of slaves from Brazil. Such phenomenal demographic growth would have had repercussions on the associative domain through an equivalent development in the associations.[141] It remains to be seen whether this was the consequence of a spontaneous attitude of the new arrivals who, upon considering the benefits that might be had from these organizations formed a society, or on the contrary, whether it was government policy that forced them into it. This question leads us to a second interpretation connecting this growth to a political phenomenon, namely that of Rosas coming to power. To explain an increase so close to Rosas taking power, however, it is necessary to find precise orders with regards to the African societies. To our knowledge, Rosas did not pass any decree or regulation specifically concerning these associations in his first years in office.

The development of new associations appears to have been, in fact, the consequence of a fragmentation of existing societies: the Conga Agunda emerged from a division in the Conga Nation; the Muchague and the Mañanbaru from a split in the Mozambique Nation; the Muchague was to suffer a further split from which the Amuera Nation would emerge in 1834. The explanation for this phenomenon must be sought less in the political context of 1830 than in existent tensions between associative logic and the ethnic community. Indeed, according to regulations these associative forms had to operate like an old-style corporation. Article 6 set out that they had to be constituted on the basis of the ethnic community: "no society may be established that is made up of individuals of a like nation in order to prevent the evils that this may cause."[142] But along with this ethnic restriction limiting development, liberal policy entailed stimulating the formalization of "tango dances" in an associative form, encouraging the propagation of associations. This contradiction explains the perplexity of the government towards the development of a movement which it had itself created, a fact which the examining commission of the African Societies refers to explicitly in an 1834 report for police captain Pedro Romero. The members of this commission warned of the unexpected and irritating effects of the government's inconsistent policy towards societies. In authorizing the creation of new societies from the division of old ones, the government contributed to insubordination within the society, something which the commission believed denaturalized the prevailing aims in the origin of the creation of the African societies, as it gave them too much freedom of action.[143]

In this perspective, what appears to be confirmation of the success of the associative model imposed by the liberals may actually cover up its failure. Indeed, it is valid to suppose that successive divisions ultimately annihilated African Societies, while indicating the extreme fragility of the ethnic solidarity network. However, the rate of development rules out this hypothesis. Divisions were produced in detriment to the associative form, which persisted continuously throughout the first half of the nineteenth century. They also tended to evolve towards a greater specialization of roles, which, in the second half of the nineteenth century, would lead to the origin of friendly societies, recreational associations and even political associations.

Rosas appears here as the heir rather then creator of a movement which he was quickly able to bring under his control to ensure the conditions for its future development. But in the dark crisis which was to sweep across the province of Buenos Aires between 1838 and 1842, taking the lives of some members of the Porteño elites, African associations would play a far from negligible role in the mobilization of support for Rosas and the Federation, which allows us to establish a prime distinction in Rosas' Rivadavian inheritance. While sociocultural associative forms which recruited members mostly from elite spheres were assimilated in opposition practices, the ethnic associations appeared as one of the types of organizations which best adhered to the values of the "Holy Federation." The distinction can be found then in a partisan logic. But the mistrust that new sociocultural associations inspired was no less justified. Not only because the malcontents began to beat the elites, who until then had been relatively spared the human cost of factional conflict but also because this type of association stimulated public discussion of social questions which had previously been the business of the authorities, be these public—in the old sense of the concept—or of the community. From this point of view, African associations appeared far less subversive, given that the very objective of the association picked up on the old idea of community administration in which existed an old representation of society and authority. Moreover, the associative principal, founded on ethnic belonging, tended to close the network of associations, hindering the identification between associative principle and foundation of the social bond. Thus, inasmuch as the sociocultural associative form tended to break or at least stretch a neighborhood sociability based around primary bonds, in introducing a contractual representation of the social bond, ethnic associative sociability reinforced community ties hidden by corporate social representations, It did this while nonetheless introducing the contractual principle which undermined old bases of authority.

The model of how African Societies were rooted in the city enforces this idea. These associations are testimony to a location based around the parishes of Monserrat and Concepción, where the majority of the free black population lived. Nonetheless, there was no strict correlation between the concentration of African inhabitants and the establishment of societies, as such societies were absent in the parishes of the center of Buenos Aires, even though there was a sizeable African-Argentine population. There are two possible explanations: either they were obliged to make this decision because land was more expensive in the center than on the outskirts, or the authorities, ever suspicious of the African population's recreational practices, encouraged them to move away from the center. Whatever the case may be, this shows above all that, unlike *pulperías*, this was not an associative form that reinforced the sociability of the neighborhood. Furthermore, the choice of the parish of Monserrat does not seem fortuitous, given that according to Miguel Ángel Rosal the price of property there was higher than in other parts of the city.[144] Their localized establishment indicated hence a topographic specificity which renewed tensions among associative values and the ethnic community.

The example of African societies shows, therefore, the complexity of transformations resulting from the establishment of new relational principles. The new associative practices opened up access to certain ties, forms of organization and a democratic ritual which took on new significance in each association through cultural practices entailing divergent social representations. But while the incidence of "democratic associations" in postcolonial Porteño society was mitigated, from a short-term perspective, the development of voluntary associations among different sectors of the urban population introduced a new representation of society as a product of voluntary ties between free individuals and equals, with unlimited consequences.

NOTES

1. M. Agulhon, *Les Cercles.*; M. Agulhon, "Généralités et antécédents lointains," in Maurice Agulhon y M. Bodiguel, *Les Associations au village* (Actes Sud, Hubert Nyssen Éditeur, 1981), 11–14. This approach is developed further by J. P. Rioux in "Structure de sociabilité et pouvoir," *Cahiers de l'Animation* 3: 46 (1984), 3–11.
2. M. Agulhon, *Les Cercles.*; R. Huart, *Le Mouvement républicain en Bas-Languedoc 1848–1881* (Paris: Presses de la Fondation Nationale des Sciences Politiques, 1982); Jürgen Habermas, *L'Espace public. Archéologie de la publicité comme dimension constitutive de la société bourgeoise*, (Paris: Payot, 1978).
3. This approach is not intended to replace or oppose the social network. They are two different approaches and to some extent complementary from a shared relationship perspective.
4. Fortunata Piselli (ed.) *Reti. L'analisi di network nelle scienze sociali* (Rome: Donzelli, 1995), presents a recent anthology of network analysis. This question is tackled below in the "Sociability and Political History" section.

5. Albert Meyers and Elizabeth D. Hopkins, preface, *Manipulating the Saints: Religious Brotherhoods and Social Integration in Post-Conquest Latin America* (Hamburg: Wayasbah, 1988). This work includes a fairly complete biography on this issue. In A. Miguel de la Cruz Espinosa, *Las confrerías de los negros en Lima*, Lima, 1985, more information can be found on brotherhoods in the city of Lima.
6. J. Torre Revello, "Fiestas y costumbres," 414–415.
7. S. Socolow, *Los mercaderes*; Lyman Johnson, *The Artisans of Buenos Aires during the Viceroyalty 1776–1810*, Ph.D. dissertation, Dept of Philosophy, University of Connecticut, 1974; Miguel Ángel Rosal, "Algunas consideraciones sobre las creencias religiosas de los africanos *porteños* (1750–1820)," *Investigaciones y Ensayos* 31 (July-December 1981): 369–382. Buenos Aires; M. A. Rosal, "Negros y pardos en Buenos Aires, 1811–1860," *Anuario de Estudios Americanos* 51: 1 (1994), 165–184.
8. These distinctions are analytical categories not an expression of successive stages in social relationships. See Ferdinand Tönnies, *Comunidad y asociación* (1887) (Barcelona: Península, 1979). I also take into account the typology used by Albert Meister, *La Participation dans les associations* (Paris: Les Éditions ouvrières, 1974); A. Meister, *Vers une sociologie des associations* (Paris: Les Éditions ouvrières, 1972; and the work of historians who have preceded us in this type of research. See M. Agulhon, *Les Cercles*; F.-X. Guerra, *Le Mexique. De l'Ancien Régime à la Révolution* (Paris: L'Harmattan, 1985), vol. 1, 126–181.
9. For an analysis of these societies, see Daniel Roche, *Le Siècle des Lumières en province. Académies et académiciens provinciaux (1680–1789)* (Paris: Mouton, 1978); D. Roche, *Les Républiques des lettres. Gens de culture de Lumières au XVIIIe siècle* (Paris: Fayard, 1988); M. Agulhon, *Pénitents et francs-maçons*.
10. On these societies in Spain, see Jean Serrailh's classic study "Les Sociétés Économiques des Amis du Pays," in *L'Espagne éclairée de la seconde moitié du XVIIIe siècle* (Paris: C. Klincksieck 1964), 223–285. On their development in the Americas, see Robert J. Shafer, *The Economic Societies in the Spanish World 1763–1821* (Syracuse: Syracuse University Press, 1958).
11. See "Lista de los señores suscriptores al Telégrafo Mercantil" in *Telégrafo Mercantil* (1801–1802) (facsimile from the Junta de Historia y Numismática Americana, Buenos Aires, 1914–1915).
12. See "Carta de Bertoldo Clak," *Telégrafo Mercantil*, 27 July 1801.
13. The same occurred in Lima, where the Academic Society of Lima was associated with the publication of the *Mercurio Peruano* (Lima, 1791–1795), and in Quito, where the Sociedad de Quito, created in 1791, began to publish in 1792 the newspaper *Primicias de Cultura* (1792), under the guidance of Francisco Javier Eugenio de Santa Cruz y Espejo.
14. The affiliation with the Societies of Friends of the Country does not appear to leave any doubt, but the differences are no less important, as these were to prove to be associations with fundamentally political objectives.
15. Daoiz V. Pérez Fontana, *La Masonería y los Masones en la organización de la República. Apuntes para la historia*, Montevideo, undated, unpublished manuscript, Grand Masonry Lodge.
16. Multiple references appear in "Carta de E. Martínez al Ministro Andrés Lamas," Montevideo, 4 October 1853, *Historia* (Montevideo) 3 (1960): 312–313. Other references in Manuel Belgrano, "Autobiografía," in *Memorias y autobiografías* (Buenos Aires: Museo Histórico Nacional, 1910), vol. 2, 91–110; Tomás Guido, "Reseña histórica

de los sucesos de Mayo," in *Memorias*, vol. 1; Manuel Moreno, *Vida y memorias de Mariano Moreno* (Buenos Aires, 1918); "Informe de los oidores," *Revista del Derecho, Historia y Letras* (Buenos Aires, 1912), vol. 43, 338–339.

17. For information on the sociocultural associations in this period see Carlos Ibarguren, *Las sociedades literarias y la Revolución Argentina (1800–1825)* (Buenos Aires: Espasa-Calpe, 1937).
18. Ricardo Piccirilli, "Rivadavia y las reformas culturales," *Boletín de la Academia Nacional de la Historia*, vol. 19, Buenos Aires, 1946, 209–228. For the Rivadavia period, see by the same author *Rivadavia y su tiempo*, 2 vols. (Buenos Aires: Peuser, 1943); on building restructuring, see F. Aliata, "Edilicia privada y crecimiento urbano."
19. On this question, see Carlos Newland, "El experimento lancasteriano en Buenos Aires," *Todo es Historia*, 244, October 1987; "La educación elemental en Hispanoamérica: desde la independencia hasta la centralización de los sistemas educativos nacionales," *Hispanic American Historical Review* 71: 2 (1991), 335–364; "El método lancasteriano," in *Buenos Aires no es pampa: la educación elemental porteña, 1820–1860* (Buenos Aires: Grupo Editor Latinoamericano, 1992).
20. José A. Wilde, *Buenos Aires setenta años atrás* (Buenos Aires: Espasa-Calpe, 1948), "Austral," 148–155; Manuel Bilbao, *Buenos Aires. Desde su fundación hasta nuestros días. Especialmente el período comprendido entre los siglos XVIII y XIX* (Buenos Aires: Imprenta de Juan A. Alsina, 1902), 405–407. According to the memoirs of Zapiola, the Philharmonic Society which appeared at the same time in Santiago de Chile was founded by one of the members of the Buenos Aires association, who was also a member of the Lancastrian society and the Valaper society, one Juan C. Lafinur. See José Zapiola, *Recuerdos de treinta años*, 59–61. For the history of lyric theater in Buenos Aires, see Mariano G. Bosch, *Historia del teatro en Buenos Aires* (Buenos Aires: Establecimiento Tipográfico El Comercio, 1910), 73–79; Vicente Gesualdo, *Historia de la música en la Argentina*, Buenos Aires, 1961. See also C. Ibarguren, *Las sociedades literarias*, 84–90.
21. *The translation of the "Confederación Peruano-Boliviana" is taken from the Dictionnaire Encyclopédique Larousse, Paris, 1965.–Translator*
22. Academia Nacional de la Historia, *Historia argentina. De los orígenes hasta la organización definitiva en 1862* (Buenos Aires: Academia Nacional de la Historia, 1939–1951), vols. 7 and 8.
23. See figure 5.
24. This continuity between the liberal Rivadavia government and the conservative Rosas government constitutes one of the most neglected aspects of Argentine historiography. Some later studies of this investigation tend to confirm this hypothesis. *Anuario IEHS* 12 gives an overview of the revision of this period.
25. A rough map is presented here with the locations of the associations for which I have been able to obtain the address of the meeting place. This may be a room or building specially rented for the member's meetings, or a private address. On methodological matters see "L'approche cartographique" in PGB, *La Création*, appendix 4, "La démarche graphique."
26. In the case of France, Daniel Gordon counts 644 references for the seventeenth century, rising to 8,294 in the following century; see Gordon, *Citizens without Sovereignty. Equality and Sociability in French Thought, 1670–1789* (Princeton: Princeton University Press, 1994), 53. A similar phenomenon is recorded for eighteenth-century Spain in P. Álvarez de Miranda, *Palabras e ideas*, 349–383.

27. An older use of this notion is found in the late seventeenth century in Spain and in a Florentine text. According to Pedro Álvarez de Miranda, the first Spanish usage of this neologism corresponds to *Hombre práctico*, by Gutiérrez de los Ríos, a work published in 1764 but written in 1680, in which the term is directly tied to social life subjected to laws. See Maurice Agulhon, "La sociabilidad como categoría histórica," in *Formas de sociabilidad en Chile 1840–1940* (Santiago de Chile, 1992), 1–10; P. Álvarez de Miranda, *Palabras e ideas*, 374.
28. The first usage in France appears in a Delamare text from 1704 and concerns a discussion on the nature of man as seen by Hobbes. But in absolutist theory, the notion of sociability is used as a social pact to show the need for and usefulness of royal sovereignty. See Delamare, *Traité de la police*, 1705, in D. Gordon, *Citizens without Sovereignty*.
29. "Sociabilité" in *Encyclopédie ou Dictionnaire raisonné...* (Paris, 1765), vol. 15, 250–251. Catherine Duprat notes that in the eighteenth century sociability and charity were used practically as synonyms; see Duprat, *Le Temps des Philanthropes* (Paris: Éditions du Comité des Travaux historiques et scientifiques, 1993).
30. In *Loi de la Nature et de la Société* (1672), Pufendorf postulates two states of nature. The movement towards society was for him the product of a rational decision. See "Sociabilité" en *Encyclopédie*; D. Gordon, *Citizens without Sovereignty*. The *Diccionario de Autoridades* confirms the existence of one of the two meanings in Spain, defining sociability as "treatment and correspondence of some people with others." See *Diccionario de la lengua castellana*, vol. 3, 133.
31. See in particular N. Elias, *La Civilisation*; R. Chartier, "Distinction et divulgation: la civilité et ses livres," *Lecture et lecteurs*; and Jacques Revel, "Les usages de la civilité," *Histoire de la vie privée*, vol. 3.
32. *Encyclopédie.*
33. In France, Philippe Ariès was the first to indicate this; see Ariès, "Pour une histoire de la vie privée," R. Chartier (ed.), *Histoire de la vie privée*. See also Dena Goodman, "Public sphere and private life: toward a synthesis of current historiographical approaches to the old regime," *History and Theory* 31: 1 (1992), 1–20.
34. "Sobre las sociedades particulares. Continuación," *El Censor* newspaper, 9 October 1817, 3–5, Senado de la Nación, *Biblioteca de Mayo* (Buenos Aires: Periodismo, 1960), vol. 8, 7199–7201.
35. "Introducción que precede las actas de la Sociedad Literaria de Buenos Aires," in Gregorio F. Rodríguez (ed.), *Contribución histórica y documental* (Buenos Aires: Casa Jocobo Peuser, 1921–1924), vol. 1, 284–288.
36. "There have been those who have claimed that the singular affection of some individuals with others which is noted in the English People comes from a political need—that is, from that of conserving harmony in order to maintain general authority—the upheaval of which will bring about the nation's ruin. But this is a confusion of principles and results. Such a motive only ties individuals to the government; but individuals love and respect each other for other principles; and one must have no hesitations in agreeing that that which has contributed essentially to inspiring in the English people this self-love, or love for each other...has been the establishment of particular societies whose fertile ramifications have spread throughout Albion." *Contribución histórica y documental* (Buenos Aires) 1 (1921–1924): 284–288
37. Tulio Halperin Donghi, *Historia de la Universidad de Buenos Aires* (Buenos Aires: Eudeba, 1962), gives a summary of the University of Buenos Aires. The main work

of reference continues to be Juan María Gutiérrez, *Noticias históricas sobre el origen y desarrollo de la enseñanza pública y superior en Buenos Aires, desde la época de la extinción de la compañía de Jesús en el año 1767 hasta poco después de fundada la Universidad de 1821* (Buenos Aires: Universidad Nacional de Quilmes, 1868).

38. Halperin Donghi disagrees, claiming that the University of Buenos Aires played a marginal role in Argentine cultural life, since unlike other Ibero-American cities, the university remained isolated from great ideological upheavals; see *Historia de la Universidad*, 86. While this may have been the case in the late nineteenth century, it was not so in the early stages of the university's history. During the period in question, there was a considerable overlap between cultural life and university teaching. This fact explains why the principal cultural associations set up during the period operated in the university. Hence it is difficult to draw a line in the city between the university milieu and "cultural life."
39. See figure 3, "Docteurs en Jurisprudence de l'Université de Buenos Aires (1826–1863)," in PGB, *La Création*, vol. 3, appendix 1, "Base de données," 701–824.
40. According to certain calculations, in Ibero-American cities the elites represented between 5 and 10% of the population. Considering the city of Buenos Aires had around 62,000 inhabitants in 1832, this would make approximately 1,100 men as heads of households (for an average 5.5 members per family), of whom 8%, according to López, followed university courses.
41. See in particular the work of Michel Forsé, "Les réseaux de sociabilité dans un village," *Population* 36: 2 (1981), 1141–1162; M. Forsé, "La sociabilité," *Économie et Statistiques* 132 (1981): 39–48; Catherine Paradeise, "Sociabilité et culture de classe," *Revue Française de Sociologie* 21: 4 (October-December 1980), 571–597; see also works on observation of social change in *Archives de l'Observation du changement social* (Paris, CNRS, 1980–1981).
42. In *Registro Oficial de la Provincia de Buenos Aires*, Buenos Aires, Imprenta del Mercurio, 1828–1851, quoted by N. Piñedo y E. Bidau, "Historia de la Universidad de Buenos Aires," *Anales de la Universidad* (Buenos Aires) 1 (1888): 79.
43. Disciplinary order was regulated by the decree of 12 July 1828. Similar legislation was in place for primary education. See C. Newland, *Buenos Aires no es pampa*.
44. This aspect should be taken into account more frequently when studying the phenomenon of "generations," since the network of sociability is one of the most important in the formation of a group which defines itself not only by age but also by shared tastes and cultural practices.
45. The only references to this association are those given by López in his autobiography; see Vicente Fidel López, "Autobiografía" (Buenos Aires, 1896) in *Evocaciones históricas* (Buenos Aires: El Ateneo, 1929).
46. *Evocaciones históricas*, 40.
47. *Evocaciones históricas*, 41.
48. Indeed, in the originators of the Salon organization were the same students who had met at Cané's home: Eduardo Acevedo, Juan María Gutiérrez, Benito Carrasco. According to Weinberg, the absence of Miguel Cané, one of the principal advocates of the association, is due to his being in Montevideo at the time; see Félix Weinberg, *El Salón Literario de 1837* (Buenos Aires: Hachette, 1977), 51.
49. On private life as an institution of the modern public sphere, see Philippe Ariès, "Pour une histoire de la vie privée," in R. Chartier (ed.), *Histoire de la vie privée: de la Renaissance aux Lumières* (Paris: Seuil, 1966); D. Goodman, "Public sphere and private life."

50. V. F. López, "Autobiografía," 39–40.
51. *La Gaceta Mercantil, Periódico comercial, político y literario*, Buenos Aires, 1823–1852, 3 February 1832.
52. "Union Library and reading room," *La Gaceta Mercantil*, 17 August 1833.
53. The business does not appear in the trade almanac for 1826, appearing for the first time in the 1829 almanac, though we have no more precise data. In his research into the world of publishing and book selling in Buenos Aires, Buonocore provides no complementary information; see Domingo Buonocore, *Libros, editores e impresores de Buenos Aires* (Buenos Aires: El Ateneo, 1944).
54. A. Isabelle, *Voyage à Buenos Aires*, 183. Félix Weinberg suggests that this information dates from 1834; see *El Salón Literario*, 19.
55. In this period the publishing business in Buenos Aires was limited to printing pamphlets and the local press. The little literary work produced locally was often published in London or Paris. Only writings of a political nature, if they were favorable towards the government of the time, had any chance of being published at the state printing works. This was particularly the case with the writings of Pedro de Angelis, published in Buenos Aires during the Rosas government.
56. A. Isabelle, *Voyage à Buenos Aires*, 195.
57. D. Buonocore, *Libros, editores*, 23–29.
58. López refers to the Literary Salon but at no time does he mention reading rooms. On the contrary, he intimates that reading was done in private libraries; see "Autobiografía," 40. Elsewhere, the Spanish bookseller and commission agent B. Hortelano reports in his memoirs of the failure of his reading room, in spite of having set this up in Buenos Aires in 1854, when the city enjoyed lively cultural and political activity, see Benito Hortelano, *Memorias* (Madrid: Espasa-Calpe, 1936), esp. 242–245.
59. With regards to culture consumption habits in France, see Françoise Parent-Lardieu, *Les Cabinets de lecture. La lecture publique à Paris sous la Restauration* (Paris: Payot, 1982).
60. Information concerning Marcos Sastre's reading room appears in the works of F. Weinberg, *El Salón Literario*, 37–44; D. Buonocore, *Libreros, editores*, 19–26; and V. F. López, "Autobiografía," 52–56.
61. Sastre was obliged to leave Montevideo in 1833, having become compromised in Lavalleja's revolution against Rivera. See Vicente Osvaldo Cutolo, *Nuevo diccionario biográfico argentino (1750–1930)* (Buenos Aires: Elche, 1968); *Almanaque de Comercio*, 1834.
62. N. Piñedo and E. Bidau, "Nómina de los graduados en la Universidad de Buenos Aires," in *Historia de la Universidad*, 407–413.
63. Reconquista is the continuation of Defensa, hence the discrepancy in the street's name. See V. F. López, "Autobiografía," 52.
64. *La Gaceta Mercantil*, 22 January 1835, reproduced in F. Weinberg, *El Salón Literario*, 40.
65. This leads Weinberg to contend that Sastre's reading room was the first of its kind in Buenos Aires; see F. Weinberg, *El Salón Literario*, 43.
66. V. Gálvez, *Memorias de un viejo*, vol. 1, 306–307.
67. The bibliographical reference for the history of this literary salon is the work of Weinberg, *El Salón Literario*; the speeches made at the first meeting were published in *Antecedentes de la Asociación de Mayo 1837–1937*, Homenaje del Honorable Concejo Deliberante de la Ciudad de Buenos Aires en el Centenario de su Fundación, Buenos Aires, Concejo Deliberante, 1937.

68. *La Gaceta Mercantil*, no. 4233, 19 July 1837, 3.
69. F. Parent, *Les Cabinets de lecture*, 78.
70. According to announcements in the local press and those published in F. Weinberg, *El Salón Literario*.
71. Both Von Shentein and Hughes lived near to the new premises of Sastre's bookstore/reading room/salon. See V. F. López, "Autobiografía," 53.
72. Émile Mangel du Mesnil, "Sastre," in *Notoriedades del Plata* (Buenos Aires: Imprenta de la Tribuna, 1862). We do not know the literacy levels for the period prior to the 1855 census, but we do know that around 7% of the population attended some kind of school, rising to 11% in 1860. If we establish a ratio between school attendance and literacy rate (in 1860, for 11% attendance there was a rate of 48%), we obtain a literacy rate of around 30% for the period in question. This calculation is of course completely arbitrary but gives us some order of importance which appears to correspond best to new data on education in Buenos Aires between 1820 and 1860. See C. Newland, *Buenos Aires no es pampa*.
73. PGB, *La Création*, vol. 3, "La base de données," shows this development.
74. This according to the paradigm of Paul Bénichou, *Le Sacre de l'écrivain 1750-1830. Essai sur l'avènement d'un pouvoir spirituel laïc dans la France moderne* (Paris: Librairie José Corti, 1973). This paradigm is contrasted with the River Plate case by Jorge Myers in "Una genealogía para el parricidio: Juan María Gutiérrez y la construcción de una tradición literaria," *Entrepasados* 3: 4/5 (1993), 65–88.
75. The archives of the Literary Society in the Archive of the Museo Mitre, Sociedad Valaper (*sic*), Book of minutes, A1 C52 C2 N2, reproduced in G.F. Rodríguez (ed.), *Contribución histórica*, vol. 1, 18–503. There were fairly close relationships between the Literary Society and the government of the time. In addition to some of its members holding posts in the government of Rivadavia, the latter decided to confer prizes to be awarded by the Society. See "Reglamento para la adjudicación de premios de la Sociedad Literaria, Buenos Aires, 4th July 1822," in P. de Angelis, *Recopilación de leyes y decretos*.
76. See for example the prospectus of the group's newspaper, "Seminario de Buenos Aires," *El Diario de la Tarde*, no. 1821, 24 July 1837, 3.
77. Fernando A. Bidabehere, *Bolsas y mercados de comercio en la República Argentina* (Buenos Aires: Talleres Gráficos I. J. Rosso, 1930), 31.
78. V. Gálvez, *Memorias*, vol. 2, 178–179. References can also be found in J. A. Wilde, *Buenos Aires*; Octavio Battolla, *Los primeros ingleses en Buenos Aires 1780–1830* (Buenos Aires: E. Muro, 1928).
79. A. Isabelle, *Voyage à Buenos Aires*, 183.
80. Taken from the hands of the church, this function was left in the hands of the women who ran the institution from the creation of the Sociedad de Beneficencia in 1823 until it was finally closed down during the Peronist administration. See Carlos Correa Luna, *Historia de la Sociedad de Beneficencia*, 2 vols. (Buenos Aires: Sociedad de Beneficencia de la Capital, 1923–1925). Other references can be found in Alberto Meyer Arana, *Rosas y la Sociedad de Beneficencia* (Buenos Aires: Impr. De Geronimo Pesce, 1923); A. Meyer Arana, *La caridad en Buenos Aires* (Buenos Aires Comisión Nacional del Centenario, 1911). A critique of this literature can be found in Carlos Newland, "La educación primaria privada bajo el gobierno de Rosas, 1835–1852," *La Nación*, 4 December 1988, sec. 4, 1–2, and *La Nación*, 11 December 1988, sec. 4, 1–2.
81. There are no examples of socioeconomic institutions during this period. Socioeconomic institutions include such bodies as the *Comisión de Inmigración*

(Immigration Commission), an association established under the initiative of the provincial government in 1854 in order to organize migratory movement from Europe to the River Plate.

82. My reference here continues to be the theory of association as laid out by Tönnies in *Comunidad y asociación*, especially the second section, which analyzes civil society and the advance of the association in the economic sphere, 80–85.
83. I will leave it to economic historians to analyze the importance of these new forms of production organization and the financing of farms in the development of a capitalist economy. From my perspective, it is important to emphasize that the transformations in relationship forms also affected economic structures. On economic organizations in the colonial period, see Jorge Gelman, *De mercachifle a gran comerciante: los caminos del ascenso en el Río de la Plata* (Universidad Internacional de Andalucía, 1996); Zacarías Moutoukias, "Réseaux personnels et autorité coloniale: les négociants de Buenos Aires au xviiie siècle," *Annales ESC* 4/5 (July-October 1992): 889–915.
84. See *Estatuto de la Sociedad Pastoril de Merinos; contrato con su empresario José Pérez* (Buenos Aires: Imprenta Argentina, 1836); *Estatuto de la Sociedad Pastoril de Amigos del País y contrato con Samuel K. Tebbets* (Buenos Aires: Imprenta de la Independencia, 1837); *Estatuto de la Sociedad Porteña y contrato con su promotor Manuel Escalada* (Buenos Aires: Imprenta de la Gaceta Mercantil, 1837).
85. See Hilda Sabato, *Capitalismo y ganadería en Buenos Aires. La fiebre del lanar, 1850–1890* (Buenos Aires: Sudamericana, 1989).
86. All existent literature on the friendly society movement in Buenos Aires indicates that the first friendly society was established in 1854.
87. See "Demanda de autorización…," in AGN. AP. X 15/10/5, folio 372.
88. See below, chapter 3. I have consulted the political correspondence in the Quai D'Orsay archives between 1829 and 1836 (from here referred to as AQO. CPA)
89. AQO. CPA. Rogers to the Minister of Foreign Affairs, Buenos Aires, 25 August 1835.
90. In *La Gaceta Mercantil* of 20 July 1833, 4, there is an announcement placed by the *Sociedad Filantrópica Francesa* to their "subscribers" in which it is announced that they may collect their diplomas. In the newspaper the results of the lottery appear, with details of the gifts presented by the ladies in contribution to the Society; see *La Gaceta Mercantil*, 17 October 1833, 4.
91. See diario *La Tribuna*, Buenos Aires, 1853–1884, 8 September 1853.
92. See C. Ibarguren, *Las sociedades literarias*; Horacio Noboa Zumarraga, *Las sociedades porteñas y su acción revolucionaria, 1800–1837* (Buenos Aires, 1939).
93. See George Reid Andrews, "Community Organizations: The Quest of Autonomy," in *The Afro-Argentines in Buenos Aires 1800–1900* (University of Wisconsin Press, 1980), 138–155; this is the only work to have attempted to establish a chronology of the development of African associations in the River Plate. Other references appear in José Luis Lanuza, *Morenada. Una historia de la raza africana en el Río de la Plata*, Buenos Aires, Schapire, 1967; Ricardo Rodríguez Molas, "Negros libres rioplatenses," *Revista de Humanidades* (Buenos Aires) 1: 1 (1961), 99–126; R. Rodríguez Molas, *La música y la danza de los negros en el Buenos Aires de los siglos XVIII y XIX* (Buenos Aires: Clio, 1957); Vicente Rossi, *Cosas de negros* (Córdoba: Río de la Plata, 1926; Buenos Aires: Hachette, 1958).
94. On the "enigma" of the disappearance of the African population, Andrews' excellent analysis is highly recommended. His study was presented as a thesis for the University of Wisconsin, entitled "Forgotten but Not Gone: The Afro-Argentines of Buenos Aires,

1800–1900." It is a pity that Andrews does not explore further the question raised in chapter 6 as to the Africans' disappearance from historical memory. In my view, as I have previously written with regards to the indigenous population of Argentina, this memory failure must be related to the imperatives of the modern nation as established by the "great men of the nation."

95. E. F. S. de Studer, *La trata de negros*; G. R. Andrews, *The Afro-Argentines*. For more on smuggling, see Hors Peitschman, "Burocracia y corrupción en Hispanoamérica colonial: una aproximación tentativa," *Nova América* 5 (1985); on the extent of this contraband in the local economy, see Z. Moutoukias, *Contrabando y control colonial* and Z. Moutoukias, "Power, corruption and commerce: the making of the local administrative structure in seventeenth-century Buenos Aires," *HAHR* 68: 4 (November 1988).
96. See R. Rodríguez Molas, "Negros libres rioplatenses."
97. See L. Johnson and S. Socolow, *Población y espacio en el Buenos Aires*, 329–349, particularly table 3 on the distribution of different ethnic groups in the population of Buenos Aires. García Belsunce argues that slaves accounted for 24.36% of the population of the city in 1810. C. A. García Belsunce (ed.), *Buenos Aires. Su gente*, 83.
98. See M. Goldberg, "Población negra y mulata de la cudad de Buenos Aires, 1810–1840," *Desarrollo económico* 16 (1976): 75–99.
99. In addition, these figures do not take into account the influx of Brazilian slaves after the war with Brazil (1825–1828) and the liberalization of trade between 1831 and 1834. See M. Goldberg, "Población negra," and a similar explanation in *The Afro-Argentines*, ch. 5. Magnus Mörner, in *La mezcla de razas en la historia de América* (Buenos Aires: Paidós, 1969) presents an analysis of prejudices affecting blacks and tackles the general problem of mixed ethnic origins in America.
100. A description of this area can be found in Francisco L. Romay, *El barrio de Monserrat* (Buenos Aires, Ed. de la Municipalidad, 1949).
101. See the analysis by Johnson and Socolow with reference to colonial society in the late eighteenth century in *Población y espacio*. For the postcolonial period, see C. A. García Belsunce (ed.), *Buenos Aires. Su gente*.
102. According to Rosal's sample, between 1821 and 1860, 58% of transactions by African-Argentines was related to the purchase and sale of land in the Monserrat parish; M. A. Rosal, "Negros y pardos."
103. The importance of this question is highlighted by Maurizio Gribaudi in *Itinéraires ouvriers*.
104. On the different ways of obtaining manumission and the different conceptions of freedom, see Rebecca Scott's recent work, *Slave Emancipation in Cuba. The Transition in Free Labor, 1860–1899* (Pittsburgh: University of Pittsburgh Press, 2000).
105. Lyman Johnson, "La manumisión en el Buenos Aires colonial: un análisis ampliado," *Desarrollo Económico* 17 (January-March 1978): 333–348.
106. Recent research into the plantation economy in Brazil has tended to show that the possibility of a slave accumulating capital was not strictly an urban specificity. See B. J. Barickman, "A bit of land, which they call roça: slave provision grounds in the Bahian Recôncavo, 1780–1860," *HAHR* 74: 4 (November 1994), 649–687.
107. C. A. García Belsunce (ed.), *Buenos Aires. Su gente*, vol. 1, ch. 2.
108. For this issue in the River Plate, see Rafael Castellano Sáenz Cavia, "La abolición de la esclavitud en las Provincias Unidas del Río de la Plata (1810–1860)," *Revista de Historia del Derecho* (Buenos Aires) 9 (1981): 55–157. With regards to the Americas in general, see David Cohen and Lack Greene, eds., *Neither Slave nor Free: The Free Man*

of African Descent in the Slave Societies of the New World (Baltimore: Johns Hopkins University Press, 1972).

109. Alberto González Arzac, *Abolición de la esclavitud en el Río de la Plata* (Buenos Aires: DAESA, 1974).

110. "Decreto reglamentando el servicio de los esclavos que introducen los corsarios, Buenos Aires, 12 de septiembre de 1827," in *Registro de la Provincia.*

111. In principle, Rosas' policy mostly entailed conserving the status quo. The governor even authorized the sale of foreign slaves with a decree in 1831; G. R. Andrews, *The Afro-Argentines*, 67.

112. See S. Socolow, *The Merchants*; S. Socolow, *The Bureaucrats of Buenos Aires, 1769–1810: Amor al Real Servicio* (Durham: Duke University Press, 1987); L. Johnson and S. Socolow, *Población y espacio*; Diana Balmori, "Buenos Aires," in D. Balmori et al., *Notable Family Networks* (Chicago: University of Chicago Press, 1984).

113. G. R. Andrews, *The Afro-Argentines.* A description of the different trades can be found in V. Gálvez, *Memorias de un viejo.*

114. For the colonial period, see references in Lyman Johnson, "The entrepreneurial reorganization of an artisan trade: the bakers of Buenos Aires, 1770–1820," *The Americas*, October 1980, 139–160; G. R. Andrews, *The African-Argentines*; José M. Mariluz Urquijo, *La industria sombrerera anterior a 1810*, (La Plata: Instituto de la Producción de la Facultad de Ciencias Económicas de la Universidad de La Plata, 1962); on the postcolonial period, see J. M. Mariluz Urquijo, "La mano de obra en la industria porteña, 1810–1835," *Boletín de la Academia Nacional de la Historia* (Buenos Aires) 32 (1962): 583–622; J. M. Mariluz Urquijo, "La comercialización de la producción sombrerera porteña (1810–1835)," *Investigaciones y Ensayos* 5 (1968): 103–129.

115. G. R. Andrews, *The Afro-Argentines*, 4; L. Johnson, "The Artisans of Buenos Aires during the Viceroyalty, 1776-1810."

116. Lyman Johnson, "The Artisans of Buenos Aires during the Viceroyalty, 1776-1810."

117. Existent research into this issue shows that the presence of slaves in the different branches of trades was the root cause of a series of crises in the organizations, which were yet to establish themselves in the region. The best-known case is that of the shoemakers' guild, which constituted one of many examples of black artisans attempting to create a guild distinct from white-dominated forms. See "The racial limits of guild solidarity: an example from colonial Buenos Aires," *Revista de Historia de América* 99 (January-June 1985): 7–26; see also G. R. Andrews, *The Afro-Argentines*, 41–46. Unlike such cities as Mexico and Lima, trade guilds in Buenos Aires had little influence. For the late eighteenth century, Lyman Johnson offers some excellent analyses, "The silversmiths of Buenos Aires: a case study in the failure of corporate social organization," *JLAS* 8: 2 (November 1976): 181–313; L. Johnson, "The impact of racial discrimination on black artisans in colonial Buenos Aires," *Social History* 6: 2 (October 1981), 301–316; L. Johnson, "Francisco Baquero: shoemaker and organizer," in David G. Sweet and Gary B. Nash, eds., *Struggle and Survival in Colonial America* (Berkeley: University of California Press, 1981).

118. Discrimination also occurred within the guilds, since at different ranks the black presence was not the same. For a more detailed analysis, see L. Johnson, "The impact of racial discrimination," as well as his as-yet-unpublished thesis, "The Artisans of Buenos Aires during the Viceroyalty, 1776–1810."

119. According to R. Bastide, the cultures of African origin were more successful in the city than in the countryside, as they were able to meet more easily at night and reformulate

their primitive communities. Roger Bastide, *Les Amériques noires. Les civilisations africaines dans le nouveau monde* (Paris: Payot, 1967), 29.

120. R. Bastide indicates this function, in addition to compensation for the humiliation of slavery, *Les Amériques noires,* 36.
121. This confusion even crops up in Andrews' book, the only one to include research into these associations. See G. R. Andrews, *The Afro-Argentines*, ch. 5.
122. *The Afro-Argentines*, 171; R. Rodríguez Molas, *La música y la danza*; V. Rossi, *Cosas de negros*, 28 and 51.
123. Benjamín Núñez, *Dictionary of Afro-Latin American Civilization* (Westport, CT: Greenwood Press, 1980), 108.
124. See references in R. Rodríguez Molas, *La música y la danza*, 7–11.
125. *La música y la danza*, 7.
126. See "Accord of 9 October 1788" in agn, Acuerdos del extinguido Cabildo de Buenos Aires, series 3, vol. 8, Buenos Aires, 1930, 623–627.
127. In this particular case this was the home of a free African-Argentine. AGN.IX 19-7-2, quoted in R. Rodríguez Molas, *La música y la danza.*
128. With regard to the black population's participation in the military, see "Estado del Ejército de la capital en octubre de 1806," in I. Núñez, *Noticias históricas de la República*, vol. 1, 97, and G. R. Andrews, *The Afro-Argentines*, ch. 7.
129. According to an 1821 report by the mayor of the neighborhood. It is interesting to point out here the terms that he uses. Note the early use of the word "tango," unmistakably connected to African dances: "the mulattos of the Conga nation who have a tango dance in barrio 15," Buenos Aires, 14 November 1821, AGN. AP. X 32.10.1, folio 62. In his etymological dictionary of the Spanish language, Corominas highlights the same meaning but dates the first usage to an 1836 document. J. Corominas, *Diccionario crítico*, 369–370.
130. See G. R. Andrews, *The Afro-Argentines*, 171.
131. *The Afro-Argentines*, ch. 9.
132. Sadly there is no literature on their history in the River Plate. In the case of African-Argentine fraternities, the only reliable references are those provided by Andrews in chapter 5 of *The Afro-Argentines*. See also the studies of M.A Rosal.
133. From research into the wills of African-Argentines in the city for the period from 1750 to 1820, Rosal, "Algunas consideraciones," shows that these practices were widespread among the black population. Of a total of 234 blacks who left wills, 174 (74%) belonged to a fraternity. In the 1820s, the proportion was still 37/61, but for the period from 1830 to 1860 there are only two known cases of African-Argentines participating in fraternities.
134. AGN. AP. X 32.10.1 folio 62. At the same time, there was an increase in blacks detained for "dancing in the street." In 1822 four decrees were passed prohibiting street dances. See AGN. AP. X 44.10.1. In a letter of 8 January 1822, the chief of police requested that the governor annul permits granted to blacks for street dancing and "limit the authorization to those points that they call *tambor,*" Buenos Aires, 8 January 1822, in AGN. AP. X 12.6.1, folio 164. Other references to detentions of blacks for dancing in the street on 5 February 1822 are found in AGN. AP. X 12.6.2, folio 225 y 228; AGN. AP. X 12.6.5, folio 198.
135. See "Reglamento dado por el superior gobierno a las naciones africanas en el año 1823," in AGN. AP. X 14.5.4.

136. See AGN. AP. X, articles 9, 12, 16, 24, 26, 27, 29, 31, 32, 33, 34, 35, and 37. David Bushnell, *Reform and Reaction in the Platine Provinces 1810–1852* (Gainesville: University Press of Florida, 1983), 26–30, details ecclesiastical reforms; a historical analysis from the point of view of the Church can be found in Cayetano Bruno, *Historia de la Iglesia en Argentina* (Buenos Aires: Don Bosco, 1966–1981), vol. 13, 411–549.
137. This is what can be deduced from article 6 and from the important role of the police (articles 10, 11, 12, and 37): restrictions on clientele (only individuals from the same nation) and indirect control of the members by the president (which did not always work, owing to solidarity between the president and members)."Reglamento dado por el superior gobierno," in AGN. AP. X 14.5.4.
138. According to the 1823 regulation, the society secretary was responsible for keeping the record of minutes, the register of associates and the accounts (article 30 of the regulation).
139. To do this I completed and compared the documentation in the police archives with that of other consulted sources: legislative documents, memoirs from the period, travel chronicles and the local press. Lastly, this corpus was compared with the results of other research into the subject. It is needful to provide some explanations as regards the data used in the graphs (figure 5). In each case I have indicated the date of appearance of the society although it was not possible to state in all circumstances whether this corresponded to the foundation date. The same is the case for the date of disappearance. As for the duration of the association, this was deduced from fragmentary information concerning each society. When references were available to the same society at two different dates, I considered by default that this society continued to operate during the period between the two dates. When only one reference was available, this was used to apply to the whole of the corresponding year. A list can be found of all of these associations in my doctoral thesis. See "Associations d'africains créées à Buenos Aires au XIXe siècle," vol. 3, appendix 4, "La vie associative."
140. See figure 6.
141. Andrews' demographic calculations confirm this theory. Andrews uses Marta Goldberg's results on the average rate of natural growth in the black population for the years 1822 and 1831. This resulting figure of 0.19% indicates a natural decrease. Andrews argues that the maintenance of this population, in spite of the decrease, was due to the influx of black slaves from Brazil between 1826 and 1827. See M. Goldberg, "Población negra y mulata," 90–94; G. R. Andrews, *The Afro-Argentines*, 90.
142. "Reglamento dado..."
143. Buenos Aires, 2 December 1834, in AGN. AP. X 33.2.2, folio 55. It is probable that the division of societies that the new regulation made possible was actually the result of an older logic. It may be that division within a nation tended to rebuild genuine ethnic groups separated by slavery.
144. M. A. Rosal, "Negros y pardos," 9.

CHAPTER 3

Politics on the Boundaries of Civility

The notion of civility refers here to the world of social exchanges in relation to the public sphere. This can be defined by the valuing of exchanges respecting certain rules of courtesy and by the importance of conversation as a form of exchange and the public use of individual reasoning. This type of sociability falls into what we call the modern public sphere as a forum of individuals meeting in "public," exercising a new power: opinion.[1] But there is no strict correlation between relationships of civility and political order. There may be a gap, indeed an abyss, between the spirit of civility and political order, even when this order is founded on democratic legitimacy. From this arise the various meanings of civility, be it urbanity (politeness, good manners, what associates urbanity with courtesan civility) or the attitude that characterizes good citizens, namely an interest in reciprocal exchanges, tolerance of others' opinions, respect for a combination of procedures and conventional rules, in which is found that civic act par excellence: the vote. From the social sphere to the political sphere, from the private to the collective, the diversity of meanings of civility requires some clarification.

When we speak of the "Republican Patria" we may refer to two things which are not necessarily related: the introduction of representative institutions or the genuine use of popular sovereignty, to which these institutions owe their legitimacy. In the first case, the political sphere may be limited to the action of a reduced number of individuals who exercise power in the name of these principles. This restriction may be explicitly recognized, such as in the case of electoral systems, or act in the absence of a defined role for new representative institutions, as was the case in nascent Ibero-American republics. In the second case, the sphere of politics is extended to the area of mediation between society and the State, and this is where the public political sphere emerges. With this, politics ceases to be the struggle for power within representative institutions but the struggle to manage society's relationships with its institutions. My hypothesis is that the background movement, found in new sociability practices and concealing new representations of the social bond based on respect for individual liberties, did not yet affect the world of politics during the period in question. It should not be ignored that the period witnessed considerable growth of the press, founded on the principle of freedom of expression, as well as the establishment of a representative republican system which, in the case of Buenos Aires—with the electoral law of 1821—was particularly advanced and implied a genuine broadening of political boundaries.[2] But while an institutional revolution is undeniable, its impact on representations of power appears to have been limited. In spite of the introduction of republican institutions, even with regard to power limited by a ratifying vote, political leaders showed a lack of respect for civil liberties which was a complementary manifestation of the scission underlying the development of new values of civility and the sphere of power. Systematic electoral fraud, heavy-handedness of the regime whenever opposition managed to control the vote, elimination of the opposition press, and the most extreme brutality against adversaries constituted the real practices of democratic politics. All of this took place as if, for the leaders of the new "Republican Patria," this brutality rather than civility was aimed at consolidating their representative power, as politics remained a field of struggle and action rather than one of opinion and negotiation. The principles of liberty and political equality, which made civility a civic culture, were consequently defined outside of the context of politics as an exercise of sovereignty. The introduction of a representative republican system appears, in this case, to owe little to the new power sphere in which, in the North Atlantic, a new notion of political representation was to emerge.[3]

The Order of Politics: The Republican Patria

The beginning of the 1820s was, for the province of Buenos Aires, the start of the "happy experience" of a government which succeeded in ensuring social peace and economic prosperity in the context of the new institutional order. This experience coincided with the definitive collapse of the territory of the Viceroyalty of the River Plate, after which the war machinery hitherto pointed towards the Spanish would be dragged along into a civil war between the provinces lasting for more than half a century. These two apparently contradictory observations share their synthesis in the notion of "representation." The problem lay less in the difficulties of establishing representative institutions than in the introduction of the new notion of representation within a society in which traditional representations of the political corpus still persisted.[4]

REPRESENTATIVE INSTITUTIONS IN THE PROVINCE OF BUENOS AIRES

The Junta de Representantes (Representative Assembly), a legislative and constituent power in the province of Buenos Aires, can be counted as part of the inheritance of the liberal government of 1821. Its origin was in the Junta Electoral de Representantes, an electoral assembly of representatives which, under the initiative of the governor Sarratea, was converted into a provincial legislative assembly in April 1820. During the ministry of Rivadavia, with the suppression of municipal power (decreed by this assembly in December of 1821) and the election law of August of the same year, the assembly ultimately became the first representative provincial institution. It was at first composed of twelve representatives from the city and eleven from the countryside, increasing in 1827 to 24 city representatives and 23 from the country.[5] The assembly functioned both as a legislative assembly elected by direct "universal suffrage" and as an electoral assembly, as it continued to elect the Governor and General of the province's armies. With its creation the representative electoral system was established in the province of Buenos Aires, defined by the election law of 14 August 1821, which gave the vote—the ability, rather than the right—to all free men "of the country" (principally the city of Buenos Aires, as the law did not yet provide for elections outside of the city) and residents over the age of twenty, although the length of residency was unspecified.[6] In accordance with the 1821 law, the people of the city and later of the countryside were to be called once a year to elect their representatives. Representation was by parish in the city and by electoral district in the countryside. According to the authorities, the reason for organizing the vote by parish in the city was purely technical, owing to the advantage of using an existent administrative structure to organize the election. The subject of representation was not the parish community but rather the individual, who was to vote in his parish to elect the city representatives, grouped together in a house of representatives for the population of the province of Buenos Aires.

This law was exceptional in various aspects. Firstly, in not placing any limits on voting it attained at once, and before many other republics, the principle of universal male suffrage: one man, one vote. Furthermore, it abandoned the previous system of indirect elections aimed at purifying the vote.[7] Lastly, and most extraordinarily, it was not later repealed. The history of the nineteenth century does contain some examples of democratic outbursts, but few were long-lasting in any sense. It is disconcerting that this democratic consensus permitted institutional stability while one of the bloodiest civil wars was developing, a war which would pit the different regions of the former viceroyalty against each other and threaten the very survival of the ruling Porteño elites.

The case of the province of Buenos Aires is all the more surprising in that it was not based on any constitutional text, nor was it the result of any considerable political or philosophical debate. It is astonishing that the institution of universal suffrage which caused so much blood and ink to run in European societies does not appear to have raised any such problems in Buenos Aires.[8] Criticism has instead been concerned with the problems of applying a text whose imprecision has been denounced as responsible for all kinds of frauds. Nevertheless, and with one exception, criticism of the vices of procedure did not imply the refutation of the principle of universal suffrage. Paradoxically, the exception was the romantic-liberal youth, who saw in electoral democracy the foundations of Rosas' conservative regime. This youth opposed the popular, blind, irrational will with the sovereignty of reason, the only legitimate foundation of democracy.[9] This did not alter the fact that after the fall of Rosas electoral democracy should be confirmed in the Constitution of the Argentine Confederation of 1853, which incidentally was proclaimed by the same liberals, no doubt more mature and also more critical of their earlier romanticism, and above all, now on the side of power.

While the principle went mostly unchallenged, the gap between representative principle and electoral practice grew in terms of how representatives were elected. According to legislation, parish authorities, justices of the peace and *alcaldes de barrio* presided over the election of the chairman and other officials of the polling place.[10] This election took place the moment the polling place opened and by the majority of the votes of those present. The task of these authorities was then to verify that the law was observed. To do so they had to ensure that the times for opening and closing the vote were respected, personally check that voters belonged to the electoral district of the parish (there were no electoral registers), verify during vote-counting that all votes were accounted for, and guarantee that the results reached the central electoral office safely. Evidently, the role of the neighborhood authorities in election results was decisive, as they held all responsibilities regarding the different aspects of the electoral act. This situation gave the neighborhood authorities a central role in the workings of the electoral machine. It is not hard to imagine the various possibilities to be had for twisting a law which they were responsible for enforcing. From the officials of the polling place, chosen with little consideration by supporters of the government who in turn were selected by neighborhood authorities, right down to the counting of the votes, these authorities effectively ran the proceedings, all the more so given that the vote was public and oral: the voter had to shout out his vote in the presence of the authorities, a feared test for civil servants whose posts often depended on their loyalty to the government. Yet even if a man of strong political convictions dared to favor any candidate other than that "suggested" by the justice of the peace, the chairman of the polling place, elected under the watchful eye of the justice of the peace, could simply feign to have forgotten to register the vote, a common occurrence. In short, as fraud was as habitual as it was widespread, the "electoral campaign" consisted mostly of ensuring the loyalty of the justices of the peace. The latter's power arose from their mediatory role between the ruling classes and the voters. They were chosen according to their loyalty to the government, for whom they were to guarantee the political discipline of the voters, which was done by ratifying vote-counting in an election whose outcome was decided elsewhere.

It can be seen then that beneath the appearance of a new ideological principle lay a continuation of nondemocratic election procedures. Indeed, although the two-round vote had been abolished, its vagueness could still be seen in the representative government. If the People existed as a principle of legitimization, and therefore their participation was required in order to bring about what François-X. Guerra calls "democratic fiction," what was really at stake at the elections was the composition of candidate lists and control of the polling place.[11] In terms which require no further comment, Tomás de Iriarte summarized the representative fiction of an act which was entirely directed and controlled by the authorities:

> The people are deceived, made to believe that they are exercising their sovereignty in the elections.... The people are dragged to the voting tables to cast a vote that others have already bought, with money or the prospect of favor, protection, or the hope of payment of an insignificant stipend.... They are the blind instruments of their patrons, who put in their hands a list of men unknown to the voters. And this act is the root of the representative system.[12]

In the absence of a political instance of mediation, electoral lists known as ministerial lists were drawn up by the government or by the faction attempting to get its foot in the political door. Voters were then limited to validating the choice of their "fellow citizens" in favor of the representatives elected by and for the latter. Even when the results were not entirely to the government's satisfaction, they could be modified. But while such fraudulent acts were admitted, the government could not disregard that other act essential to its legitimacy: the calling of elections, in which the republican pact, and therefore the social pact, was renewed. In all this there remained a novelty with regard to the system of the old *cabildos*. Voters existed and the different factions had to contend for their votes whenever the consensus of the directing class broke down, as happened in 1828–29 or 1833. In these cases, as will be seen below, fraud triggered an armed stand-off between supporters of opposing groups. In this kind of "second round," what mattered most was not the "civic act" but rather brute force. But this does not necessarily mean that citizens were mere bit-players in the political game or on the sidelines of any logical representation.

THE REPRESENTATIVES OF THE PATRIA

Half of the Assembly was reelected annually, hence every year in late April the population of the province of Buenos Aires was called to "manifest" its will by voting. The Assembly sat in Buenos Aires from its creation in 1820 until the National Constituent Congress decreed the abolition of the provincial legislature in 1826.[13] After the failed attempt at national organization in 1826 and the resignation of Bernadino Rivadavia as president of the republic in 1827, the provincial legislature was reestablished and the population of the province was once again called to elect its representatives. Until 1840 the legislature was dissolved only once, during the military coup of 1828. In December 1829 Rosas reestablished this seventh legislature, which promptly voted in the "extraordinary powers" for his government.[14]

The legal conditions required of representatives were rather vague: "to be a citizen, twenty-five years or older and possess real estate or industrial property," is a description imprecise enough to warrant all sorts of interpretations.[15] After all, there was nothing to prevent a prosperous artisan from having political pretensions, though naturally such an upstart never attained such power. The imprecision of the electoral law had to undoubtedly be related to the real impossibility of this kind of accident occurring. Nevertheless, between this fact and the reiterated idea that this was an Assembly of landlords, a kind of extension of the great property in which landowners, pretending to do politics, managed their affairs as if they were part of the private sphere, there was quite a range of possibilities whose complexity can be garnered from the prosopographic study of assembly members between 1827 and 1840.[16]

From a sample of 91 deputies, chosen on the basis of available data pertaining to the 154 members of the legislature during this period, only one sixth can be classed as owners of land and capital, belonging in most cases to the large families of Spanish traders established in the port city in the late eighteenth century. Juan J. and Nicolás Anchorena, Francisco C. Beláustegui, Miguel J. de Riglos and Mariano Sarratea were some of those mixing business with politics. Others hailed from the union of a group of families of colonial functionaries, such as José M. Escalada, José M. Rojas y Patrón and Gervasio Ortiz de Rosas. Lastly there were the beneficiaries of the *enfiteusis* law who had recently acquired land, such as José M. Baudrix and Pedro Vela.[17] While it is true that the low presence of large landowners does not imply that the interests of the economically powerful class were not represented by the Assembly, these data oppose the claim that the *Rosista* regime took landlords to the legislature[18] and even raise questions, as did Jorge Sábato for an earlier period, as to the existence of a dominant class of large landowners.[19] This is evidence, instead, of an elite with widely varying interests and power depending on a network of relationships, which was all the more effective for its diversification.[20]

In addition, the seats of the legislature were filled by individuals from sectors who had traditionally occupied administrative posts in colonial times: ecclesiasts, whose presence in the administration was considerably diminished—six out of a total of ninety-one—and members of the liberal professions, representing almost one-third of the sample, and almost all of whom were men of law.[21] Among these men were some of the members of the principal families of landowners and traders. Tomás M. Anchorena, Felipe Arana, Eduardo Lahitte, Manuel V. Maza, Laureano Rufino, and Roque Sáenz Peña were all legal professionals and owners of capital. Their means of subsistence and the basis of their social power was, naturally, agricultural production and sales. By the same token, the possession of cultural capital was hardly alien to their strategy of affirming economic and social power. In the large families there was a tradition of placing one member in the administration of the imperial State, but their legal education now played a different role in comparison with the colonial period.[22] Indeed, in a republican regime men of law enjoyed hitherto unheard-of opportunities for political action: they could make the administrative apparatus work the same way they had done in colonial times—a far from negligible advantage for the nascent State—and make public opinion be heard. These men of letters and law were an essential piece in the manifestation of the popular will, from which the representative institutions took their legitimacy.[23] However, with few exceptions, these men were not identified with this modern public sphere, not by their sociability habits, their cultural practices, nor their form of political representation.[24]

The military had a notable presence in the legislature, making up a fourth of our sample. It may be hazardous to reach a conclusion on the role of the army in the independent State, above all because towards the end of the century the army lacked the genuine, single and hierarchical command structure which might allow one to speak of a national army.[25] It can be said that with the likes of Félix de Álzaga, Miguel de Azcuénaga, Manuel Escalada and Lucio Mansilla, the presence of these members of the great families can more easily be explained by their social extraction than by their corporative characteristics. Furthermore, the army had considerable interests for those elites engaged in the process of territorial expansion.[26] This did not prevent the presence of career officers such as Tomás de Iriarte and men of somewhat dubious social origin who had gained a certain public recognition due to their role in the revolutionary army, such as Manuel Corvalán, Félix Olazábal, Ángel Pacheco, Agustín de Pinedo, Mariano B. Rolón, Juan J. Viamonte and Celestino Vidal, although there is a possibility that their public recognition was due to other types of social preeminence.[27]

Lastly, a ninth of the legislature was made up of liberal professionals. These included men promoted to government posts for their knowledge, upon which their livelihood and power depended to a great extent, which explains the presence here of the teaching staff of the recently inaugurated University of Buenos Aires. Their presence in the legislature no doubt stemmed from their qualifications in treating certain technical problems concerning the salubriousness of the city. Thus, in the absence of a municipal administration the doctors Cosme Argerich, Diego Alcorta, José Fuentes Argibel, Manuel Moreno and Ireneo Portela were invited to resolve sanitary issues arising from the growth of the city, while the engineers Felipe Senillosa and Avelino Díaz were summoned to tackle the problems of urbanism. It remains to be seen what role their academic positions played in their access to the provincial legislature. What is known is that these "technocrats" were also university professors in close contact with the young men of the associations, in whom the figure of representation appears to have been displaced by the incarnation of a power visible to the representation of an opinion.[28]

Short of sociological certainties, one can nevertheless indicate what is to be garnered from these data. Firstly, a review of the evidence: the representatives were elected from among the well-to-do, a category that grouped together different sectors of the Porteño elite. I must insist on the complexity of the political behavior of these elites, as while capital owners did not monopolize the assembly, they were not far from the political terrain, to the extent that in some cases they chose to acquire qualifications that would allow them to act better in this field. From this we can also deduce the specificity of the political field and the influence of the social field on politics.[29] Lastly, it is accurate to conclude that men of opinion associated with the new public sphere had a weak influence over representative institutions. Only one ninth of the legislature of the period was made up of men whose presence might be related to a modern kind of representation. This is all the more notable if we adopt a different approach from the biographies and classify these men according to their associative experience.

The representatives of the first provincial legislatures do not appear to have been very enthusiastic about associative experiences. Of the 156 citizens occupying posts as representatives of the province of Buenos Aires between August 1827 and April 1840, fifty-three are registered as belonging to associations, of which more than half were after 1852. With regard to membership prior to occupying a post or during the public offices, there were only three types of associations

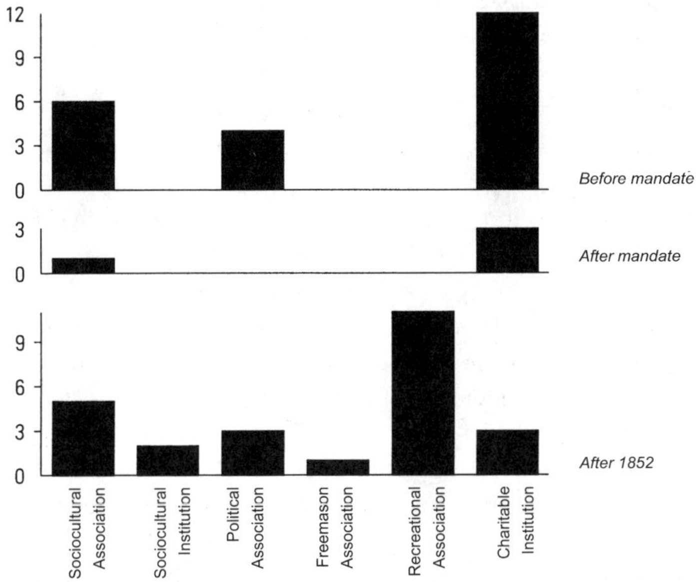

Figure 9. Association Membership Among Provincial Legislative Representatives between 1827 and 1839, in Relation to Attainment of Post

that attracted legislators: charitable institutions, sociocultural associations and political associations (figure 9). In the case of charitable institutions, almost all are registered as becoming members during their post. This can be explained above all by the fact that these "associations" were created by government initiative. It is not at all surprising, then, that among their "members" were government figures. The presence of representatives of an associative type of institution, intended for the well-being of the community which they allegedly represented, seems therefore quite natural, all the more so because this presence was an excellent means for giving their social authority a new institutional base. Furthermore, it is significant that none of the members of these two institutions joined other sociocultural associations. Their associative experience was therefore limited to the context of the institutions intended to replace old forms of community administration.

In terms of sociocultural associations, membership was in most cases prior to taking up the post and corresponded to three associations, two of which were sociocultural, the third clearly political. Two had been in operation during the

Rivadavia government: the Literary Society of 1822 and the Valaper Lodge of the same year. The third was Marcos Sastre's Literary Salon. The former two had set themselves the objective of bringing together friends from the province in order to discuss the best means to develop "the enlightenment spirit" in Argentina, and with this in mind had considered the possibility of publishing a newspaper to disseminate their ideas.[30] The Literary Society took up the model of the "Societies of Friends of the Country," while the more politically-oriented Valaper group opted for the structure of the secret societies. These associations were frequented by intellectuals connected with the Rivadavian experience and occupying political or administrative posts during their membership of the society. This was the case of Julián Segundo de Agüero, Vicente López, Felipe Senillosa, Cosme Argerich and Ignacio Núñez.[31] In all of these cases, membership of associations was closely connected to a commitment to the Rivadavian government, to the extent that it is difficult to detect whether these were "para-governmental" associations or cultural institutions designed for governmental propaganda. Whatever the case may be, in both cases these associations, instead of serving society as instruments of control and participation, worked more as instruments of government.

The third association was Marcos Sastre's Literary Salon. Although only four representatives belonged to the salon, this nevertheless suggests the presence of a cultural field which, albeit unsystematic, connected associative practices to the sphere of public power, in as much as representative power appears to have owed little at the time to the public sphere. In this respect, it is interesting that when the Literary Salon was founded in 1837, none of the former members of the Rivadavian associations joined. While this was undoubtedly a generational problem, one would have expected its members to have a similar political cultural importance to that of the members of the societies of 1822. This was not the case. Of the Literary Salon's sixty-seven members registered by Félix Weinberg, only one—the engineer Felipe Senillosa[32]—was in the House of Representatives, while such cultural personalities as the director of the public library or the authorities of the University of Buenos Aires were conspicuous by their absence.[33] The organization of Marcos Sastre's salon appears to contain the beginnings of a new relationship between public and State sociability, in which the initiatives came from "civil society," independently of the will of the men occupying government posts.[34] This may have been no more than an indirect consequence of a generational question: their absence in directorial posts can be explained by their age. Nevertheless, this placed them in a hitherto unheard-of space, that of the public political sphere. It is also needful to add that, in the four cases in question, these were professors of the University of Buenos Aires. The bond between sociability and new representation appears to have passed through university lecture theaters, or more precisely through the relational network built up from everyday encounters during courses, around the different forms of sociability previously mentioned.

Naturally, it would be over-speculative to attempt to construct any statistical reasoning from so few cases, but without considering the sample as representative it is possible to appreciate the new aspect that these associative practices brought to the relationship between citizens and politics. This handful of examples gives evidence of a new notion of representation which these men brought to the provincial legislature. The most extreme case, and equally the most exemplary, is that of Diego Alcorta, professor and mentor to the young romantic generation, who in the most dramatic moments of provincial politics—during the crises of 1828-1829 and 1833—was to occupy a seat in the provincial assembly. From what is known, it would be difficult to affirm that the election of Alcorta to the legislature was the consequence of an electoral campaign carried out by the young men of the schools, but it is evident that his presence in the House of Representatives takes on a significance quite different to that which a figure like the landowner Juan N. Terrero might have had. Not because the latter did not enjoy a certain authority, but because this kind of figure appears to have other sources of authority outside of that of opinion, at least judging by their indifference to new cultural practices in the public sphere. This could account for the lack of homogeneity in political careers, an indicator of the hybrid nature of the representative political system which would place a professor like Diego Alcorta beside a landowner and general such as Juan Manuel de Rosas, or a civil servant like B. Garcia alongside a landowner like Juan N. Terreno on the benches of the House of Representatives.

It is equally important to recognize that the webs of alliances and solidarities spun to ensure electoral success owed precious little to forms of associative sociability. Not even justices of the peace, the political intermediaries responsible in most cases for guaranteeing the triumph of the governing ticket, considered the associative network an effective or necessary means for ensuring votes. This network still did not represent a trump card for exercising power. Cultural affiliations owed more to cultural features than to political strategy. It can then be inferred that the introduction of representative institutions in the province of Buenos Aires owed very little to associative forms as institutions in the modern public sphere.

The Field of Citizen Experience: Intellectuals and Public Opinion between 1829 and 1840

If the organization of a political structure in line with the representative principle of government owed little to associative forms of organization, one must inquire into other cultural practices based around reading and discussion and the exercise of exchanging opinions with a view to ultimately editing a publication. Indeed, this period witnessed a considerable growth in "organs of opinion" which appeared to follow the rhythm of the establishment of a representative regime in the region. This correlation may suggest a connection between this growth and the practice of publicity as a founding element of modern constitutionalism.[35] However, the figure of "Opinion" includes a wide range of forms of opinion which cannot be associated so easily with the modern public sphere, even though with the breaking of colonial ties they acquired a hitherto unheard-of political potential.[36] It is necessary to see, therefore, whether there was genuine autonomy in the world of opinion with regard to the forms of authority which, until this time, included the spoken and written word.

The first answer to this question is institutional. One sees the introduction of a legal apparatus aimed primarily at the defense of a free space in which the new world of opinion might take root. One of the first measures taken by the revolutionary governments was to declare the freedom of any man to publish his ideas.[37] Initially, the new world of opinion concerned a small group of the cultural elite with the capacity to produce and consume these publications. As the political regime became established, producers and consumers multiplied, spilling over the boundaries of the world of opinion, from the traditional printing sphere, entrenched in the world of lettered elites, and into the world of popular opinion. This led the elites to raise the question of the status of these publications, an issue interwoven with that of the freedom of the press. Once opinion had crossed the boundaries of well-to-do society, the elites were forced to examine the role that these publications might play in society, which in turn implied the question of the role of society in the new political order. Thus the debate on press freedom, in which two divergent concepts of the public were intermixed, came down to the idea of a spectator public which should remain on the sidelines of public affairs, and the apprehension of the public power base. This explains the misgivings of different governments towards the declaration of press freedom. If this freedom, like suffrage, was an invaluable tool in guaranteeing the continuity of established power, it could also become a dangerous weapon against the same power. Hence, this organ of the expression of the people's will was feared far more than the electoral act, and while universal suffrage was never repealed, freedom of expression would be established and revoked time and again.

Once the principle of press freedom had been proclaimed, its application would be accompanied by a series of restrictive measures, aimed at reducing in practice the world of opinion to that of government propaganda or, in any event, at consolidating the means of control of printed opinion. Hence after the freedom of press law established by Rivadavia on 10 October 1822, Dorrego would then establish a new, more restrictive law on 8 May 1828, which in turn would be repealed by Rosas. A series of decrees then held sway in the publishing world until 1832, when the decree of 1 February imposed the principle of prior authorization for printers and publishers. This decree remained in force with sporadic interruptions until the 1852 with the arrival of a liberal government in the province. The decree of 28 February reestablished the law of 8 May 1828.[38] Leaving aside the first revolutionary period and the appearance of the first printed pages, the general atmosphere was fairly repressive. Even the 1828 regulations, considered the most liberal of the period, prohibited the discussion of religious affairs, although this did not prevent a considerable number of newspapers from appearing during this period.

THE GROWTH OF ORGANS OF OPINION IN THE CITY OF BUENOS AIRES

The first newspaper, published in Buenos Aires by royal privilege, dates from 1801. Prior to this date, and even before the introduction of the printing press in the River Plate, four handwritten newspapers are known to have existed which, with the name of *Gazeta de Buenos Ayres* and dated 1794, were aimed at providing the city's inhabitants with information on local affairs.[39] In 1781, the royal press of the Hospice for Abandoned Children edited an eight-page newspaper with the title *Noticias recibidas de Europa por el Correo de España, y por la vía del Janeyro*, but this periodical was short-lived.[40] Twenty years passed before the appearance of the first regularly published newspaper in the city of Buenos Aires.[41] Between this date and the events of 1810 three new newspapers appeared in the city, one published by the British during the occupation and another two by local elites.[42] But it was after the 1810 insurrection that periodic publications acquired a very particular status and Buenos Aires became the beacon of revolution in the united provinces of the South Atlantic. Established as an organ of insurrectional expression, the press identified itself with the need to carry out a role of providing revolutionary propaganda and as a figure for the legitimization of power, through the identification of this opinion with the will of the sovereign population (figure 10).

The growth rate of periodical publications published in Buenos Aires during the first half of the nineteenth century shows a gradual increase in the number of titles corresponding to the period, with exceptional increments coinciding with important dates in the political history of the province. After a wave of publications between 1815 and 1819, a period of much debate as to the political organization of the former colonial territory after the declaration of independence in 1816, a new wave followed the beginnings of the liberal Rivadavia government, with notable growth at the time of the second attempt at national organization in 1826, continuing to 1828 and the military coup that removed Manual Dorrego from

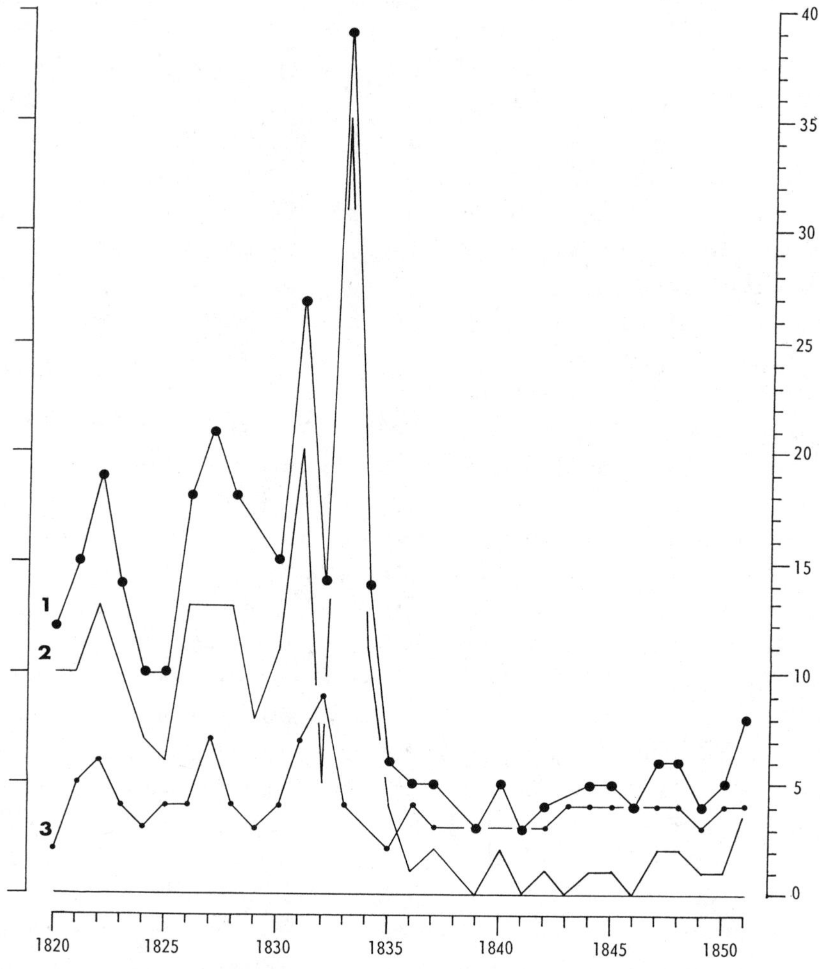

Figure 10. Periodic Publications in Buenos Aires (1829–1851)
1, Total number of publications in this year; 2, Publications appearing this year; 3, Publications founded previously and continuing to appear.

Source: Antonio Zinny, "Bibliografía periodística de Buenos Aires hasta la caída del gobierno de Rosas," *La Revista de Buenos Aires* 10–13 (1866–1867); Juan Rómulo Fernández, *Historia del periodismo argentino* (Buenos Aires: Librería Perlado, 1943).

power. The last and largest wave accompanied the struggle between two sectors of federalism with regard to the issue of constitutional organization in the province of Buenos Aires, which the October 1833 urban mobilization eventually settled. The increase in the number of publications must also be seen in relation to the political vicissitudes which led the different governments to subject the press to different laws. The fall in the number of publications in 1829 at the time of Rosas' coming to power corresponded to the repeal of the 1828 law through a decree ordering the removal of any "injurious libel," which allowed Rosas to exercise tight control over the newspapers.[43] In contrast, the repeal of the 1 February 1832 decree led to a tremendous growth of publications in 1833, which in turn was interrupted by the restoration of the 1832 restrictions in September 1834.

The simultaneity of the break in ruling class consensus and the development of the press appears to concern above all the question of the constitutional organization of an independent State. This issue visibly mobilized Porteños, especially men of law—who were also men of letters—more so than the population as a whole, who were no doubt less inclined to such rhetoric. For this population, the press of constitutional law and political philosophy was accompanied by a popular press, which was more short-lived and was intended to translate debates into the popular vernacular.

OPINION MAKERS

According to statistics, a certain enthusiasm for periodical publications can be detected in the Buenos Aires population, at least if we compare their situation with the publications of the other provinces of the former viceroyalty of the River Plate. In the 1801-1852 period, the population of Buenos Aires witnessed the appearance of 221 periodicals, while Córdoba, a seat of much learning, had only thirty-five titles and the provinces of Catamarca, San Luis, Santiago del Estero and Jujuy had to wait until the second half of the nineteenth century for their first newspapers.[44]

Is it possible to speak of a specialization of the old "learned men" in the profession of opinion? Histories of the press evoke especially the history of publishing, which in most cases is interpreted in party code, but they show little interest in the population of opinion makers.[45] The prosopographic analysis of the men of the press gives some clues as to the sociocultural characteristics of this population. In the period of 1829 to 1840, fifty people can be counted as participating more or less permanently in the production of ninety-four publications published in Buenos Aires and thirty in Montevideo by Argentines in exile. The majority of these were Porteños as the other provinces remained under-represented in the world of the press.[46] What defines them better is their cultural level, as in spite of the significant presence of popular journalism, 75 percent of cases were men of a high cultural level: in a sample of thirty-five people, two thirds were from intellectual professions. There are fewer certainties as to the social backgrounds of these intellectuals. A distinction must be made between those whose source of income was from family property, such as Mansilla and Beláustegui, and those who made a living from writing, such as Sarmiento and López. Unsurprisingly, popular journalists were mostly members of cultural elites. However, among these there were some men from popular backgrounds, as appears to be the case of Francisco Meana, writer for *El Porteño Restaurador* (1834) and Luis Pérez, author of various newspapers and flyers between 1830 and 1834, whose biography is better known, particularly due to the research of R. Rodríguez Molas.[47] There do not appear to be any doubts as to Pérez's popular origins. The same cannot be said of the autonomy of his writings with regard to the government. The correspondence between Pérez and Pedro de Angelis, the strongman in all things propagandistic, is testimony to the pact between the two. In exchange for writings favorable to the government, De Angelis promised Pérez work in the public administration, which the latter ultimately considered insignificant in comparison with his services given to the Holy Cause of the Federation.[48]

From comparing the information on membership of associations with participation in the production of a newspaper, it can be seen that eighteen of the fifty men in the press belonged to some kind of association, seventeen of them to the 1837 Literary Salon. The vast majority became journalists as a result of belonging to the Salon, while of the remaining thirty-three men, the majority wrote for publications appearing after 1837.

This graph (figure 11) shows on the right the men writing between 1829 and 1835 and whose journalistic activity was independent of any given associative experience, and on the left the publicists for whom the journalistic experience was related to the public sphere, in this particular case the 1837 Literary Salon. This leads to the idea of a new model of "men of opinion," for whom the political experience was the consequence of a cultural practice which brought to the fore exchanges of opinion and the social communication of ideas. In the first group there are more cases of writers whose activity was related to a political post, while in the second group the men were not yet in power. This confirms the table presented here. On the one hand were the publicists who were "agents" of the government, an exemplary case being Pedro de Angelis.[49] But also among the journalists we find members of the principal Porteño families and members of the provincial legislature such as Francisco Beláustegui, Manuel Irigoyen, Lucio Mansilla, and even the future Treasury Minister, José M. Rojas y Patrón. For these, participation in the press was perfectly in line with governmental activity. On the other hand,

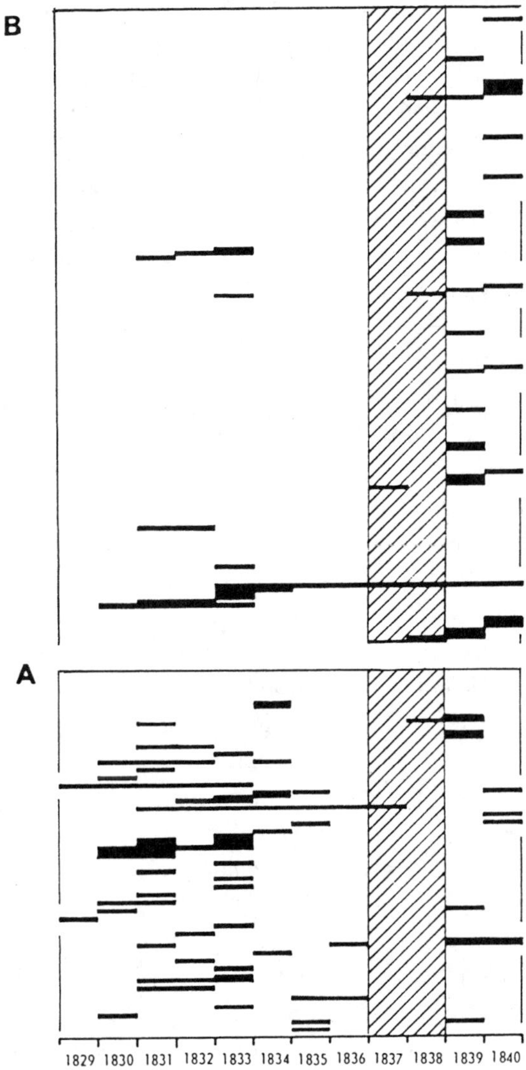

Figure 11. The Associative Experience and Journalistic Activity of Men of Opinion between 1829 and 1840: the Emergence of a New Model of the Man of Opinion

Each horizontal line or sequence of segments represents the journalistic activity of an individual. In A, the men of opinion who maintained their distance from the modern associative experience. In B, the young students who participated in Marcos Sastre's Literary Salon (for the sake of clarity, a wider vertical scale is used) In grey, the years when Sastre's Literary Salon was operating.

we find the men of the pen and associations, who, while not on the sidelines of politics, were nevertheless positioned by their activity on the borderline between cultural practice and the political experience constructed from the new public sphere institutions. Here we undoubtedly run into generational differences: one group, veterans of revolutionary politics, the other, young students attempting to find a way into this new order which appeared to offer them a place. To achieve their ambitions, they took a different path from that of their elders. Rather than the small post which could position them in the power sphere, it was through cultural practices that contact with this sphere was achieved.

THE PUBLIC OF OPINION: THE PLACES OF DIFFUSION OF PUBLIC OPINION

The public interested in opinion appears to have been quite numerous, at least from what can be deduced from the coercive policy of the government with regard to press production. It is difficult to make any advance into the knowledge of the press' influence on opinion, bearing in mind that there is no complete information available concerning the print run of different publications or the number of subscribers. Even if on an indicative level it is possible to use information on subscribers to certain newspapers, this tells us little of the public of opinion, as the written press was not the only means of communication. Indeed, it coexisted with other types of printed matter, such as posters, and other oral means: news communicated by word of mouth, news sung in popular folksongs, and in a completely different order of things but of notable importance, through rumors. In addition, the dissemination of opinion in the nineteenth century continued to be a collective act, whether in the case of reading the written press, whose subscription cost restricted the possibility of purchase, or in the verbal transmission of opinions.

With regard to the list of places where opinion was disseminated, it is necessary to indicate firstly the places where opinion was produced and consumed, which were intended for the pleasures of conversation and discussion: cultural institutions and associations, above all the University of Buenos Aires. In its lecture theaters, students discussed as much the latest theories of philosophy as matters concerning the local population. However, although the public at these encounters were the target readers of the periodic press, the university was not the established place for reading newspapers. This reading was done a few meters away, in the public library. The traveler Arsène Isabelle commented that the library was much visited and boasted a considerable number of books on history, jurisprudence, morality, exact and natural sciences, literature, etc. Isabelle estimated some twenty thousand volumes. The collection was undoubtedly modest, but what our traveler considered to have been the particular quality of the public library was the ease with which one could gain information and communicate. "It is open to the public every day except holidays. The ease with which one can read the newspapers of Buenos Aires makes it more of a reading room."[50] This is confirmed by the accounts of the library, which show subscriptions to the capital's principal newspapers in 1829.[51]

It is necessary, in addition, to mention private places entered on payment of a fee: trader circles reading rooms, cultural associations such as bookstore-reading rooms or literary associations, and so on. The public visited these places both to gain information and to exchange opinions on events. A distinction must be made between places of reading and discussion and those in which the discussion ultimately became the object of a publication. In the first case were the rooms of the trader circles, in which information was directly tied to the imperatives of the profession. This is not to imply that these associations could not become powerful centers for public opinion, as was the case of the Sala Argentina de Comercio (Argentine Commerce Room), where the principal traders of the city met. During the 1828 Lavalle coup and during the division of the liberal party in 1833, one of the objectives of combat was to gain the support of these sectors.[52] However, these associations were far from likely to publish their own means of expression. In this aspect they were distinct from the public of readers of sociocultural associations. Here reading was tied to conversation and the discussion of issues of public interest, and was directly connected to the production of a consensual opinion. But this production was not limited to these associative spaces, having an important presence in cafés, a phenomenon that can be explained both by the public who visited these places and by their location in the city. Bearing in mind that the cafés were concentrated around the cultural area of the city, consisting of the university, the public library, bookstores and publishing houses, while also home to many students, it was perfectly natural that this should become the place in which newspaper subscription proved most profitable for the owner and where clients could find valuable interlocutors.

From 1852 the traces of a trend that had been seen during the Rivadavian government and at the beginning of the Rosas government would become more evident: new forms of informal or associative sociability advocating a cultural objective such as the publishing of a literary review and as a result becoming centers of production of public opinion. The correlation between the development of associative forms of sociability and the press appears to confirm this, as it was far more evident in the 1850s than in earlier times. Indeed, during the first half of the century the associative movement had been far more hybrid and, above all, less autonomous due to the absence of legislation covering the right of association and government controls on these public sphere institutions (figure 12).

So far we have focused on the learned public of the city: the lawyers, the writers, the liberal professions, the major traders, the students; in short, those

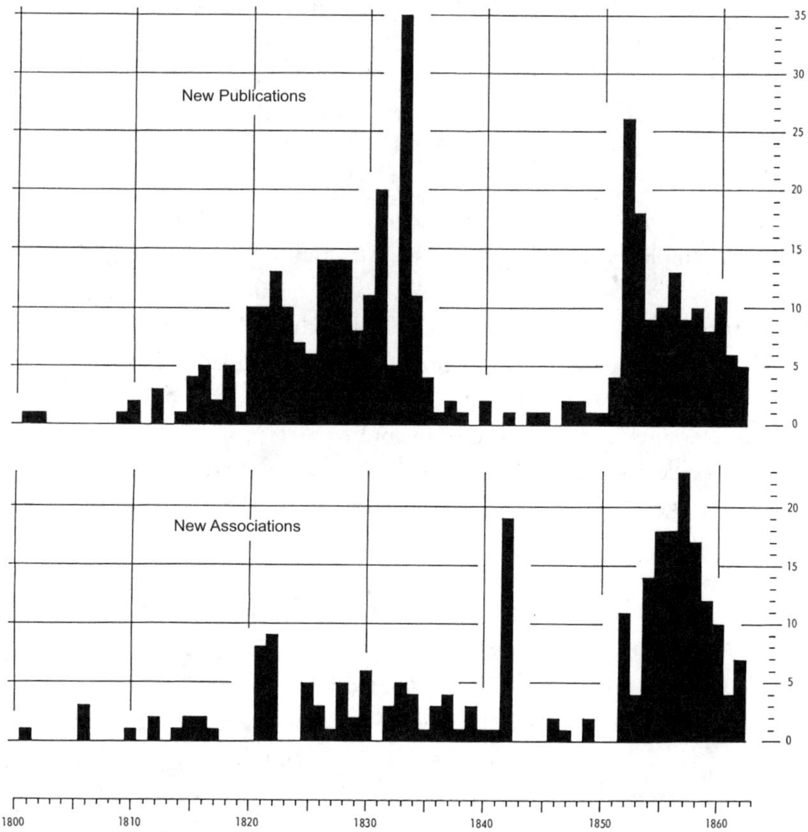

Figure 12. Development of the Associative Movement and the Press in Buenos Aires (1800–1862)

who might be classed as well-to-do and who participated in the cultural rebirth of the city. The spread of the printing press, however, goes beyond the sector of readers and writers. As can be imagined, with the development of a press written in popular language, the public of opinion which was at first restricted to a small circle of urban society began to reach other sectors of the population in the 1830s. It is known, for example, that the newspapers published by Luis Pérez were widely read by the popular sectors, and it is no surprise that one of the principal sales points was the market.[53] However, more so than being read these newspapers were heard in the city's principal places of sociability, the *pulperías*, where the written world met with popular culture. Here, guitars were used to perform *payadas* and traditional folk songs as well as the verses included with this intention in the popular press.[54] The earliest references found date from the rural uprising of 1828-1829, which suggests that the practice was already well established. Naturally, there was a distinction between the opinion expressed by the press and that which, via the *gaucho cantor*, took the form of news and rumors.[55] In one case, those who voiced the opinion were discourse "professionals." In others, as will be seen later, they were the instigators of the action. The dissemination of the written press in the popular media is then quite revealing of the development of a public sphere in which writers gained their power, and which at the same time fed other forms of representation to rival that of the men of opinion.

Limits of the Experience: Confrontation as a Model of Politicization

In spite of the widening of the political boundaries as a result of the extension of the vote and the development of spaces in which a critical opinion could be formed, the population's most frequent contacts with the sphere of power were via other paths with little connection to the new experiences of the public sphere. Indeed, the two popular mobilizations which appeared in this period were organized along different lines to those opened by the movement of opinion. However, these were vindicated as manifestations of the real will of the people against electoral fraud and a defamatory, mendacious press. This implies that a political experience was possible aside from the men and institutions of the new sphere of political power, and also means that there existed a third means of representation of the will of the people: armed opinion. And this was used when ruling class consensus broke down, as in 1828 and 1833.

PEASANT UPRISING OF 1828 AND THE TRIUMPH OF ARMED OPINION

Rosas' coming to power was directly connected to the peasant uprising in the south of the province of Buenos Aires. Rosas was able to obtain with few difficulties the cession of absolute power as a condition for leading the government of the province thanks to a critical situation, of which the disturbances were the most visible manifestation.

In a partial study into this uprising, I have found that what was presented as the insurrection of the south of the province against the Lavalle coup was in fact a set of armed actions closer in resemblance to social brigandage, to use Hobsbawm's words, than political combat.[56] The 1829 uprising was above all a manifestation of rural social tensions, the consequence of transformations in the structure of production aggravated by an explosive scenario: a critical economic situation marked by high inflation leading to a devaluation of salaries in real terms, to which was added an unforeseen imbalance in the labor market due to troops returning from the war with Brazil, and lastly one of the worst droughts in the history of the province of Buenos Aires. We will leave aside the question of the movement's autonomy, which would distract us too much from our aim, to tackle the problem of the movement's political significance.[57]

The Manifestations of Rural Anger: The disturbances began immediately after the execution of the Governor of the Province of Buenos Aires, Manuel Dorrego, in December 1828. I use the word disturbances because in fact these were different manifestations of popular discontent, some completely independent of events in the city of Buenos Aires, but coordinated by a wave of rumors circulating throughout the south of the province.[58] This instability, combined with the explosive economic, social and political situation, accounts for the generalized actions of different social and ethnic sectors, who took to all kinds of banditry. It is possible to distinguish at least three different manifestations: the attacks by "nomadic" Indians from the southern frontier, the armed actions of Rosas' men against Lavalle's troops and the acts of social banditry by *gauchos* organized in armed bands in the Salado River region.

In the three cases the mobilizations followed three traditional paths. The Indians acted through their own attack organization, the *malones*, economic ventures organized by the Indian tribes to conduct incursions into white men's lands.[59] Each raid, carried out by the men of the tribe, had its own chief and *modus operandi*. Armed groups, who figure in sources as "anarchists," operated with bands of men directed by rural leaders known as *caudillos*, such as Molina or Meta. These bands existed prior to the revolt, so when the disturbances began Molina could already count on 500 "Christians" and a similar number of Pampas Indians. Molina is a good example of the type of *caudillo* living in frontier society. An overseer under Francisco Ramos Mejía, he fled to Indian territory when Ramos Mejía was imprisoned in 1821.With deserters and some Indians he built up his own band in order to raid white property. The national government offered him amnesty in 1826 and incorporated him into the army of the southern frontier. Rosas used Molina when trying to sign alliances with certain friendly tribes. In this way Molina was to become one of Rosas' men on the southern frontier.[60] Molina's band's armed clash with Lavalle's troops can be explained entirely by Molina's connections with Rosas; with or without precise instructions from the latter, Molina acted in the context of a clientele relationship, exchanging loyalty and assistance for protection.

It is necessary to distinguish this action from that undertaken by small bands of around fifty men in the Salado River area.[61] There, the ringleaders were either subaltern army officers, such as Basualdo and Arnold, minor frontier *caudillos* like Miranda or Indian caciques like Ventura Miñaña and Benancio. These leaders were able to organize their bands as a result of the climate of discontent which incited a good number of rural inhabitants to turn to armed action, but in accordance with their clientele. Hence, the various *caudillos* became responsible for these men who in turn owed them their loyalty. However, these bands did not survive the uprising. Even earlier, around late March, many of them had joined Rosas' troops. At the same time there was a proliferation throughout the countryside and near the city of small bands of around ten people who took to general robbery. These were undoubtedly men who occasionally worked for *caudillos* and who with their bosses' incorporation into the *Rosista* army decided to continue looting *estancias*. This meant that, unlike earlier groups, their actions expressed a popular anger which went beyond the organization of *caudillo* troops. The situation was quelled in June when Rosas took on the political direction of the movement. Indians continued their attacks and *estancias* continued to be looted, but they lost their sociopolitical significance, becoming mere acts of banditry which Rosas had no hesitation in repressing.[62]

The Political Representation of the Movement: The popular mobilization of 1829 can be interpreted as one of the classic resorts to force during the outbreak of conflict among the ruling class. Rosas, who exercised posts of high military command during the two popular revolts (1829 and 1833), could mobilize his troops to impose conservative order better than anyone else. After all, his triumph over Lavalle could be explained simply by the fact that the reason of the strongest is always the greatest. This is the classic theory of Rosas' power, which John Lynch resumes with much clarity in his latest work. According to Lynch, Rosas' power arose from the control of an important and powerful client network which included a range of figures from Indian tribes to members of the provincial legislature. The resort to force or terror was a means of ensuring his absolute authority. Thus, the regime was the negation of politics, just as the social mobilizations were the negation of democratic participation. However, between General Lavalle's coup in December 1828 and the popular mobilization that took Juan Manuel de Rosas from his post of General Commander of the militias to the provincial government in 1829, there was a great difference, namely, political order. Rosas' power was founded on a popular mobilization, while Lavalle's was based on a small group of generals and intellectuals accompanying him in 1828. Against what Rosas called "the Unitarian Lodge," the 1829 uprising was presented as a real manifestation of the people's will. In this way, Rosas could pit the dubiousness of Unitarian power against the transparency of this will.

This idea of the people's transparency or authenticity is associated with the way in which the people protested, which implies a particular definition of sovereignty and the mechanisms of representation. In accordance with the political meaning which the movement assumed, the individual became a citizen when he made public use of his will, and the path taken was not the option but the action. In this confusion of the sphere of public power and the sphere of war action, the natural representatives of the people were those who directed this action, now synonymous with the sovereign will.

Established as head of the movement, Rosas thus became the legitimate representative of the people. This does not mean that the rural population was explicitly included in the context of the universe of values characterizing the modern citizen. This was a traditional society which invoked a likewise traditional authority but would enter the political field as the general will. It is then easier to understand the reason for the indifference towards a combat resolved by means of opinion or at the polls. The sphere of public power, even after the important development of the written press and the appearance of new forms of associative sociability, was devoid of popular legitimacy. This explains why one of the most feared arms of the insurrectionists was the "war of opinion." This meant the transmission of "incendiary news" which spread around the countryside. In most cases this was information and rumors transmitted from mouth to mouth; the printing press, like posters, were mostly used in the city of Buenos Aires.[63] This information circulated principally in places of popular sociability, namely rural *pulperías*. In these, the "anarchists" kept the population up to date on recent events but also gave meaning to these events.[64] In this way various rumors concerning political issues of concern to the population were spread. It is interesting to note that popular sociability in the *pulperías* was in this case one of the networks for the propagation of rural anger, which suggests the double potential of this sociability in these places. On the one hand, the *pulperías* were places where traditional collective behavior was perpetuated, while on the other hand they allowed the opening up of the popular medium towards the world of the printed word, and with it, modern political culture. According to denunciations published in the Unitarian press, religious posts were also used by the insurrectionists to disseminate the movement.[65]

This war, which the press called "more dangerous than armed conflict,"[66] proved that the population no longer believed the veracity of information broadcast by the press. This also implies the existence of an alternative medium of dissemination to that of the printing world, whose fundamental effect was to undermine the monopoly of the written press, not only as a principle organ of information but also as representative of public opinion. Thus, Rosas took advantage of the movement to "democratically" found his absolute power. While he did not challenge the democratic principle of the sovereignty of the people,

Rosas redefined the "people" and their mechanisms of representation. This allowed him, through measures such as the decree of 1 February 1832, to erode the power of journalist intellectuals, essentially the liberal opposition. The new state of affairs made such measures possible.[67]

URBAN MOBILIZATION OF 1833: PUBLIC EVIDENCE OF SOCIAL ORDER

The Buenos Aires federalism that carried Rosas to power became divided during his first term. On one side were the governor's unconditional supporters who backed the renewal of his extraordinary powers, the "Rosista" branch of federalism known as the "apostolic federals." On the other side stood the "doctrinal federals," opposed to the perpetuation of limitless powers.[68] But the differences between these two sectors of federalism did not stop there. The decisive question which continued to divide them was the constitutional organization of Argentina. The 1831 Federal League only widened the divergences.[69] While the doctrinal federals argued for a Constituent Congress to be convened, the apostolic federals sustained Rosas' anti-constitutional policies,[70] reestablishing the debate over the problem of the institutional normalization of provincial government.[71] When Rosas' mandate as governor came to an end in 1832, the legislature declared itself against the prolongation of absolute power. Rosas then refused to take up the leadership of the provincial government under these conditions and devoted himself to the organization of the expedition against the Pampas Indians. The provincial house of representatives elected the Minister of War, Juan M. Balcarce, to assume the role of governor in December 1832. Balcarce formed a conciliation government, naming two Rosista Federals, Manuel V. Maza and Victorio García Zúñiga as Ministers of Justice and Government respectively, while assigning to the Ministry of War his cousin, Brigadier General Enrique Martínez, who was distanced from the Rosista federals at the time. The entente was short-lived, with conflict breaking out during the election of representatives on 28 April 1833.

Political Confrontation at the Core of the Elites: Political hostilities began with the elections of April 1833. For this occasion, as was often the case, political leaders had previously reached an agreement to run on a joint ticket. But on the day of the election a second ticket unexpectedly appeared called the "people's ticket" and later known as the *lomos negros* ticket, the "black backs" in reference to the color of the paper on which the ticket was written. This was the work of Martínez, in coalition with the doctrinal federals, to assert their authority over the apostolic federals. The people's ticket "won" the elections, and the Rosistas denounced the fraud, preparing for a fresh electoral showdown in June.[72] For this, both sides used the figure of Rosas to gain supporters, increasing all the more the confusion at the polls.[73]

The Rosistas, or apostolic federals, believed that they would not be caught out again, and coordinated themselves in June to ensure their primacy in the fraud. As usual, the most important battle was fought during the constitution of the electoral assemblies. For this, the *lomos negros* had the army's troops at their disposal, commanded by the Minister of War, E. Martínez and seconded by Olazábal, while the Rosistas had the police, under the command of Police Chief Correa Morales. The hostilities were soon declared: by nine in the morning, both sides had already drawn their knives in the Catedral al Sur parish,[74] while in the parish of Nuestra Señora de Socorro a group of armed men threatened to cut off the ears of those who disobeyed their orders to vote for their candidate.[75] In short, the game appeared to be lost for the *lomos negros*, even with the advantage of being in the government. Yet with the Rosista federals winning the elections, the government resorted to one of their last strategies, and suspended the elections. This caused the break between the doctrinal federalists and the apostolic federalists. The Rosista ministers resigned from their government posts, while the political combat was transferred to the public sphere, facilitated by the decree of 22 June 1833, which brought back into force the press freedom law of May 1828.[76]

To mark the occasion, the doctrinal federals published a series of publications defending the politics of the government. In 1833 alone the following newspapers were published: *El Iris*, edited by José L. Bustamante, which appeared from March until August; *El Defensor de los Derechos del Pueblo*, which appeared in July and was suspended by Agrelo in October, by which time ninety-four issues had already appeared; *El Amigo del País*, edited by Marco Avellaneda, Juan M. Gutiérrez and Ángel Navarro, published from July to October; *El Constitucional*, directed by Miguel Valencia and also suspended by Agrelo; and *El Látigo Republicano*, edited by Carlos Terrada.[77] The doctrinal federals had a clear advantage over the Rosista Federals in this field, who nevertheless had *La Gaceta Mercantil* as their principal organ of expression. Not only was the practice of writing more established among young liberals, printing was also one of the practices of sociability which had been developed within the sector of doctrinal federals. Their influence on public opinion was considerable,[78] as Maza recognized in a letter to Rosas in June 1833: "The opinion, moreover, of the constitution is a torrent which is so strong that there is no human who can hold it back."[79]

This "torrent of opinion," controlled by doctrinal federals, was all the more distressing in that it concerned a broad sector of the population beyond those who read and wrote. Indeed, much printed matter now found its way to popular sectors via the *pulpería*. While these places of popular sociability, as previously mentioned, were above all a channel for broadcasting unprinted opinion (in spontaneous conversation but also in popular songs), the reading aloud of the press began to be increasingly integrated into these popular sociability practices. This explains why the debate of opinion which previously affected a very limited sector of the population gradually reached the popular sectors. The doctrinal federals, in spite of their scant influence over the urban masses, were able to win over some supporters in these sectors. In a letter to Rosas of 4 August 1833, Vicente González, one of Rosas' political go-betweens in the south of the province, wrote, "…he [a Captain of the Villamayor Squadron] assured me that Don Vicente Anastacio Echeverría spoke very badly of you and even passed round printed matter of the Schismatics. At a corner [a *pulpería*] of San José the owner there called Don Bartolo Vivot talks iniquities against you and begged me to thus make it known."[80]

González was right to mistrust the *pulpero*s. These men's capacity to mobilize others was enormous, both through spreading news and rumors and through their "translation" of the discourse of the elites with popular aims, to which can be added the distribution of the popular press which, while ephemeral, was increasingly numerous. Often, these newspapers were written in verse. The political references were present, but always translated into a popular language mixing political issues with moral foundations, frequently accompanied by religious references. Hence when the newspaper *La Negrita* explained the ideological foundations of the party it supported, it did so in these terms: "There is no longer any doubt that Juan Manual de Rosas is as apostolic as we are, as upon writing to a friend of his on San Pedro's day, he dated his letter: Río Colorado, 29 June 1833, day of my dear friend, the apostle San Pedro."[81] While references to the struggles dividing the elites were not absent, they were made on another plane to that opened up by the new cultural practices of the urban elites.

In addition to the framework of reference, the distribution networks of these newspapers differed from those of the opinion press. According to *El Amigo del País*, they were handed out free of charge in the streets, "where sometimes certain characters read them in the presence of all the people," as was the case in the *tertulias*.[82] Nor was the army excluded: according to a letter from Rosas to Guido, newspaper reading was quite widespread. Rosas' words were: "You cannot imagine their influence. The soldiers crowd round to read them, above all articles from *El Negrito*."[83] It is also feasible that printed matter circulated in African Societies, particularly newspapers aimed at blacks, such as *El Negrito* and *La Negrita*.[84] In contrast, the city's *pulpería*s were much feared by apostolic federals. According to various recovered references, Rosas and his men held *pulperos* in enormous distrust, preferring other channels such as the army.[85]

By late September, Porteño political life was intensely politicized. Each side claimed to be the voice of public opinion with the intention of undermining their adversary. The newspapers now aimed to impose opinion into popular sectors, in order to achieve their political mobilization.[86] But the absence of a strictly political field in which the elites' struggle for power might take place, combined with the fact that the so-called opinion popular press was developed in a context of references founded on infra-political terrain, led to this struggle spreading beyond both the political context and that of the cultural elites. When Tomás de Iriarte spoke of this conflict, which according to him began with the elections of 1833, he did so in a somber tone fitting of a man for whom politics was a matter for generals, which at most might interest the well-to-do, but which above all must not affect the urban masses, as the risk to social order would be too great. It is worth remembering his words with regard to the consequences of conflict among the elites:

> It encouraged the license of the press, made the press reveal even the miseries of the enemy's private life....the families entered, naturally, on the side of ill-feeling from the humiliation of their relatives, and society as a whole was split in two opposing bands; and it was not so much support or hatred of Rosas but the desire for personal vengeance which was the reason for the indecency of both contenders.[87]

Here we see once again society in danger, in a situation that much resembles that of 1828–1829. The business representative for France sums up well the prevailing climate at the time:

> In sum, we are once again atop a volcano; the parties attack each other with the pen, preparing for a more serious fight; the government, lacking in material or moral force, sits on the fence, not daring to take sides; incomplete and divided, the House of Representatives names commissions with the pretext of investigating events, but by all appearances it is far more to gain time; all the people anxiously await the attitude that General Rosas will take, so that the solution to the problem appears to depend today on the leader of a small army, separated at the moment from the capital by two hundred leagues of desert, where communication is extremely slow and difficult in the present season.[88]

Rosas and the Definition of the Federal Nation: From September, the situation was completely out of control. Balcarce decided to then intervene against the opinion movement, embarking on a trial for the abuse of the freedom of the press. On 2 October, the attorney general Agrelo presented his accusation against five apostolic newspapers and two doctrinal papers. Among these was the apostolic publication *El Restaurador de las Leyes*. The trial was to begin 10 October 1833, but the night before a "misunderstanding" triggered disturbances,[89] as some placards announced the coming trial of the Restaurador de las Leyes, which the urban population interpreted as the trial of Rosas himself, known popularly as "Restorer of the Laws," and not of the newspaper of the same name.[90]

Events happened quickly. The rumor of the detention of Rosas, probably related to the memory of the trial that had culminated in the execution of Dorrego, mobilized the urban population towards the Palace of Justice. "Many people gathered yesterday morning in the gallery of the Palace of Justice, shouts and voices in provocative tones were heard.... Those in the enclosed list repeated "Long Live...!" and "Death to...!" in the Palace of Justice. Yet as the trial did not take place, some of these individuals upon leaving continued with the same cries through the streets."[91] The news then spread of the uprising by Commander Quilmes, who had apparently seized arms in the barracks. In the city's slums, on the other side of the Puente Gálvez, there was talk of another uprising, directed by José María Benavente, Bernadino Cabrera, Bernadino Parra and Commander Montes de Oca, followed by the population of the city.[92] At noon, after the meeting in the Palace of Justice, the citizens left the center to join the movement in the suburbs. At 1 p.m. "the Restaurador General D. Agustín Pinedo was proclaimed leader of the citizens gathered there."[93] When a few days later the commission assigned by the House of Representatives to deal with the insurrectionists contacted General Pinedo, he justified his actions in these terms: "he affirmed, that when he had decided in favor of the sacrifice of acquiescing to the acclamation of the citizens who had placed themselves under his orders, so that he might be their president, it was a consequence of the armed assembly of these citizens having the sole intention of ensuring through this the use of the right to petition, which they were resolved to make known to the Honorable Assembly so that it might constitutionally remedy the grave ills that were felt..."[94]

These events sum up the episode known as the "Restorers' Revolution," which broke out on the day of the trial of the *Restaurador de las Leyes* newspaper and which could only be contained after the resignation of Balcarce from the provincial government on 3 November of the same year. During the twenty-three days until the political resolution of the conflict, an intense urban and rural mobilization was triggered which "exalted the spirit of the party."[95] In this way the public evidence of the people's will challenged the representative institutions. Once again the people's will was invoked with arms to resolve a conflict against the elites, ignoring entirely these institutions. However, unlike the 1829 uprising, the mobilization of October 1833 did not spread to the army, which is not to say that the movement was completely controlled by Rosas. To a certain extent the revolution was the consequence of an internal crisis in the army which was settled with the confrontation between those identifying with the national army, such as Balcarce, Martínez, Olazábal, Iriarte, Espinosa, etc, against those who had worked their way up from the militias, such as Pinedo, Rolón, Pueyreddón and Prudencio Rosas. Among the latter were also figures from the national army, who became followers of Rosas after 1829, such as Colonel Cortinas and General Izquierdo. While in 1833 these were the principal defenders of *Rosismo*, the revolution of October 1833 opened a new rift between Rosas' unconditional allies, such as his brother Prudencio and those who, like the mutiny leader Pinedo, intended to go their own way.

The men who mobilized "spontaneously" on the morning of 12 October were incorporated into the army. Their natural representatives were those directing the action, namely their hierarchical superiors. Politicization was reduced to a mobilization to show traditional loyalties. However, the movement was useful in defending the people's will against the arbitrariness of the Balcarce government. Hence, when Rosas was elected as governor of the province of Buenos Aires with extraordinary powers for the second time, he was sure to affirm that he was invested with the strength of opinion, the only basis on which such extraordinary power could be based.[96] Manuel Maza, a deputy and friend of Rosas, said so clearly in a letter to the governor, "if the cause of the Federation is the irresistible form of government, it is because the opinion of the masses has decided thus."[97] This opinion, as was the case in the 1829 uprising, operated as a parallel and rival power to the indecisive power of the public literary sphere.

The "Restorers' Revolution" then constituted another chapter in Rosas' crusade against the intellectuals, the professionals of politics or, in his own words, "the penpushers."[98] The place that these had arrogated in the organization of the State, constitutionally or otherwise, was a consequence of their primary identification with public opinion and later with the will of the nation, to which Rosas responded with the public evidence of the people, namely social order. Custodian of society but also its representative, Rosas cloaked his authority with a new symbolic role: the protector of the people's voice. This allowed Rosas to neutralize the sphere of public power with the establishment of the "rebel faith" which was to become one of the pillars of the regime.

NOTES

1. With regard to the new usage of the idea of opinion, see Mona Ozouf, *L'Homme régénéré. Essais sur la Révolution Française* (Paris: Gallimard, 1989). On these questions in general see Roger Chartier, *Les Origines culturelles de la Révolution Française* (Paris: Seuil, 1990).
2. Since defending this thesis, studies into electoral history in Latin America have experienced considerable development. For this period, see "Nuevo régimen

representativo y expansión de la frontera política. Las elecciones del Estado de Buenos Aires, 1820–1840," in Antonio Annino, *Historia de las elecciones en Iberoamérica, siglo XIX* (Buenos Aires: Fondo de Cultura Económica, 1995), 65–105.

3. On this question, see R. Chartier, *Les Origines culturelles.*; Keith Michael Baker (ed.), *The French Revolution and the Creation of Modern Political Culture*, 3 vols. (Oxford and New York, 1987); K. M. Baker, *Inventing the French Revolution: Essays on French Political Culture in the Eighteenth Century* (Cambridge: Cambridge University Press, 1990).
4. 'On modern representation, in addition to works cited above, see Marcel Gauchet, *La Révolution des pouvoirs. La souveraineté, le peuple et la représentation, 1789–1799* (Paris: Gallimard, 1995).
5. Saturnino Salcedo, *Las primeras formas de elegir y los actuales sistemas electorales. Régimen político de las provincias argentinas* (Buenos Aires: ETGLA, 1948), chapter 1.
6. See "Ley de Elecciones," *Registro Oficial de la Provincia*, 19–21.
7. The first electoral law dates from 27 May 1810, modeled on the 1809 decree. This established the principle of direct election but only for the "principal, healthiest part of the neighborhood." Moreover, this was not the representation of individuals but that of cities as territorial political communities; see J. V. González, *Filiación histórica*. The 1815 statute, while extending the right to vote, established the principle of vote over two rounds. See "Estatuto Provisional para la dirección y administración del Estado, dado por la Junta de Observaciones, 5 de mayo de 1815," in A. Sampay, *Las Constituciones de la Argentina (1810/1972)* (Buenos Aires: Eudeba, 1975), 212–232. Pierre Rosanvallon in *Le Sacre du citoyen. Histoire du suffrage universel en France* (Paris: Gallimard, 1992), 188–195, presents an analysis of the two-round vote in the republican representative system.
8. In a study posterior to the present study, M. Ternavasio finds a convincing explanation for this law in the elites' will to bring an end to political division. This does not however explain how such divided elites were able to reach a consensus for the solution to their conflict so easily; see M. Ternavasio, "Nuevo régimen representativo."
9. The principle of rational sovereignty would be defended by the young romantic generation of 1838, fascinated by the thinking of Guizot. See Esteban Echeverría, "Ojeada retrospectiva sobre el movimiento intelectual en el Plata desde el año 1837" (Montevideo, 1846), in *Dogma Socialista de la Asociación de Mayo* (Buenos Aires: Perrot, 1958), 26–115. On the theory of the sovereignty of reason in Guizot, see Pierre Rosanvallon, *Le Moment Guizot* (Paris: Gallimard, 1985); P. Rosanvallon, *Le Sacre*.
10. The justices of the peace were charged with trials involving insignificant sums of money, while the *alcaldes de barrio* were representatives of law and order. Some had inherited functions from the *alcaldes de barrio* of the colonial period.
11. See François-X. Guerra, "Le peuple souverain: fondements et logique d'une fiction (pays hispaniques au xixe siècle)," in *L'Avenir de la démocratie en Amérique latine* (Toulouse: CNRS, 1988).
12. Tomás de Iriarte, *Memorias*, with a preliminary study by Enrique de Gandía (Buenos Aires: Ediciones Argentinas, 1944–1969), vol. 5 , 5–6.
13. The assembly was formed in 1820 but was disbanded immediately. The first legislature dated from 1821. With the dissolution of the fifth provincial legislature in 1826, the National Congress hoped to replace the provincial institutions with a National Assembly. This aroused Porteños' localist interests, who saw in this attitude an attack on their rights and privileges, particularly the benefits of the port. This measure was one of the consequences of the 1826 "capitalization law," with which the city of Buenos Aires became the capital city. This roused Porteño opposition to national organization,

which already had few supporters in the rest of the country. All of which led to the dissolution of the National Congress, the Constitution was put aside and there was a return to provincial administration. In 1827, elections were called to establish the sixth legislature of the province. See Emilio Ravignani, "El pacto federal del 4 de enero de 1831 y la Comisión Representativa," in *Documentos para la historia argentina* (Buenos Aires: Instituto de Investigaciones Históricas, 1922), vol. 15, 1–199.

14. An exceptional measure, voted in to tackle a most critical economic, social and political situation in the province in 1828.
15. Article 3 of the electoral law. Interestingly, in the case of voters, the word "hombre" (man) is used, while in the case of representatives the word "ciudadano"(citizen) is used, a notion that appears to pick up on the colonial period idea of "neighbor."
16. See the table in the appendix to my doctoral thesis, *La Création*.
17. The enfiteusis law passed by Rivadavia to encourage smallholdings allowed, in the short term, the concentration of large tracts of lands in the hands of a small number of owners. Four years after the law was passed, sixty people held almost four hundred leagues. See Andrés Carretero, "Contribución al conocimiento de la propiedad rural en la provincia de Buenos Aires para 1830," *BIHAA-E. Ravignani* 2: 13 (1970), 146–192; Emilio A. Coni, *La verdad sobre la enfiteusis de Rivadavia* (Buenos Aires: Imprenta de la Universidad, 1927).
18. This is the classic view of the regime. See, for example, J. Lynch, *Juan Manuel de Rosas*, ch. 2, 52 92.
19. Jorge Sábato, *La clase dominante en la Argentina moderna. Formación y características* (Buenos Aires: CISEA, 1991). Some later works tend to question the existence of a large group of traders. See "Discontinuidades y permanencias," *Anuario IEHS* 12, particularly Jorge Gelman's article, "Producción y explotaciones agrarias bonaerenses entre la colonia y la primera mitad del siglo XIX. Rupturas y continuidades."
20. There have been few studies into this perspective. For the colonial period, see Z. Moutoukias, "Réseaux personnels et autorité coloniale."
21. In addition to writers (literary and journalistic) and men of science (university professors), men of law are included here among the intellectual professions, distinguished from the liberal professions. To define them, the criterion used is that of having studied law, even if the person did not later exercise this profession. This criterion differs from that used by Gaudemet, who defines jurists as those who exercised a legal profession. From my perspective, it is not possible to approach a study of the importance of jurists in political life if we rule out from the beginning all those who used this qualification as a stepping stone in their political career. See Ives Henri Gaudemet, *Les Juristes et la vie politique de la IIIe République* (Paris, PUF, 1970). On the methodologiocal question, see PGB, *La Création*, appendix 1.
22. This confirms the trend suggested by Susan Socolow for the late eighteenth century and by Diana Balmori, "Family and Politics: three generations (1790–1890), *Journal of Family History* 10: 3 (1985), 247–257. On the place of the intellectual in the strategy of the great families, see Tulio Halperin Donghi, "Intelectuales, sociedad y vida pública en Hispanoamérica a través de la literatura autobiográfica," in *El espejo de la Historia* (Buenos Aires: Sudamericana, 1987), 43–63.
23. On the similarities and differences between the colonial man of letters and the post-independence intellectual, see Tulio Halperin Donghi, "El letrado colonial como intelectual revolucionario," *Anuario* 11, segunda época (Rosario: Facultad de Humanidades y Artes, UNR) (1985), 85–101.

24. Far from corroborating the influence of economic over political power, or rather, of infrastructure over superstructure, the presence of large landowners, traders and jurists in the legislature is complementary proof of the existence of a logic of networks that the classification by socioprofessional categories barely accounts for.
25. The only history of the Argentine armed forces during the nineteenth century is that written by the Commander-in-Chief of the Army, which, as the title indicates, is a general overview of the history of the institution as it sees itself; see Comando en Jefe del Ejército, *Reseña histórica y orgánica del Ejército Argentino*, 2 vols. (Buenos Aires: Círculo Militar, 1971). I am much obliged to General Tomás Sánchez de Bustamante, who was director of the Instituto Sanmartiniano at the time and who died shortly after, for providing access to a part of the archives.
26. See D. Balmori, "Family and politics."
27. See Pilar González Bernaldo, "Producción de una nueva legitimidad: ejército y sociedades patrióticas en Buenos Aires entre 1810 y 1813," *Cahiers des Amériques Latines* 10 (1990): 177–195.
28. For the historic process of the displacement of the problem of representation in the eighteenth century see K. M. Baker, *Au tribunal de l'opinion*; also R. Chartier, *Les Origines culturelles.*
29. The theory of the dissociation between the owners and the administrators of power is Halperin Donghi's, who in fact formulated it from a period prior to ours. Nevertheless, and in the absence of an equivalent work for this period, his theory is often applied to explain the political behavior of the ruling class throughout the first half of the nineteenth century; T. Halperin Donghi, *Revolución y guerra.*
30. I have consulted the handwritten minutes of the two associations, which can be found in the Museo Bartolomé Mitre archives, and the archives of the López family in AGN. VII. There are numerous bibliographical references to these societies. See C. Ibarguren, *Las sociedades literarias*, ch. 4, and Haydée Frizzi de Longoni, *Las sociedades literarias y el periodismo, 1800–1852*, prologue by Carlos Ibarguren (Buenos Aires: Asociación Interamericana de Escritores, 1946).
31. Núñez was one of the young "Jacobins" who had joined the "Club Morenista" of 1811. In 1812 he joined the Literary Society, but then disappeared from the public stage when the society merged with the Lautaro Lodge in 1812. Evidence of his later adherence to Rivadavian liberal politics can be found in the publication of his work, aimed at promoting European immigration into the River Plate, and is confirmed by his joining the Literary Society in 1822.
32. Felipe Senillosa had been a professor of the University of Buenos Aires between 1821 and 1826, firstly (1821–1822) as a professor of Elemental Mathematics in the Department of Preparatory Studies, then as professor in Descriptive Geometry in the Department of Exact Sciences, resigning from this post in 1826. See N. Piñedo y E. Bidau, *Historia de la Universidad.*
33. F. Weinberg, *El Salón Literario*, 49–52.
34. The notion of "civil society" is used here to evoke the idea of a contract-based democracy. In Latin America, however, this democracy was not secularized. Moreover, it is difficult to find a clear distinction which, according to the definition of civil society, must be found between social order and political order. I am inclined to speak of society alone, but to distinguish this new representation of society born from a contract between free and equal individuals, subject to law, from the earlier idea of the social bond, I use the notion of "civil society."

35. See J. Habermas, *L'Espace public.*
36. On forms of opinion, see M. Ozouf, *L'Homme régénéré.*
37. The insurrectional authority of Buenos Aires passed the first legislation on freedom of the press on 20 April 1811, ratified by the Freedom of Press Decree of 26 October 1811; see "Decreto de libertad de imprenta, Buenos Aires, 26 de octubre de 1811," in *Registro Oficial de la República Argentina, comprende documentos expedidos desde 1810 hasta 1873*, Publicación Oficial (Buenos Aires: Imprenta de la República, 1879), vol. 1–2.
38. See *Registro Oficial de la Provincia de Buenos Aires*, and *Registro Oficial de la República Argentina.*
39. Juan Pablo Echagüe, "El periodismo," in *Historia de la Nación Argentina*, vol. 4, sec. 2, 59–69.
40. The newspaper is dated Buenos Aires, 8 January 1781.
41. This was the *Telégrafo Mercantil, Rural, Político-económico e Historiográfico del Río de la Plata* (1801–1802), 2 vols., facsimile reprint (Buenos Aires: Junta de Historia y Numismática Americana, 1914–1915).
42. For more on the history of the press see Oscar Beltrán, *Historia del periodismo argentino* (Buenos Aires: Sopena, 1943); Juan Rómulo Fernández, *Historia del periodismo argentino* (Buenos Aires: Librería Perlado, 1943).
43. "Ley mandando quemar los papeles injuriosos, publicados en tiempo del gobierno intruso," Buenos Aires, 24 December 1829, in P. de Angelis, *Recopilación.*
44. See Antonio Zinny, "Efemeridografía argirepatriótica o sea de las provincias argentinas," *La Revista de Buenos Aires* 16 (1868): 512–513; A. Zinny, "Bibliografía periodística de Buenos Aires hasta la caída del gobierno de Rosas," *La Revista de Buenos Aires* 9–14.
45. See O. Beltrán, *Historia del periodismo*, and J. R. Fernández, *Historia del periodismo.* However, some authors have indicated the existence of a press produced by men from a more popular background. See Ricardo Rodríguez Molas, "Elementos populares en la prédica contra Juan Manuel de Rosas," *Historia*, no. 30, 1963. Following this work, Jorge Myers proposed an entirely different and stimulating view of the press of this period, with an interest not only in opinion makers but also in examining a lesser known question, that of the discourse of the Rosista press. See Jorge Myers, *Orden y virtud. El discurso republicano en el régimen Rosista* (Quilmes: Universidad Nacional de Quilmes, 1995).
46. In a sample of 31 journalists, 21 were from Buenos Aires, five from the provinces and the remaining five from neighboring countries or Europe. PGB, *La Création*, appendix 1, "Base de données."
47. Ricardo Rodríguez Molas, *Luis Pérez y la biografía de Rosas escrita en verso en 1830* (Buenos Aires: Clío, 1957).
48. In a letter published in *El Gaucho Restaurador* of 21 March 1834, Pérez makes his discontent known: "And so it is that in spite of reiterated promises, in which I had the weakness to believe due to the poverty to which I have been reduced, I have obtained nothing more than the sad conviction that in my old age, bedeviled by sickness and poverty, I must perhaps go far from here to beg for my subsistence, while the enemies of the holy cause I have sustained enjoy the fortune they have robbed from the public treasury."
49. The case of Pedro de Angelis is certainly exemplary. A Neapolitan of bourgeois origin who defended the liberal cause in Europe, he arrived in Buenos Aires with a contract signed in Paris with Rivadavia and collaborated with the government until Rosas came to power. He was then the intellectual of Rosas' conservative regime. In addition to

his participation in periodicals, he published various writings with the objective of establishing the ideological bases of the regime. For the biography of De Angelis, see V. O. Cutolo, *Nuevo diccionario biográfico*, vol. 1; Rodolfo Trostiné, *Pedro de Angelis en la cultura rioplatense* (Buenos Aires: La Facultad, 1945); and Elías Díaz Molano, *Vida y obra de Pedro de Angelis* (Santa Fe: Colmegna, 1968). Following this work Josefa Emilia Sabor published a most useful study of the life and work of Pedro de Angelis; see Josefa Emilia Sabor, *Pedro de Angelis y los orígenes de la bibliografía argentina. Ensayo bio-bibliográfico* (Buenos Aires: Solar, 1995).

50. A. Isabelle, *Voyage à Buenos Aires*, 181–182. This observation is interesting because, for Isabelle, a reading room is defined by the ease with which one can gain information. The *Registro Estadístico* of 1822 gives the same figures.
51. "Nota con cuenta de gastos remitida por Valentín Alsina a la Contaduría General," in AGN. X. Secretaría de Rosas, 23-8-3.
52. This was the case, for example, with the newspaper *El Tiempo*, edited by Juan C. and Florencio Varela in opposition to the politics of Dorrego, or *El Lucero*, edited by De Angelis to defend the position of the Rosista federals. See *El Tiempo*, Buenos Aires, 1 November 1828 to 30 June 1829; *El Lucero*, Buenos Aires, 7 September 1829 to 31 July 1833, reedited by Pedro de Angelis.
53. See AGN. AP. X Police, 1831 file 15-10-1. Other references in *Clasificador o El Nuevo Tribuno*, 6 November 1830.
54. The verb *payar* means to improvise between two people, in contradictory verses and to the rhythm of the guitar, and on different issues. The *payador* would improvise on historical facts and recent events. In his *Facundo*, Sarmiento describes the *gaucho cantor* in this way. "The *cantor* goes from place to place, from *tapera* to *galpón*, singing of the heroes of the pampas wanted by the law, the cries of a widow whose children were stolen by Indians in a recent raid, the defeat and death of the brave Rauch, the catastrophe of Facundo Quiroga and the luck of Santo Pérez. The *cantor* candidly performs the same works of chronicle, customs, history and biography as the medieval bard." Domingo F. Sarmiento, *Facundo* (Madrid: Editora Nacional, 1975), 105. The *cancionero* was a kind of popular song in verse form, whose function was to inform the people of certain events. The study of the *cancioneros* has until now been the work of literary writers, and a historical analysis of their role in the development of a popular political culture is long overdue.
55. On the theme of rumors, see Jean-Noël Kapferer, *Rumeurs, le plus vieux média du monde* (Paris: Seuil, 1987).
56. See Eric Hobsbawm, *Rebeldes primitivos*, Barcelona, Ariel, 1968; E. Hobsbawm, *Bandidos* (Barcelona: Ariel, 1976).
57. Contrary to John Lynch, who affirms that the movement was directed and controlled by Rosas, I maintain that many of the manifestations of rural anger were autonomous. This is of course still open to debate. See P. González Bernaldo, "The 1829 uprising: social imagery and its political implications in a rural conflict," in J. Brown, *Revolution and Restructuring: The Rearrangement of Power in Argentina, (1776 1860)*, 177–207." A summary of the debate can be found in our interview with John Lynch, "Rosas visto por un historiador ingles," *Todo es Historia* 768 (October 1989): 48–52.
58. The circulation of rumors played a crucial role in the revolt. One of the mobilizing rumors, for example, was that Lavalle intended to go back to war with Brazil. This would have meant more conscription of troops and a decrease in real wages, as the deficit caused by the last war had been covered by the printing of bills. In consequence,

independently of the fact that Rosas could have ordered the propagation of these rumors, for them to circulate so rapidly throughout the countryside it was important that the people believe them and that they be founded on shared concerns.

59. For the workings of the economy of the Pampas Indians, see the works of Raúl Mandrini. See "La sociedad indígena de las pampas en el siglo XIX," in Mirta Lischetti (ed.), *Antropología* (Buenos Aires: Eudeba, 1985); R. Mandrini, "Notas sobre el desarrollo de la economía pastoril entre los indígenas del suroeste bonaerense (fines del siglo xviii y comienzos del siglo xix)," paper presented at the 8th Congress of Economic History, Tandil, 1986; R. Mandrini, "Desarrollo de una sociedad indígena pastoril en el área interserrana bonaerense," *Anuario IEHS* 2 (1987): 71–98.
60. Adolfo Saldías, *Historia de la Confederación Argentina* (Buenos Aires, 1881–1887), 3 vols. (Buenos Aires: Eudeba, 1978); Jacinto R. Yaben, *Biografías argentinas y sudamericanas* (Buenos Aires: 1952–1954); Parish to Aberdeen, letter of 12 January 1829, in J. Lynch, *Juan Manuel de Rosas*, 43.
61. P. González Bernaldo, "The 1829 uprising."
62. The decrees of 31 October and 23 December 1829, were intended to put down the *caudillos* participating in the revolt. With the decrees of September 14th and December 14th of the same year, Viamonte and later Rosas ordered the retrieval of all privately owned arms. In 1830 further measures were taken against "the crowd of extremists who call themselves Federals." See P. de Angelis, *Recopilación.*; *Registro Oficial*, vol. 2; AQO. CPA 4.
63. See P. González Bernaldo, "The 1829 uprising."
64. Prudencio Arnold, *Un soldado argentino* (Buenos Aires, 1884; Buenos Aires: Eudeba, 1970), 26–28.
65. The mobilizing power of the priests "who incite rebellion in their sermons" is referred to by Vélez Sarsfield in a letter to Lavalle dated 21 December 1828. See AGN.VII, 1-3-6, fol. 80–81. Other references to the participation of priests can be found in AGN.X, 15-1-5; newspapers *El Tiempo*, 17 March 1829, and *El Pampero*, of the same date.
66. *El Tiempo* 11 and 19 March 1829.
67. On coming to power, Rosas passed the 1828 freedom of the press law. The 1 February 1832 decree prohibited any publication without government authorization.
68. For more on political events between the first and second Rosas governments, see Enrique Barba, *Cómo llegó Rosas al poder* (Buenos Aires: Pleamar, 1972), 139–146; Víctor Bouilly, *El interregno de los lomos negros, 1830–1835* (Buenos Aires: La Bastilla, 1974); Gabriel A. Puentes, *El gobierno de Balcarce. División del partido federal (1832–1833)* (Buenos Aires: Huarpes, 1946).
69. For a political analysis of the web of projects discussed in this league, see E. Ravignani, "El pacto federal del 4 de enero de 1831."
70. The treaty of 4 January 1831, founding the Federal League, contained a clause which established "the convening of a Congress to organize the Nation." Rosas, who opposed the constitution, demanded that the Buenos Aires deputy step down from the Representative Commission meeting in Santa Fe. See E. Ravignani, "El pacto federal del 4 de enero de 1831."; Enrique Barba, "El primer gobierno de Rosas," in *Historia de la Nación Argentina* (Buenos Aires: Academia Nacional de la Historia, 1939), vol. 7, 57–62. On Rosas' political thinking, see Arturo E. Sampay, *Las ideas políticas de Juan Manuel de Rosas* (Buenos Aires: Juárez Editor, 1972), 11–85.
71. Debates concerning the need for a provincial constitution began around 1830 and intensified with the formation of the *Liga del Litoral*. In June 1833, the Assembly of Representatives designated a Commission of Constitutional Affairs to present a project

for a federal provincial constitution. The project was approved by nearly the entire house. Even Anchorena, Rosas' cousin and representative of the most conservative wing of *Rosismo*, eventually sanctioned it. In a letter dated 7 June 1833, Vicente Maza suggested to Rosas that he would do well not to oppose "the torrent invoked by the Constitution" as to do so would be to hand over victory to the opposition. See *Diario de Sesiones de la Honorable Junta de Representantes de la Provincia de Buenos Aires, Buenos Aires, 1823–1851*, sessions 3 and 18 June 1833; letter from Manuel V. Maza to Juan Manuel de Rosas, Buenos Aires, 7 June 1833, in Ernesto H. Celesia, *Rosas, aporte para su historia* (Buenos Aires: Peuser, 1954), vol. 1, 555–559. On the debate in the press, see especially *El Defensor de los Derechos del Pueblo, diario del mediodía*, Buenos Aires (June to October 1833), reedited by Bustamante, issues from 15 to 19 July 1833; *La Gaceta Mercantil*, July and August 1833, and *El Iris, Diario del Medio Día, Político, Literario y Mercantil*. Buenos Aires, Imprenta Republicana (April to August 1833), issue of 18 May 1833.

72. Many of the deputies elected by the city and in rural areas had to choose one of the two sides. Consequently, many seats remained untaken and a new election was called for in June; see *Diario de Sesiones de la Honorable Junta*, vol. 14, no. 319, sessions of 13 and 20 May 1833.
73. One poster which appeared in the parish of Monserrat read: "Viva la Federación. To you Citizens who are unfortunate enough to belong to the Company of Captain Benabento, we say today that although your Captain is a mulatto, he has been paid off by Felipe Arana to deceive you and make you believe that his ticket is the best. It is a lie, that is not the people's ticket. The ticket for which you must vote, as all citizens, is the ticket of General Rosas and General Olazábal." See E. H. Celesia, *Rosas, aporte para su historia*, 267.
74. *La Gaceta Mercantil*, 22 June 1833, 1, 2.
75. *El Defensor de los Derechos del Pueblo*, 25 June 1833.
76. P. de Angelis, *Recopilación*.
77. A. Zinny, "Bibliografía periodística."
78. On the dissemination of schismatic opinion in the cafés, see *El Gaucho Restaurador*, 30 March 1834, 4.
79. "Maza a Rosas, Buenos Aires, 7 de junio de 1833," in E. H. Celesia, *Rosas, aporte para su historia*, vol. 1, 555–559.
80. Vicente González to Juan Manuel de Rosas, Guardia del Monte, 4 August 1833, *Rosas, aporte para su historia*, vol. 1, 577–579.
81. *La Negrita*, Buenos Aires, no. 1, 21 July 1833.
82. Complaints published by *La Gaceta Mercantil*, 8 July 1833, 1.
83. E. H. Celesia, *Rosas, aporte para su historia*, vol. 1, 285. The distribution of apostolic reading matter in the army was done so via unofficial channels, as the official channels were controlled by the doctrinal federalists. In a letter from Agustín Wright to González, the former proposes obtaining newspapers so that the latter's troops could read them. See Agustín Wright to Vicente González, Buenos Aires, 4 January 1833, *Rosas, aporte para su historia*, vol. 2, 391.
84. See the reference in Rosas' letter to Arana, dated 26 August 1833, *Rosas, aporte para su historia*, vol. 2, 290.
85. See Vicente González to Juan Manuel de Rosas, Guardia del Monte, 4 August 1833; Rosas to Vicente González, Río Colorado, 20 and 26 August and 3 September 1833, *Rosas, aporte para su historia*, vol. 1, 566–613.

86. In popular newspapers there was no lack of references to Rosista loyalty. See for example the poem which appeared in *La Negrita* on 21 July 1833, entitled "Viva la Patria": "My name is Juana Peña / and by my vanity / may everybody know / I'm a very federal black / [...] / But as I've given myself away / selling these newspapers / I have to make it clear / I'm black but a true patriot. / By the *patria* we are free / and this heroic gratitude / gives us our holy obligation / to give it life and health. / [...] / I'm a patriot through and through, / and with enthusiasm and valor. / Defenders of the law / and of its Restorer. / Only by Don Juan Manuel / must you die or kill / and then by the rest. / Send me my general." See also *La Negrita*, no. 2, 28 July 1833, 2, 3.
87. See T. de Iriarte, *Memorias*, vol. 5, 7–8. The posters stuck to the doors of opponents were full of personal references. To give just one example, a poster aimed at Minister Martínez read: "Get ready Enrique / The end is nigh / You know what we want? / To play you the violin / You are evil / A dog and a traitor / To kill you would be / A very good deed / For you are the head / Of that vile faction / You will lose yours / On this occasion. / Let's see what you're worth / Against a good dagger / No matter that you're a Minister / Or a liberal. / Your blood will run / And then you will be / Dread and a lesson / For your reckless band." See E. H. Celesia, *Rosas, aporte para su historia*, vol. 1, 302.
88. "Mendeville au ministre des Affaires Etrangères," Buenos Aires, 30 June 1833, in AQO. CPA 6.
89. See E. H. Celesia, *Rosas, aporte para su historia*, vol. 1, 305–307.
90. "Yesterday morning there appeared pasted, even in the suburbs, great placards with thick red letters, announcing that at ten o'clock of the same day the jury would meet to judge the Restaurador de las Leyes." See "Juan Ramón Balcarce a la Honorable Sala de Representantes, Buenos Aires, 12th October 1833," in A. Saldías, *Historia de la Confederación*, vol. 1, 423–424.
91. A. Saldías, *Historia de la Confederación*, vol. 1, 423–424.
92. A. Saldías, *Historia de la Confederación*, vol. 1, 423–424.
93. *Los sucesos de octubre de 1833 o colección de documentos principales para la mejor inteligencia de ellos. Por un Restaurador* (Buenos Aires: Imprenta de la Independencia, 1834), 7.
94. *Los sucesos de octubre de 1833...*, 16.
95. See T. de Iriarte, *Memorias*, vol. 5, 47–48. References in AQO. CPA 6 (September-November 1833).
96. *Diario de los Anuncios*, 19 March 1835, 1.
97. Manuel Maza to Juan Manuel de Rosas, Buenos Aires, 7 June 1833, in E. H. Celesia, *Rosas, aporte para su historia*, vol. 1, 555–559.
98. "Carta de Juan Manuel de Rosas a Estanislao López, Pavón, 29 August 1831," in Enrique Barba (ed.), *Correspondencia entre Rosas, Quiroga y López* (Buenos Aires: Hachette, 1958), 137.

CHAPTER 4

The Separation of Authority and Civility (1838–1852)

The passion for the public sphere which marked the first years of Rosas' government ended tragically with a new attempt to overthrow the regime, stoked by Unitarian exiles in Montevideo and supported by the romantic liberal youth movement. The "Revolution of the Free of the South," which channeled the discontent of rural producers, came at the most critical time for the Rosista government: war with the Peruvian-Bolivian Confederation, the French blockade of the port of Buenos Aires, the alliance of the exiled opposition in Montevideo with the troops of Rivera and the French authorities, the uprising of the northeastern provinces against the Argentine Confederation, and an economic and financial crisis which led the government to authorize the printing of bills and, in turn, spiraling inflation.[1] Like the crisis in the Lavalle administration in 1828 and 1829, this economic crisis brought widespread discontent, particularly among small and medium-sized producers doubly affected by the financial crisis and the disastrous consequences wrought by the blockade of the port of Buenos Aires, forcing them to liquidate their produce in exchange for a devalued currency. The prosperity of the province of Buenos Aires, the result of an ingenious balance between the old order and the new economic circumstances resulting from independence and the establishment of the provincial system, was gravely compromised, with the risk of new winds sweeping away the delicate reconciliation of the new political institutions with the reconstruction of power after independence. In this reconstruction, vital in the organization of a stable power hitherto hindered by recent events, the romantic generation believed itself to be responsible for a historic mission: to give this new order social and cultural foundations and thus strengthen a national representative republic. In refusing to integrate this project with an inevitable austerity policy aimed at tackling the deterioration of the economic, social and political situation, Juan Manuel de Rosas opted to exclude from his regime not only a youth movement claiming not to oppose the government but also an entire sociocultural movement with which this movement identified. The governor associated the sociocultural practices of the elites primarily with a political faction and then with various groups personified by enemies of the community. Political combat therefore gradually slid into the field of collective identities, producing a break between authority and civility; in other words, between a power that believed itself to be unlimited and the traces of a nascent "civil society."

Individuals without Society

During the first years of the second Rosas government, the modern associative movement experienced modest yet significant progress. This ultimately led to the "Revolution of the Free of the South" in 1839. From then on the scarce contractual associations operating in the city of Buenos Aires mostly mobilized foreigners. Rosas imposed the need for prior authorization of any meeting, curbing considerably the associative impulse.[2] The student youth abandoned the cafés and forgot about its associative furor, while the well-to-do tended in general to return to its older forms of sociability: traditional *tertulias* in family homes, gatherings in the neighborhood, at the church entrance, during strolls along the city's avenues, and so on.[3] The abandonment of new relational practices among the elites did not entail, however, a disappearance of associative forms in the city of Buenos Aires. While the well-to-do tended to retire to the private space, the city witnessed a great intensity of public manifestations from traditional communities concerning mostly, though not exclusively, popular sectors. The disappearance of the associations, however, left the individuals they had produced without a society to belong to.[4]

THE DIVIDE BETWEEN SOCIETY AND COMMUNITY

The prohibition of all sociocultural associations was carried out in the name of the defense of society against its conspiratorial enemies, who were allegedly gathering in lodges to instigate their plots.[5] Against the opacity of these societies, the fruit of secrets and plots, Rosas set the transparency of the community. In branding these associations as "lodges," the governor denounced these perfidious associations, a point of reference for all conspirators and enemies of the "Holy Cause of the Federation," who Rosas grouped under the epithet of "filthy lodge-dwelling Unitarians." The war against these was far wider reaching than just Masonic lodges, whose very existence researchers are not unanimous on.[6] The word "lodge," used previously to refer to the political practices of certain revolutionary circles, was then used to refer to any cultural practice formerly characteristic of university students, whether these were sociocultural associations or associations based on the mere pleasure of gatherings or an enthusiasm for banquets.[7] This allowed the regime to associate certain sociability practices with a presumably negative attitude towards the community and religion, which with this objective came to be taken as the same thing. Indeed, due to the reading of anti-Masonic texts from Spain, the term "lodge" aroused ancestral fears of the infidel. Meanwhile, the press and editorials controlled by Rosas reproduced the Spanish literature on these issues.[8] The political and religious characterization of these practices, conveyed by this literature, made it possible to appeal to the ethical religious beliefs of the population, who in turn condemned them.

The Beginnings of the Break: the Proscription of the Lodges: The "lodges" appear in Rosista discourse in relation to the case of the Spaniard Jardón. According to the account of a North American diplomat, this liberal exiled on the shores of the River Plate founded the Aurora Lodge with other Spaniards in Buenos Aires in 1821.[9] In 1830 Jardón was accused by Rosas of being a "lodge instigator."[10] In his memoirs, the North American Murray Forbes recounts a conversation with Rosas on this issue: "the government studied in depth the matter of the tremendous peril to the country stemming from the Unitarian Party's identification with Spanish influences and agents. He spoke to me in no uncertain terms of the existence of certain secret lodges originally created or promoted by Spanish agents in Europe, which had spread among the classes of native society."[11] Jardón was eventually detained along with some compatriots by order of the delegated government, by virtue of its extraordinary powers. Responding to a request that Jardón be submitted to usual procedures, Minister of Government Tomás Manuel de Anchorena claimed that he had not been detained for a criminal act but "as a precautionary political measure for public safety from a secret but very real, certain and systematic attack, which has been directed for years with the greatest tenacity and firmness against the independence of the Republic in order to enslave it."[12] According to Anchorena, Spanish liberals intended to establish secret societies, "renowned for their depravity and harmful effects" among the population of the city.[13] These accusations were complementary evidence of the will of Rosas and his government to associate "Unitarians" with "liberal organizations," "secret societies," "hidden enemies," "Spanish agents," in short, all those opposed to the Federation.

These references speak volumes of the importance of the accusations against the "Masonic-Unitarian-Liberal-Spanish" plot in the Rosas regime, expressions that evince certain borrowings from Spanish anti-Masonic discourse, such as the identification of Masons with liberals and foreigners. The same occurred in accusations of a conspiracy against the State and the Church.[14] Rosas was also able to apply this stereotyped anti-Masonic discourse to local political forces. In denouncing the habits of sociability of certain groups, Rosas not only challenged the legality of these associations but also accused them of facilitating the development of enemies of the regime. This allowed Rosas to charge the Unitarians who had participated in the 1828 coup as well as liberals (among whom were the representatives of one of the branches of Federalism in opposition to Rosas) and the foreigners who had taken part in the 1828–1829 conflict. Thus, when Rosas came to redefine his alliances in the new political context after the 1829 crisis, anti-Masonic discourse enabled him to fix the boundaries between the friends and enemies of the regime, through the sociability habits that set apart members of the community. In other words, the *patria* as a political community of belonging was associated publicly with certain relational practices and values.

In this aspect, an exemplary case is that of the cacique Pincheira. A frontier cacique of Chilean Araucanian origin, Pincheira had participated in the 1929 rural uprising, during which he had raided particularly the *estancias* of the frontier zone. Lavalle had accused Pincheira, the chief of one of the "friendly Indian" tribes, of carrying out these attacks under orders from Rosas. In spite of the likeliness of these accusations, no documents have been found to prove them. Nevertheless, even though Rosas was absolved of responsibility for the exactions of Pincheira's men, there is no doubt that these actions benefited Rosas, who in any event did nothing to stop them. Once in power in the province, however, Rosas would have considerable difficulties in curbing the activities of Pincheira's band in the *estancias*.[15] It is feasible that the decision to accuse the cacique of complicity with the Spaniard Jardón and the lodge Unitarians conspiring against the independence of the republic was due to a desire to break off certain alliances that had become embarrassingly uncontrollable.[16] At first sight, it seems paradoxical that Pincheira was accused of belonging to a lodge, primarily because it was difficult to imagine any kind of relationship between the urban instigators and frontier caciques. More importantly, it would have been far easier to condemn Pincheira as a "savage Indian, enemy of civilization," an accusation easily understood by landowners. This example shows that for Rosas, factional political combat had to take place in the sphere of belonging, from a close identification between political opinions and sociability practices. Through this identification, relational codes and values would have a profound repercussion on the network of political loyalties.

The parallel between political opinion and cultural practices took in everything from associative practices to clothes, speech and more intimate sociability. When the French traveler Delacour described Porteño women in 1845, he came to the conclusion that according to his amorous senses, they were Unitarians, as if this inference were plain to see:

> They long for these young men educated in the university of the Rivadavia government, these "doctors" with syrupy voices, who can talk of love and inspire it simply by speaking of it; most distinct are they from these "out-and-out" Federals who never mention it and worry very little about inspiring it, as long as they get the real thing, to which the other part is, they say, nothing but a useless prelude.[17]

Surreptitiously, the traditional factional conflict slid into the terrain of relational values, with the result that the subject of the plot became an excellent strategy with which to reestablish relationships between a republican State and a society that on the whole still lived with traditional community values. The State, personified by Rosas, presented itself as the principal defender of this society shaken by socioeconomic transformations, which nevertheless had their origin in the State.[18]

The persecution of the lodges also provided the opportunity to curb the associative movement that threatened to develop in popular sectors. The threat originated from practices originally developed among foreign artisans and then catching on with other groups. Rosas saw in these a potential danger diffused among popular sectors of associations that he considered close to the liberals. Taking advantage of the xenophobia widespread during the 1828–1829 crisis, Rosas did not hesitate in denouncing the participation of the foreigners in the Unitarian lodge plot.[19] Mendeville, the French Consul in Buenos Aires, explained the matter thus: "They [the members of the Rosas government] claim that [the Spanish liberals] formed with this intention a kind of freemasonry; in the paragraph in which [Minister Anchorena] recalls last year's disturbances, during which foreigners took up arms, he suggests the active and audacious participation of the Spanish and the French."[20] When, in 1832, a group of French artisans applied for authorization from the government to form a friendly society, Mendeville defended the position of the authorities in Buenos Aires and sent the French minister an unfavorable report on one of the members of the association, the upholsterer Lantin, who had recently been arrested for displaying licentious engravings in his shop. Explaining the fears that this association aroused in the government, Mendeville wrote:

> Moreover, the minister complained greatly that M. Lantin endeavored to form a party among the artisans in constant opposition to the government, that he had not ceased to express his hostile inclinations since the dissolution of the famous battalion of the Friends of the Order—of which he was part—and that he never missed an opportunity to voice such inclinations. Your Excellency showed me a leaflet by way of evidence containing a speech in verse, given by M. Lantin

> at a banquet this year to celebrate the anniversary of the July revolution. He added that, with various pretexts, M. Lantin sought to form societies in his workers' faction capable of arousing disquiet in the government, whether acting against it in a subversive movement, or creating an irritating conflict between the population and foreigners.[21]

The notorious differences between Mendeville and certain French subjects had begun in 1828–1829, during the "Decembrist Revolution," when Mendeville had publicly stated his support for Rosas, while a significant number of members of the French community had joined the "Friends of the Order" battalion defending the city from attacks by Rosista troops.[22] Mendeville had to leave Buenos Aires to live in Montevideo until the end of the conflict and the rise of Rosas to the provincial government on December 1829.[23] This explains his unfavorable report on the French Artisans' Mutual Charity Society, and the creation in 1832 of a philanthropic association controlled by the Consulate and intended to replace the artisans' society.[24]

During the events of 1833, Rosas reiterated his attack on the lodge conspiracy, this time directed at the dissident factions of the Federation. In his correspondence with Vicente González, Rosas gave precise indications as to the policy to be implemented for doctrinal federals:

> I think it best not to involve our fellow countrymen, nor forget the Federal invocation. This is why I think the best name for us today is Apostolic Federals....The Schismatics should be called Unitarian Decembrists. Continue calling them this for now and I will in the meantime think about it, and I will tell the newspapers so that the name enters general usage, as I repeat that to call Anarchists only Schismatics is to confess that they are federals, and in doing so give them what is not theirs and harm our cause...[25]

In the same letter he alerted his correspondent of the rumors and defamation that the "lodge-dwellers" were spreading in rural areas.[26] Once this new political crisis was resolved, calm appears to have returned to the city. However, the basis of the break between civility and community was present in the "war of the lodges," with which Rosas intended to exercise severe control over the forms of collective life defining the community of belonging. When the Porteño youth organized with the objective of transforming the bases of this collective life, the break would be inevitable.

The Schism between Authority and Civility: The break came during the critical period of 1838 to 1839. The young liberals meeting in Marcos Sastre's Literary

Salon decided to abandon the public literary sphere to move into political action. The discord could not have been greater between a youth believing itself to be "the people's reason," and Juan Manuel de Rosas who wanted to rule his people.

The society created by the young romantic liberals saw itself as the new generation that must triumph where its elders had failed: in the reconstruction of a society from which the nation could think of itself as a political community of belonging. To do so, they extolled the virtues of a strong power that, like that of Rosas, would become the necessary step towards the regeneration of society.[27] As Juan B. Alberdi explained during the opening of the salon, Rosas had blazed a trail that they were resolved to follow:

> It is time, then, to ask of philosophy the path designated to the Argentine nation on which to walk to the common end of humanity.... Fortunately for our country, we are not the first to sense this demand; and we come only to imitate the example set by the great man who presides over our public destinies. This great capacity for intuition, a virtual habit of genius, had divined that which our faculties today work to understand and form.[28]

Like his comrades, Juan B. Alberdi had at the time the idea that the new generation would be the doctrinal guide of the power of Rosas. If the Federation was, as Sastre claimed, "the expression of the intuitive will of the people," then the youth intended to embody the "reason of the people," the only foundation of the representative system.[29] The authority of Rosas was not only the condition for social peace, without which the political cultural project of the young intellectuals could not work but also a guarantee of the industrial development of the country, as Echeverría noted during the opening of the literary salon: "I well know that the individual interest is almost always the best adviser of industry, but I also know that with a people like ours who live with little because they desire little, personal interests often lie dormant and require the stimulus of authority."[30] However, Rosas was less convinced of the advantages of associating this intellectuality with his power than the young men were of the need to align with the regime. In spite of their many attempts to win Rosas over, he remained indifferent, even distrustful.[31] Although he did not prohibit their meetings, he abstained from carrying out the role that the "new generation" claimed to reserve for him, so the salon was not to be honored by any official presence. The only member of the government who went to the meetings was the deputy Vicente López y Planes, whose son Vicente Fidel was an active member of the salon. But according to Vicente Fidel, the attitude of his father was immediately censured by Rosas, who informed him, firstly via the deputy Maza and then in person, that he disapproved of his presence among these young men and advised him to stay away from the movement.[32]

There was a fine line between reproach and repression, and this line was crossed in late 1837 when Rosas, his regime facing an increasingly critical situation, denounced this cultural movement's complicity with the enemies of the Federation. This may have been an attempt to win over more allies in conservative sectors who looked with suspicion on the "eccentricities" of youth.[33] Nine years later, Esteban Echeverría would recall this rupture in these terms: "If Rosas had not been so ignorant and had had a jot of patriotism in his soul, if he had understood his position, he would have given that repulsive mob of odious speculators and sanctimonious imbeciles surrounding him a kick up the backsides; he would have called upon and patronized these young men and set himself to work with them on the organization of the nation."[34] Pedro de Angelis gave the Rosista answer to these claims in an article published in the second edition of *Dogma socialista*:

> How extravagant was the idea of regenerating a country with a handful of young men with no credentials, no contacts, no resources, who some distrusted and others despised; Rosas must have understood how ridiculous it would have been to convert Argentina into a society of Saint Simonians and submit to the delirium of Fourier and Considérant a republic founded on the general principles of the modern organization of the States.[35]

Each side clearly illustrates the problem. When it came to choosing allies, the young men made for sorry figures next to "odious speculators" and "sanctimonious imbeciles." However, what triggered the definitive break with Rosas was not the alleged danger represented by a "socializing utopia," nor their irreverence, but rather their francophilia. The break came during the diplomatic conflict with France, which led in March 1838 to the fleet of Rear Admiral Leblanc's declaration to blockade the port of Buenos Aires.[36] The young romantics, suspicious of more than compromising sympathies from the aggressor, quickly aligned themselves with the enemies of the Federation, all the more so when contacts between the members of this movement and the French authorities were revealed. It was then that the young generation decided to abandon literary speculation and participate in political events. The principal objective of the association became to "take possession of opinion."[37] With this end, on 23 June 1838, thirty-five members of the Literary Salon met with the object of organizing "to fraternize in thought and in action,"[38] establishing an association with Esteban Echeverría as president and Juan María Gutiérrez as vice president. Fifteen days later, Echeverría presented a formula of an oath similar to that of Mazzini's Italian Youth and baptized the association Joven Argentina (Young Argentina).[39] The organization operated along regulations edited by Thompson and Barros Pazos and an action plan presented by Echeverría.[40] But the situation made public meetings difficult and, according to Echeverría, increasingly infrequent. Moreover, many members were forced into exile, most of them in Montevideo, where they associated with the Unitarians supporting the actions of the French.[41]

The force of events turned the association's plans upside down; as Echeverría writes, it was obliged to change from propaganda to armed action. Taking advantage of a favorable political situation, several members would play an active role in overthrowing the power of the Federals in the different provinces of the Confederation. In Buenos Aires, the "Club of Five" organized the insurrection that was to unite the actions of Lavalle's troops with the landowners' rebellion in the south of the province.[42] In the province of Córdoba, the members of the association participated in the organization of the revolution aimed at installing their president, Francisco Álvarez, into the government. In Tucumán the followers of the Joven Argentina had managed to extract themselves from the Federal forces allied to Rosas and were participating in the Northern League.[43] These early victories were followed by a series of failures between 1839 and 1840 which led to the defeat of the opposition forces. With Maza senior and junior murdered, the leaders of the uprising in the south executed, France retreating from the conflict and abandoning her local allies and Lavalle defeated in the north, the young generation, who had dreamed of an ideological and political direction for the regime, was forced to postpone its project and take the road to exile.

Sociability as a Nation in Exile: "You men, Argentine patriots all, for ten years you have been walking, your guns on your shoulders, prowling around the Minotaur's den of your country: Why do you fight? For the *patria*. Very well, but Rosas and his henchmen also say that they fight for the *patria*."[44] Esteban Echeverría addressed these words to his comrades in exile at a time when Rosas' regime, after five years of terror, was enjoying a growing prosperity and relative social peace.[45] With his discourse on the *patria*, Echeverría intended to recall the foundations of a political community that Rosas aimed to denaturalize. If the *patria* was one, how to explain that patriots and Rosistas fought for the same thing? If this was to be defined by a majority, which Rosas had, it had to be admitted that with this majority Rosas was the real defender of the *patria*. From this, Echeverría reached the conclusion that the *patria* could not be a number. Nor could it be a territory, otherwise how to explain why the sons of the provinces of Corrientes, Buenos Aires and Mendoza all fought for the same thing? The *patria* could not be founded on the feeling of belonging to the same place. What, then, was the reason for their combat?

"The word *patria* represents for you a social idea, or rather, it is the symbol of a Dogma common to all Argentine patriots."[46] The Social Dogma thus constituted a transcendent principle that the reason of the people, embodied by the romantic intellectuals in exile, had to profess and guarantee to future generations.[47] This dogma, embodied in the "May spirit," was what would engender the Argentine Nation. In representing the social dogma, the young intellectuals in exile were also the personification of an Argentine Nation founded on their own political and cultural values. Moreover, the dogma that they wanted to guarantee to future generations was defined by the lifestyle proscribed by Rosas.

It is significant that the first symbolic word of *Dogma socialista* should be "association." "Without association there is neither progress nor civilization," proclaimed the young generation imbued with the social ideas of that singular Saint-Simonian, P. Leroux. His idea of association, as has been seen, opposed the representation of Rosista society. According to the dogma of the Joven Argentina association published by E. Echeverría, an association could only be made up of individuals, as there could only be an association in equality and freedom.[48] But due to and within the association, moreover, the individual was to attempt to reconcile individual interests and the interests of the *patria*: association was the instance through which man, without making the absolute sacrifice of his individuality, could acquire civil customs and learn to live in society. For these young men, the importance of customs as the basis of institutional order was associated with the idea of a community of habits that supposedly established the associative practice. One of the tasks that the young men of the May Association set themselves was to carry out a radical reform of these customs in order to establish a "Latin-American sociability."[49] This was to work in various directions, principally through the promotion of associative practices. The writers of the period also built up a model of civilized sociability, in such texts as José Mármol's *Amalia*, Echeverría's *La cautiva* and *El matadero*, even Sarmiento's *Facundo*. Lastly, a tradition of courtesy reappeared that had spread during the colonial period through a literature of "civility."[50]

It is possible to see a semantic shift between the notion of civility as an attribute of a class and that of civilization as a principle of nationality.[51] This was tied to the political vicissitudes of the young romantics who ultimately opted for exile. Indeed, while at the opening of Marcos Sastre's Literary Salon these men invoked "the Great Rosas" as a principal defender of nationality, a year later they supported the French blockade of the port of Buenos Aires. This shift, which Rosas qualified as unpatriotic, was justified by these young men through the idea of civilization as the expression of national sentiment. Hence, Sarmiento had no hesitation in boasting publicly of his support for France and in committing the crime of treason against the Americas. In acting this way, Sarmiento hoped to save "European civilization, its institutions, its uses and ideas, in other words, the principle of nationality."[52] The break with Rosas brought with it this semantic shift and defined nationality as the expression of the superior culture, set against Latin Americanism as synonymous with barbarism. This aspect can be found in Echeverría and Mármol, but it was Sarmiento who would present the most definitive form in *Facundo o Civilización y barbarie*.[53] Sarmiento distinguished the community on which Juan Manual de Rosas and Facundo Quiroga based their power from that which brought about the origin of cities and was characteristic of civilized societies.[54] In his judgment, one of the explanations was sociability. He thus recognized the existence of a sociability and even forms of association typical of Rosista society, but whose distinguishing feature was that they were founded on the predominance of nature. In other words, these were forms of sociability lacking relationships of civility. It was precisely in these relationships that Sarmiento found the germ of a civil society on which a nation was to be founded as a political community of belonging.[55]

In developing these associative practices in exile, the cultural elites not only constructed a collective identity outside of the framework of sentiments of belonging to the same place but also defined it as a set of political cultural values. Thus, the *patria* in exile experienced a substantial transformation. In effect, the patriotic combat of the young intellectual Porteños, of the old Unitarian soldiers, of the exiles in Corrientes, Tucumán, Córdoba, San Juan, and so on, became the combat of the Argentine nation against a society abandoned to nature, reduced to its most barbarian and pre-civilized forms. The proscribed *patria* became a nation that did not identify itself with a State, but rather with forms of collective life that defined belonging to the political community.

THE FEDERAL COMMUNITY

Between 1839 and 1842, controls on manifestations of collective life reached paroxysmal levels. To host an evening gathering—even a family *tertulia*—it was necessary to obtain authorization from the city police chief. Meeting places such as cafés and *pulperías* were constantly monitored. Even traditional public festivities, such as carnival, were strictly regulated.[56] Associative forms were especially censured, and while no regulation was passed in this respect, there existed a de facto proscription of associative practices.[57] Associative sociability and the Unitarian party were so closely assimilated that even the Sociedad de Beneficiencia was under suspicion, a society made up of the most prominent social ladies but which had been created during the liberal Rivadavia government.[58]

In spite of this bleak panorama, which in the writings of the opposition undoubtedly aroused a reductionist vision of the regime, manifestations of collective life did not disappear. Rosas ensured that some were kept, while respecting the framework of traditional organization forms, such as civil and religious corporations.[59] Unlike the Rivadavia period, these manifestations were not politically neutral, and Rosas imposed as much intense politicization as possible on all public forms of sociability. This phenomenon was inversely proportional to the population's participation in the power sphere. A French visitor to the city in 1845 eloquently wrote, "The Federals, the pure Rosistas, voice their furious speeches in the cafés; tavern tribunes, crossroad orators, ignorant and vain, boastful and contemptible, terrible when one yields to them…, they do no more than speak of massacres."[60] These near-obligatory manifestations of Federal faith worked the same way as the electoral ritual, as ways of legitimizing absolute power, and constituted a frightfully efficient weapon.

The African Societies: In the network of urban Federal clientele that saved Rosas from apparently inevitable ruin in the crisis years of 1838 to 1840, the African population occupied a central position. Rosas established a classic clientele relationship with this group consisting of protection in exchange for loyalty, though he was not the first to recruit what were considered the most devoted soldiers of the *patria*.[61] What was special in this case was that in order to gain their support, Rosas solicited the commitment of the group via African nation societies. Thus these societies, which had developed during the liberal Rivadavia government, experienced intense public activity in the last twelve years of the second Rosas administration. Indeed, between 1840 and 1852 they were practically the only associations operating regularly in the city of Buenos Aires.[62]

There were two sides to the relationship between Rosas and the Africans. On the one hand, Rosas intervened publicly in the Africans' community life, while on the other hand the nations participated actively in public life. Rosas' participation in the life of the association took on a number of forms. Firstly, he intervened in the election of their authorities. While this was an entirely commonplace attitude in the operations of the societies, Rosas would disregard police chiefs in order to deal directly with the associations' members.[63] Secondly, he participated in festivities. On such occasions he was usually accompanied by his family, which gave these encounters an intimate tone characteristic of community relationships. There are numerous references to this, both from the opposition which denounced his demagogic attitudes and from Rosas, who had an interest in publicly proclaiming his amity with the black population, which would sometimes lend itself to a publicity campaign.[64] So it was that in 1839, facing one of the most difficult periods of his government, Rosas decided to abolish the slave trade that he himself had reestablished in 1831.[65] A little later, a painting signed by D. de Plot and dated 1 May 1841, showed the gratitude of the Africans to their liberator and symbolically ratified Rosas' alliance with the black population.[66] The canvas shows Rosas on foot and uniformed, presenting a group of slaves with a placard reading "Federation, Freedom, Down with Tyrants." At their feet are the broken chains symbolizing freedom. Behind Rosas is the Argentine flag flying in the wind, with its sky blue color replaced with a bluish red.[67] All the women wear the federal insignia of red clothes and bright red rosettes in their hair. Three of them hoist federal flags (red or red and white) with the following inscriptions: "Long Live Freedom," "Long Live the Restorer of Law," "Death to the Savage Unitarians." In the top left corner there is an angel, symbolizing spiritual order, announcing the news, "No longer shall any slave lament in the River Plate. Their bitter cries have ceased, ever since the humane Rosas, with his proud, compassionate and generous liberty, lavished this precious gift on the wretched African." The painting is testimony to the deliberate confusion between the Rosas regime and slave freedom, a confusion whose principal objective was not only to gain the loyalty of the Africans but also to show the world—especially England—that his government was one of natural law. The painting is titled "The slaves of Buenos Aires show that they are free and grateful to their noble Liberator" (a reference to the abolition of the slave trade in 1839).

The amity with the African population was not solely limited to participation in their festivities, symbolic as this undoubtedly was. It also comprised the provision of indispensable elements for the survival of the community. In recognition of their loyalty, Africans could receive a plot of land for their "nations."[68] On some occasions, nations were granted "donations" allocated for resolving the problem of members' welfare.[69] What is certain is that Africans "enjoyed" a particular and individual kind of treatment. In one case, Rosas interceded in a trial to absolve an African who had shown evidence of loyalty to the Federation.[70]

From these exchanges the Africans identified with the federal community without risking their ethnic identity, which permitted Rosas to mobilize not only the men who were old enough to carry weapons but also the group as a whole. In return, the Africans owed their loyalty to the governor and to the "Holy Cause" (the Federation). This loyalty amounted above all to a self-control which aimed to exalt the Federal fervor of society members. The president of the society was even required to inform Rosas whenever he had any doubts as to any of his members' loyalty to the Federation.[71] The society authorities also had to guarantee the rapid mobilization of the "nation" to defend the "Restorer." In records from a trial brought by the Bayombé Society against Rafael Ramos, who claimed ownership of the association's property, we discover that the conflict began "when the President of the Nation with all his associates, having received orders in the year 1840 to march to Campaña, saw fit to leave the Queen of the Nation, Mercedes Argerich…"[72] Ramos took over the society, for which the society accused him of double treason.[73] Sometimes, manifestations of loyalty did not amount to armed mobilization. The societies' demonstrations in public spaces of the city were far more effective in that the white population, especially those of Unitarian tendencies, greatly feared the Africans. The spectacle of a city "occupied" by blacks, whose repressive acts were particularly feared, became a threatening arm of persuasion.[74] The Africans demonstrated above all during the regime's most critical moments, as in 1842 when they organized a public collection for Rosas to wage war against the Unitarians.[75] In general terms, though, they showed their loyalty regularly in weekly dances and during the much feared carnival dances. The Africans not only wore federal insignia but also often recited federal propaganda in African-Argentine dialect, which was extremely hostile towards the opposition and undoubtedly inspired a fear of social upheaval in the elites.[76] However, these manifestations of federal fervor were far more controlled than the opposition's accounts would have one believe.[77]

For the Africans, the manifestations of "Federal faith" became a form of expressing their own identity, as was proclaimed in the newspaper *La Negrita* in a poem titled "Viva la *Patria*": "My name is Juana Peña / and by my vanity / may everybody know / I'm a very federal black."[78] Juana Peña's "vanity" refers both to her ethnicity and to her participation without any transition in the public political sphere, an area that previously was strictly limited to the white population. The assimilation between ethnic identity and political identity was strengthened by the blacks' participation in civic celebrations. During the festivities to commemorate the May Revolution on 25 May 25 1838, Rosas invited the Africans to participate in the festivities taking place in the central square with a spectacle based around their traditional dances with the tambour. The weight of this symbol could not have been greater and quickly provoked the indignation of the opposition and the elites in general. For them, the symbolic representation of the foundations of power could never allude to the black population, but should reflect the ideal population of the Revolution.[79] The vigorous mobilization of the Africans appears to have even carried them to the polls, as there is evidence that the parishes with greatest electoral participation during the period were precisely those with numerous African populations, Monserrat and Concepción.[80] Nevertheless, the adhesion of the Africans to the Federal cause was not unanimous. The regime's opposition also managed to win over supporters among the black population and occasionally opened up rifts in African-Rosista amity.[81] But the essential difference between each side lay in the fact that Rosas could mobilize through community associations, while the Unitarians used the army. That one appealed to the ethnic group and the other to soldier citizens naturally had consequences in the definition of the political community of belonging.

The Sociedad Popular Restauradora: The Rosas government witnessed the appearance of another form of political participation which does not seem to have arisen from the traditional community. This was the famous Sociedad Popular Restauradora (Popular Restoration Society), which for a decade intimidated a large proportion of the population. According to correspondence between Rosas and his wife, the society was born with the Revolution of the Restauradores.[82] Rivera Indarte provides some interesting data in this respect. According to him, the society was the work of Tiburcio Ochoteco, who suggested the idea of organizing a club to Rosas' wife, Encarnación Ezcurra: "Ochoteco pondered the influence that this institution would have on elevating Rosas and terrorizing his enemies, citing examples of what he had seen in Cádiz, where he had lived during the Spanish revolution of 1820."[83] The same author writes that Encarnación accepted the idea and named the club the Sociedad Popular Restauradora. Premises were rented to hold meetings. The work of the society's members consisted of eating stew and drinking wine, after which they would leave to walk drunkenly around the city yelling "death to the enemies of Rosas."[84] It is feasible that these practices were intended to become one of the persuasive forces of the regime.

The Sociedad Popular Restauradora, also known as Mazorca, apparently extended its influence during the Viamonte government, taking over sections of the countryside without actually having any written regulations. Rivera Indarte suggests that José M. Boneo proposed some, but Father Burgos rejected them, stating that, "Rosas does not want the club to have any other rules than those that he might give verbally each day."[85] From this it may be concluded that, at least by the time of Rosas' second election to the provincial government, there already existed an organization which grouped together individuals of mostly popular extraction which nevertheless had not reached the degree of formalization of the associative forms. According to testimonies, with Rosas' arrival in power the society lost part of its autonomy, becoming a kind of para-police organization. It then divided in two: the Sociedad Popular Restauradora composed of members of the Porteño elite, whose role was the dissemination of federation opinion, and the Mazorca, a kind of para-police organization intended for the repression of the enemies of the Federation and their accomplices.[86]

No documentation has been found as to the society's organization or day-to-day role, only a few references exist from its most illustrious members. However, Rosas appears to have kept a close eye on the candidates to participate in the circle of regime purging. The right to admission was in the hands of the president, who nevertheless informed Rosas after declaring any candidate's loyalty to the "Holy Cause."[87]

The society's most active period was between 1839 and 1842, a period known as the "reign of terror."[88] Its public activism then decreased before the society disappeared in 1846.[89] Judging by existing data, the influence of the Sociedad Popular Restauradora on the possible process of a politicization of popular sectors was practically nil, primarily because Rosas controlled it totally, and secondly, due to the social heterogeneity of its members. While the Mazorca was made up exclusively of members of the urban masses, its activity was limited to acts of repression directed from above. As John Lynch clearly establishes, it could not possibly be compared with a Jacobin club nor with popular political associations such as the Equality Society of Santiago de Chile or the Democratic Societies of Colombia.[90] In spite of its republican front, the Sociedad Popular Restauradora was closer to the intentions of an absolute power than that of a social democracy, and in this respect it was paradigmatic of the regime. The difficulty of understanding the nature of this form of popular public action arises from the fact that it used revolutionary symbols within a function which was the negation of any popular power. This explains the perplexity of the French Consul in Buenos Aires with regard to this singular association: "It must be understood that this society, the perfect image of our revolutionary clubs, which likewise have their core in the lower ranks of the people and share a republican aspect and principles, has by some astonishing contradiction become a column of the most complete absolutism."[91] The society itself was made up of members of the elite, and although it often operated as an organ of dissemination of opinion, it limited itself to circulating information received from Rosas.

Therefore, if the Sociedad Popular Restauradora is to be included in the associative movement which developed above all from the 1820s onwards, it is necessary to highlight certain nuances. Firstly, with regard to its formal characteristics, the society was born as an informal practice of political mobilization, and later became an institution, despite which it did not attain the specific degree of formalization common to such associative forms. It is important to highlight the specific nature of the field of social exchanges concerning a public sphere strictly identified with power, namely that the society acted within the framework of an old concept of the "public" sphere as the place of authority. Lastly, this militant action was not supported by a consensus of opinion that might imply a process of political acculturation of the popular sectors, but rather by a "rebel faith" founded on political unanimism. While the title and impression of certain symbols may suggest a modern type of association, in practice this was a traditional form of political participation.

It can be concluded that the process of politicization begun in the 1830s was hindered by this "new" form of politicization corresponding to a very different community register. Through his most zealous propagandist, Pedro de Angelis, Rosas took the precaution of defining this association via traditional community features. In an article aimed at reassuring European powers, Angelis explained that the Sociedad Popular Restauradora was neither a club nor a lodge, and that on the contrary these virtuous citizens were the most resolved enemies of secret societies. De Angelis claimed that this society was nothing more than a gathering of federal citizens, neighbors and landowners, lovers of the freedom, honor, and the dignity of their *patria*.[92] The political ideological references were the same but belonged to two types of political community. The manifestations of the federal community show that under the idea of "federation" lay a traditional vision of a social corpus by which Rosas, as the head of the community, would replace the king.

The Voiceless Opinion

The new public sphere was undoubtedly identified with practices of cultural sociability, but above all with the organ of expression of these new public spaces, namely the written press, and particularly the opinion press. During this period there was a notable decrease in these types of places and organs of expression. How was the emergent opinion of these places of sociability to identify itself with the population if it did not have the organs to listen and make its voice heard? This question is inseparable from the Rosas regime, as while the press was proscribed as the vehicle of expression of this new public, different forms of public manifestations were introduced to emit the voice of the *patria*.

OPINION IN EXILE

Organs of opinion had frequently shown their distaste for the absolute power that Rosas claimed as a condition of government. Rosas had little control over new networks of public opinion, which explains his aversion to the world of the press.[93] He twice repealed the 1828 press liberties decree, in spite of the fact that the decree was fairly repressive itself, and from 1838 he succeeded in controlling almost all of the press in the city of Buenos Aires. Between 1839 and 1851 the number of newspapers created per year fluctuated between one and two, while prior to this period the figures were far higher.[94] However, there is a distinction between the first stage, from 1839 to 1846, marked by the near total absence of a journalistic press, and the last five years of the Rosas government, which saw a weak but perceptible recovery for these publications.[95] Between 1839 and 1846 only four newspapers were published, all completely controlled by Rosas: *La Gaceta Mercantil*, *El Diario de la Tarde*, *The British Packet* and *Archivo Americano y Espíritu de la Prensa del*

Mundo. Of these, *La Gaceta Mercantil* had the greatest readership among the local population.[96] In its origins, this newspaper enjoyed the participation of various intellectuals and political men identified with the Federation, such as J. Rivera Indarte, F. de Cavia, N. Mariño and M. Irigoyen. Undoubtedly though, the figure who marked this period and the press as a whole was the Neapolitan Pedro de Angelis. In addition to his participation in *La Gaceta Mercantil*, he was the author of numerous publications supporting the Rosas government.[97] In 1840, during the diplomatic conflict with France, he published *El Espíritu de los mejores diarios que se publican en Europa y America*, a digest of articles about the River Plate region from the principal European and American newspapers.[98] He returned to the project two years later, this time focusing on international public opinion with the *Archivo Americano y Espíritu de la Prensa del Mundo*, a trilingual publication in Spanish, French and English. The publication was entirely subsidized by the government and attempted to convince European governments that the Rosas government was genuinely representative, which explains the modernity of the language and of the theoretical references in the contents of the article. The publication naturally disappeared along with the regime.[99]

With public opinion reduced to a mere instrument of official propaganda, the newspapers authorized by Rosas served to inform the population of new laws dictated by the government and to proclaim the people's unanimous support for the regime. The organs of opinion thus reverted to their original role, that of "informing the kingdom," while taking on a new role of showing the public the unanimous judgment of the community. There was a scarcity of "men of opinion" who had previously emerged from literary societies and circles, and their limited representatives alternated between the model of publicist, similar at times to the role of the intellectual of the colonial regime, and that of political man and agent of power. Pedro de Angelis corresponded to this first type, while Manuel Irigoyen, a member of the provincial legislature between 1835 and 1848, was closer to the second type. In both cases these were functionaries and writers acting according to the directives of the provincial government.

By 1847, however, the regime had evidently begun to open up. The number of publications increased and the members of the press were more greatly diversified by the reappearance of literary newspapers published by "the second romantic group of Buenos Aires," to use Félix Weinberg's words.[100] This was a group of young university students, including some future political figures such as José B. Gorostiaga, Miguel Navarro Viola, Benjamín Victorica and Juan A. García. As with the case of their elders, their intellectual inclinations led them to this kind of practice, although their cultural activities appear to have been more restricted. As one of the young students stated, not only was public political activity strictly prohibited, but the cultural life of the city continued to be rather limited:

> There were not even means with which to educate oneself. The Public Library lacked modern books, the foreign press circulated with much difficulty.... What to do in those hopeless times? There were no clubs, and the cafés were only frequented by groups of students and clerks who met there to converse.[101]

This timid cultural renewal was helped by the opening up of the repressive regime during the last five years of the Rosas government. The exiled romantics even benefited from a de facto amnesty. Thus, the bookseller Marcos Sastre was able to return to Buenos Aires in 1844. Two years later Echeverría's "Rimas" was published, while literary writings such as "Curso de bellas artes" by Vicente Fidel López circulated freely around the city.[102] But the movement remained circumscribed and was of more use to the prestige of the Rosas government than to the genuine establishment of an autonomous public opinion.

To a certain extent the expatriation of men of opinion geographically displaced the sphere of public power. The decrease in the number of journalistic publications in the city of Buenos Aires around 1835 coincided with a considerable development in the press on the other bank of the River Plate. Public opinion now took refuge in Montevideo, Santiago de Chile and Valparaíso, where the newspapers of exiled Argentines flourished, even circulating clandestinely in the city of Buenos Aires. In 1842, disturbances in the local political situation forced the departure of many Argentines exiled in Montevideo, with some returning to Buenos Aires and a considerable number emigrating to other bordering countries. There was a considerable increase in this type of publication in Santiago and Valparaíso,[103] where there was intense cultural and political activity in which Argentine émigrés played a role as active as it was controversial.[104]

The correlations between these three processes can be explained by the fact that the same men were involved (figure 13). Taking the case of the young Juan Bautista Alberdi, in 1837 he and other members of the Literary Salon founded the newspapers *La Moda* and *El Boletín Musical* in Buenos Aires. On emigrating to Montevideo in 1838, he set up *El Iniciador* with some old friends. A year later he published *La Revista del Plata* and participated in the publication of *El Grito Argentino* and *El Nacional*. He later worked on *El Comercio* and *El Talismán*. In 1843 he left for Europe, returning a year later to Valparaíso where he was reunited with Vicente F. López, Bartolomé Mitre and Carlos Tejedor. He immediately returned to journalism and participated in the publication of *El Mercurio* and

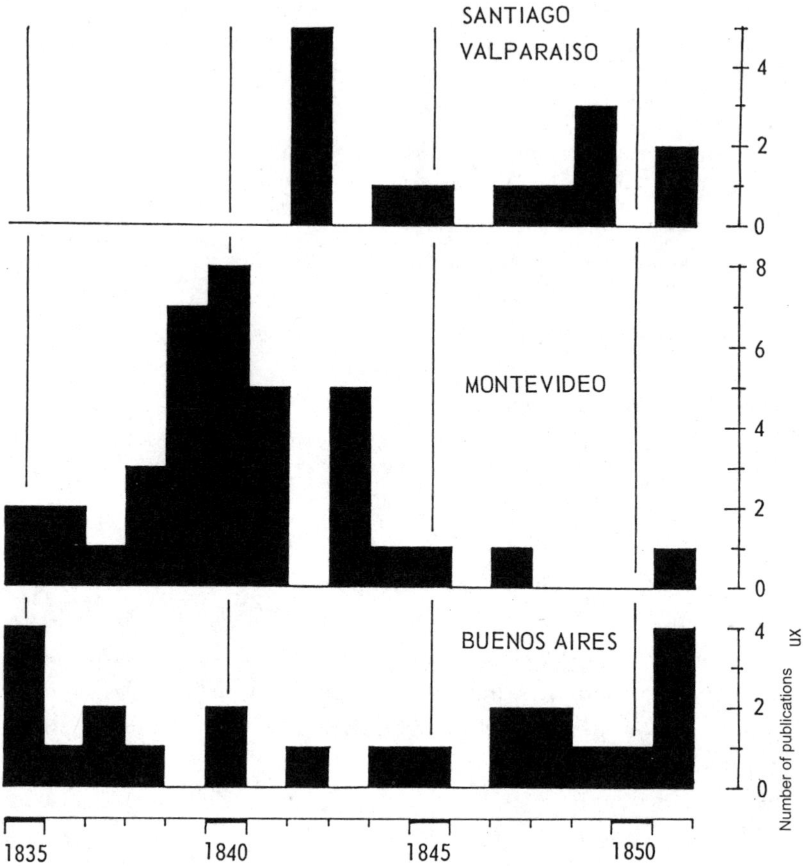

Figure 13. Evolution of Porteño Press in Comparison with the Appearance of Publications by Argentines in Exile (1835–1851)

La Revista de Valparaíso.[105] Aside from political commitments, journalism came to constitute an important or often principal means of subsistence, contributing to the formation of a group of professionals of opinion. The writings of D. F. Sarmiento or J. B. Alberdi were requested all over the city, just as the work of De Angelis was in Buenos Aires. To assimilate these three developments is to forget that the journalistic activity of Argentine exiles was not founded on a new political power originating in the public sphere, which to some extent was the case with De Angelis. This is because in the eyes of local elites the latter would always be considered a foreigner, and most importantly because he also wrote for the government, making him a functionary of the printing world rather than a spokesman for public opinion. The journalistic experience of the young romantics, first in the territory of the United Provinces and later in exile, was in contrast established in a new sphere of power. The fact that this public was expressed in exile in no way changed the political potential of their practices. On the contrary, the distance from the territory strengthened their identification with the reason of the people that they embodied and which was thus distinguished from the inconsistency of the appearances and prejudices of the people. Their identification with the new foundations of power had no other boundaries here than those of democracy, at least in the Americas, where the republican cause continued to be for many a cause which applied to the continent as a whole.

This leads us to query those who identified with and felt represented by this opinion movement. Admittedly, it is difficult to sketch a profile here due to the variety of factors implied in newspaper circulation. There was first of all the public of Argentines in exile, which went beyond the circle of writers.[106] Some publications explicitly targeted this public, such as *El Grito Argentino* and *Muera Rosas*. The former, published in Montevideo in 1839, succeeded in gaining supporters for the rebellion prepared by the exiles in Montevideo and the forces of Lavalle with the support of the French squadron. The latter publication, produced in Montevideo between 1841 and 1842, aimed to denounce the horrors of Rosas' tyranny. However, as the case of Chile shows in particular, the exiles' writings fell within the greater political objective of the period in the Americas as a whole, which implies that they would have had a large local public.[107] From the language and intellectual references of the period, it can be inferred that this public was strictly composed of members of an educated class, part of which identified with this new public sphere holding the writings of the Argentine exiles at its heart. However, in such cases as *El Grito Argentino* and *Muera Rosas*, cultural language alternated with forms of popular expression like *los cielitos*, and importance was also given to visual discourse. In proposing considerable iconography, these writers attacked Rosas in a field that only he had exploited until then: pictures.

Iconic discourse was not exclusively directed at sectors with little written press, although these appear to have been one of the main target sectors. In more general terms, it was aimed at a population which had taken a liking to pictures due to a baroque Christianity reinforced by a monarch whose physical distance made iconic representation vital, and which until now had only been used by Rosas.[108] These images presented Rosas as impious, calling himself "The Father of the Poor" while leading a life of luxury which increased the people's poverty. The image of Rosas the impostor was intended to destroy one of the axes of the relationship between the governor and the people: the duty of loyalty in exchange for protection. The caricatures denounced more so the breaches in the relationship rather than the relationship itself.[109] Other images were aimed at the well-to-do. In these cases, Rosas is shown contemplating the terrible crimes he himself has ordained with great pleasure, often with a bottle in his hand. These acts are all the more unacceptable when they lead to an inversion in the relationship between the people and the well-to-do.[110] In a caricature in *Muera Rosas*, the cruelty of the governor is symbolized in his drinking the blood of his victims:[111] a Rosas who consumed the elites who had carried him to power. Contrary to the popular image of Rosas, the exiles claimed to show the real Rosas, a cowardly man afraid even of cats and whose greatest anguish was death and the awaiting hell.[112] The caricatures might at times refer to more complex notions, though always constructed according to a simple scheme, as was the case with one caricature which aimed to denounce the contradiction between Rosas' regime and a modern representative system.[113] But as a group, and in spite of the differences in style and levels of accessibility of symbolic references, all aspired to build the counter-image of the Restaurador. This entailed reproducing representations which played a crucial role in the construction of federal identity, but shifting the meaning with the objective of revealing the real nature of the regime. This new press replete with images did not, however, abandon the rhetoric of opinion, but at the same time was evidence of a radicalization of this opinion which claimed to be judge, and its spread to the population as a whole. This explains the recourse to a condensed discourse bearing little resemblance to the individual exercise of reason, with which public opinion identified, but which now aimed to mobilize a more diverse public.

It is clear that these newspapers circulated principally in Buenos Aires, due to the network of friends and family of the exiles: in other words, always among an elite public.[114] Nevertheless, some had a more popular public, especially *El Grito Argentino*, which according to Ángel J. Carranza's account of the "Revolution of the Free of the South" was read at that time in the rural *pulperías*.[115] But the diffusion of these publications remained limited; with the departure of the writers, they became institutionalized as new forms of community expression, signaling a veritable turning point in local political life.

THE VOICE OF THE PATRIA: UNANIMITY AS THE FOUNDATION OF LEGITIMACY

The fifteen years of the Rosas government were marked by an overabundance of demonstrations in support of the Federation: from the symbolic representations of the *patria* through city adornments to their clothes, the entire community expressed its federal fervor in unison. There were numerous variations but all with a common basis: that of a community whose public recognition depended on demonstrations of apparent unanimity.[116]

This aspect of the Rosas regime has often been analyzed as one of the forms of quasi-totalitarian coercion characteristic of his government.[117] The present study does not seek to confirm or dismiss the totalitarian character of Rosista terror but rather to raise the question of the role of unanimist manifestations of community belonging within the Rosista political system. Although there is no correlation, there is nevertheless a chronological coincidence between this phenomenon and the proscription of intellectuals and men of culture, which implies that unanimism tended to replace not only the political doctrines that these men professed but also the very definition of the political community as a foundation of democratic power. In the absence of these men foreshadowing society's opinion, Rosas brought uniformity to the fore as a manifestation of the unity of a community whose social structure was still marked by corporative colonial society. This explains the insistence of the government in regulating all that could be perceived as a manifestation of belonging, beginning with the bright red ribbon which since the rural uprising of 1829 had been the symbol of the Federation.[118] According to the decree of 3 February 1832, the ribbon was to be worn visibly on the left side of the chest.[119] The measure only applied initially to administrative employees, but gradually it extended to society as a whole. The mandatory use of the red ribbon was both pedagogical and coercive. There is no shortage of accounts of its brutal application, and all affirm that until 1845 the red ribbon with the legend "Federation or Death" was imposed as a mandatory manifestation of community belonging.[120]

After the red ribbon, it was clothing that became a manifestation of belonging. Certain garments like the red Robespierre vest and the red poncho would become as fashionable as the frock coat. The Federal costume even dictated hairstyle: abundant hair with sideburns and a prominent mustache were considered symbols of the party,[121] to the extent that when Rosas' troops were to fight against the uprising in the south of the province, Prudencio Rosas ordered his men to "maintain your mustaches during the war against the Unitarian savages and their treacherous allies, the French."[122]

These manifestations of belonging had thus become symbols of community unity,. a unity represented by Rosas who also represented the soul of the federal population and its *patria*.[123] Thus, the community recognized itself in the figure of Rosas, who embodied unanimity. Those who did not identify with him had no alternative but to live outside of this community, and were therefore enemies of the *patria*. The introduction of the image of Rosas into the symbolism of the *patria* was a gradual process. As his portrait began to fill the public space, so it began to be identified with the federal community. Rosas played an active role in this process, giving detailed instructions as to the displaying of his portrait in the city's churches and in public squares during civic festivities.[124] By 1840 his image was to be found in military and civil prizes, on pocket watches and clocks, ornamental combs, fans, handkerchiefs and headscarves, decks of cards, shaving mugs, gloves, plates, jugs, and so on.[125] The overabundance of his image was in part a result of his physical absence since Rosas rarely appeared in public, and contributed to the symbolization of his image. But the shift from a "representative image of" to "the symbol of" and even "the incarnation of" no longer depended on the will or strategies of Rosas; it was a process produced within society and corresponding to collective images.[126] Its mobilizing power was all the greater for being placed in the vacant iconographic space left by the royal government.

Although Rosas occupied the symbolic place of the royal figure, he did so while introducing revolutionary symbols. In this way, he was able to associate his image with the emblem of independence, of which two of the principal icons were taken from the system instituted by the French Revolution: the Phrygian cap and the sun.[127] Rosas also introduced some innovations that allowed him to identify himself with the revolution and associate this with the Federation, one famous example being the federal flag. Rosas took the flag established in 1813 as the symbol of the nascent nation, modifying its colors and introducing new symbols to facilitate syncretism between the iconographic revolutionary system imported by the elites and popular symbols established by the Federation. Thus, the Phrygian cap adopted by the revolution allowed him to include the Federal color red in the "national" flag. Rosas described the flag in a letter to Vicente González: "Its colors are white and dark blue, a red sun in the middle and on the edges the red liberty cap. This is, by law, the National flag."[128] There is also evidence of the Federation's identification with the community of belonging in the toponymy of Buenos Aires. Under the law of 13 June 1836, the most important street in the city and the former royal road crossing the city from east to west became "calle Federación." Plaza Monserrat, where carts from the rest of the country converged and where the African societies were most densely concentrated, became "plaza del Restaurador Rosas."[129] Four years later the "calle de la Biblioteca" would also take this name.[130]

This all speaks much of Rosas' will to guarantee social unity through the unanimous manifestation of a belonging which was of a political nature but which did not pertain to a corpus of political doctrines. To be federal was to wear the federal insignia on the left lapel and be prepared to give one's life for the Federation and for its embodiment in Juan Manual de Rosas. But this identity between community, Federation and Rosas excluded the public sphere as an intermediary between representative authority and the will of the people. The young generation, in this respect, hoped to found the modern nation as a subject of sovereignty and the principle of unity over the practices and values of the time. On the periphery, not even political men had a place anymore in this triad. Moreover, Rosas was to ultimately leave them aside when he resorted to the plebiscite as a new manifestation of the will of the unanimous population.

The first plebiscite took place in 1835, to approve the variety of powers voted in by the House of Representatives. Rosas would from then on regularly turn to the people at the end of each mandate, or whenever the internal or international situation required it. Naturally, this sham democracy was to be denounced, as the liberal opposition immediately did in Tomás de Iriarte's words: "Rosas' intentions were perfectly clear. He wanted to cover up this irregular, anti-legal act, this liberticide, with popular forms, so that other countries would not believe he had used coercion in the expropriation of the people's rights."[131] Iriarte mentions the Napoleonic model, which in his opinion Rosas attempted to imitate, and which constituted evidence of the hybrid nature of his power. This does not make it any less true that the use of the plebiscite suited Rosas not only to legitimize his power in foreign eyes but also to confirm it, through a collective unanimous opinion founded more on the notion of harmony than convention. In other words, power for Rosas was not the result of political competence within republican institutions but the incarnation of a unanimous appearance of community.

The notion of unanimity of opinion is certainly contained in the idea of democratic consensus aspired to by public opinion. But between one and the other there was not only a difference of degree but also of nature, since Rosista unanimity served to associate society, which to a great extent Rosas represented as holistic, with the concept of the People as the foundation of power, when the idea of consensus implied the transformation of this society. Although the People continued to be the foundation of power, society referred to two different models of belonging. Thus, when Rosas and the liberal opposition spoke of "the Nation" they referred to two entirely distinct realities. In one case, the Nation spoke through the exacerbation of outside signs that implied the existence of one common soul, a plural society embodied in Rosas. This people-governor relationship recalled many aspects of the nation-king relationship. In the other reality, the Nation spoke through a group that represented the values of belonging of a society regarded as a group of equal individuals with diverse opinions.

Politics Under Protection

To maintain an institutional front, functionaries were needed who were capable of taking responsibility for republican institutions, even though these only had apparent authority. As was the case with the "opinion functionaries," the provincial legislature showed a tendency to operate as an annex of the executive.

THE REPUBLICAN FRONT

By a legislative decision voted in on 7 March 1835, Rosas was in possession of all powers, without restriction. The governor had enjoyed similar powers during his first mandate, but the duration of this absolute power was now in his hands, and not the legislature's. Under such conditions, the legislature no longer had any useful function. However, Rosas himself expressed his will to preserve this institution.[132] And so it was that during his government the House of Representatives continued to be elected by universal suffrage under the law established in 1821. This did not prevent Rosas from publicly establishing a system for designating candidates. As he himself announced to the House of Representatives in his 1837 opening speech, he intended to issue a list of candidates recommended by the government, for whom the population would be invited to vote.[133] This system came into effect sooner in the countryside than in the city, which already had a tradition of electoral competition, but gradually as the regime became stricter the system was also imposed in the city.[134]

Who were these candidates designated by Rosas and elected by the majority vote of a population whose electoral discipline was one of the achievements of the regime? From early 1840 to late 1851, seventy-one people held the position of representative. In comparison with the balance of the corpus between 1827 and 1840, the number of large landowners was slightly higher, a fifth of the sample.[135] However many of the same names appeared: Anchorena, Beláustegui, Piñeiro, Riglos, Rojas y Patrón, Rosas, Unzué and Vela. The most numerous of representatives, half of the sample, continued to be high functionaries and the members of the intellectual professions, although there were fewer than in the legislature of 1827 to 1840. Surprisingly, there was a presence, albeit small, accounting for a tenth of the sample, of traders and small clerks. In certain cases these were members of important Porteño families, hence the presence of the lawyer Eduardo Lahitte in the legislature can be explained more easily by his family background than by his administrative skills. In contrast, the fact that Rosas should have chosen someone like Juan José Alsina stemmed from a need to maintain a certain institutional appearance. A lawyer and doctor of jurisprudence and theology, as well as the son of a royal functionary, Alsina had all the necessary requirements to formally ensure the operations of the republican institutions.

On the whole there were few newcomers to the legislature: sixty-two of the seventy-one representatives had some previous political experience. Their political past gives some idea of the skills required to reach the legislature: above all, loyalty to Rosas, plus some knowledge of the workings of the institution obtained from prior mandates or some personal power acquired in rural districts or the army. Of the few men with no previous experience—nine in total—there was only one case in which the designation can be explained solely by clientele connections. This was Vicente González, one of the most loyal to Rosas and an important Rosista intermediary in the south of the province.[136] This inevitably caused some disgruntlement among those who associated loyalty with fortune, knowledge or social influence.[137] The case of González was quite exceptional, as the men who started out in politics with Rosas as much as those with prior experience belonged to the Porteño elite.

The institutionalization of the system of designating candidates, consequently, does not appear to have greatly changed the profile of the representatives. The principal difference with the members of the previous legislature was not of a socioprofessional nature but rather more generational. While the average age of the members of the House of Representatives between 1827 and 1840 was thirty-four, between 1849 and 1851 it was fifty-three.[138] In addition to this ageing process, these men tended to remain in their positions. Thus, the seventy-one representatives completed 247 mandates, an average of 3.5 mandates per person, while for the proceeding period the average was 2.4. This phenomenon represented a step towards political stability as Rosas saw it.

Unlike previous legislatures, there were limited cases where representatives complemented their position with the publication of a newspaper. It is hardly surprising that, as in the previous period, representatives were relatively alien to associative practices. In total there were only nine cases of representatives belonging to associations before occupying their posts, eight of seventy-one representatives. Most of these cases were individuals who participated in power during the government of Rivadavia, such as Baldomero García, Vicente F. López, José M. Rojas y Patrón and Felipe Senillosa, members of the Literary Society or the Valeper Society, both of which brought together political cultural elites associated with the Rivadavia government. In these cases, their presence in the Rosas government can be explained by their mastery of the workings of the institutions. The other three cases concerned members of the charity institution-association founded in 1833.

It can be concluded that representative politics was rare to nonexistent, rendered useless by the principle of designating candidates, which itself was similar to the notion of elector government, formulated by Natalio Botano in an earlier period.[139] Family, friendship and client ties contributed to the selection of the political group in the House of Representatives. This selection always concerned the elites and a certain generation: men born before the revolution, like Rosas, who as a result could reconcile the workings of the old social and political institutions with the new scheme of things. The regime, in contrast, excluded from representative functions the sector of the elite—another generation, who since the revolution had identified with the sphere of public power. Thus, the generational conflict tended to overlap the ideological political conflict.

THE PUBLIC FUNCTIONARIES

The case of legislature members did not differ greatly from that of public functionaries during the period. Both groups formed part of a clientele network around which power was organized in the province of Buenos Aires. Without modifying legal order, Rosas controlled different political instances of Buenos Aires and other provinces of the Federation. From diplomatic issues to questions of common law, everything was decided by Rosas, with the assistance of a personal secretary.[140]

Thus centralized, power passed directly down to his principal political intermediaries, the justices of the peace. The administrative and judicial post of justice of the peace was originally intended to replace certain functions of the old *cabildos*.[141] But under Rosas the faculties of the justices of the peace, especially in rural areas, were broadened considerably to include the posts of military commander, chief of police and tax collector. However, these functionaries, chosen according to their loyalty and their influence in their jurisdiction, held no autonomy from the governor, who exercised severe control over his men. The mandate was for one year, but like the representatives, they tended to remain in their posts longer. Between 1840 and late 1851 a total of 126 people held 395 mandates in the city and province of Buenos Aires, an average of 3.12 posts per person. This lack of renovation was an essential aspect of the power of the justices of the peace, as it allowed them to build up a broad network of clients, from landowners to producers to pampas Indians. All depended in some way on Rosas, whether to take advantage of the favors of central power, or as the principal victims of the system. These functionaries were as much the agents for transferring land confiscated from the "enemies of the Federation" as they were responsible for applying the feared vagrancy law.[142] With their powers poorly defined and only circumscribed by Rosas, the justices of the peace became a vital link between the governor and the rural population.

Aside from justices of the peace, local or provincial functionaries held no real power, apart from that of preserving the institutional form of the republican regime. The selection mechanisms of public functionaries were the same as for representatives and justices of the peace. Access to the post depended on specific capacities, but loyalty to Rosas was de rigeur. A similar longevity could be found in these posts. The stability of the regime was above all due to the perpetuation of these men. Between 1840 and 1851 a total of 198 people held 664 public posts, an average of 6.8 mandates per individual, while in the following period (1852–1862) the average was 2.38. Supposing that each mandate had an average duration of one year, each man would have had nearly eight years in their posts, a similar perpetuation to that seen in other posts. As with the case of representatives, the ties that allowed a functionary to attain a post and keep it were often primary ties—family, friendship or man-to-man solidarity—which explains why horizontal connections made from forms of associative sociability had a weak presence among functionaries of the regime. There were only a handful of individuals who joined an association before taking up a post, and three-quarters of these corresponded to the period after the Battle of Caseros.[143]

The Challenge of the Regime: a Federation without Nation

If Rosas were more skillful or less haughty, he would most carefully avoid the publication of certain acts which are indispensable for the conservation of that monstrous system, founded on the two cornerstones of terror and deceit. To sustain the latter he ought to be proclaiming liberal principles, love for republican institutions, speaking always of respect for the law, of his respect for the guarantees and rights of the citizen, while the need to sustain the element of terror contradicts daily his incessantly repeated words and protests.[144]

In this judgment of the Rosas government, Florencio Valera, shortly before his murder, once again showed his great intuition. Not only did Varela mention the economic difficulties that would bring about the end of the Rosas Federation, but he also saw the political contradictions of the system: Rosas needed to maintain an institutional front in order to gain a certain international recognition, but to do so he had to proscribe the only people capable of organizing a national representation. To confirm his power within the province of Buenos Aires, and above all in the other provinces of the Federation, Rosas had to reconcile the republican institutions with an absolute power which would permit him a supraprovincial authority. Hence the "regime of merit" denounced by Varela, a regime that undoubtedly permitted Rosas to stamp his authority on the other representative institutions. Nevertheless, this was an advantageous move only in the short term, as such a regime when faced with an insurmountable contradiction made political normalization in the province and in the country impossible. Indeed, the maintenance of Rosas' provincial power depended increasingly on the formalization of a national political and economic structure oriented towards the confirmation of Buenos Aires' economic hegemony over other regional economies. But the economic expansion of the province was founded on an authoritarian power based only on Rosas and incapable of organizing a future national power. Moreover Rosas always opposed calling a National Constituent Congress.[145] This certainly did not prevent him from enjoying his national authority, due to which he could deal with foreign powers during international conflicts, but this authority was based on a vast clientele network made up of different provincial *caudillos* and headed by himself.[146] The legitimacy of this picture of national organization depended entirely on Rosas, as no representative institution could assume the sovereignty of the nation. Although the House of Representatives of Buenos Aires had a role to play in the legitimization of its national power, in practice it was more like a symbol of this unanimous will than a genuine case of representation.[147]

Thus, during the last decade of government, while everything appeared to confirm the success of the regime, Rosas was caught in a trap of his own making. He had identified with the republican institutions and the system of symbolic references of the revolution—the independence of the United Provinces of the River Plate—but had excluded the men who could have guaranteed the transition from an exceptional authoritarian provincial power to a national republic. Once social peace had been attained, the continuity of a regime built on the exception could no longer be assured. To these institutional political difficulties were added those connected with the unanimist conception of the community of belonging. This had led Rosas to reduce the legislature power to a purely symbolic role. The House of Representatives was not only a democratic check to power but also the guarantee of civil liberties. With its neutralization, what was disassociated from the Rosista Federation was then the very idea of the nation as a society of individuals. The challenge for the regime was to separate the inseparable: the idea of a nation as a political community of belonging whose only possible political form was the representative republic, from the idea of the individual and civil society as democracy.

NOTES

1. Between 1837 and 1840, money printing increased the total of money in circulation by 283.03%. T. Halperin Donghi, *Guerra y finanzas*, 215–284.
2. See AGN. AP. X 44-10-2.
3. The memoirs of Víctor Gálvez illustrate this change well, V. Gálvez, *Memorias*, vol. 1, 362–388, and vol. 2, 79–87. I agree here with Szuchman, but it appears that this is the consequence of an interim crisis which led the regime to make a U-turn which ultimately proved fatal. In my opinion, Szuchman ignores the impact of the 1838–1842 crisis on the change of the regime and considers this change in perhaps an excessively monolithic way. See M. Szuchman, *Order, Family*.
4. In this sense I share the theory of Cochin concerning the notion of the modern individual as a product of the societies. See Augustin Cochin, *Les Sociétés de Pensée et la démocratie. Études d'histoire révolutionnaire* (Paris: Plon, 1921); republished as *L'Esprit du jacobinisme* (Paris: PUF, 1979); A. Cochin, *Les Sociétés de Pensée et la Révolution en Bretagne (1788–1789),* 2 vols. (Paris, 1925). On this question, see also François Furet, *Penser la Révolution Française* (Paris: Gallimard, 1978).

5. Jorge Myers has worked recently on the subject of conspiracy in the republican rhetoric of Rosismo. J. Myers, *Orden y virtud.*
6. On this subject there are two opposed theories. One, of Masonic origin, claims that Masonic lodges existed from the late eighteenth century. The other, defended most recently by José A. Ferrer Benimeli, sustains that the establishment of regular Freemasonry came later. The question rests on whether the expression "Masonic lodge" is limited to those possessing a constitution granted by the Grand Orient and on which documentation is available—proposed by Ferrer Benimeli—or whether a looser criterion is used whereby associations that adopted the model of Freemasonic organizations are considered even though there may not be testimony to their regularity. I have chosen the second solution, while at every opportunity alerting the reader to the nature of my data. Hence I have taken into account the lodges created by Spanish liberals exiled in the 1820s, even though Ferrer Benimeli argues that the first Masonic lodge was established in Buenos Aires in 1852. See D. V. Pérez Fontana, *La masonería.*; Alcibíades Lappas, "La logia 'Constante Unión' de la ciudad de Corrientes," *Revista de la Junta de Historia de Corrientes* 5 (1970); José A. Ferrer Benimeli, *Masonería española contemporánea* (Madrid: Siglo XXI, 1980), vol. 1 (1800–1868), 134.
7. In the nineteenth century, the majority of political associations often used the organizational form of secret societies and even named themselves "lodges." An exemplary case is that of the famous Lautaro Lodge. But even Rivera Indarte, one of the opponents of the regime exiled in Montevideo used the word "lodges" to refer to his association. See José Rivera Indarte, *Rosas y sus opositores* (1884), vol. 1 (Buenos Aires: Jackson, 1945), 110. I have developed this analysis in "La Revolución Francesa," 7–27.
8. It must be remembered that anti-Masonic repression in Spain was accentuated by the establishment of the "absolutist decade," which witnessed an abundant literature written against the Masons. Rosas published in Buenos Aires a study which enjoyed considerable popularity in Spain. See *Extracto de un papel tomado a los masones, cuyo título es como sigue: Máximas e Instrucciones Políticas que el Gran Oriente Español ha mandado poner en ejecución a todas las logias de la Masonería Egipciana*, printed in Córdoba (Spain), at the Imprenta Real, 1824; reprinted in Buenos Aires, at the Imprenta de la Independencia, 1840. The Spanish original was entitled *Españoles: Unión y Alerta. Extracto....* Newspapers also published information about the Masonic plot around the world. See *La Gaceta Mercantil*, 29 November 1830. For the history of Spanish Freemasonry in this period see J. Ferrer Benimeli, *Masonería española*, vol. 1.
9. John Murray Forbes, *Once años en Buenos Aires, 1820–1831* (London, 1871) (Buenos Aires: Emecé, 1956), 598–600.
10. It is possible that when imprisoned in 1830, Jardón was not part of a Masonic lodge. This did not prevent him from being identified with this type of practice, which in the meantime had become suspicious.
11. John Murray Forbes, "Carta a Martin van Buren, Buenos Aires, 31 de julio de 1830," in *Once años*, 598.
12. See "Informe del Sr. Ministro de Gobierno sobre la solicitud de Jardón a la Honorable Sala de Representantes," *La Gaceta Mercantil*, 23 June 1830, 1, 2.
13. *La Gaceta Mercantil*, 23 June 1830, 1, 2.
14. On the question of Pro-Masonic and Anti-Masonic literature, see the author's study "Masonería y revolución de independencia en el Río de la Plata: 130 años de historiografía," in José A. Ferrer Benimeli (ed.), *Masonería, revolución y reacción*, vol. 2 (Alicante: Instituto de Cultura "Juan Gil-Albert," 1990), 1035–1055.

15. On Pincheira's attacks on the northwest frontier, see references in *La Gaceta Mercantil*, 27, 29 and 30 October 1828 and 20 March 1829. The account of the attacks on the city of Bahía Blanca appeared in *El Tiempo*, 9 and 20 March 1829. On the presence of the cacique in Carmen de Patagones see José Biedma, *Crónicas históricas del Río Negro de Patagones, 1774–1834* (Buenos Aires: Canter, 1905), 664–669; other references in a letter from Paz to Lavalle dated 9 February 1829 in AGN.VII, 1-3-6, folio 118, and an accusation by some inhabitants of Carmen de Patagones as to Rosas' responsibility in the matter in *El Tiempo*, 13 February 1829. A biography of Pincheira can be found in Alicia Doval, "Los hermanos Pincheira," in Comando General del Ejército, *Política seguida con el aborigen* (Buenos Aires: Círculo Militar, 1973–1974), vol. 2 (1820–1852), ch. 8, 189–252
16. See J. Murray Forbes, *Once años.*
17. See Adolphe Delacour, "Le Río de la Plata. Buenos Aires, Montevideo," *Revue Indépendante* (Paris: Jicois, 1845), 38.
18. On this aspect, see the author's study "The 1829 uprising."
19. Xenophobic sentiments were fanned in particular by foreigners' participation in "Friends of the Order" battalions organized by Lavalle against the popular uprising in the south.
20. "Mendeville au ministre des Affaires Etrangères," Buenos Aires, 30 July 1830, in AQO. CPA 5. Between 1820 and 1835 Mendeville was the French business representative and General Consul. In Buenos Aires he married Mariquita Sánchez, whose house was host to the most highly reputed *tertulias* of independence supporters.
21. "Lettre de Mendeville au ministre des Affaires Etrangères," Buenos Aires, 10 November 1832, in AQO. CPA 6.
22. To make a political ideological simplification, the French liberals identified with the "Unitarians" while the monarchists with the "Federals," hence the conflict between the two groups erupted in the River Plate a year before events in France.
23. In spite of this, Mendeville's disagreements with the community were not resolved, above all after the July revolution in France. Mendeville had to leave his post definitively in 1835. See letter from Vins de Peysac dated 22 June 1835 and from M. Rogers concerning his death, 26 June 1836, in AQO. CPA 7.
24. On this conflict there is abundant documentation in the archives of the Quai d'Orsay, AQO. CPA 5.
25. Rosas to Vicente González, Río Colorado, 25 September 1833, in E. H. Celesia, *Rosas, aporte para su historia*, vol. 1, 599–604.
26. *Rosas, aporte para su historia*, vol. 2, 376, 574.
27. "Correspondencia de Juan M. Gutiérrez a Pío Tedín, Buenos Aires, 25 de abril de 1835," in *Epistolario de Don Juan María Gutiérrez*, compilation, prologue and notes by Ernesto Morales (Buenos Aires: Instituto de Cultura Joaquín V. González, 1942), 12–17.
28. Juan Bautista Alberdi, "Doble armonía," in F. Weinberg, *El Salón Literario*, 141.
29. M. Sastre, "Discurso inaugural...," in *Antecedentes*. On the matter of the sovereignty of reason, see E. Echeverría, *Ojeada*, 51–59.
30. E. Echeverría, "Discurso...," in *Antecedentes*, 83–85
31. In the opening speeches at Sastre's Literary Salon, as in the newspaper *La Moda*, there were numerous manifestations of support for Rosas. In *La Moda* there was even praise for the bright red ribbon that was a symbol of the popular component of the Federation. *La Moda*, 2 December 1837.
32. See V. F. López, "Autobiografía," 54. See also F. Weinberg, *El Salón Literario*, 107.

33. See V. F. López, "Autobiografía," 55, 62.
34. See E. Echeverría, *Ojeada retrospectiva*, 60.
35. Pedro de Angelis, *Archivo Americano y espíritu de la prensa del mundo* (Buenos Aires, 1847–1851), 28 January 1847. In this conflict there is also a generational dimensional that has yet to be the object of a systematic analysis. A pioneering study in this generational approach is that of J.-C. Schmitt and G. Levi, *Histoire de la jeunesse en Occident* (Paris: Seuil, 1996), "L'Univers Historique."
36. There is much historic literature on the two French incursions into the River Plate during the Rosas government. Rosas' attitude towards foreign powers occupies a central place in the twentieth-century historiographic dispute between nationalists and liberals. On the development of events from a nationalist point of view, see Néstor Colli, *Rosas y el bloqueo anglo-francés* (Buenos Aires: Patria Grande, 1978); Carlos Pereyra, *Rosas y Thiers, la diplomacia europea en el Río de la Plata (1838–1850)*, (Madrid: America, 1919). For a French view of the conflict see Théogène Page, "Affaires de Buenos Aires / Expédition de la France contre la République Argentine," *La Revue des Deux Mondes* (Paris) 25 (February 1841): 301–370.
37. E. Echeverría, *Ojeada retrospectiva*, 35.
38. *Ojeada retrospectiva*, 32.
39. Sympathies for the Italian republican movement had previously been expressed in the newspaper published by some members of the Literary Salon. See *La Moda,* 25 July 1837. For the ideological influence of Risorgimento thought on the young generation, see Renato Treves, "Le saint-simonisme et la pensée italienne en Argentine et en Uruguay," *Cahiers Internationaux de Sociologie*, July-December 1973, 197–216. The influence of Saint-Simonian thought has been analyzed by José Ingenieros, one of the classic authors of Argentine positivism. See José Ingenieros, *La evolución de las ideas argentinas*, 2 vols. (Buenos Aires: Futuro, 1961), especially vol. 2, ch. 7, 235–310.
40. E. Echeverría, *Ojeada retrospectiva*, 39.
41. In the second half of 1838 four branches of *Joven Argentina* were created. In Montevideo, with J. B. Alberdi, M. Cané, B. Mitre, A. Somellera and P. Bermúdez; in San Juan, M. J. Quiroga Rosas, D. F. Sarmiento, B. Villafañe, E. Rodríguez, A. Aberastain and S. Cortínez; in the city of Tucumán, the association's members included B. Villafañe, M. Avellaneda and B. Silva. Lastly, in the Córdoba branch were V. F. López, P. Paz, E. Rodríguez, A. Ferreira, R. Ferreira and F. Álvarez. The newspaper *El Nacional*, republished by Andrés Lamas and Miguel Cané, disseminated the opinion of the young generation in Montevideo. See E. Echeverría, *Ojeada retrospectiva*, 65–68.
42. A. Saldías quotes a letter from Carlos Tejedor in which he confirms that Maza's conspiracy was originally an initiative by some members of the May Association or the *Joven Argentina* association. See A. Saldías, *Historia de la Confederación*, vol. 2, 416–417. Other references in Ángel Carranza, *Bosquejo histórico acerca del doctor Carlos Tejedor y la conjuración de 1839* (Buenos Aires, 1879).
43. See E. Echeverría, *Ojeada retrospectiva*, 71–72. See Tulio Halperin Donghi, *Historia argentina. De la revolución de independencia a la confederación Rosista* (Buenos Aires: Paidós, 1972), 354–379
44. E. Echeverría, *Ojeada retrospectiva*, 91.
45. The "reign of terror" began with the formation of a coalition between internal opposition forces (the Unitarians) and foreign powers (France and England). To tackle this situation Rosas used terror as an instrument of government. During this period, known as "the black years of the regime," the governor confirmed his absolute power,

shown as the only guarantee of maintaining social order. But while the threat of external and internal enemies of the Federation was an important factor in establishing the "terror," one characteristic distinguished it from other apparently similar phenomena. Rosista "terror" was not only related to the problem of the legitimacy of the regime but also to the cohesion of the social corpus after the break with Spain. This established the Federation as a unanimous manifestation of community belonging (see below). For many years, historians of *Rosismo* left aside the question of "terror." The first to analyze it was José M. Ramos Mejía in *Rosas y su tiempo*, 3 vols. (Buenos Aires: F. Lajouane, 1907). John Lynch recently picked up on this theme in *Juan Manuel de Rosas*, 193–233.

46. E. Echeverría, *Ojeada retrospectiva*, 96.
47. *Ojeada retrospectiva*, 91–98. Under the name of romanticism there are different schools of thought, at times contradictory. This aspect is all the more surprising in Buenos Aires given that the young generation aimed to synthesize the Saint-Simonian doctrines of Leroux, nationalists like Mazzini and conservative liberals like Cousin and Gizot with the neo-Catholicism of Lamennais. According to this generation, this synthesis was to constitute the foundations of the social dogma intended to become the creed of the future nation. *Dogma socialista* was first published in Montevideo with the title "Código o declaración de los principios que constituyen la creencia social de la República Argentina," *El Iniciador*, 1 January 1839. It was also republished in book form in Montevideo, with the title *Dogma socialista de la Asociación de Mayo, precedido de una ojeada retrospectiva sobre el movimiento intelectual en el Plata en el año 37*, by Esteban Echeverría (Montevideo: Imprenta del Nacional, 1846).
48. We will not analyze here the philosophy of Echeverría, on which there is an abundance of literature; it is enough to indicate the prime position that the young generation assigned to associative life in the political community. The vast literature on Echeverría was compiled by Félix Weinberg, "Contribución a la bibliografía de Esteban Echeverría," *Universidad, Journal of the Universidad Nacional del Litoral* 5 (1960): 159–226. On the notion of the modern individual, see Louis Dumont, *Essais sur l'individualisme. Une perspective anthropologique sur l'idéologie moderne* (Paris: Seuil, 1983).
49. When these men spoke of "Latin American sociability" they did not invoke a Latin American community subject to sovereignty, but rather a community of customs, which would conserve the features of a Latin American identity defined as a counter-model to Spain: democracy, religious tolerance, industry, etc.
50. See *Cartas escritas por el muy honorable Felipe Dormer Stanhope, conde de Chesterfield, a su hijo*, 2 vols., Spanish translation by Tomás de Iriarte (Buenos Aires: Imprenta de la Libertad, 1833). Iriarte translated Dr. Gregory's edition. The same year another translation into Spanish by Rafael Zapata was published: *Consejos de Lord Conde a su hijo, y como cimiento del corazón humano explicados de un modo sencillo y familiar, y una memoria de vida del autor* (Buenos Aires, 1833). In an article from 1838, Alberdi refers explicitly to the translation and publication of *Cartas del conde de Chesterfield a su hijo Philip Stanhope* and pointed out the disadvantages implied in the diffusion of books on social education and urbanity from Europe. See Juan B. Alberdi, "Sociabilidad, costumbres," *El Iniciador* (Montevideo) 12 (1 October 1839).
51. Norbert Elias explores the question marvelously in *La Civilisation des mœurs*, where he shows the connection between the regulated customs of the court and the process of

centralization of royal power. He thus demonstrates that the customs of State are tied to a system of civilization. The interest in his results naturally exceeds modern history, as they contain an interesting idea that allows an analysis from a different perspective of the almost general identification between nation and civilization. If there was a point shared by all Ibero-American republics during the first half of the nineteenth century it was undoubtedly that the idea of nation, when this evoked something other than the State, with which there was habitual confusion, was a project of society that found its most consummate legitimacy and expression in the notion of civilization. See N. Elias, *La Civilisation des mœurs*.

52. See D. F. Sarmiento, *Civilización i Barbarie*.
53. See José Mármol, *Amalia* (Montevideo, 1851) (Madrid: Espasa-Calpe, 1978), col. "Austral"; Esteban Echeverría, *El matadero* (1871) (Buenos Aires: Centro Editor de América Latina, 1979).
54. *Civilización y barbarie* was originally serialized in the newspaper *El Progreso*. It appeared in book form for the first time in 1851, published in Santiago de Chile by J. Belin y Compañía. The life and work of Sarmiento represent some of the most important literature in existence on a public Argentine man. The work of P. Verdevoye contains a good compilation of his principal works. See Paul Verdevoye, "Domingo Faustino Sarmiento éducateur et publiciste (entre 1839 et 1852)," *Travaux et mémories de l'Institut des Hautes Études de l'Amérique Latine*, no. 12 (Paris: Institut des Hautes Études de l'Amérique Latine, 1963), 545–608.
55. See, for example, his analysis of the *pulperías* as "artificial societies," because in these, recreation was not tied to the public use of individual reason with a social interest, but purely for leisure purposes. See D. F. Sarmiento, *Facundo*, ch. 3, 108–116.
56. The 8 July 1836 decree concerning carnival festivities was repeated on various occasions. This festivity would eventually be abolished "forever" with the 22 February 1844 decree. See "Decreto proscribiendo límites al juego de carnaval, 8 de julio de 1836," and "Decreto aboliendo para siempre el juego de carnaval, 22 de febrero de 1844," in P. de Angelis, *Recopilación de leyes*.
57. See V. Gálvez, *Memorias,* vol. 1, 344; J. Rivera Indarte, *Rosas y sus opositores,* vol. 1, 109–112; Andrés Somellera, *La tiranía de Rosas* (1886) (Buenos Aires: Nuevo Cabildo, 1962).
58. In 1839 Rosas ordered the closure of the Hospice for Abandoned Children and the Orphans' School, both dependent on the Socieded de Beneficencia. See *El Grito Argentino* (Montevideo), 28 February and 14 March 1839.
59. Society's public manifestations were produced by traditional bodies. See *La Gaceta Mercantil,* 7 April 1841; Benito Hortelano's comments in *Memorias*, 205, 207, and numerous references in J. M. Ramos Mejía, *Rosas*, 319–323.
60. A. Delacour, "Le Río de la Plata," 56.
61. Their mass participation in the wars of independence and in the civil wars constitutes one of the reasons for the disappearance of the group. See G. R. Andrews, "Las legiones negras," in *Los Africanargentinos*, 137–165.
62. See figure 6. The fall in the curve of associative development corresponding to 1842 should be interpreted with caution. The curve indicates the number of associations operating in this year and about which complementary information has been found in police files. In all likelihood, the bulk of these were created previously. Nevertheless, during this period they had a very active life.
63. See "Nación Mozambique," and "Nación Argentina Federal," in AGN. AP. X 31-11-5.

64. See Vicente F. López, *Historia de la República Argentina. Su origen, su revolución, su desarrollo político hasta 1852*, 10 vols. (Buenos Aires: Carlos Casavalle, 1883), cited in J. L. Lanuza, *Morenada*, 119–120; D. F. Sarmiento, *Facundo*, 323–324.
65. This political turnabout can also be explained by the need to win British support for the conflict with France, as ending the slave trade had been one of England's demands since 1831. See J. Lynch, *Juan Manuel de Rosas*, 120.
66. The original can be found in the Museo Histórico Nacional, object no. 2540; see Ministerio de Educación de la Nación, *Catálogo del Museo Histórico Nacional*, vol. 1 (Buenos Aires, 1951), 460, no. 4278; reproduced in Juan A. Pradere, *Juan Manuel de Rosas, su iconografía* (Buenos Aires: J. Mendesky e Hijos, 1914), 139. There are no concrete references as to the identity of the artist or as to where the painting was originally exhibited, but it was probably hung in Rosas' residence, so that everybody could appreciate this evidence of the love of his people.
67. Sky blue was associated with Unitarian opinion, while bright red had become the symbol of the Federation.
68. The donation of land was not systematic. Loyalty had to be demonstrated with convincing evidence, such as in participation in a pro-governmental mobilization, the loss of nation members in an armed confrontation with the enemy, etc. Hence the government responded positively to a request from the Bayombé Society while rejecting a request from the Cabunda Society. See AGN. AP. X 31-11-5.
69. See "Carta de Rosas a su mujer Encarnación Ezcurra," Santos Lugares, 23 November 1833, in M. Conde Montero, "Correspondencia inédita de Doña Encarnación Ezcurra de Rosas," *Revista Argentina de Ciencias Políticas* 27 (October 1823–March 1824): 106–126, esp. 123; "Nación Bayombé" in AGN. AP. X 31-11-5.
70. See AGN. AP. X 33-3-3, book 100, folio 19.
71. See AGN. AP. X 33-2-6, book 85, folio 20.
72. See "Nación Bayombé," 12 August 1852, in AGN. AP. X 31-11-5.
73. AGN. AP. X 31-11-5.
74. See G. R. Andrews, "Rosas y los unitarios," in *Los Afro-argentinos*, 116–121. In his novel *Amalia*, José Mármol, one of the young romantics exiled in Montevideo, paints a fairly unfavorable picture of the African population. See J. Mármol, *Amalia*, 451–452.
75. See *La Gaceta Mercantil*, 25 June 1842. The forty participating nations succeeded in raising 4,075 pesos.
76. A complete collection of these verses can be found in Luis Soler Cañas, *Negros, gauchos y compadres en el cancionero de la Federación (1830–1848)* (Buenos Aires, 1958).
77. When Rosas felt that the manifestations were infringing on his authority, he simply abolished carnival forever; see *Registro oficial*. Ramos Mejía's account of the "carnaval de Rosas" is quite fictional. See J. M. Ramos Mejía, *Rosas*, vol. 1, 329–340.
78. *La Negrita*, 21 July 1833.
79. Such was the testimony of opposition poet Juan Cruz Varela, in a poem dedicated to the 25 May 1838: "Only by the taunts of a nation of braves / do bands of vile African slaves / through the streets and the squares go a-wandering. / Their barbarous yell, their savage rave / is on this day meditated outrage / of the new Caribbean that the South begot." In J. L. Lanuza, *Morenada*, 126–127. See also V. Gálvez's comments in *Memorias*, vol. 2, 213.
80. The data concerning electoral participation are taken from Marcela Ternavasio "Hacia un régimen de unanimidad. Política y elecciones en Buenos Aires, 1828–1850," paper presented at the "Perspectivas históricas sobre la ciudadanía política en América Latina" seminar, Bogotá, August 1995.

81. Andrews gives various examples. See G. R. Andrews, *Los Afro-argentinos*, 119–121.
82. See M. Conde Montero, "Correspondencia inédita," and E. H. Celesia, *Rosas, aporte para su historia*.
83. J. Rivera Indarte, *Rosas*, vol. 2, 129–130.
84. *Rosas*, vol. 2, 130–134.
85. *Rosas*, vol. 2, 130–134.
86. See "Lista de miembros de la Sociedad Popular Restauradora," *La Gaceta Mercantil*, 7 April 1841; J. M. Ramos Mejía, *Rosas*, 129–165; A. Saldías, *Historia de la Confederación*, vol. 2; J. Lynch, *Juan Manuel de Rosas*, 206–207. In his novel *Amalia*, José Mármol has left a rich fictional account of the opposition's perceptions during the period. Juan María Gutiérrez describes this society in terms of the aspect that appears to arouse most attraction: "This society which is commonly called *Mazorca* has the objective of inserting the delicious fruit from which it has taken its name (*"the corncob"—Translator*) up the rearguard of the Unitarian enemy." See "Correspondencia de Gutiérrez a Pío Tedín," 25 April 1835, *Epistolario de don Juan María Gutiérrez*.
87. See "Julián Salomón a Rosas," Buenos Aires, 30 September 1840, in E. H. Celesia, *Rosas, aporte para su historia*, vol. 2, 461–463.
88. In J. Lynch, *Juan Manuel de Rosas*, 214–226, there is an account of events and the participation of the Sociedad Popular Restauradora.
89. J. M. Beruti, *Memorias curiosas*, 4066.
90. See J. Lynch, *Juan Manuel de Rosas*, 206.
91. "Lettre du consul Vins de Peysac au ministre des Affaires Etrangères," Buenos Aires, 31 August 1835, in AQO. CPA 7.
92. See Pedro de Angelis, "Mazorca," *Archivo Americano*, no. 6, 31 August 1843, 56–57.
93. See "Carta de Vicente González a Antonio Reyes, campamento en el Saladillo del Rosario, 4 de noviembre de 1846," in AGN, Secretaría de Rosas, 1846, x-26-5-4.
94. See figure 10.
95. See Félix Weinberg, "El segundo grupo romántico en Buenos Aires, 1844–1852," in *Congreso Internacional de Historia de América*, vol. 6 (Buenos Aires: Academia Nacional de la Historia, 1980), 479–497.
96. A detailed analysis of the history of this newspaper can be found in Antonio Zinny, *La Gaceta Mercantil de Buenos Aires, 1823–1852*, 3 vols. (Buenos Aires: Taller Penitenciaría Nacional, 1912). For a list of the newspapers, see *La Création*, appendix 1.
97. In J. E. Sabor, *Pedro de Angelis*, there is a complete biography of this author.
98. Only two, somewhat voluminous issues were published, the first with thirty-six pages and the second with 108. See A. Zinny, "Bibliografía periodística," vol. 11.
99. According to J. Lynch, the newspaper had a print run of 1,500 copies, 400 of which were sent abroad. Lynch argues that the articles on the River Plate in the *Morning Chronicle* used the information from de Angelis. See J. Lynch, *Juan Manuel de Rosas*, 176.
100. See F. Weinberg, "El segundo grupo romántico."
101. Vicente Quesada refers here to the *Los Vampiros* society, which met in the sacristy of the Cathedral of Buenos Aires. See V. Gálvez, *Memorias*, 329.
102. See F. Weinberg, "El segundo grupo romántico," 496–498.
103. See J. R. Fernández, *Historia del periodismo*.; Benjamín Fernández y Medina, *La imprenta y la prensa en el Uruguay, 1807–1900*, Montevideo, Imprenta Artística, 1900; Ramón Briseño, "Catálogo de las diferentes publicaciones periódicas que en el país ha habido, desde 1812 hasta 1859 inclusive," *Estadística bibliográfica de la literatura chilena*, vol. 1 (Santiago de Chile: Imprenta Chilena, 1862), 473–480.

104. Lastarria's memoirs are a rich testament to the participation of Argentines in the cultural and political life of Santiago. J. V. Lastarria, *Recuerdos literarios* (1878) (Santiago: Zig-Zag, 1967), 87–171.
105. See PGB, *La Création*, appendix 1, "Base de données." For a biography of Alberdi see Jorge Mayer, *Alberdi y su tiempo* (Buenos Aires: Eudeba, 1963).
106. The Argentine community in Chile included men of letters but also members of the liberal and industrial professions. Bibliographical references to this community can be found in Pedro P. Figueroa, *Diccionario biográfico de estranjeros en Chile* (Santiago de Chile: Imprenta Moderna, 1900).
107. The problem of the introduction of representative republican institutions in societies marked by a similar colonial past was shared by the whole continent. A history of the Chilean press can be found in Raúl Silva Castro, *Prensa y periodismo en Chile, 1812–1956* (Santiago de Chile: Universidad de Chile, 1958).
108. On the place of images in Ibero-American culture, see the works of Serge Gruzinski, *La Guerre des images. De Christophe Colomb à "Blade Runner" (1492–2019)* (Paris: Fayard, 1990); S. Gruzinski, *La colonisation de l'imaginaire.*
109. See *El Grito Argentino*, 28 February and 14 March 1839.
110. *El Grito Argentino*, 4 April and 2 and 5 May 1839.
111. See *Muera Rosas*, no. 13, 1842.
112. See *El Grito Argentino*, 2, 9 and 20 June 1839
113. In the caricature which appears in issue 5 of *Muera Rosas* in 1842, the governor is depicted dressed in *gaucho* clothes as he presents his message to the House of Representatives of 27 December 1841. The legislators are drawn with donkeys' heads, a symbol of ignorance and darkness which evokes their obedience. The use of the donkey shows an attempt o reach a wider public by using popular symbols.
114. There are numerous references to methods used to distribute the clandestine press in private correspondence. See correspondence between Vicente López y Planes and his son Vicente Fidel López, in AGN, Colección de los López, room VII, 21-1-1 and 21-1-2; also J. M. Gutiérrez, *Epistolario de Juan M. Gutiérrez.*
115. See Ángel J. Carranza, *La Revolución del 39 en el sud de Buenos Aires* (1880) (Buenos Aires: Hyspamérica, 1988), 23.
116. I use the word "unanimity" to speak of a particular form of collective belonging founded on the existence of a unanimous community life, and not in the sense of the literary doctrine as understood by Jules Romains.
117. This image was principally constructed by the liberal opposition but was later adopted by a large number of historians. See J. Lynch, *Juan Manuel de Rosas*, ch. 6.
118. With the decree of 3 February 1830, Rosas made it mandatory for all public administration employees to wear the ribbon. This was reiterated in his second government. See P. de Angelis, *Recopilación.*
119. This decree was repealed on 15 February 1852. See "Decreto del 15 de febrero de 1852 declarando libre el uso de la cintilla punzó," in P. de Angelis, *Recopilación.* The reestablishment of the symbol by Urquiza triggered the revolution of 11 September. See chapter 5.
120. There are numerous reports of imprisonment for not wearing the Federal insignia, above all after 1839. See AGN.AP Index, x 44-10-2.
121. The mustache and sideburns had become symbols of the popular component of the Federation. These symbols were sufficiently rooted in the collective imagination to survive to the present day. Thus, former Argentine president Carlos Menem, born in

the same La Rioja province as Facundo Quiroga, carried out his entire first presidential campaign, in the *Partido Justicialista* primaries and then in the national elections, with large sideburns which allowed a comparison between the populist discourse characteristic of the twentieth century and the popular symbolic background of the nineteenth century. There were several allusions to the figure of F. Quiroga and it was no coincidence that Menem should choose as the first symbolic act of his government the repatriation of Juan Manuel de Rosas' ashes from England.

122. The mustache here has almost the same role as the flag. See "Prudencio Rosas da cuenta de la orden de usar 'vigotes' [*sic*] y de una acción contra unitarios de Chascomús," in E. H. Celesia, *Rosas, aporte para su historia*, vol. 2, 447.

123. Unfortunately there has been no research into the symbolic construction of the figure of Rosas. Some aspects have been analyzed in the author's article, "The 1829 uprising...," but a study of Federation imagery remains to be undertaken.

124. See A. Delacour, "Le Río de la Plata," 54–55; A. Delacour, "Voyage dans l'Amérique méridionale"; J. Rivera Indarte, *Rosas*, vol. 2, 180; *La Gaceta Mercantil*, 29 May 1840. As early as the *restauradores* revolution Rosas had given Vicente González precise instructions as to the use of his name and image. See E. H. Celesia, *Rosas, aporte para su historia*, vol. 2, 574–606.

125. See Ministerio de Educación de la Nación, *Catálogo del Museo Histórico*, vol. 1, 500–535. Some of these objects are reproduced in J. A. Pradère, *Juan Manuel de Rosas*.

126. Moreover, this process had begun in the popular semi-urban sectors during the rural uprising of 1829. See P. González Bernaldo, "The 1829 uprising."

127. On the revolutionary iconic system, see Jean Starobinski, *1789, Les emblèmes de la Raison* (Paris: Flammarion, 1979).

128. See "Juan Manuel de Rosas a Vicente González, 23 de marzo de 1836," in E. H. Celesia, *Rosas, aporte para su historia*, vol. 2, 468–469.

129. See "Ley del 30 de mayo de 1836," in P. de Angelis, *Recopilación*.

130. See Alfredo Taullard, *Nuestro antiguo Buenos Aires. Cómo era y cómo es desde la época colonial hasta la actualidad. Su asombroso progreso edilicio. Trajes, costumbres, etc.*, (Buenos Aires: Peuser), 172–174, especially appendix 3, "Plano topográfico de las calles de la ciudad de Buenos Aires, 1840–1845."

131. See T. de Iriarte, *Memorias*, vol. 5, 87–88.

132. See "Mensaje del Gobernador Juan Manuel de Rosas al abrir las sesiones de la legislatura de la Provincia de Buenos Aires," in *Registro Oficial de la Provincia*, 1837.

133. *Registro Oficial de la Provincia*, 1837, 31. See also Ezequiel Ortega, *¿Quiera el pueblo votar? Historia electoral argentina desde la Revolución de Mayo a la ley Sáenz Peña, 1810–1912* (Bahía Blanca: U. M. Giner, 1963).

134. Subsequent to this investigation, M. Ternavasio studied this issue in "Hacia un régimen de unanimidad."

135. See "Statut socioprofessionnel d'un échantillon de 47 membres de la Chambre de représentants de la province de Buenos Aires entre 1840 et 1852," in PGB, *La Création*, document no. 51, 372.

136. See the fluid correspondence between these two men in the Archivo General de la Nación, Colección Doctor Ernesto Celesia. Celesia himself published it in *Rosas, aporte para su historia*, vol. 1.

137. In a letter of 25 December 1838, Rosas responded to his cousin Anchorena's grievances with regard to the power granted to "that common man." "Rosas to Anchorena, 25th December 1838," in E. H. Celesia, *Rosas, aporte para su historia*, vol. 1, 629.

138. The average age of the members of the House of Representatives of the province of Buenos Aires increased in indirect proportion to the institution's power. Between 1827 and 1830 the average was thirty-four, reaching forty-five between 1832 and 1835, forty-eight for 1835–1840, fifty for 1841–1843 and fifty–three between 1849 and 1851. See PGB, *La Création*, appendix 1, "Base de données."
139. See Natalio Botana, *El orden conservador. La política argentina entre 1880 y 1916* (Buenos Aires: Sudamericana, 1978).
140. This explains the characteristics of the "Secretaria de Rosas" archives found in Room X of the National General Archive. The files are classified by year and make up a total of 121 files containing documents concerning twenty-three years of Rosas government. Within these files are a variety of documents on matters concering the military, politics, police, etc. See AGN's thematic index.
141. See Benito Díaz, *Juzgados de Paz de campaña de la provincia de Buenos Aires (1821–1854)* (La Plata, 1959).
142. Diaz, *Juzgados de Paz de ....*
143. Among nominative posts, those corresponding to financial administration presented the highest number of members in associations. In the rest, participation in the associative movement was almost nil.
144. Florencio Varela, "Juicio sobre el gobierno de Rosas," in *Rosas y su gobierno*, 25–28.
145. In his judgment, the promulgation of a National Constitution had to be the consequence and not the cause of union. Rosas expressed his constitutional ideas in a letter to Facundo Quiroga, dated 20 December 1834. See A. Sampay, *Las ideas políticas*, 145–149.
146. In a letter to Estanislao López, strongman of Santa Fe province, Rosas declared himself against the Representative Commission that had been established in the *Pacto del Litoral* of 1831 as supraprovincial authority responsible for organizing a Nation Federative Congress. Rosas assured López that he had no doubts as to the good intentions of the commission, but added that it was necessary that such transcendent questions, "be dealt with between us frankly and sincerely, in keeping with our friendship." See "Rosas a Estanislao López, Buenos Aires, 17 de mayo de 1832," in Andrés Carretero, *El pensamiento político de Rosas* (Buenos Aires: Platero, 1970), 86.
147. When, in 1849, Rosas rejected the reelection to the government of the province of Buenos Aires, he did so alleging that it no longer sustained the opinion of the other provinces and of the republic. The House of Representatives of Buenos Aires then had to set in motion the Rosista political apparatus in the rest of the provinces, as unanimist manifestations of the Federation. See J. Lynch, *Juan Manuel de Rosas*, 285–286.

PART II

The Nation In Power

(1852–1862)

On 2 February 1852 the Battle of Caseros put an end to the Rosista era and set the city alight with a triumphalist spirit that was as intense as it was ephemeral. No sooner had Rosas left the provincial government than the accord for the organization of the nation fell apart. The figure of General Urquiza, provincial "liberator" of Buenos Aires, arose more than reticence in the sector of exiled liberals and ultimately put them in opposition to the thirteen provinces.[1] The initial disagreements were followed by armed confrontations between Pro-Urquicistas (federalists) and Porteñistas (centralists or separatists), which threatened to submerge the city in civil war.

The way in which events occurred did not augur at all well for the city. In June 1852, General Urquiza dissolved the House of Representatives of the Province of Buenos Aires, which opposed the San Nicolás Treaty signed by the governor, Vicente López y Planes, and his peers from other provinces of the interior.[2] In July, López y Planes, a veteran of the revolution of independence who enjoyed great prestige among Porteños, was obliged to resign due to intense opposition to his national policy, judged too favorable towards Urquiza. The latter then took the helm of the provincial government and, in August 1852, nationalized the customs house of Buenos Aires. Subsequently, customs duties became the property of the nation, represented by Urquiza. With this measure, Urquiza obtained what Porteños had not attained for themselves: the union of the different sectors in conflict for power against the usurpation of the provinces of the interior. Usurpation of what? Of the nation, naturally, as both sides spoke in the name of the Argentine Nation.

On 11 September 1852, an uprising organized by the armed forces of Buenos Aires and known from then on as the Liberation Revolution rejected Urquiza's project and took over the government of the province. General Manuel Pinto, one of the heads of the movement, took over as caretaker president of the provincial legislature, restored by the September revolution. One month later, the same legislature elected the Porteñista Valentín Alsina as governor of the province of Buenos Aires. Alsina had to immediately deal with a new uprising, led this time by the Pro-Urquicista sector of troops in the "Great Army."[3] Colonel Hilario Lagos lay siege to the city from December to March 1853, when an armistice was signed between the authorities of Buenos Aires and Lagos' forces.[4] The status quo lasted barely a month. In April, with Urquiza's help, Lagos' troops established a blockade of the port of Buenos Aires which was successful at bringing about a fall in river and overseas trade.[5] The defenders of Buenos Aires finally defeated the besieging army in July 1853. Two months later, the thirteen provinces signed the Constitution of the Argentine Confederation. Buenos Aires refused to join and declared its own Constitution on 23 May 1854.[6]

This cursory overview of events occurring immediately after the fall of Rosas shows the extent to which the interests of the different provinces were still incompatible. It could not have been any other way, considering that the city of Buenos Aires intended to simultaneously direct the other provinces towards a North Atlantic economy and maintain its monopoly on the customs duties of the only Atlantic port. However, both the Argentine Confederation and the State of Buenos Aires fought to save the "Argentine Nation." Both then established legal order in the sovereignty of the people, which they assimilated with that of the nation. The deputy Bartolomé Mitre had no doubts over referring explicitly to this during discussions concerning the Constitution of the State of Buenos Aires. Mitre was opposed to the first article, which established the province of Buenos Aires as an independent State. "It is with great melancholy that I take the floor, as in spite of remnants of calm, principles of dissolution are those that dominate. If the House has a popular mandate, it is to establish a popular sovereignty. The People, just as the Nation, are indivisible principles."[7] Although the tendency represented by Mitre was a minority in the movement to vote in the Constitution, all recognized the Argentine Nation as a framework for the organization of the province. Ireneo Portela, a fierce Porteñista and minister of the government of the province of Buenos Aires, proclaimed with regards to the definition of citizenship during the debates on article 6 of the Constitution of the State of Buenos Aires:

> We declare today that the citizens of other provinces are citizens of Buenos Aires…as in including this article in the Constitution, we must declare constitutionally that we do not renounce our nationality, when all Argentines reach an agreement on our organization; but this will happen when this project is founded on the facts of reality.[8]

For Portela and for the majority of Porteños, this reality was that which recognized the primacy of the interests of Buenos Aires over the rest of the provinces of the

Republic. But the recognition of national sovereignty was indispensable for the organization of local power, hence the consolidation of the State of Buenos Aires represented in the spirit of the era an undeniable step towards the organization of nationality. The ten years of secession of the State of Buenos Aires would be, paradoxically, years of notable advances in the nation.[9] A nation with a territory of variable geometry, true, but which by a process which I will try to show here, identified with a public sphere that acquired a vigorous identity dimension. From this aspect there derived a civic representation of the nation that would prove important both in putting representative institutions into effect and in the emerging model of community belonging.

NOTES

1. On the history of this period, the most complete study continues to be James R. Scobie's *La lucha por la consolidación de la nacionalidad argentina, 1852-1862* (Buenos Aires: Hachette, 1964).
2. "Acuerdo celebrado entre los Exmos. Gobernadores de las Provincias Argentinas, en San Nicolás de los Arroyos." The text of the accord and the debates in the legislature from June 6 to 24 can be found in *Diario de Sesiones de la Sala de Representantes de la Provincia de Buenos Aires, 1852* (Buenos Aires: Imprenta Sociedad Tipográfica Bonaerense, 1864), 39–115.
3. This was the name of the coalition from the different provinces directed by General Urquiza to tackle Federation forces commanded by Juan Manuel de Rosas. The precariousness of this coalition army was well known, as shown in Domingo F. Sarmiento's account, published in November 1852; see Domingo F. Sarmiento, *Campaña del Ejército Grande* (Santiago de Chile, 1852; Buenos Aires: Kraft, 1957).
4. An account of events can be found in Ramón Cárcano, *De Caseros al 11 de septiembre*, Buenos Aires, 1918 and *Del sitio de Buenos Aires al campo de Cepeda (1852-1859)* (Buenos Aires: Coni, 1921).
5. According to the port authority's report published by the newspaper *El Progreso,* ships entering the port of Buenos Aires in December 1852 numbered 250, with a total of 17,342 tons; in May of the following year, only 83 ships and 2,713 tons. See J. R. Scobie, *La lucha*, 86.
6. The first article declared that Buenos Aires was a State possessing the free exercise of interior and exterior sovereignty, while the city did not explicitly delegate this in a federal government. See "Constitución para el Estado de Buenos Aires," in *Diario de Sesiones*, 1854, 114–119.
7. Ultimately, the Porteñista side obtained the majority in Constitutional voting This side grouped together the most radical sector of liberals with ex-Rosistas who defended provincial autonomy as a condition of economic development. See *Diario de Sesiones de la Sala de Representantes*, 23rd ordinary session of 6 March 1854, 37.
8. The difficulty that the problem of defining citizenship represented is evidence of tensions between the defense of local interests and the recognition of a superior sovereignty indispensable for the existence of a province, as the idea of province was one with the idea of nation. See the debate on this matter in *Diario de Sesiones de la Sala de Representantes*, sessions of 2–29 March 1854, 29–106.
9. On the diverse projects of national organization during this period, see Tulio Halperin Donghi's excellent analysis, "Una nación para el desierto argentino," in *Proyecto y construcción de una nación argentina, 1846-1880* (Caracas: Biblioteca Ayacucho, 1979).

CHAPTER 5

Buenos Aires and Its New Institutions of Sociability

Immediately after the overthrow of Rosas, the first English-style recreational club, The Progress Club, was founded by the Porteño population of Buenos Aires. At the same time the first regular Masonic lodge was inaugurated, the Amis des Naufragés lodge. This signaled a constantly growing wave of new associations, to the extent that it is possible to speak of an "associative boom," characterized above all as an urban phenomenon. This expansion reveals certain underlying needs, for which liberalism, benefiting from the port city's ascendancy during the ten years of the secession (1852–1861), appears to have been the trigger. "The fall of the dictatorial regime," declared the editorial of the newspaper *El Progreso* in April 1852, "has brought about a rebirth in men's desires to meet with others,"[1] desires fanned to a great degree by the government. This renovation of urban sociability can be measured not only in the number of associations but also in the increasing regularity of meetings. This sensation of social rebirth was heightened by an increase in the urban population and a notable sensation of relative political stability in the city.

The Social Reorganization of the Urban Space

With the end of what was then presented unanimously as the dictatorial Rosas regime, a sense of social rebirth gripped the city's population. Progress, measured by contemporaries by the intensity of social life, brought with it considerable modifications in the social organization of the urban space. The reactivation of exchanges was produced in the context of the disintegration of old sociability structures in the city, accompanied by the emergence of new public meeting spaces in which the development of exchanges took place through secondary, reversible ties. This phenomenon was intensified by the fact that the associative movement now tended to assume the city's administration, previously in the hands of traditional community structures.

THE GROWTH OF THE URBAN POPULATION

The transformations in the structure of sociability in the city must be considered within the context of a growing urban population. In 1838 the city had 69,400 inhabitants, rising to 82,400 in 1851 and 128,050 in 1862.[2] This demographic increase can mostly be accounted for by immigration, whether by migrants from other parts of the country attracted by the economic boom of the port city, or by increasingly numerous European immigrants. These were mostly of lower and middle class extraction, workers from the provinces selling their labor on farms and Europeans joining the secondary sector of the handicraft industry, for internal consumption, and the small business sector. The newcomers settled mostly in the northern and southern areas of the city: the parish of Nuestra Señora del Pilar in the north and the parish of San Telmo in the south (now divided between San Telmo and Barracas). Immigrants also settled in the Monserrat parish to the west of the center, where the population doubled (figure 14).

The high growth rate of these parishes in comparison with the others can be explained by the organization of economic activities in the urban space. The parishes bordering the countryside were generally home to slaughterhouse workers. Hence, the parish of Barracas saw mostly activities connected with the sale of livestock, the storage of leather and wool, meat curing and wholesale commercial exchanges in Plaza de la Constitución. The northeast area of the parish on the banks of the River Matanza, known as La Boca, was the center for river business and already home to a large percentage of inhabitants of Italian origin, specialists in river transport.[3] The artisan industry and the food trade were mostly concentrated on the west side of the city, including the parishes of Monserrat, La Piedad, San Miguel and San Nicolás, inhabited by the urban and semi-urban sector whose growth was due to the expansion of commercial activities. This area also had the highest proportion of workers of local origin, to a large extent African-Argentines, who were now registered as "natives" of Buenos Aires.[4] The historical center remained reserved for two basic functions: to the north, financial activities connected with the export trade of agricultural products, and to the south, cultural activities around the University and the nascent center of political activity. The city, especially the port area (the parishes of Catedral al Norte and Catedral al Sur), thus became the center of an important movement tied to cultural and economic exchanges with Europe,[5] and hence had the highest proportion of Europeans.

In comparison with the city during the government of Rivadavia, there was now a clearer trend towards social segregation in the urban space, with neighborhoods having a strong concentration of the same socioprofessional and ethnic groups. Far from strengthening the traditional structure of neighborhood sociability, the new model of urban establishment opened the barrio up to the city, which then became the place of public exchanges.

THE CITY AS A PLACE OF EXCHANGES

After the battle of Caseros in 1852, public gatherings and entertainment bloomed all over the city. The Chilean Vicuña Mackenna wrote that this street activity was indeed a circumstance of post-Rosista Buenos Aires: "In Buenos Aires the inhabitants seek spectacles in the street." For this writer, the difference with Santiago de Chile lay in the fact that here the notion of sociability was directly tied to gatherings outside the family circle.[6] Not only were Porteños fond of gatherings they also clearly understood that these meetings had a particular social value in the context of a public sphere extended to certain spaces in the city.

In his memoirs, published with the pseudonym Víctor Gálvez, Vicente Gil Quesada notes this bitterly. In an analysis of recent "disturbances" in "Society," he highlights this aspect in relation to the traditional network of family relationships. Now, for one to be known and appreciated by society, one's name was not enough, he laments, concluding, "if I were to frequent the Progress Club, if I were seen on the Calle Florida, if I were to gallop through the Parks of Palermo, if I were to go to the theatre, above all to the Colón, if my horses and carriages were to cross the Avenida Alvear, or Montes de Oca or Callao, the people would take an interest in Víctor Gálvez."[7]

Quesada thus evokes the loss of social prestige from the network of family sociability in a public sphere which subsequently would have its own forms and places of gathering and communications. This is not to imply that family networks lost their importance, rather that there was a notable transformation in the relationship codes identifying and defining the public sphere. Family gatherings would increasingly be confined to the private sphere, now associated with the feminine universe, while new relational habits and new public meeting places for the decent men of the city were developed. Hence when Vicuña Mackenna arrived in Buenos Aires he immediately contacted the Porteño "Society," which continued to be composed mostly of members of the same large families. In order to contact this society, "Félix Frías announced our arrival in a fragment of the editorial in his newspaper [*El Orden*], and soon we found ourselves in cordial communication with the diverse circles of Porteño society."[8] He would find these in the Progress Club, in the May Club, in the different salons,[9] and make contact with "Society" in these new institutions of sociability.

This new sociability, which chose the city and its public institutions as its stage, was in the eyes of the young Héctor Varela one of the elements that distinguished

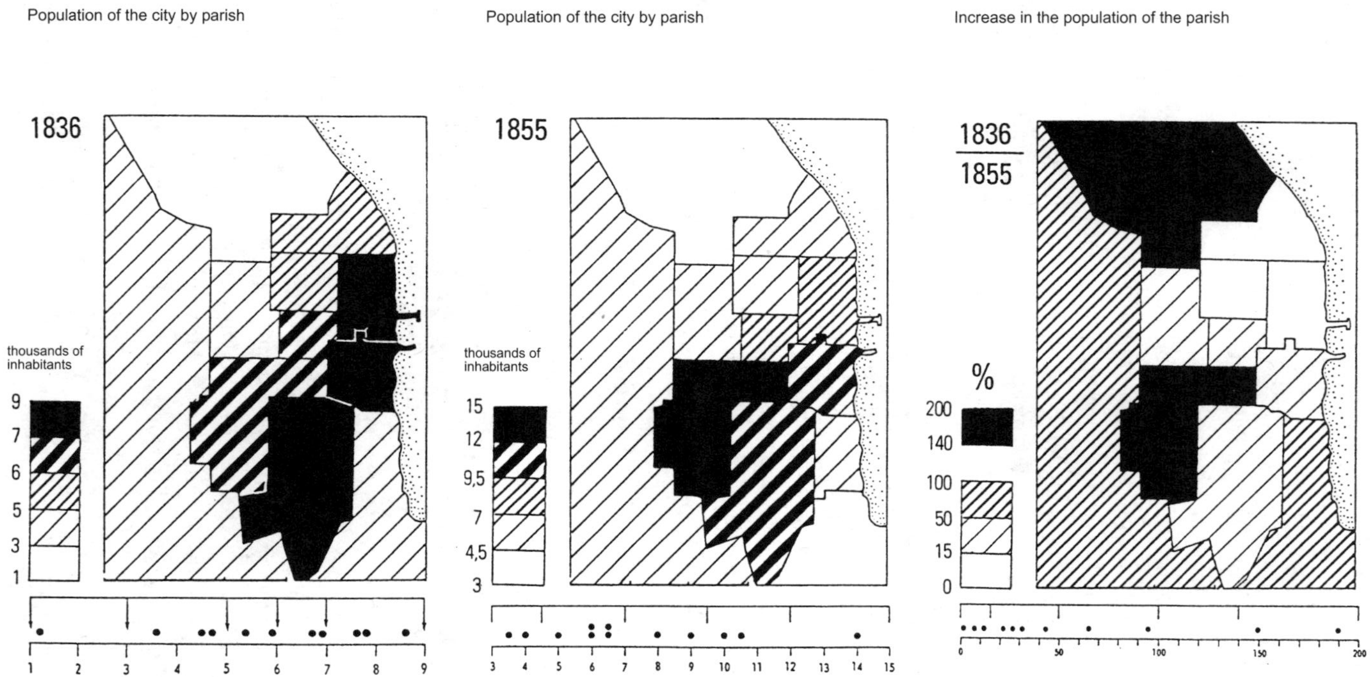

Figure 14. The Urban Population: Increase in the Urban Population of the City of Buenos Aires

A. Differential increase in the population between 1836 and 1855

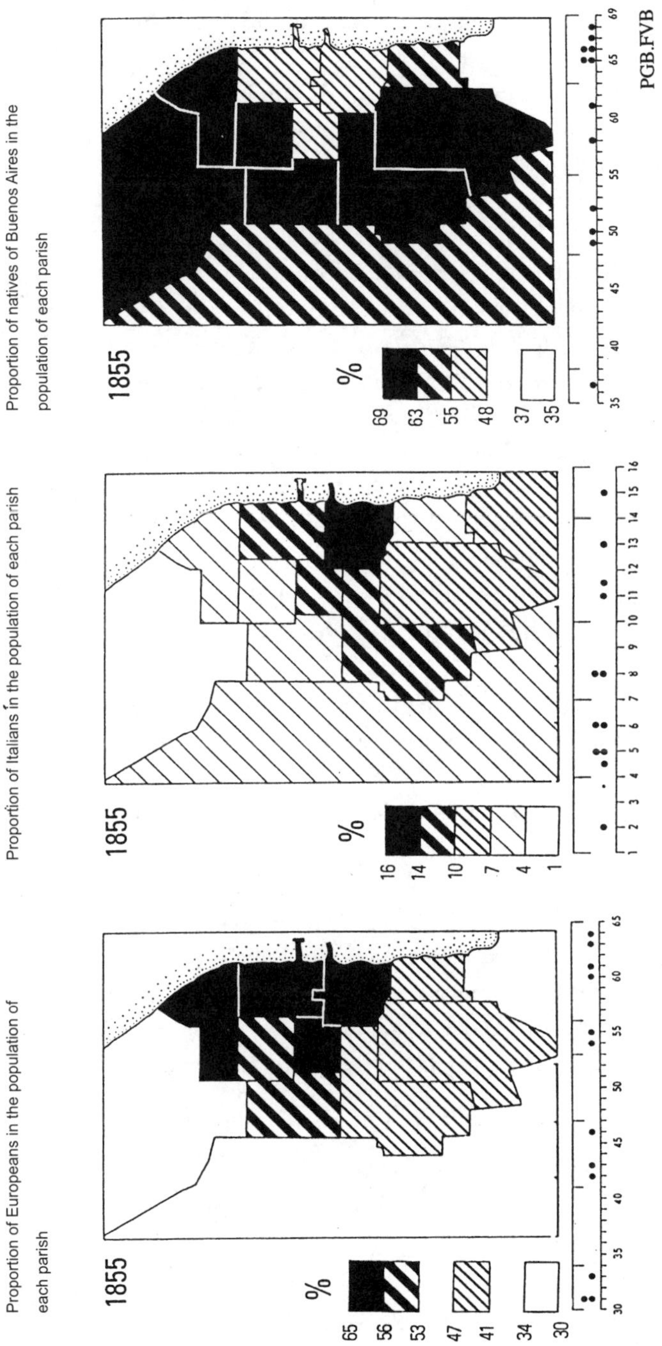

B. Effect of natives and foreigners on the increase in the population, by parish

a liberal society from the society characterized by the tyranny of Rosas. Varela gives a revealing example of events of a Sunday in the city. In his opinion, there was no comparison between the monotony of a Sunday in the 1840s and the joy and vitality of the following decade. Indeed, while in both cases the day began at the church, the social life of the post-Rosista years took place principally in the afternoon and especially away from the family home: afternoon strolls, outings to theaters or recreational salons at dusk, and gatherings in different clubs at night.[10] Varela highlights the public nature of sociability in the 1850s in comparison with the private character of the previous decade. This continued to provoke discontent among Catholics allied with liberalism. Félix Frías makes the following observation in his newspaper, *El Orden*, with regards to the unfortunate decrease in family salons (*tertulias caseras*):[11] "No doubt the sumptuous balls in the clubs do not entirely meet with the objective of nurturing social relationships as is the case in more private, frank meetings.... Ultimately, a luxury has been gained, but we believe that a real social spirit as been lost."[12] This real social spirit was, according to Frías, that of family sociability. Access to it was respected and the Church still had a say in the matter. The fact that it was Frías who introduced the conferences of Saint Vincent of Paul to Buenos Aires speaks volumes of the role that he intended for the Church in this new liberal sociability. In a public sphere predominated by forms of sociability based on a secularized notion of the social bond, Frías proposed other equally modern forms which still maintained charity as a foundation of the bond. This also explains the conflict, which from 1857, would set him against his university disciples initiated into the Freemasons.[13]

The Chilean Vicuña Mackenna corroborates this tension between old and new forms of sociability in the elites:

> There was much grumbling in all families about the detachment of youth. The houses we visited were effectively deserted, and those who have experienced the hospitality of Porteño ladies and those who admire the universal beauty of the daughters of the River Plate, will no doubt not forgive this frivolous preference for these boisterous clubs over domestic gatherings that we found most pleasant.[14]

After his many observations on Porteño sociability, Vicuña Mackenna reached the following conclusion: the particularity of the Porteños, which also accounted for the differences with the sociability of Santiago's residents, lay in the family. In Buenos Aires, families were far smaller than in Santiago, and this determined the independent and liberal spirit of a population in which there were many individuals, in comparison with Santiago, where a handful of families dominated.[15] The connection established here between the type of sociability and the importance of family size seems less original than the observation of the existence of families comprised of the sum of individuals, while others constituted a singular whole. This may suggest that, in Mackenna's judgment, one type of family would oppose the public sphere, while the other would be its complement. On this matter Vicuña Mackenna is quite perceptive.[16]

THE PUBLIC LIFE OF THE URBAN POPULATION

Clubs, associations, exhibition salons, and street theater enlivened a public life more intensely than the urban population had ever experienced. The city was seen as a place of sociability in the surveys exhibited in salons, in lithographs placed in trade almanacs and in maps that circulated in the hands of foreigners, particularly the map drawn by Grondona.[17] The inhabitants rediscovered their taste for public gatherings in squares restored to this end, along new urban and suburban avenues, in new private places intended for hosting these gatherings, such as leisure clubs and public salons, as well as during religious, secular or civic festivities.

Festivals took on a civil dimension, the likes of which had never previously been seen, just as society balls took on an undoubted political dimension.[18] This can be seen in the increase in society balls to commemorate political events.[19] The Progress Club's balls of 25 May (commemoration of the insurrection in the city of Buenos Aires) and 9 July (commemoration of the declaration of independence) became the place to be for "the crème de la crème of Buenos Aires."[20] The club even added to the calendar of commemorations a new civic festival, yet to be established by the government, to commemorate the Porteño revolution of 11 September 1852. The first public manifestation of this festivity was a ball organized by the Progress Club in December 1852, only three months after the event, with government members attending.[21] A few months later, for the anniversary of the revolution, the club organized a commemorative ball, which would later become a tradition in the dance calendar.[22] The prestige of the commemoration encouraged different clubs to participate in a dance competition to honor the event.[23] A few years later it was the government who took responsibility for organizing the festivities "of the revolution of September 11." There is no doubt as to their popularity, held as they were in the square and market of the same name, a kind of symbolic wall of the urban community. During the day the people of the city were offered *asado de cuero*, a traditional and very popular roast containing the basic foods of the rural population, and at nightfall "fireworks, balloons, and rockets set the show alight."[24]

After a long period of prohibition, carnival was reinstated, and with it, the public dances that accompanied these festivities, although the dances now clearly tended to move away from the African societies and become established in luxurious theater halls and leisure clubs. With this the well-to-do lost their aversion to carnival, mainly because the characteristics of the places where the festivities were held made a strict selection policy possible, especially in the Progress Club's balls, which could only be attended by invitation from one of the members.[25] This of course implied that with the change of clientele came a transformation of practices. Thus, with the success of the carnival balls among the elites, the formula of the masked ball appeared, which created quite a fury in the period.[26] Popular festivities did not disappear, but these celebrations also took place in private salons, at the expense of spontaneous manifestations in the street. African societies tended to lose their primacy in the organization of a festival, which at that time was celebrated in the *academias,* a kind of open-air café where the popular tango was developed and, unlike the *tambores*, was aimed at a popular multiethnic audience. Hence the fashion for public dances, which had spread among the well-to-do, also found favor among the working classes, who took advantage of the good disposition of the government towards manifestations of public entertainment to relive the old tradition of tambour dances, to which no doubt were added popular leisure practices introduced by foreigners.[27] The liberals' discourse concerning such manifestations was at times contradictory. They supported them because, for them, any manifestation of sociability was a feature of civilization, but at the same time they opposed them because these forms were considered uncivilized and were believed to cause moral degradation in the people. Héctor Varela recognized that the public dances had spread to the whole population, admitting that it would not be fair to ban the people from participating in these activities. His solution was far from original, but allowed him to solve the dilemma characteristic of young liberals: "may they be authorized but submitted to greater controls," he concluded.[28]

Aside from the differences, the masked balls of the elites and the dancing *academias* of the working classes shared the common feature of favoring gatherings in new public places, in comparison with those that had been structured around family networks and traditional social spaces.

Public Rooms, New Urban Sociability Spaces

As we have seen, during the first half of the nineteenth century, neighborhood sociability organized by parish conserved all of its vitality, to a great extent due to the *pulperías*, with neighborhood sociability cells evenly distributed over the urban space. Moreover, this organization of social space was corroborated by the topographic structure of the city. In this context, the location of cafés and associations indicated a break in the cultured community as a neighborhood sociability space. We will now see how this situation developed under the liberal government.

DECLINE OF URBAN PULPERÍAS AS PLACES OF POPULAR SOCIABILITY

In the table showing the evolution of the number of meeting places and places selling liquor in the city of Buenos Aires between 1825 and 1855, one observes that there tended to be a decrease in *pulperías* with the arrival in power of Juan Manual de Rosas.[29] While it may well be that this decrease is the result of a problem of sources, there is no doubt as to their decline in the short-term. The arrival of the liberals, which was beneficial for all forms of sociability, contributed directly and indirectly to the abandonment of these practices. Indirectly, in that due to the freedom of meeting and association *pulperías* were in competition with new forms whose novelty was often their principal attraction. The integration of new popular practices may have led to the abandonment of traditional forms of sociability. In Héctor Varela's newspaper, for example, one finds a report of various workers seeking to set up a savings account: "with the money they spend on the lottery or waste at the *pulpería*," it was possible to immediately set up "a savings account in the style of other civilized countries."[30] Naturally, "workers' letters" published in the liberal press can be regarded with suspicion. Very often this was the formula used by the liberals to transmit their message to the workers. Even so, the fact remains that there were people who received this type of message. Practices of sociability in the *pulperías* were too closely identified with the Buenos Aires of the Rosas era, which in the euphoria of the first years of the liberal government tended to be rejected entirely. This did not imply an abandonment of recreational practices, but as we will see, as these practices changed place, so too did their form and function.

The liberals had also contributed directly to the decline of *pulperías* through a policy of social control aimed at places of popular "perversion." Thus, in police archives one discovers that in 1853 there was an increase in the number of imprisonments for disturbances or organizing illegal gambling in *pulperías*.[31] The press echoed the aversion of the well-to-do to these popular places that "pushed the masses into delinquency, idleness and alcoholism."[32] The solution to the problem was in the hands of the municipalities, created by the Constitution of the State of Buenos Aires in 1854. The measures were draconian. Thus, in September 1854, *pulperos* in the town of 25 de Mayo in the southwest of the province complained of the municipal law prohibiting the sale of alcohol in *pulperías* in the area.[33] The example of 25 de Mayo was followed by other municipalities until in 1857 the municipality of the city of Buenos Aires limited, with the decree of 18 March, authorization to sell alcohol to cafés, hotels and *confiterías*, reducing *pulperías* to merely the sale of groceries. The effects of this measure where not felt immediately, firstly because the authorities had difficulties in enforcing the decree, as seen in a denunciation published in the local press of "gatherings of idle workers."[34] Gradually these reports began to turn on the *pulperías* in the suburbs, which suggests that those in the center tended to disappear or establish new relational codes to "civilize" the practice.[35] The decrease of *pulperías* in the city was not only the decrease of a place of popular sociability but also that of a cell of neighborhood sociability. With the change of place came a change in social spaces.

Parallel to the abandonment of the *pulpero's* counter as a sphere of neighborhood sociability came the emergence of new meeting spaces which took up the recreational role of neighborhood sociability. The first reference to the existence of these places dates from 1856 and shows even at this time the aversion of the well-to-do towards these practices: "The police can and must put an end to this bacchanalian behavior, closing these *academias* that only serve to demoralize the domestic class."[36] Subsequently, various newspaper articles would devote their energies to denouncing the scandalous behavior from these places: dances until dawn that disturbed the entire neighborhood, excessive spending that heightened the misery of the urban "plebs," and brawls among the participants which more often than not ended in wounds. According to the dates of the articles, the *academias* opened year-round on Saturdays and Sundays.[37] The premises had a salon for dancing and a counter for selling drinks.[38] The entrance fee went to the owner. It is not known what the fee was, but according to a newspaper article it was too high for a domestic servant.[39] It is most feasible that the success of the *academias* was due to a lack of festivities caused by the disappearance of the African societies. However, according to complaints published in the press, the practice spread rapidly among the urban population, although this type of establishment appears to have been most concentrated in certain areas. An article signed by the inhabitants of La Boca reveals that in 1859 the *academias* were already well established in the area with the largest population of foreigners, especially Italians, namely the Barracas barrio near the mouth of the River Matanza: [40]

> Fairly recently this kind of entertainment has appeared in our midst. There is nothing more harmful than this kind of entertainment, all the more so if one considers that the bulk of this population is comprised of day workers; in this respect we have heard complaints from a number of families, whose husbands, fathers or brothers have fallen into arrears due to the frequent expenditure that this kind of entertainment implies. As a result there are quarrels in the family home, excessive spending, frequent altercations, incessant brawling and

> shouting, the rest of the neighborhood is unable to sleep for part of the night, it upsets the families, it is a bad example for the children.... Moreover, crews leave their ships at night for the same reasons, jeopardizing the general interests of trade.[41]

There is no doubt as to the social extraction of the clientele. As an article in *La Tribuna* reports, they were "working class dances."[42] The *academias* were so closely identified as a popular practice that upon opening a "dance school" in the city of Buenos Aires the owner saw fit to clarify "that this school will only be open to society's decent men and classes."[43] Unfortunately, the lack of documentation prevents a more detailed investigation. Nevertheless, the limited data found constitute evidence of the existence of new forms of popular recreation.[44]

MALE SOCIABILITY IN CAFÉS

Contrary to the fate of the *pulperías*, the defeat of Rosas was rather beneficial for other drinking establishments, with cafés showing the greatest comparative growth.[45] The "geo-graph" showing the development of public places of sociability shows that their location differed from that of the 1830s.[46] They tended to leave the Manzana de las Luces and set up near the port or the new Paseo de Julio avenue. Other cafés opened along the principal streets of the city: Calle Rivadavia and Calle de la Victoria, from east to west, and Calle de las Artes and Calle del Buen Orden, from north to south. This change was related to the widening of the clientele base, which in turn modified the social function of gatherings.

As before, cafés continued to attract a clientele of aficionados of public discussions, especially young students. In addition, there were new clients from the associations that still did not have their own premises, such as the Tailors' Philanthropic Society which met at the Café del Gas.[47] Attendance at cafés also increased as a result of the appearance of a new form of sociability, the banquet, which established public discussion as an object for meeting and required premises serving food. The formula was adopted rapidly by political professionals, to whose needs the café owners quickly adapted, transforming their premises into café-restaurants.[48] One of many examples was the Café del Universo, owned by a Frenchman, announcing, "This establishment is today in a position to offer private salons for families and societies of fifty to one hundred and fifty places to those who so desire."[49] Another advertises the opening of the café and bistro Del Parral, with a meeting salon and banqueting for up to one hundred people.[50]

The success of cafés as places of urban sociability can be explained equally by the innovation of the services offered, which considerably modified the form of gathering. Indeed, with the appearance of the singing cafés came a formula that combined a place of conversation and entertainment. The first reference to this dates from April 1855, when the press announced the opening of the Café Filarmónico in Calle Chacabuco where, "for the entertainment of our clientele, every day from six to eleven there are songs with music, and on Sunday, April 22nd, Señor Montanciel will perform two shows, the first at eight o'clock with '*La Trompette de Marengo*', a military scene performed in uniform, and at nine o'clock with '*Le Travail lait à Dieu,*' a popular romance." The newspaper *La Tribuna* received favorably the innovation of "singing cafés" which increased the amount of public entertainment in the city.[51] It was then that the Café Del Siglo announced the addition of entertainment to the services offered by the establishment.[52] The Café de las Bellas Porteñas was next with an announcement of a concert in their salons.[53] The theatrical aspect of the stage design also attracted clientele, whether because the show was produced with mechanical means or with luxuriously exotic décor, or to enjoy, by dint of its location, the view of the gardens and the recreation of walking there. Hence, the Café Hotel Del Recreo, in the Plaza del Parque, published the following announcement: "The Café Del Recreo offers magnificent gardens where young people may stroll."[54] The Café Colón, near to the theatre of the same name, proposed prolonging the moment of recreation with a pause in this "new and great café which has come to beautify Buenos Aires and which is beginning to be the meeting point for the country's elegant society."[55] In all cases, the heatedness of gentlemen's discussions gave way to the benefit of a moment of varied entertainment in which the attraction of the show imposed itself on the contents of the exchange. With the emphasis now on recreation, cafés were given over to another form of entertainment, namely leisure salons.[56] In both cases, people went to see and be seen. The cafés' new role was confirmed by their location in the city, along the Paseo de Julio opposite the docks. The clientele of the new establishments was feasibly those out for a stroll in search of new forms of entertainment.

The appearance of café entertainment can also be explained by a mechanism of social differentiation. The fashion for these establishments emerged at a time when popular sectors were beginning to visit cafés in general, and there is much evidence that there was a relationship between both phenomena, all the more so in that these new fashionable cafés were more expensive. Prices were on some occasions twice those of other places, and there are numerous explicit references to the right of admission. The Café Filarmónico, for example, not only doubled its prices in the evenings but also imposed a dress code during the day, when the prices were the same as in other cafés.[57]

It would appear therefore that if the well-to-do class was seduced by this new formula, it was in order to distinguish itself from the new clientele in the cafés.

The tendency of a progressive decrease of *pulperías*, in addition to transformations in popular sociability practices, had driven the "urban masses" into the cafés. But if these replaced *pulperías* as a sphere of popular sociability, it was at the cost of a transformation in practices. The recreational role of the *pulperías* did not disappear, but conversation and discussion now took on more importance. The emergence of popular sectors in the cafés was therefore part of a general trend in popular sociability forms towards a greater specification of functions. This was only a trend, nevertheless, and very often evidence can be found of a continuing multifunctionality and often a confusion of forms, even when the popular sectors took part in associative practices. Here I have cited the case of a friendly association operating from a café, but one could also cite a contrasting example of a café that in order to attract clients offered an employment exchange for its parishioners. The establishment was called Café de los Artesanos, and in an announcement in the press, the owner states that the café, "also welcomes all kinds of laborers, working or not, who will find great comfort to rest from their labors, while those who seek laborers, cooks or servants can ask at this establishment to leave details of their house and we will send them workers of any trade; to help those who have no work and also those who need them."[58] The differences between this café's employment exchange and the "idle leisure" of the *pulperías* could not be greater. While these practices had been perceived previously as incompatible with the market economy, popular sociability now tended to be identified with the needs of the working class.

It can be concluded that a greater diversification was produced in sociability forms in cafés, which was related to the incorporation of the people—the working class—into these places. There was nevertheless a commonality between the elites' cafés, with their spectacles, and those that were meeting places for the working class. Namely, their specific establishment in a location in the urban space implied a break with the parish framework of sociability in the city. This trend, signs of which had been glimpsed in the 1830s, was confirmed by the increase of establishments and the spread of these habits among popular sectors.

THE "SALON-MANIA" OF THE ELITES

The "salons" in question here bore no resemblance to the salons of France. Porteños used the word *salón* to refer to a public room in which, upon payment of a fee, clients could enjoy themselves in good company. The deluxe furniture, the existence of a reading room with the principal newspapers of Buenos Aires and abroad, as well as the characteristics of attendance suggest bourgeois circles, with the exception that these salons allowed the presence of women and children. The location in the city, in the area with much entertainment and near to the

English-style clubs, confirms these analogies between circles and salons. But the particularity of this form of meeting lay in its role as a place of entertainment. Indeed, the principal attraction was the exhibition of "optical sights."[59] These were colored boards on different supports, which formed part of a system of an optical box with lenses and mirrors enlarging the view.[60]

The first salon created in post-Rosista Buenos Aires dates to 1854.[61] In 1855, with the name of Museo de Dioramas, it offered the well-to-do of the city "music, elegance, comfort and distinguished company."[62] It was an enormous success in "Society," which immediately began to meet in this elegant place where, along with enthusiasts of piano medleys played by a Señor Espinoza as background music, the eighteen works on display could be admired.[63] In March of the following year a new salon was opened which repeated the formula of the Café Del Recreo: comfort, good company and a visual spectacle. The particular attraction of its location near the Progress Club allowed the *clubmen* to alternate entertainment among men and recreation in the company of ladies. The proximity made the salon a kind of extension of the club, and the establishment was not long in becoming "the new meeting point" and the place to be for elegant society in Buenos Aires.[64]

Other impresarios followed this example and created new salons with visual spectacles. Soon the Nuevo Salón de Recreo, the Salón de Efectos Históricos, the Salón de las Delicias and the Salón Mecánico were all competing for the Porteño public. Their success may be accounted for by the fact that they combined two important elements: a distinguished public hoping to see and be seen and a spectacle which united luxury consumption with visual culture. While the success of the salons can be explained principally by the same mechanism of social differentiation that had led to the first singing cafés, their development should be considered in the context of the appearance of new visual forms created and disseminated during the revolution. The break with Spain had brought a crisis of symbolic systems which affected the symbols of royal power, and religious iconography was restricted due to the secularization of culture. This system was only partially replaced by new visual forms originating from the iconographic system established by the French Revolution.[65] There remained a vacuum of visual language, which would be partially filled during the twenty years of Rosas' government through the over-representation of his portrait. But the visual monopoly imposed by Rosas was far from translating a democratization of society images and tended more to substitute than to dethrone the symbolic system of royal power.[66]

Immediately after the defeat of Rosas there was a rich period of visual expansion of social imagery. History scenes and *scènes de moeurs* (scenes of local customs) constituted the new visual forms through which society was represented and exhibited publicly, and the salons were the first networks for the dissemination and consumption of this imagery. A wide variety of subject matter was exhibited in these views between the opening of the first salon and the end of our period, including[67] views of famous cities and breathtaking landscapes, great images from world history, the Bible and local history. The choice of visual consumption owed much, no doubt, to the arrival of images that began to circulate in the market. This did not alter the fact that the repeat exhibitions of certain views and the introduction of local themes expressed a reworking of the most common images on the local market. These could fulfill a considerable role in Porteños' identification with republican values. In historical themes, for example, there was a reiteration of views of events that affirmed these values. Salons would show images such as "Defense of the Port of Saint Denis in 1830," "The 1848 Revolution in France," "Exhumation of the Martyrs of Freedom in France," and "Garibaldi attacking French Troops in the Battle of 30 April 1849." While these cases may suggest that Porteño tastes counted for little in the selection of views that the European market had to offer, there is no doubt influence in selecting views showing local events, which accounted for nearly 50 percent of images on show.[68]

Rosas no doubt had the unfortunate privilege of primacy in subject matter. Except in the case of a natural disaster produced by an earth tremor, the qualification of "hideous" and other equivalents were reserved for him.[69] The tyranny of Rosas remained a subject of common identity and common disgust, to later become one basis for national identity. The victims would define the characteristics of the heroes in the period after independence. Two unifying themes appeared: that of independence and its deified heroes, such as San Martín, and that of the glory of Buenos Aires, from the valiant defense of the city against the British invasions of 1806 and 1807 to the "glorious battle of Pavón," the last armed conflict between the troops of Buenos Aires and the Confederation.[70]

At a time when liberals tended to revise earlier theories that idealized the autochthonous population of the Americas and understood them as victims of a Spanish State responsible for three centuries of "American slavery," another subject that deserves attention—representing around 30 percent of the sample—is that of the conquest and the Indians. It is important to remember that at the time when these images were displayed, Buenos Aires was going through one of its most difficult periods in the conflict with different Indian tribes in Patagonia. This accelerated the process of redefining the components of collective identities. The dissemination of these images, some of which pertained to choices made elsewhere, contributed to displacing the representation of the Indians in social imagery. The European theme of reviving memories of the conquistadors in a Europe at the height of imperial expansion was combined with images of rebellious Indians, enemies of the construction of a nation. Thus images such as: "The expedition led by Christopher Columbus sets sail from the port of Palos in search of the New World," "Columbus discovers America," "Triumphant landing of Christopher Columbus," and "Isabel I names Columbus Viceroy of the New World,"[71] were exhibited together with the likes of "The Indians punished by Washington for their alliance with the English against the North American people," "Combat between Washington's troops and some Indians," "A North American family ambushed by Indians," or with images of the conflict between the State of Buenos Aires and the Indians of the south: "The Indians' last invasion of Pergamino," "Great battle in the desert against the Indians, under the command of General Manuel Rosas,"[72] and "A family of Indians is caught by the lions." Next to these images of "barbarians" and "primitivism" are images of the latest progress from an industrial civilization which dazzled the ruling elites of Buenos Aires, such as "Grand Universal Exhibition in the Palace of Industry in Paris in 1855," "Crystal Palace of New York for the exposition of the industry of all nations," and "Universal Exhibition of Paris 1858."

The case of the salons shows the important role that the urban visual culture occupied in the creation of social imagery. As we have seen, there were principal themes that fixed certain images in the collective memory and gave a new identity to the city and urban culture. Common identity was only a step away from national history, which would be taken up by the historians of the liberal revolution in Buenos Aires. But long before this, images circulated in the Porteño salons supported the construction of a common memory.

The Association Boom

The renovation of the city as a place of sociability would be accompanied by a boom in associations, which was not only permitted, but encouraged by the authorities. Indeed, under the liberal government the restrictions concerning public meetings ended at the same time as limitations on press freedom were repealed. In 1854 the Constitution of the State of Buenos Aires made explicit reference to the right to peaceful meeting, which was now enjoyed by all of the province's inhabitants (article 149) and announced a future law with this respect.[73] After 1854, the associative form became the success formula for the urban population's sociability exchanges.[74]

Along with the rate of associative development the practice also became notably more institutionalized. Unlike in the earlier period, associations were not only more numerous but also more durable. This was especially the case with Freemasonry and some leisure clubs. The institutional stability can be accounted for by both the climate of freedom prevalent in Buenos Aires and by the tendency of these forms towards regularization and specialization. With the institutionalization of the practice, the period was distinguished by a greater diversity of associations: sociocultural associations, leisure clubs, esoteric associations, friendly societies, charity and aid associations, political associations, and so on. There was also a notable development of popular associative forms, in addition to the African societies. Friendly societies enjoyed considerable success, if their rate is compared with that of other forms already established in the region.

TAKING ROOT IN THE CITY SPACE

A cursory comparison of the map of cultural life in Buenos Aires between 1829 and 1852 and between 1852 and 1862 (figure 7) shows continuity in the organization of social and cultural space. However, on closer examination the document reveals more. Firstly, social and cultural exchanges tended to be centered around Plaza Mayor, modifying the nature of these acts. Theaters, which during our first period were outside of the central area, near the old Plaza de Toros (where bullfights were held), now regrouped around the city center. Parallel to this spatial recentering came the disappearance of popular elements such as circus attractions, dances, mimes, and comedy plays, as the theater became more clearly associated with literary culture.[75] The same occurred with leisure activities, which began to regroup in the cultural and economic center of the city.

Two areas can be observed to have been established in the center. In the southeast was a concentration of places of culture and power: the university, with the new Hall of Representatives, attracted an increasingly greater public (from street N to street S from north to south, between streets 02 and 09 from east to west). In the northeast a concentration of economic activities connected to the port and foreign trade emerged, including the stock exchange and the banking area (from street N to street J to the north, between streets 1 and 5 from east to west). The specialization of these areas in turn circumscribed certain regroupings of associations around these poles. Sociocultural associations were situated mostly in the center, in the parish of Catedral al Sur, around the culture barrio. Three of these operated on the premises of the university, next to the public library. The others were distributed fairly homogenously around the university, on the streets Rivadavia (N), Potosí (P) and Belgrano (R). In the same area was another form of association previously unknown to Argentine society: English-style leisure clubs. The city's clubs were situated in an area between the streets Rivadavia (N), Chacabuco (06), Moreno (Q) and Defensa (03), in which the university and the largest concentration of bookstores and publishing houses were found. Entertainment and cultural consumption were, at least geographically, two closely related functions defined by their common urbanity. For nature lovers there were the clubs on the outskirts of the city. Here, the city and the countryside catered to similar tastes and needs for bourgeois sociability. When meetings were among men and for discussions, they were held in the luxurious salons of the city, while when they were with the family and for recreation, they took place in clubs in the villages near to the city, namely Flores and Belgrano six miles away and San Isidro twelve miles away.[76]

On the north side of the central area were concentrated socioeconomic associations and clubs connected with port activity, meeting centers for traders which brought together bourgeois leisure and business. Also to be found here were foreign traders' associations in operation since the Rosas period, such as the Foreign Residents' Club and the English Chamber of Commerce. This was also the area where two of the city's three theaters were located, the Colón and the Argentino. The combination of business and pleasure is confirmed by the location of the Supreme Council and the Grand Orient on the first floor of the prestigious Colón Theater (3 between N and M).[77] Towards the west, half a mile from the port, were concentrated the friendly associations who organized the artisans of the city, to a considerable extent of foreign origin. Further southwest of the center were the African societies, far less numerous than during the Rosas government but located in the same area on the edge of the city. The existence of concentrated areas can be interpreted as a similarity or even multifunctionality in certain associations. Thus, the function of entertainment was related to the consumption of culture while bourgeois circles were associated with the business world. Two associative forms were distinguished by their fairly homogenous distribution around the city: religious associations (fraternities and Third Orders) and electoral clubs. With regards to the former, available data are too scarce to attempt any kind of analysis. In contrast, the latter will be seen more extensively in studying political sociability. It is significant, nevertheless, that these associations had the same spatial organization as the religious community. This could constitute an indication of the weight of neighborhood sociability in these two types of organization.

How can the uneven distribution of associations in the urban space be explained? This imbalance suggests that these associative forms constituted, with regards to traditional forms of sociability, an alternative model situated by necessity outside of the framework of neighborhood sociability. Were these parish residents or an urban population which moved around the city in order to satisfy different sociability needs? To answer this question the addresses of the associations' members are needed. As this information is lacking, I will try to infer it through other means. With this end, I compare the map of association distribution with a series of maps containing demographic and sociocultural data.[78]

Figure 15 clearly highlights the different concentrations of associations by parish. The parish with the most associations was Catedral al Sur, followed by Catedral al Norte and Monserrat. It is possible that the greater number of associations was due to a greater number of inhabitants. However, if this map is collated with density of population, it can be observed that the parishes with greatest population density were not those with the highest concentration of associations. Therefore, although population distribution had consequences on association location, there was no close correlation between the number of inhabitants and the number of associations.

The map of literacy by parish shows, on first reading, a correlation between literacy and the establishment of associations. The parishes with the highest level of literacy were those with the greatest concentrations of associations: Catedral al Norte and Catedral al Sur. But where does this leave the parishes of San Miguel and Nuestra Señora del Socorro, with a proportion of literate population varying between 60 and 65 percent and a limited number of associations? Besides, it can be seen that on the whole the population of the city had a high level of literacy, the lowest percentage still being over 30.[79] In reality, the disadvantage of this correlation is that literacy is not itself an indicator of the cultural fusions that imply the development of associative relationships. While it was a necessary condition for reading newspapers, by itself it tells us little of the nature of the level of education, which conditioned the choice of reading. Hence it is difficult to explain the topographic organization of one of the first friendly societies, due to the fact that, because of their trade, these artisans had a level of education that set them apart from other manual workers.[80] What distinguished them from the others was not the level of education but rather its nature.

It appears more productive to collate the map of association distribution with that of population distribution according to ethnic-cultural origins. The associations may have been established where the concentration of European populations was greater. In order to prove this hypothesis, we have deliberately distinguished the percentage of Europeans in relation to the European population of the city and in relation to the population of each parish. This shows that associations were not necessarily established where the foreign population was a majority. Hence, the parish of Barracas, with a strong concentration of Italian immigrants, had few associations even while the Italian population was one of those most affected by the associative movement.[81] The same was the case of residents originally from the province, who were concentrated outside of the city's cultural and political center, in places in which the establishment of associations was almost nil. Elsewhere, the map of the proportion of natives of Buenos Aires in the population of each parish represents a similarly insignificant figure in terms of establishment of associations.

In short, the element that appears to determine most the establishment of organizations is the presence of a mixed population, with a considerable percentage

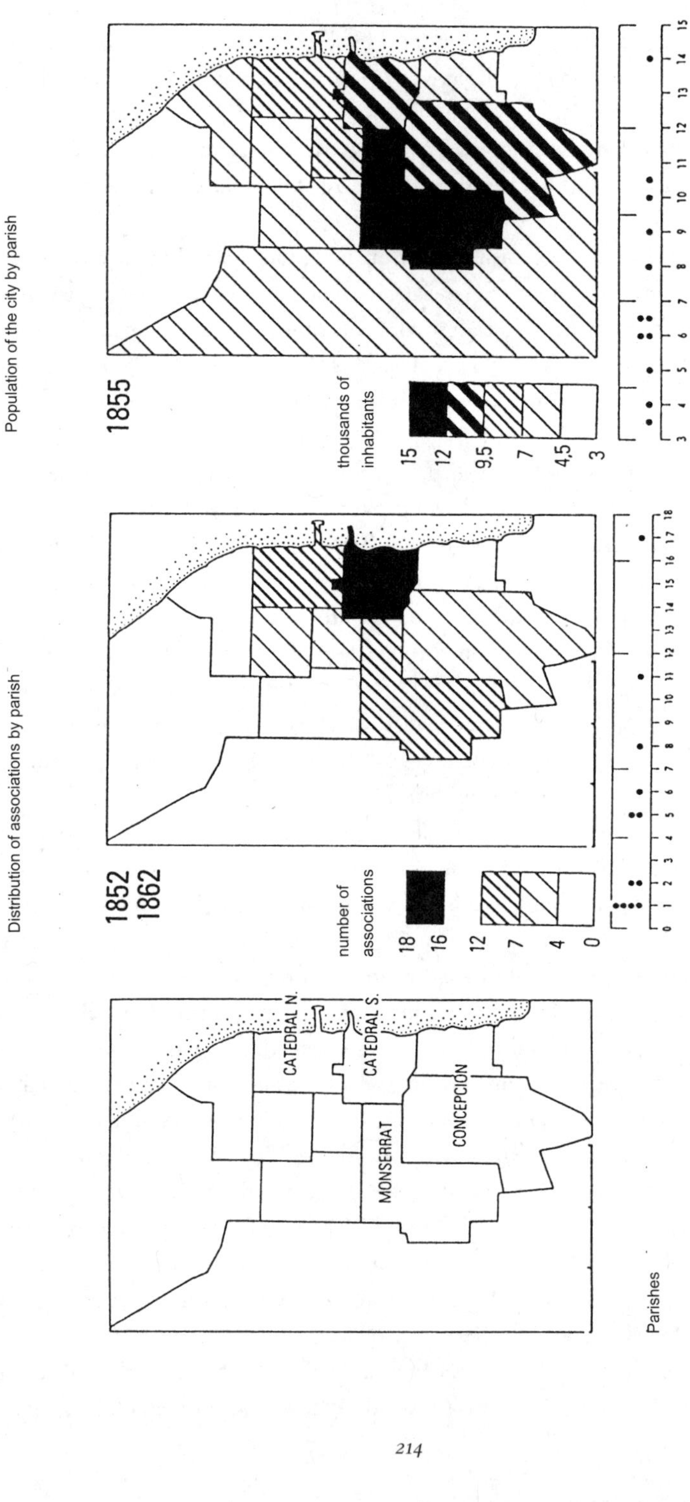
Population of the city by parish
1855
thousands of inhabitants
15
12
9,5
7
4,5
3
Distribution of associations by parish
1852
1862
number of associations
18
16
12
7
4
0
Parishes
CATEDRAL N.
CATEDRAL S.
CONCEPCIÓN
MONSERRAT

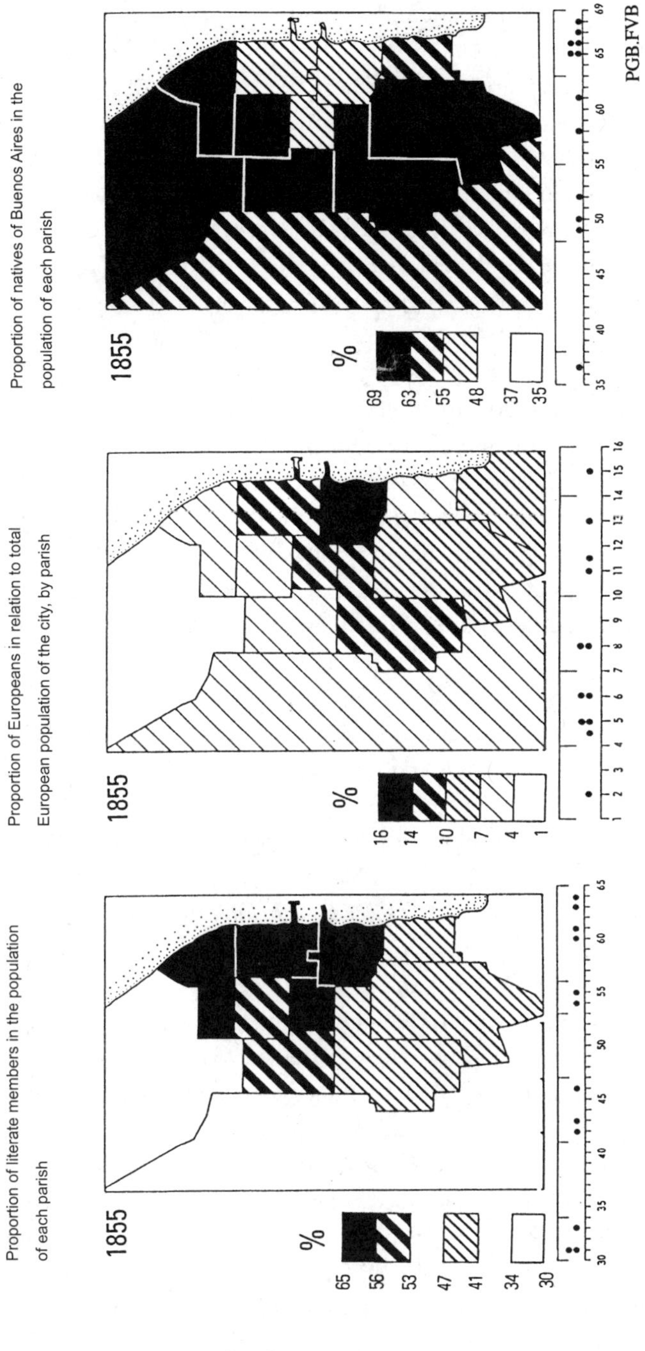

Figure 15. Distribution of Associations in Relation to Ethnic-Cultural Origins of the Population of the City

of residents of European origin. To this can be added the attraction of the political, economic, and cultural institutions found in the historic city center. Moreover, while the sociocultural origins of the population conditioned the location of certain associations in comparison with others (for example, African societies established in the Monserrat parish with its strong concentration of blacks, just as friendly societies grouped together in the parish of San Miguel where the artisans of European origin were the most numerous) the model of establishment tended to break with the organization of the urban space through neighborhood sociability and fixed to the parish. The association did not attract inhabitants of the barrio, but individuals with a series of shared interests and values. We will return to this later.

THE AGENTS OF DISSEMINATION OF THE LIBERAL ASSOCIATIVE MODEL

Associative relationships were nothing new for the inhabitants of Buenos Aires. However, until 1852, the phenomenon concerned a highly restricted sector of the population. For the rest, relational practices were limited to the network of informal relationships woven around primary ties or traditional organization forms. From 1852, associative forms multiplied and diversified. The liberal government no doubt contributed to the development of the associative movement, which in its judgment generated values fitting of a free republican society.[82] Nevertheless, it would be naïve to claim that the rise in associations was due to the city inhabitants' explicit will to align themselves with the liberals. Associative practices were effectively in line with ideology, and much can be found from analyzing the nature of this relationship, but we cannot reduce this analysis to political history. The actors were not necessarily conscious of the ideological commitment involved in learning new relational practices. On the contrary, the act should be related to fashionable phenomena, often tied to mechanisms of social differentiation in which imitation was imposed on a previously discussed choice. In any event, it was necessary for agents to introduce and propagate new practices by their own example. However, the observation of the movement's chronology highlights the role of foreigners in the rise of the associative movement, as figure 16 illustrates.

In the different columns of the figure, the same model is produced: appearance of the associative form among foreigners and considerable development, from 1852, among Argentines. While, as the French writer Delacour wrote with regards to French Basques in Montevideo, "the enthusiasm for pleasure and society perpetuated the union of the Basque population,"[83] these men, while remaining faithful to their old customs, were important agents in the dissemination of new relational practices beyond the Basque community. Hence it was foreigners who, in reproducing practices from their own countries, introduced innovations in the social life of the society receiving them. In spite of this, the model of dissemination was not the same. Above all there are notable variations in the chronology of their appearance. Hence foreign lodges appeared later than in Europe, but they did appear before friendly societies established themselves in Buenos Aires and after they appeared in the old continent. We also find differences and even inversions in the social model of propagation of practices.

This was the case with freemasonry, which contrary to the process in Europe, was developed principally among foreign artisans and later become established among the local elites. While it is true that some lodges had operated in Buenos Aires during the first half of the nineteenth century, these were somewhat short-lived. With some exceptions, the local population ignored their activity. In 1850 a French vessel was shipwrecked on the western banks of the River Plate. Among the crew were various Freemasons, who organized a lodge and immediately appealed to Freemason solidarity for assistance. The circumstances of the creation of this lodge were described by its Venerable in a letter written to the Grand Orient in France: "Given that a work of fraternity was necessary, above all in a foreign country..., we joined together and established a lodge, which took the distinctive name of 'Amie des Naufragés' [Friend of the Shipwrecked]. Shortly after founding the lodge it fell into a state of lethargy due to the lack of interest from the government of the time." After the defeat of Rosas, the Venerable Ferdinand Bayan would petition the Grand Orient of France to concede them Masonic constitutions.[84] Of the 13 brethren making up the list of members of the Amie des Naufragés lodge in 1853, only two were from the Les Amis de la Patrie lodge in Montevideo. The others had been initiated into French lodges in Paris, Strasbourg and Sète, among others.[85] No Argentine would take part in the lodge, although in theory this was not prohibited. The reason for this "indifference" was undoubtedly due to the socioprofessional extraction of its members. Of the 182 brother Masons on the lists of the lodge between the date of its constitution and 1862, 40.6 percent were artisans. However, the handicraft profession in Buenos Aires was still greatly marked by socioethnic divisions, a result of racial prejudices tied to the considerable presence of a black, former slave labor force. Consequently, associative practices had notable difficulties in overcoming the stigmas of the old caste societies. Hence those in Buenos Aires who were more susceptible to being attracted to this new practice—the cultural elite of the city, some of whom had already been initiated into the Masonry in exile—were no doubt discouraged by the presence of low social classes.[86] Shortly later, certain members of the English community created the Excélsior Lodge No. 617, with the constitution of the Great United Lodge of England. I have not been able to consult the archives of this organization, but according to documents published by the Masons, the

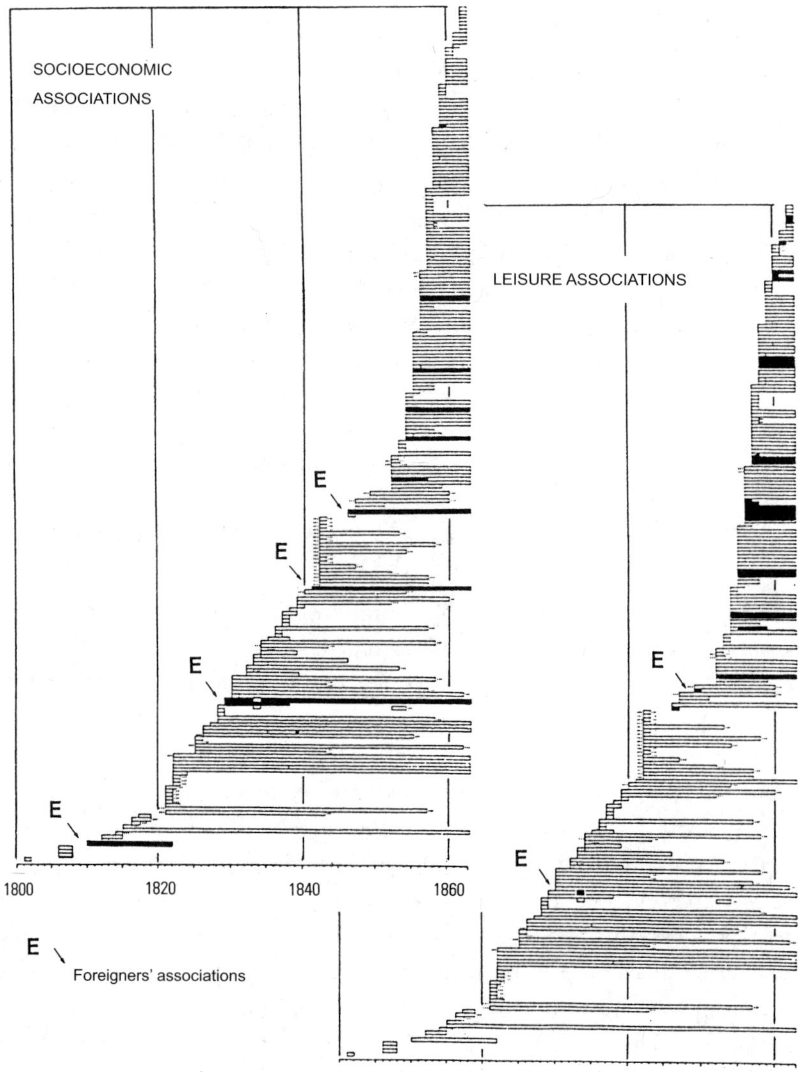

Figure 16. Presence of Foreigners' Associations in the Associative Movement

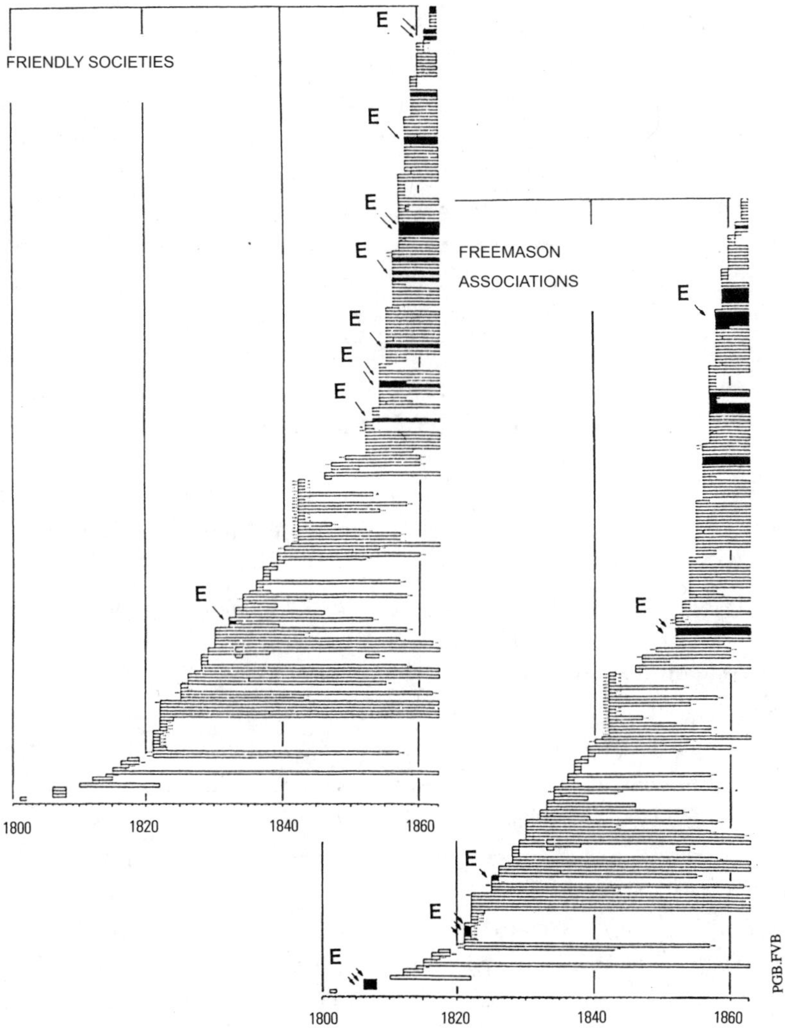
FRIENDLY SOCIETIES
E
1800
1820
1840
1860
FREEMASON
ASSOCIATIONS
E
1800
1820
1840
1860
PGB.FVB

lodge did not recruit its members from the local population.[87] Only three years later the first national lodges appeared, made up almost entirely of the well-to-do. Between 1856 and 1862, only 5.37 percent of the members of the national lodges were artisans or storekeepers.[88] This then was an inverse model: foreign artisans introduced Freemason lodges, which were later developed by local elites.

The associationist potential of foreigners can be explained by the confluence of two circumstances: above all, their earlier associative experience, as some reproduced in their adoptive country practices learnt elsewhere.[89] There was also a lack of primary ties, and without connections in local society they managed to create a network of relationships that could replace these ties.[90] Thus, in most cases what drove foreigners to form organizations was the need for ties of solidarity, although the stated objectives may not have been mutual welfare. The tendency appears to have been towards the recreation of community ties in the adopted country through associations of fellow countrymen, which rather than reproducing past ties, in fact created an ethnic identity.[91] But to replace primary ties they turned to the associative form, founded on secondary ties, with which they introduced notable innovations in their relational universe and in that of the society receiving them. In choosing the associative form of relationship, foreigners positioned themselves outside of the context of the traditional educated community, which contrary to what might be supposed, facilitated exchanges with the local population as relationships between foreigners and nationals could be struck up outside of traditional forms of collective life. This was done not necessarily through the effective integration of the latter into the associations of the former, but through the development of the associative model which implied the existence of shared relational codes and values, from which the associationist metaphor of the nation as a community of belonging could be constructed. This was expressed by the president of the Buenos Aires Typographic Society, himself of foreign origin: "Under the sky of America and on the soil of the republic, speaking a different language and deriving from different customs, I feel today that I am a son of the century, equal under the rules of modern civilization and, most surprisingly, united with the men around me by ties of brotherhood and of the supreme communion of mutual aid."[92] Luis Pinto's words are unequivocal. Even when the objectives of the association were strictly social, the practice implied a set of common values identified with by all those who shared them. Pinto speaks of modern civilization, of brotherhood, of the century, to evoke what united all men, even though they spoke different tongues, under the American sky: republican values. It is interesting to see that he uses a term which defined the traditional community, the soil, to distinguish a new belonging which competed with the principles of this community: the Republic.

Among the agents of propagation it is necessary to make a special mention of the role of those exiled by the Rosas regime. Due to this condition and their political commitments, they tended to develop associative practices in exile. On returning to Argentina, they reproduced these practices among their companions in misfortune. For example, Bartolomé Mitre, who was part of the Historical and Geographic Institute of Uruguay, established in Montevideo on 25 May 1843, would later in 1854 found the Historical and Geographic Institute of the River Plate, formed by exiles of the Rosas regime.[93] A similar example is that of Domingo Faustino Sarmiento, who in 1854 was initiated into a Freemason lodge in Chile, The Unión Fraternal lodge of Valparaíso, with the Porteños Francisco Álvarez de Toledo, Mariano E. Sarratea, Javier Villanueva and Jacinto Rodríguez Peña.[94] On their return to Buenos Aires, many of them went on to found with others the first Porteño lodge, the Unión del Plata. While exiles at first favored meetings with fellow exiles, they shortly incorporated a vast sector of the Porteño elite into their relationship network. In the Unión del Plata, for example, there was a group of thirteen Masonic brethren, of whom at least seven were initiated in exile.[95] Of the new members, those like the Portuguese trader A. Alves Pinto arrived in the country already holding a high rank in the institution. Traders and landowners such as Miguel Martínez de Hoz and Carlos Casares entered the Freemasons through men such as Alves Pinto. Although at first the lodge was composed mostly of political exiles, in a short time the proportion of former exiles to businessmen and traders with no notable political past was reversed. Freemasonry spread rapidly in a wide sector of the well-to-do, which easily exceeded the sphere of the intellectual elites. Within six years, a handful of exiles who decided to reproduce in Buenos Aires an associative practice acquired elsewhere formed a network of 924 Masons.

DIFFUSION OF THE ASSOCIATIVE MODEL AMONG THE LOCAL POPULATION

The favored sphere for the diffusion of new associative practices was that of the sectors of the local population who maintained frequent contacts with foreigners, particularly traders and intellectuals. In a sample of 1,215 members of different associations created in Buenos Aires between 1829 and 1862, from a corpus of 2,248 people, the individuals connected with trade made up 30 percent. If businessmen and traders are grouped together, the results are all the more striking:[96] 39 percent of members of associations were traders, followed by intellectual and liberal professions, which made up 25.5 percent. In contrast, the sector of major landowners only accounted for 8 percent of the sample. According to MacCann, their reticence may have been due to the fact that this sector was divided into two categories, "those who want to adopt European habits, which they imitate, and those who prefer to preserve the customs of the country....Generally the

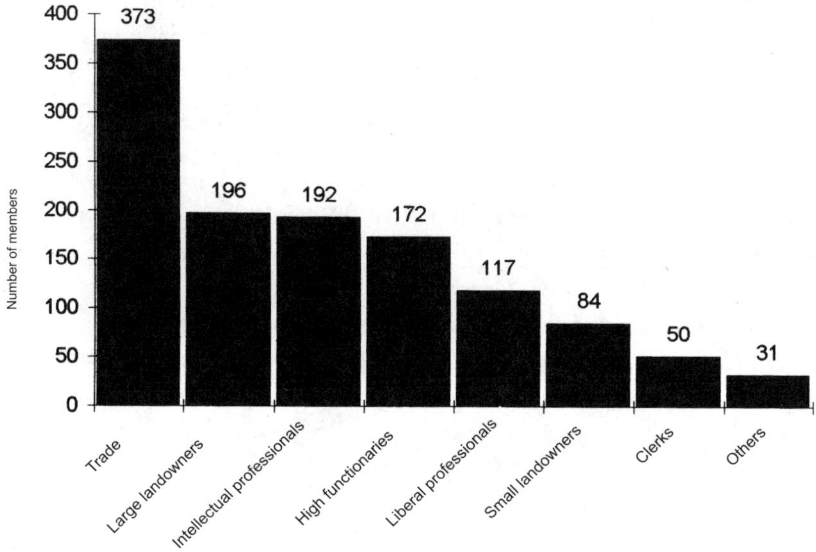

Figure 17. Socioprofessional Status of a Sample of 1,215 Members of the Associations in Buenos Aires between 1829 and 1862

landowners who wish to adapt their customs to European life are those who, accidentally or on purpose, have connections with Buenos Aires' foreigners."[97]

The popular sectors, however, were not left out of the associative movement, although their practices were developed above all with the aims of solidarity, philanthropy and social security. This was the case with friendly associations, which experienced growth among this sector during this period.[98] The first experience in this sphere was that of French artisans in 1832, without sequel until 1853, when the same artisans created the Philanthropic Charitable Society of the Hairdressers of Buenos Aires.[99] From then on, the development of friendly societies occurred at a more regular rate: one each in 1854, 1855 and 1856, four in 1857, three in 1858, one in 1859 and 1860, two in 1861 and one in 1862, according to the information found in police archives and the press of the period.[100] Most of these associations were formed by and made up of foreign artisans, more often bringing together workers from the same geographic region than from the same trade. Their function was the same as in Europe: charging a monthly fee, the societies aimed to raise funds in order to help its members. They guaranteed sick pay and support for the family of the member in the event of death. Other functions included a savings account for members and providing means for the development of centers of instruction and training in manual arts in order to improve the worker's condition. At times the statutes of the association even included the creation of cultural centers.[101] The success of the formula can be explained by the fact that the mutualist model of common welfare responded very well to the needs of its affiliates, such as workers and immigrants. These associations thus assumed two entirely compatible objectives: solidarity and philanthropy among natives of the same country, in connection with protective organization aimed at improving the worker's condition, all the more difficult in the case of a foreigners. According to the French traveler Martin de Moussy, who traveled around Argentina until the late 1850s, these associative forms had difficulties in developing among Argentine workers. This republican, who was close to Argentine liberals, observed with regards to friendly societies: "They are made up principally of foreign workers. Few nationals have so far entered them, as until now they do not appear to have realized their usefulness. Furthermore, as we have previously intimated, the spirit of association is not yet particularly developed in the country."[102]

De Moussey's observations are not entirely exact, however, as the mutualist movement also spread to the natives, alongside the growth of popular sociability forms that were already established in the local population. This was the case of African societies, which already provided mutual assistance to the members of the same ethnic group (nation), and which in this period would evolve towards more clearly mutualist forms of organization.[103] The earliest example can be found in 1855 in the documentation concerning the Abaya society.[104] Without abandoning the organization of dance gatherings, this society gave priority to its aid role.[105] The second reference is the Brazilian Protection Society, created in Buenos Aires in 1856 in the mould of African societies. In the first article of its regulations we find a significant modification: while the objective of African societies was to "emancipate with its funds those members who prove themselves to be proud by their morality and industry," the Brazilian Protection Society declared that its objective was to "promote the spirit of association and mutual protection."[106] Contrary to Andrews' suggestion, festivals and dances did not disappear, but became a parallel activity and generally were no longer financed with the society's funds. This was established by article seventeen of the regulations: "The funds of the society are intended for charitable work. In the case of the commission approving the organization of a dance or extraordinary festival, it is authorized to invite members to contribute voluntarily to such organization."[107] Gradually, sociability around ties of solidarity abandoned the recreational role with its strong ethnic connotation, favoring the aspect of mutual aid among workers. Certain features of the fraternities-associations persisted, hence members were obliged to accompany the ill and go to members' funerals. Another sign of these features can be found in the name of the societies—for example, the Carmelo Friendly

Society—and in the date chosen for its establishment—"Easter Sunday, the day of the resurrection of Jesus Christ"—while the Typographers' Friendly chose to begin on May 25th, a visibly more political and secular symbol. The third example of the growth of black associative forms is the recently mentioned Carmelo Friendly Society, created by African-Argentines in 1858. Like previous associations, it was mixed, and according to the only document in our possession, retained many features of African societies,[108] but as in other cases certain innovations made the ethnic associative form evolve towards a friendly society.

It is most probable that the evolution of African societies towards mutualist forms was related to the propagation of friendly societies among foreign artisans. That they appeared simultaneously is significant. It is feasible that the African-Argentines, with a vigorous associative tradition and knowing the benefits of new practices, introduced new functions without abandoning their much-liked acts. The fact that these associative forms developed above all among the black population might constitute, moreover, a response to the limited development of the mutualist movement among Porteño workers. However, this movement managed to establish itself outside of the context of ethnic solidarity. In this period, we find examples of friendly associations born from a more corporative than philanthropic initiative. The best known case is that of the Buenos Aires Typographic Society, founded in 1857 by publishing artisans: printers, lithographers, bookbinders, and national and foreign booksellers.[109] This society had two fundamental differences from previously known forms: it was organized strictly by trade and included both nationals and foreigners. From these first forms of workers' organizations were born the first expressions of the workers' movement. According to documentation found by Falcón, this typographic society would be the first to make contact with the International Workers Association in 1860.[110] The institution had significant characteristics distinguishing it from other mutualist societies. It incorporated functions typical of sociocultural associations heretofore specific to the Porteño elite: the establishment of a meeting place, the publication of a newspaper, and the creation of a public library. Article 21 of their regulations established that: "absence from meetings is unforgivable, as they are the basis of any association." In turn, the importance of sociability relationships in the associative context would be highlighted by the society's different chairmen.[111] Mariano Varela, the first chairman, announced in a speech the commission's intention to collect the principal newspapers of the capital in order to facilitate reading said papers on the society's premises. Later, the commission decided to found a library, a project that appears to have been successful. The *Diccionario de Buenos Aires* of 1862 informs us that a library functioned within the society, "which is visited every night and on Sundays by members but also those who wish to visit and members' guests."[112] In

1858, Varela announced in *La Tribuna* the future appearance of the newspaper *El Tipógrafo Argentino*, an organ of the society which was not eventually published.[113] Here we discover, along with the corporative objectives, the enthusiasm for public meetings and discussions tied to forms of intellectual entertainment previously seen in the elites. These practices constituted a bridge in a society polarized by the new practices of the elite and traditional sociability forms which still characterized the practices of the urban masses.

With regards to post-Rosista social life we can conclude Buenos Aires was a city whose inhabitants multiplied their relationship forms. It is not only the number and plurality of forms that can be highlighted. The particularity of each area of attraction meant the displacement of inhabitants in order to satisfy their sociability needs. From the club to the salon, passing through the theater and public dances, the elites crossed the city to meet among peers rather than among neighbors. Popular sectors did likewise: *academias* and cafés were meeting points, which indicates the displacement of this group. To be sociable it was not enough to walk in the neighborhood plaza or attend a *tertulia* of one of the principal Porteño families. Those who wished to be among the well-to-do had to go to Plaza San Martín, walk along the Paseo de Julio and the docks, attend the Colón Theater and the salons and, naturally, frequent the fashionable clubs as often as possible. For the working class, the map of obligatory sociabilities was not as precise, as the institutionalization of the places of sociability was less important, due to various reasons. Firstly there was the problem of controls on popular practices. Meeting places were more feared by the authorities and as a result were controlled more strictly. Secondly there were the disadvantages of the clients' low economic level. The owners of liquor stores aimed at a popular clientele found it harder to make a reasonable profit from their businesses, all the more so as the economic data appear to begin to change and the specialization of these places tends to distinguish between sales of merchandise and liquor, which reduced one of the oldest sources of income: debt. Hence these businesses aimed at entertaining the popular sectors generally had a short life: a small investment to set up shop, but ultimately small profits. In these conditions, meeting habits were formed and abandoned more rapidly, but this is not to say that the associative wave did not reach the population as a whole.

We see consequently that the urban structure built around the sociability of the neighborhood was juxtaposed with another, organized according to the consumption of culture and new forms of entertainment, which did not entirely entail a phenomenon of social segregation in the urban space. One implied primary ties of community based on place, the other contractual ties connected to exchanges and the consumption of certain forms of culture (press, discussions, cultural spectacles). These new social ties based on cultural exchanges, often through associative sociability relationships, would prove to be suitable for the diffusion of new sentiments of belonging to a community defined in cultural and political terms.

NOTES

1. "Asociación," *El Progreso. Diario guvernativo*, Buenos Aires, Imprenta del Estado, 7 April 1852.
2. According to N. Besio Moreno's calculations in *Buenos Aires*, 428–429.
3. See Nicolo Cuneo, *Storia dell'emigrazione italiana in Argentina, 1810–1870* (Milan: Garzanti, 1940); J. C. Chiaramonte, "Notas sobre la presencia italiana en el Litoral argentino en la primera mitad del siglo XIX," in Fernando Devoto (ed.), *L'Italia nella società argentina* (Roma: Centro Studi Emigrazione, 1988); José Carlos Moya, *Spaniards in Buenos Aires: Patterns of Immigration and Adaptation, 1852–1930*, Ph.D. dissertation, University of New Jersey, 1988.
4. The so-called "disappearance" of the African-Argentine population may in part have been the consequence of their inclusion among the "local population," which would explain why, during the same period, blacks apparently disappeared from the city and the number of natives increased. We have used the results of the census of 1855, published by Manuel R. Trelles in *Registro Estadístico*, vol. 2 (1857), 1–17; see also A. E. Lattes and R. Poczter, *Muestra del censo de la población de la ciudad de Buenos Aires de 1855* (Buenos Aires: Cuadernos del Instituto Torcuato Di Tella, 1968), vol. 5. See figure 8.
5. Haydée Gorostegui de Torres, *La organización nacional* (Buenos Aires: Paidós, 1972).
6. Benjamín Vicuña Mackenna, *Páginas de mi diario durante tres años de viaje, 1853-54-55* (Santiago de Chile, 1856), 367.
7. V. Gálvez, *Memorias*, vol. 1, 28.
8. See B. Vicuña Mackenna, *Páginas de mi diario*, 367–368.
9. The salon referred to by Vicuña Mackenna was not the same as the kind of aristocratic salon such as was found in France. In this case it was a kind of café that put on spectacles, frequented by the elites. See *Páginas de mi diario*.
10. "El domingo," *La Tribuna*, 19 October 1856.
11. It is interesting that Frías should add the word *casero* (home) when he speaks of *tertulias*, which suggests that public *tertulias* had developed considerably since the Battle of Caseros.
12. "Sociabilidad," *El Orden*, 21 February 1856.
13. This question is explored in greater length in chapter 7.
14. B. Vicuña Mackenna, *Páginas de mi diario*, 376.
15. *Páginas de mi diario*, 370.
16. On the question of the family and the institutionalization of a public bourgeois sphere, see Habermas, *L'Espace public*, 54–61.
17. Grondona was the first to include in his map a legend that in addition to the names of streets and principal churches also indicated the location of salons and leisure clubs. "Plano de Buenos Aires de Grondona, 1856," in AGN, Map archive, 11-2-16. There is a reproduction of this map in PGB, *La Création*, vol. 3, 930.
18. The difference between society balls and public balls was that the former were by invitation, while the latter were in theory open to all. For an analysis of public balls,

see François Gasnault, *Guinguettes et lorettes. Bals publics à Paris au XIXe siècle* (Paris: Aubier, 1986), 16.

19. With regards to the question of the political uses of festivals, see A. Corbin, N. Gérôme, and D. Tartakowsky (eds.), *Les Usages politiques des fêtes au XIXe-XXe siècles* (Paris: Publications de la Sorbonne, 1994).
20. Leisure clubs offered various examples of the political dimension that public life acquired, even in recreation. Thus, the founders of the Progress Club chose May 25th as the date of their inauguration banquet, the most Porteño of civic festivities. Moreover, the names of the two other clubs founded in Buenos Aires during the decade evoked political events: the May Club (the revolution) and the July Club (the declaration of independence).
21. "Baile del Club en conmemoración del 11 de septiembre," *El Progreso*, 6 December 1852.
22. See "Baile en el Club," *La Tribuna*, 13 September 1853; *El Progreso,* 13 September 1854.
23. At the time of the creation of the May Club, the authorities of the Progress Club reproached the former for attempting to attract their clientele by organizing a September 11 ball on the same date. See *La Tribuna*, 11 September 1855.
24. See *La Tribuna*, 18 September 1859. The well-to-do, in contrast, would celebrate it in Palermo, already the place to be for the "crème de la crème of Buenos Aires." An account of the period can be found in José Luis Bustamante, *Bosquejo de la historia civil y política de Buenos Aires desde la batalla de Monte Caseros* (Buenos Aires, 1856), 155–159.
25. Membership of the Progress Club was limited. By statute, there could only be two hundred members, giving it an aristocratic character that distinguished it from other clubs. To attend one of its parties was a good way to show that one participated in the "chosen" network of two hundred great Porteño families. This question is explored further below.
26. There is a notable chronological gap in comparison with public balls in Paris. In Buenos Aires the fashion took hold just as such practices were going into decline in Paris. See F. Gasnault, *Guinguettes et lorettes.*
27. While vigilant, the government evinced a certain tolerance towards these practices. Between 1852 and 1862 I have found only one reference to imprisonment for "holding a dance without permission." The rest of the cases concerned imprisonment for prohibited gambling. See AGN. AP. X.L 333.
28. *La Tribuna*, 2 July 1858.
29. See figure 3.
30. *La Tribuna*, 13 March 1861.
31. AGN, Police, General Index, 1851–1859, 44-10-3
32. *La Tribuna*, 15 December 1853.
33. To defend their trade, the *pulperos* invoked the irreplaceable role of the *pulpería*, which contributed as much as the Church to the development of the region. See *La Tribuna*, 7 September 1854.
34. This suggests that for the liberal elites the role of recreation and the leisure associations were incompatible with the sociability of the *pulperías*. In the case of these gatherings, recreation became idleness, even when they took place outside working hours. See *La Tribuna*, 21 December 1858.
35. See *La Tribuna*, 9 February 1861; *La Tribuna*, 8 March 1861. This subject is explored further in "Pedagogía societaria y aprendizaje de la Nación en el Río de la Plata," in A.

Annino, L. Castro Leiva and F.-X. Guerra, *De los Imperios a las Naciones: Iberoamérica* (Zaragoza: Ibercaja, 1994), 451–469.

36. "Las Academias," *La Tribuna*, 3 April 1856. See also 4 March and 22 April 1856.
37. In addition to articles previously cited, other references can be found in *La Tribuna* of 3, 4 June 1857, 17 February, 2 July and 23 November, 1858 and 14 June 1861.
38. By extension, the term "academia" could refer to a dance gathering, even if it took place in a private residence. Hence, for example, the news that informs officials of the First Regiment of National Guards "that tonight there is an *academia* in the residence of Commander Emilio Castro." *La Tribuna*, 14 May 1859; the same usage is seen in the issue of 6 July 1861.
39. See *La Tribuna*, 22 April 1856.
40. See figure 15.
41. See "Bailes públicos," *La Tribuna*, 8 May 1859.
42. "Un baile deshecho por un pillo," *La Tribuna*, 6 December 1859.
43. "Escuela Danzante," *La Tribuna*, 26 August 1857.
44. This contradicts Ricardo Falcón's claims. He does not take these meeting places into account, leading him to claim that popular recreational life was limited until the early twentieth century. See Falcón, *L'Immigration, les travailleurs et le mouvement ouvrier en Argentine: 1870–1912*, doctoral thesis, École des Hautes Études en Sciences Sociales, Paris, 1985, 310–315.
45. See figure 3.
46. See figure 4.
47. *See La Reforma Pacífica*, 24 October and 29 November 1857.
48. This is evinced by the advertisements placed by the café owners in the local press, which referred explicitly to the number of people that the salons could accommodate.
49. *La Tribuna*, 21 August 1853.
50. *La Tribuna*, 9 August and 13 October 1853.
51. For the announcement of the opening night, see *La Tribuna*, 22 April 1855. See also Varela's comments in *La Tribuna* 30 March 1856.
52. *La Tribuna*, 4 June 1856.
53. *La Tribuna*, 24 December 1858.
54. *La Tribuna*, 7 October 1857.
55. *La Tribuna*, 28 May 1857.
56. This is explored further below.
57. See *La Tribuna*, 29 March 1856.
58. *La Reforma Pacífica*, 30 December 1858.
59. In a later work, Robert Amigo and Ana María Telesca refute this identification of salons with elite sociability practices. In my judgment, they are right to raise the question in terms of urban visual culture, as well as in insisting on the existence of a diverse audience. Nevertheless, even when the formula of the visual spectacle was extended to a "less select" public, a good number of salons appear to have identified with a form of bourgeois entertainment which assimilated these places of cultural consumption within elite sociability spaces. Naturally, this did not prevent the practice from spreading to a wider sector of the population; on the contrary, this identification could prove to be a considerable trump card for the propagation of the practice and to the advantage of the proprietors. Nor does this mean that visual culture was the private property of the elites (we have already seen that it was one of the pillars of Rosas' popular support) but it is important to distinguish it here from

sociability. See Roberto Amigo and Ana María Telesca, "La curiosidad de los Porteños. El público y los temas de las vistas ópticas en el Estado de Buenos Aires (1852–1862)," in V Congreso de Historia de la Fotografía en Argentina, Buenos Aires, 1996. I am particularly grateful to Roberto Amigo for his attentive reading of my text and his valuable comments, which helped me to rework some of these questions.

60. See V Congreso de Historia de la Fotografía en Argentina.
61. Visual spectacle was already known in Buenos Aires. The first exhibitions of magic lanterns date, according to Gesualdo, from the late eighteenth century. From 1843 various projections of optical views were presented in the Teatro Mecánico y Gabinete Óptico. See Vicente Gesualdo, "Los salones de vistas ópticas. Antepasados del cine en Buenos Aires y el interior," *Todo es Historia* 248 (1988): 70–80.
62. *La Tribuna*, 4 July 1855
63. *La Tribuna*, 13 October 1855.
64. *La Tribuna*, 18 August 1858.
65. See José E. Burucúa et al., "Influencia de los tipos iconográficos de la Revolución Francesa en los países del Plata," in *Imagen y recepción de la Revolución Francesa en la Argentina*, Jornadas Nacionales por el Bicentenario de la Revolución Francesa (Buenos Aires: Comité Argentino para el Bicentenario de la Revolución Francesa/Grupo Editor Latinoamericano, 1990), 129–140.
66. In this respect, see J. A. García Martínez, *Orígenes de nuestra crítica de arte. Sarmiento y la pintura* (Buenos Aires: Ediciones Culturales Argentinas, 1963).
67. Documentation consists of announcements in newspapers in Buenos Aires.
68. The list is presented in chronological order according to their showings in the salons.
69. To cite some examples: "The unfortunate execution of Camila O'Gorman"; "The death of Maza, murdered in the House of Representatives while writing his resignation, in the presence of the tyrant Rosas"; "The taking of Catamarca by order of Oribe under the command of Mariano Maza and Juan Balbao, deputy of Rosas, who ordered the decapitation of the province's principal functionaries and their representatives, among whom were Commander Espeche and the ministers Gregorio Dulce and Gregorio González, whose heads were displayed on pikes in the square, and at the foot of these was a pyramid with the heads of six hundred massacred prisoners"; "Doctor Florencio Valera, an Argentine journalist murdered on the night of the 20 March 1848 in Montevideo by order of Manuel Oribe"; "Death of the liberator hero Juan Lavalle in Jujuy, murdered by Rosas' soldiers, who fired through the door as he crossed the courtyard of the house where he had spent the night"; "Manuelita Rosas presents on a platter the head of the Tucumán colonel Juan Zelarrayán to his widow, who beseeches Manuelita's Rosas' father, the tyrant Juan Manuel de Rosas, the grace to bury him on consecrated land"; "Hideous murder of the Spaniard Martínez Eguilaz, burnt alive in a barrel of tar by the executioners Silveira and Moreira in 1840, under the tyranny of Rosas."
70. Hence: "Principal persons who fought for independence"; "Battle of Maipú, won by General San Martín on the 5 April 1818"; "Great battle of Cepeda, with the portraits of the military chiefs"; Departure from Cepeda of the Army of the State of Buenos Aires"; "Naval combat off the coast of the town of San Nicolás between the fleets of Buenos Aires and of the Confederation"; "Invasion of Buenos Aires by the British and its total failure: defeat and surrender of General Beresford"; "The funeral parade of the Argentine hero Juan Lavalle passing through the Plaza del Retiro, 21 January 1861"; "Beautiful painting depicting the glorious battle of Pavón, won by the

invincible infantry corps and the valiant artillery corps of Buenos Aires and by the brave Argentine Legion against the forces of the Argentine Confederation." See below for a further exploration of this question.

71. We might also recall that the impresarios who had financed the construction of Buenos Aires' luxurious theater decided to name it the "Colón" (Columbus). The Uruguayans constructed an imposing theater named the "Solís," after the Spanish explorer who "discovered" the River Plate. In the following list the chronological order of their exhibition has been respected.
72. This is the only picture where the image of Rosas is not negative. Alongside the Indians, "the tyrant Juan Manuel de Rosas" becomes simply General Manuel Rosas. The change of direction that Rosas would bring to the conquest of the territories of the Patagonian Indians and their extermination was already clearly under way.
73. "Constitución para el Estado de Buenos Aires," in *Diario de Sesiones de la Sala de Representantes de la Provincia de Buenos Aires* (Buenos Aires: Imprenta de la Sociedad Tipográfica Bonaerense, 1865), 114–119.
74. See figure 5 on the chronology of the associative movement in Buenos Aires, in which two major periods are highlighted: from the creation of the first associations in the city until 1852 and from this date until 1863, as far as our investigation goes.
75. See Raúl H. Castagnino, *El teatro en Buenos Aires durante la época de Rosas* (Buenos Aires: Ed. Nacional de Estudios del Teatro/Comisión Nacional de Cultura, 1944), 252–279
76. This double role of a club for men's meetings and family entertainment would later be found in one of the most traditional aristocratic clubs, the Jockey Club, founded in 1882. In the building on the Calle Florida, men met in the library and the drawing rooms. Later, the club would buy land to the north of the city, in San Isidro, where facilities were built to receive families.
77. The first location of the Supreme Council and Grand Orient of the Argentine Republic was on the south side, on the Calle Bolívar on the corner of the church of San Ignacio and a few yards from the university. In 1860 they moved to the first floor of the Colón Theater, in the parish of Catedral al Norte. Their move may be explained by the prestige of the new location, but perhaps also because the northern barrios had a greater relationship with the public of the Masonic network. The establishment of the conferences of Saint Vincent of Paul and their location in the buildings of the church of San Ignacio might also explain their move away from the barrio of Catedral al Sur.
78. In the map, we have placed all those whose locations are known.
79. The first data on literacy are from the census of 1855 and give a proportion of 48% of literate people. Carlos Newland corrects these figures, proposing 55.55%. See C. Newland, *Buenos Aires no es pampa*.
80. R. Falcón, *L'Immigration*, 333.
81. On the first wave of Italian immigration settling in the neighborhood of La Boca, see Fernando Devoto, "The origins of an Italian neighborhood in Buenos Aires in the mid-nineteenth century," *The Journal of European Economy History* 18:1 (Spring 1989).
82. During the first ten years of the secession, the newspapers of Buenos Aires, particularly *La Tribuna*, *El Nacional* and *La Reforma Pacífica*, published many articles extolling the virtues of the associative spirit.
83. A. Delacour, "Voyage dans l'Amérique méridionale."
84. "Lettre du Vénérable Bayan au Grand Orient de France demandant la régularisation de leur loge, Buenos Aires, 12 août 1852," in Bibliothèque Nationale (Paris), Argentine, loge "Amie des Naufragés," FM2, 843.

85. Archivos de la Gran Logia Argentina, Amie des Naufragés lodge, 1852–1860, box 761.
86. Only the Chilean Francisco Bilbao was a member of this "artisan lodge." His presence illustrates the differences between Chilean liberals and Argentines. The former tended to seek in the organization of artisan associations a popular base for political combat, while their Porteño counterparts held these sectors in deep distrust, above all after the Rosist and Chilean experience. Bartolomé Mitre, who had encouraged the experience of the Equality Society of Santiago de Chile, was later highly critical when Nicolás Calvo invited artisans of Buenos Aires to organize against the antinational politics of Porteño liberals. Mitre's disapproval was no doubt due to the fact that artisans were mobilized against his "party," but it is nevertheless significant that he made no attempt to mobilize them himself. See *La Tribuna*, 22 February and 16–18 March 1859. For the organization of the Artisans' Club, see *La Reforma Pacífica*, March 1859. On the participation of Bilbao in the organization of the Equality Society, see José Zapiola, *La Sociedad de Igualdad y sus enemigos* (Santiago de Chile: Guillermo Miranda, 1902); also Luis Alberto Romero, *La Sociedad de Igualdad. Los artesanos de Santiago de Chile y sus primeras experiencias políticas,* Serie Historia (Buenos Aires: Instituto Torcuato Di Tella, 1978).
87. See "El centenario de la logia Excélsior," *Símbolo* (Buenos Aires) 9:36 (1954).
88. See chapter 6.
89. In the associative experiences of foreigners very different forms could be found, from guild organizations to gatherings in cafés. But there were trends according to the country of origin. Among Italians, some of whom were political exiles, the experience of secret political associations was more common than among the population of British or North American origin.
90. Foreigners did not however arrive in complete isolation, and most of the time the choice of country of immigration was dictated by the existence of ties with relatives who had already settled in the country. But while these ties helped to cross the Atlantic and set up home, they did not alone satisfy all the relational needs of an individual. On the question of migratory chains, see J. S. MacDonald and L. D. MacDonald, "Chain migration, ethnic neighborhood formation and social networks," *Milbank Memorial Fund Quarterly* 12:42 (1964), 82-95. On this perspective, and on the case of the River Plate, see Fernando Devoto, "Las cadenas migratorias italianas: algunas reflexiones a la luz del caso argentino," *Estudios Migratorios Latinoamericanos* (1988), 103–122; J. C. Moya, *Spaniards in Buenos Aires*; and more recently, César Yáñez Gallardo, *Saltar con red. La temprana emigración catalana a América, 1830–1870* (Madrid: Alianza, 1996).
91. Frequently the ethnic tie was more the effect than the cause. See F. J. Devoto and E. J. Míguez, *Asociacionismo, trabajo e identidad étnica. Los italianos en América Latina en una perspectiva comparada* (Buenos Aires: CEMLA/CSER/IHES, 1992). A critical review of this issue can be found in Fernando Devoto, *Movimientos migratorios: historiografía y problemas* (Buenos Aires: Centro Editor de América Latina, 1992).
92. See "Sociedad Tipográfica Bonaerense," *La Tribuna*, 1 June 1859.
93. See Instituto Histórico y Geográfico, "Conmemoración del Centenario," *Revista del Instituto Histórico y Geográfico* (Montevideo) 17 (1943); Ricardo Levene, *Los estudios históricos de la juventud de Mitre* (Buenos Aires: Emecé, 1946).
94. See Bibliothèque Nationale (Paris), Chile, Union Fraternelle lodge, FM2, 845, "Tableau des membres de la loge Union Fraternelle," 24 June 1855.
95. See chapter 7.
96. We have no data as to the socioprofessional status of the other 1,035 members.

Although these selection criteria might be refuted by a more detailed analysis, they are nevertheless indicative of a trend.

97. William MacCann, *Two Thousand Miles' Ride through the Argentine Provinces* (London, 1853).
98. According to the figures of the 1914 census, reproduced by Ricardo Falcón, between 1854 and 1870, 41 friendly societies registered in Argentina. Between 1870 and 1880 the number increased to 107, and 220 in the following decade. See R. Falcón, *L'Immigration*, 180.
99. Sociedad Filantrópica de Beneficencia de los Peluqueros de Buenos Aires, Regulations and request for authorization in AGN. AP. X 31-11-5.
100. See "Développement du mouvement associatif," in PGB, *La Création*, vol. 3, appendix 3.
101. See "Reglamento de la Sociedad Filantrópica de Beneficencia de los Peluqueros de Buenos Aires"; "Reglamento de la Sociedad de la Unión y Socorros Mutuos," in AGN. AP. X 31-11-5; Sociedad Tipográfica Bonaerense, *Estatutos*, Buenos Aires, 1858. For the *Unione e Benevolenza* society there is a more extensive bibliography. In addition to Samuel Bailey, "Las sociedades de ayuda mutua y el desarrollo de una comunidad italiana," *Desarrollo Económico* 21:84 (January–March 1982), 485–514, see Ema Cibotti's studies, "Mutualismo y política en un estudio de caso. La sociedad Unione e Benevolenza en Buenos Aires entre 1858 y 1865," in *L'Italia nella società argentina*, 241–265, and "Notas para el análisis del desarrollo político de Unione e Benevolenza entre 1858 y 1865. Historia de dos escisiones" (unpublished).
102. Martin de Moussy, *Description géographique et statistique de la Confédération Argentine*, vol. 2 (Paris, 1860–1864), 622.
103. See "Reglamento de la sociedad que instala la Nación Argentina dirigida a la Virgen del Luján," reproduced in PGB, *La Création*, vol. 3, appendix 3, document 41.
104. Andrews mentions as the first African-Argentine mutualist society the Society of Union and Mutual Aid created in 1855, but this society, founded in 1854 by a group of Frenchmen, was made up of Europeans. See G. R. Andrews, *Los afroargentinos*, 179.
105. The regulation reads as follows: "In order to aid and to help each other in the case of illness or death of one of the members, and to enjoy ourselves together on festive days, we have brought together a considerable number of people of color and of both sexes." See "Demanda de autorización que dirigen los individuos de la nación Abaya al jefe de policía," in AGN. AP. X 31-11-5.
106. The society maintained features of ethnic societies, but with a notable innovation: while it was organized according to ethnic principles, it took into account other criteria of identity. Thus, instead of calling itself "Conga" or "Angola" society, it defined itself as "African-Brazilian." See "Sociedad Protectora Brasilera," in AGN. AP. X 31-11-5.
107. See AGN. AP. X 31-11-5.
108. See AGN. AP. X 31-11-5.
109. This is established in article 1 of the regulations. See Sociedad Tipográfica Bonaerense, *Estatutos.*
110. Falcón quotes a letter from Raymond Wilmart to Karl Marx dated 27 May 1873. See R. Falcón, *L'Immigration*, 325.
111. See "Memoria del presidente en su primer aniversario," and "Discurso con motivo al tercer aniversario," in Sociedad Tipográfica Bonaerense, *Estatutos*; also *La Tribuna*, 1 June 1859,
112. *Diccionario de Buenos Aires.*
113. See *La Tribuna*, 6 January 1858. The society would not publish its newspaper, *Anales de la Sociedad Tipográfica Bonaerense*, until 1872.

CHAPTER 6

New Modalities of Social Exchanges

The "associative boom" implied not only the establishment and triumph of an organizational form but also a renewal of urban sociability based on a new notion of "public" as a privileged space of exchange. It was no doubt more than a mere historical coincidence that these two phenomena occurred simultaneously. The hypothesis of this investigation is that associative practices contributed to the reorganization of urban sociability. With this in mind, I have mentioned the model of the establishment of associations and their effect on the social organization of the urban space. This question of the spatial organization of sociability relationships is less peripheral or anodyne than it may seem, as it leads us to the social representations fixing the similarities and distances between individuals.

Associative practice, in the strictest sense of the word tied to the administration of the association, concerned a limited number of members. But within this small circle of active leaders and the rest of the members an associative tie was developed, as seen in such places as general assemblies or extraordinary meetings. We have distinguished this type of tie and exchange from a greater, more tenuous set of bonds, by means of the notion of associative sociability. However, the association also stimulated sociability itself, respecting a series of behavior codes and values which the movement had institutionalized, which often exceeded the objectives and formal framework of the organization, whether this enthusiasm for social exchange was developed in the antechamber of the association (the reading and meeting rooms that some organizations provided) or exceeded and prolonged the association in other such meeting places as cafés or salons.

Freemasonry: A Society of Reflection and a Leisure Club

We have seen the extent to which the arrival of the liberals coincided with a renewal of meeting habits in the local population. Of the variety of forms developed—

sociocultural, socioeconomic, commercial, corporative, recreational—freemasonry occupied one of the most important places, in terms of the number of societies created, its establishment in the country and its appeal to the ruling class of the State of Buenos Aires. In spite of the importance that it acquired after 1854, there are no reliable studies of this institution. The wealth of literature available concerns the ethical-ideological controversy among its defenders and its detractors, and in all cases the arguments used tend to obscure any attempt at historical analysis. Moreover, Latin American university historians have shown total indifference to this question, which, judging by their attitude, is yet to acquire the status of a historical object.[1] This appears to be in part explained by the fact that the freemasonry question has been monopolized by the dispute between liberals and nationalists. In addition there is the problem of the "inexistence" of Masonic archives, making any approach to this already difficult and unexplored issue a minefield due to its ideological challenge.[2] Without claiming to overcome this deficit here, some references to the history of the establishment of the institution in the region can be asserted.

THE ESTABLISHMENT OF FREEMASONRY IN THE RIVER PLATE BASIN

After the defeat of Rosas, freemasonry grew rapidly in the city of Buenos Aires. The rate at which it was established, in time and in space, to some extent matched the pace of political life in the State of Buenos Aires, but it can only be entirely understood from a regional perspective. The creation of an Argentine freemasonry in effect constituted a stage of Masonic diffusion along the Atlantic coast of South America. The institution entered the continent via Brazil, where the first independent Masonic power on the whole continent was created in 1822. It then descended to Uruguay on two occasions, eventually leading to the definitive creation of the Supreme Council and Grand Orient of the Republic of Uruguay in 1855. In turn, this branch would expand the order into Argentine territory and give the constitution to the Supreme Council and Grand Orient of the Argentine Republic in 1858.

This dissemination was influenced both by internal factors within the institution and the political situation of each of the countries. Thus, the descent of freemasonry from Brazil to Uruguay occurred in two stages. The first was during Brazil's occupation of Uruguay (1817–1828) when the Brazilian authorities used the organization to consolidate their armed invasion. This was a similar phenomenon, albeit smaller, to that of Spain during the Napoleonic invasion of 1808.[3] The success of the first lodges can also be explained by the characteristics of the local population.[4] After the retreat of Brazilian troops and the constitution of the Republic of Uruguay, the Brazilian lodges disappeared.[5] Other lodges still operated in the territory, but they depended on North American and French Masonic powers without acquiring the constitution of an independent authority.[6] The second Brazilian descent into Uruguay was in 1854, after the Great War, which put an end to regional conflict over river traffic. This time, the Brazilian Masonic powers legalized the creation of the Grand Orient of the Republic of Uruguay.

The appearance of the first regular Freemason lodges for the population of the River Plate, or more precisely within the creole elite, dates from the mid-nineteenth century, with the December 1854 establishment in Montevideo of the Misterio y Honor lodge, dependent on the Grand Orient of Brazil.[7] The lodges spread rapidly, with three new ones established in 1855: Sol Oriental, Hisperia and Honor y Patria. With the exception of the latter, which operated intermittently, the others had a constitution from the Grand Orient of Brazil. The Les Amis de la Patrie lodge notified the Grand Orient of France of "the enthusiasm for Freemasonry seen for some months in the population…meetings taking place in various places…perhaps the promoters of these meetings have other objectives unknown to the majority and even to us but the fact is that in three months in this country, where there had been no other regular lodge but our own for the last fifteen years, a Grand Orient has been established including six lodges."[8] The lodge referred here to the first schism occurring between February and March 1855, when two Masonic authorities claimed recognition from the Grand Orient of Brazil: the Grand Orient of Montevideo and the Supreme Council of the Republic of Uruguay.[9]

In this sudden growth of Uruguayan Freemasonry there is an unarguable correlation with political history, as its establishment coincided with the pre-electoral period and with liberals and conservatives preparing for the coming elections.[10] Various attempts at political organization then appeared: The Society of Friends of the Country established by the conservatives and the National Party founded by Lamas, which later signed the "Liberal Union" with a group of *colorados* and *blancos*. Meanwhile, Flores consolidated an alliance with the old *caudillo* Oribe by means of the Pact of the Union, which supported the candidacy of the liberal Gabriel Antonio Pereira.[11] It is necessary to include in this context the appearance of Masonic lodges, whose organizational structure appears to have been especially used by liberals.[12]

The French lodge maintained a fairly critical attitude towards Uruguayan Freemasonry, due to the irregularity of its proceedings. As the Grand Orient of France indicated a few months later,

> they give to the Masonic world the strangest spectacle, that of having three or four different Masonic authorities comprising members decorated with

> the highest ranks and forming alone the whole Uruguayan Masonry...in Montevideo there soon will be no more than thirtieths and thirty-third ranks, something akin to the unlikely situation of an army with no more than generals, colonels and officers, and no soldiers.[13]

At the same time, the authorities of the French lodge made no secret of their preference for the Supreme Council of the Republic of Uruguay, established by the Supreme Council of Brazil in June 1855: "This new authority provides more guarantees than the other, given that it comprises honorable and illustrious people, most of whom have occupied high positions in the State."[14] Indeed, various members of the government joined the Freemasons and did this so publicly that in 1855 it triggered the first conflict between the Church and a public power accused of being an accomplice to the Freemasons. Lamas, a vicar apostolic in Montevideo, wrote to the Secretary of State (and Mason) Salvador Tort to denounce the laxity of the government in allowing the lodges to make their work public.[15]

In 1856 twelve lodges were founded in Uruguay and the movement continued to grow. By 1862 there were twenty-six lodges in Uruguay depending on the Grand Orient of the Republic of Uruguay. The Masonic zeal spread to Buenos Aires and the Mesopotamia region, where some lodges had already been established. Thus, while before March 1856 the Porteño population kept its distance from the first manifestations of Freemasonry on the east bank of the Plate, after 1856 Freemasonry spread as rapidly as it had done in Uruguay.[16]

The first reference to the will to establish a lodge in Buenos Aires dates from 1856. In a letter sent to Gabriel Pérez, the founder of the Supreme Council of Uruguay, Miguel Valencia requested his support in establishing a lodge in the city of Buenos Aires, enclosing the diplomas of thirteen Masonic brethren wishing to form a part of it. Pérez, who was in Buenos Aires and had been authorized to found Masonic lodges, inaugurated the Unión de la Plata on 9 March of the same year, following the Scottish Rite.[17] The letter says nothing of the origin of this administration. According to an anti-Masonic satire in Buenos Aires in 1858, the idea of creating a lodge arose from gatherings in the bookstore of one Hortelano, where intellectuals and young students would meet to read the newspapers and discuss literature and politics.[18] According to the author, in these years the opposition to the government met in Hortelano's reading room. Presumably it was here that Dr. Alsina proposed that his supporters should organize against the government by forming a Masonic lodge.[19] The author of the satire denounced the political objective of these proceedings: "the emergence of Freemasonry stems from the need of some men dominated by a thirst for power to use all means necessary to obtain it," which is confirmed by a tip-off from a member of the

Unión del Plata lodge: "Their objective, if truth be told, was to establish a meeting place where forgotten or unappreciated men could satisfy their needs and protect each other."[20] However, and in spite of the logic of his arguments, the name Alsina is not found among the founders of the Unión del Plata lodge.[21]

Besides the problem of the Alsina origin of the first Masonic lodges, their growth rate suggests a secure relationship with politics.[22] In 1856 three lodges were set up, two in the city of Buenos Aires and the third in Confederation territory. All three depended on the Grand Orient of the Republic of Uruguay. In the course of 1857, a year of great political agitation due to the fact that the election of the governor depended on the results of the legislative elections, six new lodges appeared, all in the city of Buenos Aires. Two Masonic powers then disputed their authority over the others.[23] However, faced with the possibility of armed conflict with the Confederation, the liberals, divided during the elections, put aside their differences to organize against the enemy. This explains why there was no opposition to the government's candidate in the legislative elections of 1858, with the exception of the pro-Urquista sector. That year the number of lodges founded in Buenos Aires decreased to four, but another two were established in the province of Buenos Aires and another in Confederation territory. 1859 saw the preparation for armed conflict which would end in the war between Buenos Aires and the Confederation, a situation which moderated the growth of Freemasonry. The total number of lodges created was lower than the previous year, but the proportions between city and country lodges was evened out by the establishment of two in each. In 1860 the Masonic expansion movement was sluggish, although with greater growth in Confederation territory than in the province of Buenos Aires. A new armed conflict in 1861 postponed the unification that would eventually be cemented at the start of the following year. The extremely tense situation experienced throughout Argentina led to a general decrease in the rate of lodge growth. Eventually, from 1862 and the organization of a national State between Buenos Aires and the Confederation, Freemasonry would experience a decade of some of its greatest growth in its history in the region.

During its first six years of expansion, the establishment of Masonic lodges was not limited to an exclusively urban sphere. The city ports of Montevideo and Buenos Aires held greater concentratons, but lodges were also found in the small towns along the Paraná and Uruguay rivers, connecting the Mesopotamia region with the Atlantic ports. The presence of the lodges in these small towns cannot be explained in any way by their political or cultural scope, but rather by their location in a river trade network including Paraguay, southwest Brazil, Mesopotamia and Uruguay.[24] The institution offered the possibility of a network of relationships and information that facilitated transactions, at a time when the vicissitudes of political life tended to hinder them.[25] This suggests that the Porteño leaders who joined the Masons took advantage of this network, which was well established in the commercial sphere, to affirm their national politics. Indeed, by means of the Supreme Council and Grand Orient of the Republic of Argentina, the province of Buenos Aires, being separate from the Argentine Confederation and established as an independent State, controlled the most important commercial network connecting the regional economy with the international market and making the city of Buenos Aires the political and economic center of exchange.

Towards the end of the period in question (figure 18, 1858–1862 map) it is possible to note another phenomenon that amplifies the model of establishment shown above: the creation of military lodges. In the southwest of the province of Buenos Aires, on the frontier with Indian territory in Guaminí, the Luz del Desierto lodge was created in 1859.[26] This strange positioning of Masonry in the middle of the pampas can be explained by the important presence of military figures among the Masonic brethren. At the time, some officers who were already initiated in the order and sent to the southern frontier of the province decided to create a lodge in the camp. The formula was undoubtedly successful during the whole period of advance across the frontier and operated as an extraordinary factor of diffusion in the newly populated regions.

RECRUITMENT

Although theoretically open to all, membership in Freemasonry is attained through the meeting of the requirements of initiation. These conditions are established in the general regulations of all lodges. In Buenos Aires, the first lodges followed, in theory, the General Regulations of the Asilo de la Virtud lodge in Montevideo, which set out as a condition of entrance the possession of "moral and financial qualities."[27] Each interpreted this prerequisite in its own way and, judging by the complaints of some brethren, tended to act rather liberally in initiations, a liberality that came to be a source of conflict. When the admission of a new brother was voted on, any interpretation was possible, and the most divergent positions came to be established in the regulations. For this reason, in 1858 the Regeneration lodge proposed a list of entrance conditions applicable to all lodges: belief in God, age 25 or over, moral conduct, good health and sufficient means of subsistence.[28] In spite of these efforts irregularities persisted, and eventually in 1859 the Supreme Council was obliged to send out a circular ordering all lodges to observe greater moderation in the admission of nonbelievers, as "the abuses carried out in this lodge, with nonbelievers who lack the considerations required by our regulations being admitted to the initiation into the sacred mysteries, has led us to demand that there be greater circumspection in the admission of nonbelievers."[29]

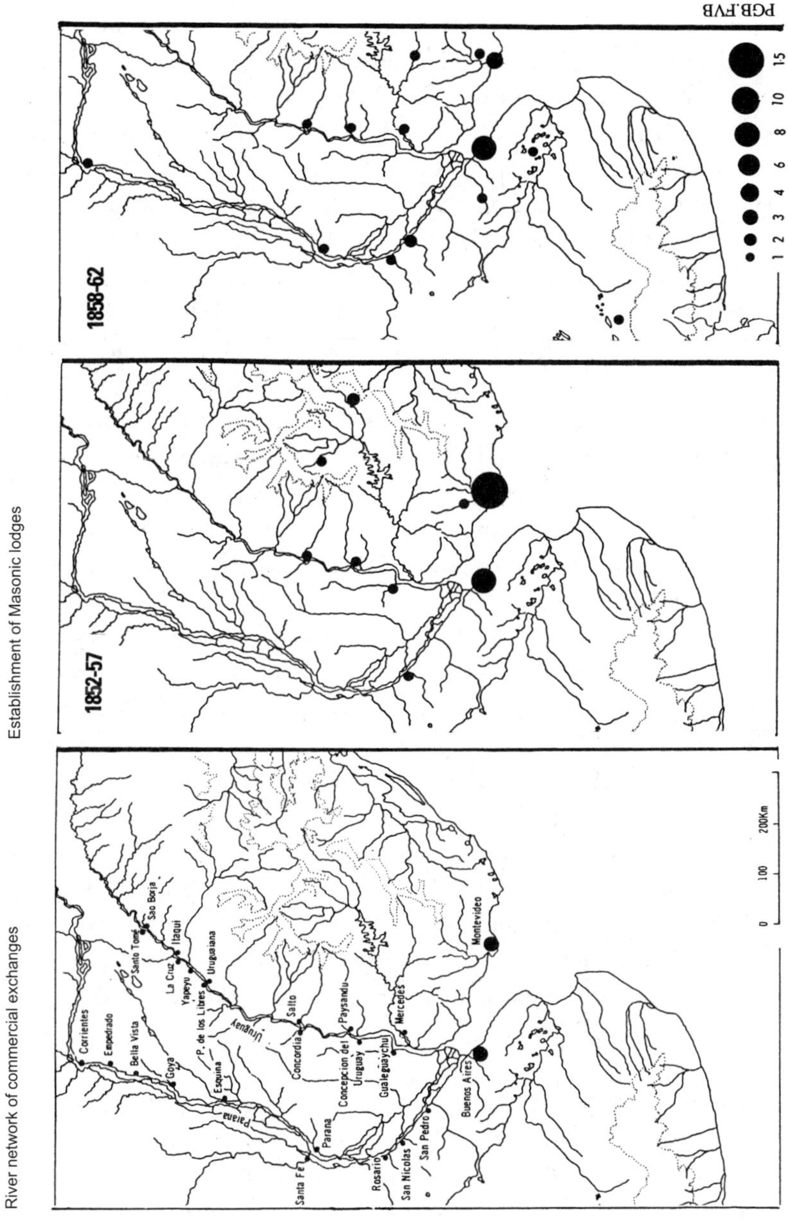

Figure 18. Model of Establishment of Masonic Lodges in the River Plate Region

Naturally, divergent interpretations were more abundant in terms of "moral qualities" than in socioeconomic criteria. Hence, on moral grounds lodges rejected the initiation of such politicians and intellectuals as Santiago Calzadillas, Adolfo Saldías, Leandro N. Alem, Martín Beruti, Federico Barbará and Héctor Varela.[30] But in terms of belief in God, requirements were not always respected, as seen in the proceedings against the nonbeliever Pelegrín Baltazar, found in the archives of the Grand Central Lodge. During his initiation, Baltazar had declared himself an atheist, which led lodge Venerable Master Nicanor Albarellos to refuse his initiation.[31] As a consequence of this, the Central Lodge opened proceedings. During the trial, Baltazar confessed that he "had gone that day under the false impression that the society which he intended to enter was an extremely liberal society, and that wishing to appear extremely liberal, had claimed to hold ideas and principles which he in fact was far from professing." It is difficult to verify the sincerity of his words, though it is evident that this prerequisite was not always respected, which explains Baltazar's clumsiness.[32] In contrast, although it was not prohibited, blacks and individuals of lower social extraction were rarely admitted.[33] At times the social segregation that the lodges implicitly applied could be questioned by the brethren, but as will be seen later, manual laborers would be accepted for initiation on scarce occasions during the first stage of the establishment of the order.[34]

Apart from regulations, what tells us the most about Freemasonry recruitment policy is the analysis of the individuals who were actually able to join. Between 1856 (the creation of the first regular Masonic lodge in Buenos Aires) and the end of the period in question (1862), 924 members can be counted in Argentine lodges (under Uruguayan jurisdiction until 1858 and thereon under Argentine jurisdiction). In a sample of 595 people, or 64.39% of the total membership, it can be seen that the majority of the members worked in some commercial activity (figure 19). These were followed by functionaries (mostly in the army), then intellectual and liberal professionals. Individuals of low social extraction were, as mentioned earlier, very much in the minority. Thus, lodges recruited their members principally from among the well-to-do and, within this, from individuals with commercial occupations.

MODALITY OF EXCHANGES

The formal framework of exchanges among Freemasons was rigorously established by a whole body of regulations and constitutions that the lodge had to respect if it was to belong to the order. While differing from other sociocultural associations due to the initiation aspect, Freemasonry had some features in common with these associations, typical of secondary groups of belonging. Firstly, there was

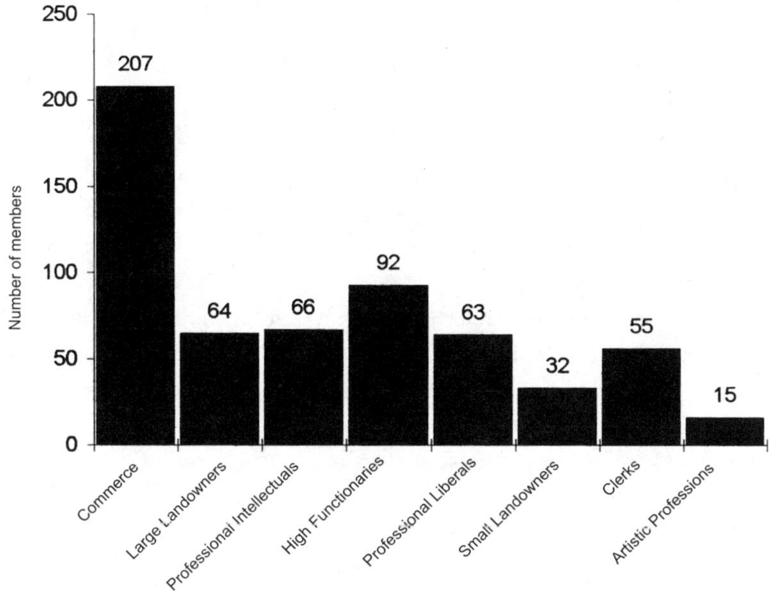

Figure 19. Socioprofessional Status of a Sample of 595 Members of the Freemasonry

the voluntary and revocable nature of membership, founded on the principle of social equality.[35] Apart from strictly symbolic activity, the goal of work within the lodge was, like in other associations, the intellectual formation of its members. This formation entailed, as elsewhere, exchanges of information and opinion on problems concerning society as a whole, and particularly the issues of education, health and public welfare, to which can be added questions affecting the institution directly, related to its place in society. The regulations only strictly prohibited political or religious discussions.[36] Generally, the discussion began after the reading of a paper sent by either one of the members of the workshop, by another lodge or a Masonic authority. After this reading, the members discussed its contents and reached a common agreement—let us say a shared opinion—recorded by the minutes and often reported in a paper to the Obedience. Unlike other associations, this communication between men, which sought a social consensus through acts and words, established secrecy as a condition of opinion, hence public debates among Masons outside of the lodge were tightly controlled.

Various incidents give evidence of the limits of this experience in the public sphere. The Freemason authority intervened, for example, to moderate the conflict between the Chilean brother Francisco Bilbao and a large part of the brethren implicated in the separatist policy of the State of Buenos Aires.[37] The controversy began with a debate between Sarmiento and Bilbao in the Buenos Aires press in 1858, which the Supreme Council opposed.[38] The discord continued in January 1859 when Bilbao, in an article published in Calvo's *La Reforma Pacífica* newspaper, alluded to his friendship with Santiago Albarracín, a Freemason and former representative of the province of Buenos Aires, and at the time a city councilor. Héctor Varela, a councilor, deputy and Freemason, then publicly denounced the alliance between Albarracín, Bilbao and Calvo.[39] The Masonic Obedience considered it unacceptable that Freemasons use newspapers to make their political differences public. Consequently, the Supreme Council sent out a circular to the lodges under its jurisdiction recommending tighter controls over the secular conduct of its members, reminding them "any manifestation of disagreements between Masonic brethren is to your enemies' advantage."[40] Tactical as the measure may seem, it is nevertheless true that the space for the exchange of public opinions within the lodge was reduced. Thus, while Freemasonry was considered one of the principle institutions in the modern public sphere, in order to preserve itself it tended to maintain the space for opinion within the restricted context of the lodge. Other institutions, founded on the principle of publicity, would act as halfway houses between the lodge and the public sphere.

Indeed, Masons intended to act in this sphere, specifically via the intermediaries of other associations. To do so, they created secular associations in order to intervene above all in two spheres very dear to the institutions: public welfare and education. The first of these initiatives concerned the creation in July 1857 of the Institute for the Deaf and Mute.[41] Three months later the Alsina government declared the enterprise to be in the public's interest and granted it a monthly subsidy of one thousand pesos.[42] The event passed almost unnoticed but numerous comments in the press show that the initiative was well received.[43] A year later Héctor Varela, speaker of the Lealtad lodge, deputy and councilor, proposed the creation of a poorhouse.[44] Unlike the first project, this one ran into lively opposition from ecclesiastical authorities and the Catholic sector close to the *La Religión* newspaper, who qualified Freemason philanthropy as "false charity."[45] The reasons for this disagreement are evident. By means of their philanthropy, Freemasons intended to rationalize the type of individual assistance, which jeopardized the place that the Church had hitherto occupied in public welfare.[46] The fact that the Catholic Félix Frías opened the Conferences of Saint Vincent of Paul at the same time that Freemasons established the poorhouse was no doubt not coincidental, but was an attempt to hinder the Masons' progress in this field.[47] The conflict reached its climax during the opening of the poorhouse. The Masonic commission organized a public ceremony for the occasion attended by 150 Freemasons and members of the government and municipality.[48] The ecclesiastical authorities refused to participate and accused the government of endorsing, by the mere presence of its representatives, the ceremony and Freemasonry, and thus promoting the order's activities in society.[49]

For the Masons, charity only served a purpose if it was accompanied by education, as Sarmiento stated: "The moral and intellectual elevation of man is the target of modern Masonic charity...Masonic charity must spread science, truth and moral doctrine in order to walk in harmony with the principles of the political economy that disapprove of the charity that rewards idleness and moral degradation, freeing its victims from the punishment that the Great Designer of the Universe has placed on the offense itself, sickness on disorder, destitution and misery on lack of foresight and vice..."[50] Sarmiento was the first Mason to speak of this objective.[51] The Constancia lodge responded to the initiative with a project to create a School of Arts and Trades in the town of Merlo, thirty miles from the city of Buenos Aires, with the objective of promoting an applied industrial education for people with scarce resources.[52] In connection with the question of education and public welfare, the Masons also showed interest in immigrants' problems of integration into local society. Hence, five months after the creation of the Unión de la Plata lodge, the guardian Santiago Albarracín reminded his Mason brethren of the need to assist immigrants arriving in the country with no means of subsistence. By means of a subscription, his lodge managed to raise five hundred pesos, which was donated to the Immigration Commission.[53]

In spite of its closed nature, the Masonic institution occupied a public place, whether directly or via an intermediate association. It also operated as a charitable association and friendly society. There is no doubt that these roles account for the institution's success among the local population, but their rapid growth in the city of Buenos Aires cannot be fully comprehended without bearing in mind the fact that it also operated as a men's recreation society. It could not have been any other way, as one of the most appreciated values of the order was that of fraternity. Thus, the exchanges among brethren were stimulated by both the Masonic ritual and the sociability practices that accompanied and prolonged them. The traditional Masonic banquets, while a ritual obligation, were also a sociability practice increasingly common in society. The purely social aspect, or the mere function of sociability, which these practices implied in Freemasonry even appear to have taken on considerable importance in Buenos Aires, to the extent that this "secular" aspect at times prevailed over the more philosophical, esoteric or philanthropic aspect, as can be inferred from a debate among some Masons following the luxurious *tenida (A meeting of a masonic lodge–Translator)* of 21 July 1860 in the salons of the Colón Theatre. Certain brethren wondered whether the aim of Freemasonry was philanthropy or the organizing of luxurious feasts, as was increasingly the case in Buenos Aires.[54] The same observation appears in the article by an anonymous occasional Mason appearing in the *La Reforma Pacífica* newspaper. In it, the author gave his reasons for not being a regular member. Porteño Freemasonry, he confessed, ignored the true Masonic principles, and had no philosophical or social tendency: "Masonry among us has come to be a fashion, to be a Mason is like being a member of the Progress Club or the July Club."[55] This implies that Freemasonry served to channel the sociability needs of the local population. But while offering a meeting place and a network of relationships, it also established as the foundation of these connections a set of values based on an individual and contractual representation of society which, as will be seen below, had endless consequences.

The importance of the entertainment role in the lodges' recruitment might explain why men belonged both to the lodges and the clubs; in total 128 Masons can be counted as having dual memberships (13.8% of all Freemasons). Most first joined a club and went on to be initiated into the Freemasons (ninety of 128 cases), while thirty-four joined a club after joining the Masons. It is feasible then that recreational exchanges between men constituted an important aspect in the attraction of the lodge. In these specific cases, at least, the enthusiasm for a sociability practice tied to the role of recreation among men might explain the movement from one form to another. The fact that the Great Lodge, like many workshops, operated from the first floor of the Colón Theatre is undoubtedly not a coincidence but in fact most significant.[56] The shared location may indeed be interpreted as a closeness of roles.

Cultural Recreation as a New Social Need

The rate of the establishment of sociocultural associations followed that of the emergence of the former Spanish colonies into the "democratic era." It is not therefore surprising to find that in Buenos Aires the arrival of the liberals was accompanied by a blooming of these forms of associative sociability with sociocultural goals. These also, however, showed signs of a growth in the type of exchanges and in their clientele. The associations, which originated in the needs of some men to discuss "Society," now contributed to satisfying a generalized need for cultural diversion, which served to define community belonging. As will be seen below, these sociohistorical variations had notable consequences for the political significance of cultural practices.

GROWTH TOWARDS A FORM OF CULTURAL ENTERTAINMENT

Sociocultural associations were one of the first contractual forms of relationship established in the River Plate. I have shown how the traces of a mutation (1800–1827) were confirmed from the 1830s on, to a great extent due to university students and the dissemination of new cultural practices tied to the development of the written press. As the trend was confirmed the public increased. Thus, after the first sociocultural associations, strictly composed of members of the intellectual elite, there was a move towards forms that were developed among a wider public: students, journalists and businessmen.

When sociocultural associations reappeared in 1852, they took root in the area of the city that was socially established as the place for cultural exchanges, the Manzana de las Luces university area. This does not alter the fact that this physical space now received a clientele belonging to a wider sociocultural space. The cultural associations which developed tended to accentuate increasingly the entertainment function of the cultural exchange, which therefore implies a widening of their clientele as they now attracted individuals previously uninterested in associative practices. Thus the Philharmonic Society, created in 1852 by music lovers, soon had three hundred members, and the same was the case of the May Philharmonic Society. These associations used the associative organization model (open forms, revocable ties, elected authorities, participation of all members in general assemblies, etc.) to formalize meetings that previously took place intermittently. People also met here to attend performances and be seen. To participate it was necessary to have sufficient income to pay the membership fee and to respect the codes of civility which gave access to this wide cultural universe.

In some of these associations spectacle predominated over literary or political discussion, as was the case in philharmonic societies. Conversation, in cases where it did not disappear, was no longer de rigeur. The role of these bodies, moreover, was very similar to that of recreational associations and this similarity often led to a confusion of the forms, as seen in the case of the May Philharmonic Society, which took on one of the principal roles of recreation clubs: the organization of a members' monthly ball. The confusion was so great that this sociocultural association would eventually choose outright the entertainment form, becoming the May Club just one year after its foundation.[57] Vicuña Mackenna gives evidence of the fusion between the activities of sociocultural societies and recreational clubs.[58] It is not surprising that many members belonged at once to both kinds of clubs and associations. The figures speak for themselves. In a sample of 217 members of cultural associations during this period, sixty-eight of them, almost a third, were also members of a recreational club. Of these, a 53% majority first joined a cultural association to later join a club, while 35.2% did the opposite.[59] These data reveal how much this function could attract new members. Indeed, these associations were the stage on which civility and the good graces of the city's inhabitants were extolled. People did not intend to present themselves here as courteous and sociable by means of the public use of individual reason, but by a certain enthusiasm for offering themselves as a spectacle. In this sense, these associations were tied to the "salon-mania" discussed above, but with the distinction that the formal context that organized the gatherings now formed part of the exaltation of the civility of the members. Varela notes this in his newspaper: "these associations, with liberal republican regulations, found a civilized people through the development of democratic customs."[60]

THE ASSOCIATION AS AN IDENTITARY MECHANISM

Unlike Masonic lodges, the formal framework of cultural exchanges showed variations related to the particular objectives of each society. But of all the associations, those that stood out in number and importance were those that emphasized the nation as foundation and objective of the relationship. This was the case with literary societies, which attracted a more select public with a more professional attitude towards cultural activities: men of letters and of law, principally, who met together to reflect on society's questions. In comparison with similar associations created previously, it is possible to clearly distinguish a sensibility that focused on society as a political community of belonging. In other words, the question of the nation was now at the center of its cultural exchanges.

Some associations were born of a common interest among cultured men to publicly establish the memory of the nation.[61] Their promoters, to a great extent former companions in exile, connected the birth of nationality to the restoration of the public sphere, the source of their own power. The Instituto Histórico-Geográfico del Río de la Plata, for example, was created under the initiative of some of the better-known political figures, who fought in the political terrain for the creation of a national State: Valentín Alsina, Bartolomé Mitre, Dalmacio Vélez Sársfield, Carlos Tejedor, Domingo Faustino Sarmiento, Rufino de Elizalde, and Juan María Gutiérrez among others.[62] These men represented the different tendencies of the national organization project: the "nationalists" like Bartolomé Mitre, the "autonomists" like Valentín Alsina, and the "Urquizists" like Miguel Valencia, Mariano Fragueiro, and Nicolás Calvo. However, while there were some differences as to the conditions for the organization of the Nation State, all agreed on recognizing that the Nation was the foundation of the community of belonging. For this reason, the men gathered in associations which assigned a very particular importance to the creation of a national memory. The Institute, which functioned as an association with regulations similar to other bodies, set itself the following objective: "the study of history, geography and statistics in all its relationships and applications, limiting ourselves to the River Plate, where it is possible to explore advantageously for the first time its rich materials, which are yet to be classified." But as they suggest, their mission did not consist solely of cataloguing the heritage of the nation but also of making sense of it: "we must take pride in making order in the chaos of documents which our historical inheritance constitutes."[63] From this order, they intended to institutionalize the memory of the nation. Therefore, the investigating members met regularly to "order" the accounts that made up the national past, with the aim of creating the Nation through the socialization of recounting the origins. Héctor Varela, a member of the organization, announced to public opinion that "every people has in its own annals a treasure to defend, not as ancient priests guarded the sibylline books, but as the sacred tie between generations which perpetuates memories."[64] Bartolomé Mitre edited at the same time his *Historia de Belgrano* and participated in the *Galerías de Celebridades Argentinas* with Domingo F. Sarmiento, Luis Domínguez, Juan María Gutiérrez, and Manuel Moreno. In addition, Domínguez wrote his *Historia argentina* and Alejandro Magariños Cervantes his *Biblioteca americana*, a project to publish an anthology of texts "of the principal Statesmen of the Argentine Republic."[65]

At roughly the same time that the Historical-Geographical Institute was established the Association of Friends of the Natural History of the Plate was founded. Unlike the former, this organization was set up under the initiative of the government and its statute established by the rector of the University of Buenos Aires, José Barros Pazos.[66] The objective of this institution-association was the "conservation and development of the Museum of Buenos Aires."[67] To this end, the statute provided that the society should be made up of thirty principal members, including the four founders, the university rector and the museum director, who would choose the remaining members. The statute also established the presence of honorary and corresponding members. The society's collections came from the State or from private donations, with which the commission was to provide the growth of the museum's exhibits, primarily a collection of minerals, pieces of anatomy, physics instruments and a notable collection of artistic, modern medals that the government of Buenos Aires had acquired in 1823.[68] Barros Pazos and Trelles' project was to make the Natural History Museum an institution for cataloguing the vestiges of national history and geography. For this reason, they created the Friends of the Museum association, comprising learned men who were to take responsibility for geological research in order to attain better knowledge of the local natural environment. Scientific activity placed itself thus at the service of the nation, as the recovery of the vestiges "of the local nature and history" became a masterpiece of the construction of a shared past, with the museum the essential instrument for the conservation of these remnants. The association set itself the mission of making the Natural History Museum a place of memory, which citizens could visit to give themselves over to the cult of the Nation. This explains why, from 1854, there was a gradual increase in pieces of historical memory classified as "art, antiques, diverse objects, and other rubrics."[69] And although in our period these were far less numerous than zoological pieces, proportionally they increased more rapidly. Thus, of the 5,439 pieces of zoology in the museum's possession by the end of the period in question, 67.45% had been acquired after the foundation of the association of friends of the museum. In contrast, the objects that were historical vestiges had been obtained almost entirely (96.6%) after 1854. For these men of culture and power, the scientific and cultural project merged with the political project of the nation.[70]

There were other associations operating as idea circles, with the objective of consecrating the memory of the nation. We can cite the case of the Ateneo del Plata and the Liceo Literario, established in 1858, which grouped together the principal journalists and intellectuals of the period with a view to developing the arts and national history. In both cases these were associations created by the initiative of men of letters, financed by the contributions of its members. The Ateneo del Plata, which displayed political tendencies close to those of the province of Buenos Aires, could count on the benevolence of the government, which provided the association with the university's lecture halls. The Liceo Literario, an association made up of such figures as Bilbao, Calvo, Viel Castel and Fajardo, recognized its differences with the politics of Buenos Aires and had to make do with holding meetings in the homes of its members. In spite of political differences, culture was the object of exchanges for both institutions, in so far as it was national culture. Thus, the Ateneo del Plata established, through its commissions on history, literature and poetry (directed by D. F. Sarmiento, M. Cané and L. Domínguez) themes of common interest which favored the development of a national culture. At the first meeting, the theme of a monthly poetry contest on "The historic novel: the discovery and the conquest of the River Plate" was proposed.[71] Miguel Cané, responsible for the literature section, gave the following possibilities as themes for a historic novel: "the death of Crámer and Castelli," "the Liniers drama," and "accounts of the death of Solís."[72] Sarmiento, responsible for the history section, inaugurated studies with a reading of his memoir on "the spirit and conditions of a history of America."[73] The cultural exchanges were no doubt part of a device to identify the redefinition of the community of belonging.

For the promoters of the Ateneo, the important factor was that "the indications of the masters, in the form of lectures, should illustrate our intellectual world and develop for the younger generation something approaching the learning of the Sorbonne, the College of France, the great universities of Germany and Italy."[74] The comparison is a curious one, as the two institutions mentioned were famously different from the University of Buenos Aires. While in France, as Pierre Rosanvallon shows, the "resurrection" of scientific institutions was linked to the presence of a national State and associated with a new figure of the learned intellectual, in Buenos Aires the responsibility of literary circles as places of culture originated from a private initiative and evoked more the romantic image of the intellectual philosopher.[75] The cultural institutions of the elites aimed, on the contrary, at occupying the place of the State's nonexistent scientific institutions. In addition, the structure of associative sociability of the elites preceded the State in its role of imposing on society an institutional presence of the nation.

The new associations were not limited to a strictly cultural aspect of social exchanges. There were also some which highlighted the corporative scientific aspect of these exchanges. This was the case with associations with members from the liberal professions who hoped to form an organization for their personal benefit but also to provide a service for the community. These adapted the friendly society model, but were founded on criteria of cultural belonging. Thus, the Buenos Aires Pharmaceutical Association,[76] the Dolores Association of Doctors and the Association of Doctors of Buenos Aires combined mutual aid with public discussions on issues of general interest, which were also issues of their professions. Because of this, a role in the development of knowledge that responded to the needs of the country can be attributed to them. This was then another aspect of the identitary mechanism: the association of individuals for the development of science that while not national, was adapted nevertheless to the needs of the nation.

RECRUITMENT IN SOCIOCULTURAL ASSOCIATIONS

Far from representing contradictory phenomena, the different types of association presented above manifested a like tendency for widening the clientele base in cultural exchanges, as can be gathered from the analysis of the associations' members.[77] It is difficult to say whether the 217 registered members were representative of the group as a whole. Nevertheless, it is possible to say fairly certainly that they were representative of the elites of sociocultural associations, as these appeared most frequently in documents and in the local press. According to these data, the cultural associations were made up of a majority of intellectuals and members of the liberal professionals, while large landowners still distrusted these organizations, or at least their direction. Perhaps more surprising was the scarce presence of commercial professions, a sphere in which associative habits had already developed. The reason for this indifference might be found in the associations' considerable specialization and their lesser focus on strictly cultural objectives, which limited the clientele and as a result may have made the relationship network less attractive.[78]

In the case of some associations, the student population still represented a considerable number of members, as appears to have been the case in the Ateneo del Plata, according to a notice published in the local press announcing that "as the most part of the members of the Ateneo are students of the University and will be taking exams from the first of the coming month, many gentlemen have made efforts to suspend the session that would take place on this day."[79] But it would appear that in addition to intellectuals and the inevitable students, new sectors began to take an interest in these associations. Administrative clerks, most notably, made up almost a fifth of the total of members. Although these figures must be considered with extreme precaution, they nevertheless are quite significant and allow us to conjecture the way the associations spread. The widening of the clientele would thus occur due to the conduct of the middle class, which was closest to the cultural and political elites. This was due to the provincial State's dependence on administration but also because these sectors, being intermediaries between elite culture and popular culture, saw in associative belonging a way of incorporating the cultural model of the political elites, which might have opened the doors to a certain amount of social climbing.

In comparison to the preceding period, sociocultural associations were more highly specialized in their roles, tending to be limited strictly to the cultural and scientific sphere. As shown above, this restricted their clientele to the sector of intellectuals and politicians interested in cultural policy. However, they were not alien to this pronounced taste for social exchanges respecting certain relational codes and values, founded on an individual and contractual representation of society. But their members would manage to satisfy this need for pure sociability and the need to be connected with a wide relational network through attending leisure associations.

Sociability as the Object of Associations: Leisure Clubs

The recreational society was certainly not an English invention. The population of the city and the countryside had more or less established their own forms of entertainment in the colonial period. In the countryside, the *pulpería* was the principal place of leisure, while in the city there were various places and forms, from bathing in the river, through numerous family *tertulias,* to dances to the rhythm of the tambour, inhabitants constantly manifested their need for pure sociability. Although it is necessary to distinguish between popular entertainment and that of the well-to-do, urban colonial sociability was characterized by its spontaneous forms, which often arose from family ties. The entertainment function was then developed through modern forms of sociability, which presaged a fundamental trend in corresponding collective life, as Maurice Agulhon clearly showed, towards the expansion of bourgeois civilization.[80] Shared entertainment then became the object of the association.

THE ORGANIZATION OF NEW PLACES OF RECREATION

To enjoy good company with a certain amount of merrymaking increasingly became the generalized model of sociability among the well-to-do. As we have seen, informal relationships in both cafés and associations of various kinds developed this form of pure sociability. But what we have been able to identify as common features of certain associative forms ultimately brought about the origin of a specific form: the leisure society or English-style club.

The first leisure clubs were established by the city's foreign population. These were at first forms that combined the pleasure of the gathering with a need for information. This was the case with the traders' rooms or circles seen above. But as the trend for organizations took shape, specific leisure forms began to appear, namely social and sporting recreational associations. The first of these was the Foreign Amateur Racing Society, founded in Buenos Aires in 1849 by members of the Foreign Residents' Club.[81] The commission met in the club's facilities in the city, but the men met on a strip of land in the Belgrano area, five miles from the center, where races were held. Three years later, members of the local population established the Progress Club, which was rather more a form of leisure club, combining cultural recreation, society games and sporting entertainment. The formula caught on immediately, with twelve similar clubs appearing between 1853 and 1858. The form developed progressively until 1856, with one association founded in 1854, three in 1855 and four in 1856, before gradually diminishing up to 1858 and further still up to 1862. This curve can be easily explained. After the establishment of this practice in the local population, there was a brief phase of expansion during the early years of the constitutional government, from the declaration of freedom of association in 1854 until 1856–1857. After this, the domestic situation and particularly the development of armed conflict with the Confederation accounted for this deceleration in the establishment of new clubs, all the more so considering that the war coincided with the economic crisis which affected intensely the export sector of the provincial economy. These economic difficulties explain to a great extent the decrease in places of entertainment.

The mode in which the clubs were established was very similar to that of the Masonic lodges, originating in the foreign population of the capital before being developed by the native population and spreading to towns in the countryside (figure 20). The status of these towns was fairly heterogeneous, but what they all had in common was the importance of agricultural production in their economies: livestock in the south, in San Miguel, San Nicolás, and Chascomús; farming in the north and west, in Flores, Mercedes, Belgrano, San Isidro and Zárate. In certain cases these were already places of leisure for the urban population, Flores and Belgrano being visited on Sundays by the well-to-do of Buenos Aires, while San

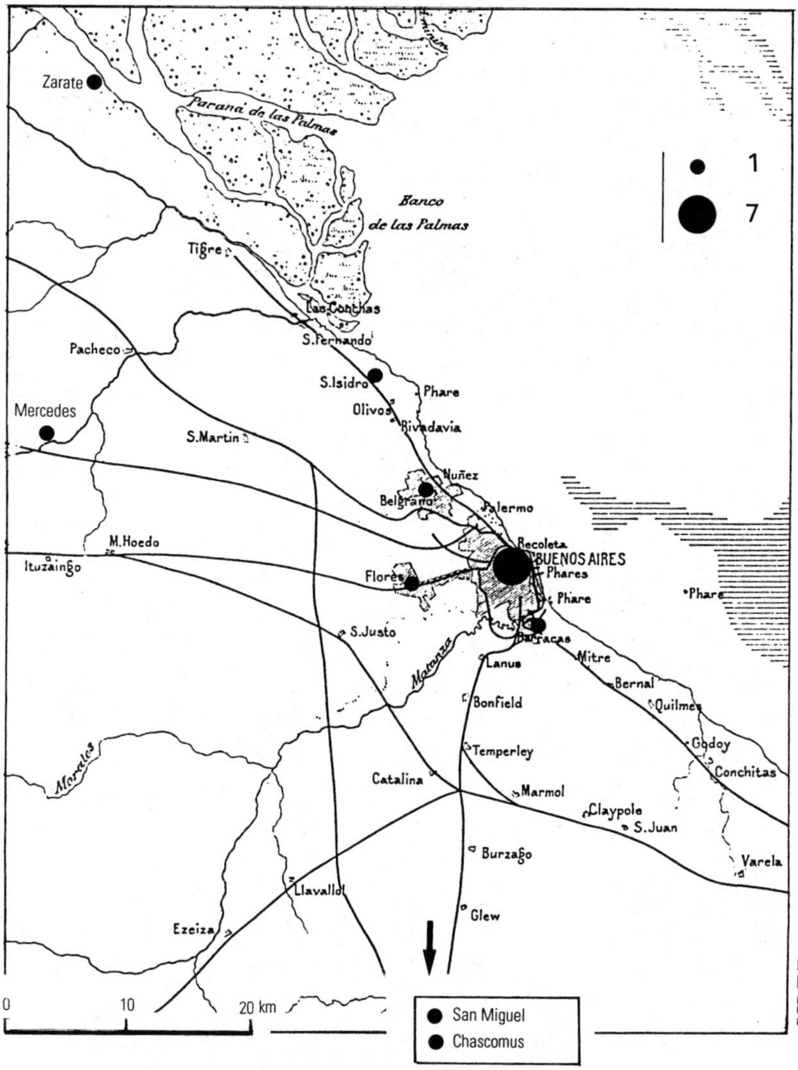

Figure 20. The Establishment of Recreation Clubs in the State of Buenos Aires (1852–1862)
Source: *Nouvelle GU* (1891)

Isidro, fifteen miles from the capital, was a summer resort for Porteño families. In others, the elites of the city who moved to the countryside spread the new forms of sociability among the local population. In many cases, recreation clubs were the first modern associations to be developed in rural areas.

RECRUITMENT

Who were the members of these clubs? The practice was first developed among the urban elites closest to the English population. In principle there were no restrictions to participating in these, as long as the candidate could afford the entrance fee and monthly subscription. The cost varied from one club to the next. Thus, at the first club created among Argentine nationals, the cost of admission was as much as 1000 pesos with a monthly subscription of 100 pesos.[82] Clubs founded subsequently targeted a less wealthy clientele and fees were considerably lower, varying between 25 pesos in the national guards' club and 70 in the Club del Plata. From these figures it is possible to infer pronounced differences in the socioprofessional origin of the members. The Chilean Vicuña Mackenna, who visited Buenos Aires at the height of the clubs' growth, left us the following testimony: "The chief club is the Progress Club, being the most expensive and the most aristocratic. It has 280 members who pay 50 pesos [*sic*] per year. Its immediate rival, although rivalry of this class of establishment is for the club's betterment, is the May Club, which might call itself the *cercle bourgeois* of the population."[83]

What was this difference that Vicuña Mackenna mentions? In theory, the Progress Club was open to all, as it was only necessary to be presented by three members and obtain a minority of votes in the directive commission.[84] This effectively facilitated the recruitment of family members and friends. Besides, the cost of the fee worked as an effective selection mechanism. The club's clientele can therefore be defined as the more comfortable section of the population. But what constituted its aristocratic nature in comparison to other clubs with equally bourgeois clientele were the restrictions on the number of members for whom access to the facilities was strictly reserved. According to the statutes these could number no more than 210, in other words the principal families of Buenos Aires.[85] This naturally aroused the displeasure of those excluded from "the most select of Buenos Aires," as is affirmed by an "indignant citizen" with regards to a ball in the salons of the club organized by Pastor Obligado, one of the members but also the Governor of the State of Buenos Aires, in honor of the Paraná Commission:

> what surpasses in originality all that is said, is that the Progress Club should be the official and aristocratic representative of the whole population of Buenos Aires, who pay their taxes with which public festivals are celebrated, without any right to enjoy them....There are, we believe, approximately two hundred members of the Progress Club and to hold a ball of this kind seems correct and consequent to the rank that Buenos Aires assumes in the world, but may the guests be not the individuals of a club determined by society lists, but the citizens and their families from diverse circles albeit always the first of Buenos Aires...[86]

Who was this aristocracy that claimed to represent the population of Buenos Aires? One can count 573 individual members of the club from between 1852 and 1863, and information corresponding to the socioprofessional status of 262 of them is available.[87] The best represented sector was that of large land and capital owners, constituting 32% of the total. Until this time, this group had a small presence in the elite's other forms of sociability. This means that in sectors considered more traditional the cultural mutation was produced by means of commercial societies and recreational associations. More than conversation and discussion, these men sought company among peers in order to widen their network of relationships.[88] The presence of the intellectual professions was as important as that of the large landowners, and in the majority of cases the former also held political positions. Moreover, a third of the club's members occupied a position in the administration of the provincial State. The percentage was much higher than in Freemasonry, where these accounted for only 13.8 percent of members. Frequently the great initiatives of the period were conceived and decided in the salons of the club: the construction of the first railroad, the installation of the gas company, the foundation of the Stock Exchange, and so on.[89]

Unfortunately, the archives of the May Club have not been found, which might have allowed us to compare the data of the Progress Club with those of the institution that Vicuña Mackenna defined as the *"cercle bourgeois."* Some names have been garnered from the local press. These are individuals who made up the directive commission, twenty-seven in total. Although it may be difficult to draw any conclusion from such scant figures, these might show a trend which could be later confirmed. Land and capital owners were again the most dominant group, accounting for a third, but subsequently two groups can be seen to have increased their representation, namely liberal professions, who constituted a fifth of all members, and traders, accounting for almost a sixth. This suggests that the more bourgeois character was due to the fact that the club was open to a clientele of a social prestige less recognized by the community as a whole. It also appears that the political class had a greater presence here. Almost half of the twenty-seven members held a public position, and a sixth were journalists. But it is most likely that these were over-represented as in most cases this was the ruling elite of the club. Be that as it may, the great difference between one club and the other was that the May Club did not set a limit on the number of members.

With regards to clubs in country towns, it is easy to imagine that the clientele was made up of producers of a foreign origin who were accustomed to these leisure practices, new agricultural producers from the city, and those of older stock, all of whom probably tended to join the new network of socioeconomic exchanges. However, once again the lack of archives leaves this question unanswered for now.

MODALITY OF EXCHANGES: RECREATION AND POLITICS

Clubs were recreation associations whose aims were pure sociability. Ties were made from common activities that brought members together: social leisure activities and sports. The modality of the exchanges depended on the type of activity developed by the association. When this was social recreation, leisure forms were similar to those of sociocultural associations, while in contrast the first forms of sporting recreation presaged an entirely new associative model in the shape of sports clubs.

The Progress Club, the first of its kind created at the heart of the Porteño population, set itself the following objective: "to promote the spirit of association which has completely disappeared, through periodic meetings of the most respectable men, whether national or foreign; to dispel unfounded prejudices, generated by isolation and distrust, unifying inasmuch as this is possible political opinions with discussions; to unite the strengths of all for the good of the moral and material progress of the country."[90] Thus expounded, the purpose of the club was the same as that of the Society of Friends of the Country, to which new political objectives were added. But aside from explicit economic and political goals, the club was founded to satisfy a need for public sociability among the well-to-do. During the inaugural banquet, G. Posadas clarified that: "This association, new in our land… has the special objective of arousing among one thousand fellow countrymen the need to meet together to pool their ideas towards the development of our national industry; also the need to fraternize with foreigners from friendly countries."[91]

The confusion between politico-economical and recreational objectives arose initially from the use of the word "club," until then used in the French sense.[92] It is therefore difficult to say whether or not at first the name concealed a will for explicit political action. In any event, there was no such consensus among members. This explains why in the book of minutes the word "club" was written in inverted commas more often than not. With regards to the objectives of the meetings, there was not even unanimity between the secretaries taking the minutes. For some, the denomination "club" was evidence of the initial will of the founders to constitute a kind of society of ideas, a will which had subsequently been betrayed. For others, the "club" had adopted the forms of English-style recreational associations. This misunderstanding was the cause of some friction among members, as seen in the discontentment of "Argentines of the defense" made public by Varela's newspaper:

> In establishing that association the previous year, with the pompous title that it carries, all believed that politics and social progress would be the principal objectives to be followed preferentially. Politics because it is shockingly absurd and ridiculous to give the name Club to an association of dances, gastronomy

> and billiards where coffee and all is sold at a higher price than in the finest hotel in Paris...the aristocratic nature that the society has taken repels all idea of sociability, frankness and good taste which should always prevail in meetings of this class.[93]

The reproach could not be clearer: the fostering of the spirit of association was for them inseparable from a civility that was to develop a public political space. Comfort and recreation were still identified with aristocratic forms of sociability which could bring nothing useful to republican society. Diego de Alvear, president of the club, took no time in responding to this accusation. After listing extensively the benefits of sociability that "reestablish the ties of the *patria*, friendship and even family," promote the spirit of association and industry and stimulate the memory of the great men of the country, Alvear concluded: "If in spite of all this it is considered that our Progress Society has been sterile in its results, because it was not constituted as a revolutionary lodge to hoist a purely political and bellicose standard, the anonymous author can seek out converts to his club." Alvear ends by reiterating that all forms of recreation cultivated by the club and which aroused reproach were essential for the realization of great objectives.[94] In other words, the relationships typical of recreational societies were the most apt to carry out successfully the political project of the elites. The institutional and economic reconstruction of the nation came here from the establishment of a civilized society, whose model would be the clubs of the elites.

This implied an important change, perhaps even a mutation, in the political sphere. While politics heretofore had been associated with action (mobilizations, riots, coups d'état, revolutions) or with power, it was now identified with certain cultural practices which defined the community of belonging as "civil society" and as a nation. At the same time, banquets and balls permitted civility to be established as the foundation of the social bond and civic festivals to be commemorated; the monthly *tertulias* served to build ties of friendship and contemplate the portraits of the principal heroes of the *patria*, which imprinted in the memory of the association's members the political components of national identity; lastly, libraries were the place par excellence of urbanity and the space where public space was established as the foundation of power.[95]

The ball calendar also reflected the identity between civility and politics. Whether to celebrate the oath of the Constitution,[96] to commemorate Independence Day, to applaud the end of the conspiracy against the government of Buenos Aires,[97] or to celebrate the meeting of the Congress of the Argentine Republic,[98] balls were organized in which good form blended with civic spirit. This trend was confirmed by the organization of banquets in honor of those individuals and events considered favorable for the citizen's progress and freedom.[99] Varela refers explicitly to this in his newspaper, when he informs the population of Buenos Aires of the banquet in honor of the national guard: "The custom of political banquets is essentially one of free people. Democracy has always made banquets a powerful indicator of public opinion. Freedom could not fail to give Buenos Aires one of its most beautiful and fertile practices."[100]

The new political sphere was also related to the décor. The salon of the club contained busts and portraits of Rivadavia, San Martín, Belgrano, Varela, Lavalle, Paz and Alvear.[101] There was also in the context for certain occasions, such as the banquet in honor of the National Guard, a veritable symbolic portrait of the nation: "An allegoric trophy, in the Roman style, representing strength with the national flag at the peak, formed the center of the banquet flag, with two triumphant arches at each end, with inscriptions of the National Guard from the interior and from the capital, symbolizing the triumph of the people, who were thus solemnified."[102] In forming part of the meetings, visual representations contributed to the club members' construction of identity. Alvear was indeed not wrong when he affirmed that recreational forms were the best channel for the realization of great political objectives.

The second activity around which relationships of sociability were developed was sport. This phenomenon only began to appear during our period. Some social clubs included this new activity in their calendars. The Progress Club, for example, added an arms room to its facilities where members could practice fencing. But the most novel phenomenon was the creation of associations specifically organized for sports trials. This was the case of the Shooting Club, which at the time of its foundation in 1855 had fifty members who met on Admiral Brown's estate, where today the National History Museum is located.[103] The organization of races was also a motive for the creation of associations. Following the example of the Amateur Racing Society, in 1855 the local population established the Argentine Racing Association.[104]

Aside from their differences, the rise of associations can be interpreted as a valuation of certain sociability relationships which were produced in the context of what we might call "civil society." This leads us to the question of the political scope of this belonging.

NOTES

1. There are exceptions, especially in the Mexican case, where secret societies have famously played a political role. Yet, few studies into Freemasonry have been based on a study of the institution's archives.
2. I am indebted to the authorities of the Great Argentine Lodge and the Great Masonic Lodge of Uruguay, who opened their archives to me. I am grateful particularly to the

former grand secretary of the Great Argentine Lodge, Víctor Curi, and to Humberto Escardino, a member of the historical commission of the Great Masonic Lodge of Uruguay, who assisted me tirelessly during my research. A critical list of the literature can be found in my article, "Masonería y Nación: la construcción masónica de una memoria histórica nacional," *Historia, Review of the Instituto de Historia, Pontificia Universidad Católica de Chile* 25 (1990): 81–101.

3. Bonapartist freemasonry was official and almost a part of the state. In the hands of the French troops, it worked as a kind of ideological political instrument in the occupation. On Spanish freemasonry, see J. A. Ferrer Benimeli, *La masonería*.

4. According to figures reproduced by Martha Marenales Rossi and Guy Bourdé, in 1843 the population of Montevideo was 63% foreign. Towards the end of the century these figures decreased, but still remained high. See Martha Marenales Rossi and Guy Bourdé, "L'immigration française et le peuplement de l'Uruguay, 1830–1860," *Cahiers des Amériques Latines* 16 (1977): 7–21.

5. The Los Aristócratas lodge and Perfeita Amistade lodge (both founded in 1822) operated in Brazil with the constitution of the Grand Orient of Brazil. See D. V. Pérez Fontana, *La masonería*; A. Fernández Cabrelli, *Presencia masónica en la Cisplatina* (Montevideo: América Una, 1986). (A. Lappas does not mention these lodges.) Moreover, patriotic groups opposed to the Portuguese-Brazilian occupation appealed to the same type of organization. This was the case with the Caballeros Orientales society, founded by Carlos María de Alvear, a former member of the Lautaro lodge. This association, while not strictly Masonic, reproduced the organization of the secret societies with the distinction of three grades of membership. See "Constitución Orgánica del Orden Caballeros Orientales," in Marta Campos and Theverin de Garabelli, *La revolución oriental. Su génesis* (Montevideo: Junta Departamental, Biblioteca José Artigas, 1973). On the history of this association there are references in Antonio Díaz, *Memorias inéditas del general oriental don César Díaz* (Buenos Aires, 1878); T. de Iriarte, *Memorias*, vols. 1 and 3.

6. The minute book of the Les Amis de la Patrie lodge in Montevideo reveals that a French lodge, Les Enfants du Nouveau Monde, was operating in the city in 1829. See Archive of the Great Masonic Lodge of Uruguay (AGMLU), Minute Book of the Les Amis de la Patrie lodge. According to Pérez Fontana, this lodge was already in operation in 1827. See D. V. Pérez Fontana, *La masonería*. At almost the same time, the Asilo de la Virtud lodge was founded, which, according to Pérez Fontana, comprised foreigners who were members of the Estrella Sureña lodge. According to the minutes, this lodge of modern rites was created with the constitution of the Grand Orient of Pennsylvania. See "Minute book," in D. V. Pérez Fontana, *La masonería*. The lodge operated regularly until 1837. After this date it continued but with strictly political ends, as Giuseppe Garibaldi testified on joining the Les Amis de la Patrie. See Bibliothèque Nationale (Paris), Uruguay, Les Amis de la Patrie lodge, FM2, 586. In 1842, the latter lodge obtained a constitution from the Grand Orient of France. In 1847 some Englishmen organized The Pilgrims lodge, requesting a constitution from the Grand United Lodge of England. One year later, the Les Amis de la Patrie lodge advised of the existence of a lodge named Los Hijos del Secreto operating in the Orient of Montevideo. See AGMLU, minutes of the Les Amis de la Patrie lodge.

7. Naturally this was not the first lodge to operate in Montevideo, but the first regularly operating lodge whose archives we possess. See AGMLU, Minute Book of the Misterio y Honor lodge.

8. Correspondence from the Les Amis de la Patrie lodge to the Grand Orient of France, Montevideo, 1 August 1855, in Bibliothèque Nationale (Paris), Montevideo, Les Amis de la Patrie lodge, FM2, 867.
9. The archives of the Great Masonic lodge of Uruguay have not retained any testimony concerning this schism. The only references are from correspondence between the Les Amis de la Patrie and the Grand Orient of France. See Bibliothèque Nationale (Paris), Les Amis de la Patrie lodge, FM2, 865; FM2, 867.
10. To briefly summarize the main features of this history, after the end of the Great War in 1851, the two parties that had fought each other for eight years were faced with the challenge of transforming their war practices into political practices. The conservatives aligned themselves behind the political program of the Society of Friends of the Country, an economic society created in Montevideo in 1852. The liberals encountered difficulties in organizing themselves for the elections and held a minority in parliament. The conservative, or *blanco,* Francisco Giró then assumed the presidency. One year later a revolution led by the *caudillo* Flores forced him to abandon power and dissolve the two houses. A provisional triumvirate then took charge of the government until the new elections in February and March 1854. Flores was elected until the end of Giró's mandate (1856). It was at this time that Freemasonry made its appearance.
11. See the classic work by Juan E. Pivel Devoto, *Historia de la República Oriental del Uruguay, 1830–1930* (Montevideo: Raúl Artagareytia, 1945); J. E. Pivel Devoto, *Historia de los partidos políticos uruguayos, 1811–1897*, 2 vols. (Montevideo, 1942). The history of Uruguayan Masonry is yet to be written. There are some important works that have prepared the groundwork, such as the research of Arturo Ardao. Although Ardao's interest lies in the philosophical aspects of the Masonic order, he has sketched the political growth (closely related to philosophical growth) of Freemasonry in Uruguay. See Arturo Ardao, *Racionalismo y liberalismo en el Uruguay* (Montevideo: Universidad de la República, 1962). On the relationship between Freemasonry and liberalism in Uruguay, there is a fairly useful work by Manuel Claps, "Masones y liberals," *Enciclopedia Uruguaya* 27 (1969). See also Alfonso Fernández Cabrelli, *Masonería y sociedades secretas en las luchas emancipadoras de la patria grande* (La Paz: América Una, 1975); A. Fernández Cabrelli, *Masonería, morenismo, artiguismo: presencia e influencia de la francmasonería en los movimientos independentistas del Río de la Plata* (Montevideo: América Una, 1982); and A. Fernández Cabrelli, *Presencia masónica.* The latter author is the director of the review *Hoy es Historia* (issue 1 appeared in 1983), in which there are frequently articles on issues close to Freemasonry. With regards to Freemasonry, it is necessary to cite the works of D. V. Pérez Fontana, *La masonería*; Aldo Ciasullo, "Reseña histórica de la masonería uruguaya," *Revista Gran Lodge de la Masonería del Uruguay* 2 (April 1985).
12. In the Spanish translation of the anti-Masonic writings of Louis Gaston Sécur, which appeared in Montevideo in 1877, there is a dedication to the Society of Friends of the Country in Montevideo, in which the translator, the priest Francisco Javier Quintanilla, reminds the members of this organization of their role in society: "Your first duty, Friends of the Country, is to fight against Freemasonry, which with the most perfidious means firmly aspires to the extermination of religion and the imbalance of social order, and which is inexorably making itself a place in governments and impregnating the atmosphere of the people." See Louis Gaston de Ségur, *Los franc-masones, lo que son, lo que hacen, lo que quieren* (Buenos Aires: Igon, 1877).

13. See Bibliothèque Nationale (Paris), Uruguay, Les Amis de la Patrie lodge, correspondence with the Grand Orient of France, Montevideo, 20 February 1856, FM2, 867.
14. Bibliothèque Nationale (Paris), Uruguay, Les Amis de la Patrie lodge, correspondence with the Grand Orient of France, Montevideo, 10 June 1856, FM2 867.
15. The conflict began with the celebration of the Feast of St. John organized by the Sol Oriental lodge in 1855, which was reported by the press of Montevideo. See "Carta de Lamas al ministro secretario de Estado," *El Nacional*, 23 July 1855; "Carta de lectores," 28 July 1855. See also "Carta de lectores," *La Nación*, 7 July 1855, 3; "Un enemigo de las logias," *La Nación*, 11 July 1855, 3; "Carta a Salvador Tort," *El Comercio del Plata*, 22 July 1855.
16. See figure 18 on the model of establishment of Masonic lodges.
17. "Carta de Miguel Valencia a Gabriel Pérez," 4 March 1856 (the diplomas do not appear in the correspondence), in AGLMU, "Antecedentes de la fundación del Gran Oriente Argentino." The authorities of the Grand Masonic Lodge of Uruguay brought together in this file all of the documentation concerning the creation of the Grand Orient of the Republic of Argentina. In it one finds lists of members, decrees and Masonic correspondence pertaining to Argentina. There are also references in AGLA, Actas 1856–1861, Minute Book, Unión del Plata lodge, book 3. According to Chaparro, Valencia was already running an ad hoc workshop where Argentines who had become initiated into Freemasonry in exile would meet. See Félix Chaparro, *José Roque Pérez, un héroe civil argentino* (Rosario: Multicarta, 1951), 122.
18. See Mugiense, *Farsa de la francmasonería en Buenos Aires* (Buenos Aires: Imprenta de la Revista, 1858). Hortelano created the Bibliographic Casino. On the same premises were the Spanish Hall of Commerce and the Spanish Charitable Society. See B. Hortelano, *Memorias.*
19. *Farsa de la francmasonería*, 15.
20. *Farsa de la francmasonería*, 34.
21. The founders were Miguel Valencia, Santiago Albarracín, Federico Álvarez de Toledo, Domingo Faustino Sarmiento, Palemón Huergo, José María de Uriarte, A. L. Alves Pintos, Francisco Albarracín, Julián Vélez, José M. Lagos, Carlos Cáceres, Esteban Señorans and Miguel Martínez de Hoz. See AGLA, Minute Book, Unión del Plata lodge, 1858–1861, book 3.
22. See chapter 7.
23. For more on this question, see chapter 8.
24. On trade in the region, see Thomas Lyle Whigham, *The Politics of River Commerce in the Upper Plata, 1780–1865*, Ph.D. dissertation, Stanford University (Ann Arbor: University Microfilms International, 1986).
25. On the usefulness of Masonic networks to people involved in the trade, see M. Agulhon, *Pénitents et francs-maçons*, 168–179.
26. The archives of this lodge can be found in AGLA, Minute Book, Luz del Desierto lodge, box 37 (1860–1879). This does not contain documentation concerning the foundation or the first two years.
27. See *Reglamento interno de la Resp Log de San Juan de Esc. regularmente constituida la Or..., de Montevideo en el año de la V. L. 5830, bajo el título distintivo Asilo de la Virtud, Montevideo,* Imprenta del Telégrafo, 5836, ch. 6, art. 72.
28. The requirement of good health can be accounted for by the fact that the Masonry had some of the functions of friendly societies. See AGLA, Minute Book,

Regeneración lodge, box 36, session of 10 November 1858. In later regulations this condition disappeared. The criteria of age, morality, education and level of income were maintained. See *Constitución para la Orden Masónica en la República Argentina* (Buenos Aires: Imprenta Litográfica Jacobo Peuser, 1891).

29. The institution was experiencing its first schism and it is most likely that these two authorities twisted the rules in order to win over the greatest possible number of people from the secular world. See Circular 114 of 7 April 1859, in AGLA, Minute Book, Constancia lodge, book 2.
30. They would later join the Masons. See AGLA, Minute Book, Unión del Plata lodge, book 2.
31. See AGLA, Minute Book, Consuelo del Infortunio lodge, book 27, session of 4 January 1859.
32. See AGLA, Central Grand Lodge, box 3, proceedings against Pelegrín Baltazar.
33. There is only one documented case to our knowledge of an African-Argentine being admitted into the Freemasonry. The case was so unheard of that the Venerable Master of the Unión del Plata lodge, Mariano Billinghurst, cited the example to demonstrate his own democratic vocation when his leadership of the Supreme Council was called into question. See AGLA, Minute Book (1856–1861), Unión del Plata lodge, book 3, session of 25 August 1860.
34. Hence, in the Obediencia a la Ley lodge there was some argument as a result of the rejection of the initiation of a brother who had been accepted by vote. The reason for this rejection was the social status of the candidate. The brother speaker of the lodge, Martín Beruti, retorted that "to refuse an initiation went against the regulations," and reminded his brethren "that Freemasonry was essentially a humanitarian and philanthropic association and that with such actions it would become an aristocracy; if Freemasonry accepted anyone, it must not be for money but for moral good and knowledge." See AGLA, Minute Book, Obediencia a la Ley lodge, book 586, session of 8 February 1860.
35. On this question see Ran Halévi, *Les Loges maçonniques dans la France d'Ancien Régime. Aux origines de la sociabilité démocratique* (Paris: A. Colin, 1984).
36. Naturally, this does not mean that such discussions never occurred in the lodges, but the minutes rarely recorded them.
37. Bilbao was quite an ambiguous figure for the Porteño ruling class. Liberal and republican, he professed an anticlericalism quite uncommon among Hispano-American liberals, which explains why he was little understood in his time. A companion of Argentine liberals during their exile in Chile, Bilbao was left of the progressive sector of the liberal party. However, in supporting the national federalist organization advocated by Urquiza he was at odds, like J.B. Alberdi, with Porteño liberalism and a considerable number of Freemasons committed to the government. The numerous conflicts among these would ultimately lead to Bilbao being isolated from the liberals and the federals. Even today he continues to be a controversial figure. The best biography of Bilbao is Armando Donoso's *Bilbao y su tiempo* (Santiago de Chile: Zig-Zag, 1913).
38. See *La Tribuna*, 10 June 1858. Sarmiento wrote to all the lodges of Buenos Aires to inform them that he "had accepted in a spirit of fraternity the invitation dispatched to him, in order to settle the unpleasant situation between him and brother Bilbao." See AGLA, Minutes, various documents, Unión del Plata lodge, box 21, session of 14 June 1858.

39. See *El Nacional*, 19 January 1859; *La Reforma Pacífica*, 20 January 1859; *La Tribuna*, 21 and 22 January 1859. The differences between the Porteño Freemasons were of a political and religious nature. In the political aspect, Varela represented the "Porteñista party" against Francisco Bilbao who was aligned with Nicolás Calvo and his newspaper *La Reforma Pacífica* (the voice of the pro-Urquizista party). With regards to differences over religious issues, the positions were reversed. The two extremes were represented on the one hand by the Freemasons Bilbao and Pescs, both fiercely anticlericalist, and on the other hand by the Catholic Freemasons. Varela and Sarmiento were positioned in the center of the religious issue. See *La Reforma Pacífica*, 10 January and 18 November 1858; *La Tribuna*, 1 February 1859; Alejandro Pesce, *Roma y la Franc-masonería. Refutación de algunas palabras contra la Franc-masonería vertidas por D. Martín Avertino Piñero* (Buenos Aires, 1858); Francisco Bilbao, *La contra-pastoral* (Buenos Aires: Imprenta y Litografía Berheim y Boneo, 1862). The response to this writing can be found in Estrada y Gelpi's leaflet *El catolicismo y la Democracia. Refutación de la América en Peligro* (Buenos Aires); see also Félix Frías, "La sepultura eclesiástica," *El Pensamiento Argentino* (Buenos Aires, 1863).
40. Circular of the Grand Orient of the Republic of Argentina of 15 February 1859. One copy in AGLA, Correspondence, Fraternidad y Beneficencia lodge, book 21.
41. This was an initiative of the Regeneración lodge. See AGLA, Minute Book, Regeneración lodge, box 36, session of 19 August 1857.
42. See *La Reforma Pacífica*, 28 October 1857, 2; *El Orden*, 25 November 1858, 3.
43. See *La Reforma Pacífica*, 28 October 1857, 2; *El Orden*, 25 November 1858, 3.
44. The creation of a poorhouse was an idea that Varela had been toying with for some time. On various occasions he wrote articles in this respect in his newspaper. See "Un asilo para los pobres," *La Tribuna*, 12 May 1855, 2; "Asilo para los pobres," *La Tribuna*, 130 November 1855, 2; "Indigencia y hospicio," *La Tribuna*, 1 28 February 1856, 2; "Asilo de mendigos,"*La Tribuna*, 13 April 1858, 2. The project was presented to the lodge at the session of 10 June 1858. See AGLA, Minute Book (1857–1860), Lealtad lodge, book 41, sessions of 10 and 26 June 1858.
45. See "La caridad de los masones," *La Religión*, 30 October 1858, 1–3; "Caridad masónica," 13 November 1858. Relationships between Freemasonry and the Church in the province of Buenos Aires constitute an enormous area that is yet to be the object of research. It is impossible here to grant it the space it deserves. I will limit myself to mentioning the rich bibliography that I have consulted on this issue. See *Historia, Doctrina y Fin u Objeto de la Franc-masonería. Por un franc-masón que no lo es más. Dedicada a las gentes honradas*, translated from the second French edition by "an Argentine concerned for the good of his country" (Buenos Aires: Imprenta de Mayo, 1858); Antonino Fulias, *Farsa de la Francmasonería en Buenos Aires por El Mugiense* (Buenos Aires: Imprenta de la Revista, 1858). This satire provoked the response from Pesce mentioned above: *Roma y la Franc-masonería*. Fulias would reply with *Refutación de los errores filosóficos dogmáticos del Dr. Pesce contenidos en su folleto Roma y la Franc-masonería por el Rev. P. Lector y Examinador Sinodal* (Buenos Aires: Imprenta de la Revista, 1859); see numerous articles in the press of the period, particularly the newspaper *La Religión, periódico teo-social* (Buenos Aires, 1853–1861).
46. To my knowledge, there have been no historical investigations of this issue. The only existent work with regards charitable institutions in Buenos Aires does not note the appearance of this new notion of public welfare. See A. Meyer Arana, *La caridad en Buenos Aires*.

47. The opening act took place at the Merced church on 24 April 1859. See *La Religión*, 30 April 1859, 1. The first hostilities between the ecclesiastical authorities and the Porteño Freemasons began in February 1857, when the Bishop of Buenos Aires, Mariano José de Escalada, published in the press a pastoral letter aimed at all the faithful, reminding them of the bulls to excommunicate the Freemasons, *In eminenti*, by Clemente XII (1738), and *Providas*, by Benedict XIV (1751). This provoked a sharp reaction from the Freemasons. Spirits were pacified for a time, until September 1858, when the same bishop prohibited the giving of Christian burial to members of the order. The Freemason Alejandro Pesce then published an inflammatory piece that stoked hostilities between these two institutions. At this precise moment the project for the creation of a poorhouse was made public. See AGLA, Minute Book (1858–1870), Unión del Plata lodge, box 21, session of 26 February 1857; *El Orden*, 19 September 1858, 2; *La Tribuna*, 19 and 29 September de 1858; A. Pesce, *Roma y la Franc-masonería*. The majority of Freemasons considered Pesce's standpoint too extreme. However, a rift had been opened between the Church and Freemasonry, and in spite of numerous attempts by the latter to stem the order's anticlerical tide, the ecclesiastical authorities would always play the confrontation card.
48. See *El Orden*, 18 October 1858, 3; 19 October 1858, 2.
49. "El púlpito," *La Religión*, 23 October 1858, 5.
50. Letter of 23 March 1859 to the Great Venerable of the Grand Orient of the Republic of Argentina. In the same missive, Sarmiento urged the lodges of Buenos Aires to promote education as a necessary compliment to charity. See AGLA, Minute Book, Confraternidad Argentina lodge, box 14. From 1856 to 1862, Sarmiento was in charge of the General Schools Department. In 1857 he was elected councilor and joined the education commission. He directed the special commission for the creation of a model parish school, which was opened in 1860. The project was well received by the press, who applauded the initiative. Sarmiento left the municipality in 1858 but would continue with his policy through the General Schools Department. See *Memoria de la Municipalidad de Buenos Aires correspondiente al año 1859* (Buenos Aires: Imprenta de la Revista, 1859), 121–122.
51. Sarmiento requested that the lodges allocate half of their funds to the purchase of books and to helping rural schools. See Ibid. The Confraternidad Argentina lodge approved the "granting of five thousand medals for the purchase of books, in order to distribute them among the needy children of the countryside." See AGLA, Minute Book, Confraternidad Argentina lodge, box 14, session of 19 March 1859.
52. Thus, the program specifies "young students must belong to the needy class" and would be entirely under the care of the school administration. But it was only at the end of the period in question here that Freemasonry would create a series of institutions for the development of public instruction. See "Carta dirigida al Gran Secretario General del Gran Oriente de la República Argentina en respuesta al proyecto educativo de Sarmiento, en Buenos Aires, a 16 de May de 1859," in AGLA, Constancia lodge, book 2. In a letter from November 1860, the lodge wrote to the Grand secretary to request that he intercede against the Governor and Freemason Bartolomé Mitre in order for the latter to grant free of charge the installations of the Merlo chapel. See AGLA, Great Central Lodge (1860–1864), box 24, session of 3 November 1860. The French Freemason Adolphe Vaillant proposed a project similar to the Les Amis de la Patrie lodge. See Bibliothèque Nationale (Paris), Uruguay, Les Amis de la Patrie lodge, FM2, 867, correspondence with the Grand Orient of France, January 1860.

53. See AGLA, Minute Book (1856–1861), Unión del Plata lodge, book 2, session of 28 August 1856. In the same period, the French Freemason Vaillant, Venerable of the Les Amis de la Patrie lodge, presented to the Grand Orient of France an emigration project to rationalize and make more profitable Freemasons' aid for new immigrant brothers. This project had the same aim as the education policy: to provide the means to supply sufficient education to guarantee their entry into the labor market. It is not known whether Albarracín knew of Vaillant's project, but the coincidence of dates is quite significant. See Bibliothèque Nationale (Paris), Uruguay, Les Amis de la Patrie lodge, FM2, 867, correspondence with the Grand Orient of France 10 June 1856.
54. See AGLA, Minute Book, Consuelo del Infortunio lodge, box 27, sessions of 21 and 28 August 1860
55. See "Un masón que no es aquí masón," signed "Un fusionista," *La Reforma Pacífica*, 10 October 1858.
56. The lodges never referred to their location in the city. However, from the 1857 conflict between the two rival Masonic powers we know that the Grand Orient of the Argentine Confederation was on Calle San Martín. Alcibíades Lappas informs us of the location of the other Masonic power. See A. Lappas, "Pellegrini, Carlos Enrique," in *La masonería*, 307; AGLA, Minutes, various documents, Fraternidad y Beneficencia lodge, box 665, correspondence of 22 January 1859.
57. The decision was made by the General Assembly on 8 March 1855. The entrance fee was set at three hundred pesos and the monthly fee ten pesos. See *La Tribuna*, 10 March 1855.
58. See B. Vicuña Mackenna, *Páginas*, 48.
59. See PGB, *La Création,* appendix 1, "Base de données."
60. See *La Tribuna*, 28 August 1854.
61. In spite of the differences between the historical constitution process of the old European nations and the process that established the creation of the young Hispano-American states, the nineteenth century witnessed in both cases the birth of the "nation memory," as expounded by Pierre Nora. See Pierre Nora, "La nation-mémoire," in Pierre Nora (ed.), *Les Lieux de mémoire II, La Nation* (Paris: Gallimard, 1986), 647–658.
62. There has been no research into this association-institution. There are some references in R. Levene, *Los estudios históricos*, 89, and in Rodolfo Trostiné, *Manuel Ricardo Trelles, historiador de Buenos Aires* (Buenos Aires, 1947), 29.
63. See *Bases orgánicas del Instituto Histórico-Geográfico del Río de la Plata* (Buenos Aires: Imprenta de La Tribuna, 1856).
64. See "Instituto Histórico-Geográfico," in *La Tribuna*, 1 May 1855, 2.
65. See *Galería de Celebridades Argentinas. Biografía de los personajes más notables del Río de la Plata* (Buenos Aires: Imprenta Americana, 1857); Juan María Gutiérrez, *Pensamientos, máximas, sentencias, juicios, etc., de escritores, oradores y hombres de estado de la República Argentina* (Buenos Aires: Biblioteca Americana, 1859); Luis Domínguez, *Historia argentina* (Buenos Aires: Imprenta del Orden, 1861). This question is considered in chapter 8.
66. See *Estatuto de la Asociación de Amigos de la Historia Natural del Plata, creada por superior decreto del 6 de Mayo de 1854* (Buenos Aires: Imprenta de la Revista, 1855).
67. *Estatuto de la Asociación de Amigos de la Historia Natural del Plata*, art. 1.
68. According to Trelles, the original collection was made up of 1,505 medals from a collection of father Casone, guardian of the medals of the Vatican. The collection was

bought by the Rivadavia government in 1823. See M. R. Trelles, *Registro estadístico*, vol. 2 (1858), 135–149. Arsène Isabelle makes some comments on the museum's collection, which he calls a "cabinet of curiosities," *Voyage à Buenos Aires*, 161–162.

69. A list of these objects can be found in PGB, *La Création*, appendix 1, document 4, "Nombre d'objets acquis par le Musée d'Histoire Naturelle entre 1854 et 1861."
70. A nation which, as the associations' names suggest, was classed within a territory of variable geometry.
71. See "El Ateneo del Plata," *La Tribuna*, 2 October 1858.
72. "El Ateneo del Plata," *La Tribuna*, 2 October 1858.
73. This work was published in *El Nacional,* 21 and 25 October 1858.
74. Minutes of the Ateneo del Plata, second preparatory meeting, published in *La Tribuna*, 29 June 1858, 2.
75. See P. Rosanvallon, *Le Moment Guizot*, 155–162.
76. See Francisco Cignoli, *Historia de la Asociación Farmacéutica y Bioquímica Argentina* (Buenos Aires, 1947); F. Cignoli, *Historia de la Farmacia Argentina* (Rosario: Librería Renz, 1953), 198–225; F. Cignoli, "Mitre y la Asociación Farmacéutica Bonaerense," *Investigaciones y Ensayos*, vol. 11 (Buenos Aires: Academia Nacional de la Historia, 1971), 297–304.
77. Unfortunately, the different associations examined here did not leave behind any archives. I have tried to piece together lists of members from the information published in the local press, in addition to using the regulations and statutes of the associations, which often contained a historical introduction with a list of members. Thus, in the case of the Philharmonic Society, which had more than 300 members, we only have the names of the directive commissions. In contrast, our lists are quite complete in terms of members of the History Institute, the Ateneo del Plata and the Liceo Literario. With this information I have been able to draw up a list, albeit incomplete, of 217 members of these associations. This list can be found in PGB, *La Création*, vol. 3, appendix 1, "Base de données."
78. It is difficult, nevertheless, to form conclusions from incomplete lists. Even if the complete membership lists were available, the socioprofessional classification would be debatable and it would be necessary to treat any conclusions with extreme prudence.
79. See *La Tribuna*, 30 November 1858, 2.
80. See M. Agulhon, *Les Cercles*.
81. See Ricardo Hogg, *Yerba vieja*, vol. 1 (Buenos Aires: Casa Editora July Suárez, 1940), 232; Jorge Navarro Viola, *El Club de Residentes Extranjeros (1841–1941)* (Buenos Aires: Coni, 1941), 35–38.
82. The entrance fee alone represented at least three months' salary of a mid-level functionary. The monthly fee was the equivalent of 34% of this salary. Agricultural laborers' wages were around 200 pesos, while city wages were a little higher. See Hilda Sabato, "Salarios rurales en la provincia de Buenos Aires, 1842–1895," in *Capitalismo y ganadería*, 112–113.
83. *"Cercle bourgeois"* [bourgeois circle] is in French in the text. The figure of 50 pesos per year is wrong. It is possible that Vicuña Mackenna meant 50 pesos per month, but according to club documents, the fee was at first 70 pesos, rising to 100 in 1856. It is possible that, as a guest, Vicuña Mackenna was charged 50 pesos. See B. Vicuña Mackenna, *Páginas*, 376.
84. I have consulted the documentation in the archives of the Progress Club, including the minute book and the members' book. I are grateful here to Lucía Gálvez, a member

of the club's culture commission, who enabled me to access the archives and library. The documentation was completed by the use of the written press, especially the association's newspaper, *El Progreso*, as well as the newspaper of various members of the club, the Varela brothers' *La Tribuna*.

85. Article 1: "In accordance with that established by its founders, the society mass of the 'club' may not exceed two hundred and ten members, and once this figure has been reached, new members will only be admitted in the case of places becoming vacant." The clause was repealed on various occasions. In 1855 the directive commission allowed the number to be increased to 250. In 1856, when the club began to have difficulties paying the cost of the luxurious décor purchased in Europe, the commission accepted the raising of the number to 300, at the session of 7 July. On 30 May 1862, at the request of 105 members, the number was increased again to 350. See Archives of Progress Club, Minute Book, sessions of 8 September 1852, 7 July 1856, and 30 May 1862.
86. See "Protesta de un ciudadano," *La Tribuna*, 26 January 1855, 3.
87. The lists are complete. See PGB, *La Création,* appendix 1, "Base de données."
88. The Progress Club enabled rich foreign traders to attain blood ties with the local ruling class. Mariano Acosta married his son to the daughter of the businessman Adolphe Van Pratt, one of the shareholders in the first railroad, and his daughter to the son of Daniel Gowland, a wealthy English trader. Manuel H. Aguirre married his son to the daughter of one of the largest sheep producers, Claudio F. Stegmann. Federico Elortondo married the daughter of Tomás Amstrong, one of the richest foreign businessmen, a landowner, industrialist and financier and one of the founders of the Stock Exchange; all were members of the club.
89. See Club del Progreso, *Datos históricos sobre su origen y desenvolvimiento. Apuntes coleccionados por la comisión directiva en este centro con motivo del 50º aniversario de su fundación* (Buenos Aires, 1902); Héctor José Iñigo Carreras, "El Club del Progreso, de Caseros a la *Belle Époque,*" *Todo es Historia* 57 (January 1972).
90. Thus Diego de Alvear resumes the objectives established in the statutes. The original 1852 regulations have not been found. See "Carta del presidente del Club, doctor Diego de Alvear, al director del diario *La Tribuna,*" *La Tribuna*, 3 September 1853.
91. See *El Progreso*, 27 May 1852.
92. Until the foundation of the Progress Club, the word designated almost exclusively a political association.
93. See *La Tribuna*, 26 August 1853.
94. *La Tribuna*, 3 September 1853.
95. At the Progress Club there were two copies of each of the principal newspapers, in an incredibly well stocked library room. The library also had copies of foreign magazines well known in Argentina, such as *Revue des Deux Mondes*, the *Correo de Ultramar* and *El Mundo Ilustrado*. See Progress Club archives, Minutes of 4 May 1858, 15 September 1859, 16 June 1861, and 29 March 1862.
96. See *La Tribuna*, 25 May 1854, 3.
97. *La Tribuna*, 12 July 1855, 3.
98. *La Tribuna*, 27 May 1862.
99. The reasons for the banquets are evidence of fluctuations in the political commitment of the club's members. Thus, from banquets in celebration of the liberator Urquiza we pass to those in honor of Bartolomé Mitre and other leaders who contributed to the

extermination of the *Mazorca* (a contemptuous name for supporters of Urquiza). See *El Progreso*, 7 September 1852, 2; *La Tribuna*, 8 February 1856, 3.

100. See *La Tribuna*, 14 February 1856, 2, 3.
101. Miguel J. Azcuénaga, a member of the directive commission in 1855, had asked Mariano Balcarce, who was in Paris, to have busts sculpted of San Martín, Belgrano, Rivadavia and Moreno. It is not known if these busts were exhibited in the club. In any event, and to our knowledge, that of Mariano Moreno was never exhibited. This is explained by the fact that the memory of Moreno evoked the most extreme tendencies of the revolution. See *La Tribuna*, 3 September 1853 and 30 May 1855; Progress Club Archives, Minute Book, sessions of 25 June and 7 and 22 July 1862.
102. See *La Tribuna*, 14 February 1856, 2.
103. *La Tribuna*, 18 January and 23 February 1855.
104. See J. Navarro Viola, *El Club*, 35–38.

CHAPTER 7

The Public Sphere and Representative Government

Associative practices introduced a new representation of the individual and of the social bond, the consequences of which can be evaluated through the incidence of associative movement in local society. This was nevertheless a slow process, its speed corresponding to the deep cultural mutation of the modern era that led to representative republican governments. The coordination of these two processes was more or less harmonious and often unnoticeable in the eyes of the historian. Still, there were moments that cast light on events and allowed phenomena to be seen, whether from the introduction of discourse intended to make sense of practices, or from the growth and impact of these modifications on the relational universe of the population.

The ten years of secession of the State of Buenos Aires, with the rise of the associative movement and the reappearance of vigorous discourse in the political contract, provide us with one of the few times when connections between social representations and political institutions came to the surface. In this movement of common trends, associative practices diffused a contractual representation of society as the sum of individual legal subjects, while at the same time participating directly in breathing new life into representative institutions.

Towards a New Political Approach: The Public Sphere as the Threshold of Government

Political activity arrived on the public scene in Buenos Aires with the end of the Rosas government in the province of Buenos Aires. This period witnessed the appearance of "the freedom party," whose most famous leaders were the romantic liberals exiled during the Rosista regime. Between March and December 1852, political life took on a rare vitality: the resurgent opinion press, the reappearance of participation forms in public life, and the creation of new forms of political organization tied to the practice of "universal suffrage," breathed new life into republican institutions, which had never been fully repealed.

The resurgence of public political activity owed much to the freedom of assembly, which made the rise of the associative movement possible. Associations multiplied and diversified, with a clear tendency towards specialization in one area of action. At the same time, however, the "associative boom" expanded the political sphere into the intermediate space between the individual and government, which brought about a modification in relationships between society and its institutions. The innovation of the period lay less in the presence of institutional reforms or transformations in socioeconomic relationships than in this extension of the political sphere accompanying the renewal of republican institutions. In this intermediate sphere between private life and power, a new concept of representation appeared to connect with old power bases and networks.

RENEWAL OF POLITICAL LEADERSHIP AFTER THE BATTLE OF CASEROS

After three months of triumphal agreement, conflicts with Urquiza's politics led Porteño leaders to split from the Argentine Confederation. The theories of the old Unitarian party then found a wide range of sympathizers among Porteños, from their natural heirs (the intellectual liberal elites) to large land and capital owners able to curb the demands of interior provinces. One week after the revolution of 11 September 1852, Lorenzo Torres, one of the major figures of Rosismo, and Valentín Alsina, one of the young romantic liberals exiled in Montevideo, sealed with a symbolic embrace the new Porteñista front. This alliance, surprising only on the surface, revealed a continuous line between Rosas' conservative politics and the politics of the exiled liberals: to defend the interests of Buenos Aires.[1] This was founded on the development of free exchange with international trade and the province's exclusive access to duties from the port of Buenos Aires.

This continuity of Porteñista interests did not translate, however, into a perpetuation of the leading Rosista class in the provincial government. Only eighty-seven men from the Rosas government (9.3% of the administration of the State of Buenos Aires) remained in their posts after Caseros. However, the Rosista past did not hinder excessively the political rise of those who remained in the administration. Thus, thirty-two of the eighty-seven men, a full third, had a successful political career after 1852, in spite of having participated in the previous administration. Some of these were men who, due to their prestige and administrative competence, served under various governments. Without doubt, an exemplary case is that of Vicente Fidel López, whose political career dated from the revolution and independence.[2] But with few exceptions, the majority were men setting out in their careers, and for whom the Rosista experience did not appear to be a disadvantage. Thus, one in two justices of the peace, representing 38 percent of former Rosista men, had a successful political career after Caseros. In some cases, promotion up the political ranks was gradual: Felipe Botet, for example, was a rural justice of the peace until the end of the Rosas regime, when he was elected councilor of San Telmo. Similarly, Juan Carranza, a justice of the peace during the 1833 revolution, would later, in 1860, become councilor of the wealthy parish of Catedral al Sur. Others rose more rapidly, as was the case of justices of the peace who became deputies in the House of Representatives of the province of Buenos Aires, such as Luis Gómez, Manuel J. Guerrico, and even José M. Otamendi, elected senator in 1859. The case of Plácido Obligado is quite singular. The father of Manuel Obligado, he worked as a justice of the peace during the early years of the second Rosas government (1835–1836), before subsequently disappearing from the political scene. His election to the legislature in 1860 can be explained more easily by the career of his son, ex-governor of the province, than by his own political track record.

Rosista representatives constituted a fairly limited number of deputies in the liberal legislature, totaling only five, and only fourteen continued in political activity. Of these, the cases of Nicolás Anchorena, Juan B. Peña and Lorenzo Torres are of interest due to the importance of their Rosista past on their future careers. Nicolás Anchorena, a rich landowner, Rosas' cousin and related by marriage to one of the most important families of the Rosista period, held the position of representative during the latter years of the Rosas government, going on to hold various other positions in the liberal administration, including Minister of the Interior in 1852 and deputy and senator of the city of Buenos Aires on various occasions. Anchorena's presence in the liberal government was no doubt part of an effort by the provincial government to ensure the support of one of the most important sectors of local elites. Juan B. Peña, a man of finance, with kinship ties to the powerful Lezica, Ramos Mejía, Ortiz Basualdo, and Díaz de Vivar families, had also participated in the first Rosas government.[3] He was later involved in the revolution of the "Free of the South" in 1839, which took him away from power in the last decade of Rosas' government. With the liberals' arrival in 1852, he was made Minister of the Treasury. He later held various positions in the State of Buenos Aires administration, standing out especially as a conciliator. In 1857 he was one of the candidates for the government of the province in the moderate sector of the Porteñista liberals. The case of Lorenzo Torres, in contrast, is quite different. A lawyer and one of the first graduates of the University of Buenos Aires, where he was also professor between 1829 and 1832, he moved away from the liberal youth movement in 1835. In 1839 he defended Rosas during the revolution initiated by the youth movement along with Unitarian opposition in Montevideo and certain landowners and producers from the south of the province. He later became one of the major figures of Rosismo. His political career after Caseros was to be marked by his past: a man of Porteñista continuity, he was also one of the heirs of Porteño federalism, making him a crucial element in relationships between the province of Buenos Aires and the Confederation. In 1857 Urquiza's supporters even singled him out as a possible candidate for the provincial government.

The cases cited here clearly illustrate the transition between Rosista order and the liberal government. The men continuing in power enjoyed a social authority stemming from family networks or from a strong influence over the urban and rural masses. In incorporating these men into the "freedom party," the liberal party was able to associate itself with the maintenance of Rosista order. But the presence of these representatives of continuity, ensuring institutional renewal, could not hide the transformations taking place at the very heart of the provincial ruling class. This was less a change in the social make-up of the political elites than a generational renewal tied to the introduction of new methods of accessing political institutions.

A New Generation of Representatives. The first manifestations of a rebirth in public political life were seen in the first "free" elections of March 1852. The inhabitants of the province were invited to elect their representatives to the provincial legislature. From this moment and until 1862, 234 people would occupy the benches of the assembly, from 1852 to 1854 in the House of Representatives and then, after the 1854 Constitution of the State of Buenos Aires, in the House of Deputies of the Legislative Assembly. With regards to the representatives of the legislatures of 1827–1839, there were no fundamental differences, except that the "skilled classes" were now better represented, with a third of legislators belonging to the intellectual professions, of whom an overwhelming majority (90%) were lawyers.[4] This situation translated into a greater number of deputies with a university degree, around 75 percent of those on whom we have information concerning level of studies.[5] Some of these combined degrees with other sources of power, as appears to have been the case of Federico Anchorena, Félix Sánchez de Zelis and Norberto de la Riestra, who belonged to rich landowning families. But generally it was a matter of men using their cultural capital as a source of power. While previously men had gained prestige through a career in the colonial administration, naturally accompanied by a suitable family strategy, they now entered a political career that increasingly required new skills that would guarantee their rise through the political ranks.

Let us consider the example of the Escalada family. Antonio José de Escalada, born in Buenos Aires in 1754, was a functionary of the crown. His sons were among the ranks of the independence army, in the first steps towards a new career in honor and power. Antonio José married his daughter, María Remedios, to José de San

Martín, while his son Manuel became a general of the revolutionary army. As a general, Manuel would hold various positions in the administration of the State of Buenos Aires, in which he was three times Minister of War. His son, Manuel María, continued along this path, but unlike his father, achieved his promotion with new skills. Graduating in law from the University of Buenos Aires in 1844, he first occupied positions in the justice administration, before beginning his political career as a deputy in the legislature of 1852. In 1856 he was made a minister in the Obligado government. Manuel María did not marry, but nevertheless established ties with the principal Porteño families by joining the Progress Club. The change of strategy for political success is evident: firstly as functionaries of the crown, then as members of the revolutionary army, and lastly by obtaining a university degree, which appears to have smoothed the way to a new political career, consolidated by a position in powerful relational networks that associative practice apparently ensured.

This interesting example would demand an exhaustive study of family groups' professional strategies in political promotion. This issue is undoubtedly essential, but exceeds the objectives of this investigation. Nevertheless, what is clear is that from 1852 university graduates began to be more numerous in the House of Representatives and in the provincial State administration. In the majority of cases, these were graduates of the city and province's only university.[6] In my judgment, this increase in degrees awarded by the University of Buenos Aires can be explained by the fact that, since its foundation in 1821, this university had attained a certain institutional stability and above all an undoubted importance in local political life, as not only did the number of graduates tend to increase but also, as figure 21 shows, so did the percentage of graduates acquiring positions of power.[7]

Figure 21 shows that of seventy-five degrees recorded, twenty-seven, or one-third, were obtained between 1841 and 1850. Graph B confirms the idea of an influx of university graduates after the Rosista period. The area in gray indicates three generations of students/colleagues, the most homogenous of which is that of 1841 to 1852, which suggests that the new political class was not formed exclusively in exile. A large number of its members were formed in Rosista institutions, but in a system that excluded them from power, a circumstance that explains their incorporation into the cause of the regime's exiles, as well as the failure of the attempt at "national" Rosista organization.

It can be noted furthermore that representatives' ages varied. While Rosas-era representatives tended to get older, as observed earlier, the legislature now tended to get younger. From an average of fifty-three for the representatives of the last years of Rosismo, in the first years after Caseros the average fell to forty-five, then forty-three in the case of legislators from 1856 to 1858.[8] There is a temptation to

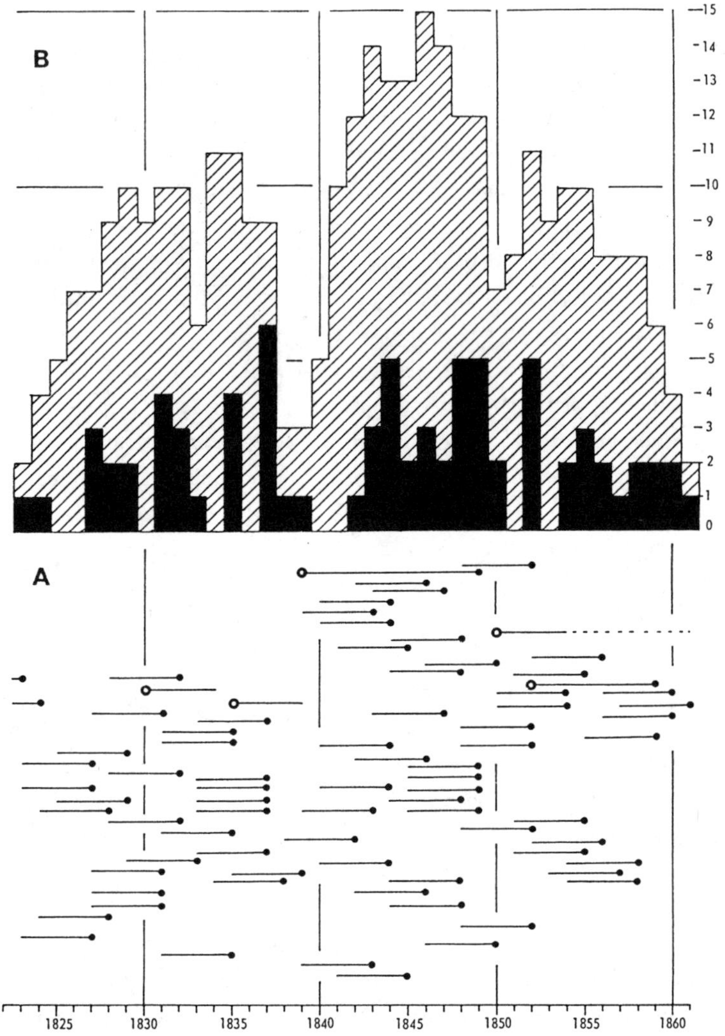

● Date when degree was obtained

O Year of registration in the university

—— Duration of studies (we calculate four years on average, from the date of registration or obtaining the degree)

- - - - Interruption of studies

Figure 21. University Careers (at the University of Buenos Aires) of the State of Buenos Aires' Representatives between 1852 and 1862 (sample of 109 people)

A, Each point preceded or followed by a line represents the university record of one deputy (the order of lines along the vertical is random, following the order of the data table); B, In black, the number of degrees obtained per year. In gray, the number of deputies studying at the university in the same period.

conclude that nothing appears to distinguish more clearly these new representatives from the old "functionaries" of Rosista representation than their age. However, there were also notable differences in selection criteria for positions of power. The end of Rosismo coincided with the appearance of professionals in politics, above all lawyer-publicists who tended to extend their sphere of political action to the public sphere. In order to reach power, the mere family network or traditional social authority were no longer enough. These forms of renown and power now had to be based around a new concept of representation that appears to have been the key to the vault of institutional stability.

The New Mechanisms of Power: While the social extraction of representatives did not vary significantly for the duration of our period, the same cannot be said of associative practices. Indeed, one of the major differences that characterized the representatives of the legislature after Caseros lay in the intensity and nature of their associative sociability practices. The figures speak for themselves: between 1828 and 1852 only 12 percent of legislators formed part of an association before or during their mandate, while in the period in question the proportion reached 66 percent. Figure 22 allows us to observe this in greater detail. In 92 percent of cases, deputies were affiliated with an association before or during their mandate, while in the 1840s this was true of only 21 percent.[9] This confirms the idea of a relationship between associative affiliation and political activity, whether belonging to an association constituted an inroad to the political sphere, or whether politicians aimed to join networks of public sociability in order to consolidate and extend their representative power

Not all associations attracted deputies in equal number. Logically, those most frequented by deputies were political associations, and 40 percent of memberships among deputies were in electoral clubs.[10] After this came classic forms of associative belonging: sociocultural associations, Masonic associations, and leisure clubs, representing 20 percent of affiliations. Contrary to current theory, Freemasonry showed a relatively low level of memberships (11%) in comparison with other associative forms, which makes it necessary to play down the idea of Freemasonry's supposed prime position in local politics. From a quantitative perspective at least, membership of the Masons continued in this period to be a practice restricted to a relatively small number of deputies. On the whole, deputies opted for other associative forms.[11] In all cases it appears to be clear that for the representatives of the provincial legislature, associative practice was already an acquired cultural activity: between 1852 and 1862, 72 percent of deputies were members of an association. Moreover, this aspect exceeded the context of provincial legislators. Again the figures speak for themselves: in the same years, 64 percent of the ruling

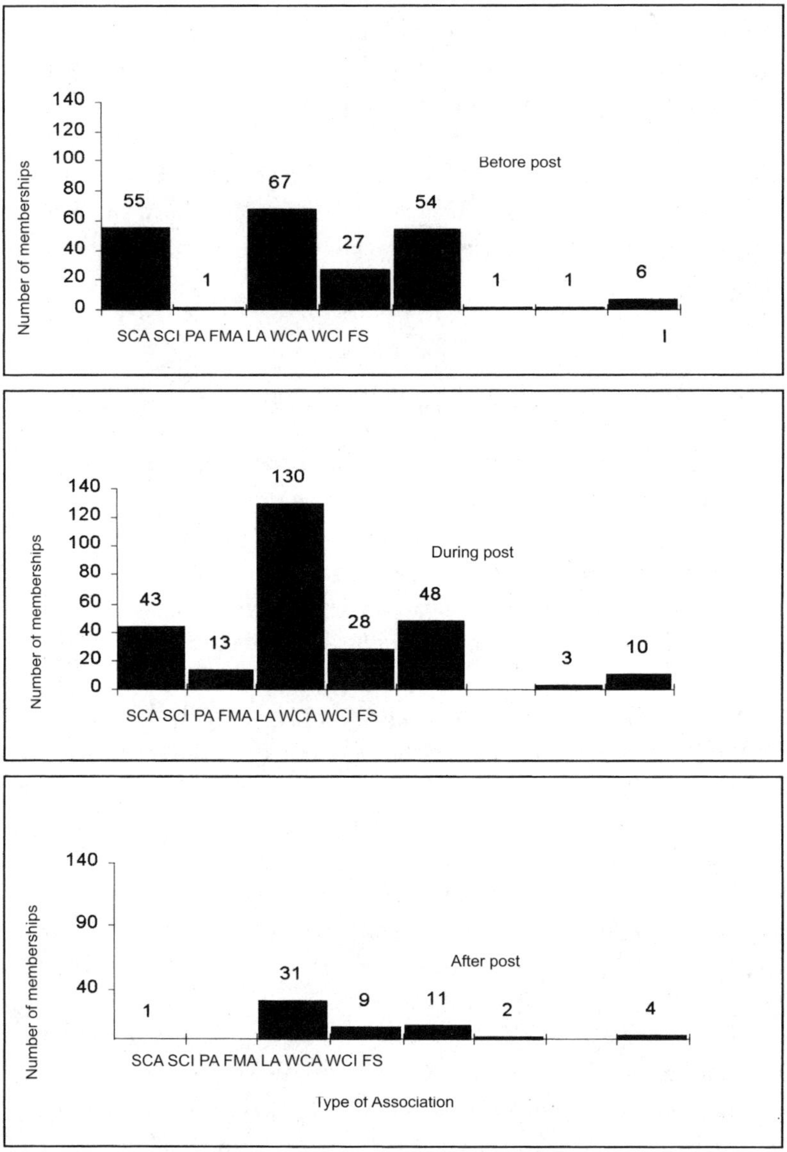

Figure 22. Type of Associative Belonging of 234 Representatives of the Legislature of the Province of Buenos Aires between 1852 and 1862, in Relation to the Attainment of a Post

Note: For type of association, see figure 24

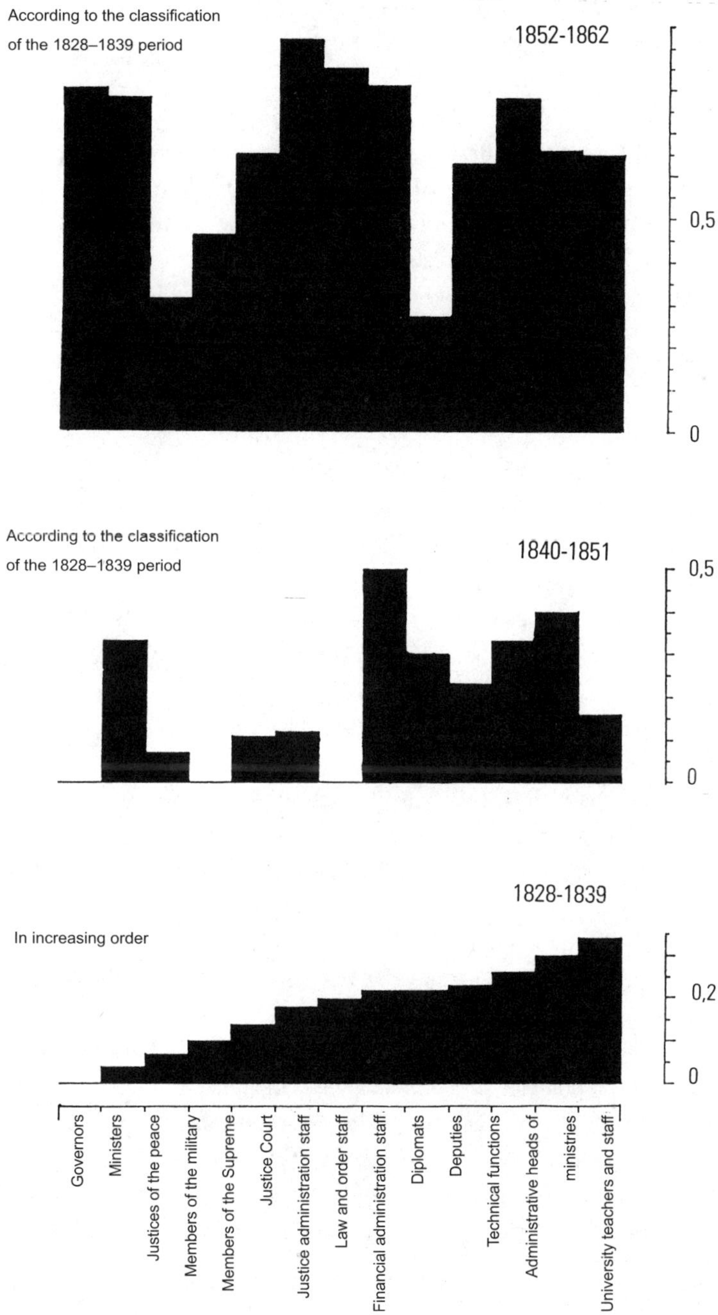

Figure 23. Average Growth in Associative Belonging in the Porteño Ruling Class, According to Post

class participated in at least one association. This clearly shows that the case of the deputies was by no means an exception. Even higher percentages can be found in certain positions: of twenty-seven people occupying a post in the justice system, twenty-five were members of an association, an average of 0.92 per person; in positions of law and order, in which there were no affiliations between 1840 and 1852, there was now an average of 0.86 per person. In contrast, academic and diplomatic posts, which stood out before for their adhesion to this kind of cultural practice, were now part of the average of associative practices. In both cases, the scarce political influence of the post might explain this low level.

The data are all the more significant if we take into account figure 24 on the type of association that most attracted the different posts. This illustration allows us to distinguish three models of membership. First, there were the posts with a majority of affiliations to sociocultural associations. This was the case of 50 percent of posts, which shared in common the demand for professional competence, such as in the case of the members of the Supreme Justice Court, technical, academic, judicial and diplomatic posts, in addition to ministers and ministerial administrative heads. With the exception of governors, who were elected by the legislature, these were all nonelective posts. Of these eight categories, we can distinguish five with a second kind of membership: governors, members of the Supreme Court, ministerial administrative heads, diplomatic posts and technical posts combined the cultural association with an electoral club. The former association was probably to consolidate alliances within the ruling class, while the latter was to be in touch with the voters. Ministers, those in judicial posts and those in academic posts alternated sociocultural practice with leisure associations. The two forms were similar in terms of indirect relationships with political activity, but differed in terms of the network of relationships that each one provided: in the sociocultural association these functionaries were able to make contact with the government *intelligentsia*, while in the clubs members could rub shoulders above all with the socioeconomic elite.

The second model of membership corresponds to posts that primarily favored membership in a political association. These included military posts, law and order, and justice administration, in addition to deputies, senators, councilors, conventional posts and national congressmen, in other words, posts directly affected by the electoral act, whether proceeding from election by "universal suffrage" or from intervention on the day of voting. Belonging to a club was in these cases a means of reaching voters through the staging of the representative act. Participation in an electoral club was combined in the majority of cases with affiliation to a leisure club, for reasons mentioned above. One exception was military members who affiliated, in order of priority, with electoral clubs and the Freemasons.

	SCA	SCI	PA	FMA	LA	WCA	WCI	SEA	SEI	CS	RA	FS	TOTAL
Deputies	99	14	228	64	113	3	4	11	–	6	6	20	568
Senators	39	7	48	11	44	–	4	2	–	2	1	8	166
Councilors	27	–	100	45	54	1	4	16	–	2	4	20	273
Conventional posts	24	6	31	13	22	–	1	–	–	–	–	3	100
Governors	10	1	6	2	6	–	–	–	–	1	1	3	30
Supreme Court of Justice	20	6	10	6	8	–	–	1	–	–	2	2	55
Ministers	32	7	16	8	17	–	2	–	–	2	1	12	97
Administrative ministerial heads	6	–	4	2	6	–	–	–	–	–	–	1	19
Military posts	9	1	35	25	15	–	–	3	–	–	–	3	91
Justice administration	18	6	11	14	17	1	–	1	–	–	2	–	70
Diplomats	5	–	3	1	3	–	–	1	–	–	–	1	14
University teachers and staff	36	6	15	17	18	1	–	1	–	–	2	7	103
Financial administration	16	2	32	10	49	–	6	31	–	6	2	12	166
Technical posts	12	1	11	1	3	–	–	–	–	–	–	–	28
Justices of the peace	11	–	114	39	64	–	–	4	–	–	3	–	235
Law and order	4	1	6	–	6	–	1	–	–	–	–	2	20
Total	368	58	670	258	445	6	22	71	–	19	24	94	2,035

Figure 24. Type of Associative Belonging in the Porteño Ruling Class between 1852 and 1862, According to Posts

SCA: sociocultural association ; SCI: sociocultural institution; PA: political association; FMA: Freemason association; LA: leisure association; WCA: welfare and charity association; WCI: welfare and charity institution; SEA: socioeconomic association; SEI: socioeconomic institution; CS: commercial society; RA: religious association; FS: friendly society

Lastly were those posts that favored membership in associations whose principal objective was sociability among peers. Thus, men in high posts in the finance administration mostly chose "aristocratic" or "bourgeois" leisure clubs. These were individuals whose social extraction, as much as their professional post, accounted for this associative affiliation, although this does not appear to have been at odds with their presence in the government, whether because it allowed them to climb the different rungs of an administrative career or because it gave certain social foundations vital to institutional stability.

In terms of the date of entering the association in comparison with the date of assuming the post (figure 25), the majority of men (47.9%) of the ruling class were members of an association some time before occupying a post, while 32.3 percent joined an association while in their post. Both situations account for the memberships of men in a political career. In the remaining cases, membership came after their mandate, but not necessarily at the end of their political career; of this 20 percent, a clear majority remained active after 1862.

In certain cases, membership prior to the mandate was considerable enough as to create the impression of a kind of "electoral campaign" within the political organization in question. Thus, 75 percent of associative affiliations of conventional and national congress posts were made prior to their election, as were 60 percent of councilor posts and 57.3 percent of deputies. The incorporation into these relationship networks appears to have been directly tied to obtaining the post, all the more so in the case of first and second degree electoral posts. The same phenomenon can be found in financial administration and technical posts. In total, we find 3,653 associative memberships in Buenos Aires between 1829 and 1862. For the period that concerns us, more than half were of men holding posts in the State administration, while previously this was less than 50 percent of the total.[12] This leads us to conclude that if obtaining a university degree had become a means of accessing power, it was thus as much due to the qualification, which corresponded to new selection criteria of the political leadership, as it was to relationship networks which these men joined due to their sociability practices, given that the main difference with the previous period lay in the creation of new associative forms of organization developed from cultural practices in the intellectual sphere connected to the University of Buenos Aires acting as anterooms to power. To have a successful political career, it was increasingly indispensable to participate in the associative world.

WIDENING OF THE POLITICAL SPHERE: THE CASE OF FREEMASONRY

Freemasonry was the first sociability institution with a network of relationships in harmony with the imperatives of Porteño politics, which suggests that the

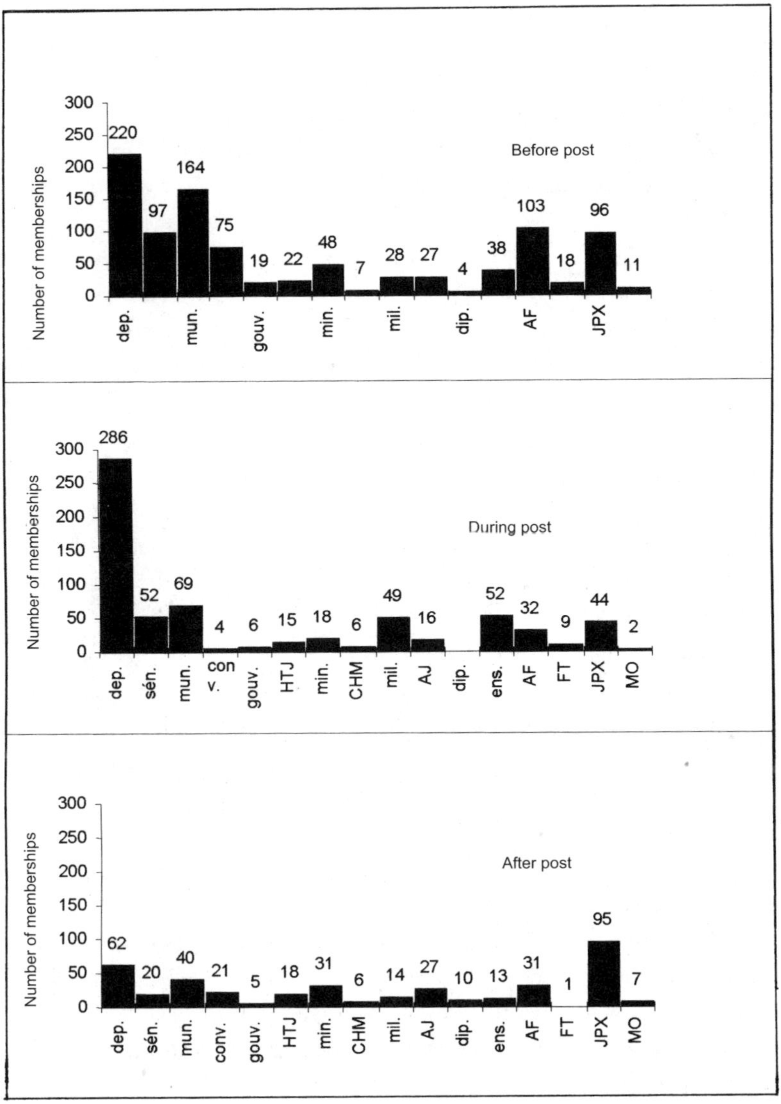

Figure 25. Association Membership Among the Ruling Porteño Class between 1852 and 1862, in Relationship to Obtaining a Government Post

dep.=deputies; sen.=senators; mun.=councilors; conv.=conventional; gouv.=governors; HTJ=members of Supreme Justice Court; min.=ministers; CHM=administrative ministerial heads; mil.=members of the military; AJ=Justice Administration Staff; dip.=diplomats; ens.=university teachers and staff; AF=financial administration staff; FT=technical posts; JPX=justices of the peace; MO=maintainers of law and order

political use of the Masonic organization would naturally occur. It has even been sustained that Freemasonry was the principal agent in national organization.[13] Due to this, the case is of double interest.[14] It is intrinsic to the association, above all, as it is imperative to clarify the relationship often claimed between Masonry and power. Likewise, such study permits an analysis of the political role of the new contractual practices in the establishment of a new social tie as a product of the contract between individuals who were rational beings and legal subjects.

The chronology of Masonry's development might justify the assimilation between Freemasonry and power. Indeed, the first Porteño lodge was created in March 1856, at a time of great political enthusiasm due to the proximity of the elections called for 30 March and aimed at renewing a good half of the provincial legislature's seats. These were important elections, as they would decide the assembly that, in turn, was to designate the governor. At this time, a group of "progressives," identifying with the Varela brothers' *La Tribuna* newspaper, began to unite against the politics of a government that in their judgment granted too many concessions to the Confederation.[15] This translated into a rapid increase in informal meetings, the organization of electoral clubs, and the publication of opinion periodicals.

All this suggests that the establishment of Freemasonry at this precise moment could not have been a simple coincidence. However, when it comes to finding any coherence between the creation of this lodge and the organization of an opposition to the Obligado government, the certainties are fewer. Firstly, almost all the founding brethren were secondary figures in Porteño politics. With the exceptions of Sarmiento and Valencia, the remainder were not men committed to public political life. In the case of some, the political career began later, while others would keep their distance from the public scene. The exceptions were former deputy Mariano Billinghurst, acting in the elections of that time, and others such as Federico Álvarez de Toledo and Carlos Casares, who were already considering the possibility of presenting their candidacy for the provincial legislature. In this case it is feasible that their affiliation to Freemasonry had ulterior political motives. However, if we focus on the quantitative aspect, it can be seen that of the seventy-three brethren who formed the Unión del Plata lodge in 1856, fourteen would go on to participate in the activities of electoral clubs, and of these, only two, Billinghurst and Juan M. Gutiérrez, would do so in the same year as joining the Masons. Consequently, it is difficult to infer, as many authors claim, that the first lodge served to organize the opposition's campaign. Furthermore, the initiation of Lorenzo Torres shortly after complicates the matter further. How can the theory of an Alsinista Freemasonry be reconciled with Torres' presence?[16] It is therefore difficult to deduce a political trend among any group of founding brethren. For example, if we take the members of the 1857 assembly who voted for Valentín Alsina as governor of the province, the results contradict the classic theory on the Alsinista origin of Freemasonry. Masons voted equally for Alsina and for opposition candidates.[17] These figures say more about an Alsinista liberal party that recruited its political allies in the Progress Club and confirmed its alliances in electoral clubs. In fact, these men of power on the whole preferred to join a political club or a leisure club than be initiated into the Masons, as the latter was probably less effective in political activity connected to electoral practice. However, one must not lose sight of the fact that the electoral act was in this period nothing but the confirmation of decisions made elsewhere, and in this aspect Freemasonry could help men to access new power networks.

Let us examine the principal Masons that reached government after 1852. 128 of them held a post in the provincial government, of which, only ten had done so before Caseros. The other 118 represented 12.7 percent of the total of members of the order. If these are compared with the percentage of members of the Progress Club who also had a post in the government, these figures appear most modest. Of 573 club members between 1852 and 1862, 182 held an official post, or rather 31.8 percent against 12.7 percent. There was therefore a wide Masonic base that remained on the periphery of power.[18] This suggests that while the Masonic network facilitated access to power, this was almost always limited to individuals of like social extraction. Belonging to the order only brought difficulties in accessing other social spheres, although these were well represented at a grass roots level. This was the primary feature of the Masons: a minority of members of the elite who attained governmental posts, a majority made up of traders and salesmen who remained on the periphery of elective or nominative posts in the State of Buenos Aires. The details of the posts occupied by individuals initiated into Freemasonry give a more precise idea of the importance of Masonic affiliation in access to a high position in the State administration.

It can be seen that the presence of Masons was not the same in all posts. While they were entirely absent from posts dedicated to the maintenance of law and order, they held a fourth of military posts. This can be explained on the one hand by the considerable percentage of military members in the Freemasons but also by the characteristics of the military career that, due to the hierarchical structure, was more suited to Masonic organization than elective posts. Among the latter, there was nevertheless a reasonable number of Masons, both in the House of Representatives and as councilors. Thus, the average of Masonic affiliation, which for the total of posts was 15.5 percent, increased to 31 percent in elective posts. In addition, 42 percent of Masonic affiliations by the ruling Porteño class were prior to obtaining posts, 36 percent during the mandate and the remaining 22 percent

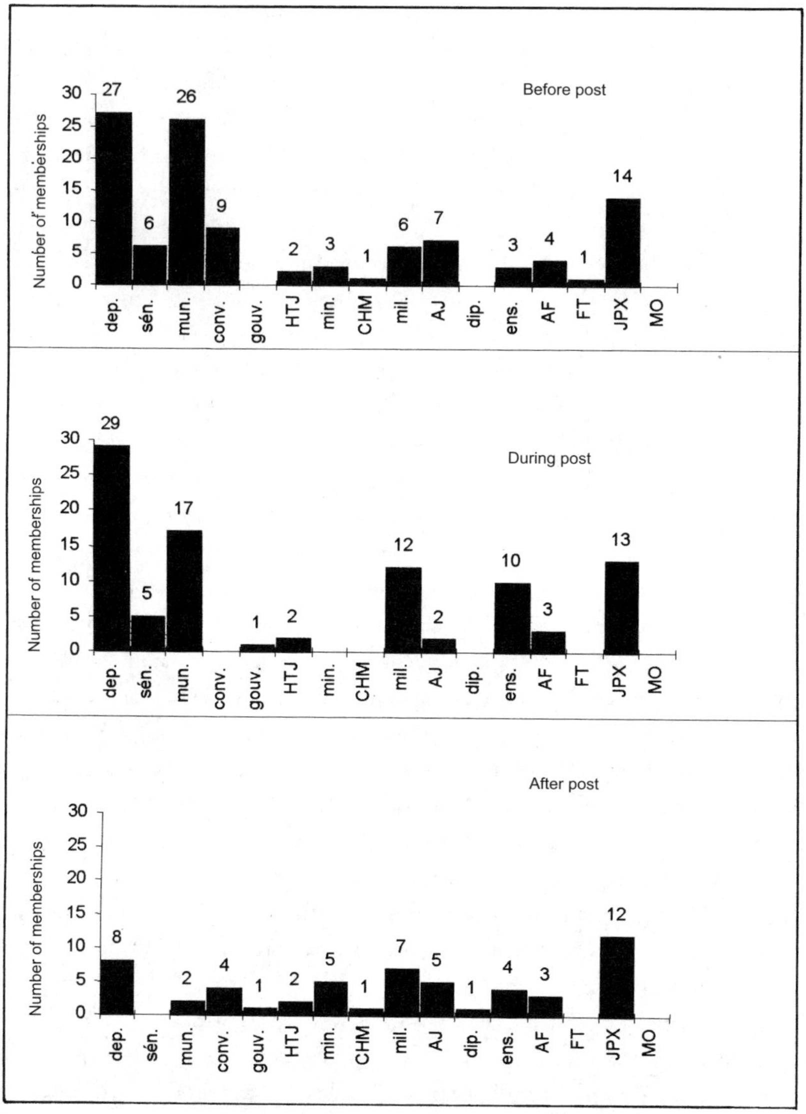

Figure 26. Number of Freemasonry Affiliations Among the Porteño Ruling Class between 1852 and 1862, in Relation to Obtaining the Post

dep.=deputies; sen.=senators; mun.=councilors; conv.=conventional; gouv.=governors; HTJ=members of Supreme Justice Court; min.=ministers; CHM=administrative ministerial heads; mil.=members of the military; AJ=Justice Administration Staff; dip.=diplomats; ens.=university teachers and staff; AF=financial administration staff; FT=technical posts; JPX=justices of the peace; MO=maintainers of law and order

afterwards, which suggests that this affiliation may have had some influence in access to positions. This can be analyzed through a few examples.

The lawyer Juan J. Alsina, son of the Spanish surveyor Juan de Alsina, had begun his political career in 1829 as a deputy in the House of Representatives of the provincial legislature, at the age of thirty. He held various posts in the financial administration during the first Rosista government, before falling from favor in 1837 with the break between Rosas and the young intellectuals. The activity of his brother Valentín, exiled in Montevideo, had also left him out of favor, as Valentín Alsina participated in the Argentine Commission that organized combat against Rosas. In spite of some years of misfortune, he retook his bench in the legislature in the last years of the Rosista government, which could have counted against him. He may have been trying to regain his position when he joined two of the local elites' principal meeting centers, the Progress Club in 1854 and Freemasonry in 1858, but without any apparent success given that after Caseros he did not occupy any political post. This then is a case of affiliation to Freemasonry that did not apparently play any role in the political career or situation of one of its members.

In contrast, the Freemasonry experience was quite favorable for the Torres brothers. Unlike Juan J. Alsina they held principal positions in the order. Initiated with the creation of the first lodge in 1856, both brothers were involved in much activity and rapidly rose through the organization's hierarchy, although there was no immediate relationship between this affiliation and their political combat. As in the case of Domingo F. Sarmiento, Masonry allowed them to consolidate a career that was already in motion, but which nevertheless required confirmation from the new Porteño powers. For the same reason, the Torres brothers did not disregard other associative networks, such as the Progress Club, and sociocultural associations, such as the Historical-Geographical Institute, of which they were members along with Mitre and Sarmiento.

There were of course cases where membership in the Masons was more decisive in access to power, as was the case with Dr. Guillermo Rawson, born in the province of San Juan to an American father. He studied at the University of Buenos Aires where he obtained a degree in medicine in 1844. At this time he established his first contacts with the Porteño elite. He returned to his native province and then was back in Buenos Aires in 1856, when he joined the Unión del Plata lodge with his friend from San Juan, Domingo F. Sarmiento. Unlike other cases mentioned, Freemasonry was Rawson's only association during our period. Just as Sarmiento had done in favor of his educational projects, Rawson used the Masonic networks to carry out a sanitation campaign, with the aim of establishing a public hygiene policy. His activity during the yellow fever epidemic of 1857 brought him great prestige in the eyes of the secular public, while the

Masons granted him a privileged place in all commissions of public welfare and hygiene. Rawson thus became a public figure before arriving on the political scene in 1858. This arrival was no doubt connected to his Masonic activity, as it was this that allowed him to attain political stature. Thus, after initiation into Freemasonry and without participating in other power networks nor in any electoral campaign, Rawson nevertheless rose through the political ranks: a deputy of the provincial legislature in 1856, then a senator of the same legislature in 1861, he was then designated a minister of the Government of the Argentine Republic in 1862 by President Bartolomé Mitre, also a Freemason.

Rawson's case differs from those who, like Carlos Durand, Juan A. García, and Antonio Pillado combined Masonic membership with political activity in the electoral clubs. Durand, for example, was also a doctor and graduate of the University of Buenos Aires. Like Rawson, he participated in different Masonic commissions dedicated to public welfare. In addition to the advantage of being a Porteño, Durand associated Masonic work with more specifically political activity. A member of the San Nicolás electoral club in 1857, a parish to which he would be elected councilor in 1858, Durand was part of the directive commission of the Liberty Club from 1860 to the end of our period.

These examples show a Masonic organization that, in terms of its recruitment and values, was very close to the liberal government. The specific role that this affiliation played in political careers varied from one individual to another. Freemasonry did not replace any political party, in fact its importance was of another kind. In these associations, men could connect to new power networks, founded in the social and economic authority of the individuals composing the association, the extension and institutionalization of such connections, and in the representative power that appeared in this intermediate space between the individual and the State.

In this regard, we can recall the exemplary case of Domingo F. Sarmiento, one of a limited number of Masons of conviction who had a parallel and successful career in the Masonic order and political life. He thus came to be president of the nation in 1868 and the director of the Argentine Grand Orient in 1882. The two careers were closely related, to the extent that some affirm that Sarmiento was the prototype Masonry-produced politician.[19] A journalist of repute from the province of San Juan, Sarmiento began his public career in 1839, editing the *El Zonda* newspaper. At the same time he made contact with the young romantic Porteño movement in the shape of the Argentine Youth association. During his exile, he collaborated on various newspapers in Chile and Uruguay.[20] He also published various political writings, with which he gained a certain fame among Rosas' adversaries. In 1854, while in Chile, he was elected deputy of the Buenos Aires legislature, a seat that he ultimately did not take. One year later he moved to the city of Buenos Aires, where he was made director of the *El Nacional* newspaper. A few months later he assumed his first public role in the Buenos Aires municipality, moving up the political ladder that would take him to the presidency. A senator of the Buenos Aires legislature in 1857, he was named minister of Bartolomé Mitre's government in 1860.[21] In 1862 he was elected governor of the province of San Juan, resigning in 1864 to take the post of business attaché to the United States government. In 1868, while working in the USA, he was elected as the second constitutional president of the Argentine Republic.

The success of Sarmiento's career is difficult to explain in terms of traditional mechanisms. Sarmiento was a man from the provinces, with no resources and, to make matters worse, self-taught. In addition, unlike other liberals he did not have an influential network of family ties at his disposal to help him in his career.[22] For these reasons he well embodied this new sphere of political power, taking from it his principal power source. Indeed, Sarmiento was one of the most eminent journalists to make the pen his fundamental political weapon. It is no surprise then that he was also a faithful follower of the associative movement. In 1836 he joined the Dramatic and Philharmonic Society of his native province. In 1837 he came into contact with Sastre's Literary Salon group and in 1839 participated in the foundation of the provincial branch of the May Association. He joined the Freemasons in 1854, at the Unión Fraternal lodge in Valparaíso. In the same year Bartolomé Mitre invited him to join the Historical-Geographical Institute of the River Plate. In 1856, when he was beginning his political career, he joined the aristocratic Progress Club, founding at the same time as the first Masonic lodge in Buenos Aires, the Unión del Plata. In 1860, as minister of the Mitre government, he obtained the thirty-third degree of the Freemasons. He then occupied various positions of authority before taking that of the Grand Master of the Grand Orient of the Argentine Republic.

A close look at Sarmiento's life as a Mason reveals a Freemason of conviction who worked constantly within and without the lodge in two fields of particular Masonic interest: education and public welfare. Sarmiento was undoubtedly one of the politicians who most benefited from this organization in the first years of its existence. Hence, as a councillor in 1857 he demanded the lodges' support for his efforts in developing public and secular education. The success of the model school of the parish of Catedral al Norte was to a great extent due to the economic contribution of the lodges and the support of the municipality, whose education commission regularly featured Masons: Sarmiento in 1856 and 1857, Héctor Varela in 1858 and 1859, and Antonio Pillado in 1860 and 1861. But Freemasonry was of more use to Sarmiento in affirming a public renown acquired in the secular world. His efforts in education, furthermore, did not date from his initiation into the Freemasons.[23] All the same, the order gave him the support and recognition of the Masonic world, some of the members of which formed part of the powerful Porteño elites. Freemasonry was to Sarmiento a trump card, of use to him in consolidating a power proceeding from the new and growing idea of representation.

New Citizen Practices: From Opinion in Arms to Electoral "Armies"

The "associative boom" introduced a veritable innovation in Porteño political sociability. The reestablishment of representative institutions was accompanied by the creation of "electoral clubs," with the aim of bringing into force an electoral act organized at the time in two stages: firstly, they sought the consensus of elites for the various candidates, for whom these new associative networks, coordinated along old forms of power and authority, intervened. Secondly, the clubs produced political movement to ensure the victory of the candidate chosen by the elites, which required the participation of other sectors of the urban population who did not take part in the earlier consensus. Although the profile of the chosen candidates barely changed, the mechanisms that took them to power brought important modifications in old structures. This change gave new life to the "old" institutions and, in spite of an extremely delicate economic and political situation, made an institutional stability possible that set the foundations of future national power.

THE REESTABLISHMENT OF SUFFRAGE

The electoral law of 1821 was never repealed by Rosas. It was the extraordinary powers that permitted Rosas to institute the regime of fixed elections, which he presented as a legal guarantee of authority.[24] After the fall of Rosas, the Porteño liberals who in 1837 had repealed the same law, not only now accepted it but also applied it with a vitality heretofore unheard of. The Constitution of the Argentine Confederation in turn confirmed the republican government founded on the principle of electoral democracy. The Porteños, who refused to ratify this, nevertheless did the same in passing the first constitution of the province of Buenos Aires, now an "autonomous state." Article 7 of this constitution ratified the 1821 law, adding new parts aimed generally at widening the vote. The vote was now given to minors enrolled in the National Guard and married men over 18. The only condition was that of being born in Argentine territory (in Buenos Aires or the provinces of the Confederation) or being naturalized. There were no cultural or economic restrictions for voters, but there were certain conditions expected of the representatives. In order to be a deputy it was necessary to possess capital of 10,000 pesos per year, or exercise a profession or trade that would produce a similar amount, in order to guarantee the independence and availability of those elected. In the case of senators, the required capital was 20,000 pesos.[25] Aside from these restrictions there were no other conditions.[26] The governor was still elected by the legislature. On the whole there were few changes, and those that were made tended to confirm electoral democracy.

However, the Constitution of the State of Buenos Aires had barely been voted in when debates on the need for electoral reform began. Various criticisms were made of the existing legislation, above all concerning the vices of procedure.[27] Claims of fraud, always presented by the defeated side, had no impact on electoral practices, not even in 1857 when new legislation was brought into effect.[28] The electoral law of this year introduced new mechanisms concerning the composition of voter lists and the election of authorities in the electoral assemblies. The principle of universal male suffrage remained intact. This provincial law was later used to draw up the national election law, passed by the national Congress in 1863.[29] At the same time new modifications were introduced in order to restrict and control the vote. The constitutional reform of 1853, voted in by Buenos Aires in 1860, began by establishing the indirect voting of senators and the president of the republic.[30] Nonetheless, until the end of our period, legislation confirmed the principle established by the 1821 law.

ELECTORAL CLUBS: FROM COMMUNITY ORGANIZATION TO THE PUBLIC SPHERE

After 17 years of Rosas, in 1852 the population of the province was called to elect its representatives. During the first "free" elections, new associative forms appeared aimed at "organizing" opinion. Five days before the election of the legislators and two months after the defeat of Rosas, the newspaper *El Progreso* reported that "the diverse electoral clubs met Saturday and set about organizing a list of candidates to represent the city. We are pleased to see this solemn rehabilitation of public spirit in our country. During the dictatorship, and even after, there were no more candidates than those of the government".[31] The newspaper thus evoked the practice used by Rosas to replace representative authorities, with perhaps a hint of a warning to Urquiza, who intended to reestablish this practice after his "liberating campaign."[32] The Porteñista opposition, comprising to a great extent exiled liberals, rejected Urquiza's "suggestions" and organized "electoral clubs," in order to draw up a different list of candidates. In this way the "parish electoral clubs" were born.

If this explains the reasons why clubs were used, it leaves one question: how was this organizational structure introduced? Indeed, this new political organization spread quickly and effectively.[33] Is it feasible to imagine a kind of spontaneous generation of the politicization of the citizens, who in no time at all organized Porteño political life?[34] Undoubtedly not, and rightly so in that, until 1857, these associations functioned without any apparent regulations, as if a structure of this type could be regulated spontaneously. While it is true that in 1852 the existence was mentioned of regulations for the parish of San Miguel, it would be five years before the regulations of 1857, signed by members of civil and political society, put an end to this statutory vagueness.[35] The norm established that each parish must compile, before the elections, a complete list of representatives for the city. The list was drawn up according to the opinion of each parish, that is, by the parish representatives participating in the commission of the club. Next, a central commission had to compile the definitive list, with the candidates who figured most frequently on parish lists.[36] Lastly, the population ratified "its will," already expressed in drawing up the list, in the electoral act.[37]

Why was the parochial structure chosen to standardize opinions? The first answer would be that parish lines were the limits set by the 1821 law.[38] Thus, given that electoral assemblies were established by parish, it was logical that in each of these a club should be organized to guarantee the triumph of the candidate "agreed on" by each assembly. This would explain the territorial division into clubs (although it would still be necessary to explain why the election law opted for the parochial framework) but does not resolve the problem of the rapid establishment of this associative form. A plausible explanation for this accelerated parochial organization, which the *El Progreso* newspaper placed in the context of the public sphere, is that it was created from a previous parochial sociability structure, which was now used to political ends. The clubs thus took advantage of a community structure, with its connections and authorities, which contributed both to organizing the campaign to "standardize opinion" around candidate lists and to guaranteeing electoral discipline in each parish on voting day.

During the debate on the electoral law project for the State of Buenos Aires in 1856, both those who advocated the creation of electoral districts and those who opposed it mentioned the existence of strong community ties influencing a theoretically individual vote. The deputy Carlos Tejedor thus supported the project, highlighting the positive aspect of community ties: "Among neighbors in the same parish everyone respects one another, because everyone knows each other; and although there may be some unruly persons, I believe that they would think twice before committing in their parish that which is generally committed by those who do not belong to it."[39] One year later, Senator Vélez Sarsfield opposed the law, alluding to the harmful influence of community ties in exercising political rights: "The word 'parish' among us means having a justice of the peace, it means having a priest, very influential persons in the elections, authorities who carry much weight and are a hindrance in the elections. Let us not then make a territorial division that so restrains the citizens' free exercise of this right."[40]

It is these community ties and authorities mentioned above by the elected representatives of the people that we find during the organization of parish clubs, especially in the election process of the the parish commissions responsible for drawing up the list of candidates. According to some references, it was apparently the outgoing commission that had to call a "parochial assembly" to elect the new commission.[41] The press, which held a privileged place for accounts of associations, particularly those referring to political life, informed the parishioners of these meetings.[42] For the election to be legitimate, the parish assembly had to bring together a minimum of thirty individuals resident in the parish.[43] However, the newspapers' numerous public denouncements suggest that the calling of assembly elections was not always public and even that it was common for these affairs to become meetings of friends and members of the same faction, to confirm a decision made beforehand and elsewhere.[44]

Let us now see some examples of the existence of networks that preceded parochial assemblies. In the parish of Concepción, some neighbors complained of the priest Mariano Marín who, having come face to face with a group of opponents, called the assembly on a different day than the one planned in order to avoid the attendance of opponents to his candidates.[45] This incident came about when the justice of the peace of the parish, opposed to Marín, called a new assembly in his home. Marín then set out on a campaign "with his cronies Solá, José M. Dantas, Amoedo, Luis Beláustequi (catechist) and others to beg votes from door to door in the parish."[46] The progressive opposition then did likewise. In the parish of San Miguel, Manuel Trelles, a notable neighbor who since 1852 had participated in the electoral commissions, was accused by Varela "of having secretly made the elections of the persons who must make up the electoral commission of 1856."[47] In the parish of Catedral al Norte, the group of those excluded published a manifesto in the *El Orden* newspaper to protest "not having been invited by the justice of the peace to elect the parochial commission."[48] According to the group's allegations, the assembly was made up of fifty people, all political acquaintances of the justice of the peace. The same newspaper accused Carlos Casares, president of the Catedral al Sur parish commission, of having been elected by an assembly that did not contain the required number of people present as established by the regulations.[49]

There are various other quotes, all referring to clubs whose relationship networks existed prior to the constitution of the association. It was these that prevailed in the election of parochial electoral authorities, who in turn would determine the list of candidates. The parish authorities (priest, justice of the peace, notable persons) then used traditional ties and authorities to organize a practice that, theoretically, was founded on the negation of these community forms.[50] From this point of view, parish electoral clubs represented a typical case of modern political organization imposed on a traditional community structure. Established in order to ensure the political representation of "citizen-individuals," the parochial clubs confirmed the place of traditional community authorities in the representative system. This suggests that the public space where the campaign took place had far less to do with the modern public sphere than with an older public space occupied by traditional authorities. This appears to be confirmed by the positioning of the electoral clubs in the city. Of a total of twenty-three references concerning meeting places, seventeen mention meetings taking place in the parish church, half of them in the presbytery and the other half in the sacristy. The other six mention meetings in the home of the justice of the peace or of the notable men of the parish.[51] Nevertheless, the adoption of these new associative forms introduced an innovation in the organization of political life. While the first clubs were meetings of notable men, as the political game opened up (to a great extent due to the systemization of fraud) the nature and function of these organizations changed. By 1853 clubs could be found that were organized outside of the parish framework and which nevertheless followed the dynamic that had led to their origin in 1852, but were now created by those excluded from parochial commissions. In 1854 two new "opinion clubs" were formed, the Constitucional and the Argentino, to oppose the ministerial candidates backed by the parochial clubs.[52] While these first hints of political organization were indicative of the growth of the political sociability structure in the city, in the 1856 elections particularly, the year that the political class split into "progressives" and "conservatives," the "opinion clubs" established themselves definitively as forms of extra-parochial organization. During the new electoral campaign, the list of "progressives" was supported by the *La Tribuna* newspaper and the electoral club of the national guards, while the "conservatives" used the structure of the parish clubs and broke, to use the *La Tribuna* expression, "the neighborly pact," as they "annulled the preexisting agreement, and gave a kick up the rear to the established conciliation of old."[53] With these accusations, Varela sought to justify the new electoral associations organized outside of the parish community, which would multiply during the electoral campaign of 1857. There was even a mention of the possibility of creating a central commission of "opinion clubs."[54]

One of the great opinion clubs, the Liberty Club created in 1857, immediately distanced itself from the parochial clubs, considering them mere electoral coteries. The club announced that its objective was not to propose candidates but to bring about the victory of those who genuinely represented the will of the people.[55] Varela enumerates the benefits that the new clubs would bring, in terms that are worth quoting:

> The education of public opinion, which is the essence of democracy, has special schools in the form of clubs, has unbiased teachers in the form of popular orators, has libraries in the pages of free publications...a club means a serious meeting between men who individually comprise all their dignity as citizens and seek to make the club effective through their support of patriotic initiatives due to the union and unity that they carry in their preparatory work in order to exercise democracy.[56]

In spite of the convincing declarations of civic-mindedness, the "opinion clubs" bore more in common with clientele organizations than "civic schools," to a great extent because the "individual-citizen" to whom Varela refers only existed in a few circles of society, when in reality the 1821 law granted citizenship to the male population as a whole.

Nevertheless, the new clubs defined themselves as a framework of representation. This was also of course the basis of the parochial clubs, but the "opinion clubs" were distinguished by a veritable representative image that began with active participation in the press during the clubs' electoral campaign. Together with parochial clubs, which had become quasi-government institutions, each newspaper set up its own club or joined an already existing one. Newspaper editors would often sit on the commission of the club. In this way opinion clubs came into contact with the new public sphere constructed since 1852 by the development of the opinion press. It was not entirely a coincidence that clubs should choose the facilities of the city's theaters for the organization of clientele.[57] On the stage, the club directors represented, in both senses of the word, general opinion, and not that of a "circle" or parish. In the meeting hall, the people/audience saw for the first time this representative staging. This people/audience continued to grow. In 1856, the National Guards club managed to attract around six hundred to seven hundred people to the Victoria Theater.[58] One year later, the Liberty Club brought together around 1,300 citizens at the Argentino Theater.[59] The same club gathered some 2,000 citizens together in 1861 in the Colón Theater.[60] These were quite considerable figures. Even taking into account the small assemblies, the meetings over the whole period brought together an average of five hundred people. After the nationalization of Porteño political life, this first representative staging appears to have lost followers; in the 1860s attendance at meetings fluctuated between sixty and 150 people, according to Hilda Sabato's figures.[61] It goes without saying that this representative force translated into mobilizing capacity. The first battle, before the voting, broke out among the elites and consisted of measuring the "dissuasive" forces in order to make a decision as to future electoral alliances. However, the fact

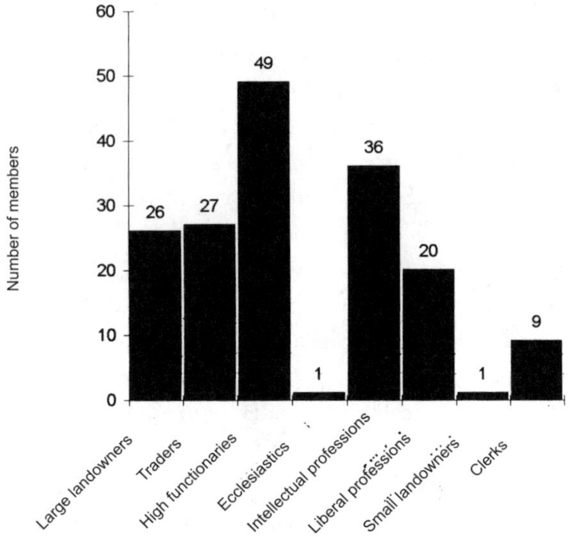

Figure 27. Socioprofessional Status of Electoral Club Directive Commission Members between 1852 and 1862 (Sample of 169 People)

that they took opinion as the foundation of the association was in itself a break with parochial clubs, which were defined in relation to their belonging to the community of the place.

The road from the parish to the public sphere was neither unequivocal nor irreversible. The same men would quite often act at the same time in both contexts. As indicated above, these were organizational forms that were established and thus joined together two power structures that for this author, as for the intellectuals of the past, were theoretically contradictory, but which coexisted on the historic plane. Furthermore, there is enough evidence to believe that political life was established in this space wherein it was possible to confuse the two registers: communal and individual.

THE ELECTORAL DIRECTORS

So far we have seen the electoral irregularities within club commissions, and the influence of traditional authorities and the heads of factions in their constitution. But we still know little of this population of "first electors" who, for a limited time, would represent the parish and the city. According to our sources, 359 individuals participated in the commissions of the electoral clubs between 1852 and 1862. Their socioprofessional extraction did not much differ from that of the ruling class (see figure 27). It is true that, as in the case of the Freemasons, commercial professions, and those of administration employees were better represented than in the ruling class. But on the whole these were well-to-do people, and often those who were already close to power: the military, intellectuals, and the liberal professions. The political intermediaries responsible for recruiting and mobilizing the bases had scarce access to ruling positions.

Nearly half of these (41.5%) also held a position in the administration of the State of Buenos Aires, which suggests that the activity of the club was not alien to the political careers of the directors (see figure 28). The posts that attributed most importance to the activity of the clubs were those that were more or less directly related to the elections (senators, deputies and councilors), in addition to the military and justices of the peace, who played a central role on election day. Logically, members of parochial clubs had more means of accessing power than those of opinion clubs. As the former were controlled by the government and had more chances of victory, they were in a better position to hand out posts after the elections. Thus, of the 149 members of clubs who held posts in the government and administration of the State, seventy were members of the parish clubs, forty-one belonged to opinion clubs and thirty-eight participated in both forms of electoral organization.[62]

Of the total of club directors who held representative roles, two types of political careers appear to stand out: that of the representatives participating in commissions after having occupied a seat in the legislature or Municipal Council (more than half, 59 of 106), and that of representatives whose election appears to have been the consequence of their participation in clubs' commissions (47 of 106). These figures suggest that the clubs played one of the essential roles of political parties in the nineteenth century, which were born as political forces of electoral action, tied to the parliamentary institution: that of giving the Public institutional recognition through Parliament.[63] This aspect appears to be confirmed by the other half of the directors, who did not occupy posts during the period and whom could be qualified as individuals from "civil society." It is true, however, that some young men, who were setting out at this time in political life, would hold a privileged place after 1862, such as Luis Elordi, Carlos D'Amico, Dardo Rocha, etc. Others, men of letters, did not hold posts at this time but did play important roles in the public sphere. The exemplary case is undoubtedly that of Mariano Varela, but we can also mention other such figures as José M. Estrada, Manuel Rocha, Carlos Terrada and the young Adolfo Saldías, who did not yet have the fame he would gain later.

This associative belonging is also evidence of transformations in Porteño political life. Indeed, of 359 leaders, 158 (44%) had at least one affiliation to a leisure club, Masonic lodge or cultural association. This was an aspect that culturally

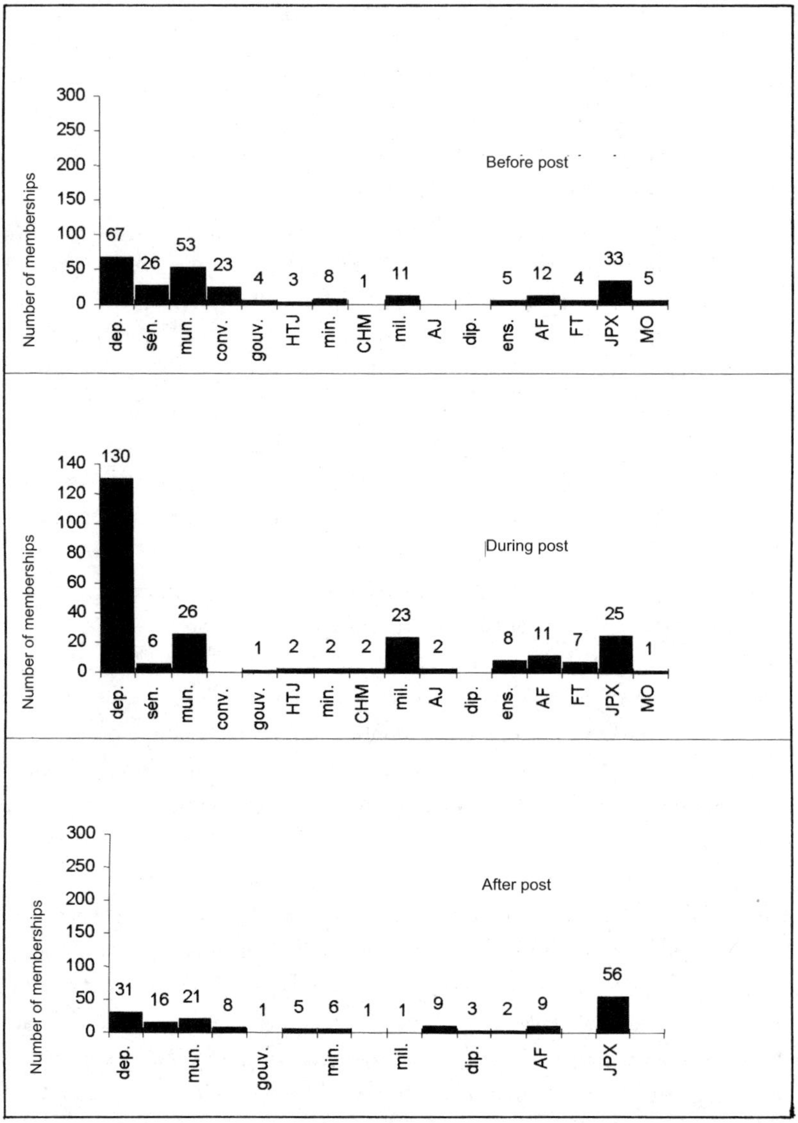

Figure 28. Number of Affiliations of Porteño Ruling Class with Electoral Clubs between 1852 and 1862, in Relation to Obtaining the Post

dep.=deputies; sen.=senators; mun.=councilors; conv.=conventional; gouv.=governors; HTJ=members of Supreme Justice Court; min.=ministers; CHM=administrative ministerial heads; mil.=members of the military; AJ=Justice Administration Staff; dip.=diplomats; ens.=university teachers and staff; AF=financial administration staff; FT=technical posts; JPX=justices of the peace; MO=maintainers of law and order

characterized the Porteño elites as a whole, but the large percentage of affiliations among members of electoral commissions suggests that the associative boom was not alien to the political sphere. Thus, of 106 leaders of clubs who occupied an elective post, seventy-two (68%) were members of another association. We could even add to this figure the eight cases of deputies not affiliated personally but who had in their nuclear family a member who was. At the heart of the running of the clubs participating in associative networks, we can find key figures in Porteño political life such as B. Mitre, A. Alsina, C. Tejedor, N. Calvo, C. Casares, R. Elizalde, Juan M. Gutiérrez, J. Mármol, P. Obligado, E. de la Riestra, H. Varela, etc. It is true that these associations only committed themselves on limited occasions to political infighting, but they were also a springboard for certain political ambitions and even to obtaining institutional recognition through access to representative posts, including the management of the electoral club itself. The most evident case, above all due to the fact that records exist, which is not the case of all the associations, is that of Freemasonry. While for the ten years of secession we can only find one case of electoral orders from the authorities of the order in the Masonic archives, in contrast there are numerous examples of lodges pressing the government on the institution's sensitive issues: health, education and culture.[64] It is no coincidence at all that the public posts corresponding to these spheres were occupied by active Freemasons, such as Sarmiento in education and Rawson and Durand in health.

Equally significant was the presence of Masons in the management of men's clubs connected to the world of publishing, particularly the written press. Among these were the principal political figures of the period, such as Adolfo Alsina, Nicolás Calvo, Juan A. García, Juan M. Gutiérrez, José Mármol, Bartolomé Mitre and Héctor Varela. Although from a quantitative point of view the participation of these men of the press in the running of the clubs was still in a minority (of 359 individuals, only 31 worked in newspaper editing), of these men half went on to hold an elective role, and this only up to 1862. These were men who played an essential role in factious political life, among whom were the leaders of the two principle parties: Adolfo Alsina and Bartolomé Mitre. Why did both these faction leaders attribute importance to the campaign in the public sphere, when this type of activity did not directly translate into many votes at the polls, given that it was aimed at an apparently abstemious sector of the population? Furthermore, club commissions did not exactly reproduce the networks that influenced their election. In this period there were fewer electoral *caudillos* than might have been expected, and a massive presence of men whose action was defined in the context of the public sphere. Of the seventy-nine men comprising the central club commissions between 1857 and 1862, only six held this post twice. In ten years, from a total of

	# of cases					
# of times	**CP**	**%**	**CCP**	**%**	**CO**	**%**
1	210	85	73	92	175	92
2	30	12	6	8	15	8
3	5	2				

Figure 29. Repeat Participation of Electoral Club Leaders
CP: parish club; CCP: central commission; CO: opinion club
Source: PGB, *La Création,* appendix 1, "Base de données."

359 individuals who joined the management of electoral club commissions, only five managed to be on the same club's commission three times. The renewal of these leaders worked better in the opinion clubs than in the parishes (figure 29).

The Republican "Balance": The Coordination of Two Logics of Political Representation

Let us return to the moment when the clubs' commissions were set up. These organisms were intended to draw up the list of candidates for representation, thus the establishment of the commissions was a fundamental moment in the representative process, through which the population would elect their candidates at elections. This gave the commissions a representative dimension that the actors recognized explicitly.[65] What was their role in the electoral process? The first answer would be that they effectively replaced primary assemblies, which the Provincial Statute of 1815 had established as a form of indirect election, which was later revoked by the 1821 electoral law.[66] It is true that unlike the major electors chosen by primary assemblies, parochial commissions only designated "candidates" for representation. This list then had to be ratified on election day, but by precisely those who the principle of indirect voting turned away from the polls, while the well-to-do tended to triumph in the election of major electors. This would explain the apparent contradiction in Porteño political life: on one hand, an intense politicization of public life, on the other, scarce participation in voting on election day. The indifference of the elites and of those who identified with the new public culture was perhaps due to the fact that this second instance of representation was not particularly aimed at them. For them, the essential part had already been done, namely the election of the candidates whom the elites delegated to draw up the lists. In this way, the structure of the club allowed competition to be regulated by the lists and resolved the difficult problem of consensus among notable men, a problem first raised by the establishment of the 1821 law. To do so, these elites were assigned a representative dimension they had not previously possessed and which originated in the parochial assemblies' vote.

The Foreigners' Club, founded in Buenos Aires in 1859 to support the Artisans' Club, is an example of the representative potential of these associations. The initiative met with lively criticism from the opposition, who alleged that foreigners should not meddle in electoral matters. The club's president, the French businessman St. Guilly, replied that "the club's program is that of discussing our interests and expressing our opinions, although as foreigners we do not have the right to vote."[67] The foreigners intended to take advantage of the right to association established by the Constitution of the State, to publicly represent their interests. This then was a new form of representation that used the organization of the electoral clubs but did not lead to the vote. The club's president clearly states as much in an article published in Calvo's *La Reforma Pacífica*:

> As foreigners we can openly express our preference for the candidates whose presence in the legislature would suit most both our interests and those of the sons of the country.... We will give our support in electoral matters to those representatives of Buenos Aires who prove themselves to be willing to support our rights, but we have no business at the polls.[68]

It goes without saying that this support meant both a favorable strength of opinion and mobilizing forces for the elections. But it is clear that the foreigners delegated the authority for drawing up a list of candidates for representation to Calvo, and the public show of support increased Calvo's authority, the origin of which lay precisely in the representative power which this delegation implied.

Once authority for drawing up the lists had been delegated to commission members, these members negotiated a joint list with other clubs. The public support that these different lists attained was a fundamental aspect in the negotiating power of the leaders of the different clubs. In general, an agreement was usually reached which reduced the total number of lists to two. The decision then lay in the hands of the voters. But then other practices came into play that had little in common with the modern idea of voting: partiality in the constitution of the assemblies, falsification of the electoral register, and diverse forms of electoral coercion were all common currency, and although regularly denounced by the defeated candidate's supporters they did not jeopardize the regime's institutional stability.

The clubs would serve the Porteño liberals in the 1850s in organizing this type of fraudulent practice, which was on the whole improvised at this time. Héctor Varela, a liberal with profound republican convictions, had nothing but praise in public for what he saw as a form of democratization of the electoral act. In his judgment, one of the advantages of the clubs, aside from guaranteeing the prior agreement of candidacies, was that they provided a strike force to be imposed at the moment when electoral assemblies were formed on election day, "as in our imperfect electoral system the result of the elections almost always depends on them."[69] How exactly was this electoral army organized? At this point it is necessary to make a distinction between the networks formed on the parochial structure and those organized from opinion clubs. Although in both cases it was connections and not the "individual's rational will" that determined the election of the candidate, in the parochial networks there may have remained a traditional notion of community representation that opinion clubs attempted to suppress, principally because to organize themselves they had to break with the cultural foundation of traditional ties, as was seen in the mobilization of African-Argentines.

During the 1857 electoral campaign, the Liberty Club created a branch for "colored citizens."[70] The political function that Rosas had imposed on African societies was now taken up by this club, which at its first meeting managed to attract three hundred African-Argentines. The existence of strong community ties may have made the political mobilization of this sector of the population a little easier and less frightful. To do so, the liberals designated one Rosendo Mendizábal as the head of the branch, a 37-year-old of mixed race and a musician by profession, who instead of establishing "bilateral" ties with the Conga, Benguela or Mondongo nations, as Rosas had done, created an organization aimed at bringing together African-Argentines in their entirety. To gain their loyalty, he censured ethnic organizations and attempted to create ties that would adapt better to the type of representation required by liberal constitutionalism.

However, the problem of African-Argentine representation had been raised a year earlier, when *La Tribuna* highlighted the risk of promoting a community vote. At the time Varela criticized the opportunist attitude of the "conservatives" who refused to include Colonel García in their list and proposed in his place the mixed-race Colonel Domingo Sosa.[71] According to this newspaper, Sosa could only be the representative of a "caste" and not of the "People." Varela then recalls the case of Rosendo Mendizábal, who had just been admitted into the National Guard Club: "serious and influential men cried to the heavens: they proclaimed that there should be no more mulattoes: that Medizabal would only represent a caste, which was highly dangerous, inasmuch that it was a disadvantage that a seat in the legislature should be occupied by a man who might become an organ of the exaggerated claims of a caste..."[72] One year later, however, those who had previously been horrified would now turn to Mendizábal to create a branch of the Liberty Club. From his first speech, Mendizábal was clear of his intentions: "The cause that we have come together for, as you well know, is that of principles, laws and general progress.... Let us remember, friends, and let us place in the hearts of our friends, of those less learned men unaware of the decades of revolution and history of our country, that it is not the party or the circle that we are seeking to combat, to whom we owe citizenly guarantees and equality for all before the law."[73] This is not to say that the club transformed this sector of the population into citizen-individuals who exercised a political right. The club appeared to modify the community vote through clientele ties, thus eliminating the problem of "caste" representation. Mendizábal's political career is evidence of this. In spite of facing strong racial prejudices, he managed to become a part of the associative elite network: a member of electoral club commissions on two occasions, he joined the Freemasons in 1858.[74] In 1859 he joined the parochial clubs' central commission. The same year he obtained a post in the State administration, as a member of the office for fiscal land, a post that was hardly within the orbit of a musician. Mendizábal undoubtedly owed his political success to his participation in the elites' associative network, where he was accepted due to his ability to mobilize others. Associative activity made Mendizábal an indispensable political intermediary in the electoral battle.With the case of the National Guard Club we can evoke another classic example of an electoral club functioning as an organizational structure of political clientele.[75] The club was founded in 1855 on ties within the army community, which undoubtedly constituted a complementary guarantee of electoral discipline. In 1856, in a meeting of eight hundred people in the Victoria Theater, Nicasio Biedma, a member and commander of the National Guard, took the floor to offer the club "four hundred men to support the candidate," an offer that received the instant applause of José Barros Pazos (a National Guard deputy candidate) and Nicolás Calvo, editor of the newspaper *La Reforma Pacífica*, who at the time supported the same candidate.[76] The club was successful in the elections, with a clear superiority over the "carters and farm workers with their ponchos and knives," who were apparently highly disorganized.[77] In the San Miguel parish, the national guards interrupted the meeting and clashed with "the armed rabble...the compact wall that the people and their knives formed, led by *serious men*, mayors and deputy mayors," destroyed the voting table and the ballot papers to begin a second election with the vote of political acquaintances.[78] The inhabitants of Concepción, according to the account of the defeated, heard that the national guards were approaching and locked themselves in the church with the ballot papers. After a violent stone-throwing battle the army of the National Guard managed to remove the table and the voting lists. The same was the case in other parishes.[79] These accounts may suggest that the means employed by the national guards in no way differed from those of the opposition. However, when a year earlier Héctor Varela announced the creation of a club in his newspaper *La Tribuna*, he indicated that this club represented true public opinion as "it

Figure 30. The Two Facets of Representation, from El Mosquito *(1863)*

brings together citizens from different parishes."[80] True public opinion was thus defined as that which broke with the local framework of belonging and that which guaranteed the freedom of the vote.

It remains to be seen what importance is to be given to the participation of popular sectors in these fraudulent electoral practices. To tackle this issue suitably other types of sources would undoubtedly be required. We can nevertheless approach the question from the perspective of the elites writing in the newspapers, speaking in meetings and managing clubs. It is surprising and even paradoxical, however, that the elites should have resorted at the last minute to an election whose results depended on the mobilization of a clientele that left much to chance, although the risks were incomparable to those they would run in the same circumstances towards the end of the century, as in this case it was a matter of a fight between factions of the elites who already directed the first instance of drawing up lists of candidates.

How did these elites justify the fraud? In 1854, *La Tribuna* disagreed with the list proposed by the San Miguel Club, reaching the following conclusion on the strategy to be followed: "if unfortunately we cannot arrive at any transaction with the San Miguel Club we will have to descend to the field of struggle to see if it declares itself the victor in the field."[81] As Varela recalls in an article cited above, given the imperfection of the electoral system, force could constitute a guarantee of representation, therefore the citizens were to mobilize in order to impose their will on election day.[82] Calvo said much the same in inciting artisans to mobilize to change their fate. This was, of course, a discursive strategy to justify the flagrant contradiction between the institutions they claimed to venerate and the practices that supposedly led them to them. But why should these not be taken literally? If the idea worked (given that the institutional stability of local political life was, in spite of everything, undeniable) why should it not be imagined that this discourse, which concealed a flagrant contradiction, translated a political reality? We are indeed far from the "citizen-individual" figure to whom the liberals ceaselessly referred, while it is also true that this call to active participation had more similarities with the war dynamics prevalent during the crisis period of the local ancien régime than with the exercising of new political rights. But there is also no doubt that this dynamic was indicative of the birth of political life in the region and played an important function in the establishment of new bases of political legitimacy.[83] Furthermore, for the popular sectors it was very often their only contact with politics, in a society that lived through half a century of civil war. Rosas was able to use this "force of opinion" that was written with guns and translated into warring acting, with which he believed he would be able to do without the political elites associated with representative institutions and guarantees of fundamental liberties. In my judgment, this was to prove harmful for Rosas.

The electoral clubs, founded after Rosas' fall to bring representative institutions into operation, appear to have related this type of relationship with politics, which paved the way for such institutions. This sheds light on declarations such as that of *La Tribuna* in 1854, announcing the triumph of its candidates thusly, "we have the principal element: force. We have the support of public opinion."[84] In this electoral mobilization there was not only clientele action but also a representative logic, that of a will manifesting itself through war. It is true that the 1821 electoral law proposed a model of citizenship intended to put an end to this militarized society, but the long period of Rosas' government, which associated the concentration of powers with permanent civil war, turned this law into dead letters. The Porteño elites appear to have found in the organization through clubs of "electoral armies," a solution to the problem of the political representation of certain sectors of society, a solution that does not appear to have aroused the unanimity of these elites, judging by D'Amico's criticism of Bartolomé Mitre's policies: "It was Mitre who, in order to oppose the vote of Urquiza's soldiers in 1852, invented fraud instead of using arms, because the abuse of force has no other honored remedy than force."[85] In other words, instead of leading his soldiers to the battlefield, Mitre led them to the polls. This was no coincidence. From 1852, electoral practice combined the force of opinion with the force of arms on election day. Thus, in a meeting of the National Guard Club in 1856, Biedma could offer "four hundred men" and not "four hundred votes," as if these were two equivalent forms of representation.

In introducing significant modifications to local political life, the electoral clubs played an important role in the renewal of representative institutions. At the same time they made it possible to regulate the confrontation between notable men over candidacies and amplify representation through the more vigorous participation of institutions of the public sphere in drawing up candidate lists. But the clubs brought with them a third innovation that contributed greatly to the institutional stability of the period: they extended the representation of society, introducing new logics of political representation.

NOTES

1. On this point, see Tulio Halperin Donghi's excellent analysis, "Una nación."
2. For a biography of López, see Ricardo Piccirilli, *Los López. Una dinastía intelectual. Ensayo histórico-literario, 1810–1852* (Buenos Aires: Eudeba, 1972).
3. See Carlos Calvo, *Nobiliario del Antiguo Virreinato del Río de la Plata*, vol. 2 (Buenos Aires: Librería y Editorial La Facultad, 1936), 186–187.
4. Figures obtained from a sample of 182 people, 78% of the total. See PGB, *La Création,* appendix 1, "Base de données." With regards to the geographic origin of the members, again there were few major differences with the members of the Rosista legislature. In a

sample of 162 people, 85% were from Buenos Aires, 12% from the interior, principally the province of Córdoba, and 3% from neighboring countries, particularly Uruguay. See PGB, *La Création,* appendix 1, "Base de données."

5. We have data on 115 deputies out of 234 (approximately half of the total). Of these 115, eighty-seven (75%) had a university degree. These figures would decrease to 37% if those on whom we have no information did not hold a degree. See PGB, *La Création,* appendix 1, "Base de données."
6. See document 89, "Lieu d'étude des 108 diplômés de la Chambre de représentants de la province de Buenos Aires entre 1852–1862," in PGB, *La Création*, vol. 2, 583.
7. The total number of university graduates is eighty. We have only used seventy-five of these in the graph, as the other five either exceed the chronological scope established or their corresponding data are not entirely certain.
8. See PGB, *La Création,* appendix 1, "Base de données."
9. See "Appartenance associative des représentants de la province de Buenos Aires entre 1840 et 1852," in PGB, *La Création*, vol. 1, document 56, 380.
10. See below, "New citizen practices…"
11. This question is developed further below.
12. Figures refer to total memberships and are not accumulative. The same person might be counted three times. Of a total of 3,653 memberships, 202 were from the 1828–1839 period, 109 from 1840–1851 and 1,038 from the ten years of secession of the State of Buenos Aires. See PGB, *La Création,* appendix 1, "Base de données."
13. This is affirmed by Freemasonry itself. Some authors highlight the primary role of the Masonic Order, while others speak of the work of the Freemasons. In the first case are the works of Antonio Zúñiga and Martín Lazcano, and in the second above all are the investigations of Alcibíades Lappas. See Antonio Zúñiga, *La Logia "Lautaro" y la independencia de América* (Buenos Aires: Ed. Gráf. J. Estrada, 1922); Martín Lazcano, *Las sociedades secretas, políticas y masónicas en Buenos Aires*, 2 vols. (Buenos Aires: El Ateneo, 1927); Alcibíades Lappas, *La masonería argentina a través de sus hombres* (Buenos Aires: self-published, 1966). For an analysis of Masonic work, see my work "Masonería y Revolución de Independencia."
14. It is impossible to analyze in detail here all of the associations in question. I have decided to view just one case, not with the purpose of finding "the model," but rather to present a historic case that clearly shows the new relationships between the public and private spheres.
15. The only existent study on these elections is that of Alberto Armando Mignanego, "La elección de marzo de 1856 en Buenos Aires," *Boletín de la Universidad Nacional de La Plata* 19: 6 (1935), 123–142; also A. A. Mignanego, *El segundo gobernador constitucional de Buenos Aires y el proceso electoral de 1856–1857* (Buenos Aires, 1938).
16. Valentín Alsina was the principal adversary of the "conservative" politics of Manuel Obligado and was the "progressive" candidate for the provincial government. Lorenzo Torres, in contrast, was the candidate of the more radical "conservative" sector close to Urquiza. According to the anti-Masonic farce referred to above, the creation of the Unión del Plata was the work of Alsina. See *Farsa.*
17. See document 100 in PGB, *La Création*, vol. 2.
18. Nevertheless, Freemason traders had more possibilities of attaining a post in government than traders without such an affiliation. The latter accounted for 8.4% of the ruling class, while the proportion of Freemason traders was 12.9% The same was the case of administrative clerks, for whom the Masonic affiliation doubled the chances of access

to a post in the administration of the State of Buenos Aires. In contrast, the percentage of Freemason university graduates was similar to that of deputies. The majority of these, 66.6% of graduates, were former students of the University of Buenos Aires. The age did not differ in the leading group. See PGB, "Statut socioprofessionnel de la classe dirigeante *porteña* entre 1852 et 1862 (échantillon de 427 personnes, 46% du total)," in *La Création*, appendix 1, document 2.

19. This is naturally the opinion of Freemasons but also of those who denounced the influence of the order over the nation. This criticism corresponds above all to authors of the nationalist right, whose combat against Freemasonry was rather muddled with their combat against liberalism. See for example the works of Jordán Genta, *Sarmiento y la masonería* (Buenos Aires, 1949); J. Genta, *La masonería en la Argentina* (Buenos Aires, 1949 and 1951); J. Genta, *La masonería y el comunismo en la revolución del 16 de septiembre* (Buenos Aires, 1956); and J. Genta, *La masonería argentina en la historia argentina. A propósito del centenario de la muerte del General San Martín (1850–1950)* (Buenos Aires, 1949).
20. On this period of Sarmiento's life, the most documented work continues to be P. Verdevoye's thesis, *Domingo Faustino Sarmiento*.
21. A post from which he resigned in 1861 because of events in his native province. In the same year that he was named minister, 1860, he participated in the two national conventions.
22. It is true that he was related to some of the principal families of San Juan, but in spite of his insistence in trying to make of this a source of social prestige (his *Recuerdos de provincia* [Santiago de Chile, 1850] aimed to rehabilitate his ancestry), his branch of the family had in fact seen better days.
23. Sarmiento's efforts in public education date from long before his joining the Masons. His wrote on the subject for the first time in 1839 when he was 28. In 1849 he published *De la educación popular*, in which he developed his ideas on secular education, in Santiago de Chile.
24. See "Mensaje de Rosas a la Junta de Representantes de la provincia de Buenos Aires," in Heráclito Mabragaña, *Los mensajes. Historia del desenvolvimiento de la Nación Argentina (redactados cronológicamente, 1810–1910)*, vol. 1 (Buenos Aires: Comisión Nacional del Centenario, 1910), 322–345.
25. Articles 23 and 31 of the *Constitución del Estado de Buenos Aires*, 1854.
26. During the debate, Nicolás Anchorena pointed out the disadvantages of this "vagueness." See Sala de Representantes de la Provincia de Buenos Aires, *Diario de sesiones*, session of 14 March 1854, 80.
27. Héctor Varela even took the trouble to enumerate all of the legal institutions that the law placed at the disposal of politicians to guarantee fraud: the method of registering voters, constitution procedures in electoral assemblies, the place of voting at church entrances, the form of election by complete candidate lists, etc. See "Ley de elecciones," *La Tribuna*, 22 July 1854.
28. See Cámara de Senadores del Estado de Buenos Aires, *Diario de sesiones de la Cámara de Senadores del Estado de Buenos Aires* (Buenos Aires: Imprenta El Orden, 1858), session of 1 October 1857, 435–441. Varela mentions this law in *La Tribuna*, 16 and 18 June 1857.
29. Passed by the Congress of the Argentine Confederation, law 140 established three days of elections, which facilitated fraud enormously. It was replaced by law 75, which followed the Porteño formula of holding elections on a single day. See Legislación Argentina, *Colección completa de leyes nacionales sancionadas por el Honorable Congreso durante los años 1852 a 1917*, vol. 1 (Buenos Aires: 1918), 158–167, 284–295.

30. Senators were elected by deputies, and the president and vice-president by electoral college. See article 78 of the Constitution of the Argentine Confederation of 1853, and article 80 of the Constitution of the Argentine Republic, reformed in 1860. See A. Sampay, *Las Constituciones*.
31. *El Progreso*, 6 April 1852, 3.
32. *El Progreso*, 6 April 1852, 3.
33. On the rate of its growth, see figure 6.
34. The question arises all the more in that no author has so far elucidated the phenomenon of the birth and growth of this new power system.
35. The regulations established for the city of Buenos Aires "an association comprised by its parishes, with the name of parochial clubs." See article 1 of the "Reglamento de los clubes electorales," *La Tribuna*, 28 February 1857. At the foot of the document are the signatures of the nineteen persons who participated in drawing up the statute. These were members of the Porteño elites: four were justices of the peace, of which three were working as such at the time, seven were functionaries (representatives and councilors) elected by the people, one was a parish priest, another from the military, five belonged to "civil society" and two were unidentified. The list gives us an approximate idea of the authorities who intervened in parochial community life: civil authorities, ecclesiasts and the military, as well as notable figures.
36. See "Reglamento de los clubes electorales."
37. "Reglamento de los clubes electorales," article 6.
38. This was not, however, a matter of electoral districts, as the population voted in their parish of residence for the representatives of the city as a whole.
39. See "Sesión de la Cámara de diputados del 8 de octubre de 1856," in Cámara de Diputados de la Provincia de Buenos Aires, *Diario de la Cámara de Diputados de la Provincia de Buenos Aires, 1854–1862* (Buenos Aires, 1857), 483.
40. See "Sesión de la Cámara de Senadores del 26 de septiembre de 1857," in Cámara de Senadores del Estado de Buenos Aires, *Diario de sesiones*, 415.
41. The justice of the peace could also apparently do this. See "Pública solicitada," *La Tribuna*, 16 March 1856, 3; "Hechos locales," *La Tribuna*, 16 February 1856, 3.
42. The section concerning associative life was called "Local News" and often appeared in the third column of the second page in the press. At times, and frequently so in *La Reforma Pacífica*, it appeared on the first column of the third page. It is possible to imagine that there were replacements for this means of communication, which targeted the population with less regular access to the press, all the more so given that under electoral law the illiterate also enjoyed political rights. These substitutions can be found precisely in a fundamentally parochial sociability structure.
43. Héctor Varela complained about this clause on numerous occasions, considering that even when this number of people was found, it was far from representative of the general will of the parish. See *La Tribuna*, 28 May 1855, 1, and 2 March 1856, 2.
44. According to regulations, the parish commission had to dissolve itself after the electoral act, which meant that the clubs did not have a prolonged institutional life and that at the time of voting, therefore, whoever participated in the election of their authorities was not the associative hierarchy but another kind of authority.
45. See "Pública solicitada," *La Tribuna*, 16 March 1856, 3; "Los vecinos de la Concepción y su protesta," *La Tribuna*, 19 March 1856, 2.
46. See "Pública solicitada," *La Tribuna*, 16 March 1856, 3.
47. See "Pública solicitada," *La Tribuna*, 3–4 March 1856, 1. The parish of San Miguel was

one of the first to organize an electoral club, founded by R. Trelles, Ramón Basavilbaso, Manuel Insiarte, Bruno González and Pedro Vernet. See AGN, Manuscripts BN, file 526, document 8634.

48. See *El Orden*, 22 February 1857, 3.
49. See *El Orden*, 1 March 1857; "Reglamento de los clubes electorales," *La Tribuna*, 28 February 1857.
50. This is not to say that these authorities confirmed the power of the Church as an institution or the predominance of the State through the justices of the peace. The authority of these notable men appears to have been based more on a logic similar to that described by Giovanni Levi to explain the authority of Giulio Cesare Chiesa: it lay less in the representative institution than in its mediation capacity between the community and the institutions. See Giovanni Levi, *Le Pouvoir au village. Histoire d'un exorciste dans le Piémonte du XVIIe siècle* (Paris: Gallimard, 1989).
51. See "Avisos," *La Tribuna*, 17 March 1855, 4; "Hechos locales," *La Tribuna*, 4 May 1855, 2; "Hechos locales," *La Tribuna*, 19 February 1856, 3; *El Orden*, 19 February 1856, 3; *El Orden*, 22 February 1856, 2; *El Orden*, 29 February 1856, 3; "Avisos," *La Tribuna*, 14 February 1857, 3; *La Tribuna*, 16 March 1856, 2; *La Tribuna*, 28 March 1856, 3; *El Nacional*, 18 February 1857; *La Tribuna*, 18 February 1857, 2; *El Orden*, 21 February 1857, 2; *La Tribuna*, 6 March 1858, 3; *La Tribuna*, 19 March 1862.
52. The Constitutional Club, created by the initiative of the Varela brothers, held their meetings on the premises of *La Tribuna*. In a joint meeting that brought together around 100 people, both clubs reached a political pact to propose a joint list of candidates. See *La Tribuna*, 28 April 1854, 2.
53. Varela declared: "the list presented [by the parish clubs] is neither that of the parishes nor that of the people, but that of a circle who have compiled the list in the shadows, excluding from the discussion of candidates all those who would not submit to their clique's appointments." See "Usurpación de nombre," *La Tribuna*, 27 March 1856.
54. The newspaper *El Orden* reported that the previous evening the commissions of seven "dissident" clubs had met in the El Porvenir Theater, with the aim of establishing a central commission to unite them. Marín, Pirán, Cuenta and Casares were then elected as members of this commission. See *El Orden*, 14 March 1857.
55. "The Liberty Club rarely proposes a candidate, but it seeks to have the representative of the will of the people voted for and triumphant." See "La opinión pública en evidencia," *La Tribuna*, 17 February 1857, 2.
56. See "Educación de la democracia," *La Tribuna*, 19 March 1858, 2.
57. Participation in these meetings required the presentation of an invitation card. See *El Orden*, 11 March 1856, 3. *La Tribuna* includes a missive "informing the members of the National Guard Club that on Sunday, March 16th, the general meeting will take place in the Victoria Theater at 12 o'clock. Entrance cards must be shown." *See* "Hechos locales," *La Tribuna*, 14 and 15 March 1856, 3. In 1857, the Liberty Club announced that nobody would be authorized to enter without an invitation, but that "whoever so wishes to enter the Liberty Club may request such documentation from the house at no. 37 of Calle Merced, every day." See *La Tribuna*, 20 February 1857, 2.
58. See *El Orden*, 18 March 1856.
59. See *La Tribuna*, 14 March 1857, 2.
60. See *La Tribuna*, 5 March 1861, 2.
61. Confirmation can be found here of the modifications that the nationalization of Porteño power brought to political life in the city of Buenos Aires. See H. Sabato,

"Citizenship, political participation, and the formation of the public sphere in Buenos Aires, 1850s–1860s," *Past and Present* 1992.

62. See PGB, *La Création,* appendix 1, "Base de données."
63. On the proto-parties, see the classic studies by Robert Michels, *Les Partis politiques* (1911) (Paris: Flammarion, 1971), and Moisei Ostrogorski, *La Démocratie et les partis politiques* (Paris: Calmann-Lévy, 1912).
64. The case of electoral orders concerns the councilor elections of 1861. At the request of the Unione Italiana lodge, the Regeneración lodge called Freemason brethren to vote for brother Salvarezza in order to prevent the candidates of the Saint Vincent of Paul Society from gaining a foothold in the municipality, as "education would then fall into the hands of this society." The lodge invited the members of the national workshop to vote on the 25th with Masonic energy and fervor to prevent the triumph of the Jesuits. Brother Keil stated that it would be advisable that the Supreme Council give a list of municipalities, in order to create a group vote. Mariano Billinghurst, Venerable Master of the lodge, accepted the idea and declared that it was possible to make up a list of candidates, although this question had not yet been studied. But in his judgment any vote was good, as long as it was not for the Jesuits. In the following session, Billinghurst, who formed part off the Supreme Council, reported that all Masons would be invited to a grand session to discuss the coming municipal elections, with the aim of defeating the Jesuits. He then invited "foreign brethren to register in their respective parishes, to cast their vote on the 25th." See AGLA, Minute Book, Regeneración lodge, box 36, session of 7 November 1860.
65. This was the essence of the denouncements of vices in the calls for candidates in the parochial assemblies.
66. An analysis of the different electoral forms and of the 1815 statute can be found in S. Salcedo, *Las primeras formas de elegir.*
67. See "Club de los estranjeros," *La Reforma Pacífica*, 1 March 1859.
68. See "El derecho de asociación y la circular a los agentes extranjeros," *La Reforma Pacífica*, 2 March 1859.
69. See "Elecciones," *La Tribuna*, 11 March 1855, 2.
70. See "Un nuevo club patriótico," *La Tribuna*, 15 March 1857, 2.
71. A. E. Rodríguez also refers to Domingo Sosa, a black man and, according to Beruti, a former slave. See J. M. Beruti, *Memorias curiosas*, 4112; Adolfo Enrique Rodríguez, *El régimen electoral en el lapso 1827-1828* (Buenos Aires, 1965).
72. "Por qué tomáis nuestras armas," *La Tribuna*, 29 March 1856.
73. See "Un nuevo club patriótico," *La Tribuna*, 15 March 1857, 2.
74. According to Mariano Billinghurst, when voting on his request to join there were many nays on the grounds of the color of Mendizábal's skin. See AGLA, Minute Book, Unión del Plata lodge, box 21, session of 25 August 1860.
75. The National Guard was created in March 1852 to "sustain the legitimate authorities." In September of the same year Bartolomé Mitre was designated as its head, which ensured his triumph over Urquiza's army in 1853. During the period of secession of the State of Buenos Aires, the National Guard was the principal combat force of the separatist State. See Comando en Jefe del Ejército, *Reseña histórica*, vol. 1.
76. See *La Tribuna*, 18 March 1856, 2, 3.

77. See "Elecciones del domingo," *La Tribuna*, 1 April 1856, 2.
78. See "Adolfo Alsina al Sr. Jorge Atucha," *La Tribuna*, 2 April 1856.
79. *La Tribuna*, 2 April 1856. The account of events differs from that of the national guards' supporters. See "Aparición de la Mas-horca," *La Tribuna*, 1 April 1856, 2.
80. See "Asamblea popular," *La Tribuna*, 18 March 1855, 2.
81. See *La Tribuna*, 26 April 1854.
82. See "Elecciones," *La Tribuna*, 11 March 1855, 2.
83. I have explored this question in "Producción de una nueva legitimidad."
84. See *La Tribuna*, 30 April 1854.
85. See Carlos D'Amico, *Buenos Aires, sus hombres, su política (1860-1890)* (Mexico, 1890) (Buenos Aires: Editorial Americana, 1952), 103–104.

CHAPTER 8

The Nation and New Social Ties

The Catholic Félix Frías was one of the first to see in the new associative forms not only the principal challenge to the primacy of the Church in its running of certain common interests but also a potential danger in the terrain of political identities.[1] In an article published in *El Progreso*, Frías vindicated Christian universalism faced with what he called "pure reason emancipated from God and the religious authority, so fatal for society's peace and order."[2] He thus disapproved of his companions in exile who had closely associated their sociability practices with the nation. Frías intended to denounce the contractual representation of the social tie as a foundation of the nation, as this representation established itself in the spirit, or at least in the spirits of those cultural elites who had taken responsibility for the leadership of the city and the province.

The Nation as Condition of Association: The National Imperatives of Freemasonry

In spite of the political incertitude of the time, rendering the Argentine nation a project of random success, the associative movement more or less explicitly demanded a jurisdictional framework, or at least a cultural framework, in the nation as a condition of its development. This would make the associative network an invaluable tool in the creation of a national political structure, as seen once again in the example of Freemasonry.

In effect, since the foundation of the first lodges, Freemasonry appears to have been profoundly influenced by the problem of national organization. In October 1854, only a few months after the creation of the Unión del Plata lodge, and while the State of Buenos Aires had set itself a different constitution to that of the Argentine Confederation, nine members of the workshop decided to found a new lodge with the name of Confraternidad Argentina,[3] inspiring Miguel Valencia to observe that "the new lodge carries a great recommendation in its distinctive name.... We can only hope that the repetition of this blessed name contributes to making the importance felt of us all living in complete union and as good brethren! This name and program obliges all those who have risen to work with zeal and constancy."[4] During the opening ceremony, Idelfonso Islas evoked the role of Freemasonry in the region: "to diffuse new light among the sons of these beautiful regions, infusing in them the virtues of tolerance and charity. These healthy examples will bring the disappearance of this hatred and rage, the rotten fruit of the evil passions that have driven us so far from our path and that unfortunately still operate today."[5] José R. Pérez was more explicit in speaking of the role that the institution was to play in the crisis wrought by the secession of the province of Buenos Aires: "Freemasonry is today the only society that can save us from this one hundred-headed monster."[6]

In spite of these explicit references to the political unification of the provinces, there is nothing to suggest that the creation of the lodge stemmed from a strictly political maneuver. While Eustaquio Torres' move to the Confraternidad Argentina lodge, for example, suggests a schism caused by the possible candidacy of his brother Lorenzo, the latter's continued presence in the Unión del Plata lodge, along with Domingo F. Sarmiento and Palemón Huego, contradicts this hypothesis.[7] However, it must be noted that while at first there were no visible tensions between the two lodges, differences soon appeared. According to the testimony of José Roque Pérez, it all began with an internal conflict in the Unión del Plata lodge during the election of the workshop's authorities, on 5 January 1857. Miguel Valencia, the founding father of the lodge and the holder of the highest degree among Porteño Freemasons, was replaced by José R. Pérez, a recent initiate in the order who at the time only held the degree of Master Mason. According to Pérez, this most unexpected change was the consequence of the absolutist nature in which Valencia had directed the lodge.[8] The enmity between both parties was accentuated when the March 1857 electoral campaign led to the division of the liberal party. The political situation in the secular world, furthermore, was tense enough for José Roque Pérez, Venerable Master of the Unión del Plata lodge, to decide to suspend Masonic work until 6 April, "due to the agitated situation in the country."[9]

After the storm of electoral brawling had passed, however, dissidence in the Masonic world raged on. The election of Valentín Alsina as governor of the province appears even to have accentuated this. On 2 June, José R. Pérez sent a personal letter to Jayme Vinent, Grand Assistant Secretary of the Grand Orient of Uruguay, detailing the conflict with Valencia and the latter's subversive conduct in attempting to establish himself as an autonomous authority.[10] Some days later, by means of a circular dated 20 June 1857, Esteban Señorans announced to the lodges of Buenos Aires the creation of the Grand Orient for the Argentine Confederation, with a constitution from the Supreme Council and Grand Orient of the Empire of Brazil [*sic*], and invited all brethren to the inauguration of the Supreme Council on Tuesday, 23 June.[11] The reaction was swiftly evident. At the 22 June session, the Venerable Master of the Unión del Plata lodge, José Roque Pérez, qualified this act as one of "anarchist rebellion," quickly warning the other lodges dependent on the Grand Orient of Uruguay of the illegality of Valencia's authority.

Surreptitiously, in a conflict that strictly concerned the order's problems of legality, the question of the national legitimacy of the new Masonic authority crept in, as with the constitution of the Supreme Council and Grand Orient for the Argentine Confederation, Miguel Valencia proclaimed the independence "of Argentine Freemasonry."[12] As Supreme Council member Idelfonso Islas indicated in a letter to the Supreme Council of Uruguay in defense of Valencia, the legitimacy of the act arose from the fact that he had emancipated national Masonry: "The Mason is a free man, who owes himself above all to his country. It is not rational to maintain him always under foreign power and interests." José R. Pérez responded to these accusations:

> With regards to the preposterous intention of dominating this State and the Argentine Confederation, it must be said that you must not fear the just reproach for such disloyal ambition, in conserving at all costs your Empire in some of our lodges. These provinces you call *neighbors* are not under your jurisdiction, and since a Supreme Council has been established in them, you must show deference and abnegation.[13]

Islas explicitly refers here to the fact that the Grand Orient of Uruguay protected the "dissident" lodges: the Unión del Plata and two others created during the first half of 1857, namely Consuelo del Infortunio and Tolerancia. Under these circumstances and in order to "emancipate Argentine Masonry," Valencia needed to establish new workshops, so as to operate in line with regulations.[14] Hence, he granted a constitution to the four new lodges established between June and November 1857: Regeneración, Lealtad, Constancia and Verdad.[15] The Masonic world then split in two: the "independentists" under Valencia and the "legalists" under Pérez. By October, spirits were waning. Pérez and Valencia met and began to discuss a possible accord.[16] However, in November the legalists decided to enter by force the temple of the Supreme Council of the Argentine Confederation, located on Calle San Martín. They limited themselves to symbolic attacks, though not without intimidating the independentist brethren there.[17] Such was the hot-headedness of their actions that police intervention was required in the lodges.[18] With this the events became part of the public domain. According to the Amie des Naufragés lodge, the events "even shook the secular public of Buenos Aires."[19] As a consequence, the *La Tribuna* newspaper published on its first page a manifesto of the Grand Orient of the Argentine Confederation denouncing "the arbitrary and anti-Masonic attitude of the Grand Orient of Uruguay."[20]

The "independentists" continued to maintain the same arguments: "any independent country or nation has the right to a Supreme Council according to the bases outlined in the Statutes and Constitutions decreed in 1786 by Federico II."[21] The problem was that in what nation's name did they speak, given that at the time there was no State with jurisdiction over the national territory? Valencia based Freemasonry on a virtual jurisdiction, which at the time aroused strong political differences. While remaining in the strictly Masonic sphere, the consolidation of his authority implied a commitment to national politics. José Roque Pérez, who questioned the totality of Valencia's conduct, held the same national Masonic pretensions. Hence, from the creation of the independent authority, he requested from Montevideo, in exchange for his loyalty, the foundation of a new Masonic power for the "Argentine Republic."[22] The name gives some idea of how events later developed. In August, the Supreme Council of Uruguay informed of the possible promotion of the degrees of the brethren of Buenos Aires lodges, from whom would be selected the future dignitaries of the new Masonic power of the Argentine Republic. José Roque Pérez, after only one year in the order, received the thirty-third degree, along with Nicanor Albarellos, Fernando C. Cordero, Eustaquio Torres, Federico Álvarez de Toledo, Santiago Albarracín and Antonio A. Pinto. Another sixteen brethren were promoted to thirtieth and eighteenth degrees.[23] On 24 November, José Roque Pérez, Nicanor Albarellos and Fernando C. Cordero reached an agreement with Pedro Díaz de Vivar, Esteban Señorans and Alejandro Brown, members of the Supreme Council and Grand Orient of the Argentine Confederation, who decided to finally leave Valencia and establish themselves as a Masonic power under the protection of Montevideo.[24] The Supreme Council and the Grand Orient of the Argentine Republic was established solemnly in the city of Buenos Aires on 22 April 1858,25 with Brown, Señorans and Díaz de Vivar now forming part of the high ranks of the new national authority.

The Grand Orient of the Argentine Confederation, with Valencia and Islas, continued to exercise its authority over a few lodges now declared irregular and established primarily in Confederation territory.[26] In June of 1858 they created the Constante Unión lodge in the city of Corrientes and the Bien Social lodge in Rosario.[27] Various testimonies from Freemasons even mention other irregular workshops founded in Confederation territory, but given the absence of archives it is very difficult to ascertain the true extent of "Valencian" Freemasonry in the territory.[28] Denunciations of a reconciliation between Valencia and the Confederation government are nevertheless an indication of the political territory with which his Masonic power was identified.[29] It is quite likely that the type of recruitment in these lodges also contributed greatly to their identification with the Confederation's cause. While the lodges qualified as "regular" and aligned with Pérez attracted members mostly from the spheres of large traders, the military and men of letters, Valencia appears to have appealed more to small traders and artisans. Unfortunately, on this point the problem of sources arises once again. Nevertheless, the few available references indicate a significant presence of artisans in the lodges dependent on Valencia's authority. In a personal letter to Jayme Vinent, José Roque Pérez writes of Valencia "his only hope lies in organizing the French lodge to give us (as he says) *a Grand Orient of hairdressers*. This artisans' lodge is fitting for the intrigue he uses…"[30] The anti-Masonic satire published in 1858 also alludes to the differences in social extraction of the two Masonic powers.[31] However, the artisan sphere was seen to be most favorable to an economic policy that looked after the interests of local producers. On this point, the Porteño artisans agreed with the provinces of the interior in a common demand for a protectionist policy. Valencia would undoubtedly have fought fervently for the cause of a national Masonry based on the common interests of Freemason brethren and the provinces of the Confederation, all the more so in that the lodges of the other power were composed to a great extent of businessmen with ties with the export trade, and therefore ardent defenders of reducing port duties and of free trade with Europe.

By March 1860 the two Masonic powers still co-existed.[32] The Grand Orient of the Argentine Confederation was then able to gain recognition from the English Masonic power and requested the same of the Grand Orient of France.[33] This happened immediately after Urquiza's military triumph at the Battle of Cepeda had brought a temporary solution to the conflict between Buenos Aires and the Confederation. But it also corresponded to a particularly uncertain moment in relations between the two. In spite of the pact of San José de Flores of 11 November 1859, there was a rumor of a new armed confrontation. It is feasible then that the foreign Masonic powers acted with the same incertitude in recognizing one of the two Masonic organizations as the authority of the order in Argentina.[34] But the relationship of forces changed when the Supreme Council of the Argentine Republic granted the thirty-third degree to the governor of the province of Buenos Aires, Bartolomé Mitre, to his interior minister Domingo F. Sarmiento and war minister Juan A. Gelly y Obes, to the president of the Argentine Confederation, Santiago Derqui and to the head of the Confederation armies, Justo José de Urquiza.

This episode is cited frequently as evidence of Freemasonry's essential role in the organization of the Argentine nation, and admittedly it is at least memorable.[35] The ceremony was held on 21 July 1860, eight months after the Battle of Cepeda. After the incertitude of the first months, Bartolomé Mitre brought to the Confederation new hope for peace.[36] On 6 June, the heads of the State of Buenos Aires and of the Confederation signed an accord for the future unification of the two. But as James Scobie has indicated, the façade of progress towards nationality concealed potential conflicts which would be triggered as soon as Buenos Aires felt its preponderance over the rest of the provinces threatened.[37] In the meantime, Buenos Aires and the Confederation relaxed in the climate of détente, fed by the hope of a definitive constitution for the Argentine Nation. In June, Bartolomé Mitre invited the president of the Confederation, Santiago Derqui, and the governor of the province of Entre Ríos, Justo José de Urquiza, to the celebrations to commemorate the Independence of the United Provinces of the River Plate, to be held in the city of Buenos Aires on 9 July. The two Confederation men accepted the invitation and traveled to Buenos Aires in July, where a veritable climate of jubilation prevailed, intoxicating the Porteño population. The press reflected the great hopes reborn among the city's inhabitants. At the time, various gatherings, dances and banquets were organized in honor of Derqui and Urquiza. The Progress Club's Directing Commission, for example, agreed to spend 8,000 pesos—three times the usual amount—on a ball in honor of Justo José de Urquiza.[38] It is in this context that the actions of the Supreme Council must be considered, but with the small but important detail that the Masonic authority contributed to this reconciliation by granting the highest degree of the order to the men who held the power to put an end to the secession of Buenos Aires and the Confederation. This meant that, contrary to the fundamental principles of any initiatory order, the Supreme Council conceded by decree something which had to be reached by strict rites of passage,[39] a decision which aroused vigorous objections among Masonic bases.[40]

It might be argued that Freemasonry was one step ahead of the State in the organization of a national structure. However, this is not to imply that it directed the process of national organization. The Masonic schism shows that the development of political affairs was uncertain for the Freemasons, to such an extent that they put their faith in different national authorities but also in that it was imperative to tether the order's fate to that of the nation. The consolidation of a Masonic network implied a certain identification with a national power, which explains the political role undertaken by Freemasonry in processes of national organization as diverse as those of the former Spanish colonies and that of the Risorgimento in Italy.[41]

Naturally, it remains to be explained why Mitre and the others accepted entry to Freemasonry. Some of the advantages they could garner from this organization are evident: with it they had at their disposal a network of relationships which could prove extremely useful for the future organization of the State. It must be remembered that the institution had quite a network of traders who controlled exchanges between the *litoral* region and European markets.[42] The integration of these men into the structure of national power was the *sine qua non* in the construction of a national market organized around Porteño interests. In addition, some members of the ruling classes belonged to Freemasonry, from military men and lawyers to wealthy landowners and traders. Thus, the order could be useful in consolidating a kind of "national network" which would serve as a basis of the new ruling class. The Masonic organization made it possible to replace the old political system, founded on family ties and social solidarities which did not necessarily coincide with the jurisdictional territory of the new State, with alliances fit for modern political practices, formed in a new territorial context. In addition, Masonic values adapted well to liberal Porteño*s'* national project. It is no surprise, therefore, to find that Mitre, who was probably advised by his Minister of the Interior, Domingo F. Sarmiento, should try to consolidate the march towards unification by bringing in an association which was already based on the principles of nationality. Furthermore, the Masonic schism ended with the unification of the nation. In 1862, after the definitive integration of Buenos Aires into the Confederation, the "dissident brethren" joined the Grand Orient of the Argentine Republic.[43] The Grand Orient of France and the Grand Lodge of England then recognized the Supreme Council and the Grand Orient of the Argentine Republic as the only regular Masonic power. By this time the Masonic organization could offer the elites of the different provinces now making up the "Argentine Nation" a network of relationships which would allow the first ties to be made with the new national ruling class in Buenos Aires.

It is undoubtedly difficult to generalize the history of the establishment of Freemasonry during the secession of the State of Buenos Aires with that of the associative movement as a whole, and it cannot be said that all the associations claimed a national jurisdiction as a framework for their development, although some may have been established to vindicate a national representation, as was the case seen above with the Lancastrian societies or the May Association. But even when their development was limited to the city of Buenos Aires, the identity between association and nation did not disappear. This identity was seen, for example, in the calendar of meetings to mark the great symbolic dates of the nation. The same occurred in the names of the societies, often evoking values that defined the political community, such as *mayo*, *julio*, *septembrista*, *constitucional*, *argentino*, *confraternidad argentina*, *libertad*, and so on, And even when the nation was not explicitly evoked, it remained a condition of association, as Varela reminds us with regards to the establishment of the May Philharmonic Society in 1854. *El Nacional* then mentioned a National Philharmonic Society, a name that Varela rejected, arguing that the adjective "national" implied that the other societies were not, which for him constituted an inadmissible claim.[44] All these associations shared in fact the same identification with a public sphere, due to which the new nation could be envisaged and represented.

Sociability and National Imagery

Studies of imagery have been greatly developed in the last twenty-five years.[45] In this period the encounter between political history and research in the terrain of imagery have born fruit, although innovative research into the subject has involved above all the study of signs and symbols of power.[46] Even in the late 1980's the "nation" was called into question, associated with the intensely ideological nationalist debate or with a "soul" or ahistoric body typical of a "historicizing history," to use Lucien Febvre's term, which in the River Plate was identified with the Ricardo Levene's "new historical school."[47] It is true that Anderson published his *Imagined Communities* in 1983, and in the same year Ernest Gellner's *Nations and Nationalisms* appeared, but these works would only have repercussions on becoming known considerably later, when the disintegration of the Soviet empire called for an urgent understanding of the phenomenon of "nationalisms."[48] That the nation is an imaginary creation is an idea that today arouses scarce objections. Pierre Nora concludes his monumental project on the places of the memory affirming that "the 'Nation', in its unitary sense, retains its belonging and its legitimacy with regards to the memory, and only the memory."[49] But what could be more imaginary than this "common" historical memory? As Cornelius Castoriadis clearly stated, "this history is neither past nor common, and what serves as support for this collectivizing identification in the people's conscience is on the whole mythical."[50] In contrast, historiography has focused far less on the fact that this imaginary creation was established socially due to the intensity and nature of sociability exchanges. However, the equation of the nation, at least for Porteño intellectuals, passed in part for sociability. The intensity and nature of new social relationships were not only experienced as the manifestation of a social renaissance but were represented as the place of institution of the nation as a society of sovereign individuals.

The first question that arises is how sociability practices can also account for national imageries. Until the present day, historical studies of social imagery were undertaken essentially via the analysis of certain social institutions such as language or iconographic forms.[51] However, nobody can argue that, as in these social institutions, sociability discourse and practice are only produced in the context of a universe of imaginary representations organizing and defining them in relation to others. Without these representations, any society would be inconceivable.[52] Therefore, if imagery as a creative instance implies the capacity to imagine, to bring into existence something that did not exist before, then that something can be produced both by language and by sociability practices.[53] The type of bonds, the characteristics of the network, and the nature of organizational forms were favored here to show the particular ways in which these men imagined society and their relationships with others.

In spite of the differences between the forms analyzed thus far, it is a fact that these associations shared certain common characteristics:[54] they were organized on contractual, egalitarian relationship forms which implied the notion of the modern individual and developed a specific type of tie, that of associative sociability. This was a secondary tie, revocable and therefore contractual, which implied the sharing of a number of values that brought together and identified the members of all associations apart from the specific objectives of each one. In reality, these exchanges pertained to the same representation of the rational individual-being, sociable due to civility and social through a voluntary act. In the association—one might even say "because of the association"—man became a social being. The association only existed in the context of these rational, free, and equal individuals-beings who decided to formalize their exchanges with a common agreement. With this, the encounter became a social value, with the only condition that it be produced respecting certain norms belonging to the same register defining the social tie in a representative republican regime.

The intensity of the exchanges, verified by the growth of the associative movement during our period, implied the development of values that defined the members of this movement, but who also brought with them a new representation of society. In this universe of reading, the image transference of associative values was made towards society. The process came into play through a double imagery operation: sociability as a social value was the origin of a new type of collective belonging, implying a new associative representation of society which then became the framework for the realization of these values. The nation as society thus took on this "reality" in and because of these relationships.

THE NATION AS "CIVIL SOCIETY"

The deputy Ignacio Gorriti lucidly specified, in a speech in the Constituent Assembly of 1825, the problem arising from the organization of a national power in the region:

> The nation can be considered in two ways, either as people who have the same origin and the same language, although different states are formed from them, or from a society already constituted under the regime of a single government. Greece was a nation in the first sense, notwithstanding its division into a multitude of small states, which made other numerous particular governments, with the same laws as the rest of the nation. The same is also true of Italy: all of her land is considered a nation, even though she is divided into a multitude of different states. The Americas might also be considered, at least all of the South, as a single nation, even though it has different states that while having a common interest have their own particular interests, which are quite different, but not in the sense of a nation, ruled by the same law and with the same government. And I ask, what is a free nation? It is a society in which men give themselves, their property and all that results from this to the greater good.... When they cede and put at the benefit of society this portion of property, it is because the considerations with which they cede them and the conditions that they demand are more advantageous to the individual than the conservation of his full rights in the natural state. It is then in this sense that I have said, and I repeat, that we have no nation: there is none. Yes, gentlemen, there is none. To throw off the yoke of Spain we have united: but this union does not form a nation.[55]

Like all his compatriots, Gorriti excluded the possibility of founding a nation on a community of culture and making Spanish America a single nation. He differed from other orators in not only affirming that there was no national power that could justify the creation of an army but declaring instead that the absence of a political contract jeopardized the very existence of a civil society that would form a nation. The question lies at the center of modern political thought, but in the River Plate this profound cultural mutation, which made society appear the result of a pact dragging individuals from their natural state to a social state, it is striking because of the impossibility of confusing the State with the nation. Therefore, what allows a better understanding of the configurations of the imagery of the nation as a political community of belonging is the failure of the political project. Thus, while the birth of the nation was identified in almost all America with the State, the dawn of this birth in the River Plate made society the territory of the nation. To imagine the nation in the River Plate is to imagine the social tie that legitimized the political project, constantly put off until a later date, of organizing the State.

It is difficult today to construct a precise chronology of the genesis of this new society-nation. Nevertheless, there are two elements that appear to be crucial:

firstly, the end of the war of independence accompanied by the first failures in the political organization of the former colonies. During the war, the question of the foundation of the social tie was not imperative, as the very dynamic of war provided an answer. There was then a supposed community of objectives, namely the break with Spain and the creation of an independent government, which led to a momentary consideration of the unity of the social body. The war also worked to consolidate territorial communities, above all around the organization of an army. Although there were abundant contradictions in the conceptions of the question of sovereignty, the nascent "nation" was clearly associated with the project of political organization of the *pueblos* fighting for freedom. Ten years later, after the failure of this attempt at constitutional organization, and when the United Provinces had broken up into different, autonomous provinces, José Ignacio Gorriti described the nation in quite different terms: "What is a free nation? It is a society in which men give to the greater good themselves, their property and all that results from this."[56] The nation of 1815 was a State, while by 1825 it had become a society based on a contract between rational individuals. These two aspects, associated with modern political thinking, became two distinct stages in the River Plate as a result of circumstances. The second element that appears to have been decisive in the displacement of the meaning of nation, a system of political unity and then a society born of a rational and individual will, lies in the formation of a group of young romantic intellectuals who, from their reading and culture practices, would associate the nation with the new relational forms, whose principal function was to rethink the social tie as outside of the context of the Catholic monarchy.

The study of the associative tie informs us most particularly of two identifying figures of political imagery that, in the River Plate, were clearly associated with the nation. The first of these is the notion of "sociability" as the very foundation of society, whose principal function was tied to the idea of community—which in the Hispanic world is often confused with the Christian community—and the idea of the contractual tie, from which was founded the associationist metaphor of the nation as a political community of belonging. It is true that this metaphor, intended to replace the metaphor of the body, is one of the topics of modern political thought, but it is all the more widespread in that it has vigorous pedagogical support: the associative practices. Thus, the new cultural associations, created with the aim of exchanging knowledge and opinions on matters of "public interest," developed a contractualist discourse and practice from which it is possible to think of this society-nation. In assimilating association and nation, these men created an imaginary sphere from which one could think of an individual without previous ties entering into relationships freely and consentingly, and society as the product of these new social ties. It is no surprise to find then that whenever one speaks of this nation, which did not manage to establish itself but existed as a foundation of power, one always resorts to the associationist metaphor.[57] In addition to "sociability," "civility" occupied a preferential place as a practice of community belonging and joined contractual ties with courteous language. Thus, the notion of "civility," which tended to be widespread among the sociability practices of the elites, had a double function in the region, as a criterion of social distinction for the elites who claimed to embody the nation, and at the same time in permitting the idea of the national tie through the acquisition of civil behaviors which in turn contributed to pacifying society—an indispensable condition for the establishment of a national State—and associating the nation with the movement of civilization.[58] The principal advocates of the associative movement, both conservatives and liberals, sustained that any relationship with the other, entered into with an associative spirit, obligatorily placed society on the road to civilization. C. Calvo declared this explicitly on entering the 1858 Liceo Literario: "In the end, what is civility but the accumulation of social improvements, and never are these improvements transmitted through hatred and isolation, but through love and sociability."[59] In turn, Diego de Alvear recalls the North American example: "That life in common, that immediate contact among the men, that active and effective cooperation for all enterprises for the common good, is the secret of the prosperity and greatness to which the North American Confederation has risen in a few years."[60] Civility even became a condition of equality.[61] The selective nature of the audience at the Colón Theater, for example, did not prevent H. Varela from highlighting the democratic nature of Porteño sociability: "the theaters put on shows twice a week and their audiences show us that, in this country, there is no disinherited class. While they are in general the place of elegance, salons and parks can also be of entertainment to the people."[62] Sociability was egalitarian in that it became a universal form of relationship shared by the population as a whole, an aspect that was inseparable from the fraternal and cordial attitude in exchanges, as well as in the sense that urbanity and tolerance were indispensable conditions of this.[63]

These identifying figures associated the nation with a political community of belonging to "civil society" as a society of natural law. It appears that this was one of the specificities of national imagery in the region, built up by the rhythm of constitutional failures. It is true that this civic representation of the nation was the very foundation of the modern idea of nation, born with the French Revolution and confused with the representative republic.[64] But this political idea of the nation is almost always combined with the "ethnic" and historical community.[65] However, in the River Plate, civic representation of the nation was the only kind that would allow the constitutional bases of a national State to be founded. The nation, the only legitimate source of power, could only be invoked in its civic representation. In my judgment, this was one of the reasons for the failure of a Rosas regime faced with a liberal opposition who ultimately monopolized the identitary nation. The difficulty for Rosas in proposing a viable national alternative to that of Porteño liberalism came down to the obstacles arising in conceiving of the nation as a society of individuals. The liberal opposition, in contrast, not only had a discourse that assigned a preferential place to the individual but which associated it to a relational practice which worked as a principal foundation of the civic nation. It must not be forgotten that Rosas would only become the emblem of the nation in the early twentieth century, when the nationalist movement took up the conceptual tools needed to question the principal foundations of liberal democracy, which until then had been enough to define the identitary nation. Then, and only then, would the national scope of Rosas' regime appear irrefutable.

THE NATION AT THE HEART OF REPRESENTATION

The public sphere was not only the space from which it was possible to imagine the nation but it was also, as the analysis of the "opinion clubs" shows, the space towards which the problem of representation shifted from the embodiment of power to the representation of an opinion.[66] The associative practice thus allowed the establishment of the new social tie as a constitutive principle of a political representation that was only conceived in the national context. This did not prevent, as we have recalled various times, the coexistence of other forms of political representation, but strengthened the association between new relational practices and the nation as a political community of belonging. In this sense, public sphere institutions as a whole functioned as extraordinary agents of diffusion for national imagery of the political community.

The model of establishment in the city is a prime indicator of the norms introduced by the associations, which tended to break with the traditional structure of neighborhood sociability built around the parish community. This aspect is revealed clearly in the organization of electoral clubs, in which there was a more transparent distinction between the parochial clubs, organized on the basis of the religious community, and the so-called "opinion" clubs. Recall that in announcing the creation of the National Guards Club in his newspaper, Héctor Varela indicated that this represented true public opinion because it brought together citizens from different parishes.[67] In breaking with traditional references to the people as a territorial community, "citizens" in opinion clubs could only be recognized in the context of this great community of values and foundation of legitimacy that was the modern nation. The representative function of the new associations, thus, held the nation as the foundation of the political tie.

In this regard, the debate concerning Article 6 of the Constitution of Buenos Aires is most illustrative. In defining citizenship, Bartolomé Mitre refused to accept Alsina's expression "Porteño citizenship." Mitre was opposed to Buenos Aires legislating citizenship, as this idea could not be considered aside from the nation: "I understand that, as has been done until now, all of the sons and daughters of the provinces, as Argentines, are true citizens in Buenos Aires, but this is not in virtue of this local resolution which we have reached here, but in virtue of national sociability, in virtue of which we all form the same family, and part of a nation."[68] This "national sociability" was above all that which joined the citizen to the public sphere. While for the members of the elite it existed in multiple forms, for the popular sectors it principally concerned the electoral clubs, in which a new representative logic was established. The clubs constituted, therefore, a form of civic pedagogy, in the sense that they promoted new feelings of community belonging based on political cultural values specific to the republican nation.

This can be seen in the names of the clubs: Constitutional, Argentine, National Guard, Freedom, Independence, Impartial, The People, 25th May, Union, Peace, General Lavalle, General Belgrano, The Free of the South, Buenos Aires, Democracy, 25th September, 11th November, National, and so forth. Some evoked constitutive events of the political community, such as the 25th May, The Free of the South, 25th September, and 11th November clubs. Others evoked individuals who embodied this nationality, such as the General Belgrano and General Lavalle clubs. In the remaining cases the clubs evoked values-concepts that defined the political community: Constitutional, Argentine, Freedom, Independence, Impartial, Union, Peace and Democracy. All alluded to a collectivity which was defined through a number of political and cultural values able to unite the different provinces as a great community, but as Bartolomé Mitre recalls in the House of Representatives: "I have not seen the need thus far. Without a need for a constitution, citizenship has defined itself well. It has been defined who are citizens, where their obligations and responsibilities lie, and yes, obligatorily, as we also all have duties as citizens of Argentina within our own territory, because we represent a part of the Argentine Republic, a part of its great thought, a part of the revolution."[69] In rehabilitating representative institutions via institutions in the public sphere, the city and province of Buenos Aires positioned the nation, along with the new representative logic, as the context for representation.

City and Nation, a Porteño Equation

The history of the nineteenth century in Argentina, and more particularly that of the process of nation-building, cannot be understood without taking into account the geopolitical objectives hatched around the port city of Buenos Aires.

An abundant historical bibliography recalls the specific difficulties in organizing the nation for a port city intent on monopolizing the benefits of its position at the expense of a territory that it imagined as a vast tributary interior. Prolonged and bloody civil wars were also testimony to a submissive fate, at the time far from arousing unanimity in regional elites. From this political seesaw of constitutional projects and military conflicts this new representation of the nation was built, conceived not only as a democratic society but also as a sociability associated with an urban culture whose framework had in the meantime come to be the city of Buenos Aires. Thus, the equation of the nation not only took place in the public sphere but also in a precise physical space associated with civic culture: the city of Buenos Aires.

While the association between the city and the nation had been present since the insurrectional movement of Buenos Aires, which claimed to represent all of the cities of the Viceroyalty of the River Plate, during the secession years, the antinational period *par excellence*, a device would be introduced to create from the urban community as a whole a model of cultural belonging, from which the building of the Argentine nation could be conceived.

THE URBAN VOCATION OF THE PORTEÑO RULING CLASS

The liberals' return governing the province of Buenos Aires in 1852 put the finishing touches on a renewal in the urban tradition of the Argentine elites. In the city a two-pronged process began: power was taken by the young liberals who claimed the capital city's control over the vast interior, and a municipal structure was put in place over the urban space. The Porteño ruling class' double urban vocation, founded on the city-nation pairing, brought the division of the liberals into "autonomists" placing the city-province at the foreground as a sovereign subject, and the "nationalists" invoking the power of the city as the head of the nation.[70] But all shared the urban vocation founded on the conviction that in a territory of variable geometry, the attributes of power were in a city which associated the tradition of power with the economic supremacy provided by the port. To this was added an urban cultural tradition which all liberals recognized as the foundation of the modern nation.

In spite of the divisions of the "liberal party," there was a common effort to confirm this "capital" destiny of the port city. To do so, the Porteños created a new municipal institution to replace the old *cabildo* abolished by the liberal government of Bernardino Rivadavia on 24 December 1821.[71] This initiative aimed to reestablish a municipal tradition which had been broken by the liberals themselves, but which they now considered indispensable in confirming the process begun with the May Revolution of 1810. Although the "discovery" of the benefits of this institution dated from the 1830s, it was only after the Rosas government that the urban elites associated its disappearance with the real loss of their own power.[72] Its reestablishment was no doubt aimed at restoring an institution within which the elites had found an undisputed place but also at confirming an urban political culture that reinforced the idea of the modern nation. The profiles of the city and the nation and of two opposing political traditions were intermingled at the heart of a municipal institution that through its operation became a kind of extension of the government of the State of Buenos Aires.

This particularity of the new Municipality of Buenos Aires was above all a consequence of the way the city's representative government worked. As the government held the monopoly on fraud, it was best placed to "manage" the representative institutions and impose its candidates more easily on the government and the Municipal Council. But Article 1 of the Municipalities Law confirmed the control of central power over the municipality, establishing that the minister of the interior would be president of the body, with not inconsiderable prerogatives.[73] It should then be no surprise to discover that municipal action was confused with the politics of the State of Buenos Aires. This situation was confirmed by the fact that a large number of councilors—66% of 166 men in the post between 1855 and 1862—were men committed to the politics of the provincial State. In the majority of cases these were deputies from the House of Representatives. Only a few of those making up the remaining 34%, who started their political careers as councilors, would remain out of national politics. In contrast, for the others the municipal responsibilities marked the beginning of a political career which would carry them from the city government to the national government.[74]

All this gives a better understanding of what was at stake in urban politics between 1852 and 1862. It was a matter of highlighting the economic role of the port city, as it was from the superiority of this role that the Porteño elite claimed the "historic destiny" of their city as head and capital of the territory.[75]

URBAN SPACE, THE BIRTHPLACE OF NEW BELONGINGS

Considerable public works took place during the secession years. The building of the new customs house, the construction of a wharf to facilitate disembarkation in the port of Buenos Aires and the laying of the first railroad for activating trade exchanges between the city and the surrounding countryside were some of the city's new services. It also set about ordering the urban space around this reactivation of exchanges, in particular installing a gasworks for the city's lighting and repairing the city's rudimentary and deteriorating public roads.[76] The renovation of urban amenities was accompanied by a considerable growth in construction, which in little time extended from the city into the suburban area.[77]

The reactivation of exchanges produced other transformations in the city, given that for the liberals this reactivation had more functions than accelerating exchanges: it also had to civilize them, consolidating rules of conduct in a public life from which it became a privileged place. This was seen above all in the transfer of the most important places of exchange to outside of the nucleus of the city. Thus, Once de Septiembre square and market and Constitución market centralized city-countryside exchanges on the edges of the city. With this, wholesale trade was facilitated and the city was saved of carts passing through it, deteriorating the public streets and giving Buenos Aires the rustic appearance that the urban elites so lamented. Later the old market squares were overhauled with a view to making them spaces of civility. During the period in question extensive work was carried out to urbanize these centers of public life. Logically, attention was focused primarily on the west side of the Plaza Mayor, on Plaza de la Victoria.[78] Only a few months after the revolution which separated the province of Buenos Aires from the Argentine Confederation, the first paving works were begun in this square, where the city's only public monument was located. The flagstones of the square were intended to give the city an urban profile, just as larger works would do in the years to come. Thus, in 1857 during the inauguration of the railroad towards the west of the province, the municipality, with the collaboration of the railroad's shareholders, lay gardens and built a music kiosk in Plaza del Parque.[79] This novelty brought an important change in the urban landscape and broke with the traditional model of squares in the Spanish-speaking world and the associated tradition of sociability.[80] From this followed initiatives to landscape other public squares, with the bulk of works beginning in 1860, during the Bartolomé Mitre government with Sarmiento as Minister of the Interior and President of the Municipality.[81]

The chronology of renovations in places of public sociability can be easily explained by political events. Let us recall that after an armed clash between Buenos Aires and the Confederation in October 1859, the former signed a peace treaty to put an end to its secession. In April 1860, the Convention of the State of Buenos Aires examined the Constitution of the Argentine Confederation, which in September became the Constitution of the Argentine Nation. The climate of peace and prosperity then prevalent in Buenos Aires can account for the beginning of such works, but perhaps these were due less to a surplus of funds left over at the end of the war that could then be allotted to "superfluous" needs than to the demands imposed by the new role of capital that the city was set to assume. With this objective, "men of the national organization" such as Sarmiento and Mitre intended to make the urban community a paradigm of national sociability.

It may be unnecessary to cite here Sarmiento's thoughts on the role that the city was to play in the triumph of civilization, but perhaps it is necessary to recall the conception of "national sociability" that he shared with Mitre. In *Civilización y barbarie*, Sarmiento distinguishes the community on which Juan Manuel de Rosas and Facundo Quiroga founded their power from that which gave rise to cities and was characteristic of civilized societies. Sociability was one of the explanations. Sarmiento thus recognized the existence of a sociability and even associative forms typical of Rosista society whose distinguishing feature was that they were based on the prevalence of nature. In other words, for Sarmiento these were forms of sociability in which relationships of civility were missing. It was precisely in these relationships that Sarmiento saw the basis of a civil society on which the nation as a political community of belonging was to be founded. His idea was clear: civility constituted the sociability of the republic, and therefore the principle of national sociability. This then was not only a rule of *savoir-vivre* but also an identifying value. Bartolomé Mitre, who in this aspect shared Sarmiento's point of view, included in the third edition of his biography of Manuel Belgrano a first chapter on "Argentine sociability." In his analysis, he placed prime importance on the municipal government and therefore on the urban community as one of the principal historical forerunners of Argentine sociability.[82]

These authors' policy of urban renovation fell within this line of thought. From squares remodeled as places of public sociabilities to the construction of large boulevards—places of social encounters—their acts tried to favor civil relationships in the public sphere, as from here was born the national representation of collectivity. This accounts for the attention given to the decoration of places of sociability during the years of secession.

THE CITY, A PILLAR OF NATIONAL MEMORY

In the establishment of a new urban decoration, two stages can be distinguished, corresponding to two attempts to define the city's relationship with the nation. In the first stage, primarily between 1856 and 1857, the city emphasized political cultural values which made it the paradigm of national community. In the second stage, approximately between 1860 and 1862, urban decoration recalled the capital destiny of the national city.

The years 1856 and 1857 in effect signaled the first moment when Porteño national memory crystallized. During the governments of Pastor Obligado and Valentín Alsina an important memory device was introduced, principally with the initiative of modifying the only civic monument in the city of Buenos Aires. The municipality, with government backing, decided to raise a statue of Liberty on the pyramidal column commemorating 25 May. The choice of location for the first civic statue was significant, above all because the pyramid confirmed the republican nature of the new monument,[83] but also because Plaza de la Victoria,

Figure 31. The Remodeling of Plaza de la Victoria

A. Plaza de la Victoria seen from east to west. In the center, the May Pyramid (1811) with the statue of Liberty (1856) seen from behind. In the background and to the left is the Colón Theater (1855). Lithograph by A. Vallardi, 1859

B. Marianne. Photo by Esteban Marco

B. Plaza de la Victoria from southeast to northwest. The statue of Liberty is seen from front, with the Cabildo in the background. Daguerrotype, 1860.

a place of civic concentration, was a place of remembrance. Previously identified with royal power, it recalled the British invasions of 1806 and 1807, events that would forever mark the population of the city.[84] After the event, the central square was named "de la Victoria" in commemoration of the triumph over the British following General Whitelocke's surrender in July 1807.[85] Moreover, the urban toponymy confirms the importance of this event in the memory of the revolutionary city, even though it was an event that showed Buenos Aires' loyalty to its king.[86] Its influence was so great that when the *cabildo* decided in 1811 to raise a monument to the memory of the events of 1810, it proposed the addition of an inscription commemorating the recapture of 12 August 1806, the defense of 5 July 1807 and the establishment of the first insurrectionary government, the Primera Junta, on 25 May 1810.[87]

The memory of this heroic and loyal defense of the city and of the Crown served as a "pedestal" for the monument commissioned from the Frenchman Joseph Dubourdieu by the Municipality of Buenos Aires.[88] The statue was a woman standing, with a serene appearance, with an old-fashioned drape and the left breast exposed, finished with a Phrygian cap, broken chains at her feet, the coat of arms of the *patria* in her left hand and a pike in her right. On the four sides of the pyramid the scene was completed by four female statues representing industry, commerce, science and the arts.[89] But why was this allegory to Liberty and the Republic chosen to decorate the city?[90] It could be said that the municipality left the decision in Dubourdieu's hands, who being conditioned by the French iconographic system preferred an abstract representation of the Republic to the bust of one of its great men. But in fact this answer sidesteps the question, because it is always possible to question why the Porteño authorities chose a sculptor whose tastes but also his ideological inclinations, were not unknown to them.[91] To account for this, we can refer above all to the prestige of an artist who represented the new wave of an urbanism in the making. Thus, the press celebrated both the choice of the symbol and the remodeling of the urban landscape with civic statues, a policy it considered typical of civilized societies.[92] But while the iconic model was famously borrowed from France, the will to associate the memory of the city to one of the greatest values of modern political culture was part of the Porteño elite's political strategy, consistent in legitimizing by all means possible the creation of an autonomous State in the province of Buenos Aires.[93]

In spite of the pomp with which the statue was celebrated, the government of Buenos Aires preferred the cult of its great men to abstract representations of the Republic, perhaps because this facilitated the diffusion of abstract values covering a varied and dangerous array of possible interpretations.[94] Whatever the case, Bartolomé Mitre emphasized the pedagogical objective of this action on announcing his intention to create "a rational memory" aimed at replacing oral memory.[95] He thus presented the foundations of a liberal historiography aimed at affirming collective memory in a historical civic-mindedness whose goal was to forge, through the lives of the great men, a model for the republican population. The literary and iconographic monuments raised in memory of the great men of the nation were intended to personify the Republic.[96] In this context, the 1857 publication of the *Galería de Celebridades Argentinas* appeared, directed by Juan María Gutiérrez.[97] The government of the province moved further in this direction by deciding to introduce the cult of Bernadino Rivadavia, one of the early liberals, associated with the economic and cultural boom period in the city of Buenos Aires and with the attempt at national organization in 1826.

Between 1856 and 1857, with the collaboration of the Municipality of Buenos Aires and the Sociedad de Beneficiencia the government organized the return of Rivadavia's ashes. Sarmiento, representing the municipality, depicted the great man of the State above all as founder of the House of Representatives and of universal suffrage. The profile of the "Great Republican" was completed with the evocation of his acts in the sphere of culture and science. Carried away by his own enthusiasm, Sarmiento proclaimed Rivadavia as the "founder of Buenos Aires and of the representative system of the Argentine Republic...father of Buenos Aires and of the Argentine Republic."[98] Other speeches in memory of the illustrious Argentine bore much resemblance, placing the accent on the Porteño and republican nature of the figure, rendering him an emblem of the Republican City.[99] If the press is to be believed, the city was far from indifferent to the ceremony to mark the return of the ashes: sixty thousand people attended it, meaning that almost 70% of the population lined the streets.[100] Was this figure so popular? For the French republican Arsène Isabelle, he was in 1835 to liberal Porteños.[101] His national policy in 1826 had alienated a large number of the Porteño ruling class, and the popularity of his first years of government had been blemished by his intervention in General Lavalle's 1829 coup. Twenty years of Rosas government had, however, changed many things. Principally, the failure of the Rosista regime had had the result of resurrecting the careers of anyone who appeared to oppose the regime. Added to this was the fact that the Porteño ruling class now had to unite its efforts in order to tackle the Argentine Confederation. To do so, it needed federative symbols. The republic was one, while Rivadavia, the symbol of the modern, prosperous city—in short, of a civilizing city, in Sarmiento's words—could certainly become another.[102] He also had the advantage of allowing the personification of power.[103] The organization of the ceremony to mark the return of the ashes was accompanied by many other devices aimed at uniting the city of Buenos Aires in the evocation of Rivadavia.[104] With the 12 February 1857 decree, the main street of the city, called "Camino del Rey" and "Federación" under Rosas, was christened "Rivadavia," a name it retains to the present day. The same decree announced the future installation of a statue of Rivadavia in the House of Representatives of the State of Buenos Aires. The press went so far as to propose that Dubourdieu's young *Libertad* be dethroned and replaced with a statue of Bernardino Rivadavia.[105]

The years 1857 and 1858 were thus the beginning of the urban decoration campaigns associating the city of Buenos Aires with the great republican values: Liberty, Progress, Representative Government but also the *Patria*—in its strictest sense—and the Nation, conceived as a political cultural community with imprecise spatial contours. Between 1860 and 1862, urban décor would witness another important turning point related to political events. In effect, during these two years the city set out on a policy of urban remodeling, some aspects of which are mentioned above. As in the preceding period, the government and the municipality launched various projects for the improvement of the urban space, with the difference that this time the initiatives were more numerous. However, what distinguished the two moments was not a mere quantitative difference. From here on, decoration would reflect a city reconciled to its national destiny. Public spaces increasingly became places of national sociability insofar as they were populated by statues intended to pay homage to the nation. While the formula was already well-known, what now constituted the main difference was the choice of figures, above all two of them, who from now on would occupy the first row in the national pantheon: José de San Martín and Manuel Belgrano.

The idea of building a memorial to San Martín was not Mitre's own, but during his government and in spite of the difficult situation arising from a new armed conflict with the Confederation, the initiative resulted in the erection of a bronze equestrian statue, unveiled by Mitre on 13 July 1862.[106] The chosen location was the Campo de Marte, a place where San Martín had trained his grenadier troops, and where one of the streets leading to the square already carried his name. The square appears to have been the natural place to pay homage to this hero of the war of independence. Moreover, the slightly off-center location gave the advantage of allowing the overhaul of a place for walks, with fountains, public benches, a bandstand, and the equestrian statue in the middle.[107] But the choice of this decentralized location might also reflect, to some extent, the secondary place that San Martín occupied in the city's memory.[108] San Martín was not originally from Buenos Aires, and although he had by marriage become part of one of the most honorable Porteño families, the Escaladas, he spent most of his life abroad. His military campaign, furthermore, took him away from his family and from the political life of the city, and in spite of a few brief stays he never participated in the affairs of Buenos Aires. But this distance proved beneficial to San Martín, making him appear as the hero who was "above internecine rivalries." Nevertheless, it was only later, and due to Bartolomé Mitre, that San Martín would occupy an unarguable place in the national pantheon.

To enthrone the memory of San Martín in the city of Buenos Aires, the choice of the image took on considerable importance. In his commemoration, the city was to raise an equestrian statue that coincided with the tradition of representation of power on horseback.[109] But the pose of San Martín and his horse recalls a rather popular lithograph of the governor of Buenos Aires, Juan Manuel de Rosas.[110] Although both are part of the same iconographic tradition, to which we can add the engraving of General San Martín by Núñez de Ibarra (Buenos Aires, 1818) and that of Belgrano by Géricault (Paris, 1819), the similarity with Rosas had its consequences. Undoubtedly. The choice of an image that already evoked a popular representation of the power of Buenos Aires was not unintentional. Furthermore, Sarmiento admits in his biography of San Martín that the statue borrowed the image from a popular engraving.[111] The iconic relationship perhaps served to incorporate a man of the nation to the memory of the city, constructing the cult of San Martín over the memory of Rosas.

The case of Manuel Belgrano is different. Belgrano was a Porteño, a member of one of the major trading families, and participated in the political life of the city, starting with the creation of the Consulate of Commerce in 1794. He participated in the defense of the city during the British invasions and played an important part in the Porteño insurrection of May 1810. He therefore had a hand in the principal events that marked the population of Buenos Aires. Furthermore, he died in the city and his mortal remains lay in the church of Santo Domingo, which was already a place of memory in the city.[112] It is true that his death was treated with complete indifference by a city in the throes of all-out anarchy, and that on the day of his death three different governments came into power, but this act of ingratitude aroused in Porteños a need for redress towards the man who ultimately became "one of the most noble figures of our history." The new liberal government of the province of Buenos Aires did not forget him, and in this period Mitre dedicated to him an important biography.[113] But it was not until 1860 that a commission of city inhabitants was set up to promote the construction of a statue of the founding father. The idea arose again with the unveiling of the statue of San Martín, but the project would take some time to be completed.[114]

The Mitre government also carried out an old project which had been in waiting since the Rivadavia era, namely the decoration of the tympanum of Buenos Aires Cathedral, incomplete since 1822. Various attempts at completing the work had failed, until 1860 when the government of Buenos Aires commissioned the sculptor

Figure 32. The Modeling of Plaza San Martín
Top, Equestrian statue of General San Martín. Louis J. Daumas
Bottom, Lithograph of General Juan Manuel de Rosas. Anonymous

J. Dubordieu.[115] The government decided to give evidence of the devotion of the city to the Unity of the Nation through a monumental action. But while Buenos Aires decided to represent part of the scenographic space of Plaza de la Victoria, a theme that evoked its withdrawal and repentance on the façade of the cathedral, it did so with a biblical allegory with significant connotations for the city.

To celebrate the national unification of 1860, Dubordieu chose the meeting of Joseph and Jacob, when the former "flung his arms around him and wept endlessly while embracing him," a fitting allusion to Buenos Aires' reconciliation with the nation and its other sons, the thirteen provinces of the interior. Joseph, who under "the protection of Yahveh made all his enterprises prosper," clearly represents the destiny that the city has assigned itself.[116] Despised and betrayed by his brothers, Joseph recognizes them even though they do not recognize him. What we find in this allegory is also a Buenos Aires as head and soul of the nation. Joseph, sold as a slave by his brothers, proves to be the one who saves his father, his brothers and all his family from starvation. Here was a marvelous warning for those considering a solution that excluded Buenos Aires. In short, it was a biblical allegory that stamped on the decoration and on the people's spirits the destiny of a city and of a nation. The period press saluted the work but did not go so far as interpretations of this type.[117] In any event, the choice of subject matter did not trigger any kind of controversy, while the statue of liberty, a creation of the same artist, had aroused some objections,[118] perhaps for the simple reason that for a Porteño this destiny was taken for granted. Even more surprising is the indifference with which historians have considered a representation that is one of the major works of political Porteño art.[119]

These last two years of the secession therefore marked a pivotal point in urban memory. The city, which had previously sought legitimacy by presenting itself as a bastion of republican values, now associated itself with its historic destiny and introduced the principal that would later serve to constitute a national memory. Consequently, the objective of memory was important in Buenos Aires during the years of secession. Indeed, while in certain aspects the city's situation "unburdened" by the gap between city and nation was comfortable, this raised serious problems for the legitimacy of its power.[120] It was therefore a matter of associating it, along with the action of the Porteño ruling class, with the tradition of May 1810. The strategy was clear: in this iron hand between Buenos Aires and the Confederation, power must correspond naturally to who best embodied the nation. A policy for the development of national symbols had a certain usefulness and appeared in any event complimentary to armed combat. In this combat, Buenos Aires triumphed to a certain extent. While Confederation policy was almost nonexistent in this sphere, its success in Buenos Aires was all the greater

Figure 33. A New Urban Scenography: the City's "Devotion" for the Nation

The decoration of the tympanum of Buenos Aires Cathedral, by the sculptor Joseph Dubordieu (1860). Allegory of national unity based on the biblical theme of the encounter between Joseph and Jacob.

See Diccionario de Buenos Aires. Guía del forastero, 1864

for being founded on a colonial tradition of the city as the place of institutional memory, and was in harmony with a transformation of sociability structures that facilitated the development of new sentiments of collective belonging. Urban remodeling associated new civility relationships with a historic civic-mindedness which would make the city its place of worship. Thus, during the last six years of secession there was a resurgence in the public space of the principal figures on whom the historical identity of the nation would be founded. These figures were then more or less clearly associated with the history of the city: Rivadavia, San Martín, Belgrano but also Lavalle, Paz and Varela. An equivalence was thus established between City and Nation which would have considerable consequences on the construction of a national memory. Among these consequences was that of accelerating the process of remodeling memory in the urban community. Hence, the statue of Liberty and the Republic crowned the May Pyramid in Plaza de la Victoria. The places of traditional sociability, based on the "community of place," aimed to evoke the great men of the nation. In turn, the city stamped its features on memory, in short urbanizing it. The national community was thus defined by means of a form of collectivity characteristic of the urban way of life typical of the Porteño elites. It would not be until the late nineteenth century that the national memory would incorporate the rural space and the society that it comprised as components of collective identity. But in serving as a basis of national memory, the city revitalized a feeling of "localist" belonging, founded on an old tradition as sovereign city. Far from resolving the enormous problem of the transference of belonging of the Spanish nation to the Argentine nation, the city added that of sovereign identities. City of Janus, Buenos Aires gave shape to a nation founded on an antinomic memory.

NOTES

1. Frías mentions this danger in the 1852 article cited in the following footnote, but the vindication of the religious nature of national identity appears in his historical writings of 1866. See Manuel Estrada, "Lecciones sobre la historia de la República Argentina," *Revista Argentina* 4 (1866).
2. See El Progreso, 7 July 1852, 1, 2. Frías would not cease from then on in doing battle with Freemasonry and all the new secularized forms of organization of community life.
3. The founding brethren were Alejandro Brown, Pedro Díaz de Vivar, Idelfonso Islas, José M. Miró, Juan Miller, Adolfo Saldías, Pablo Santillán, Esteban Señorans and Eustaquio Torres. The minute book of the lodge was only begun in June 1858, when the Masonic schism triggered by the foundation of this lodge ended. I have found documentation pertaining to this period in the archives of the Gran Logia de la Masonería del Uruguay. The list of members was reconstructed from Masonic correspondence. See AGLMU, "Antecedentes."
4. See "Discurso del delegado del Todo Poderoso Supremo Consejo y Gran Oriente del Uruguay en el acto de inauguración de la logia 'Confraternidad Argentina,' al Oriente de Buenos Aires, el 22 de noviembre de 1856," in AGLMU, "Antecedentes."

5. AGLMU, "Antecedentes."
6. José Roque Pérez, "Discurso en la inauguración de la logia 'Confraternidad Argentina,' el 22 de noviembre de 1856," AGLMU, "Antecedentes."
7. In a well-documented, if deeply anti-Masonic study, Aníbal Rottjer sustains that the Confraternidad Argentina lodge was born from political divisions among the pandilleros and the chupandinos, but gives no evidence whatsoever to corroborate this claim. In fact, Rottjer merely takes up the old anti-Masonic phobia theory denouncing the presence of the Freemasons everywhere. See Aníbal Atilio Rottjer, *La masonería en la Argentina y en el mundo (historia de los hermanos Tres Puntos)* (1957) (Buenos Aires: Nuevo Orden, 1976), 230.
8. See The personal letter from Roque Pérez to Jayme Vinent of 2 June 1857 in AGLMU, "Antecedentes."
9. See AGLA, Minute Book, Unión del Plata lodge, box 21, session of 23 March 1856.
10. See Letter cited in footnote 8.
11. Circular addressed to the Venerable Master of the Unión del Plata lodge, in AGLMU, "Antecedentes." This was the Brazilian Supreme Council, chaired by Paulino José Soares de Souza, Viscount of Uruguay.
12. The Unión del Plata lodge denounced the irregularity of the Brazilian authority that had granted the constitution to the Grand Orient for the Argentine Confederation. Furthermore, it challenged the legality of the seven so-called regular lodges established during this period because, in accordance with the regulations on establishing a Grand Orient, this number of lodges was required as a minimum, while at the time there were only four lodges, of which three were opposed to the new authority.
13. See "Carta del Sop. Gr. Ins. del Sup. Cons. de Buenos Aires al Sup.. Cons. del Uruguay," Buenos Aires, 11 July 1857, in AGLMU, "Antecedentes." "Neighbors" is underlined in the text.
14. According to these regulations, seven Masons were required to establish a lodge and seven lodges to establish a Grand Orient.
15. The Verdad lodge was created by Frenchmen who had separated from the Amie des Naufragés lodge. On its creation, see "Correspondance de la loge Amie des Naufragés," in Bibliothèque Nationale (Paris), Argentina, correspondance, FM2, 843.
16. See "Carta de Fernando C. Cordero a Jayme Vinent, Buenos Aires, 21 de octubre de 1857," in AGLMU, "Antecedentes."
17. See "Circular del Gran Oriente para la Confederación Argentina a las logias del Oriente de Buenos Aires," Buenos Aires, 6 November 1857, in AGLA, various documentation 1852–1860, Amie des Naufragés lodge, box 761.
18. The reference to this intervention appears in a letter from A. Vaillant, Venerable Master of the Les Amie de la Patrie lodge in Montevideo to the Grand Orient of France. See Bibliothèque Nationale (Paris), Uruguay, Montevideo, Les Amis de la Patrie lodge, FM2, 867, correspondence of 1 October 1857.
19. See letter of 28 March 1858 addressed to the Grand Orient of France, in Bibliothèque Nationale (Paris), Argentina, Buenos Aires, Amie des Naufragés lodge, correspondence with the Grand Orient of France, FM2, 843.
20. See "Pública solicitada," *La Tribuna,* 16 December 1857, 1.
21. Article 10 of the Constitution and Regulations of Freemasonry establishes: "every rite, in its territorial jurisdiction, has a single sovereign authority." Article 11 specifies the terms: "By territorial jurisdiction of a rite we refer to the extent of the territory of any one political State and its territorial dependencies." See *Constitución y Reglamentos*

Generales de la Masonería Escocesa para la Confederación Argentina y Valle de Buenos Aires (Buenos Aires: Imprenta Americana, 1857), 8.

22. See "Carta de Jayme Vinent a Roque Pérez," Montevideo, 2 July 1857; "Carta de Gabriel Pérez a Roque Pérez," Río de Janeiro, 12 July 1857; in AGLMU, "Antecedentes."
23. Mariano Billinghurst, Juan A. García, Juan F. Gutiérrez, José Martínez de Hoz, Manuel Langenheim, Mariano Cabral, José M. Uriarte and José M. Lagos received the thirtieth degree. Lorenzo Torres was one of the brethren who received the eighteenth degree. See "Informe sobre aumentos de salarios del 6 de agosto de 1857," in AGLMU, "Antecedentes."
24. Fernando C. Cordero informed Jayme Vinent in the following terms: "In line with your indication, we have decided to form a Masonic Power and we wish to thank you in advance for the support you might offer us". See "Carta de Fernando C. Cordero a J. Vinent," Buenos Aires, 28 November 1857, in AGLMU, "Antecedentes."
25. See AGLA, various documentation, Amie des Naufragés lodge, box 761.
26. There are many gaps in available data, as unfortunately the archives of the Grand Orient of the Argentine Confederation have not been preserved.
27. Constante Unión operated until 1860, when it was closed by the police. It resumed activities in 1867, but under the patronage of the Grand Orient of the Argentine Republic. Bien Social was one of the "irregular" lodges and was "regularized" in September 1860 by the Supreme Council and Grand Orient of the Argentine Republic. See AGLA, Minute Book (1858–1862), Constante Unión lodge, 23, box 54; Gran Logia Central, 1860–1864, book 24.
28. See AGLA, Minute Book, Unión del Plata lodge, box 21.
29. See *La Tribuna,* 20 October 1858.
30. See "Carta de José R. Pérez a Jayme Vinent, Buenos Aires, 2 de junio de 1857," in AGLMU, "Antecedentes." The phrase "a Grand Orient of hairdressers" is underlined in the text.
31. See *Farsa de los francmasones,* 28.
32. There is a reference to the Masonic *tenida* (meeting) of 13 March 1860 at the Consuelo de Infortunio lodge in AGLA, Minute Book (1857–1861), Consuelo del Infortunio lodge, box 27.
33. Letter from the Amie des Naufragés lodge to the Grand Orient of France, Buenos Aires, 27 January and 29 August 1860, in Bibliothèque Nationale (Paris), Argentina, Amie des Naufragés lodge, correspondence with GOF, FM2, 843.
34. There is no doubt that English Freemasonry had considered that the situation was uncertain enough to give a chance to the Grand Orient of the Argentine Confederation. The Grand Orient of France, on the other hand, showed great prudence, postponing on various occasions demands for recognition from the two Argentine Masonic powers. The French Amie des Naufragés lodge recommended: "We admit that the Grand Orient of France has acted with characteristically deep wisdom in delaying this recognition until peace and calm have been reestablished in these areas; in the interests of the order, we believe that it would be wise and prudent to also demand an end to the Masonic division which still reigns here, producing the worst results". See correspondence from the Amie des Naufragés lodge to the Grand Orient of France, Buenos Aires, 29 August 1860, in Bibliothèque Nationale (Paris), Argentina, Amie des Naufragés lodge, correspondence with GOF, FM2, 843.
35. This reference is shared by Masonic authors. See *Diccionario Enciclopédico de la Masonería,* edited by Lorenzo Frau Abrimes and Rosendo Arús Arderiv (Buenos Aires:

Kier, 1962); see also M. V. Lazcano, *Las sociedades secretas,* vol. 2, 351–354; L. Hurcade, "Misión de la masonería argentina en la organización nacional," *Símbolo* 1:1 (July 1946), 18–27.

36. Mitre was elected governor of the province of Buenos Aires on 2 May 1860, immediately announcing his intention to merge it with the Argentine Confederation.
37. See J. Scobie, *La lucha por la consolidación,* 284–296.
38. See Archives of the Progress Club, Minute Book, session of 3 July 1860.
39. Sarmiento and Gelly y Obes already belonged to lodges under the obedience of the Supreme Council and may have suggested this idea to Bartolomé Mitre. Derqui and Urquiza were initiates in Freemasonry, but were not to our knowledge active in the order during this period. Nor was Mitre a part of the order. Lappas claims that Mitre had been initiated in Bolivia and then joined the Confraternidad Argentina lodge, while also enjoying honorary membership of the Unión del Plata lodge. However, we have found no data as to his participation in them. On the contrary, in Pedro Palacios' participation in the Unión del Plata lodge in July 1860 there is an explicit reference to Governor Bartolomé Mitre as profane. At the same time, Palacios denounced the unacceptable attitude of the Confraternidad Argentina lodge, which had granted by decree and in a single day the first three Masonic degrees. See AGLA, Minute Book, Confraternidad Argentina lodge, box 14, session of 21 July 1860; A. Lappas, *La masonería argentina,* 282.
40. See AGLA, Minute Book, Unión del Plata lodge, box 21, session of 25 August 1860; Minute Book, Confraternidad Argentina lodge, box 14, session of 21 July 1860; Minute Book, Consuelo del Infortunio lodge, box 27, session of 28 August 1860.
41. On this question, see in particular studies by the Centro de Documentazione Massonica de Turín. For an overview of the question of Freemason studies in Italy see Aldo Alessandro Mola, "Orientaciones actuales de los estudios de la historia de la masonería en Italia," in José A. Ferrer Benimeli (ed.), *La masonería en la historia de España del siglo xix,* vol. 1 (Junta de Castilla y León, 1987), 411–427.
42. See figure 18.
43. With circular no. 556, the Supreme Council informed the lodges of the Orient that the differences among Masonic brethren had ended. We have found a copy of the circular in the minute book of the Tolerancia lodge, though nothing was found in the archives of the Grand Lodge. The document refers exclusively to Idelfonso Islas, Pedro Caleixas and Eugenio Felsicon, without mentioning Valencia. Nevertheless, Lappas affirms that the latter too was one of the dissident brethren joining the Supreme Council of the Argentine Republic. Might Lappas have had access to other documents? Whatever the case, in his study he quotes no sources. See AGLA, Minute Book, Tolerancia lodge, box 30; A. Lappas, *La masonería argentina,* 387–388.
44. See *La Tribuna,* 12 March 1854, 3. The society was inaugurated on 25 May with a concert to celebrate liberty and the constitution. See *La Tribuna,* 18 May 1854.
45. The various disciplines of the social sciences have a particular interest in this concept, which opens new research perspectives, hence the multiple meanings given to the term, the diverse disciplinary approaches, and the innumerable works on the subject. It would be impossible to make a summary here of this research, and more difficult still to decide on the exact definition of the term. Interdisciplinary studies are sadly lacking and frequently each discipline uses the notion of imagery according to its own analysis registers. There have been some individual attempts, such as the research of Gilbert Durand. See *Les Structures anthropologiques de l'imaginaire* (1960) (Paris: Bordas,

1984). On imagery as a historic object, see Evelyn Patlagean's article, "L'imaginaire," in Jacques Le Goff, Roger Chartier and Jacques Revel (eds.), *La Nouvelle histoire* (Paris: Retz, 1978), 249–269; an overview of the different research sources appears in the collective work *Histoire et imaginaire* (Paris: Poiesis, 1986; distributed by Payot); Pierre Ansart, "Marx et la théorie de l'imaginaire social," *Cahiers internationaux de sociologie* 45 (1968): 99–116; Bronislaw Baczko, *Les Imaginaires sociaux. Mémoires et espoirs collectifs* (Paris: Payot, 1984).

46. It was Marc Bloch who sketched a study model of political attitudes in *Les Rois thaumaturges* (Strasburg, 1924). Thirty years later, this path was well signposted because of Kantorowicz's capital work in the field of the cult of the monarchy. See Ernst Kantorowicz, *The King's Two Bodies. A Study in Medieval Political Theology* (Princeton: Princeton University Press, 1957). Specialists in ancient Greece and Rome and medieval history opened the way to the modernists. Specialists in the contemporary age, from the very characteristics of social imagery, expressed an obstinate distrust with regards to the new problems of history. In this respect, Raoul Girardet's book was an important contribution and to a large extent helped to extend the boundaries of contemporary history. See Raoul Girardet, *Mythes et mythologies politiques* (Paris: Seuil, 1986). See also an updated view of the problem of concepts and sources in Jacques Le Goff, *L'Imaginaire medieval* (Paris: Gallimard, 1985).

47. See Tulio Halperin Donghi, "Un cuarto de siglo de historiografía argentina (1960–1985)," *Desarrollo Económico* 25: 100 (January-March 1986), 487–520.

48. Since then, an abundant literature has enhanced our understanding of the historical process of constructing modern nations. The bibliographical references can be found in Eric Hobsbawm, *Nations and Nationalism since 1780* (Cambridge: Cambridge University Press, 1990).

49. See Pierre Nora, "La nation-mémoire," in *Les Lieux de mémoire,* 653.

50. Cornelius Castoriadis, *L'Institution imaginaire de la société* (Paris: Seuil, 1975), 207–208.

51. This applies especially to Michel Vovelle's first works into the imagery of death. See Gaby Vovelle and Michel Vovelle, *Vision de la mort et de l'au-delà en Provence d'après les autels des âmes du Purgatoire, xve-xxe siècles* (Paris: A. Colin, 1970). Since then, this type of analysis has multiplied. See M. Vovelle's work on the French Revolution, "L'iconographie: une approche de la mentalité révolutionnaire," in *Recherches sur la Révolution. Un bilan des travaux scientifiques du Bicentenaire* (Paris: La Découverte, 1991), 149–163.

52. Has not Jean-Pierre Vernant already shown that such material processes as work cannot be understood without the whole of social representations which organize community life? Before him, Max Weber had admirably opened up this path. See Jean-Pierre Vernant, *Mythe et pensée chez les Grecs: études de psychologie historique,* 2 vols. (Paris: Maspero, 1974); Max Weber, *L'Éthique protestante et l'esprit du capitalisme* (Paris: Plon, 1967). In a study of ideology, Godelier also advanced in this direction. See Maurice Godelier, "La part idéelle du réel. Essai sur l'idéologie," *L'Homme* 18:3/4 (July-December 1978), 155–187.

53. When we speak of imagery as a whole of significant representations, in no case do we understand this as the platonic idea of image, reflex, deformation of reality. We follow C. Castoriadis when he defines imagery as a creative instance, "the originary faculty of postulating or assigning, in the modality of representation, a thing or relation that does not exist." He thus distinguishes radical imagery, "the last condition of what can be represented and what can be conceived," as a common root of effective and

symbolic imagery. When we speak of national imagery we refer to this secondary, socially instituted imagery. See C. Castoriadis, *L'Institution,* 177.

54. The existence of a "family" of forms is a factor mentioned by nearly all recent investigations. Nevertheless, there are variations on the element that defines the group. Thus, forms of sociability might be spoken of as "traditional or modern," of the "Ancien Regime" or "democratic," "aristocratic" or "bourgeois." At the root of these distinctions we find the paradigm of classic sociology: Tönnies' "community-association" and Durkheim's "mechanic and organic solidarities." See F. Tönnies, Comunidad y asociación; Émile Durkheim, *De la division du travail social* (Paris: PUF, 1967).
55. This was Gorriti's speech during the discussion on the law for the creation of a national army. See *Asambleas Constituyentes,* vol. 1, 1325.
56. *Asambleas Constituyentes,* vol. 1, 1325
57. In opposing the creation of a national army, Deputy Ignacio Gorriti used this metaphor: "If it were a matter of forming a company [association] in which commercial interests or private funds were dealt with, and only with the project of forming the association one of the entrepreneurs demanded from the company the funds needed to raise the capital for it before the conditions had been accepted, and before knowing the benefit...could one look on this project as rational? ... Well sir, if we do not yet know if the parts will be agreed on in the articles needed to found the association, nor if they will ultimately separate from this association, how are we going to raise a national army?" See *Asambleas Constituyentes,* vol. 1, 1325.
58. Civility, in effect, is a value in the sense that in developing contacts between men, it contributes to the progress of civilization as a dynamic of superior culture. I have developed this question elsewhere in "Pedagogía societaria y aprendizaje de la Nación en el Río de la Plata, 1820–1862," in A. Annino et al., *De los Imperios.*
59. See *La Reforma Pacífica,* 15 October 1858.
60. See *El Progreso,* 7 April 1852, 2.
61. The democratic nature of these forms has been studied at length, thus it is unnecessary to focus on it here. In addition to the works of Maurice Agulhon previously cited, see also the different approaches by R. Halévi, *Les Loges maçonniques,* 9–16, and F. Furet, *Penser,* 58–62.
62. See *La Tribuna,* 28 February 1861, 2.
63. See above, chapter 6', "New Modalities of Social Exchanges."
64. Dominique Schnapper has worked on this question in *La Communauté des citoyens.*
65. Even Renan highlights the overlap between these two representations of the nation as a community of belonging. See E. Renan, "Qu'est-ce qu'une nation?"
66. On the history of this process, see K. M. Baker, *Au Tribunal de l'opinion,* and R. Chartier, *Les Origines culturelles.*
67. See "Asamblea popular." *La Tribuna,* 18 March 1855, 2.
68. See House of Representatives of the Province of Buenos Aires, Diario de sesiones de la Sala de Representantes, 27th session of 10 March 1854, 65.
69. See House of Representatives of the Province of Buenos Aires, Diario de sesiones de la Sala de Representantes, 27th session of 10 March 1854, 65.
70. This situation brought about a resurgence in the confusion of powers and sovereignties in the origin of the independence movement in the city of Buenos Aires: a capital city of a viceroyalty which claimed authority as the head of a vast territory, and an urban community which, by means of its *cabildo,* acted as sovereign body. A penetrating

analysis of the connections between these two political models in Mexico can be found in Antonio Annino, "Prácticas criollas y liberalismo en la crisis del espacio urbano colonial el 29 de noviembre de 1812 en Ciudad de México," *BIHAA E. Ravignani* (Buenos Aires) 6 (third series, second semester, 1992): 67–97.

71. See "Ley de municipalidad para la ciudad," 11 October 1854, *Registro Oficial del Gobierno de Buenos Aires* (Buenos Aires: Imprenta Americana, 1851–1862).
72. Particularly *Echeverría in Ojeada retrospectiva.*
73. See the 11 October law cited in note 71. Municipality memoirs often mention tensions between it and the government. See *Memoria de la Municipalidad,* 1859, 3–4.
74. See PGB, *La Création,* appendix 1, "Base de données."
75. With scarce exceptions, the liberals shared the idea that unity in the national space arose from natural conditions as a whole. There were a few men who, like Juan Bautista Alberdi, developed the idea of a national space built from a policy of regulation and coordination of commercial flow.
76. Both works represented respectively an average of 16% and 11.4% of the municipality's spending between 1858 and 1862, while between the same dates spending on public schools was on average 5% and public works 2.8%. See *Memoria de la Municipalidad.*
77. In 1849, the number of land surveys carried out for the construction of new buildings was around 300. By 1854 the figure had doubled. See M. R. Trelles, *Registro estadístico,* vol. 2, 109. The increase in the built area can be garnered from the observation of different maps of the city. These are detailed in PGB, *La Création,* vol. 3, 915–921.
78. Plaza Mayor had a market in the middle, dividing the square in two: Plaza de la Victoria and Plaza 25 de Mayo (see figure 1).
79. See *La Tribuna,* 27 October 1857.
80. The mutation of the dry public squares into landscaped squares was seen later in Spain, which may confirm the idea of relationships between political imagery and urban landscape. See Antonio Bonnet Correa, "Le concept de Plaza Mayor en Espagne depuis le XVIème siècle," in *Publicaciones de la Casa de Velázquez, Forum et Plaza Mayor,* 79–105.
81. In 1860 palm trees were planted in Plaza Victoria and Plaza 25 de Mayo. The former also boasted an *alameda* from 1858. In the same year a parish residents' commission was set up to renovate Plaza de la Libertad. The insalubrious and indecent Plaza de Monserrat in the African neighborhood became around the same time a square with trees and public benches, while there was also a project to raise a statue of Belgrano. In Plaza Lorea two rows of trees were planted, while in the same year the commission of Campo de Marte began preliminary work to transform this place for military maneuvers into a place for strolling. The Avenida Julio was also renovated with the same end. See *La Tribuna,* 1860, "Hechos locales"; *Memoria de la Municipalidad,* 1860.
82. See B. Mitre, *Historia de Belgrano,* prefacio de la tercera edición (1876–1877). For a historiographical analysis of this preface, see Natalio Botana, "El capítulo introductorio a la Historia de Belgrano," *La libertad política y su historia* (Buenos Aires: Sudamericana, 1991), 37–44.
83. On the elements defining the republican character of a monument and particularly on its role in a pedagogy of urban appearance, see Maurice Agulhon, *Marianne au combat. L'imagerie et la symbolique républicaines de 1789 à 1880* (Paris: Flammarion, 1979); M. Agulhon, "Architecture républicaine," *Monuments historiques, La République* 144 (April–May 1986): 7–11.

84. The importance of these events in urban memory is undisputed. One need only see the significance assigned to the invasions in the first national histories by Domínguez, Mitre and López. Some indirect references also suggest that the events of 12 August and 5 July were the reason for popular commemorations during the nineteenth century, though unfortunately the inexistence of research into this subject obliges us to remain here on the side of mere conjecture.
85. See B. Mitre, *Historia de Belgrano,* vol. 1, 248. Mitre cites here an inscription placed during the funerals in honor of the dead soldiers, and giving evidence of the use of the word "Argentine" to refer to the inhabitants of Buenos Aires: "To the Argentine Warriors, insulted by the land of their birth, who gave their lives gloriously for their homes, their children and their wives," in *Breve descripción de las exequias en honor de los soldados que murieron por la defensa de Buenos Aires* (Buenos Aires: Imprenta de los Niños Expósitos, 1807).
86. During this period Plaza Monserrat in the African neighborhood was called "Plaza de la Fidelidad" in commemoration of the loyalty of the black population during combat with the British. The Plaza Nueva was later called "De la Unión" in memory of the place of the first meetings of the inhabitants of Buenos Aires to organize the recapture of the city. Plaza de la Piedad was at the time named "Plaza Lorea," in honor of the local Isidoro Lorea, murdered with his wife by the British in July 1807. The Plaza del Retiro was rechristened "Campo de Gloria" to recall how the recapture began there in 1807. See La Tribuna, 14 May 1861. In addition, two French travelers confirmed on two different dates the strong impression that these events left on the urban memory. See A. Isabelle, *Voyage à Buenos Aires,* 157–160; A. Delacour, "Le Rio de la Plata," 15.
87. See *Acuerdos del extinguido Cabildo* (series 4), vol. 3, 443–444. The government authorized the construction of the commemorative pyramid column but with a plaque alluding only to events of 1810, evidence of the existence of two memories disputing the same place.
88. The scarce information available on this artist was obtained by Julio E. Payró in *Prilidiano Pueyrredón, Joseph Dubourdieu. La Pirámide de Mayo y la Catedral de Buenos Aires* (Buenos Aires: Facultad de Filosofía y Letras, Biblioteca de Historia del Arte, 1972), serie argentina no. 5. According to the author, Dubourdieu may have trained under Pierre-Jean David d'Angers, a significant factor as we will see below.
89. Originally, the woman had a civic crown on her head and carried in her right hand the pike, with the Phrygian cap at the end of the pike. Some days later, for unknown reasons but whose significance is clear, the author decided to crown her with the Phrygian cap. The description of the first version appeared in the period press. See *El Nacional,* 23 May 1856. According to Maurice Agulhon's typology, the definitive sculpture was closer to the bourgeois image of the Republic, although it incorporated two popular elements in the exposed breast and the Phrygian cap. See M. Agulhon, *Marianne au combat,* 110.
90. These words are a little controversial given that all authors affirm that it was a statue of Liberty and not of the Republic. But even if for the government the Patria-Liberty pairing did not evoke the Republic—something that remains to be proven—what is true is that it did so for the sculptor. From its signs and chronology, this monument is part of the history of feminine representation of the Republic. That said, the population of Buenos Aires only saw in it a statue of Liberty. This raises the problem of the translation of signs, which classical theory settled too rapidly.

91. The fact that he had trained under Pierre-Jean David d'Angers was itself an indication of a preconceived aesthetic idea, the political connotations of which were clearly known to the Porteño elites. See J. E. Payró, *Prilidiano Pueyrredón.*
92. See *La Tribuna*, 10 January 1858.
93. However, the strangeness of the emblem in the "Argentine" iconographic tradition was recognized later by two of the period's most important political figures: Bartolomé Mitre and Domingo F. Sarmiento. When the Municipality of Buenos Aires asked their advice in 1883 with regards to a possible demolition of the monument, Mitre responded that "the statue can and must be pulled down because it is no more than a false decoration with no historic significance." Sarmiento argued likewise, approving the demolition and accusing the statue of profaning the national tradition, "because it obliged the people to worship an idol devoid of meaning in the history of the nation." But during this period the forms of memory were manifestly different. Texts cited by Rómulo Zavala, *Historia de la Pirámide de Mayo* (Buenos Aires: Academia Nacional de la Historia, 1962), 79–82.
94. Let us not forget that the Phrygian cap, dear as it was to the liberals, had helped the conservative Rosas in associating the bright red of the "Holy Federation" with the revolutionary symbol. The memory of the Rosista experience was too fresh and is evidence that republican values could be used for any interpretation.
95. B. Mitre, "Preámbulo a la biografía de Manuel Belgrano," in *Historia de Belgrano*. It is notable the proximity of this analysis with that which leads Pierre Nora to distinguish and oppose historical memory to memory itself. See P. Nora, "Entre Mémoire et Histoire. La problématique des lieux," in *Les Lieux de mémoire*, vol. 1, xvii–xlii.
96. From an iconographic point of view, the civic statues had the advantage of filling the representative vacuum left by the figure of the king, which Rosas had filled so well.
97. It was here that Bartolomé Mitre published his first biography of Manuel Belgrano. The *Galería* also included biographies of Rivadavia, San Martín, Varela, Moreno, Funes, Brown, Guido, García, and Lavalle. Juan María Gutiérrez was also the promoter of other publishing projects along the same lines. See J. M. Gutiérrez, *Pensamientos, máximas*; J. M. Gutiérrez, *Apuntes biográficos de escritores, oradores y hombres de Estado de la República Argentina*, Buenos Aires, Imprenta de Mayo, 1860. The *Galería de Celebridades* project was still part of the Enlightenment tradition. In 1788, the Real Calografía had launched a project to publish *Retratos de españoles ilustres* (portraits of illustrious Spaniards), a collection that by 1814 had reached 114 portraits and which continued to appear, with some interruptions, until the end of the nineteenth century. But while in the case of Spain the project allowed the Enlightenment to be founded on Spanish origins, in the Argentine case the oldest personalities date from the revolution for independence. On the Spanish case, see *Summa Artis. Historia general del arte* (Madrid: Espasa-Calpe, 1987), vol. 31, *El grabado en España*, 524–558.
98. See *La Tribuna*, 21 August 1857.
99. See *La Tribuna*, 21 and 28 August 1857; *Rasgos biográficos sobre D. Bernardino Rivadavia por D. R.* (Dardo Rocha?) (Buenos Aires: Imprenta de las Artes, 1857). In his introduction to *Galería de Celebridades* Juan María Gutiérrez presents Rivadavia as the first of the great men of the patria (in the sense of the *"patria chica,"* Buenos Aires). In the same work, Sarmiento suggests that San Martín was to the nation what Rivadavia was to the city of Buenos Aires.

100. See *La Tribuna*, 6 September 1857. There are five lithographs by A. Clairaux with a drawing by A. Durand which serve as evidence of this popular event. The documents can be found in the Museo Histórico Nacional, items 9352, 9353, 9354, 9355 and 9356. See Ministerio de Educación de la Nación, *Catálogo del Museo Histórico*, vol. 2, 391.
101. A. Isabelle, *Voyage à Buenos Aires*, 153.
102. With few exceptions, the adoption of Rivadavia as a symbol of the Republican City was unanimous and opponents had difficulty in making themselves heard. In this respect see *Refutación Solemne de los Rasgos Biográficos y Discursos Escritos y Pronunciados en Buenos Aires por los Señores Gutiérrez, Alsina, Mitre y otros, con motivo de los funerales de Don Bernardino Rivadavia. Escrito por un Porteño de Nota* (Buenos Aires, 1857).
103. It is feasible that some attempt was made in this respect, in order to replace the highly popular figure of Rosas with that of Rivadavia. This is the interpretation that can be made from the minting of medals adorned with his bust, provided by the government and the municipality. See "Rivadavia en la medalla," *Numismática* 4.
104. See decrees of 12 February and 14 and 26 August 1857, in *Registro Oficial del Gobierno*. In spite of conflicts between the Sociedad de Beneficencia, the municipality also participated in the organization of the event. See *Actas del Concejo Municipal*, 1857, sessions of 11 March and 4 May 1857.
105. See *El Nacional*, 28 May 1857.
106. The statue was commissioned in 1859 to the French sculptor Louis Joseph Daumas. For a more detailed analysis, see Eduardo Schiaffino, *La pintura y la escultura en Argentina (1783–1894)*, Buenos Aires, Edición del autor, 1933; Academia Nacional de Bellas Artes, *Historia general del arte en la Argentina*, vol. 4 (Buenos Aires: Academia Nacional de Bellas Artes, 1985).
107. See "Paseo de Marte" in *Memoria de la Municipalidad*, 1861.
108. Naturally, this was not Bartolomé Mitre's opinion, being the author of the most famous biography of San Martín. In his preface to the first edition of the biography of Belgrano, Mitre affirms that San Martín was equally popular. See B. Mitre, "Preámbulo a la biografía de Manuel Belgrano," in *Historia de Belgrano*.
109. The iconography of the equestrian image stems from the *velazqueña* tradition of the Spanish Golden Age. According to certain authors, in the River Plate this type of image may also have ties with the iconography of Théodore Géricault. See Academia Nacional de Bellas Artes, *Historia general del arte*, vol 3 (1984); Bonifacio del Carril, *Las litografías argentinas de Géricault* (Buenos Aires: Emecé, 1991).
110. See "Retrato ecuestre con uniforme, litografía en negro, autor anónimo," cited by J. A. Pradère in *Juan Manuel de Rosas*, 69; "Estatua de San Martín," in *Diccionario de Buenos Aires. Guía del forastero* (Buenos Aires: Imprenta del Porvenir, 1863). Many thanks to Roberto Amigo for his advice on the analysis of this question.
111. Sarmiento says that this was an engraving of San Martín. See Domingo Faustino Sarmiento, "Biografía de José de San Martín," in *Galería de Celebridades*. Did he do this in good faith or did he deliberately confuse him with Rosas? In the engraving by Nuñez de Ibarra, San Martín is not in the same position as in the equestrian monument, which bears much resemblance to Rosas.
112. This church witnessed one of the bloodiest confrontations between the British, entrenched in the tower, and the Porteños during the 1807 invasion. The cannonballs which can still be seen in the tower and the flags taken from the British, which are displayed inside the church, were a source of pride for Porteños, who made the church

and its tower a commemorative place. See, for example, "La torre simbólica," *La Tribuna*, 17 December 1853.

113. In December 1855, the government of Buenos Aires gave the name of Manuel Belgrano to the town that had just been founded in the district of San José de Flores. In 1857, Mitre published his "Biografía de Belgrano" in *Galería de Celebridades*. A second revised edition in 1858 and especially the third, from 1876–1877, make up a biography which is one of the capital pieces in liberal historiography.

114. See *La Tribuna*, 24 August and 13 November 1862. The statue would eventually be unveiled in 1879, in the place where supposedly the statue of Bernadino Rivadavia was to be positioned. See Academia Nacional de Bellas Artes, *Historia general*, vol. 4.

115. Joseph Debourdieu had already suggested to Rosas in 1851 that the work be completed, but urban decoration was not the priority of the government of that period, even though at that time the city was going through an unarguable period of growth. See Alberto S. J. de Paula, "La autoría del frontis de la catedral de Buenos Aires," *Anales del Instituto de Arte Americano e Investigaciones Estéticas* 24 (1971): 93–97.

116. See Genesis 39:3.

117. See *La Tribuna*, 14 December 1860.

118. See *La Reforma Pacífica*, 6 February 1859.

119. We have found few references as to this decoration. Even classical art histories barely allude to it. See J. Payró, *Prilidiano Pueyrredón*; Paula, "La autoría"; Academia Nacional de Bellas Artes, *Historia general*.

120. Bartolomé Mitre developed the finest analyses on this question during the debate on the Constitution of the State of Buenos Aires in the Porteño legislature. See *Diario de sesiones de la Sala de Representantes*, sessions of 6 and 24 June, 39–115.

CONCLUSION

The Creation of a Nation in the River Plate during the Nineteenth Century

In spite of the title, this investigation does not set out to give an answer to the question of where to place the origins of the Argentine nation. It reveals, in contrast, the manifestations of a new representation of the social tie that fed the imagery of the nation, an imagery which gave the nation unity at the price of a recasting of society. This allows us to conclude that in the Porteño elites, the equation of the nation included civility and politics which, as a result, were found in the origins of the nation. This unequivocal formula of the problem conceals a number of questions affecting in varying degrees the issue at stake here.

The City of Buenos Aires, Birthplace of Nationality

Originally chosen as a scale of observation, this investigation into sociability practices in the city of Buenos Aires led me to reflect on the urban space and the city as a place of power. The above analysis highlights the permanence and even vitality, until the mid nineteenth century, of neighborhood ties woven around old community ties, structured over the community of place or of the parish, data which might draw a modification of the view of the city, and more generally of the construction process of the national State in Buenos Aires.

The work shows firstly that certain aspects of the process of creating a national representation of the collective being competed for the occupation of space. Hence we can see that while traditional relationship forms were situated in the traditional context of the religious community and place community (the parish) or through blood ties (the family), associative forms were part of a different organization of the urban social space. This leads us to postulate that the breakup of the traditional context of belonging was related to the development of the national reference point for collectivity. However, the chronology of transformation in community structure not only did not correspond to that of the political institutional process of the creation of a nation State but the modernity introduced by to be adjusted to traditional community structures, something which gives this process a very different sense from that assigned to it by legal texts. This aspect allows, for example, a new view of the problem of political representation in the city. Thus, the use of the parish structure to organize the electoral campaign and voting gave a community sense to the vote which, in principle, clearly contradicted the very notion of the citizen individual.

The demonstration of the permanence of traditional spaces of belonging also helps us to better understand the very process of creating a national reference point for the community. This is firstly because it reveals the relational forms and values of a population whose only description until this time came from authors with elite origins, and secondly because these elites, while tending to make this "archaic" permanence disappear from the texts, had to harmonize traditional belonging with the nation as a new community of belonging. Something which might bring a better understanding of the configurations of national imagery is the study of the relationship between new points of reference and old structures which, furthermore, concerned the elites themselves. Lastly, the demonstration of the vitality of the parochial community is testimony to another kind of permanence, that of an old public space which was still not secularized. There is another aspect, with multiple consequences, which underlines the need to review the process of establishing republican nations in societies far less transformed than their institutions. This aspect can account for the importance that religion would have in the young Hispano-American republics, not only concerning the Church as an institution and religion as dogma but also the latter as a common belief around which all community ties were structured. This confirmation raises questions as to the relationship in the city between these two "public" registers: the republican public sphere which implied the individual citizen exercising control of power by means of opinion, and the old sphere in which there persisted the idea of the public sphere as a place of one authority and where politics and religion were extensively interwoven. This study shows, in brief, that parochial communities could be the most relevant units of investigation for understanding as definitively as possible the complex dynamic between a traditional society and the birth of new structures in which modern political action held a clearer influence.

The analysis of the organization of the social urban space led us to reflect on the city as a place of power. We have seen that with the development of associative civility the urban space acquired a completely new sense, because the mode of relationship defining the urban community was now related to the city as the framework of the "public sphere." However, it was in this sphere that the national representation of collectivity was born. An implicit equivalence is hence established between the urban sphere and the modern nation, which means that the genesis of the Argentine nation can be attributed to the urban space, and more precisely to the city of Buenos Aires. This shows the importance of the urban remodeling of Buenos Aires during the secession years. The liberal elite intended to consolidate the public spirit which carried the national sentiment by means of the reorganization of the urban space around the new values defining the nation as a political community of belonging. It is no surprise to see how the elements that would connect in the collective memory the city of Buenos Aires with the Argentine nation were fixed in the decoration of the city. In hindsight we know that from this identification with the nation, the city would not escape unharmed, naturally losing its autonomy but also part of its leading role in the nation it claimed to embody.

The Question of Rosismo

It is impossible not to include Rosismo in any investigation of the city of Buenos Aires during the first half of the nineteenth century, and in this case the question was particularly unavoidable. Nevertheless, I did not make Rosismo the crux of this work. The reader will see that both the chronological limits adopted and the perspective of the investigation show signs of an undeniable heterodoxy with regards to the habitual approaches to the problem. Some, no doubt, will reproach me for examining Rosas via one of his less specific aspects, others for having placed everyday practices within a political question which denaturalizes them. I have, in effect, intended to deliberately introduce other dimensions of the problem.

This investigation refutes the monolithic nature of Rosismo. Thus, we have shown how the mutation of the Porteño sociability structure, whose original manifestations date from the beginning of the century, perpetuated throughout the first Rosas government and the early years of the second. This may appear to be an anodyne aspect, but these new practices postulated the public sphere as the new frame of reference of the relationship, upon which would develop a public culture that functioned as one of the principal channels of diffusion for the new representations of the social tie and the nation as a civil society. This process was not interrupted, therefore, by Rosas' arrival in the government of the province of Buenos Aires. On the contrary, in refusing to throw himself once more into the constitutional adventures which had brought about the fall of Rivadavia, Juan Manuel de Rosas accepted the new forms of community identity tied to cultural renewal in the city. This was indeed a phenomenon which principally concerned a class of a certain age among the cultural elites, but which introduced the identification between public sphere and nation.

When Rosas broke with the liberal youth, he proscribed any form of organization and action identified with "unitarian opinion," which meant that the modern nation was thought of as the subject of law and principle of unity in relation to practices and values characteristic of this instance. In spite of everything appearing to confirm the success of the regime, Rosas was up against an insurmountable contradiction. In effect, without revoking republican institutions nor the revolution's system of symbolic references, he excluded the men who had guaranteed the connection between authority and the nation as new foundations of power. How could Rosas assure his continued presence in the provincial government or in Buenos Aires' de facto preponderance over the rest of the Federation, when his power rested on personal loyalties? In this type of power no genuinely representative institution was in a position to assume the sovereignty of the nation. The cultural elites who would be able to guarantee the continuity of the regime presented themselves as Rosas' principal opponents, identifying in exile with the constitutive principals of the Argentine nation. Thus it seems that the reason for the Rosista political system sinking was as much in its refusal to give a constitutional form to the Federation as it was in the exclusion of the men who could guarantee future organization in the continuity of Rosista power. With this exclusion, Rosista proscribed any space where this question could be identified with the Argentine nation.

Naturally, the regime was not made up solely of sociabilities. It would be frankly unreasonable to reduce the fate of a whole balance of multiple forces down to a problem of freedom of association. As a result, we do not know how much economic tensions weighed, whether with other regions or with sectors of local producers, nor what influence stemmed from the opposition's war of attrition which obliged Rosismo to maintain a permanent war as the only future for his power. Nor must we forget the dimension of international pressure, which produced incessant conflicts, ultimately bringing out the diverse hostilities of an armed coalition that would bring a military end to the regime. All these questions had a bearing on power and may go some way to explaining Rosas' fall. It is not a question of substituting these explanations but of adding other elements to the understanding of the historic process of the creation of a national State in the region. Nor should we exaggerate and give sociability the status of primary cause, as this would amount to a monolithic view of the regime. The approach adopted does not seek to replace the latter "canonical" interpretation of Rosas's power, but rather highlights certain relatively unknown aspects of sociocultural and political life, which allow us to reveal other lines of continuity and breaks between Rosas' power and that of the representative republican institutions.

The Experience of Politics

Throughout our analysis we have seen man's encounter with politics, be it by the most classical means of mobilization of individuals in armed confrontation to gain political rights, or via the less common route of the public sphere. These were questions that concerned problems, approaches, different actors, but which permitted a common reflection on politics as the field of social action. This history unveils a society which symbolically appropriated power, and the diversity of forms of action was testimony to the nature of a power which had been converted in a vacant place. Behind all these actions is the question of representation, a notion whose polysemy obscures the complexity of the problems it contains. In effect, while with the breakup of the colonial tie the republic was the only legitimate political form, in linking its destiny to that of the nation, the problem of representation arose at the very heart of the social tie. This work shows, for example, that within the associative experience, practices could be used for identification with a public opinion appealing to an individual representation, or for an urban mobilization in search of a plebiscite which concealed an ancient notion of political representation, or lastly, for the organization of the electoral act in which individualist representation went hand in hand with corporative representation.

Novel as they were, associative contractual practices brought significant modifications to the political experience. This was firstly because these sociability forms were associated with cultural practices which established discussion as the foundation of an association which, by means of the printing press, became public opinion. Secondly, these changes occurred because of the scope of a phenomenon which extended the public sphere to sectors that still operated according to an old logic of authority and representation. And lastly, these modifications were a consequence of these innovations, all data on political practices appear to have been modified. Comparative study of biographies has allowed us particularly to discover the appearance of a new type of man in power, defined with regards to the public sphere. Inasmuch as the socioprofessional extraction of men who held a position in the power structure of the State of the province of Buenos Aires did not evince considerable differences during all of the period studied, it was a different matter in experiences in the public sphere. This allows us to conclude, primarily, that neither Rosas' arrival nor that of the liberals, significantly changed the sociological bases of political power. The same family groups were always present, the members of which had various forms of power, but whom could hardly be designated as large landowners. The present study also shows to what extent it is difficult to oppose categories such as "landowners," "large traders," or "lawyers," and propose a sociological theory of the provincial State.

We have noticed, in contrast, notable differences with regards to the political experience of these men of power. While there were few political men in the Rosista era who began their political career editing a newspaper or participating in a cultural movement, many of those who came to power after 1852 did have such experience. Sociability practices allowed, in particular, a significant distinction to be established between the ruling class of the period. Before 1852 what few associations existed were connected to religious practices or ethnic solidarity. The scarce affiliations by members of the ruling class to lay associations were rarely put down to a career strategy. The cultural mutation implied by associative practice was still manifested beyond the sphere of power. In contrast, after 1852 one of the particularities characterizing the ruling class was the intensity of its associative life. These practices could induce a new form of power which brought a new kind of politics to the forefront, a kind of professional of political representation. This amounts to saying that before 1852, political activity linked to the establishment of a representative republic owed very little to forms of association connected to the public sphere, as politics was still more the field of confrontation than negotiation, of action rather than opinion. The rise of the associative movement and its success among the members of the ruling class was therefore the sign of a significant transformation of the power structure. Furthermore, associative practices could play a fundamentally important role in the building of a national political structure. Associations such as the Progress Club, the May Club or Freemasonry helped to build ties outside of the traditional framework of family and clientele networks. The politicians who identified with the national public sphere but who, like Mitre and Sarmiento, did not have a powerful family, could through the associative network become a part of the different family groups who possessed, at provincial level, socioeconomic, political, or cultural power. The associative networks also had the advantage of being situated on the sidelines of the provincial framework, which explains the help they provided to the organization of a national political structure, as seen in the case of Freemasonry.

The Nation as Preeminence of Civility

Ultimately we must surrender to the evidence. We must not forget that this is a study of the representations of the nation in the urban elites of Buenos Aires. The different popular sectors tied to rural production or urban handicrafts, the immigrants open to all occupations, the recently emancipated African Porteños, in short, all of this urban population, did not need the elites' sociability at all. Courteous sociability was not for them, if the republic was often a trick and the Argentine nation an immaterial design. This analysis tells us little of their representations of the community of belonging, although from their urban sociability practices the vitality of the parochial community can be inferred. The development of contractual associations was not, as we have seen, a phenomenon which concerned exclusively the world of the elites. Rather, this type of contractual tie went beyond civil codes of conduct that functioned in the elites as a criterion of social and national belonging.

What then was this nation, whose criteria of belonging not only were not shared by the population as a whole but which also paved the way to exclusion? The Porteño elites do not appear to have asked themselves such a question, or in any event not in these terms, because the nation we speak of is the society to be constructed, of which these elites believed themselves to be the sole architects. Indeed, to postulate association as the basis of the social tie is a way of thinking of this tie in a totally different context to that of traditional society. In other words, it is a means of thinking of another society, a society which as the result of a contract allowed the individual to pass from a natural state to a social state. A society that, as we have seen, was also the product of a civilized sociability, an aspect which Sarmiento had already indicated in 1845 as indispensable in the eradication of the *caudillos'* power, whom he held responsible for the weakening of national power. Furthermore, Sarmiento found in associative civility relationships the nucleus of a civil society on which the nation was to be founded as a political community of belonging. In this way, civility was the sociability of the republic, which after the failure of the political regime installed by Juan Manuel de Rosas, was converted into the principle of national sociability.

The nation's criteria of belonging oscillated between civic-mindedness and civility, and I hoped to go deeper here into the extent of this ambivalence when it was this that fed the identity of the nation. The question is not merely of speculative interest. In Argentina, The identification of the civic nation with civilized sociability facilitated the resolution of a great political problem, namely that of conciliating the new principle of sovereignty, which legitimized independence from Spain, with the inheritance of the right of conquest and colonization which granted the Argentine elites a social and political preeminence, in situating them naturally at the head of public affairs. With the identification between civilization and national sociability, the elites could sustain the process consolidating a State which would be the expression of a "nationality," without jeopardizing its own power, because the principle of nationality which helped to legitimize the power of the State was associated with a series of relational codes identified with the urban elites. The confirmation of civilization as the expression of a national identity thus legitimized the elites' civilizing role, which led them to the conquest of national territory, firstly against the "barbaric" *caudillos* and then against the "savage" Indians. Furthermore, the diffusion of codes of civil conduct, previously aimed at regulating relationships between the well-to-do, functioned as an important self-control mechanism aimed to guarantee a monopoly on force and securing the centrality of coercive power for the State. It is worth mentioning that these behaviors, which brought courtesy and good manners to the foreground as mechanisms of social control, at the same time made discussion one of the principal means of exchange. While strengthening the State's coercive power, civility as a relational value, due to the practice to which it was associated, opened up a space in which the emergence of a critical opinion was possible. A strong State, yes, but to a certain extent a State under surveillance.

In closing, we might ask why the political community of belonging is thought of as a product of a sociability. Throughout the analysis I have said that this situation follows at least two reasons. The first is connected to the difficulty of conceiving it from the available "models" for nation. The second is concerned with the political process in the region and the resulting difficulty of building the State over the old colonial administrative structure. But perhaps there is a deeper reason which concerns the cultural mutation I mentioned at the beginning of my analysis. Independence, like modernity, provoked the breakup of the collective conscience that western society had known since the Reformation and its religious wars, of which the Hispanic world had remained on the margins. The revolution, so to speak, repaired this breach. It may be no coincidence that men then sought answers in the notion of sociability. But this fragmentation of the collective conscience is all the more frightful here in occurring at the same time as the disappearance of the king figure, whose principal function was, for Hobbes, to make unity possible. This might allow an understanding of the deep reasons which led the cultural elites to imagine the nation firstly as a society state, given that in all probability, independence not only raised the problem of the foundation of political power but more importantly the foundation of the social tie.

SOURCES & BIBLIOGRAPHY

Manuscripts

GENERAL ARCHIVE OF THE NATION (AGN)

Police

POLICE, GENERAL INDEX

1836–1836	x 44-10-1
1850–1850	x 44-10-2
1859–1859	x 44-10-4

POLICE

1856–1856	x 32-4-4
1856–1856	x 13-3-4
1827	x 14-5-4
1827	x 14-5-6
1828	x 14-8-7
1828	x 14-9-1
1829	x 15-1-5
1829	x 15-1-6
1830	x 15-6-7
1836–1836	x 47-7-5
1837	x 15-10-1
1831	x 15-10-2
1831–1840	x 31-10-1
1832	x 15-10-5
1832	x 15-10-6
1833	x 16-3-4
1833	x 16-3-5
1834	x 16-4-7
1835	x 16-7-3
1853	x 18-9-2

POLICE, JAILS

1832–1852	x 31-10-2

POLICE, ARMY

1833	x 40-2-6

POLICE, CIVIC FESTIVITIES, PUBLIC JAIL

1829	x 36-2-9

POLICE, SUPERIOR ORDERS

1821–1836	x 32-7-1
1829	x 32-11-5
1830	x 32-11-7
1836	x 33-2-6
1836	x 33-2-7
1837	x 33-3-2
1837	x 33-3-3
1838	x 33-3-6
1839	x 33-3-8
18402	x 33-4-2
1840	x 33-4-3
1840–1841	x 33-4-4
1839–1842	x 33-4-5
1851	x 33-7-4
	x 33-7-5
	x 33-7-6
	x 33-7-7
	x 33-7-8
1857	x 33-11-5
	x 33-11-6

POLICE, PARTS OF THE CITY

1833	x 33-1-9
1833	x 33-2-2
1834	x 33-2-2
1836	x 33-2-8

POLICE, PARTS OF THE COUNTRYSIDE

1829	x 32-11-6

POLICE, ROSAS' SECRETARIAT

1830–1850	x 23-9-9
1833	x 16-3-4
1833	x 16-3-5

POLICE, AFRICAN SOCIETIES

1845–1864	x 31-11-5

Colección López, Room VII

Files consulted: 21–1–12; 21–1–13; 21–1–1; 21–1–2; 21–1–6; 21–1–7; 21–1–16; 21–1–17.

National Library Manuscript Collection

Files consulted: 1825–1855.

Colección Casavalle

Gutiérrez, Juan María, "La Sociedad Literaria y su obra," files 7–8.

Archivo Tomás Guido

VII 16–1–10

Archivo Lavalle

VII. Files consulted: 1–3–6; 7–1–6.

Map Archive

Map of the city of Buenos Aires with ecclesiastical division into 12 parishes, 1859.

Map of the city and administrative and statistical table of the State, with arrangement of best data. The map according to the new nomenclatures of the streets and the demonstrative and statistical table according to most recent measurements and the best data from recent years on population, wealth, etc. of the areas of the countryside. Buenos Aires, 1858.

Map of the city of Buenos Aires with police division into 13 sections, 1859.

Map of the city of Buenos Aires with division into 12 courts, by Solveira, 1862.

ARCHIVE OF THE MUSEO MITRE

Administrative map of the Capital of the State of Buenos Aires, by N. Grondona, 1856.

Map of the city according to the new nomenclature of its principal streets, 1860.

Topographic map of the names of the principal streets of the city of Buenos Aires and of its temples, squares, public buildings and barracks in the year 1822.

Topographic map of the city of Buenos Aires and its surroundings, dedicated to his Excellency and Illustrious Restorer of Laws Don Juan Manuel de Rosas (property of the Printer's of the Commerce and Lithography of the State), 1836.

ARCHIVE OF THE GRAND LODGE OF ARGENTINA (AGLA)

Unión del Plata Lodge
Actas. Documentos varios (1858–1875): box 21.
Libro de matrículas 1856–1859: book 2.
Libro de actas 1856–1861: book 3.
Libro de actas 1861–1867: book 4.

Consuelo del Infortunio Lodge
Correspondencia 1858–1873: box 8.
Libro de actas 1857–1861: box 27.
Actas de compañeros 1857–1868: box 28.
Actas 1861–1867: box 29.

Tolerancia Lodge

Libro de actas 1860–1867: box 30.

Regeneración Lodge
Libro de actas 1857–1860: box 36.
Libro de actas, compañeros 1858–1883: box 38.
Libro de actas, maestros 1858–1887: box 39.

Lealtad Lodge
Correspondencia 1858–1861: box 27.
Libro de actas 1857–1860: book 41.
Libro de asistencias 1859–1861: book 42.

Constancia Lodge
Copiador de cartas 1858: box 474/475.
Registro de diplomas s.f.: box 477.
Libro negro s.f.: box 478.
Nómina de miembros s.f.: box 480.

Asistencia 1858–1864: box 483.

Sol de Mayo Lodge
Libro de actas 1860–1863: book 45.
Actas de compañeros s.f.: book 49.
Actas de maestros s.f.: book 50.
Libro de beneficencia: book 53.
Correspondencia: book 4.

Unidad y Amistad Lodge
Documentos varios 1858–1865: box 665.
Documentos varios 1858–1870: box 760.

Unione Italiana Lodge
Libro de Actas 1858–1874: box 25.
Documentos varios (undated): box 748.

Obediencia a la Ley Lodge
Documentos 1859–1870: box 8.
Asistencia 1859–1882: book 571.
Libro negro 1858–1894: book 583.
Copiador 1859–1885: book 584.
Copiador 1860–1878: book 585.
Libro de actas 1859–1865: book 586.

Verdad Lodge
Documentos 1859–1882: box 21.

Dios y Libertad Lodge
Correspondencia al GOA: book 21.

Les Amis de la Verité Lodge
Documentos 1860–1878: box 31.

Unión Lodge
Correspondencia: box 401.

Verdadera Iniciación Lodge
Libro de actas 1858–1859: box 21.

Constante Unión Lodge
Libro de actas 1858–1862: box 54.

Unión y Filantropía Lodge
Libro de actas 1858–1878: box 21.

Fraternidad y Beneficencia Lodge
Actas y documentos varios 1858–1865: box 665.
Correspondencia: book 21.

Amie des Naufragues Lodge
Matrículas 1856–1896: box 710.
Matrículas 1852–1856: box 711.
Libro de actas 1852: box 712.

Libro de actas 1857–1863: box 713.

Asistencias 1854–1859: box 755.

Inventario archivo 1854–1864: box 772.
Documentación varia 1852–1860: box 761.

Luz del Desierto Lodge
Book 1860–1879: box 37.

Grand General Secretariat
1858–1871: cajas no. 24 y 30.

Grand Central Lodge
1860–1864: box 24.

Various Lodges
1858–1876: box 40.

ARCHIVE OF THE GRAND MASONIC LODGE OF URUGUAY (AGLMU)

Minute books (unnumbered))
Logia Les Amis de la Patrie 1842–1862.
Logia Les Enfants du Nouveau Monde 1862.
Logia Misterio y Honor 1854–1860.
Logia Constante Amistad 1856–1862.
Logia Unión y Beneficencia 1856–1862.

Membership Lists (unnumbered)
Logia Les Amis de la Patrie.
Logia Asilo de la Virtud.
Logia Constante Amistad.
Logia Santa Rosa de Lima.

Archive of the Grand Central Lodge (unnumbered))
Correspondencia con logias de Buenos Aires.

Antecedentes de la fundación del Gran Oriente de la República Argentina.

BIBLIOTHÈQUE NATIONALE, PARIS. MASONIC COLLECTION

Argentina, Buenos Aires, loge Amie des Naufragés
Correspondance avec le GOF 1852–1875: FM2, 843.
Tableaux 1852–1875: FM2, 844.

Uruguay, Montevideo, loge Les Amis de la Patrie
Correspondance avec le GOF 1842–1850: FM2, 589.
Tableaux 1842–1850: FM2, 589.
Correspondance avec le GOF 1851–1905: FM2, 867.
Tableaux 1851–1875: FM2, 868.

Chile, Valparaíso, loge Union Fraternelle, loge Etoile du Pacifique
Tableaux: FM2, 845.

ARCHIVE OF THE PROGRESS CLUB (UNNUMBERED)
Libro de entradas y salidas de socios 1852–1863.
Memorias 1852–1863.

ARCHIVES OF THE MINISTRY OF FOREIGN RELATIONS, PARIS
Correspondance politique argentine 3 (1828); 4 (1829); 5 (1830–1832); 6 (1832–1833); 7 (1834–1836).

ARMY GENERAL ARCHIVE
The author has consulted the files concerning the military careers of Ángel Pacheco, Manuel J. García, Manuel de Irigoyen, Manuel Escalada, José M. Flores, José M. Paz y Weil, Bartolomé Mitre, Matías Zapiola, Juan A. Gelly y Obes, Benito Nazar, Pastor Obligado, José B. Gorostiaga, Francisco Pico, Manuel Hornos, Lucio Mansilla, Lucio V. Mansilla, José M. Zapiola, Santiago Albarracín, Antonio Lezica, Tomás de Iriarte, José M. Morales, Emilio Mitre, Domingo F. Sarmiento, Carlos Terrada, Félix Olazábal, Cruz Gorondo, Julián Martínez and Miguel de Azcuénaga.

Publications

PUBLIC DOCUMENTS AND COMPILATIONS OF PUBLIC SOURCES

Actas del Concejo Municipal de la Ciudad de Buenos Aires, 1856–1919, Buenos Aires, 1911–1921.

Acuerdos del extinguido Cabildo de Buenos Aires, Archivo General de la Nación, serie IV, tomo III, libros LXII, LXIII, LXIV, 1808–1809, tomo IV, 1810–1812, Buenos Aires, G. Kraft, 1927.

Almanaque de comercio de la ciudad de Buenos Aires para el año 1826, por J. J. Blondel, Buenos Aires, Imprenta del Estado, 1825. Reedición: Buenos Aires, Ediciones de la Flor, 1968.

——, 1829, 1830, 1833, 1834, 1836.

Almanaque de la ciudad de Buenos Aires, Buenos Aires, 1851.

Almanaque comercial. Guía del forastero para el estado de Buenos Aires, Buenos Aires, Imprenta de La Tribuna, 1855.

Almanaque Agrícola e Industrial de Buenos Aires. Prontuario de Agricultura, Jardinería, Ganadería, Economía Doméstica, Hijiene, Medicina, Buenos Aires, P. Morta Editor, 1861.

Angelis, Pedro de, *Recopilación de Leyes y Decretos promulgados en Buenos Aires desde el 25 de mayo de 1810 hasta el fin de diciembre de 1835*, Buenos Aires, Imprenta del Estado, 1837.

Antecedentes de la Asociación de Mayo, 1837–1937, Homenaje del Honorable Concejo Deliberante de la Ciudad de Buenos Aires en el Centenario de su Fundación, Buenos Aires, Concejo Deliberante, 1937.

Barba, Enrique (comp.), *Correspondencia entre Rosas, Quiroga y López*, Buenos Aires, Hachette, 1958.

Bases del Instituto Histórico–Geográfico, Montevideo, Imprenta Nacional, 1843.

Bases Orgánicas del Instituto Histórico–Geográfico del Río de la Plata, Buenos Aires, Imprenta de La Tribuna, 1856.

Cámara de Senadores del Estado de Buenos Aires, *Diario de sesiones de la Cámara de Senadores del Estado de Buenos Aires*, Buenos Aires, Imprenta El Orden, 1858.

Candiotti, Marcial, *Bibliografía doctoral de la Universidad de Buenos Aires y catálogo cronológico de las tesis del primer centenario, 1821–1920*, Buenos Aires, Talleres Gráficos, 1920.

Canter, Juan, "Algunos impresos raros de la época de Rosas," *Boletín del Instituto de Historia Argentina y Americana* 1:25, 257–271.

Carril, Bonifacio del, *Monumenta Iconográfica. Paisajes, tipos, usos y costumbres en la Argentina, 1536–1860*, Buenos Aires, Emecé, 1964.

——, *Las litografías argentinas de Géricault*, Buenos Aires, Emecé, 1991.

Carril, Bonifacio del, et al., *Iconografía de Buenos Aires. La ciudad de Garay hasta 1852*, Buenos Aires, Municipalidad de Buenos Aires, 1982.

Celesia, Ernesto N., "Anexo documental," in *Rosas, aporte para su historia*, Buenos Aires, Peuser, 1954.

Colección de leyes y decretos militares concernientes al Ejército y Armada de la República Argentina, 1810–1896, con anotaciones de derogaciones, modificaciones, etc., por E. Domínguez, Buenos Aires, Compañía Sur Americana de Billetes de Banco, 1898.

Conde Montero, M., "Correspondencia inédita de Doña Encarnación Ezcurra de Rosas," *Revista Argentina de Ciencias Políticas* 28 (October 1923 – March 1924): 106–126.

Constitución para la Orden Masónica en la República Argentina, Buenos Aires, Imprenta Litográfica Jacobo Peuser, 1891.

Constitución y Reglamentos Generales de la Masonería Escocesa para la Confederación Argentina y Valle de Buenos Aires, Buenos Aires, Imprenta Americana, 1857.

Diario de Sesiones de la Cámara de Diputados de la Provincia de Buenos Aires, 1854–1869, nine vols..

Diario de Sesiones de la Convención del Estado de Buenos Aires, Buenos Aires, Imprenta del Comercio del Plata, 1860.

Diario de Sesiones de la Honorable Junta de Representantes de la Provincia de Buenos Aires, Buenos Aires, 1823–1851.

Diario de Sesiones de la Sala de Representantes de la Provincia de Buenos Aires, 1852–1854, Buenos Aires, Imprenta de la Sociedad Tipográfica Bonaerense, 1864–1865.

Diccionario de Buenos Aires. Guía del forastero, Buenos Aires, Imprenta del Porvenir, 1863.

Digesto de ordenanzas, reglamentos, acuerdos, etc., de la Municipalidad de Buenos Aires, Buenos Aires, Imprenta de la Sociedad Anónima, 1873.

Documentos para la historia argentina, vol. 17, *Relaciones interprovinciales. La Liga del Litoral, 1829–1833*, Buenos Aires, Instituto de Investigaciones Históricas, 1922.

Espinosa, Gervasio, "Apuntes autobiográficos," in José Juan Biedma, *Vida militar del general Gervasio Espinosa*, Buenos Aires, 1894, 123–139.

Estatuto de la Asociación de Amigos de la historia natural del Plata, creada por superior decreto del 6 de mayo de 1854, Buenos Aires, Imprenta de La Revista, 1855.

Estatuto de la Sociedad Pastoril de Amigos del País y contrato con Samuel K. Tebbets, Buenos Aires, Imprenta de la Independencia, 1837.

Estatuto de la Sociedad Pastoril de Merinos; contrato con su empresario José Pérez, Buenos Aires, Imprenta Argentina, 1836.

Estatuto de la Sociedad Porteña y contrato con su promotor Manuel Escalada, Buenos Aires, Imprenta de la Gaceta Mercantil, 1837.

Estatutos, Reglamentos y Constituciones argentinas (1811–1898), Buenos Aires, Universidad de Buenos Aires, Departamento Editorial, 1956, col. "Documentos para la Historia Argentina," no. 23.

Fernández Latour, Olga, *Cantares históricos de la tradición argentina*, Buenos Aires, Peuser, 1960.

"Informe sobre pulquerías y tabernas el año de 1784," *Boletín del Archivo General de la Nación* (Mexico City) 18 (1947): 3/4,198–236, 368.

Instituto de Estudios de Administración Local, *Planos de ciudades iberoamericanas y filipinas existentes en el Archivo de Indias*, Madrid, Instituto de Estudios de Administración Local, 1951.

Irazusta, Julio, *Vida política de Juan Manuel de Rosas a través de su correspondencia*, eight vols., Buenos Aires, Albatros, 1970.

Lattes, Alfredo E., and R. Poczter, "Muestra del censo de la población de la ciudad de Buenos Aires de 1855," *Cuadernos del Instituto Torcuato Di Tella* (Buenos Aires) 5 (1968).

Legislación Argentina, *Colección completa de leyes nacionales sancionadas por el Honorable Congreso durante los años 1852 a 1917*, 19 vols., compiled by Augusto Da Rocha, Buenos Aires, Librería de la Facultad, 1918.

Leguizamón, Martiniano, *Papeles de Rosas*, Buenos Aires, 1935.

Mabragaña, Heráclito, *Los mensajes. Historia del desenvolvimiento de la Nación Argentina (redactados cronológicamente, 1810–1910)*, six vols., Buenos Aires, Comisión Nacional del Centenario, 1910.

Memoria de la Municipalidad de Buenos Aires, Buenos Aires, Imprenta de La Revista, 1859–1861.

Mitre, Bartolomé, *Bases orgánicas del Instituto Histórico–Geográfico*, Buenos Aires, Imprenta de La Tribuna, 1856.

——, *Reglamento consultivo del Instituto Histórico–Geográfico*, Buenos Aires, 1856.

Moores, Guillermo H., *Colección cronológica de vistas de Buenos Aires*, Buenos Aires, Instituto Bonaerense de Numismática y Antigüedades/Editorial Kraft, 1939.

——, *Estampas y vistas de la ciudad de Buenos Aires, 1599–1895*, Buenos Aires, Peuser, 1945.

Outes, Félix, *Cartas y planos de los siglos XVII, XVIII y el primer decenio del siglo XIX*, Buenos Aires, Instituto de Investigaciones Geográficas de la Facultad de Filosofía y Letras, 1930.

——, *Iconografía de Buenos Aires*, Buenos Aires, Museo Etnográfico/Imprenta Coni, 1940, publications series B, no. 2, twenty pages.

Ravignani, Emilio (comp.), *Asambleas Constituyentes Argentinas*, seis vols., Buenos Aires, Instituto de Investigaciones Históricas, 1937–1939.

Registro Oficial de la Provincia de Buenos Aires, Buenos Aires, Imprenta del Mercurio, 1828–1851.

Registro Oficial de la República Argentina; comprende documentos espedidos desde 1810 hasta 1873, oficial publication, Buenos Aires, Imprenta de la República, 1879.

Registro Oficial del Gobierno de Buenos Aires, 1851–1862, Buenos Aires, Imprenta Americana, 1851–1862.

Reglamento de la Asociación Farmacéutica Bonaerense, sancionado el 30 de junio de 1859, reformado sobre el originario del 16 de octubre de 1856, Buenos Aires, 1859.

Reglamento de la Bolsa de Comercio sancionado en Asamblea General de socios, Buenos Aires, 1858.

Reglamento de la Sala Española de Comercio, Buenos Aires, Imprenta y Librería de B. Hortelano, 1852.

Reglamento interno de la Resp. Log de San Juan de Esc. regularmente constituida la Or. de Montevideo en año de la V. L. 5830, bajo el título distintivo Asilo de la Virtud, Montevideo, Imprenta del Telégrafo, 5836.

Reglamento para la Sociedad de las Escuelas de Lancaster, Montevideo, Imprenta de Pérez, 1822.

Rodríguez, Gregorio F. (comp.), *Contribución histórica y documental*, three vols., Buenos Aires, 1921–1924.

Sampay, Arturo, *Las Constituciones de la Argentina (1810–1972)*, Buenos Aires, Eudeba, 1975.

Sociedad Nuestra Señora del Carmen, *Estatutos*, Buenos Aires, 1862.

Sociedad Tipográfica Bonaerense, *Estatutos*, Buenos Aires, 1858.

Taullard, Alfredo, *Los planos más antiguos de Buenos Aires, 1580–1880*, Buenos Aires, Peuser, 1940.

Trelles, Manuel R., *Registro estadístico del Estado de Buenos Aires*, three vols., Buenos Aires, 1854–1859.

Vilaseca, Clara (comp.), *Cartas de Mariquita Sánchez. Biografía de una época*, Buenos Aires, Peuser, 1952.

MEMOIRS, TRAVEL CHRONICLES, POLITICAL WRITING

Agrelo, José Pedro, "Autobiografía, 1810–1816," in *Memorias y autobiografías*, vol. 2, Buenos Aires, Museo Histórico Nacional, 1910, 223–262.

Alberdi, Juan Bautista, *Fragmento preliminar al estudio del derecho* (1837), Buenos Aires, Biblos, 1984.

——, "Doble armonía entre objeto de esta institución, con una exigencia de nuestro desarrollo social; y de esta exigencia con otra general del espíritu humano" (1838), in *Antecedentes de la Asociación de Mayo, 1837–1937*, Homenaje del Honorable Concejo Deliberante de la ciudad de Buenos Aires en el Centenario de su Fundación, Buenos Aires, Concejo Deliberante, 1937.

——, *La República Argentina, treinta y siete años después de su Revolución*, Valparaíso, 25 May 1847.

——, *Bases y puntos de partida para la organización política de la República Argentina* (1852), Buenos Aires, Eudeba, 1966.

——, *Escritos póstumos*, Buenos Aires, 1895–1901.

Arnold, Prudencio, *Un soldado argentino* (1884), Buenos Aires, Eudeba, 1970.

Bacle & Co., *Trajes y costumbres de Buenos Aires*, facsimile edition with prologue by Alejandro González Garaña, Buenos Aires, Vian, 1947.

Beaumont, John, *Travels in Buenos Aires, Entre Ríos and Uruguay* [*Viajes por Buenos Aires, Entre Ríos y la Banda Oriental (1820–1827)*.

Belgrano, Manuel, "Autobiografía." in *Memorias y autobiografías*, vol. 2, Buenos Aires, Museo Histórico Nacional, 1910, 91–110.

Beruti, Juan Manuel, *Memorias curiosas de los sujetos que han sido gobernadores y virreyes de las provincias del Río de la Plata*, in *Biblioteca de Mayo*, vol. 4, Buenos Aires, Senado de la Nación, 1960, 3647–4150.

Biedma, José Juan, "La revolución de los restauradores de 1833. Diario de las operaciones del ejército restaurador de las leyes llevado por su segundo jefe, general M. B. Rolón," *Revista Nacional* (Buenos Aires) 19:37, 1904.

Bilbao, Francisco, "Sociabilidad chilena," *El Crepúsculo*, 20 June 1844.

——, *La contra–pastoral*, Buenos Aires, Imprenta y Litografía Berheim y Boneo, 1862.

——, *La América en peligro* (1863), Santiago de Chile, Ercilla, 1941.

Bilbao, Manuel, *Historia de Rosas*, Buenos Aires, Imprenta de Buenos Aires, 1868.

——, *Tradiciones y recuerdos de Buenos Aires*, Buenos Aires, 1934.

——, *Buenos Aires. Desde su fundación hasta nuestros días. Especialmente el período comprendido entre los siglos XVIII y XIX*, Buenos Aires, Imprenta Juan A. Alsina, 1902.

Breve descripción de las exequias en honor de los soldados que murieron por la defensa de Buenos Aires, Buenos Aires, Imprenta de los Niños Expósitos, 1807.

Bustamante, José Luis, *Bosquejo de la historia civil y política de Buenos Aires desde la batalla de Monte Caseros*, Buenos Aires, Imprenta J. A. Bernheim, 1856.

Calzadillas, Santiago, *Las beldades de mi tiempo* (1891), Buenos Aires, Estrada, 1944.

Cartas escritas por el muy honorable Felipe Dormer Stanhope, conde de Chesterfield, a su hijo, two vols., translation by Tomás de Iriarte, Buenos Aires, Imprenta de la Libertad, 1833.

Cinco años en Buenos Aires, 1820–1825, por un inglés (London, 1825), prologue by Alejo B. González Garaño, Buenos Aires, Solar, 1942.

D'Amico, Carlos, *Buenos Aires, sus hombres, su política (1860–1890)* (Mexico City, 1890), Buenos Aires, Americana, 1952.

Darwin, Charles Robert, *Diary of the Voyage of HMS Beagle* [Spanish translation *Diario del viaje de un naturalista alrededor del mundo en el navío de S. M. "Beagle"*], two vols., Madrid, Espasa–Calpe, 1921.

Delacour, Adolphe, "Voyage dans l'Amérique Méridionale: Buenos Aires, Montevideo," *Revue Indépendante* (Paris), 10 June 1844, 3–27.

——, "Le Rio de la Plata, Buenos Aires, Montevideo," *Revue Indépendante*, Paris, Jicois, 1845.

D'Hastel, Adolfo, *Doce litografías coloreadas de la Plata, 1839–1840*, Buenos Aires, Kraft, 1944.

"Diario de Juan José Echevarría," *Revista del Instituto de Investigaciones Históricas* 16 (1933): 55–57.

Diario de un soldado, Buenos Aires, Archivo General de la Nación / Comisión Nacional Ejecutiva 150° aniversario de la Revolución de Mayo, 1960.

Díaz, Antonio, *Historia política y militar de las Repúblicas del Plata desde el año 1828 hasta 1866*, Montevideo, 1877.

——, *Memorias inéditas del general oriental Don César Díaz*, Buenos Aires, 1878.

Díaz, Ramón, *La Lira Argentina*, Buenos Aires, 1824.

Domínguez, Luis, *Historia argentina*, Buenos Aires, Imprenta El Orden, 1861.

D'Orbigny, Alcide, *Voyage dans les deux Amériques, publié sous la direction de...*, Paris, Furne et Cie, 1853.

Dumas, Alexandre, *Memorias de José Garibaldi* (1861), Barcelona, Muñoz Moya y Montevedra, 1985.

Echeverría, Esteban, *La cautiva* (1837), Buenos Aires, Centro Editor de América Latina, 1979.

——, "Ojeada retrospectiva sobre el movimiento intelectual en el Plata desde el año 1837" (Montevideo, 1846), in *Dogma socialista de la Asociación de Mayo*, Buenos Aires, Perrot, 1958.

——, *Dogma socialista de la Asociación de Mayo, precedido de una ojeada retrospectiva sobre el movimiento intelectual en el Plata en el año 37*, Montevideo, Imprenta del Nacional, 1846.

——, *El matadero* (1871), Buenos Aires, Centro Editor de América Latina, 1979.

Esteves Sagui, Miguel, *Apuntes históricos*, Buenos Aires, Academia Nacional de la Historia, 1980, col. "Biblioteca de Publicaciones Documentales."

Estrada, Manuel, "Lecciones sobre la historia de la República Argentina," *Revista Argentina* 4 (1866).

Estrada y Gelpi, *El catolicismo y la Democracia. Refutación de la América en Peligro*, Buenos Aires, undated

Extracto de un papel tomado a los masones, cuyo título es como sigue: Máximas e Instrucciones Políticas que el Gran Oriente Español ha mandado poner en ejecución a todas las logias de la Masonería Egipciana, Córdoba (España), Imprenta Real, 1824; reedition, Buenos Aires, Imprenta de la Independencia, 1840.

Farsa de la Francmasonería en Buenos Aires, por el Mugiense, Buenos Aires, Imprenta de La Revista, 1858.

Frías, Félix, "La sepultura eclesiástica," in *El pensamiento argentino*, Buenos Aires, 1863.

Fulias, Antonino, *Farsa de la Francmasonería en Buenos Aires, por el Mugiense*, Buenos Aires, Imprenta de La Revista, 1858.

——, *Refutación de los errores filosóficos dogmáticos del Dr. Pesce contenidos en su folleto "Roma y la Francmasonería," por el Rev. P. Lector y Examinador Sinodal*, Buenos Aires, Imprenta de La Revista, 1859.

Galería de Celebridades Argentinas. Biografía de los personajes más notables del Río de la Plata, por los señores B. Mitre, J. M. Gutiérrez, M. Lozano, M. García, T. J. Guido, M. Moreno, L. Domínguez, M. Lacasa, Buenos Aires, Imprenta Americana, 1857.

Gálvez, Víctor, *Memorias de un viejo. Escenas y costumbres de la República Argentina* (1888), three vols., Buenos Aires, Peuser, 1889.

Guerra, capitán José María, *Memoria histórico–militar del capitán de inválidos Don José María Guerra, actuante en la Revolución de los Restauradores (1833) y en la campaña libertadora del General Lavalle contra Rosas*, introduction, notes and review by Agustín Rivero Astengo, Buenos Aires, Ed. de la Comisión de Homenaje a los Libres del Sur, 1939.

Guido, Tomás, "Reseña histórica de los sucesos de Mayo," in *Memorias y autobiografías*, Buenos Aires, Museo Histórico Nacional, 1910.

Gutiérrez, Juan María, *Pensamientos, máximas, sentencias, juicios, etc., de escritores, oradores y hombres de estado de la República Argentina*, Buenos Aires, Biblioteca Americana, 1859.

——, *Apuntes biográficos de escritores, oradores y hombres de Estado de la República Argentina*, Buenos Aires, Imprenta de Mayo, 1860.

——, *Noticias históricas sobre el origen y desarrollo de la enseñanza pública y superior en Buenos Aires, desde la época de la extinción de la compañía de Jesús en el año 1767 hasta poco después de fundada la Universidad de 1821*, con noticias biográficas, datos estadísticos y datos curiosos inéditos o poco conocidos, Buenos Aires, 1868.

——, "La primera sociedad literaria y la primera revista en el Río de la Plata," *Revista del Río de la Plata*, vol. 1, Buenos Aires, 1871.

Head, Francis Bond, *The Pampas and the Andes*, London, 1826, Spanish translation *Las Pampas y los Andes*, Buenos Aires, Hyspamérica, 1986.

Historia, Doctrina y Fin u Objeto de la Franc–masonería. Por un franc–masón que no lo es más. Dedicada a las gentes honradas. Traducida de la 2da. ed. francesa por un argentino ansioso del bien del país, Buenos Aires, Imprenta de Mayo, 1858.

Hogg, Ricardo, *Yerba vieja*, vol. 1, Buenos Aires, Casa E. Julio Suárez, 1940.

Hortelano, Benito, *Memorias*, Madrid, Espasa–Calpe, 1936.

Iriarte, Tomás de, *Ante el tribunal de la opinión pública*, Buenos Aires, Imprenta Republicana, 1833.

——, *Memorias*, 11 vols., preliminary study by Enrique de Gandía, Buenos Aires, Ediciones Argentinas, 1944–1969.

Isabelle, Arsène, *Voyage à Buenos Aires et à Porto Alegre de 1830 à 1834*, Havre, Imp. de J. Morlent, 1835 [Spanish translation: *Viaje a Argentina, Uruguay y Brasil, en 1830*, Buenos Aires, Americana, 1943].

Isola, Albérico, *Usos y costumbres de Buenos Aires*, Buenos Aires, 1844.

King, John Anthony, *Twenty–four years in the Argentine Republic covering the adventures of the autor, the civil and military history of the country and a comparison of its political conditions before and during the administration of the Governor Rosas* (London, 1852), [Spanish translation: *Veinticuatro años en la República Argentina que abarcan las aventuras del autor, la historia civil y militar del país y una relación de sus condiciones políticas antes y durante la administración del gobernador Rosas*] Buenos Aires, La Cultura Argentina, 1921.

Lamas, Andrés, *Apuntes históricos sobre las agresiones del dictador argentino Don Juan Manuel de Rosas contra la independencia de la República Oriental del Uruguay*, Montevideo, 1849.

La revolución de 1833. Exposición del Gobernador y Capitán General de la Provincia de Buenos Aires, a que dan lugar los documentos presedentes, Buenos Aires, October 1833.

Lastarria, José Victoriano, *Recuerdos literarios* (1878), Santiago de Chile, Zig–Zag, 1967.

López, Lucio V., *La gran aldea (costumbres bonaerenses)*, Buenos Aires, Imprenta de Martín Biedma, 1884.

López, Vicente Fidel, *La revolución argentina. Su origen, sus guerras y su desarrollo político hasta 1830*, Buenos Aires, Carlos Casavalle Editor, 1861.

——, *Historia de la República Argentina. Su origen, su revolución, su desarrollo político hasta 1852*, ten vols., Buenos Aires, Carlos Casavalle, 1883.

——, "La gran semana de 1810. Crónica de la Revolución de Mayo" (1885), in *Evocaciones históricas*, Buenos Aires, Jackson, 1945.

——, "Autobiografía" (Buenos Aires, 1896), in *Evocaciones históricas*, Buenos Aires, El Ateneo, 1929.

Mac Cann, William, *Two Thousand Miles' Ride through the Argentine Provinces* (London, 1853), translation by José Luis Busaniche *Viaje a caballo por las provincias argentinas*, Buenos Aires, Imprenta Ferrari, 1939.

Mangel du Mesnil, Émile, *Notoriedades del Plata*, Buenos Aires, Imprenta de La Tribuna, 1862.

Manual de Buenos Ayres. Explicación del plano topográfico que manifiesta la distribución y nuevos nombres de las principales calles de esta ciudad, plazas, edificios públicos y cuarteles. Con agregación del sistema que se ha seguido en la nueva numeración. 1823, manuscrito anónimo, 1823. First edition, with preface and paleographic transcription by Professor Jorge Ochoa de Eguileor, Buenos Aires, Municipalidad de Buenos Aires, 1981.

Marmier, Xavier, *Buenos Aires y Montevideo en 1850* (1851), translation and prologue by José Luis Busaniche, Buenos Aires, El Ateneo, 1948.

Mármol, José, *Amalia* (Montevideo, 1851), Madrid, Espasa–Calpe, 1978, col. "Austral."

Martínez, E., "Carta al ministro Andrés Lamas, Montevideo, 4 de octubre de 1853," *Historia*, vol. 3, 1960, 312–313.

Miers, John, *Travels in Chili and La Plata* (London, 1826), Spanish translation *Viaje al Plata, 1819–1824*, Buenos Aires, Solar Hachette, 1968.

Mitre, Bartolomé, "Biografía de Belgrano," in Gutiérrez, Juan María (dir.), *Galería de Celebridades Argentinas*, Buenos Aires, 1857. The third edition, revised and extended, was published with the title *Historia de Belgrano y de la Independencia Argentina*, Buenos Aires, 1876–1877.

——, *Historia de San Martín y de la Emancipación Sud–Americana*, Buenos Aires, Félix Lajouane, 1890.

——, *Diario de juventud: 1843–1846*, Buenos Aires, Instituto Mitre, 1936.

Morales, Ernesto (comp.), *Epistolario de Don Juan María Gutiérrez*, Buenos Aires, Instituto Cultural J. V. González, 1942.

Moreno, Manuel, *Vida y memorias de Mariano Moreno*, Buenos Aires, 1918.

Moussy, Martin de, *Description géographique et statistique de la Confédération Argentine*, three vols., Paris, 1860–1864 [Spanish translation: *Descripción geográfica y estadística de la Confederación Argentina*, Buenos Aires, Ediciones Culturales Argentinas, 1963].

Murray Forbes, John, *Eleven Years in Buenos Aires* [Spanish translation *Once años en Buenos Aires, 1820–1831*], compilation, translation and annotations by Felipe Espil, Buenos Aires, Emecé, 1956.

Núñez, Ignacio, *Noticias históricas, políticas y estadísticas de las Provincias Unidas del Río de la Plata, con apéndice sobre la usurpación de Montevideo por los gobiernos portugueses y brasileros* (London, 1825), Buenos Aires, La Cultura Argentina, 1952.

Page, Theogène, "Affaires de Buenos Aires / Expédition de la France contre la République Argentine," *La Revue de Deux Mondes*, vol. 25, Paris, February 1841, 301–370.

Parchappe, Narciso, *Expedición fundadora del fuerte 25 de Mayo en cruz de guerra, año 1828*, Buenos Aires, Eudeba, 1977.

Parish, Woodbine, *Buenos Aires and the provinces of the River Plate since their discovery and conquest by the Spanish* (London, 1838), [Spanish translation *Buenos Aires y las provincias del Río de la Plata desde su descubrimiento y la conquista por los españoles*], preliminary study by J. L. Busaniche, Buenos Aires, Hachette, 1958.

Pellegrini, Carlos E., *Recuerdos del Río de la Plata*, Buenos Aires, Litografía de las Artes, 1841.

Pesce, Alejandro, *Roma y la Franc–masonería. Refutación de algunas palabras contra la Franc–masonería vertidas por D. Martín Avertino Piñero*, Buenos Aires, 1858.

Poucel, Benjamin, *Les Otages de Durazno, souvenirs du Río de la Plata pendant l'intervention anglo–française de 1845 à 1851*, Paris, A. Faure, 1864.

Rasgos biográficos sobre D. Bernardino Rivadavia por D. R. (Dardo Rocha?), Buenos Aires, Imprenta de las Artes, 1857.

Refutación Solemne de los Rasgos Biográficos y Discursos Escritos y Pronunciados en Buenos Aires por los Señores Gutiérrez, Alsina, Mitre y otros, con motivo de los funerales de Don Bernardino Rivadavia. Escrita por un Porteño de Nota, Buenos Aires, 1857.

Reyes, Antonio, *Ubicaciones y memorias*, Buenos Aires, 1883.

Rivera Indarte, José, *Rosas y sus opositores* (1884), Buenos Aires, Jackson, 1945.

Ruano, Agustín Gerónimo, "Memoria sobre la revolución de octubre de 1833," *Revista del Instituto de Historia y Geografía del Uruguay*, vol. 14, Montevideo, 1938, 287–304.

Saavedra, Cornelio, "Instrucción que dió don Cornelio Saavedra a sus apoderados en el juicio de residencia," in Zimmermann Saavedra, *Don Cornelio Saavedra, presidente de la junta de gobierno de 1810. Bosquejo histórico documental*, Buenos Aires, J. Lajouane, 1909.

——, *Memorias y autobiografías*, Buenos Aires, Emecé, 1944.

Sarmiento, Domingo Faustino, *Civilización i Barbarie. Vida de Juan Facundo Quiroga, i aspecto físico, costumbres, i ábitos de la República Argentina*, Santiago de Chile, Imprenta del Progreso, 1845.

——, *De la educación popular*, Santiago de Chile, J. Belin i Cía., 1849.

——, *Recuerdos de provincia* (Santiago de Chile, 1850), Buenos Aires, Kapelusz, 1966.

——, *Argirópolis o la capital de los Estados Confederados del Río de la Plata*, Santiago de Chile, J. Belin i Cía., 1850.

——, *Campaña del Ejército Grande* (Santiago de Chile, 1852), Buenos Aires, Kraft, 1957.

Ségur, Louis Gaston de, *Los franc–masones, lo que son, lo que hacen, lo que quieren*, Buenos Aires, Igon, 1877.

Senado de la Nación, *Biblioteca de Mayo. Diarios y crónicas*, Buenos Aires, Senado de la Nación, 1960.

——, *Biblioteca de Mayo. Periodismo*, vols. 7–9, Buenos Aires, Senado de la Nación, 1960.

Somellera, Andrés, *La tiranía de Rosas* (1886), Buenos Aires, Nuevo Cabildo, 1962.

Un Restaurador (A Restorer, pseudonym), *Los sucesos de octubre de 1833, o colección de los documentos principales conexos con los Restauradores*, Buenos Aires, Imprenta de la Independencia, 1834.

Valencia, Miguel, *Manual de los Masones Libres del Río de la Plata*, Buenos Aires, Imprenta Americana, 1856.

Varela, Florencio, *Escritos políticos, económicos y literarios* (1859), Buenos Aires, Freeland, 1975.

Vicuña Mackenna, Benjamín, *Páginas de mi diario durante tres años de viaje, 1853–54–55* (Santiago de Chile, 1856), Buenos Aires, Revista Americana de Buenos Aires, 1936.

——, *El ostracismo de O'Higgins*, Valparaíso, Imprenta del Mercurio, 1880.

Wilde, José Antonio, *Buenos Aires desde setenta años atrás*, Buenos Aires, Espasa–Calpe, 1948.

Wright, Agustín, *Los sucesos de octubre de 1833, o colección de los documentos principales conexos con los Restauradores. Por un Restaurador*, Buenos Aires, Imprenta de la Independencia, 1834.

Zapiola, José, *Recuerdos de treinta años, 1810–1840*, Santiago de Chile, Guillermo Miranda Editor, 1902.

——, *La Sociedad de Igualdad y sus enemigos*, Santiago de Chile, Guillermo Miranda Editor, 1902.

PERIODIC PRESS

Amigo del País (El), Buenos Aires, 1833.

Archivo Americano y Espíritu de la Prensa del Mundo, Buenos Aires, 1847–1851.

Avisador (El), Buenos Aires, 1833 (one issue only.)

Constitucional (El), Buenos Aires, 1833.

Defensor de los Derechos del Pueblo (El), Diario del mediodía. Buenos Aires, Buenos Aires, 1833.

Gaceta Mercantil. Periódico comercial, político y literario (La), Buenos Aires, 1823–1852.

Gaucho (El), Buenos Aires, 1830.

Gaucho Restaurador (El), Buenos Aires, 1834.

Grito Argentino (El), Montevideo, 1839.

Iris (El), Diario del Medio Día, Político, Literario y Mercantil, Buenos Aires, 1833.

Lucero (El), Buenos Aires, 1829–1833.

Moda (La.) Gacetín semanal de música, de poesía, de literatura, de costumbres, Buenos Aires, 1837–1838. Facsimile from the National Academy of History with introduction and notes by José Oria, Buenos Aires, Kraft, 1938.

Nacional (El), Buenos Aires, 1852–1893.

Negrita (La), Buenos Aires, 1833.

Orden (El), Buenos Aires, 1855–1858.

Pampero (El), Buenos Aires, 1829.

Progreso (El), Diario guvernativo, Buenos Aires, Buenos Aires, 1852–1853.

Reforma Pacífica (La), Diario político, literario y mercantil, Buenos Aires, 1856–1861.

Religión (La), Periódico teo–social, Buenos Aires, 1853–1861.

Telégrafo Mercantil (El), Rural, Político–económico e Historiográfico del Río de la Plata, Buenos Aires, 1801–1802. Facsimile published by the Junta de Historia y Numismática Americana, Buenos Aires, 1914–1915.

Tiempo (El), Buenos Aires, 1828–1829.

Tribuna (La), Buenos Aires, 1853–1884.

REFERENCE WORKS

Abad de Santillán, Diego, *Gran Enciclopedia Argentina*, nine vols., Buenos Aires, Ediar, 1956.

Archivo General de la Nación, *Índice temático general de unidades archivonómicas del período nacional. Gobierno*, Buenos Aires, AGN, 1977.

Biblioteca Nacional, *Un siglo de periódicos (políticos). Catálogo con fechas, 1800–1899*, Buenos Aires, Imprenta de la Biblioteca Nacional, 1935.

Biedma Pillado, Juan J., *Diccionario biográfico argentino*, Buenos Aires, AGN.

Briseño, Ramón, "Catálogo de las diferentes publicaciones periódicas que en el país ha habido, desde 1812 hasta 1859 inclusive," *Estadística bibliográfica de la literatura chilena*, Santiago de Chile, Imprenta Chilena, 1862.

Calvo, Carlos, *Nobiliario del Antiguo Virreinato del Río de la Plata*, six vols., Buenos Aires, Librería y Editorial "La Facultad," 1936.

Cámara de Diputados de la Nación, *Nómina de diputados de la nación por distrito electoral. Período 1854–1987*, four vols., Buenos Aires, Secretaría Parlamentaria, Dirección de Archivos, Publicaciones y Museo, Secretaría de Publicaciones e Investigaciones Históricas, 1988.

——, *Nómina alfabética de diputados de la nación. Período 1854–1987*, Buenos Aires, Secretaría Parlamentaria, Dirección de Archivos, Publicaciones y Museo, Secretaría de Publicaciones e Investigaciones Históricas, 1988.

Candiotti, Marcial, *Bibliografía doctoral de la Universidad de Buenos Aires y catálogo cronológico de las tesis del primer centenario, 1821–1920*, Buenos Aires, Talleres Gráficos, 1920.

Casares, Julio, *Diccionario ideológico de la lengua española*, Barcelona, Gustavo Gili, 1988.

Chandler, Tertius, and Gerald Fox, *3000 Years of Urban Growth*, London, Academic Press, 1974.

Cibotti, Ema, *Nómina de miembros de la comisión directiva de Unione e Benevolenza, 1858–1862* (unpublished typewritten edition.)

Corominas, José, *Diccionario crítico etimológico de la lengua castellana*, Berna, Francke, 1954.

Cutolo, Vicente Osvaldo, *Argentinos graduados en Chuquisaca*, Buenos Aires, Elche, 1963.

——, *Nuevo diccionario biográfico argentino (1750–1930)*, six vols., Buenos Aires, Elche, 1968.

Diccionario de la lengua castellana en que se explica el verdadero sentido de las voces, su naturaleza y calidad y las fraces o modos de hablar, los proverbios o refranes y otras cosas convenientes al uso de la lengua (Madrid, 1737), facsimile edition, Madrid, Gredos, 1969.

Diccionario enciclopédico de la masonería, reedited by Lorenzo Frau Abrimes and Rosendo Arús Arderiv, two vols., Buenos Aires, Kier, 1962.

Dictionnaire Universel d'Antoine Furetière (Le), facsimile edition, Paris, SNL Robert, 1978–1984.

Encyclopédie ou Dictionnaire raisonné..., vol. 15, Paris, 1765.

Figueroa, Pedro, *Diccionario biográfico de estranjeros en Chile*, Santiago de Chile, Imprenta Moderna, 1900.

Hardoy, Jorge Enrique, "Guía de colecciones de planos de ciudades iberoamericanas," in Francisco de Solano (coord.), *Estudios sobre las ciudades iberoamericanas*, Madrid, CSIC/ Instituto Gonzalo Fernández de Oviedo, 1983, 881–935.

Helguera, María del Carmen, *Nómina de miembros de la Tercera Instancia en la provincia de Buenos Aires (1812–1854)*, La Plata, Cámara de Apelaciones, Departamento Histórico Judicial de la Suprema Corte de Justicia de la Provincia de Buenos Aires, 1990.

Lappas, Alcibíades, *La masonería argentina a través de sus hombres*, Buenos Aires, author's edition, 1966.

Legislatura de Buenos Aires, *Poder legislativo de la provincia de Buenos Aires, 1854–1989. Composición de sus cámaras*, La Plata, Legislatura de Buenos Aires, 1989.

Le Mée, René, "Les villes en France et leur population de 1806 à 1851." *Annales de démographie historique*, 1989, 321–393.

Ligou, Daniel (dir.), *Dictionnaire de la Franc–Maçonnerie*, Paris, PUF, 1987.

Ministerio de Educación de la Nación, *Catálogo del Museo Histórico Nacional*, two vols., Buenos Aires, Ministerio de Educación de la Nación, 1951.

Museo Histórico Nacional, *Catálogo del periodismo e imprenta argentina*, Buenos Aires, 1960.

Museo Mitre, *Catálogo de la Biblioteca*, Buenos Aires, Ministerio de Justicia e Instrucción Pública/Imprenta Biedma, 1907.

Newton, Jorge, *Diccionario biográfico del campo argentino*, Buenos Aires, 1972.

Nouvelle Géographie Universelle. La terre et les hommes, by Elisée Reclus, vol. 19, *Amérique du Sud. L'Amazonie et la Plata*, Paris, Librairie Hachette, 1894 [Spanish translation: *Nueva geografía universal. La tierra y los hombres*, Madrid, El Progreso Editorial, 1888–1893].

Pagano, Nora, *Nómina de diputados de la Junta de Representantes, 1829–1852* (unpublished.)

Pradeiro, Antonio, *Índice cronológico de la prensa del Uruguay, 1807–1852*, Montevideo, Universidad de la República Oriental del Uruguay, 1862.

Provincia de Buenos Aires, Ministerio de Educación, Subsecretaría de Cultura, *Índice de la Sala de Representantes de la Provincia de Buenos Aires, 1821–1852*, La Plata, Publicaciones del Archivo de Historia de la Provincia "Dr. Ricardo Levene," catalogue of documents and archives III, 1970.

Provincia de Buenos Aires, Ministerio de Gobierno, Secretaría de Asuntos Legislativos, *Provincia de Buenos Aires. Aporte a la cronología de sus autoridades*, La Plata, Dirección de Bibliotecas, Información Legislativa, 1983.

República Argentina, Ministerio de Economía, Hacienda y Finanzas, Departamento de Bibliotecas, *Compilación cronológica de los Presidentes, Vicepresidentes de la Nación Argentina, Ministros de Hacienda, de Economía, Secretarios de Estado de Hacienda y/o Finanzas, Secretarios de Estado de Programación y Coordinación Económica y sus respectivos secretarios, 1854–1978*, Buenos Aires, 1981.

Revista del Instituto Argentino de Ciencias Genealógicas, nos. 1–12, Buenos Aires, 1942–1957.

Robinson, Arthur H., *Early Thematic Mapping in the History of Cartography*, Chicago, The University of Chicago Press, 1982.

Santons Gómez, Susana, *Bibliografía de los viajeros a la Argentina*, two vols., Buenos Aires, Fundación para la Educación, la Ciencia y la Cultura/Instituto de Antropología e Historia Hispanoamericana, 1983.

Serryn, Pierre, *Nouvel Atlas Général*, Paris, Bordas, 1962.

The Times, Atlas of the World, vol. 5, *The Americas*, London, 1957.

Touring Club Italiano, *Atlante Internazionale del Touring Club Italiano*, Milan, Touring Club Italiano, 1956.

Udaondo, Enrique, *Diccionario biográfico argentino*, Buenos Aires, 1938.

Universidad Nacional de La Plata, *Catálogo de los periódicos sudamericanos (1791–1861)*, La Plata, 1934.

Vizoso Gorostiaga, Manuel, *Diccionario y cronología histórica americana*, Buenos Aires, Ayacucho, 1947.

Yaben, Jacinto R., *Biografías argentinas y sudamericanas*, Buenos Aires, 1952–1954.

GENERAL BIBLIOGRAPHY

Abad de Santillán, Diego, *Historia institucional argentina*, Buenos Aires, Tea, 1966.

Academia Nacional de Bellas Artes, *Historia general del arte en la Argentina*, Buenos Aires, Academia Nacional de Bellas Artes, 1985.

Academia Nacional de la Historia, *Historia de la Nación Argentina. De los orígenes hasta la organización definitiva en 1862*, Buenos Aires, Academia Nacional de la Historia, 1939–1951.

Agulhon, Maurice, *Pénitents et francs–maçons de l'ancienne Provence* (1966), Paris, Fayard, 1984.

——, "Les Chambrées en Basse–Province: histoire et ethnologie," *Revue Historique*, 497, Paris, January–March 1971, 337–368.

——, "La sociabilité, la sociologie et l'histoire," *L'Arc* 65, 1976, 76–84.

——, *Les Cercles dans la France bourgeoise, 1810–1848. Étude d'une mutation de sociabilité*, Paris, Armand Colin, 1977.

——, "Vers une histoire des associations," *Esprit* 18, June 1978, 13–18.

——, *La République au village. Les populations du Var de la Révolution à la IIème République*, Paris, Seuil, 1979.

——, *Marianne au combat. L'imagerie et la symbolique républicaines de 1789 à 1880*, Paris, Flammarion, 1979.

——, "La sociabilité est–elle objet d'Histoire," in E. François (comp.), *Sociabilité et société bourgeoise en France, en Allemagne et en Suisse (1750–1850)*, Actes du Colloque de Badhomburg, 1986, 13–22.

——, "Architecture républicaine," *Monuments Historiques*, "La République," 144, April/May 1986, 7–11.

——, *Histoire vagabonde I. Ethnologie et politique dans la France contemporaine*, Paris, Gallimard, 1988.

——, "La sociabilidad como categoría histórica," in *Formas de sociabilidad en Chile, 1840–1940*, Santiago de Chile, 1992, 1–10.

Agulhon, Maurice, and M. Bodiguel, *Les Associations au village*, Actes Sud, Hubert Nyssen Éditeur, 1981.

Agulhon, Maurice, and Maurice Crubellier, "Les citadins et leur culture," in Georges Duby (dir.), *Histoire de la France urbaine. La ville de l'âge industriel*, vol. 4, Paris, Seuil, 1980, 435–444.

Aliata, Fernando, "La ciudad regular. Arquitectura edilicia e instituciones durante la época rivadaviana," in *Imagen y recepción de la Revolución Francesa en la Argentina*, National Conferences for the Bicentenary of the French Revolution, Buenos Aires, Buenos Aires, Comité Argentino para el Bicentenario de la Revolución Francesa/Grupo Editor Latinoamericano, 1990, 159–179.

——, "Ciudad o aldea. La construcción de la historia urbana del Buenos Aires anterior a Caseros," *Entrepasados*, vol. 2: 3, 1992, 51–70.

——, "Edilicia privada y crecimiento urbano en el Buenos Aires posrevolucionario, 1824–1827," *BIHAA– E. Ravignani*, third series, first semester 1993, 59–92.

Allende, Andrés R., "Un juez de paz de la tiranía. Aspectos de la vida de una parroquia durante la época de Rosas," *Investigaciones y Ensayos*, vol. 14, Buenos Aires, Academia Nacional de la Historia, 1973, 167–204.

Álvarez, Juan A., *Las guerras civiles argentinas* (1912), Buenos Aires, Eudeba, 1984.

Álvarez de Miranda, Pedro, Palabras e ideas: el léxico de la ilustración temprana en España (1660–1760), Madrid, *Boletín de la Real Academia Española*, 1992.

Amigo, Roberto, and Ana M. Telesca, "La curiosidad de los porteños. El público y los temas de las vistas ópticas en el Estado de Buenos Aires (1852–1862)," in *V Congreso de Historia de la Fotografía en la Argentina*, Buenos Aires, 1996.

Amunátegui Solar, Domingo, *El sistema de Lancaster en Chile*, Santiago de Chile, 1895.

Andrews, George Reid, *The Afro–Argentines of Buenos Aires, 1800–1900*, University of Wisconsin Press, 2000.

Annino, Antonio (coord.), *Historia de las elecciones en Iberoamérica, siglo XIX*, Buenos Aires, Fondo de Cultura Económica, 1995.

Annino, Antonio, et al., *America Latina: dallo Stato coloniale allo Stato nazione (1750–1950)*, two vols., Milan, Franco Angeli, 1987.

Annino, Antonio, Luis Castro Leiva & François–X. Guerra, *De los Imperios a las Naciones: Iberoamérica*, Zaragoza, Ibercaja, 1994.

Ansart, Pierre, "Marx et la théorie de l'imaginaire social," *Cahiers internationaux de sociologie*, vol. 45, 1968, 99–116.

Ardao, Arturo, *Racionalismo y liberalismo en el Uruguay*, Montevideo, Universidad de la República, 1962.

Ariès, Philippe, "L'enfant et la rue, de la ville à l'antiville" (1979), in *Essais de mémoire 1943–1983*, Paris, Seuil, 1993, 233–255.

Ariès, Philippe, and Georges Duby (dirs.), *Histoire de la vie privée*, III, *De la Renaissance aux Lumières* (Roger Chartier, coord.), Paris, Seuil, 1986.

Arrieta, Rafael, *La ciudad y los libros. Excursión al pasado bibliográfico argentino*, Buenos Aires, Librería del Colegio, 1955.

——, "Esteban Echeverría y el romanticismo en el Plata," in *Historia de la literatura argentina*, vol. 2, Buenos Aires, Peuser, 1958, 17–112.

Artola, Miguel, *La burguesía revolucionaria (1808–1874)*, Madrid, Alianza, 1973.

Assadourian, Carlos Sempat, "Integración y desintegración regional en el espacio colonial. Un enfoque histórico," in *El sistema de la economía colonial*, Lima, Instituto de Estudios Peruanos, 1982.

Auza, Néstor Tomás, *El periodismo en la Confederación, 1852–1861*, Buenos Aires, Eudeba, 1978.

——, *Los católicos argentinos: su experiencia política y social*, Buenos Aires, Claretiana, 1984.

Baczko, Bronislaw, *Les Imaginaires sociaux. Mémoires et espoirs collectifs*, Paris, Payot, 1984.

Baily, Samuel, "Las Sociedades de Ayuda Mutua y el desarrollo de una comunidad italiana." *Desarrollo Económico*, vol. 21: 84, January–March 1982, 485–514.

Baker, Keith Michael (comp.), *The French Revolution and the Creation of Modern Political Culture*, three vols., Oxford and New York, 1987.

——, *Au Tribunal de l'opinion. Essais sur l'imaginaire politique au XVIIIe siècle* (1990), Paris, Payot, 1993.

Balmori, Diana, *Casa y Familia. Spatial Biographies in Nineteenth–Century Buenos Aires*, Ph.D. dissertation, University of California, 1973.

——, "Family and politics: three generations (1790–1890)," *Journal of Family History*, vol. 10: 3 1985, 247–257.

Balmori, Diana, et al., *Notable Family Networks in Latin America*, Chicago, The University of Chicago Press, 1984.

Baranger, Joseph, "The historiography of the Río de la Plata since 1830," *HAHR* 39, 1959.

Barba, Enrique, *La organización del trabajo en el Buenos Aires colonial. Constitución de un gremio*, La Plata, Centro de Estudios Históricos, Facultad de Humanidades y Ciencias de la Educación, 1944.

——, *Unitarismo, federalismo, rosismo*, Buenos Aires, Pannedille, 1972.

——, *Cómo llegó Rosas al poder*, Buenos Aires, Pleamar, 1972.

Barcia, José, *Los cafés*, Buenos Aires, 1982.

Barickman, B. J., "A bit of land, which they call roça: slave provision grounds in the Bahian Recôncavo, 1780–1860," *HAHR* 74–4, November 1994, 649–687.

Bastide, Roger, *Les Amériques noires. Les civilisations africaines dans le Nouveau Monde*, Paris, Payot, 1967.

Battolla, Octavio, *Los primeros ingleses en Buenos Aires, 1780–1830*, Buenos Aires, E. Muro, 1928.

Beccar Varela, Adrián, *Plazas y calles de Buenos Aires: significación histórica de sus nombres*, two vols., Buenos Aires, Talleres Gráficos, 1910.

Beltrán, Oscar, *Historia del periodismo argentino*, Buenos Aires, Sopena, 1943.

Benavente, fray Marcelino, *Homenaje a su memoria. De la venerable Orden Tercera de Santo Domingo*, Buenos Aires, 1911.

Bénichou, Paul, *Le Sacre de l'écrivain, 1750–1830. Essai sur l'avènement d'un pouvoir spirituel laïc dans la France moderne*, Paris, Librairie José Corti, 1973.

——, *Les Temps des prophètes. Doctrines de l'âge romantique*, Paris, Gallimard, 1977.

Besio Moreno, Nicolás, *Buenos Aires. Puerto del Río de la Plata. Capital de la República Argentina. Estudio crítico de su población, 1536–1936*, Buenos Aires, Tacuarí, 1939.

Best, Félix, *Historia de las guerras argentinas de la Independencia, internacionales, civiles y con el indio*, two vols., Buenos Aires, 1960.

Beverina, Juan, *Las invasiones inglesas (1806–1807)*, two vols., Buenos Aires, Círculo Militar, 1939.

——, *La reconquista y la defensa de Buenos Aires*, Buenos Aires, Publicaciones del Instituto de Estudios Históricos sobre la Reconquista y la Defensa/Peuser, 1947.

Bidabehere, Fernando A., *Bolsas y mercados de comercio en la República Argentina*, Buenos Aires, Talleres Gráficos L. J. Rosso, 1930.

Biedma, José, *Crónicas históricas del Río Negro de Patagones, 1774–1834*, Buenos Aires, Canter, 1905.

Bilsky, Edgardo, *Contribution à l'histoire du mouvement ouvrier et social argentin. Bibliographie et sources documentaires de la région parisienne*, Nanterre, CNRS, 1983.

Bolsa de Comercio, *La Bolsa de Comercio en su centenario*, Buenos Aires, Ed. La Bolsa, 1954.

Borah, Woodrow, "Trends in recent studies of colonial Latin American cities," *HAHR* 64–3, August 1984, 535–554.

Bosch, Mariano G., *Historia del teatro en Buenos Aires*, Buenos Aires, Establecimiento Tipográfico El Comercio, 1910.

Bossio, Jorge A., *Los cafés de Buenos Aires*, Buenos Aires, Schapire, 1968.

——, *Historia de las pulperías*, Buenos Aires, Plus Ultra, 1972.

Botana, Natalio, *El orden conservador. La política argentina entre 1880 y 1916*, Buenos Aires, Sudamericana, 1978.

——, *La tradición republicana*, Buenos Aires, Sudamericana, 1984.

——, *La libertad política y su historia*, Buenos Aires, Sudamericana, 1991.

——, *Domingo Faustino Sarmiento*, Buenos Aires, Fondo de Cultura Económica, 1997.

Bouilly, Víctor, *El interregno de los lomos negros, 1830–1835*, Buenos Aires, La Bastilla, 1974.

Bourricaud, François, "Civilité," *Encyclopédie Universalis*, corpus 5, 1989, 948–951.

Brown, Jonathan, *A Socioeconomic History of Argentina, 1776–1860*, Cambridge, Cambridge University Press, 1979.

Bruno, Cayetano, *Historia de la Iglesia en la Argentina*, 12 vols., Buenos Aires, Don Bosco, 1966–1981.

Buisson, Inge, et al., *Problemas de la formación del Estado y de la nación en Hispanoamérica*, Bonn, Inter Nationes, 1984.

Buonocore, Domingo, *Libros, editores e impresores de Buenos Aires*, Buenos Aires, El Ateneo, 1944.

——, *Libros y bibliófilos durante la época de Rosas*, Córdoba, Universidad Nacional de Córdoba, 1969.

Burgin, Miron, *Aspectos económicos del federalismo argentino* (1946), Buenos Aires, Solar, 1975.

Burucúa, José E., et al., "Influencia de los tipos iconográficos de la Revolución Francesa en los países del Plata," in *Imagen y recepción de la Revolución Francesa en la Argentina*, National Conferences for the Bicentenary of the French Revolution, Buenos Aires, Buenos Aires, Comité Argentino para el Bicentenario de la Revolución Francesa/Grupo Editor Latinoamericano, 1990, 129–140.

Bushnell, David, "El sufragio en la Argentina y en Colombia hasta 1853," *Revista del Instituto de Historia del Derecho*, vol. 19, 1968, 11–29.

——, *Reform and Reaction in the Platine Provinces, 1810–1852*, Gainesville, University Press of Florida, 1983.

Caillet Bois, Ricardo, *Rosas y la Comisión Representativa creada por el Pacto Federal del 4 de enero de 1831*, Buenos Aires, Talleres Jacobo Peuser, 1941.

Campos Theverin de Garabelli, Marta, *La revolución oriental. Su génesis*, two vols., Montevideo, Junta Departamental/Biblioteca José Artigas, 1973.

Canal i Morell, Jordi, "El concepto de sociabilidad en la historiografía contemporánea (Francia, Italia y España)," *Siglo XIX*, second period, 13, January–June 1993, 5–25.

Canter, Juan, "La logia Lautaro y Mendoza," *Revista de la Junta de Estudios Históricos de Mendoza*, vol. 2, 1936.

Carbia, Rómulo, *Historia crítica de la historiografía argentina (desde sus orígenes en el siglo XVI)*, Buenos Aires, Coni, 1940.

Cárcano, Ramón, *De Caseros al 11 de septiembre*, Buenos Aires, 1918.

——, *Del sitio de Buenos Aires al campo de Cepeda (1852–1859)*, Buenos Aires, Coni, 1921.

Caroux, Jacques, "La démocratie par l'association?," *Esprit* 18, June 1978, 3–8.

Carranza, Ángel J., *Bosquejo histórico acerca del Doctor Carlos Tejedor y la conjuración de 1839*, Buenos Aires, 1879.

——, *La revolución del 39 en el sud de Buenos Aires* (1880), Buenos Aires, Hispamérica, 1988.

Carretero, Andrés, "Contribución al conocimiento de la propiedad rural en la provincia de Buenos Aires para 1830," *Boletín del Instituto de Historia Argentina y Americana*, vol. 2: 13, 1970, 146–192.

——, *El pensamiento político de Rosas*, Buenos Aires, Platero, 1970.

——, *La llegada de Rosas al poder*, Buenos Aires, Pannedille, 1971.

Castagnino, Raúl H., *El teatro en Buenos Aires durante la época de Rosas*, Buenos Aires, Ed. Nacional de Estudios del Teatro/Comisión Nacional de Cultura, 1944.

Castan, Yves, *Honnêteté et relations sociales en Languedoc, 1715–1780*, Paris, Plon, 1974.

Castellán, Ángel A., "Las ideas sociales de Juan A. García," *Boletín de Sociología* 3, Buenos Aires, 1944, 155–178.

Castellano Sáenz Cavia, Rafael, "La abolición de la esclavitud en las Provincias Unidas del Río de la Plata (1810–1860)," *Revista de Historia del Derecho* 9, Buenos Aires, 1981, 55–157.

Castelli, José Blas, *Mutualismo y mutualidades*, Buenos Aires, Intecoop, 1958.

Castoriadis, Cornelius, *L'Institution imaginaire de la société*, Paris, Seuil, 1975.

Celesia, Ernesto H., *Rosas, aporte para su historia*, Buenos Aires, Peuser, 1954.

Celestino, Olinda, and Alberto Meyers, *Las cofradías en el Perú: región central*, Frankfurt, Klaus, 1981.

Centre de Recherches d'Histoire Sociale de l'Université de Picardie, *Oisivité et loisir dans les sociétés occidentales au XIXe siècle*, pluridisciplinary colloquium, Amiens, 19 & 20 November 1982, Abbeville, Imp. F. Paillart, 1983.

Céspedes, Conrado, "La prensa en Mendoza. Sus primeros establecimientos tipográficos y primeros órganos de publicidad," *Revista de la Junta de Estudios Históricos de Mendoza*, vol. 3, nos. 9–10, 1936, 13–34.

Céspedes del Castillo, Guillermo, *Lima y Buenos Aires. Repercusiones económicas y políticas de la creación del Virreinato del Plata*, Seville, Escuela de Estudios Hispanoamericanos, 1947.

Chamboredon, Jean-Claude, "Compte-rendu à l'ouvrage de Maurice Agulhon et Maryvonne Bodiguel: *Les Associations au village*," *Annales ESC* 1, Paris, January–February 1984, 52–58.

Chaparro, Félix, *José Roque Pérez, un héroe civil argentino*, Rosario, Multicarta, 1951.

Charles, Christophe, *Les Élites de la République, 1880–1900*, Paris, Fayard, 1987.

Chartier, Roger, *Lecture et lecteurs dans la France d'Ancien Régime*, Paris, Seuil, 1987.

——, *Les Origines culturelles de la Révolution Française*, Paris, Seuil, 1990.

Chiaramonte, José Carlos, *Nacionalismo y liberalismo económico en la Argentina, 1860–1880*, Buenos Aires, Solar, 1971.

——, "La cuestión regional en el proceso de gestación del estado nacional argentino. Algunos problemas de interpretación," in Marco Palacios (comp.), *La unidad nacional en América Latina. Del regionalismo a la nacionalidad*, Mexico City, El Colegio de México, 1983, 51–85.

——, "Organización del Estado y construcción del orden social: la política económica de la provincia de Corrientes hacia 1821–1840," *Anuario de la Escuela de Historia*, Facultad de Humanidades y Artes de la Universidad Nacional de Rosario, second period, no.11, Rosario, 1984–1985.

——, "Legalidad constitucional o caudillismo: el problema del orden social en el surgimiento de los Estados autónomos del litoral argentino en la primera mitad del siglo XIX," *Desarrollo Económico*, vol. 26: 102, July–September 1986, 175–196.

——, "Notas sobre la presencia italiana en el Litoral argentino en la primera mitad del siglo XIX," in Fernando Devoto (comp.), *L'Italia nella società argentina*, Roma, Centro Studi Emigrazione, 1988.

——, "Formas de identidad en el Río de la Plata luego de 1810," *BIHAA – E. Ravignani*, third series, no. 1, first trimester,1989, 71–92.

——, "El federalismo argentino durante la primera mitad del siglo XIX," in Marcello Carmagnani (comp.), *Federalismos latinoamericanos: México, Brasil, Argentina*, Mexico City, El Colegio de México/Fondo de Cultura Económica, 1993, 81–132.

Chombart de Lauwe, Paul–Henry, et al., *Paris et l'agglomération parisienne*, Paris, 1952.

Ciasullo, Aldo, "Reseña histórica de la masonería uruguaya," *Revista Gran Logia de la Masonería del Uruguay* 2, April 1985.

Cibotti, Ema, "Mutualismo y política en un estudio de caso. La sociedad Unione e Benevolenza en Buenos Aires entre 1858 y 1865," in Fernando Devoto (comp.), *L'Italia nella società argentina*, Roma Centro Studi Emigrazione, 1988, 241–265.

——, "Notas para el análisis del desarrollo político de Unione e Benevolenza entre 1858 y 1865. Historia de dos escisiones" (undated), unpublished work.

Cibotti, Ema, and Hilda Sabato, "Hacer política en Buenos Aires: los italianos en la escena pública porteña, 1860–1880," *BIHAA – E. Ravignani*, third series, no. 2, first semester 1990, 7–46.

Cicerchia, Ricardo, "Vida familiar y prácticas conyugales. Clases populares en una ciudad colonial, Buenos Aires, 1800–1810," *BIHAA – E. Ravignani*, third series, no. 2, first semester 1990, , 91–109.

Cignoli, Francisco, *Historia de la Asociación Farmacéutica y Bioquímica Argentina*, Buenos Aires, 1947.

——, *Historia de la Farmacia Argentina*, Rosario, Librería Renz, 1953.

——, "Mitre y la Asociación Farmacéutica Bonaerense," *Investigaciones y Ensayos*, vol. 11, Buenos Aires, Academia Nacional de la Historia, 1971, , 297–304.

Claps, Manuel, "Masones y liberales," *Enciclopedia Uruguaya* 27 (1969).

Claval, Paul, *La Logique des villes. Essai d'urbanologie*, Paris, Litec, 1981.

Club del Progreso, *Datos históricos sobre su origen y desenvolvimiento. Apuntes coleccionados por la comisión directiva en este centro con motivo del 50° aniversario de su fundación*, Buenos Aires, 1902.

Cochin, Augustin, *Les Sociétés de Pensée et la démocratie. Études d'histoire révolutionnaire* (1921), reedition with the title *L'Esprit du jacobinisme*, Paris, PUF, 1979.

——, *Les Sociétés de Pensée et la Révolution en Bretagne (1788–1789)*, two vols., Paris, 1925.

Cofradía del Santísimo Rosario de Mayores, Buenos Aires, 1918.

Cohen, David, and Lack Greene (comps.), *Neither Slave nor Free: The Free Man of African Descent in the Slave Societies of the New World*, Baltimore, 1972.

Colli, Néstor, *Rosas y el bloqueo anglo–francés*, Buenos Aires, Patria Grande, 1978.

Comando en Jefe del Ejército, *Reseña histórica y orgánica del Ejército Argentino*, two vols., Buenos Aires, Círculo Militar, 1971.

Comando General del Ejército, *Política seguida con el aborigen*, two vols., Buenos Aires, Círculo Militar, 1973–1974.

Comité Internacional de Ciencias Históricas, Comité Argentino, *Historiografía argentina, 1958–1988. Una evaluación crítica de la producción histórica argentina*, Buenos Aires, 1990.

Coni, Emilio A., *La verdad sobre la enfiteusis de Rivadavia*, Buenos Aires, Imprenta de la Universidad, 1927.

"Conmemoración del Centenario," *Revista del Instituto Histórico y Geográfico*, XVII, Montevideo, 1943.

Corbin, Alain, Noëlle Gérôme and Danielle Tartakowsky (dirs.), *Les Usages politiques des fêtes au XIXe–XXe siècle*, Paris, Publications de la Sorbonne, 1994.

Corcuera de Mancera, Sonia, *El fraile, el indio y el pulque. Evangelización y embriaguez en la Nueva España (1523–1548)*, Mexico City, Fondo de Cultura Económica, 1991.

Correa Luna, Carlos, *Historia de la Sociedad de Beneficencia*, two vols., Buenos Aires, 1923–1925.

Cortazar, Augusto Raúl, *Poesía gauchesca argentina*, Buenos Aires, 1969.

Corvalán Mendilaharsu, Dardo, *Apuntes sobre la vida universitaria e intelectual bajo la dominación de Rosas*, Buenos Aires, Ed. M. Gluza, 1929.

Cruz Espinosa, Miguel de la, *Las confrerías de los negros de Lima*, Lima, 1985.

Cuneo, Nicolo, *Storia dell'emigrazione italiana in Argentina, 1810–1870*, Milan, Garganti, 1940.

Cutolo, Vicente O., *Buenos Aires. Historia de las calles y sus nombres*, two vols., Buenos Aires, Elche, 1988.

Delille, Gérard, *Famille et propriété dans le royaume de Naples (XV–XIX)*, Paris, EHESS/École Française de Rome, 1985.

Descimon, Robert, and Jean Nagle, "L'espace parisien. Les quartiers de Paris du Moyen Âge au XVIIIe siècle. Évolution d'un espace plurifonctionnel," *Annales ESC* 34 (September–October 1979): 5, 956–974.

Devoto, Fernando, "Las sociedades italianas de ayuda mutua en Buenos Aires y Santa Fe. Ideas y problemas," *Studi Emigrazione* (Roma, Centro Studi Emigrazione) 21 (September 1984): 84, 320–342.

——, "Las cadenas migratorias italianas: algunas reflexiones a la luz del caso argentino," *Estudios Migratorios Latinoamericanos*, 1988, 103–122.

——, "The origins of an Italian neighbourhood in Buenos Aires in the mid–XIX century," *The Journal of European Economy History* 18 (Spring 1989): 1.

——, *Movimientos migratorios: historiografía y problemas*, Buenos Aires, Centro Editor de América Latina, 1992.

——, "Idea de nación, inmigración y cuestión social en la historiografía académica y en los libros de texto en Argentina," *Estudios Sociales* 2/3 (1992): 9–30.

Devoto, Fernando, and Eduardo Míguez, *Asociacionismo, trabajo e identidad étnica. Los italianos en América Latina en una perspectiva comparada*, Buenos Aires, CEMLA/CSER/IHES, 1992.

Díaz, Benito, *Juzgados de Paz de campaña de la provincia de Buenos Aires (1821–1854)*, La Plata, 1959.

Díaz, Rogelio, *Síntesis histórico–cronológica del periodismo en la provincia de San Juan, 1825–1937*, San Juan, Junta de Estudios Históricos de San Juan, 1937.

Díaz Molano, Elías, *Vida y obra de Pedro de Angelis*, Santa Fe, Colmegna, 1968.

Donoso, Armando, *Bilbao y su tiempo*, Santiago de Chile, Zig–Zag, 1913.

Doval, Alicia, "Los hermanos Pincheira," in Comando General del Ejército, *Política seguida con el aborigen*, vol. 2, Buenos Aires, Círculo Militar, 1973–1974.

Duby, Georges, "France rurale, France urbaine: confrontation," in *Histoire de la France urbaine*, vol. 1, *La Ville antique*, Paris, Seuil, 1980, 1–35.

Dumont, Louis, *Homo hierarchicus. Le système de castes et ses implications*, Paris, Gallimard, 1966.

——, *Essais sur l'individualisme. Une perspective anthropologique sur l'idéologie moderne*, Paris, Seuil, 1983.

Duocastella, Rogelio, *Cómo estudiar una parroquia*, prologue by Dr. Casimiro Morcello, Barcelona, Nova Terra, 1965.

Duprat, Catherine, *Le Temps des Philanthropes*, Paris, Éditions du Comité des Travaux historiques et scientifiques, 1993.

Durand, Gilbert, *Les Structures anthropologiques de l'imaginaire* (1960), Paris, Bordas, 1984.

Durkheim, Émile, *De la division du travail social* (1893), Paris, PUF, 1967.

Duroselle, Jean Baptiste, *Les Débuts du catholicisme social en France jusqu'en 1870*, thesis for doctorate in arts, Paris, PUF, 1951.

Echagüe, Juan Pablo, "El periodismo," in Academia Nacional de la Historia, *Historia de la Nación Argentina. De los orígenes hasta la organización definitiva en 1862*, Buenos Aires, Academia Nacional de la Historia, 1939–1951, vol. 4, second section pp. 59–69.

"El Centenario de la logia Excélsior," *Símbolo* (Buenos Aires) 9 (1954): 36.

"El Diario," *La Prensa Argentina*, special issue, Buenos Aires, 1932.

Elias, Norbert, *La Civilisation des mœurs* (vol. 1 of *Über den Prozess der Zivilisation*, 1st ed. of 1939), Paris, Calmann-Lévy, 1973.

——, *La Société de cour* (1969), Paris, Calmann-Lévy, 1974.

"Estudios sobre el mundo rural," *Anuario del IEHS* 2, Tandil, Universidad Nacional del Centro de la Provincia de Buenos Aires, 1987, 23–70.

Evolución institucional del municipio de la ciudad de Buenos Aires, Buenos Aires, Ediciones del Concejo Deliberante, 1963.

Falcón, Ricardo, *L'Immigration, les travailleurs et le mouvement ouvrier en Argentine: 1870–1912*, 3rd cycle doctorate thesis, Paris, École des Hautes Études en Sciences Sociales, 1985.

Farge, Arlette, *Dire et mal dire. L'opinion publique au XVIIIe siècle*, Paris, Seuil, 1992.

Fernández, Juan Rómulo, *Historia del periodismo argentino*, Buenos Aires, Librería Perlado, 1943.

Fernández Burzaco, Hugo, "La venerable Orden Tercera de Santo Domingo en Buenos Aires," *Revista Historia*, 31, 121–144.

Fernández Cabrelli, Alfonso, *Masonería y sociedades secretas en las luchas emancipadoras de la patria grande*, La Paz, América Una, 1975.

——, *Masonería, morenismo, artiguismo: presencia e influencia de la francmasonería en los movimientos independentistas del Río de la Plata*, Montevideo, América Una, 1982.

——, *Presencia masónica en la Cisplatina*, Montevideo, América Una, 1986.

Fernández y Medina, Benjamín, *La imprenta y la prensa en el Uruguay, 1807–1900*, Montevideo, Imprenta Artística, 1900.

Ferrer Benimeli, José A., *Masonería española contemporánea*, two vols., Madrid, Siglo XXI, 1980.

——, "Bolívar y la masonería," *Revista de Indias* (Seville) 43 (July–December 1983): 172.

Fitte, Ernesto, "La revolución de los restauradores," *Investigaciones y Ensayos* (Buenos Aires, Academia Nacional de la Historia) 23 (July–December 1977): 199–222.

Forsé, Michel, "Les réseaux de sociabilité dans un village," *Population* 36 (1981): 2, 1141–1162.

——, "La Sociabilité," *Économie et Statistiques* 132 (1981): 39–48.

Forum et Plaza Mayor dans le monde hispanique, Publicaciones de la Casa de Velázquez, "Recherches en Sciences Sociales," no. 4, Paris, E. de Boccard, 1978.

Fradkin, Raúl, Juan Carlos Garavaglia, Jorge Gelman and Pilar González Bernaldo, "Continuidades y rupturas en la primera mitad del siglo XIX en el Río de la Plata (mundo rural, Estado, cultura)," *Anuario IEHS* 12, Tandil, Universidad Nacional del Centro de la Provincia de Buenos Aires, 1997.

François, Étienne (dir.), *Sociabilité et société bourgeoise en France, en Allemagne et en Suisse (1750–1850)*, Paris, Ed. Recherches sur les Civilisations, 1986.

François, Étienne, and Rolf Richardt, "Les formes de sociabilité en France," *Revue d'histoire moderne et contemporaine*, vol. 34, July–September 1987, 453–472.

Frizzi de Longoni, Haydée, *Las sociedades literarias y el periodismo, 1800–1852*, prologue by Carlos Ibarguren, Buenos Aires, Asociación Interamericana de Escritores, 1946.

Furet, François, *Penser la Révolution Française*, Paris, Gallimard, 1978.

Galván Moreno, Carlos, *El periodismo argentino*, Buenos Aires, Claridad, 1944.

Gálvez, Jaime, *Rosas y la libre navegación de los ríos*, Buenos Aires, Instituto de Investigaciones Históricas Juan Manuel de Rosas, 1944.

Garavaglia, Juan Carlos, "El Río de la Plata en sus relaciones atlánticas: una balanza comercial (1779–1784)," *Moneda y Crédito* 141 (1977): 75–101.

——, *Mercado interno y economía colonial*, Mexico City, Grijalbo, 1983.

Garavaglia, Juan Carlos, y José Luis Moreno (comps.), *Población, sociedad, familia y migraciones en el espacio rioplatense, siglos XVIII y XIX*, Buenos Aires, Cántaro, 1993.

García Belsunce, César A. (dir.), *Buenos Aires. Su gente, 1800–1830*, two vols., Buenos Aires, Emecé, 1976–1977.

García Martínez, J. A., *Orígenes de nuestra crítica de arte. Sarmiento y la pintura*, Buenos Aires, Ediciones Culturales Argentinas, 1963.

Gasnault, François, *Guinguettes et lorettes. Bals publics à Paris au XIXe siècle*, Paris, Aubier, 1986.

Gauchet, Marcel, *La Révolution des pouvoirs. La souveraineté, le peuple et la représentation, 1789–1799*, Paris, Gallimard, 1995.

Gaudemet, Ives Henri, *Les Juristes et la vie politique de la IIIème République*, Paris, PUF, 1970.

Gelman, Jorge, *Économie et administration locale dans le Rio de la Plata du XVIIe siècle*, third cycle doctorate thesis, Paris, EHESS, 1983.

——, "El gran comerciante y el sentido de la circulación monetaria en el Río de la Plata colonial tardío," *Revista de historia económica* 5 (Autumn 1987): 3, 485–508.

——, "Venta al contado, venta a crédito y crédito monetario en América colonial: acerca de un gran comerciante del Virreinato del Río de la Plata," *Jahrbuch für Geschichte von Staat, Wirtschaft und Gesellschaft Lateinamerikas* 27 (1990): 101–126.

——, *De mercachifle a gran comerciante: los caminos del ascenso en el Río de la Plata*, Universidad Internacional de Andalucía, 1996.

Gemelli, Giuliana, y Maria Malatesta, *Forme di sociabilità nella storiografia francese contemporanea*, Milan, 1982.

Genta, Jordán, *Sarmiento y la masonería*, Buenos Aires, 1949.

——, *La masonería en la Argentina*, Buenos Aires, 1949 and 1951.

——, *La masonería y el comunismo en la revolución del 16 de septiembre*, Buenos Aires, 1956.

——, *La masonería argentina en la historia argentina. A propósito del centenario de la muerte del General San Martín (1850–1950)*, Buenos Aires, 1949.

Gesualdo, Vicente, *Historia de la música en la Argentina*, three vols., Buenos Aires, Beta, 1961.

——, "Los salones de vistas ópticas. Antepasados del cine en Buenos Aires y el interior," *Todo es Historia* 248 (1988): 70–80.

Girardet, Raoul, *Mythes et mythologies politiques*, Paris, Seuil, 1986.

Giusti, Juan Carlos, "Los cafés," in *Lugares y modos de diversión*, Buenos Aires, Centro Editor de América Latina, 1985, col. "Cuadernos de Historia Popular Argentina," 1–20.

Godelier, Maurice, "La part idéelle du réel. Essai sur l'idéologie," *L'Homme* 18 (July–December 1978): 3/4, 155–187.

Goldberg, Marta, "Población negra y mulata de la ciudad de Buenos Aires, 1810–1840," *Desarrollo Económico* 16 (1976): 61, 75–99.

Goldman, Noemí, and Pilar González Bernaldo, "Treinta años de historiografía política argentina," in Comité Internacional de Ciencias Históricas, Comité Argentino, *Historiografía argentina, 1958–1988. Una evaluación crítica de la producción histórica argentina*, Buenos Aires, 1990, 293–302.

González, Julio C., *La proyectada modificación de la Real Audiencia en 1812*, Buenos Aires, 1942.

González, Julio V., *Filiación histórica del gobierno representativo argentino*, two vols., Buenos Aires, 1937.

González Arzac, Alberto, *Abolición de la esclavitud en el Río de la Plata*, Buenos Aires, 1974.

González Bernaldo, Pilar, "El levantamiento de 1829: el imaginario social y sus implicaciones políticas en un conflicto rural," *Anuario del IEHS* 2, Tandil, Universidad Nacional del Centro de la Provincia de Buenos Aires, 1987, 137–176.

——, "Producción de una nueva legitimidad: ejército y sociedades patrióticas en Buenos Aires entre 1810 y 1813," *Cahiers des Amériques Latines* 10 (1990): 177–195.

——, "La Revolución Francesa y la emergencia de nuevas prácticas de la política: la irrupción de la sociabilidad política en el Río de la Plata revolucionario (1810–1815)," in Ricardo Krebs and Cristián Gazmuri, *La Revolución Francesa y Chile*, Santiago de Chile, Editorial Universitaria, 1990, 111–135.

——, "Masonería y Revolución de Independencia en el Río de la Plata: 130 años de historiografía," in José A. Ferrer Benimeli (coord.), *Masonería, revolución y reacción*, vol. 2, Alicante, 1990, 1035–1054.

——, "Pedagogía societaria y aprendizaje de la nación en el Río de la Plata, 1820–1862," in Antonio Annino et al., *De los Imperios a las Naciones: Iberoamérica*, Zaragoza, Ibercaja, 1994.

Goodman, Dena, "Public sphere and private life: toward a synthesis of current historiographical approaches to the Old Regime," *History and Theory* 31 (1992): 1, 1–20.

Gordon, Daniel, *Citizens without Sovereignty. Equality and Sociability in French Thought, 1670–1789*, Princeton, Princeton University Press, 1994.

Gorostegui de Torres, Haydée, *La organización nacional*, Buenos Aires, Paidós, 1972, col. "Historia Argentina."

Greenow, Linda, "Microgeographical analysis as an index to family structure and networks," *Journal of Family History* 10 (1985): 3, 272–283.

Grenier, Philippe, "Structure et organisation de l'espace argentin," *Mappemonde*, "Amérique Latine," no. 88–4, 36–46.

Gribauldi, Maurizio, "A proposito di linguistica e storia," *Quaderni Storici* 46 (1981).

——, *Itinéraires ouvriers: espaces et groupes sociaux à Turin au début du XXe siècle*, Paris, Éditions de l'École des Hautes Études en Sciences Sociales, 1987.

Gruzinski, Serge, *La Colonisation de l'imaginaire. Sociétés indigènes et occidentalisation dans le Mexique espagnol, XVI–XVIIIe siècle*, Paris, Gallimard, 1988.

——, *La Guerre des images. De Christophe Colomb à "Blade Runner" (1492–2019)*, Paris, Fayard, 1990.

Guerra, François–X., *Le Mexique. De l'Ancien Régime à la Révolution*, two vols., Paris, L'Harmattan, 1985.

——, "Lugares, formas y ritmos de la política moderna," *Boletín de la Academia Nacional de la Historia* (Caracas) 31:284 (October–December 1988), 2–18.

——, "Le peuple souverain: fondements et logique d'une fiction (pays hispaniques au XIXème siècle)," in *L'Avenir de la démocratie en Amérique Latine*, Toulouse, CNRS, 1988.

——, "Révolution Française et révolutions hispaniques: filiation et parcours," *Problèmes d'Amérique Latina. Notes et études documentaires* (Paris, La Documentation Française) 94 (1989): 3–26.

——, "Les avatars de la représentation en Amérique hispanique au XIXème siècle," in *Reinventer la démocratie: le défi latino–américain*, Paris, Presse de la Fondation Nationale des Sciences Politiques, 1992, 49–84.

——, *Modernidad e independencias. Ensayos sobre las revoluciones hispánicas*, Madrid, Mapfre, 1992.

Gutton, Jean–Pierre, *La Sociabilité villageoise dans l'ancienne France*, Paris, Hachette, 1979.

Habermas, Jürgen, *L'Espace public. Archéologie de la publicité comme dimension constitutive de la société bourgeoise*, Paris, Payot, 1978.

——, *Écrits politiques*, Paris, Cerf, 1990.

Halévi, Ran, *Les Loges maçonniques dans la France d'Ancien Régime. Aux origines de la sociabilité démocratique*, Paris, Armand Colin, 1984.

Halperin Donghi, Tulio, *El pensamiento de Echeverría*, Buenos Aires, Sudamericana, 1951.

——, *Historia de la Universidad de Buenos Aires*, Buenos Aires, Eudeba, 1962.

——, "El surgimiento de los caudillos en el cuadro de la sociedad rioplatense posrevolucionaria," *Estudios de Historia Social*, vol. 1: 1, Buenos Aires, Facultad de Filosofía y Letras, 1965, 121–149.

——, *Revisionismo histórico argentino*, Buenos Aires, Siglo XXI, 1970.

——, *Revolución y guerra. La formación de la élite dirigente en la Argentina criolla*, Buenos Aires, Siglo XXI, 1972.

——, *De la revolución de independencia a la confederación rosista*, Buenos Aires, Paidós, 1972, col. "Historia Argentina."

——, "La expansión ganadera de la frontera de Buenos Aires, 1820–1852," in Marcos

Giménez Zapiola (comp.), *El régimen oligárquico. Materiales para el estudio de la realidad argentina (hasta 1930)*, Buenos Aires, Amorrortu, 1975.
——, *Proyecto y construcción de una nación argentina, 1846–1880*, Caracas, Biblioteca Ayacucho, 1979.
——, *Guerra y finanzas en los orígenes del Estado argentino (1791–1850)*, Buenos Aires, Editorial de Belgrano, 1982.
——, *Reforma y disolución de los imperios ibéricos, 1750–1850*, Madrid, Alianza, 1985, col. "Historia de América Latina."
——, "El letrado colonial como intelectual revolucionario," *Anuario*, second period, no.11, Rosario, Facultad de Humanidades y Artes de la Universidad Nacional de Rosario, 1985, 85–101.
——, "Un cuarto de siglo de historiografía argentina (1960–1985)," *Desarrollo Económico* 25 (January–March 1986): 100.
——, "Intelectuales, sociedad y vida pública en Hispanoamérica a través de la literatura autobiográfica," in *El espejo de la historia*, Buenos Aires, Sudamericana, 1987, 43–63.
Hardoy, Jorge E., "La cartografía en América Latina durante el período colonial. Un análisis de fuentes," in *Ensayos histórico–sociales sobre la urbanización en América Latina*, Buenos Aires, Sociedad Interamericana de Planificación/Comisión de Desarrollo Urbano y Regional de CLACSO, 1978, 19–58.
——, "Las formas de la ciudad colonial," in *Estudios sobre la ciudad iberoamericana*, Madrid, CSIC/Instituto Gonzalo Fernández de Oviedo, 1983, 319–322.
Hébrard, Véronique, *Le Venezuela indépendant. Una nation par le discours, 1808–1830*, Paris, L'Harmattan, 1996.
Heras, Carlos, "Antecedentes sobre la instalación del régimen municipal en la provincia de Buenos Aires," *Trabajos y Comunicaciones* (La Plata, Universidad Nacional de La Plata) 1 (1949): 75–107.
——, "Nuevos antecedentes sobre la instalación del régimen municipal en Buenos Aires," *Trabajos y Comunicaciones* (La Plata, Universidad Nacional de La Plata) 3.
Hernando, Diana, *Casa y Familia. Spatial Biography in Nineteenth Century Buenos Aires*, Ph.D. dissertation, University of California, Los Angeles, 1973.
Histoire et imaginaire, collective work, Paris, Poiesis, 1986 (distribution Payot.)
Hoberman, Louisa Schell, and Susan Socolow, *Cities and Society in Colonial Latin America*, Albuquerque, University of New Mexico Press, 1988.
Hobsbawm, Eric J., *Rebeldes primitivos*, Barcelona, Ariel, 1968.
——, *Bandidos* (1969), Barcelona, Ariel, 1976.
——, *Nations and Nationalism since 1780. Programme, Myth, Reality*, Cambridge, Cambridge University Press, 1990.
Horas, Alberto Plácido, *Esteban Echeverría y la filosofía política de la generación de 1837*, San Luis, Universidad Nacional de Cuyo, 1950.
Horkheimer, Max, *Crítica de la razón instrumental*, Buenos Aires, Sur, 1969.
Huard, Raymond, *Le Mouvement républicain en Bas–Languedoc, 1848–1881*, Paris, Presse de la Fondation Nationale de Sciences Politiques, 1982.
Hurcade, Luis, "Misión de la masonería argentina en la organización nacional," *Símbolo* 1 (July 1946): 1, 18–27.

Ibarguren, Carlos, "Las primeras sociedades político–literarias argentinas," in *2nd International Congress of American History*, Buenos Aires, July 1937.

——, *Las sociedades literarias y la Revolución Argentina (1800–1825)*, Buenos Aires, Espasa–Calpe, 1937.

Informatique et prosopographie, mesa redonda realizada en el CNRS, Paris, 1984; Paris, Éditions du CNRS, 1985.

Ingenieros, José, *La evolución de las ideas argentinas* (1918–1920), Buenos Aires, Futuro, 1961.

Iñigo Carreras, Héctor José, "El Club del Progreso, de Caseros a la *Belle Époque*," *Todo es Historia* 57, January 1972.

Jesualdo, Artigas, "La Escuela Lancasteriana. Ensayo histórico–pedagógico de la escuela uruguaya durante la dominación luso–brasilera (1817–1825), en especial del método Lancaster, acompañado de un apéndice documental," *Revista Histórica*, vol. 20, year XLVII, nos. 58–60, Montevideo, 1954.

Jitrik, Noé, *Esteban Echeverría*, Buenos Aires, Centro Editor de América Latina, 1967.

Johnson, Lyman, *The Artisans of Buenos Aires during the Viceroyalty, 1776–1810*, Ph.D. diss, University of Connecticut, 1974.

——, "La manumisión en el Buenos Aires colonial: un análisis ampliado," *Desarrollo Económico* 17 (January–March 1978): 333–348.

——, "The entrepreneurial reorganization of an artisan trade: the bakers of Buenos Aires, 1770–1820," *The Americas*, October 1980, 139–160.

——, "The racial limits of guild solidarity: an example from colonial Buenos Aires," *Revista de Historia de América* 99 (January–June 1985): 7–26.

——, "The silversmiths of Buenos Aires: a case study in the failure of corporate social organization," *JLAS* 8 (November 1976): 2, 181–313.

——, "The impact of racial discrimination on black artisans in colonial Buenos Aires," *Social History* 6: 2 (October 1981), 301–316.

——, "Francisco Baquero: shoemaker and organizer," in David G. Sweet and Gary B. Nash (comps.), *Struggle and Survival in Colonial America*, Berkeley, University of California Press, 1981.

Johnson, Lyman, and Susan Socolow, "Población y espacio en el Buenos Aires del siglo XVIII," *Desarrollo Económico* 20:79 (October–December 1980), 329–349.

Kantorowicz, Ernst, *The King's Two Bodies. A Study in Medieval Political Theology*, Princeton, Princeton University Press, 1957.

Kapferer, Jean–Noël, *Rumeurs, le plus vieux media du monde*, Paris, Seuil, 1987.

Kinsbruner, Jay, *Petty Capitalism in Spanish America. The* Pulperos *of Puebla, Mexico City, Caracas and Buenos Aires*, Dellplain Latin American Studies no. 21, Boulder, CO, Westview Press, 1987.

Kusnesof, Elizabeth, "The history of family in Latin America: a critique of recent work," *LARR* 24 (1989): 2.

La arquitectura en Buenos Aires (1850–1880), Buenos Aires, Instituto de Arte Americano, Facultad de Arquitectura y Urbanismo, 1965.

Langle, Henry–Melchor de, *Le Petit monde des cafés et débit parisiens au XIXe siècle*, Paris, PUF, 1990.

Lanuza, José Luis, *Morenada. Una historia de la raza africana en el Río de la Plata*, Buenos Aires, Schapire, 1967.

Lappas, Alcibíades, *La masonería argentina a través de sus hombres* (1958), Buenos Aires, author's edition, 1966.

——, "La logia «Constante Unión» de la ciudad de Corrientes," *Revista de la Junta de Historia de Corrientes* 5, 1970.

——, *La masonería en la ocupación del desierto*, Buenos Aires, Instituto Histórico de la Organización Nacional, 1981.

Lazcano, Martín, *Las sociedades secretas, políticas y masónicas en Buenos Aires*, two vols., Buenos Aires, El Ateneo, 1927.

Le Goff, Jacques, *L'Imaginaire médieval*, Paris, Gallimard, 1985.

Lemieux, Vincent, *Réseaux et appareils. Logique des systèmes et langage des graphes*, Quebec, Edisem, 1982.

Lepetit, Bernard, *Les Villes dans la France moderne (1740–1840)*, Paris, Albin Michel, 1988.

Levaggi, Abelardo, *Manual de historia del derecho argentino*, vol. 2, Buenos Aires, Dellepiane, 1987.

Levene, Ricardo, *Los orígenes de la democracia en Argentina*, Buenos Aires, 1911.

——, "Los gremios en la época colonial," *Anales de la Facultad de Derecho de Buenos Aires*, vol. II, third series, 1916.

——, "El Instituto de Sociología de la Facultad de Filosofía y Letras," *Boletín del Instituto de Sociología* (Buenos Aires) 1 (1942): 3–8.

——, *Los estudios históricos de la juventud de Mitre*, Buenos Aires, Emecé, 1946.

Lugares y modos de diversión, Buenos Aires, Centro Editor de América Latina, 1985, col. "Cuadernos de Historia Popular Argentina."

Lynch, John, The Spanish–American Revolutions 1808–1826 (1976).

——, *Juan Manuel de Rosas, 1829–1852* (1981), Buenos Aires, Emecé, 1984.

——, "Los caudillos como agentes del orden social: Venezuela y Argentina, 1820–1850," in Antonio Annino et al., *America Latina: dallo Stato coloniale allo Stato nazione (1750–1950)*, two vols., Milan, Franco Angeli, 1987.

MacDonald, John, and Leatrice MacDonald, "Chain migration, ethnic neighborhood formation, and social networks," *Milbank Memorial Fund Quarterly* 12:42 (1964), 82–95.

MacFarlane, Alan, "History, anthropology and the study of community," *Social History* 5 (May 1977).

Maeder, Ernesto J. A., *Evolución demográfica argentina desde 1810 a 1869*, Buenos Aires, Eudeba, 1969.

Maguire, Patricio José, *La masonería y la emancipación del Río de la Plata*, Buenos Aires, Imprenta de la Universidad, 1969.

——, "La masonería como instrumento en la lucha de influencias durante el período de la independencia y organización de los países hispanoamericanos," *BIHAA– E. Ravignani* 13 (second series, 1970): 22–23,.

Mandrini, Raúl, "La sociedad indígena de las pampas en el siglo XIX," in Mirta Lischetti (comp.), *Antropología*, Buenos Aires, Eudeba, 1985.

——, "Notas sobre el desarrollo de la economía pastoril entre los indígenas del suroeste bonaerense (fines del siglo XVIII y comienzos del siglo XIX)," *8th Conference on Economic History*, Tandil, 1986.

——, "Desarrollo de una sociedad indígena pastoril en el área interserrana bonaerense," *Anuario IEHS*, 2, Tandil, Universidad del Centro de la Provincia de Buenos Aires, 1987, 71–98.

Mantila, M., *Bibliografía periodística de la provincia de Corrientes*, Buenos Aires, Imprenta y Librería de Mayo, 1887.

Marenales Rossi, Martha, and Guy Bourdé, "L'immigration française et le peuplement de l'Uruguay, 1830–1860," *Cahiers des Amériques Latines* 16 (1977): 7–21.

Mariluz Urquijo, José M., *La industria sombrerera anterior a 1810*, La Plata, Instituto de la Producción de la Facultad de Ciencias Económicas de la Universidad de La Plata, 1962.

——, "La mano de obra en la industria porteña, 1810–1835," *Boletín de la Academia Nacional de la Historia* 32 (1962): 583–622.

——, "Las sociedades anónimas en Buenos Aires antes del Código de Comercio," *Revista del Instituto de Historia del Derecho* 16 (1965).

——, "La comercialización de la producción sombrerera porteña (1810–1835)," *Investigaciones y Ensayos* 5 (1968): 103–129.

——, *Estado e industria, 1810–1860*, Buenos Aires, Macchi, 1969.

——, "Notas sobre la evolución de las sociedades comerciales en el Río de la Plata," *Revista del Instituto de Historia del Derecho* 22 (1971).

Marín, María H., Alberto de Paula and Ramón Gutiérrez, *Los ingenieros militares y sus precursores en el desarrollo argentino (hasta 1930)*, Buenos Aires, 1976.

Márquez Miranda, Fernando, *Ensayo sobre los artífices en la platería en el Buenos Aires colonial*, Buenos Aires, 1933.

Mayer, Jorge, *Alberdi y su tiempo*, Buenos Aires, Eudeba, 1963.

Mayo, Carlos, "Aspectos de un período crítico en la historia de la masonería argentina (1902–1906)," *Investigaciones y Ensayos* 18 (1975).

——, *La masonería en crisis*, Buenos Aires, Centro Editor de América Latina, 1988.

Meister, Albert, *Vers une sociologie des associations*, Paris, Les Éditions Ouvrières, 1972.

——, *La Participation dans les associations*, Paris, Les Éditions Ouvrières, 1974.

Mendras, Henri, "Éléments de problematique pour l'étude de la sociabilité," *Archives de l'Observation du changement social*, vol. 1, Paris, CNRS, 1978.

Meyer Arana, A., *La caridad en Buenos Aires*, Buenos Aires, Comisión Nacional del Centenario, 1911.

——, *Rosas y la Sociedad de Beneficencia*, Buenos Aires, 1923.

Meyers, Albert, and Elizabeth Hopkins, preface to *Manipulating the Saints: Religious Brotherhoods and Social Integration in Post–Conquest Latin America*, Hamburg, 1988.

Michels, Robert, *Les Partis politiques* (1911), Paris, Flammarion, 1971.

Mignanego, Alberto Armando, "La elección de marzo de 1856 en Buenos Aires," *Boletín de la Universidad Nacional de La Plata* 19:6 (1935), 123–142.

——, *El segundo gobernador constitucional de Buenos Aires y el proceso electoral de 1856–1857*, Buenos Aires, 1938.

Mitchell, Clyde (comp.), *Social Networks in Urban Situation*, Manchester, Manchester University Press, 1969.

Mola, Aldo Alessandro, "Orientaciones actuales de los estudios de la historia de la masonería en Italia," in José A. Ferrer Benimeli (coord.), *La masonería en la historia de España del siglo XIX*, two vols., Valladolid, Consejería de Educación y Cultura, 1987, 411–427.

Mörner, Magnus, *La mezcla de razas en la historia de América* (1967), Buenos Aires, Paidós, 1969.

Morse, Richard, *Las ciudades latinoamericanas*, vol. 2, Mexico City, Sep. Setentas, 1973, chapter 2, "Argentina," 59–79.

——, "The city–idea in Argentina, a study in evanescence," *Revista de História de São Pablo* 52:104 (year XXVI, 1975), 783–802.

——, "La cultura política iberoamericana. De Sarmiento a Mariátegui," in *De historia e historiadores. Homenaje a José Luis Romero*, Mexico City, Siglo XXI, 1982, 225–257.

Moutoukias, Zacarías, "Power, corruption, and commerce: the making of the local administrative structure in seventeenth–century Buenos Aires," *HAHR* 68:4 (November 1988).

——, *Contrabando y control colonial. Buenos Aires entre el Atlántico y el espacio peruano en el siglo XVII*, Buenos Aires, Centro Editor de América Latina, 1989.

——, "Réseaux personnels et autorité coloniale: les négociants de Buenos Aires au XVIIIème siècle," *Annales ESC* 4/5 (July–October 1992): 889–915.

Moya, José Carlos, *Spaniards in Buenos Aires: Patterns of Immigration and Adaptation, 1852–1930*, Ph.D. dissertation, 1988.

Myers, Jorge, "Una genealogía para el parricidio: Juan María Gutiérrez y la construcción de una tradición literaria," *Entrepasados* 3 (1993): 4/5, 65–88.

——, *Orden y virtud. El discurso republicano en el régimen rosista*, Quilmes, Universidad Nacional de Quilmes, 1995.

Navarro Viola, Jorge, *El Club de Residentes Extranjeros (1841–1941)*, Buenos Aires, Imprenta Coni, 1941.

Newland, Carlos, "El experimento lancasteriano en Buenos Aires," *Todo es Historia* 244 (October 1987).

——, "La educación primaria privada bajo el gobierno de Rosas, 1835–1852," *La Nación*, 4 December 1988, section 4, 1–2, and 11 December 1988, section 4, 1–2.

——, "La educación elemental en Hispanoamérica: desde la independencia hasta la centralización de los sistemas educativos nacionales," *HAHR* 71/2 (1991): 335–364.

——, *Buenos Aires no es pampa: la educación elemental porteña, 1820–1860*, Buenos Aires, Grupo Editor Latinoamericano, 1992.

Nicolet, Claude, "Prosopographie et histoire sociale: Rome et l'Italie à l'époque républicaine," *Annales ESC* 5 (September–October 1970): 1209–1228.

——, *L'Idée républicaine en France. Essai d'histoire critique*, Paris, Gallimard, 1982.

Noboa Zumárraga, Horacio, *Las sociedades porteñas y su acción revolucionaria, 1800–1837*, Buenos Aires, 1939.

Nora, Pierre (dir.), *Les Lieux de mémoire. La République*, Paris, Gallimard, 1984.

——, *Les Lieux de mémoire. La Nation*, Paris, Gallimard, 1986.

Núñez, Benjamín, *Dictionary of Afro–Latin American Civilization*, Westport, Greenwood Press, 1980.

Ortega, Ezequiel, *¿Quiera el pueblo votar? Historia electoral argentina desde la Revolución de Mayo a la ley Sáenz Peña, 1810–1912*, Bahía Blanca, U. M. Giner Editor, 1963.

Ostrogorski, Moisei, *La Démocratie et les partis politiques*, Paris, Calmann–Lévy, 1912.

Oszlak, Oscar, *La formación del Estado argentino*, Buenos Aires, Editorial de Belgrano, 1985.

Ozouf, Mona, *L'Homme régéneré. Essais sur la Révolution Française*, Paris, Gallimard, 1989.

Palcos, Alberto, *Sarmiento, la vida, la obra, las ideas, el genio*, Buenos Aires, El Ateneo, 1936.

——, *Historia de Echeverría*, Buenos Aires, Emecé, 1960.

Palomar, Francisco, *Primeros salones de arte en Buenos Aires*, Buenos Aires, Cuadernos de la Ciudad de Buenos Aires no. 27, 1972.

Panilla, Norberto, *La polémica del romanticismo en 1842: Vicente F. López, D. F. Sarmiento, S. Sanfuente*, Santiago de Chile, Editorial América, 1943.

Paradeise, Catherine, "Sociabilité et culture de classe," *Revue Française de Sociologie* 21:4 (October–December 1980), 571–597.

Parent–Lardeur, Françoise, *Les Cabinets de lecture. La lecture publique à Paris sous la Restauration*, Paris, Payot, 1982.

Patlagean, Evelyn, "L'imaginaire," in Jacques Le Goff, Roger Chartier and Jacques Revel (dirs.), *La Nouvelle histoire*, Paris, Retz, 1978, 249–269, col. "Les Enciclopédies du Savoir Moderne."

Paula, Alberto S. J. de, "La autoría del frontis de la catedral de Buenos Aires," *Anales del Instituto de Arte Americano e Investigaciones Estéticas* 24, Buenos Aires, 1971, 93–97.

Payró, Julio E., *Prilidiano Pueyrredón, Joseph Dubourdieu. La Pirámide de Mayo y la Catedral de Buenos Aires*, Buenos Aires, Facultad de Filosofía y Letras, Biblioteca de Historia del Arte, 1972, Argentine series no. 5.

Peitschman, Hors, "Burocracia y corrupción en la Hispanoamérica colonial: una aproximación tentativa," *Nova América* 5, 1985.

Peña, Enrique, *Estudio periodístico y revistas existentes en la Biblioteca Enrique Peña*, Buenos Aires, Amorrortu, 1935.

Pereyra, Carlos, *Rosas y Thiers, la diplomacia europea en el Río de la Plata (1838–1850)*, Madrid, Editorial América, 1919.

Pereyra, Horacio, *Competencia entre puertos. Buenos Aires, Montevideo y la ley de aduanas de 1835*, Buenos Aires, Macchi, 1984.

Pérez Baltazar, Dolores, *Buenos Aires, un ejemplo de urbanismo ilustrado*, tesis doctoral, Madrid, Facultad de Geografía e Historia, Universidad Complutense de Madrid, 1981.

Pérez Fontana, Daoiz V., *La Masonería y los Masones en la organización de la República. Apuntes para la historia*, Montevideo, undated (unpublished typewritten copy.)

Petrecca, Francisco, *El cancionero histórico popular argentino. Un approche méthodologique*, third cycle doctorate thesis, Paris, Université de Paris III, 1982.

Piccirilli, Ricardo, *Rivadavia y su tiempo*, two vols., Buenos Aires, Peuser, 1943.

——, "Rivadavia y las reformas culturales," *Boletín de la Academia Nacional de la Historia* 19 (1946): 209–228.

——, *Los López. Una dinastía intelectual. Ensayo histórico–literario, 1810–1852*, Buenos Aires, Eudeba, 1972.

Piñedo, N., and E. Bidau, "Historia de la Universidad de Buenos Aires," *Anales de la Universidad* 1 (1888): 363–413; 539–552.

Pivel Devoto, Juan E., *Historia de los partidos políticos uruguayos, 1811–1897*, two vols., Montevideo, 1942.

——, *Historia de la República Oriental del Uruguay, 1830–1930*, Montevideo, Ed. Raúl Artagareytia, 1945.

Ponton, Rémy, "Une histoire de la sociabilité politique. À propos de l'ouvrage de Maurice Agulhon *Les Cercles dans la France bourgeoise, 1810–1848*," *Annales ESC* 6 (1980): 1269–1280.

Pradère, Juan A., *Juan Manuel de Rosas, su iconografía*, Buenos Aires, J. Mendesky e Hijos, 1914.

Prieto, Adolfo, *El discurso criollista en la formación de la Argentina moderna*, Buenos Aires, Sudamericana, 1988.

Puentes, Gabriel A., *El gobierno de Balcarce. División del partido federal (1832–1833)*, Buenos Aires, Huarpes, 1946.

Ramos, Juan P., *Historia de la instrucción primaria en la República Argentina, 1810–1910*, two vols., Buenos Aires, Peuser, 1910.

Ramos Mejía, José M., *Rosas y su tiempo*, three vols., Buenos Aires, F. Lajouane, 1907.

Ravignani, Emilio, "El cuerpo de plateros en el Río de la Plata, 1769–1809. Una corporación histórica," *Nosotros* (Buenos Aires) 23 (year X, September 1916): 305–315.

——, "El Pacto Federal del 4 de enero de 1831 y la Comisión Representativa," in *Documentos para la historia argentina*, vol. 15, Buenos Aires, Instituto de Investigaciones Históricas, 1922, 1–199.

——, "La liga litoral (1829–1833)," in Facultad de Filosofía y Letras, *Documentos para la historia argentina*, vol. 17, Buenos Aires, Taller Jacobo Peuser, 1922.

——, "Primeras disidencias entre federales triunfantes: elección de Juan Manuel de Rosas, 1829," *Boletín de la Junta de Historia y Numismática Americana* (Buenos Aires) 9 (1936): 5–23.

Renan, Ernest, "Qu'est–ce qu'une nation?," lecture given at the Sorbonne, 11 March 1882, in *Discours et conférences*, Paris, C. Lévy, 1887, 277–310.

Revel, Jacques, "Les usages de la civilité," in Philippe Ariès and Georges Duby (dirs.), *Histoire de la vie privée, III, De la Renaissance aux Lumières* (Roger Chartier, coord.), Paris, Seuil, 1986.

Rioux, Jean–Pierre, "Structure de sociabilité et pouvoir," *Cahiers de l'Animation* 3:46 (1984), 3–11.

"Rivadavia en la medalla," *Numismática* 4.

Rivera, Adolfo L., *El retrato en Buenos Aires, 1580–1870*, Buenos Aires, Universidad de Buenos Aires, 1982.

Roberts, Carlos, *Las invasiones inglesas del Río de la Plata, 1806–1807*, Buenos Aires, Talleres Gráficos Jacobo Peuser, 1938 [reedition: Buenos Aires, Emecé, 2000].

Roche, Daniel, *Le Siècle des Lumières en province. Académies et académiciens provinciaux (1680–1789)*, Paris, Mouton, 1978.

——, *Les Républiques des lettres. Gens de culture de Lumières au XVIIIe siècle*, Paris, Fayard, 1988.

Rodríguez, Adolfo E., *El régimen electoral en el lapso de 1827–1828*, Buenos Aires, 1965.

——, *Cuatrocientos años de policía en Buenos Aires*, Buenos Aires, Editorial Policial, 1981.

Rodríguez Molas, Ricardo, *Luis Pérez y la biografía de Rosas escrita en verso en 1830*, Buenos Aires, Clío, 1957.
——, *La música y la danza de los negros en el Buenos Aires de los siglos XVIII y XIX*, Buenos Aires, Clío, 1957.
——, "La pulpería rioplatense en el siglo XVII (ensayo de historia social y económica)," *Universidad* (Santa Fe, Universidad Nacional del Litoral) 49 (1961): 99–134.
——, "Negros libres rioplatenses," *Revista de Humanidades* 1:1 (1961), 99–126.
——, "Elementos populares en la prédica contra Juan Manuel de Rosas," *Historia* 30 (1963): 69–101.
——, *Historia social del gaucho*, Buenos Aires, Centro Editor de América Latina, 1968.
——, "Las pulperías," in *Lugares y modos de diversión*, Buenos Aires, Centro Editor de América Latina, 1985, col. "Cuadernos de Historia Popular Argentina."
Rojas, Ricardo, *Historia de la literatura argentina*, Buenos Aires, 1917–1922.
Romay, Francisco L., *El barrio de Monserrat*, Buenos Aires, Editorial de la Municipalidad, 1949.
——, *Historia de la Policía Federal Argentina*, Buenos Aires, Publicaciones de la Biblioteca Policial, 1963–1978.
Romero, José Luis, *Las ideas políticas en la Argentina*, Buenos Aires, Fondo de Cultura Económica, 1975.
——, *Latinoamérica, las ciudades y las ideas*, Buenos Aires, Siglo XXI, 1976.
Romero, José Luis, and Luis Alberto Romero, *Buenos Aires, historia de cuatro siglos*, two vols., Buenos Aires, April, 1982.
Romero, Luis Alberto, *La Sociedad de Igualdad. Los artesanos de Santiago de Chile y sus primeras experiencias políticas*, Buenos Aires, Instituto Torcuato Di Tella, 1978, history series.
Rondanina, Esteban F., *Liberalismo, masonería y socialismo en la evolución nacional*, Buenos Aires, Libera, 1965.
Rosa, José María, *Del municipio indiano a la provincia argentina, 1580–1852*, Madrid, Instituto de Estudios Políticos, 1958.
Rosal, Miguel Ángel, "Algunas consideraciones sobre las creencias religiosas de los africanos porteños (1750–1820)," *Investigaciones y Ensayos* 31, July–December 1981.
——, "Artesanos de color en Buenos Aires (1750–1910)," *BIHAA – E. Ravignani*, 1982, 331–346.
——, "Negros y pardos en Buenos Aires, 1811–1860," *Anuario de Estudios Americanos* 51:1 (1994), 165–184.
Rosanvallon, Pierre, *Le Moment Guizot*, Paris, Gallimard, 1985.
——, *Le Sacre du citoyen. Histoire du suffrage universel en France*, Paris, Gallimard, 1992.
"Rosas visto por un historiador inglés," *Todo es Historia* 268 (October 1989): 48–52.
Rosemblat, Ángel, *El nombre de la Argentina*, Buenos Aires, Eudeba, 1964.
Rossi, Vicente, *Cosas de negros* (1926), Buenos Aires, Hachette, 1958.
Rottjer, Aníbal A., *La masonería en la Argentina y en el mundo (historia de los hermanos Tres Puntos)* (1957), Buenos Aires, Nuevo Orden, 1976.
Rucquoi, Adeline, "Des villes nobles pour le Roi," in *Realidad e imágenes del poder. España a fines de la Edad Media*, Valladolid, Ámbito, 1988, 195–214.

Sabato, Hilda, *Capitalismo y ganadería en Buenos Aires. La fiebre del lanar, 1850–1890*, Buenos Aires, Sudamericana, 1989.

——, "Citizenship, political participation, and the formation of the public sphere in Buenos Aires, 1850s–1880s," *Past and Present*, 1992.

Sabato, Hilda, and Elías Palti, "¿Quién votaba en Buenos Aires? Práctica y teoría del sufragio, 1850–1880," *Desarrollo Económico* 30:119 (October–December 1990), 395–424.

Sabato, Jorge F., *La clase dominante en la Argentina moderna. Formación y características* (1979), Buenos Aires, CISEA, 1991.

Sabor, Josefa E., *Pedro de Angelis y los orígenes de la bibliografía argentina. Ensayo bio-bibliográfico*, Buenos Aires, Solar, 1995.

Sáenz Valiente, José María, *Régimen municipal de la ciudad de Buenos Aires. Su organización y funcionamiento desde 1810*, jurisprudence thesis, Buenos Aires, Adolfo Grau, 1911.

——, *Bajo las campanas del Cabildo*, Buenos Aires, Kraft, 1952.

Salas, Alberto M., *Diario de Buenos Aires, 1806–1807*, Buenos Aires, Sudamericana, 1981.

Salcedo, Saturnino, *Las primeras formas de elegir y los actuales sistemas electorales. Régimen político de las provincias argentinas*, Buenos Aires, ETGLA, 1948.

Saldías, Adolfo, *Historia de la Confederación Argentina* (1881–1887), three vols., Buenos Aires, Eudeba, 1978.

Salvadores, Antonio, "La enseñanza primaria y universitaria hasta 1830," in Academia Nacional de la Historia, *Historia de la Nación Argentina. De los orígenes hasta la organización definitiva en 1862*, Buenos Aires, Academia Nacional de la Historia, 1939–1951, vol. 7, part 1, ch. 8.

Sampay, Arturo E., *Las ideas políticas de Juan Manuel de Rosas*, Buenos Aires, Juárez Editor, 1972.

——, *Las Constituciones de la Argentina (1810–1972)*, Buenos Aires, Eudeba, 1975.

Scenna, Miguel Ángel, "Los cafés, una institución porteña," *Todo es Historia* 21 (1967): 48–56.

Schiaffino, Eduardo, *La pintura y la escultura en la Argentina, 1783–1894*, Buenos Aires, author's edition, 1933.

Schmitt, Jean–Claude, and Giovanni Levi, *Histoire de la jeunesse en Occident*, Paris, Seuil, 1996, col. "L'Univers Historique."

Schnapper, Dominique, *La Communauté de citoyens. Sur l'idée moderne de nation*, Paris, Gallimard, 1994.

Scobie, James R., *La lucha por la consolidación de la nacionalidad argentina, 1852–1862*, Buenos Aires, Hachette, 1964.

——, *Argentina, a City and a Nation*, New York, Oxford University Press, 1971.

Scott, Rebecca, *Slave Emancipation in Cuba. The Transition in Free Labor, 1860–1899*, Princeton, Princeton University Press, 1985.

Sereni, Emilio, *Capitalismo y mercado nacional* (1966), Barcelona, Crítica/Grijalbo, 1980.

Serrailh, Jean, *L'Espagne éclairée de la seconde moitié du XVIIIe siècle*, Paris, Librairie C. Klincksieck, 1964.

Sesquicentenario de la Contaduría General y Tesorería General de la Provincia de Buenos Aires, La Plata, 1971.

Shafer, Robert J., *The Economic Societies in the Spanish World, 1763–1821*, Syracuse, Syracuse University Press, 1958.

Shils, Edward, "Ideology and civility," in *The Intellectuals and the Powers and Other Essays*, Chicago, University of Chicago Press, 1972, 42–70.

Silva, Carlos Alberto, *El poder legislativo de la Nación Argentina*, five vols., Buenos Aires, Cámara de Diputados de la Nación, 1937.

Silva Castro, Raúl, *Prensa y periodismo en Chile, 1812–1956*, Santiago de Chile, Universidad de Chile, 1958.

Simmel, Georg, "La sociabilité. Exemple de sociologie pure ou formale," in *Sociologie et épistémologie* (1918), Paris, PUF, 1981, 121–136.

Slatta, Richard, *Los gauchos y el ocaso de la frontera*, Buenos Aires, Sudamericana, 1985.

Sociabilité, pouvoirs et société, Actes du Colloque de Rouen réunis par F. Thelamon, Rouen, Publications de l'Université, 1987.

Socolow, Susan, *The Merchants of Viceregal Buenos Aires: Family and Comerse*, London, 1978.

——, *The Bureaucrats of Buenos Aires, 1769–1810: Amor al Real Servicio*, Durham, Duke University Press, 1987.

Soler Cañas, Luis, *Negros, gauchos y compadres en el cancionero de la Federación (1830–1848)*, Buenos Aires, 1958.

Starobinski, Jean, *1789, Les emblèmes de la Raison*, Paris, Flammarion, 1979.

Stone, Lawrence, "Prosopografía," in *El pasado y el presente*, Mexico City, Fondo de Cultura Económica, 1986, 61–94.

Strickon, Arnold, "Estancieros y gauchos: clase, cultura y articulación social," in Esther Hermitte and Leopoldo J. Bartolomé (comps.), *Procesos de articulación social*, Buenos Aires, Amorrortu, 1977.

Studer, Elena F. Scheuss de, *La trata de negros en el Río de la Plata durante el siglo XVIII*, Buenos Aires, Facultad de Filosofía y Letras, 1958.

Summa Artis. Historia general del arte, Madrid, Espasa–Calpe, 1987.

Subercaseaux, Bernardo, *Cultura y sociedad liberal en el siglo XIX. Lastarria, ideología y literatura*, Santiago de Chile, Aconcagua, 1981.

Szuchman, Mark, *Order, Family and Community in Buenos Aires, 1810–1860*, Stanford, Stanford University Press, 1988.

Tandeter, Dora, Pablo Yankelivich et al., *Bibliographie de l'Université de Buenos Aires*, Buenos Aires, Eudeba, 1990.

Tau Anzoátegui, V., *Formación del Estado federal argentino (1820–1852)*, Buenos Aires, Instituto de Historia del Derecho, 1965.

——, *Manual de historia de las instituciones argentinas*, Buenos Aires, Macchi, 1975.

Taullard, Alfredo, *Historia de nuestros viejos teatros*, Buenos Aires, Imprenta López, 1932.

——, *Nuestro antiguo Buenos Aires. Cómo era y cómo es desde la época colonial hasta la actualidad. Su asombroso progreso edilicio. Trajes, costumbres, etc.*, Buenos Aires, Jacobo Peuser, 1927.

Taylor, William B., *Drinking, Homicide and Rebellion in Colonial Mexican Villages*, Stanford, Stanford University Press, 1979.

Terán, Oscar, *Alberdi póstumo*, Buenos Aires, Puntosur, 1988.

Ternavasio, Marcela, "Nuevo régimen representativo y expansión de la frontera política. Las elecciones del Estado de Buenos Aires, 1820–1840," in Antonio Annino, *Historia de las elecciones en Iberoamérica, siglo XIX*, Buenos Aires, Fondo de Cultura Económica, 1995, 65–105.

Tirart, Jean–Yves, "Problèmes de méthode en histoire sociale," *Revue d'histoire moderne et contemporaine* 10 (1963): 211–218.

Tönnies, Ferdinand, *Comunidad y asociación* (1887), translation by José Francisco Ivars, Barcelona, Península, 1979, col. "Homo Sociologicus."

Torre Revello, José, "Fiestas y costumbres," in Academia Nacional de la Historia, *Historia de la Nación Argentina. De los orígenes hasta la organización definitiva en 1862*, Buenos Aires, Academia Nacional de la Historia, 1939–1951, vol. 14, sec. 1, 409–420.

Treves, Renato, "Le saint–simonisme et la pensée italienne en Argentine et en Uruguay," *Cahiers Internationaux de Sociologie*, July–December 1973, 197–216.

Trostiné, R., *Pedro de Angelis en la cultura rioplatense*, Buenos Aires, La Facultad, 1945.

——, *Manuel Ricardo Trelles. Historiador de Buenos Aires*, prologue by Guillermo Furlong, Buenos Aires, 1947.

Tudesq, André–Jean, *Les Grands notables en France (1840–1849). Étude historique d'une psychologie sociale*, two vols., Burdeos, Imprimerie–Librairie Delmas/PUF, 1964.

Udaondo, E., *Crónica histórica de la venerable Orden Tercera de San Francisco de la República Argentina*, Buenos Aires, 1920.

——, *Reseña histórica del monasterio de Santa Catalina de Siena*, Buenos Aires, Talleres Gráficos San Pablo, 1945.

"Un entretien avec Maurice Agulhon," *Sport Histoire* 1, Toulouse, 1988, 11–15.

Verdevoye, Paul, "Domingo Faustino Sarmiento éducateur et publiciste (entre 1839 et 1852)," *Travaux et mémories de l'Institut des Hautes Études de l'Amérique Latine* 12, Paris, Institut des Hautes Études de l'Amérique Latine, 1963, 545–608.

Vergneault–Belmont, Françoise, *L'Œil qui pense. Méthodes graphiques pour la recherche en sciences humaines,* Paris, L'Harmattan, 1998.

Vernant, Jean–Pierre, *Mythe et pensée chez les Grecs: études de psychologie historique*, two vols., Paris, Maspero, 1974.

Viqueira Albán, Juan Pedro, "Diversiones públicas y cultura popular en la ciudad de México durante el siglo de las luces," *Anuario de Estudios Americanos* 44 (1987): 195–228.

Vovelle, Gaby, and Michel Vovelle, *Vision de la mort et de l'au–delà en Provence d'après les autels des âmes du Purgatoire, XVe–XXe siècle*, Paris, Armand Colin, 1970.

Vovelle, Michel, *Idéologie et mentalités*, Paris, Maspero, 1982.

——, "L'iconographie: une approche de la mentalité révolutionnaire," in *Recherche sur la Révolution. Un bilan des travaux scientifiques du Bicentenaire*, Paris, La Découverte/ Institut d'histoire de la Révolution Française/Société d'études robespierristes, 1991, 149–163.

Weber, Max, *Gesammelte Aufsätze zur Religionssoziologie*, 1947.

Weinberg, Félix, "Contribución a la bibliografía de Esteban Echeverría," *Universidad* (revista de la Universidad Nacional del Litoral) 5 (1960): 159–226.

——, *El Salón Literario de 1837*, Buenos Aires, Hachette, 1977.

——, "El segundo grupo romántico en Buenos Aires, 1844–1852," in *Congreso Internacional de Historia de América* (Buenos Aires, Academia Nacional de la Historia) 6 (1980): 479–497.

Whigham, Thomas Lyle, *The Politics of River Commerce in the Upper Plata, 1780–1865*, Ph.D. dissertation, Stanford University, Ann Arbor, University Microfilms International, 1986.

Yáñez Gallardo, César, *Saltar con red. La temprana emigración catalana a América, 1830–1870*, Madrid, Alianza, 1996.

Zambrano, Fabio, "Las sociabilidades modernas en Nueva Granada, 1820–1848," *Cahiers des Amériques Latines* 10 (1990): 197–203.

Zabala, Rómulo, and Enrique de Gandía, *Historia de la ciudad de Buenos Aires I (1536–1718)*, Buenos Aires, Municipalidad de la Ciudad de Buenos Aires, 1937.

——, *Historia de la Pirámide de Mayo*, Buenos Aires, Academia Nacional de la Historia, 1962.

Zavala, Iris M., "Organizaciones secretas en el destierro, 1823–1834," in *Masones, comuneros y carbonarios*, Madrid, Siglo XXI, 1971, 123–165.

Zavalía, Clodomiro, *Historia de la Corte Suprema de Justicia de la República Argentina en relación con su modelo americano*, Buenos Aires, Jacobo Peuser, 1920.

Zinny, Antonio, "Bibliografía periodística de Buenos Aires hasta la caída del gobierno de Rosas," *La Revista de Buenos Aires* 10/13 (1866–1867).

——, "Efemeridografía argirepatriótica, o sea de las provincias argentinas," *La Revista de Buenos Aires* 16 (1868).

——, *Historia de la prensa periódica de la República del Uruguay, 1807–1852*, Buenos Aires, Imprenta de Mayo, 1883.

——, *Historia de los gobernadores de las provincias argentinas*, Buenos Aires, La Cultura Argentina, 1910.

——, *La Gaceta Mercantil de Buenos Aires, 1823–1852. Resumen de su contenido con relación a la parte americana y con especialidad a la historia de la República Argentina*, three vols., Buenos Aires, Taller Penitenciaría Nacional, 1912.

Zorraquín Becú, Ricardo, "La Corte Suprema y sus grandes presidentes," *Boletín de la Academia Nacional de la Historia* 34 (1964): 247–263.

Zúñiga, Antonio, *La logia "Lautaro" y la independencia de América*, Buenos Aires, Establecimiento Gráfico J. Estrada, 1922.